BUSINESS PRINCIPLES AND MANAGEMENT

12e

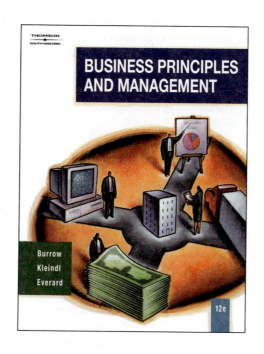

JAMES L. BURROW, PH.D

BRAD KLEINDL, PH.D.

KENNETH E. EVERARD, ED.D

THOMSON

SOUTH-WESTERN

Australia · Brazil · Canada · Mexico · Singapore · Spain · United Kingdom · United States

Business Principles and Management, Twelfth Edition
James L. Burrow, Brad Kleindl, and Kenneth E. Everard

VP/Editorial Director:
Jack W. Calhoun

VP/Editor-in-Chief:
Karen Schmohe

Executive Editor:
Eve Lewis

Developmental Editor:
Karen Hein

Sr. Marketing Manager:
Nancy Long

Marketing Coordinator:
Angela Glassmeyer

Content Project Manager:
Diane Bowdler

Manager of Technology, Editorial:
Liz Prigge

Technology Project Editor:
Sally Nieman

Web Coordinator:
Ed Stubenrauch

Manufacturing Coordinator:
Kevin Kluck

Production House:
Pre-PressPMG

Art Director:
Tippy McIntosh

Internal Designer:
Lou Ann Thesing

Cover Designer:
Lou Ann Thesing

Cover Images:
© Image Bank

Photo Researcher:
Darren Wright

Printer:
Quebecor World
Dubuque, IA

For more information about our products,
contact us at:

Thomson Higher Education
5191 Natorp Boulevard
Mason, Ohio 45040
USA

Career Cluster icons are being
used with permission of the:
States' Career Clusters Initiative,
2006, www.careerclusters.org

Reviewers

Brenda Albright-Barnhart
Teacher, Business Department
Bolton High School
Alexandria, LA

Janice Goddard
Teacher, Business & Information
    Technology
Norcross High School
Norcross, GA

Stephanie Hezekiah
Business Teacher
Lowndes High School
Valdosta, GA

Kimberly H. Orrick
Teacher, Business Department
Seminole County Middle/High School
Donalsonville, GA

Ernest H. Powers
Business/Marketing Teacher
South Charleston High School
South Charleston, WV

Jennifer L. Wegner
Business & IT Department Chair
Mishicot High School
Mishicot, WI

About the Authors

James L. Burrow, Ph,D., has a background in marketing and human resource development. He works regularly with the business community and other organizations as a consultant on marketing and performance improvement strategies. He recently retired from North Carolina State University where he served as the coordinator of the graduate Training and Development Program for over 15 years. Dr. Burrow received degrees from the University of Northern Iowa and the University of Nebraska in marketing and marketing education.

Brad Kleindl, Ph.D., is Dean of The Robert W. Plaster College of Business Administration at Missouri Southern State University. He has taught courses in marketing, international business, entrepreneurship, and Internet marketing and has presented at conferences and industry meetings across the U.S., Europe, Africa, and Asia. In the Spring of 2003, Dr. Kleindl was a Senior Fulbright Scholar in South Africa lecturing on Internet marketing, e-business, and e-commerce.

Kenneth E. Everard, Ed.D., is Professor Emeritus at The College of New Jersey, where he served as professor of management and as developer and administrator of graduate programs in business education, office administration, human resources management, and management.

Contents

Unit 4   Management Responsibilities   268

Unit 5   Financial Management   386

Unit 6 Production and Marketing Management 510

Unit 7   Human Resources Management   614

Work with a Powerhouse of Practical Business Expertise

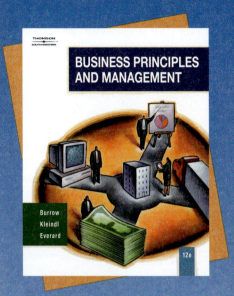

Introduce your students to today's critical business management concepts and principles in a realistic, investigative, and enriching manner with *Business Principles and Management, 12E*. Business operations are approached from the entrepreneurial and management perspective. All the functions of business management are covered extensively, including the use of technology and communication as tools of business. Explore the global dimension of business and possible career opportunities and bring the world of business to the classroom.

Student Text   Written specifically for high school students, *Business Principles and Management* combines fundamental concepts with a strong lesson-based instructional design, weaving in research opportunities, creative methods of assessment, interesting real-world features, mathematical calculations, case studies, and academic connections.

Annotated Instructor's Edition   Comprehensive teaching notes at point of use in the margins help you create a dynamic learning environment with minimal preparation. Solutions, background information, and projects address different learning styles and abilities.

Instructor's Resource CD   Find all the resources you need on one convenient CD. Never be without your teaching materials if there's a computer available.

Exam *View*® Assessment Software   Assessment is a snap with this electronic testing and grading software.

Web Site   You and your students can access this free Web site for a wealth of online learning tools. Visit thomsonedu.com/school/bpmxtra today.

Student Activity Guide   Ideal for additional review and reinforcement of text concepts.

Adobe eBook   Enhance learning with this eBook, complete with photos, graphics, and rich fonts.

DVD   Get students' attention and involve them in learning with the accompanying video on DVD.

Now You See It

Take a look for yourself at how this dynamic text brings business concepts to life for your students day after day with proven learning features and unmatched teaching support. It's everything you need for today's classroom and the understanding that extends well beyond.

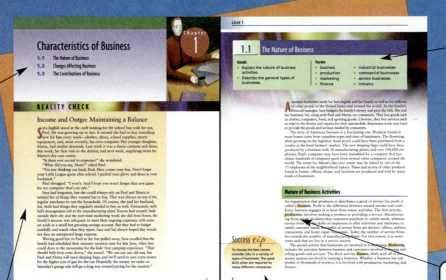

Prepare students to READ each lesson effectively by previewing Goals and Terms.

Chapters are broken into several class-length *Lessons*. The Lesson Numbers and Titles provide an overview of the chapter content.

Reality Check presents a story written to introduce concepts in the chapter using real-world examples.

Success Tips present insightful, practical tips on behavior and skills that lead to success.

Key Terms, first introduced in the Lesson Openers, are bold and highlighted with yellow in the text, emphasizing their importance and allowing students to find them easily.

Career Cluster presents the needed skills, education, work experience, and industry opportunities for a variety of business-related career paths.

Focus On... takes a look at current events, technology topics, international trends, innovation, change, and other important issues that impact the business environment.

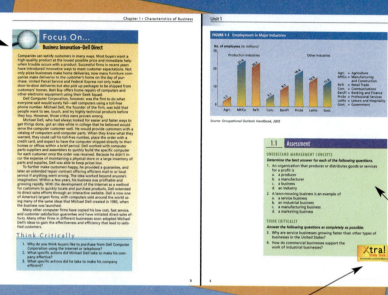

Figures provide a summary of important information, graphically organizing information for the student and visually detailing the links and associations between data and corresponding analysis.

Xtra! Study Tools, available on the free Web site are flash-based game reviews for every Lesson.

Assessment ends every Lesson, allowing you to evaluate student comprehension and progress frequently. Think Critically evaluates higher-order thinking skills.

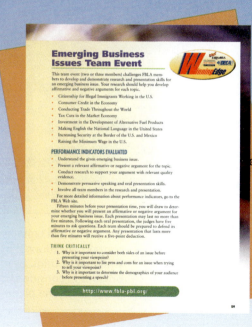

Winning Edge prepares students for BPA, DECA, and FBLA competitive events, while encouraging critical-thinking and decision-making skills.

Student-Focused Features for Hands-on Practice

NET Bookmark encourages students to use the Internet for research. The Web Site provides a safe portal for students to gather real data for analysis.

Facts & Figures presents interesting information, including statistics and numerical representations, that helps students understand the breadth and scope of business enterprises and activities.

Business Note asks students to relate what they've learned to a real business setting and provides tips for business success.

Career tip

Many people entering the computer field in the United States have moved from programming to information management. Software programming has been outsourced to countries such as India where there are highly qualified software engineers who work for low wages. Designing, building, and managing computer systems is more difficult to outsource.

Career Tips present helpful insights into a variety of business related career opportunities.

American car producers have learned to equal or exceed foreign car makers in the quality of their products. Is quality an important factor when you buy a car or other expensive product?

The photos and captions contain questions that ask students to think beyond the obvious in considering what's going on in the picture.

Integrated Assessment Puts Practical Knowledge to the Test

Xtra! Quiz Prep provides online chapter review, immediate feedback for students, and a report on results to teachers.

Chapter Concepts provides a brief review of the key topics from every lesson in the chapter.

Review Terms and Concepts assesses knowledge of basic chapter content and vocabulary.

Make Connections cross-curricular assessment activities connect business principles to math, communication, writing, reading, technology, research, and other academic subjects.

Case in Point presents in-depth scenarios related to the chapter content and then asks students to analyze the cases using critical-thinking skills.

My Business, Inc. is an ongoing project in which students apply the concepts they've learned while running a juice bar. In every chapter, students build on previous knowledge as they build their business.

CHECKPOINT

Why must companies be concerned about both effectiveness and efficiency?

Checkpoints throughout the chapter provide opportunities for informal evaluation of learning.

Business and Its Environment

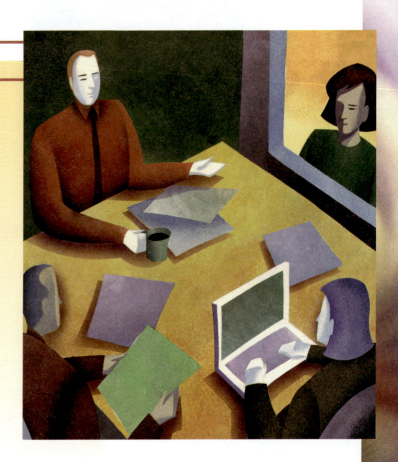

" . . . in developing countries, the central challenge is no longer to make manual work productive—we know, after all, how to do it. The central challenge will be to make knowledge workers productive. Knowledge workers are rapidly becoming the largest single group in the work force . . . It is on their productivity, above all, that the future prosperity and indeed the future survival of the developed economies will increasingly depend. "

Peter F. Drucker

Characteristics of Business

REALITY CHECK

Income and Outgo: Maintaining a Balance

Sara Inglish stood at the curb waiting for the school bus with her son, Paul. He was growing up so fast. It seemed she had to buy something new for him every week—clothes, shoes, school supplies, sports equipment, and, most recently, his own computer. Her younger daughter, Marta, had similar demands. Last week it was a dance costume and shoes; this week, her first visit to the dentist; and next week, supplying treats for Marta's day-care center.

"Is there ever an end to expenses?" she wondered.

"What did you say, Mom?" asked Paul.

"I'm just thinking out loud, Paul. Here comes your bus. Don't forget your Little League game after school. I packed your glove and shoes in your backpack."

Paul shrugged. "I won't. And I hope you won't forget that new game for my computer that's on sale."

Sara had forgotten, but she could always rely on Paul and Marta to remind her of things they wanted her to buy. That was always on top of the regular purchases to run the household. Of course, she and her husband, Sal, both had things they regularly needed to buy as well. Fortunately, with Sal's management job at the manufacturing plant Toyota had recently built outside their city and the part-time marketing work she did from home, the family's income was adequate to meet their ongoing expenses, with some set aside in a small but growing savings account. But they had to budget carefully and watch what they spent. Sara and Sal always hoped they would not face an unexpected large expense.

Waving good-bye to Paul as the bus pulled away, Sara recalled that the family had scheduled their summer vacation time for late June, when they could drive to the mountains for the kids' first camping experience. "That should help keep costs down," she mused. "We can use our old tent, but Paul and Marta will need sleeping bags, and we'll need to save extra money for the higher cost of gas for the car. Hopefully the money we make on Saturday's garage sale will go a long way toward paying for the vacation."

1.1   The Nature of Business

Goals
- Explain the nature of business activities.
- Describe the general types of businesses.

Terms
- business
- production
- marketing
- finance
- industrial businesses
- commercial businesses
- service businesses
- industry

American businesses work for Sara Inglish and her family as well as for millions of other people in the United States and around the world. As the family's financial manager, Sara budgets the family's money and pays the bills. She and her husband, Sal, along with Paul and Marta, are consumers. They buy goods such as clothes, computers, food, and sporting goods. Likewise, they buy services such as trips to the dentist and repairs for their automobile. Businesses work very hard to provide the goods and services needed by consumers.

The story of American business is a fascinating one. Products found in most homes come from countless types and sizes of businesses. The flowering plant growing on the Inglishes' front porch could have been purchased from a vendor at the local farmers' market. The new sleeping bags could have been produced by a business with 10 manufacturing plants and over 100,000 employees. Paul's computer may have been assembled by a company that purchases hundreds of computer parts from several other companies around the world. The treats for Marta's day-care center may be baked by one of the 15 employees of the neighborhood bakery. These and scores of other products found in homes, offices, shops, and factories are produced and sold by many kinds of businesses.

Nature of Business Activities

An organization that produces or distributes a good or service for profit is called a **business**. Profit is the difference between earned income and costs. Every business engages in at least three major activities. The first activity, **production**, involves making a product or providing a service. Manufacturing firms create products that customers purchase to satisfy needs, whereas service firms use the skills of employees to offer activities and assistance to satisfy customer needs. Examples of service firms are doctors' offices, airlines, restaurants, and home repair businesses. Today the number of service firms far exceeds the number of manufacturing firms. For this reason, it is sometimes said that we live in a service society.

The second activity that businesses are involved in is marketing. **Marketing** includes the activities between business and customers involved in buying and selling goods and services. The third activity, **finance**, deals with all of the money matters involved in running a business. Whether a business has one worker or thousands of workers, it is involved with production, marketing, and finance.

Success tip

To choose the best career, consider jobs in a variety of types of businesses. The same skills often are required by many different companies.

The price that Sara Inglish pays for Paul's computer game will be based in large part on supply and demand for the game. Supply of a product refers to the number of similar products that will be offered for sale at a particular time and at a particular price. If there are many similar products available, the price is likely to be lower. Demand, on the other hand, refers to the number of similar products that will be bought at a given time at a given price. If there are many people looking to buy the same computer game, the price is likely to be higher.

CHECKPOINT

What is the difference between a manufacturing firm and a service firm?

Types of Businesses

This book will focus on the various types of businesses and business activities and what it takes to manage a business successfully. But before beginning that study in detail, let's take a look at the general nature of business.

Generally, there are two major kinds of businesses—industrial and commercial. **Industrial businesses** produce goods used by other businesses or organizations to make things. Companies that mine coal or ore and that extract oil and gas from the earth provide resources for use by other companies and consumers. They are important industrial businesses. So are companies that construct buildings, build bridges, manufacture airplanes, or assemble televisions. Farmers and other agricultural producers are considered industrial businesses because they grow crops and raise livestock needed for the food we eat and used in the manufacture of a variety of products we use every day.

Unlike industrial businesses, **commercial businesses** are engaged in marketing (wholesalers and retailers), in finance (banks and investment companies), and in providing services (medical offices, fitness centers, and hotels) as their primary business activities. **Service businesses** are a type of commercial business that use mostly labor to offer mostly intangible products to satisfy consumer needs. For example, lawn mowing is a service. Figure 1-1 shows the number of people employed in selected types of production and commercial industries including services.

Industry is a word often used to refer to all businesses within a category doing similar work. For example, the publishing industry includes any business that deals with producing and selling books, magazines, newspapers, and other printed documents prepared by authors. The automotive industry includes all manufacturers of automobiles, trucks, and other vehicles as well as the producers of related automotive products. Even government can be considered an industry, because it provides fire and police protection, libraries and schools, and many other services required by the citizens the government serves. This industry would include all services provided by local, state, and federal governments.

CHECKPOINT

List an example of an industrial business, a commercial business, and a service business.

FIGURE 1-1 Employment in Major Industries

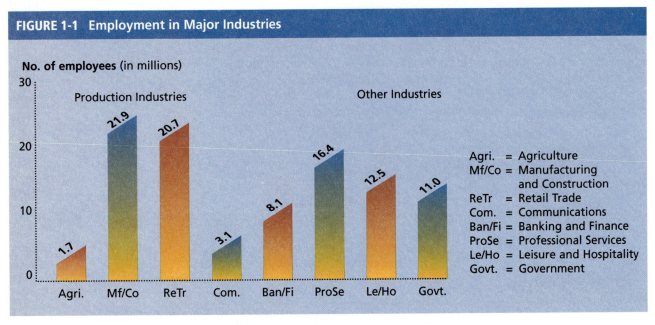

No. of employees (in millions)

Production Industries   Other Industries

Agri. 1.7
Mf/Co 21.9
ReTr 20.7
Com. 3.1
Ban/Fi 8.1
ProSe 16.4
Le/Ho 12.5
Govt. 11.0

Agri. = Agriculture
Mf/Co = Manufacturing and Construction
ReTr = Retail Trade
Com. = Communications
Ban/Fi = Banking and Finance
ProSe = Professional Services
Le/Ho = Leisure and Hospitality
Govt. = Government

Source: Occupational Outlook Handbook, 2005

1.1 Assessment

UNDERSTAND MANAGEMENT CONCEPTS

Determine the best answer for each of the following questions.

1. An organization that produces or distributes goods or services for a profit is
   a. a producer
   b. a manufacturer
   c. a business
   d. an industry
2. A lawn-mowing business is an example of
   a. a service business
   b. an industrial business
   c. a manufacturing business
   d. a marketing business

THINK CRITICALLY

Answer the following questions as completely as possible.

3. Why are service businesses growing faster than other types of businesses in the United States?
4. How do commercial businesses support the work of industrial businesses?

Xtra! Study Tools
thomsonedu.com/school/bpmxtra

1.2 Changes Affecting Businesses

Goals
- Describe how innovations affect businesses.
- Identify the impact global competition has had on U.S. businesses.
- Discuss ways in which businesses can improve their business practices.

Terms
- innovation
- global competition
- effectiveness
- efficiency
- domestic goods
- foreign goods
- output
- productivity
- downsize
- empowerment

An important characteristic of business is that it is dynamic, or constantly changing. To be successful, businesses must react quickly to the changing nature of society. For instance, horses were the principal means of transportation until the invention of steam power. Then, with the emergence of the first cross-country railroad in 1869, goods and services traveled mainly by rail for about 50 years. When the gasoline engine arrived, travel patterns shifted from train to car, bus, and truck. Shortly thereafter, airplanes glided along at 100 miles an hour but were soon replaced by jets, crisscrossing countries and oceans and carrying people and products to their destinations in a matter of hours.

Innovation

An **innovation** is something entirely new. Innovations affect the kinds of products and services offered for sale by other businesses. For example, clothing used to be made from only natural fibers, such as cotton and wool. Then chemical researchers developed synthetic fibers, such as rayon, nylon, and polyester. Now consumers have more choices in clothing and other fabric products.

Innovations also affect business operations. For example, since Apple Computer built one of the first personal computers about 35 years ago, computers operated by individual employees have increasingly influenced the way businesses do business. Computers help businesses design and manufacture products as well as keep track of billing, inventory, and customer information. Computers are now involved in most key business functions. The Internet is an innovation that has literally changed the relationships between businesses and their customers. Customers have 24-hour access to businesses without leaving their homes. Small businesses can compete with large businesses for customers from all over the country and even around the world.

CHECKPOINT
What are two ways that innovations affect businesses?

Impact of Global Competition on Business

For hundreds of years, American businesses led the way in producing new goods and services for sale around the world. Consumers worldwide eagerly purchased exciting new products that were invented and made in the United States. Factories hummed with activity, workers from other countries arrived by the thousands to find jobs, and people spent their wages buying the goods that the firms produced. Many businesspeople and government leaders from foreign countries also arrived to find out how American businesses were managed.

During the past half-century, however, other countries have become more industrialized and have learned how to invent and produce new products for consumers. Often the products were cheaper than similar products produced in the United States and, over time, many of the products were judged to be of equal or better quality. Americans gradually began to purchase these foreign products.

Foreign companies learned to produce innovative designs for products ranging from cell phones to MP3 players and flat-screen televisions. American business leaders soon realized it was time for change. They had to find ways to use the abundant resources of the United States and the human talent of their managers and employees to meet the challenge of global competition. **Global competition** is the ability of businesses from one country to compete with similar businesses in other countries. One of the biggest challenges facing American businesses today is competing in the global economy.

business *note*

Learning a foreign language offers an important career advantage. Most companies that compete in the global economy prefer employees who understand other cultures and can communicate comfortably in their customers' language. Use the Internet to identify the languages spoken by the most people around the world. If you chose to learn a second language to help you with an international business career, which one would you choose and why?

CHECKPOINT

Identify two major types of changes that present challenges to business.

In what types of consumer goods does the U.S. face serious global competition?

PHOTO: © DIGITAL VISION.

Focusing on the Right Things

Businesses often study their own operations to determine whether they are doing the right things and doing the right things well. Two terms are used to describe the best business practices. First, **effectiveness** means making the right decisions about what products or services to offer customers and the best ways to produce and deliver them. Second, **efficiency** means producing products and services quickly, at low cost, without wasting time and materials. Firms that provide products at the lowest cost while maintaining the quality customers expect will usually succeed. Some companies are extremely efficient but very ineffective, whereas others are effective but inefficient. Good managers focus on both effectiveness and efficiency and are able to achieve both.

ACHIEVING EFFECTIVENESS

Making the right decisions requires both common sense and skill. Knowing what customers want is critical to business success and to achieving effectiveness. What kind of sleeping bags, for example, will best satisfy the needs of the Inglish family when they take their summer vacation in the mountains? In the early days of manufacturing, customers bought whatever was available because there were few brands, colors, and styles from which to select. Today, the choices for most products have increased because many businesses provide similar products. Consumers can usually choose among the products offered by both domestic and foreign firms. **Domestic goods** (products made by firms in the United States) must compete with **foreign goods** (products made by firms in other countries).

Businesses today focus efforts on gathering information from consumers, studying their buying habits, testing new products with prospective customers, and adding new features to existing products. New designs, different materials and colors, understandable instructions, and ease of product use are features customers like. Large businesses spend millions of dollars examining customers' preferences. Equally important, businesses also invest heavily in keeping customers satisfied after products are sold. Product guarantees and follow-up with customers to make sure the product is working well help keep customers loyal.

To meet their needs, customers increasingly are concerned about the quality of products they buy. They want them to work well and last a long time. A growing emphasis of American producers is to improve the quality of the products they produce. Japanese car makers are an excellent example of how foreign producers captured a large portion of the market worldwide by providing customers with reliable and attractive cars. In the past, American car producers were not meeting quality needs as well as Japanese producers in the view of many buyers. Too many new cars had defects that required numerous trips to car dealers to correct.

American car producers have learned to equal or exceed foreign car makers in the quality of their products. Is quality an important factor when you buy a car or other expensive product?

PHOTO: © GETTY IMAGES/PHOTODISC.

On the other hand, Japanese cars had fewer initial problems and required little service.

American producers learned important lessons about quality from the Japanese. Today, American car producers are building products that are equaling their Japanese and European counterparts. American car manufacturers and producers of many other products vigorously stress to their workers the importance of using procedures that result in the highest quality. The concept is called *total quality management (TQM)*, which is a commitment to excellence that is accomplished by teamwork and continual improvement of work procedures and products. Where TQM is practiced, managers and employees receive a great deal of training on the topic of quality from experts. The result is a return to what customers want—well-made products.

ACHIEVING EFFICIENCY

Not only must firms do the right things, such as offering high-quality products, but they must also produce their products efficiently. Efficiency is measured by output—the quantity produced within a given time. Productivity, on the other hand, refers to producing the largest quantity in the least amount of time by using efficient methods and modern equipment. Workers are more productive when they are well equipped, well trained, and well managed. Employee productivity in the United States has grown over the years in manufacturing firms, but the growth has not been as rapid as in a few other industrialized nations.

Efficiency—including improved productivity—can be achieved in three ways:

1. Specialization of effort
2. Better technology and innovation
3. Reorganization of work activities

Competition based on quality has grown in importance worldwide. In the United States, the Malcolm Baldrige National Quality Award program is managed by an agency of the federal government. Each year, hundreds of firms apply for this distinctive national honor. Organizations that win an award usually notice an upturn in demand for their products. Quality awards are also offered in other countries. The Japanese offer the Deming Award, which is named after an American who was an expert on quality.

SPECIALIZATION In any business with more than a few employees, work can be performed more efficiently by having workers become specialists. In a large automobile repair shop, for example, not all workers are general mechanics. Rather, some workers specialize in body repair work whereas others specialize in repairing transmissions or engines. When workers specialize, they become expert at their assigned tasks. As a result, specialization improves quality while increasing the amount produced. Because specialization improves efficiency, it is no wonder that businesses hire or train employees for many specialized jobs.

Efficiency can also be improved through mass production. Mass production is a manufacturing procedure actually started in the early 1900s. It combines the use of technology, specialized equipment, and an assembly line. Employees perform efficient repetitive assembly methods to produce large quantities of identical goods. Through mass production, the cost of goods manufactured decreases because it is possible to produce more items in less time. Today, computer-driven equipment and robots make it possible to mass-produce large numbers of items with fewer workers.

TECHNOLOGY AND INNOVATION Efficiency can also be improved through the application of advanced technology. Technology includes equipment, manufacturing processes, and materials from which products are made. Because of new discoveries and inventions, better-quality goods and services are built at a faster pace and often at a lower cost. Improved materials, for example, may weigh less, last longer, and permit faster product assembly. Examples of new technology are found in everyday items such as cars, clothing, computers, and electronic appliances. Advanced technology helps companies stay ahead of competitors. And because technology has a significant impact on productivity, businesses spend billions of dollars annually on inventing, buying, and using new technology.

REORGANIZATION OF WORK The third and quite challenging way to increase efficiency is through reorganizing the way work gets done. From the late 1970s through the early 1990s, companies experienced slow growth, for reasons related to the U.S. and worldwide economy. However, one key reason for the slow growth arose from the competition from other industrialized nations. The typical reaction to slow growth caused by global competition was to try to cut back on production costs by laying off workers. A business would **downsize** by reducing the amount and variety of goods and services produced and the number of employees needed to produce them. By laying off workers, dropping unprofitable products, or even increasing the use of technology, firms were able to cut their costs. But the problem of producing the right products inexpensively still existed. Better ways were needed to compete with foreign firms, many of which had lower labor costs and equal or better quality and productivity. Some firms boldly decided to move in a direction that was similar to tearing down the business and rebuilding it.

Many firms arrived at the conclusion that employees were their most important resource. Further, managers learned that by empowering workers, the firm could become more productive. **Empowerment** is letting workers participate in determining how to perform their work tasks and offer ideas on how to improve the work process of the company. Empowerment dramatically changed the role of the worker.

In the past, workers performed narrow tasks on assembly lines and had little decision-making power. After empowering workers, firms found that the quality of work often improved, as did the efficiency of production. Although better-trained and highly skilled workers were required, fewer managers were needed. Companies were able to reduce the number of levels of management by pushing down the day-to-day decisions directly to workers rather than to managers. Workers were taught to use computers, to work in teams, and to be responsible for quality.

While practicing empowerment, some managers were also redesigning the work flow throughout their organizations—a concept sometimes called *re-engineering*. Instead of typical assembly lines found in factories and offices, production steps were eliminated, abbreviated, or placed entirely in the hands of a team of employees. Customer complaints dropped. Fewer well-trained workers, with the help of advanced technology and streamlined work processes, could better satisfy customers than could more workers using outdated methods and equipment. Most major firms—and many smaller ones—adopted these newer practices and are finding that customer satisfaction has risen along with productivity.

American firms are renewing their position as strong competitors in world business as a result of restructuring their work processes and a more intensive focus on quality and customers' needs. Empowering workers has contributed a great deal to the rebuilding of the image of American business. U.S. businesses are now doing the right things well. Furthermore, both large and small businesses are no longer thinking only about customers in their own countries. They see prospective customers located all around the country and around the world. American factories operate in other countries, and businesses in other countries make and sell products in this country. Business today is complex, challenging, and very exciting.

CHECKPOINT
Why must companies be concerned about both effectiveness and efficiency?

Investing in advanced technology helps businesses achieve greater efficiency. How does technology contribute to greater customer satisfaction?

PHOTO: © COMSTOCK IMAGES.

1.2 Assessment

UNDERSTAND MANAGEMENT CONCEPTS

Determine the best answer for each of the following questions.

1. The ability of businesses from one country to compete with similar businesses in other countries is known as
   a. domestic competition
   b. foreign competition
   c. global competition
   d. fair competition

2. Which of the following is **not** one of the ways companies can achieve efficiency?
   a. Specialization of effort
   b. Reducing prices charged to customers
   c. Better technology and innovation
   d. Reorganization of all work activities

THINK CRITICALLY

Answer the following questions as completely as possible.

3. Why were Japanese automobile manufacturers able to compete effectively with U.S. manufacturers who were considered world leaders?

4. What are some reasons that quality increases when employees are empowered to make decisions about their work?

Xtra!
Study Tools
thomsonedu.com/school/bpmxtra

Focus On...

Business Innovation–Dell Direct

Companies can satisfy customers in many ways. Most buyers want a high-quality product at the lowest possible price and immediate help when trouble occurs with a product. Successful firms in recent years have introduced innovative ways to meet customer expectations. Not only pizza businesses make home deliveries; now many furniture companies make deliveries to the customer's home on the day of purchase. United Parcel Service and Federal Express not only make door-to-door deliveries but also pick up packages to be shipped from customers' homes. Best Buy offers home repairs of computers and other electronic equipment using their Geek Squad.

Dell Computer Corporation, however, was the first to do what everyone said would surely fail—sell computers using a toll-free phone number. Michael Dell, the founder of the firm, was told that people want to see, touch, and try highly technical products before they buy. However, those critics were proven wrong.

Michael Dell, who had always looked for easier and faster ways to get things done, got an idea while in college that he believed would serve the computer customer well. He would provide customers with a catalog of computers and computer parts. When they knew what they wanted, they could call his toll-free number, place the order with a credit card, and expect to have the computer shipped directly to their homes or offices within a brief period. Dell worked with computer parts suppliers and assemblers to quickly build the specific computer for each customer once the order was received. Because he didn't incur the expense of maintaining a physical store or a large inventory of parts and supplies, Dell was able to keep prices low.

To further make customers happy, he provided a guarantee, and later an extended repair contract offering efficient mail-in or local service if anything went wrong. The idea worked beyond anyone's imagination. Within a few years, his business was profitable and growing rapidly. With the development of the Internet as a method for customers to quickly locate and purchase products, Dell extended its direct sales efforts through an interactive website. Dell is now one of America's largest firms, with computers sold around the world using many of the same ideas that Michael Dell created in 1983, when the business was launched.

Many other computer firms have copied his low cost, fast service, and customer satisfaction guarantee and have initiated direct-sales efforts. Many other firms in different businesses soon adopted Michael Dell's ideas to gain the effectiveness and efficiency that lead to satisfied customers.

Think Critically

1. Why do you think buyers like to purchase from Dell Computer Corporation using the Internet or telephone?
2. What specific actions did Michael Dell take to make his company effective?
3. What specific actions did he take to make his company efficient?

1.3 The Contributions of Business

Goals
- Identify two ways a nation measures its economic growth and prosperity.
- Describe the benefits of business ownership to the nation and individuals.

Terms
- gross domestic product (GDP)
- underground economy
- entrepreneur
- franchise
- franchisor
- franchisee
- intrapreneur

Business Growth and Prosperity

Overall, the United States is a prosperous nation. Much of its prosperity is due to business growth. Around the world, people admire and envy this country's economic strength. Let's look at two ways in which a nation measures its economic wealth and its benefits to citizens.

GROSS DOMESTIC PRODUCT

The chief measure of a nation's economic wealth is the **gross domestic product (GDP)**. The GDP is the total market value of all goods and services produced in a country in a year. Whenever products or services are purchased, the total dollar amount is reported to the federal government. The GDP of the United States is compared from year to year and is also compared with the GDP of other countries. These comparisons provide an ongoing measure of economic success.

Certain types of transactions, however, are never included in the GDP. These transactions are not recorded because they are unlawful or do not occur as part of normal business operations. For example, when a student is hired by a homeowner to mow lawns, formal business records are not normally prepared and the income is usually unrecorded. Some adults work part- or full-time for cash and never report that income or pay taxes on it. When drugs or counterfeit merchandise are sold illegally, such transactions are of course unreported. Income that escapes being recorded in the GDP is referred to as the **underground economy**. Business transactions that occur in the underground economy have increased in recent years in relation to the total GDP. Estimates range between 5 percent of the GDP during a brisk economy to 20 percent during a slow economy. The size of the underground economy concerns government officials due to its illegal nature and because the activities are not taxed although the people involved still require government services.

In 2005, the total known and recorded GDP for the United States reached the staggering $12.4 trillion mark, as shown in Figure 1-2. As a comparison, the GDP of the United States is slightly more than the combined total GDP of the 25 countries that make up the European Union (EU). The only single country that comes close to America in terms of GDP is China. That country's rapidly growing economy produces a GDP now totaling over $8 trillion. The rate of growth and the current size of the U.S. GDP indicate, in a rather striking way, its economic strength.

FIGURE 1-2 Countries with the Largest GDPs

	World	$59,380,000,000,000
1	United States	$12,370,000,000,000
2	European Union*	$12,180,000,000,000
3	China	$ 8,158,000,000,000
4	Japan	$ 3,867,000,000,000
5	India	$ 3,678,000,000,000
6	Germany	$ 2,446,000,000,000
7	United Kingdom	$ 1,867,000,000,000
8	France	$ 1,816,000,000,000
9	Italy	$ 1,645,000,000,000
*Combined GDP of all EU countries		

Source: The World Fact Book, 2005

INDIVIDUAL WELL-BEING

A second measure of a nation's wealth is the individual well-being of its citizens. Although GDP figures are helpful in judging the overall growth of an economy, such figures by themselves tell little about the economic worth of individuals. However, the U.S. Department of Commerce gathers information that reveals the financial well-being of U.S. citizens.

With increased income, an average family improves its level of living. Over 65 percent of all families live in homes they own. Many families now own items that less than 50 years ago were considered luxuries by most households. For example, almost all homes have refrigerators and more than one television. Sixteen percent of homes have two or more refrigerators and over one-third own a large-screen television. The number of homes with access to cable or satellite televisions has grown rapidly, with over 75 percent having that type of access. Over half of all adults in the United States carry cell phones today and some families give cell phones to their children before they are 10 years old.

In addition to consumer products, Americans also invest money in self-improvement, including education, exercise and fitness, and personal-care products. They participate in life-enrichment activities by attending the theater and concerts and by traveling in this country and abroad. Despite these large expenditures on material goods and services, Americans also put some of their money into savings. The amount of savings varies from year to year, with total annual savings by Americans averaging over $100 billion.

Even though the typical American has done well financially compared to people in other countries, economic and social problems still exist. For example, slow economic

business note

According to the Census Bureau, the average annual income of a person without a high school diploma is about $25,000, and earnings frequently decline. Completing high school raises that figure to $37,000, and obtaining a college degree results in an average yearly income of over $65,000. If a person with each level of education works for 30 years and earnings increase on average 3 percent each year, calculate how much each will earn in their lifetime. What is the percentage difference in the lifetime earnings between the lowest and highest paid individual?

periods may create job shortages, layoffs, and reduced incomes. Some people cannot find employment because of inadequate skills or reductions in the supply of jobs caused by business failures or relocation of companies to other states and other countries. When incomes drop, it becomes more difficult to buy homes, to send children to college, and to save for retirement. Increasing costs for medical care, insurance, gasoline, and electricity put pressures on many people, especially those with low or fixed incomes. Although the United States is a prosperous nation, many people live in poverty. In recent years, over 10 percent of all American families had incomes below the poverty level of about $18,000 for a family of four. Among the results of poverty are poor housing conditions, inadequate nutrition, and lack of access to health care and quality education. You will learn more about these and similar problems in later chapters. The health and well-being of both a country's businesses and its citizens are important to its long-term success.

CHECKPOINT
What does gross domestic product (GDP) measure?

Business Ownership

The successful growth of business in the United States has resulted from many factors. Two reasons for business growth are the strong desire by individuals to own their own businesses and the ease with which a business can be started. Someone who starts, manages, and owns a business is called an **entrepreneur**.

POPULARITY OF SMALL BUSINESS

Many small businesses are one-person or family operations with few employees. Can you name some examples in your community?

It is the tradition of this country to encourage individuals to become entrepreneurs. Few government controls, for example, prevent a person from launching a new business. Almost anyone who wishes to do so may start a business. Some require almost no money to start and can be operated on a part-time basis. As a result, many new businesses spring up each year. These new businesses may have physical facilities, such as a store in a mall or a small rented space used for manufacturing or service activities. On the other hand, new business owners may work from home offices or even operate businesses that exist only on the Internet.

Small business is a term used to describe companies that are operated by one or a few individuals. Small businesses have always been an important part of our economy. By far the largest number of businesses operating in the United States are considered small, and about half of all employed people work for small businesses. In a recent economic

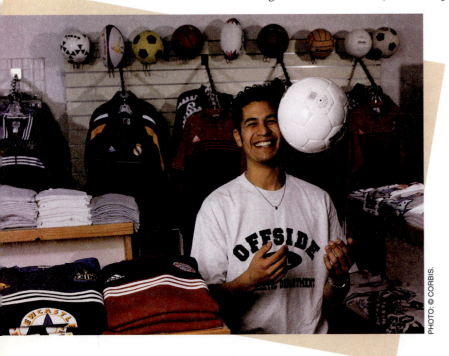

PHOTO: © CORBIS.

slowdown when many large firms were laying off thousands of workers, small businesses were hiring in large numbers. Often the new entrepreneurs were highly skilled managers who had been displaced by large firms that were downsizing. During that time, the number of applicants hired by small firms exceeded the number laid off by large firms. It is often believed that small businesses pay lower wages than larger businesses. Contrary to that belief, many of these small firms, especially those providing technical and professional services, were offering high-paying jobs.

Many small businesses are one-person or family operations with only a few employees. Examples include restaurants, gift shops, gas stations, and bakeries. Computers have made it possible for small businesses to operate from homes and on the Internet. For example, consultants working from their homes can do much of their work by e-mail with clients, and craftspeople can offer their products for sale on the Internet, without the expense of a storefront.

Most large businesses today began as very small businesses. Because they were well managed and supplied products and services consumers desired, they grew larger and larger. For example, Subway began as a small business and now has over 25,000 restaurants in 83 countries. The first Kinko's copy center was opened by a new college graduate in 1970 to serve students and faculty at the University of California at Santa Barbara. Due to its popularity and success, it expanded into more than 1,200 locations with 20,000 employees. In 2003, it was purchased by FedEx for over $2 billion.

GROWTH OF FRANCHISE BUSINESS

For the person with an entrepreneurial spirit, a popular way to launch a small business is through a franchise. A **franchise** is a legal agreement in which an individual or small group of investors purchases the right to sell a company's product or service under the company's name and trademark. Wireless Zone, Supercuts, and Bruegger's Bagels are examples of franchises operated by small-business owners under such agreements. The two parties to a franchise agreement are the **franchisor**, the parent company of a franchise agreement that provides the product or service, and the **franchisee**, the distributor of a franchised product or service.

In a typical franchise agreement, the franchisee pays an initial fee—often $100,000 or more—to the franchisor, and a percentage—usually 3 to 8 percent—of sales. In return, the franchisee gets assistance in selecting a location for the store or building and exclusive rights to sell the franchised product or service in a specified geographic area. The franchisor also provides tested policies and procedures to follow as well as special training and advice in how to operate the franchise efficiently. These services are particularly valuable to inexperienced business owners. They give a franchise business a far greater chance of success than a firm starting on its own has. Although 5 to 10 percent of franchised businesses fail, the failure rate is far lower than the failure rate of nonfranchised new businesses.

Prospective franchisees should carefully check out the franchisor. Fraudulent dealers have deceived many innocent people. Franchise agreements may require franchisees to buy all items needed to operate the business from the franchisor, often at a price substantially higher than available elsewhere. Some franchisors have been charged with allowing other franchisees to open businesses too close to each other, reducing the amount of possible revenues. To avoid these problems, some states have passed laws to protect franchisees. Potential franchisees should seek the help of lawyers and accountants and even experienced business-people before signing franchising agreements.

Over 25 million businesses currently exist in the United States. They vary in size from one part-time employee to over 1 million employees worldwide and in assets from a few dollars to billions of dollars. Some of these businesses have only a few customers, whereas others have millions of customers located throughout the world.

FIGURE 1-3 You can find all types of businesses represented by franchises.

Franchises from A to Z

Agway	Nathan's Famous, Inc.
Budget Rent-A-Car	Orange Julius of America
Century 21	Pizza Hut
Denny's	Quik Print, Inc.
Eureka Specialty Wood Products	Roy Rogers
Fairfield Inn by Marriott	Sbarro, Inc.
Goodyear Tire Centres	TCBY Systems
Howard Johnson	Uniclean Systems
International Dairy Queen	Virtual Window Fashion Store
Jiffy Lube	Wendy's Old Fashioned Hamburgers
Kwik Copy	
Lawn Doctor, Inc.	Yogi Bear's Jellystone Park
Midas International Corp.	Ziebert Tidycar

In spite of the possible dangers, the number of franchises has grown steadily. Although they make up fewer than 5 percent of all businesses, there are more than 500,000 franchise businesses in the United States. Figure 1-3 lists the variety of businesses operating under franchise agreements. Franchising is especially popular in the retail and service industries. Franchise businesses account for over 35 percent of all retail and service revenues each year.

RISKS OF OWNERSHIP

The success of a business depends greatly on managerial effectiveness. If a business is well managed, it will likely earn an adequate income from which it can pay all expenses and earn a profit. If it does not earn a profit, it cannot continue for long. An entrepreneur assumes the risk of success or failure.

Risk—the possibility of failure—is one of the characteristics of business that all entrepreneurs must face. Risk involves competition from other businesses, changes in prices, changes in style, competition from new products, and changes that arise from economic conditions. Whenever risks are high, the risk of business failure is also high.

Businesses close for a number of reasons. One out of every four to five businesses fails within three years, and about half cease operations within six to seven years. However, those figures include firms that voluntarily go out of business, such as by selling to someone else or by changing the type of ownership. The results of one study indicated that only 18 percent of all small firms failed within eight years of opening, whereas 28 percent closed voluntarily. The reported causes of business failure are shown in Figure 1-4. Most often, economic and financial factors cause businesses to fail.

OBLIGATIONS OF OWNERSHIP

Anyone who starts a business has a responsibility to the entire community in which the business operates. Customers, employees, suppliers, and even competitors are affected by a single business. Therefore, a business that fails creates an economic loss that is shared by others in society. For example, an unsuccessful

FIGURE 1-4 Causes of Business Failure

PRIMARY REASONS FOR FAILURES	PERCENT OF FAILURES
ECONOMIC CAUSES	64.1
Industry weakness, low profits, and low sales	
FINANCE CAUSES	23.9
Heavy expenses and burdensome debts	
DISASTER AND FRAUD	6.7
Hurricanes, floods, and theft	
NEGLECT CAUSES	3.7
Business conflicts, family problems, and poor work habits	
STRATEGY CAUSES	0.9
Overexpansion and difficulty collecting from customers	
EXPERIENCE CAUSES	0.8
Inadequate planning and inexperience	

Source: Adapted from *Business Failure Record. The Dun & Bradstreet Corporation, 1992.*

business probably owes money to other firms that will also suffer a loss because they cannot collect. In fact, a business that cannot collect from several other businesses may be placed in a weakened financial condition and it, too, may fail.

Successful businesses also have economic and social responsibilities. The privilege of operating a business with the potential of making a profit also carries a number of obligations to a variety of groups that serve and are served by the company. Many years ago, an executive of a major business association described the many responsibilities of business owners:

- TO CUSTOMERS: That they may have the best at the lowest cost, consistent with fairness to all those engaged in production and distribution
- TO EMPLOYEES: That their welfare will not be sacrificed for the benefit of others, and in their employment relations, their rights will be respected
- TO MANAGEMENT: That it may be recognized in proportion to its demonstrated ability, considering always the interest of others
- TO COMPETITORS: That there will be avoidance of every form of unfair competition
- TO INVESTORS: That their rights will be safeguarded and they will be kept so informed that they can exercise their own judgment respecting their interests
- TO THE PUBLIC: That the business will strive in all its operations and relations to promote the general welfare and observe faithfully the laws of the land.

Just as every business has an obligation to the community, the community has an obligation to each business. Society should be aware that owners face many risks while trying to earn a fair profit on the investment made in the business.

Success tip

To demonstrate their commitment to social responsibility, most businesspeople are very active in community and civic organizations. You should find ways to donate your time and abilities to activities that assist others and that help address community needs. You will feel very good about the service you provide.

Consumers should realize that the prices of goods and services are affected by expenses that arise from operating a business. Employees should realize that a business cannot operate successfully, and thereby provide jobs, unless each worker is properly trained and motivated to work. The economic health of a community is improved when groups in the community are aware of each other's obligations.

INTRAPRENEURSHIP

Sometimes large businesses are not viewed as places that encourage the creativity that leads to new ideas and opportunities. Some talented employees leave to start their own businesses when they believe they are not able to use all of their talents. To keep their businesses on the cutting edge and to encourage their creative employees, some larger employers are supporting intrapreneurs. An **intrapreneur** is an employee who is given funds and freedom to create a special unit or department within a company in order to develop a new product, process, or service. Although the main company finances the new venture, intrapreneurs enjoy the freedom of running their operations with little or no interference from upper managers.

Some of the largest corporations in the United States provide intrapreneurship opportunities that allow valuable employees to provide the company with innovative products and services. IBM and other major corporations such as 3M (which makes Scotch tape, Post-it Notes, and a variety of other products) and General Electric have also captured the innovative and entrepreneurial talents of employees.

Employees benefit because they risk neither their salaries nor their savings to launch a new business. Employers benefit by keeping creative employees who might have started successful competing businesses. Furthermore, employers and consumers benefit because new and better products, processes, and services are introduced at a quickened pace through intrapreneurships.

In recent years, businesses that struggled for survival in a global economy looked for ways to increase employee productivity and commitment. Two methods were sharing profits with employees and offering employees the opportunity to become owners of the company through the purchase of stock. These programs provide an extra incentive for employees to increase their efficiency and effectiveness. As a business becomes more successful and profits increase, the employees benefit by receiving a percentage of those profits or a higher value for the stock they own. Companies benefit by obtaining funds from employees who buy shares and by having a loyal, productive workforce.

NETBookmark

The free-enterprise economy of the United States has demonstrated remarkable growth. That growth is highlighted in data prepared by the U.S. Bureau of Economic Analysis. Point your browser to www.thomsonedu.com/school/bpmxtra. Review the information illustrating changes in the U.S. economy from 1990 to 2005. Analyze the information and draw two conclusions you believe are the most interesting or surprising. Using data from the table, prepare a graph or chart to support each of your conclusions. What are some reasons you believe the U.S. economy has been so successful?

www.thomsonedu.com/school/bpmxtra

STUDYING BUSINESS PRINCIPLES AND MANAGEMENT

Whether you plan to operate a business of your own, move into a top management position in a large company, or work as a valuable and valued employee for a company, you benefit from being well informed about the production, marketing, and financial activities of the business. As an owner, you must have a complete understanding of all phases of business operations, including employee relations and government regulations. This knowledge will also give you many advantages as an employee in organizations that empower their personnel to take greater responsibility for managing their own work and participating in employee teams. Moreover, if you expect to become a supervisor or an executive of a company, you must fully grasp how the activities of all departments are coordinated in a smoothly operating business. Even organizations that are not profit-making businesses, such as the government and charitable organizations, operate in a manner similar to businesses. Business knowledge will help you contribute as an employee or as a manager in these organizations as well.

CHECKPOINT

What is the main difference between an entrepreneur and an intrapreneur?

1.3   Assessment

UNDERSTAND MANAGEMENT CONCEPTS

Determine the best answer for each of the following questions.

1. An example of income that would be included in the underground economy but not included in the GDP is
    a. small-business profits
    b. income generated by oil and gas production
    c. income from the sale of services
    d. cash paid for work that is not reported on taxes

2. Which of the following is *not* offered to a franchisee by a franchisor?
    a. help in finding a location for the business
    b. operating procedures and policies
    c. a guaranteed minimum profit
    d. the use of the company's name and trademark

THINK CRITICALLY

Answer the following questions as completely as possible.

3. What factors do you believe have contributed to the very large GDP of the United States compared to that of most other countries?

4. What are a business's responsibilities to the community in which it operates? What are the community's responsibilities to businesses?

Xtra!
Study Tools
thomsonedu.com/school/bpmxtra

CHAPTER CONCEPTS

- Industrial businesses produce goods used by other businesses or organizations to make things. Commercial businesses engage in marketing, in finance, and in providing services. Every business engages in at least three major activities: production, marketing, and finance.

- The increased global competition of recent years has required firms to become more efficient and effective at providing goods and services of high quality at low prices to customers around the world. Innovations such as computer technology and the Internet have changed the way businesses run.

- A country's economic growth is seen in a continuously expanding GDP and the variety of goods and services that people are able to afford. The ease of starting a small business has allowed many people to become either entrepreneurs or intrapreneurs. Although many small firms fail, many others are highly successful as independent enterprises, franchisees, or large international firms.

REVIEW TERMS AND CONCEPTS

Write the letter of the term that matches each definition. Some terms will not be used.

a. business
b. commercial businesses
c. downsize
d. efficiency
e. entrepreneur
f. foreign goods
g. franchisee
h. franchisor
i. global competition
j. gross domestic product (GDP)
k. industrial businesses
l. industry
m. innovation
n. output
o. production
p. productivity
q. service businesses

1. Businesses that produce goods used by other businesses or organizations to make things
2. Organization that produces or distributes a good or service for profit
3. Producing products and services quickly, at low cost, without wasting time and materials
4. Something entirely new
5. Businesses that use mostly labor to offer mostly intangible products to satisfy consumer needs
6. Activity that involves making a product or providing a service
7. Ability of businesses from one country to compete with similar businesses in other countries
8. Parent company of a franchise agreement that provides the product or service
9. Quantity produced within a given time
10. All businesses within a category doing similar work
11. Total market value of all goods and services produced in a country in a year
12. Products made by firms in other countries
13. Someone who starts, manages, and owns a business
14. To reduce the amount and variety of goods and services produced and the number of employees needed to produce them

DETERMINE THE BEST ANSWER

15. The difference between earned income and costs is
    a. finance
    b. start-up costs
    c. profit
    d. revenue

16. Coal-mining and construction companies are examples of
    a. industrial businesses
    b. commercial businesses
    c. service businesses
    d. domestic businesses

17. When Apple Computer built a personal computer it was an example of
    a. global competition
    b. a new-product franchise
    c. a marketing activity
    d. an innovation

18. A result of global competition on the U.S. auto industry was that
    a. laws were passed to prevent foreign auto sales in America
    b. U.S. manufacturers improved quality and efficiency
    c. consumers preferred U.S. brands over foreign brands of cars
    d. no companies were able to make a profit

19. A company that is committed to total quality management
    a. hires managers with college degrees
    b. asks employees to emphasize efficiency rather than effectiveness
    c. uses teamwork and improved work procedures
    d. all of the answers are correct

20. Efficiency can be achieved in all of the following ways **except**
    a. specialization of effort
    b. setting a lower price than competitors
    c. using better technology and innovation
    d. reorganizing work activities

21. The gross domestic product (GDP) of the United States is approximately equal to that of
    a. China
    b. all of the countries in the European Union
    c. England and France
    d. the rest of the world

22. An important measure of individual well-being is
    a. the poverty rate
    b. average family income
    c. the standard of living
    d. all of the answers are correct

APPLY WHAT YOU KNOW

23. Why is the supply and demand of products important to both businesses and consumers?

24. Why do you believe some innovations are successful whereas others are not?

25. Do you believe that most U.S. businesses are getting better at meeting the challenges of global competition? Why or why not?

26. Do you believe it is more important for a business to be more effective, be more efficient, or try to balance both? Justify your choice.

27. Why do you believe employees would want to work in a business that believes in empowerment even when it often means more work and responsibility?

MAKE CONNECTIONS

28. **Research** Use your school library or the Internet to identify the top 10 industries in the United States based on the number of businesses in the industry. Prepare a bar chart to report your findings. Make sure to carefully label all of the information.

29. **Math** Use the U.S. GDP figures shown below to answer these questions: (a) What is the actual number of dollars for 1970? Show all the necessary digits. (b) What is the percent of increase for each decade? (c) Calculate the total percent of increase from 1970 to 2000. (d) Determine the average yearly increase in the GDP for the period shown.

Year	GDP ($)
1970	1.036 trillion
1980	2.784
1990	5.744
2000	9.963

30. **Technology** Use a word-processing or desktop publishing program to create a historic timeline that illustrates every decade from 1950 to the present. Use the Internet to identify an important innovation that had a major impact on businesses and consumers for each decade. Complete the timeline by listing the innovation, the inventor of the innovation, and the year it was developed.

31. **Speaking** You are a manager at a company that is implementing a program to empower employees. Prepare a speech that could be presented to the employees that will inform them about the program and the benefits to them and to the business. You may want to prepare a slide presentation using a computer to support your speech.

32. **Writing** At a library or on the Internet, find a recent article about problems a U.S. company or industry is having in competing with foreign companies. Write a report describing the problems and what the U.S. companies are doing to compete more successfully.

CASE IN POINT

CASE 1-1: Staying Competitive

The Kirk family came to this country early in the 20th century and made a bicycle that soon developed a reputation for its quality. Through much of the century, Kirk was the "Cadillac" of American bicycles. In the 1980s, it ran circles around numerous competitors; one in four bikes was a Kirk. Throughout this time, three generations of the Kirk family managed the company.

The success of Kirk's line of bicycles gave the company great confidence—perhaps too much confidence. During the last three years sales dropped, slipping from 1 million bikes sold yearly to 800,000 the next year and 650,000 last year. Three major competitors with well-designed but much lower-priced bikes who sold through discount stores and large sporting goods stores were stealing customers. When the Kirks saw competitors offering new and innovative bicycle styles, they ridiculed them as fads that only added to the companies' costs.

To compensate for the lower sales, Kirk began to cut costs. Some long-time employees were let go and lower-quality parts were bought from foreign firms. The company tried to keep its higher prices even as customers complained, believing that people who really knew bikes would want to buy Kirks as they always had done. Kirk managers made no attempt to talk to biking customers. Neither did the managers listen to the hundreds of dealers who sold Kirk bicycles in specialty shops. Loyal dealers started adding competitors' products to survive. Bike deliveries were running late. The changes made to cut costs did not correct the situation. For the last three years, Kirk operated at a loss. Something drastic had to occur.

Recently, Kirk was purchased by another company. Headquarters for the company were set up in Colorado, where biking is popular. Kirk's new managers talked to customers and dealers. As a result, new products rolled off the assembly line that satisfied loyal dealers and older bikers who recalled the excellent quality of the Kirk two-wheelers. But can the new Kirk adequately rebuild itself to compete in a tough market? Quality Kirk bikes sold only at specialty shops cost $550 to $2,500, which is far more than most bikes purchased at discount stores cost. Plenty of persuading will be needed to convert price-conscious casual bikers or more serious riders who put on 25 to 100 miles a week.

Signs of success appear on the horizon. A small profit is expected this year for the struggling firm. Whether the new managers can re-establish Kirk's earlier lead in the marketplace is yet to be determined.

THINK CRITICALLY

1. What was the main reason the old Kirk company failed? Explain your answer.
2. What should the new managers do to help improve Kirk's effectiveness?
3. What might the company do to help improve its efficiency?
4. Form a group with two other students to discuss and make recommendations for how the Kirk company might regain its former success.

CASE 1-2: Know Your Franchise

Fast Snacks is a food franchise that sells outlets to entrepreneurs interested in opening their own businesses. The business sells a variety of healthy snacks and drinks that can be prepared rapidly. It requires only a small, inexpensive location for the food preparation area and a sales counter. The franchisees are usually quite successful because of the strict rules set by the franchisor. Start-up costs are not as high as those of sandwich shops and small restaurants. Because the franchisor is very careful about who owns a Fast Snacks franchise in order to maintain a low failure rate, many applications are rejected.

Emi Tanaka and Rosa Lopez, two friends who have known each other for years, decided they would like to quit their jobs and go into business for themselves. Neither friend had been a manager or run a business before, but Rosa had worked several years at a large full-service restaurant and Emi's parents ran a small clothing shop where she had worked part-time until she graduated from high school. Both agreed that a new, unique fast-food business would be an excellent idea for their community and even agreed on a downtown location. Both liked to cook at home and had visited many restaurants. They agreed that a nice place in the business district of their town would attract shoppers, workers, and others. Both believed they could raise enough money to get started.

Emi and Rosa believed that a franchise business would be the best choice, and both seemed to have adequate money to invest. They checked the local library and Internet resources for franchising information and found a long list of possibilities. They studied the list and decided Fast Snacks was their favorite. They gathered as much information as possible, contacted the Fast Snacks headquarters, and obtained and mailed an application. They were excited when the manager called them for a meeting. However, they were surprised to learn that although the start-up costs were low, the franchisor collected 8 percent of sales. After thinking about it for a few days, they decided that because the franchise business had a great reputation, it could not fail. There was no need to check with other franchisors.

THINK CRITICALLY

1. Did Emi and Rosa make any mistakes in how they made their decision to select Fast Snacks? Give reasons for your answer. (With directions from your instructor, you may prefer to form groups of three to five students. Half the groups should argue that Emi and Rosa made the right decision, whereas the others should argue that they made the wrong decision. Each group should then provide reasons for the decisions.)

2. What advice would you give Rosa and Emi as they prepare to open their business to help them become successful and make adequate profits?

3. The franchisor of Fast Snacks is considering selling franchises in locations that are much nearer to each other in order to have more franchises. That might result in lower sales and profits for each franchisee, but higher franchise fees as well. What are the advantages and disadvantages of the current policy for new franchise locations?

project: MY BUSINESS, INC.

FIRST DECISIONS

Throughout this course, you will participate in a continuing project in which you will plan your own business—a juice bar. This project will require you to gather and analyze information and make decisions about your new business. The section called "Project: My Business, Inc." at the end of each chapter will guide you through the next step in business planning, as you apply what you learned in the chapter to a realistic new business venture. Develop written answers to each of the Data Collection and Analysis activities identified by your teacher, using a computer if possible. After you have completed each chapter's activities, save your work in the notebook you have prepared.

Juice bars are a part of two industries—fast food and health foods. Although juice bars are popular today, you will want your business to be successful in the future. It is not practical to start a business that may not be needed in a few years. In this project, you will study information to help you determine the future of your business and make the first specific decisions about it.

DATA COLLECTION

1. Gather information about the size and growth of the health and fitness market as well as the fast-food industry from newspapers, magazines, and other publications.
2. In your city or neighborhood, identify the types of businesses that exist in the areas of fast food and health foods. (Try to include the very small businesses that operate as part of a larger business such as a supermarket or health club.) List the name of each business, a brief description of the business, the type of products offered, and the business location.
3. Find information that identifies the failure rate of new fast-food businesses and health and fitness businesses.
4. Using the Internet and the library or by visiting businesses in your area, identify the common types of products offered by juice bar businesses.

ANALYSIS

1. What factors have led to the growth of juice bars? Is there any evidence that this type of business may not be as successful in the future?
2. What are the advantages and disadvantages of starting a small juice bar business in your community?
3. Create a name for your business. A good business name is short and easy to remember. It should relate to the type of business being operated, should be appealing to prospective customers, and should be different from other similar businesses. You may want to create an interesting design for your business name that could be used on signs and in promotion.
4. Develop an initial business concept—a one- to two-paragraph statement that describes the business and a possible location, the most likely customers, and the primary products and services that could be offered.

Social and Ethical Environment of Business

2.1 Human Resources

2.2 Societal Values

2.3 Ethical Issues

REALITY CHECK

The Supervisor's Secret

Tyler Eastman picked up the file folder and walked to his supervisor's office. He had finally saved enough money for the down payment and closing costs for a small stone house on the lake that he had long wanted. He now needed his supervisor's signature on several documents that the bank required in order to approve the loan money.

The Quest Company, where Tyler worked, was the main employer in this small Ohio town. Because the firm paid high wages, the town had nice stores and good restaurants. Taxes paid by the company supported the police and fire departments, the public school, and the recreation center.

Recently, however, Quest had fallen on hard times. Sales declined and unsold goods piled up. Some employees were let go. To survive, Quest had to cut costs. Rather than continue operations in Ohio, Quest decided to relocate to Georgia, where costs for taxes, wages, utilities, and raw materials were lower.

Only yesterday, Tyler's supervisor, Rayshawn Clark, had been informed that the town's factory would shut down over the next 12 months. He was being promoted but would move to the new Georgia plant. Many workers, like Tyler, would lose their jobs.

Therefore, when Tyler excitedly asked Rayshawn to sign the bank papers for his new home, Rayshawn was disturbed. Should he sign the loan papers when he knew Tyler's job would barely last a year? If he didn't sign, everyone would soon find out why. Morale among the employees would drop, and they would look for jobs elsewhere. It was important to keep the plant closure decision a secret as long as possible. The town would be devastated when it learned that its main employer would be relocating. Rayshawn pondered the dilemma he was in.

2.1 | Human Resources

Goals
- Describe the changing nature of the U.S. population and how this impacts businesses.
- Explain the issues that businesses face with the U.S. labor force.

Terms
- baby boom
- baby bust
- Frost Belt
- Sun Belt
- Rust Belt
- labor force
- labor participation rate
- glass ceiling
- sticky floor syndrome
- comparable worth

Since its establishment more than 225 years ago, the United States has become the world's leading economic, technical, and political power. The country has the world's largest economy and relies on highly sophisticated and modern means of production, transportation, and communication. Americans enjoy a very high standard of living. All these achievements can be attributed to the enormous resources that the country possesses: the ingenuity of its people, a democratic form of government, a social system that rewards individual initiative, and public policies that encourage innovation.

Despite the many successes, problems persist with regard to discrimination, crime and violence, environmental protection, ethical conduct, and social responsibility. Because businesses are a part of the total society in which they operate, social changes affect how they operate. Similarly, businesses affect society in different ways, as Tyler Eastman will soon discover. Thus, one cannot study business principles and management without also having an understanding of the social forces that shape business.

People are a firm's most important resource. A recent study of top managers found that finding and retaining qualified workers was more important than finance, technology, product innovation, or international business. The workers help businesses achieve their organizational goals. The challenges faced by businesses are closely interwoven with those experienced by the workers. In particular, such issues as those caused by changes in population and lifestyles have a direct bearing on business operations and on the well-being of the nation.

Population

The gross domestic product (GDP) of a country cannot increase unless there are enough people to provide the necessary labor and to purchase the goods and services produced. Population statistics enable businesses to plan how much and what kinds of goods and services to offer. However, the GDP of a country must grow at a faster rate than its population in order to improve living standards. Both the size and the characteristics of the population are important in business planning. Information about the size and characteristics of the American population can be found at the Web site of the U.S. Census Bureau, www.census.gov.

GROWING POPULATION

The population of the United States has grown steadily over the years, as shown in Figure 2-1. The growth rate is largely determined by the birth rate, the death rate, and the level of immigration into the country. Generally, as the standard of living increases, the birth rate falls, and this has been the case in the United States. At the same time, because of better health care and an improved public health system, people are living much longer.

Much of the population increase takes place through immigration. The United States annually accepts more legal immigrants than any other country in the world, with large numbers coming from Asian and Latin American nations. Many immigrants also enter the country illegally to seek a better life.

CHANGING POPULATION

The nature of the population has been changing, too. Currently, more than 80 percent of Americans can be racially classified as Caucasian. Because of higher birth rates among nonwhite Hispanics and African-Americans, and recent immigration, their proportions in the population have been growing. This growing diversity of the workforce increases the need for better cross-cultural communication and sensitivity to the interests and concerns of various groups.

Changes in the birth rate have caused shifts in the number of people in different age groups. For example, because of the high birth rate during 1945–1965, there are more people in the 42–62 age group. Because of this **baby boom**, the number of people aged 55 and over today has increased substantially. The low-birth-rate period that followed the boomer period is called the baby bust period.

facts & figures

In 2004, Hispanic purchasing power in the United States was approximately $700 billion; by 2010, it is estimated to be at least $1 trillion. By the year 2050, the Hispanic population will reach nearly 100 million, representing almost 25 percent of the U.S. population.

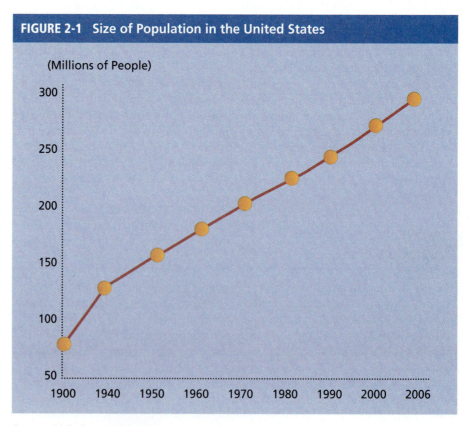

FIGURE 2-1   Size of Population in the United States

(Millions of People)

Source: U.S. Census Bureau

The **baby bust** period has created a shortage of young workers, called "busters." This shortage will continue to create serious problems, especially when the boomers retire in large numbers.

Businesses must be prepared to offer the kinds of goods and services needed by people of different age and racial groups. For instance, because of the increase of Spanish-speaking people, some newspapers and magazines publish Spanish-language editions. As people live longer, food companies continue to develop special foods and products for the elderly.

PHOTO: © GETTY IMAGES/PHOTODISC.

MOVING POPULATION

Americans are people on the move. Every year, on average, one out of five Americans changes his or her address. People move short distances, often from cities to suburbs. They also move long distances, such as from the **Frost Belt**, the colder northern half of the country, to the **Sun Belt**, the warmer southern half of the nation. As businesses relocate to where customers are located, they affect where other people move to in order to find jobs. For example, factories have relocated to the southeastern states, where wage rates are lower than in the **Rust Belt**—the north central and northeastern states where the major manufacturing firms once dominated. As illustrated at the beginning of this chapter, the Quest Company decided to move from Ohio to Georgia to lower its labor and other costs.

The continuing movement of people from the city to the suburbs and from the north to the south has led to many unintended consequences. When families and businesses leave cities in large numbers, the cities lose the financial ability to provide high-quality services. As a result, crime and poverty have increased in some large cities. Many southern states such as Georgia and Florida have experienced rapid economic and industrial growth. When businesses move from the Rust Belt, they leave behind unemployed workers, closed factories, decaying towns, and homeless people. However, in recent years, political and business leaders have taken bold steps to revitalize cities and communities in the northern states.

How has the "baby bust" period affected the supply of young workers in business?

CHECKPOINT
What factors are influencing shifts in the U.S. population?

Labor Force

As the population grows, so does the labor force. The **labor force** includes most people aged 16 or over who are available for work, whether employed or unemployed. Of course, many of the people in the labor force may be available for work but are not actively seeking employment, such as students and full-time homemakers. In a recent year, the Bureau of Labor Statistics reported that the

Success *tip*

Job competition can be very intense. Consider yourself to be a bundle of skills that businesses will buy. Identify the skills that make you unique and appealing to a business.

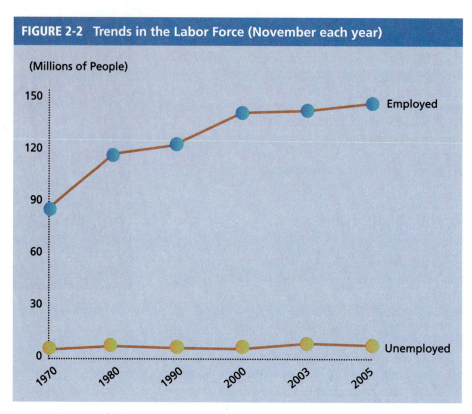

FIGURE 2-2 Trends in the Labor Force (November each year)

Source: Bureau of Labor Statistics

size of the American labor force was almost 140 million. Figure 2-2 shows the growth of the labor force.

The **labor participation rate** is the percentage of the labor force that is either employed or actively seeking employment. In the last three decades, the labor participation rate increased primarily because many more women took jobs outside the home. In 1975, around 46 percent of women worked outside the home. By 2005, the figure had risen to nearly 60 percent. Some reasons for the increase are that women have been choosing not to marry, to delay marriage, or to marry and pursue careers before or while raising children. Figure 2-3 shows the trend in the labor participation rates for males and females. The expansion of the economy through much of the 1990s coaxed many people, such as retirees, people with disabilities, and homemakers, to enter the labor force.

The growth of the economy, changes in the population and where people live, and technological advances have created a variety of new jobs. One of the great strengths of the American economy has been its ability to create new jobs. Most new jobs are in the service industries, such as computer programming, banking and insurance, leisure, food services, and health care. The growing use of computers has created a large number of technical jobs in areas such as computer applications and programming. The Internet has influenced how firms conduct business, and e-commerce is rapidly emerging as a new way to sell and buy goods and services. The rapid growth in the computer industry has led to a shortage of qualified workers and, in turn, has led to high wages for those with the necessary education and skills. To meet the demand for such high-tech workers, the government allows firms to hire workers from foreign countries.

Many of the new jobs require more skills, which means workers have to be educated. As a result, more people are going to college or acquiring training

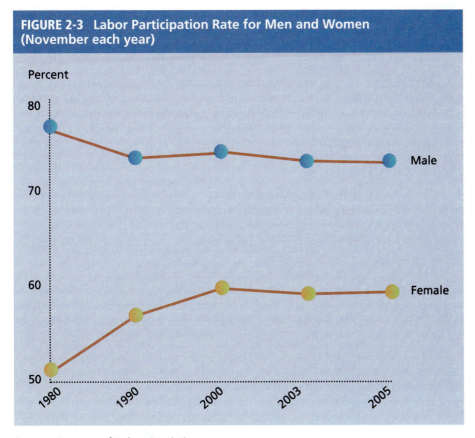

FIGURE 2-3 Labor Participation Rate for Men and Women (November each year)

Percent

Male

Female

Source: Bureau of Labor Statistics

in new skills. As technology changes and old jobs disappear, many workers need retraining. At the same time, technology has simplified jobs, such as short-order cook or bank teller. These jobs now require little training and therefore pay low wages. Some jobs, such as telephone operator, have been eliminated since the work has been automated. A large number of workers are in dead-end jobs and are not earning an adequate income to maintain a reasonable standard of living.

For various reasons, including lack of financial resources, public schools in many areas are failing to provide the quality of education historically expected of high school graduates. High school graduates are particularly deficient in math, computer, social, and communication skills. Businesses are sometimes forced to provide remedial education in basic skills for newly hired workers.

POVERTY

The prosperity of Americans is not equally distributed among the population. According to the Bureau of the Census, between 12 and 15 percent of the population in any given year live in poverty. This means that these people are poorly housed, clothed, and fed. Many live in inner-city slums or in rural areas. Statistics suggest that the richest 20 percent of American families have continued to earn more over the past 30 years, whereas the income of the lowest fifth has remained about the same. Thus, the gap between the rich and poor is widening.

Due to such programs as Social Security, poverty among elderly people is much lower today than previously. However, many children live in poverty because they

In 1966, women earned 58 cents for every dollar earned by men for comparable work. That gap has closed by an average of half a penny each year since then. In 2004, women earned 76.5 cents for every dollar earned by men for comparable work. Nearly every year the difference in earnings narrows somewhat.

reside in households where one or more parents do not have the education and skills to hold high-paying jobs. Many parents cannot participate fully in the labor force because they don't have access to good-quality, affordable child care. The strongest influence on increased income is increased education.

The government has several programs to reduce poverty. Minimum wage rates, unemployment benefits, financial or food aid, and subsidized medical care provide a basic safety net for the economically disadvantaged. Businesses increasingly offer training programs to provide skills that enable people to find and hold jobs.

EQUAL EMPLOYMENT

Equality for all is one of the basic principles on which the United States was founded. Yet, some groups of Americans have found it difficult to obtain jobs or be promoted on an equal basis. Several laws have been passed to outlaw discrimination on the basis of race, gender, national origin, color, religion, age, handicap, and other characteristics.

In many occupations, the numbers of women and racial minorities are few. Even when they find jobs, people in these groups may encounter difficulties in being promoted above a certain level. This has come to be known as the **glass ceiling**—an invisible barrier to job advancement. The barriers are often difficult to detect. For example, if employees expressed discomfort with having a female or African-American supervisor, this may make promotion of women and African-Americans less likely. Employers are now legally obligated to provide equal employment opportunities for all.

Many women and members of racial minority groups are employed in entry-level positions with little hope for career advancement. These are low-paying jobs requiring little skill and education, such as restaurant server, sales clerk, or nurse's aide. The inability of these workers to move up from these jobs is referred to as the **sticky floor syndrome**. Higher education and redesigning the jobs offer the best opportunities for workers to escape from this predicament.

COMPARABLE WORTH

Studies show that men tend to earn more than women do. It is not clear if this difference is due to discrimination against women or to the nature of the jobs women do. There are a few professions in which women predominate. Wages tend to be lower in jobs that employ lots of women than in jobs held primarily by men. For instance, most dental hygienists are women, whereas most airline pilots are men. Pilots tend to earn more money than dental hygienists.

But what happens when the jobs are not the same but require similar levels of training and responsibility? **Comparable worth** means paying workers equally for jobs with similar but not identical job requirements. The concept is also called "equal pay for comparable work." Jobs compared may be distinctly different, such as legal secretary and carpenter. However, if it can be determined that the two jobs require about the same level of training and responsibility, the pay scale for the two jobs should be the same. That is, legal secretaries should be paid more than what they currently earn to bring their pay up to that of carpenters. To determine whether work is of equal value, analysts compare factors such as special skills, physical strength, job dangers, responsibility, and education.

However, it is not easy to determine the specific factors that measure the worth of jobs. Should physical strength, for instance, be used to compare the worth of a legal secretary to a carpenter? And if few applicants are available for the carpenter's position and many are available for legal secretaries, is it fair to pay legal secretaries more than carpenters? These and other factors make it difficult for employers to design and implement comparable worth plans. But businesses are trying. Many states have passed laws that promote using comparable worth for determining wages in government jobs.

CHECKPOINT
List the factors influencing the U.S. labor force.

2.1 Assessment

UNDERSTAND MANAGEMENT CONCEPTS

Circle the best answer for each of the following questions.

1. The U.S. labor force includes
   a. people aged 16 and over who are available for work
   b. employed people aged 16 and over
   c. unemployed people aged 16 and over
   d. all of the above

2. When people encounter difficulties in being promoted to management above a certain level they have encountered
   a. a glass ceiling
   b. a promotion ceiling
   c. a sticky floor
   d. a legal barrier

THINK CRITICALLY

Answer the following questions as completely as possible.

3. What factors are contributing to the growth of the U.S. population?

4. What has caused the decline in the number of young workers in recent years?

thomsonedu.com/school/bpmxtra

2.2 | Societal Values

Goals
- Discuss how the values of Americans have changed.
- Explain how businesses have adapted to changing values.
- Describe the dilemma posed by the need for business to grow and the need to protect the natural environment.

Terms
- Generation X
- Net Generation
- telecommute
- recycling

Change is constant in our society. We produce a steady stream of new products, new ideas, new ways of doing things, and new attitudes. In recent decades, societal values have been undergoing change at a fast pace.

Changing American Values

An especially striking development has been the transformation of the family. The number of children living with both parents continues to fall because of rising divorce rates and the rising number of single mothers. The birth rate, too, has declined, as women delay marriage and pursue careers outside the home. The traditional definition of "family" consisting of a working husband, a homemaker wife, two children, and a dog is now the exception. Fewer than one fourth of America's families fit this picture. Often, both parents work to support the family, as must single parents. Businesses have responded to the needs of today's fast-paced family life with a whole array of time-saving products and services from fast food of every description to dry-cleaning delivery services to day care.

Because of increased competition in the economy, businesses are striving to produce more while keeping costs low. Employers have increased their demands on employees. Many employees find the pace and demands of work stressful. For dual-career couples and especially those with children, the quality of home life often suffers. Job insecurity discourages workers from taking vacations or time off, and instead they work longer hours to meet their job requirements. Factors such as these have strained the employer–employee relationship. Workers from the post-baby-boom generation, called Generation X, feel less loyal to a particular employer than did earlier generations. They expect to change jobs many times during their careers, as does the Net Generation—those born between 1977 and 1997. Also, competent women stopped by the glass ceiling often quit their jobs to start their own businesses. Women now operate a majority of new small businesses.

With so many men and women working side by side, workplace romance has blossomed, but so have incidents of sexual harassment. As the number of single adults and working couples has grown, dining at home is being replaced by dining out. American consumers spend more on restaurant meals than on groceries.

People are placing more emphasis on safety and active lifestyles. This is reflected in airbags in cars, larger cars, and sporty vehicles.

A disturbing aspect in some parts of contemporary American society is the incidence of unpredictable and unprovoked violence through the use of guns, often by young people. Workplaces, schools, churches, and transportation systems are all susceptible to the random gunfire killing and injuring of innocent people. This concern over violent crime has led to an expanding personal-security business in the form of personal and home protective gadgets, guns, guards, gated communities, and prison construction.

The United States also has the dubious distinction of being lawsuit-happy. Individuals, groups, and organizations are quick to file lawsuits. Damage awards can run into millions of dollars. To avoid such expensive legal liabilities, businesses try to be very careful with respect to the safety of their products and the impact of their operations on employees, customers, and the overall society.

Ethics *tip*

Businesses are concerned about hiring ethical employees. A business could conduct a police check, use a lie detector, conduct an Internet search, or use personality tests when evaluating potential employees. Explain why it is important for young people to act ethically. Explain how unethical activity could hurt future employment.

Employer Responses

A changing society affects individuals as well as organizations. Many social issues transfer to work settings. Employees leave home each workday thinking about personal problems. Responsibilities may be enormous for workers with preschool children, aging parents, family illnesses, and financial burdens. Concerns such as these follow employees to their work sites and affect their job performance. Competition for quality employees can be intense. To attract and retain competent workers, employers have responded to these social changes by taking action to improve the way work is done, to assure healthier and safer working conditions, and to help workers deal with some personal problems.

REDESIGNING JOBS

As you will learn in other chapters, when jobs consist of mainly repetitive tasks, workers get bored, productivity drops, and morale declines. Many workers come late to work, call in sick, or even quit their jobs to find more interesting jobs elsewhere. Thus, to retain workers, employers redesign jobs to make them varied and challenging. In some cases, employees learn a variety of jobs and regularly switch jobs within the same organization. Such job rotation increases workers' interest in their jobs and enables employees to fill in for coworkers who may be absent.

Workers now often participate in job decisions, provide suggestions, and serve on committees that look for ways to improve work quality. Today's employees often work in teams. Work teams can improve morale as well as the quality of work. Businesses also try to improve job satisfaction through empowering workers to make important decisions.

IMPROVING HEALTH AND SAFETY

The United States is facing an obesity epidemic that is negatively affecting employees' health. In response to concerns over health and safety, businesses operate wellness and fitness programs. A physically unfit employee is absent more and is less productive than a fit employee. Many businesses encourage a healthy lifestyle by providing incentives to smokers to quit, membership to health clubs, counseling services where workers can receive support for stress or emotional problems, and payment for treatment of drug, alcohol, and other forms of addiction. Employers thereby reduce medical and insurance costs.

PHOTO: © GETTY IMAGES/PHOTODISC.

FAMILY-FRIENDLY PRACTICES

Given the changes in the family structure, employers are making efforts to address this aspect of their employees' lives. By law, employers provide unpaid leave to employees to take care of their sick children or parents, or to give birth to, adopt, or take care of newborn children. Many progressive businesses provide day-care facilities for the young children of employees. Some employers provide flexible scheduling so that workers can avoid commuting to and from work during hectic rush hour traffic as well as accommodate their family needs and lifestyle. Advances in communication technology in the form of the Internet, e-mail, mobile phones, and fax have led many businesses to allow workers to telecommute. Telecommuters work from home or on the road, staying in contact with their employers electronically.

Telecommuting is becoming more common in the U.S. What are the advantages to employers of allowing workers to telecommute?

CHECKPOINT

Describe how employers are reacting to changing societal issues.

Natural Resource Issues

A growing population means more people to buy more things. More purchases mean more packaging, boxes, and worn-out products to throw away. Discarded plastic, chemical, and metal products take many years to break down in landfills. Moreover, some products (such as medical waste) may be harmful if not disposed of properly. The increasing demand for products places great pressure on natural resources, such as land, water, air, minerals, and forests. It also affects the habitats of wild animals and the lives of native peoples. Both business and society have to address these resource issues.

business note

Personal values have a direct impact on the type of jobs a person will take and how managers run their businesses. List the values you find important. Identify how they may change over time. List the jobs you think will match your personal values and why.

MANAGING THE ENVIRONMENT

Preserving the natural environment and properly disposing of consumer and industrial waste have become major concerns in our society. As landfills become full, we have shifted our focus to reducing the growth of waste and to recycling—reusing products and packaging whenever possible. We are trying to conserve nonrenewable resources, such as oil, natural gas, and iron ore. At the same time, we are using more renewable resources, such as electricity generated from the sun (solar power), from water, and from wind.

At times, pollution-control goals, such as improvement of air quality, may be at odds with energy conservation goals. For example, the use of coal, which is currently in great supply, generally pollutes air more than natural gas, which is in short supply. A business changing from coal to natural gas meets environmental goals but violates conservation goals. In contrast, a business changing from natural gas to coal conserves natural gas but creates pollution. In time, scientists may discover ways to use coal without creating a great deal of pollution. Until then, people have to decide how best to conserve natural resources and protect the environment.

Pollution dangers have become more and more apparent. Large cities are often covered by smog that contains pollutants from motor vehicles. As a result, many residents suffer from breathing problems. In numerous rivers and lakes, pollutants have killed fish and other marine life. Chemical products used to destroy insects and plant life have especially endangered waterways and farmlands, and in some places entered the food chain.

In 2004, more than 44 million Americans worked as full-time or part-time telecommuters. Increasing numbers of employees are conditioning their acceptance of new jobs on approval from the employer to telework.

CONTROLLING ENVIRONMENTAL POLLUTION

Many groups have pressured governments and employers to tighten pollution standards and to conserve natural resources. The federal government created the Environmental Protection Agency (EPA) in 1974 to help control and reduce pollution in the basic areas of air, water, solid waste, pesticides, noise, and radiation. The EPA enforces such laws as the Clean Air Act, Clean Water Act, Resource Recovery Act, Federal Water Pollution Control Act, Federal Environmental Pesticide Control Act, Noise Control Act, and Resource Conservation and Recovery Act. For instance, laws have been passed that require engines in cars to be both fuel-efficient and less polluting.

New waste disposal rules, especially for hazardous materials like medical and nuclear waste, are very strictly enforced and often costly to carry out. These high costs also encourage illegal dumping in bodies of water or on remote land areas. To conserve resources and to protect the environment, more and more companies are using recycled materials in their production processes.

In the aftermath of the Exxon Valdez accident, which spilled oil along coastal Alaska in 1989 and killed large numbers of marine life, environmentalists and socially minded groups formed the Coalition of Environmentally Responsible Economies to encourage companies to behave responsibly. The Coalition developed a list of 10 environmental guidelines, named the CERES Principles. The Coalition asks organizations to follow the principles voluntarily; they are not legally required to do so. Sun Oil Company (Sunoco) was the first major company that promised to follow the CERES Principles listed in Figure 2-4 (see p. 40).

Laws against pollution and demands for conserving natural resources are costly to businesses. An issue arises when foreign countries have weaker laws, law enforcement is lax, or public concern over pollution and conservation is not as strong as in the United States. As a result, companies in these foreign countries can make goods more cheaply than companies in America. One of the objections to increasing trade with Mexico, for example, is that pollution laws in Mexico are much weaker than in the United States.

CHECKPOINT
List natural resources issues impacting businesses and describe how these businesses are reacting to them.

FIGURE 2-4 The CERES Principles

1. Protect the environment from the release of pollutants, especially hazardous substances that may damage the environment.
2. Conserve nonrenewable natural resources through efficient use and careful planning.
3. Minimize the creation of waste, especially hazardous waste, and dispose of such materials in a safe, responsible manner.
4. Make every effort to use environmentally safe and sustainable energy sources to meet organizational needs.
5. Reduce environmental, health, and safety risks to employees and surrounding communities.
6. Sell products that cause as little damage to the environment as possible and are safe to use.
7. Accept responsibility for any harm the company causes to the environment, correct damages made to the environment, and compensate injured parties.
8. Keep the public informed of incidents relating to operations that harm the environment or pose health or safety hazards.
9. Appoint one person to represent environmental interests to serve on the highest-level decision-making committee that represents owner interests.
10. Produce and publicize a yearly self-evaluation of progress toward implementing these principles and meeting all applicable laws worldwide.

Source: www.ceres.org. Adapted from CERES: 1990. The 1990 CERES Guide to the Valdez Principles, The Social Investment Forum, Boston, MA.

2.2 Assessment

UNDERSTAND MANAGEMENT CONCEPTS

Circle the best answer for each of the following questions.

1. Which of the following is *not* true for the Net Generation?
   a. They expect to change jobs many times during their careers.
   b. They were born between 1977 and 1997.
   c. They are the post-baby-boom generation.
   d. They feel less loyal to a particular employer.

2. Pollution can, in part, be controlled through
   a. recycling
   b. EPA regulations
   c. following the CERES Principles
   d. all of the above

THINK CRITICALLY

Answer the following questions as completely as possible.

3. Identify a list of employer practices that have enhanced the quality of work life for employees.

4. Give at least two examples of how environmental goals can be at odds with energy conservation goals.

Xtra! Study Tools
thomsonedu.com/school/bpmxtra

2.3 Ethical Issues

Goals
- Describe how ethics relates to business practice.
- Suggest ways in which businesses can be socially responsible.

Terms
- ethics
- business ethics
- code of ethics
- social responsibility
- stakeholders
- nongovernmental organizations (NGOs)

Laws provide a minimum standard of behavior for people and businesses to follow. However, many behaviors are neither allowed nor disallowed by law. The guide that then comes into play is ethics. **Ethics** refers to standards of moral conduct that individuals and groups set for themselves, defining what behavior they value as right or wrong.

Ethical behavior is closely linked to personal values—underlying beliefs and attitudes that individuals or groups possess. To decide whether a particular action is ethical or not, we have to ask questions such as: Is the action right or is it wrong, regardless of what the laws state? Therefore, ethical conduct goes beyond state and federal laws.

Business Ethics

A collection of principles and rules that define right and wrong conduct for an organization is called **business ethics**. Any action that does not conform to these moral principles is unethical behavior. Not all firms have the same rules of ethical conduct, however. Notions of right and wrong vary from manager to manager, business to business, and country to country. Generally, moral conduct that is favorable to the largest number of people is considered ethically desirable.

The business scandals at companies such as Tyco International, Enron, and MCI have placed considerable importance on business ethics. This has led some companies to hire chief ethics officers. Their job is to ensure that workers are trained in how to comply with a company's ethics policies. Many businesses have created codes of ethics to guide managers and workers in their behavior. A **code of ethics** is a formal, published collection of values and rules that reflect the firm's philosophy and goals. Having such a code removes or reduces opportunities for unethical conduct. These codes deal with such issues as accepting business gifts, respecting employee privacy, using company property for personal use, and maintaining confidentiality. Business confidentiality means keeping sensitive company information secret.

Ethical codes are communicated to employees through memos, newsletters, posters, and employee manuals. Organizations establish procedures to handle situations that arise when employees violate the codes. To be effective, codes of ethics must have the full support of the organization's top-level managers. Codes are ineffective if they are not enforced.

ETHICAL DILEMMAS

The issue of ethics often arises when it is not clear whether a particular action is legal or illegal. As the opening story illustrated, the supervisor, Rayshawn Clark,

PHOTO: © GETTY IMAGES/PHOTODISC.

Offshore drilling is an important source of crude oil. Can you name some environmental drawbacks of offshore drills?

is caught in the dilemma of revealing the future plans of the company versus ensuring business as usual. Philosophers have debated the issue of right and wrong for centuries. One well-known approach is to ask the question: What is the value or worth of a specific behavior for society as a whole? The best behavior is that which does the most good for the most people. For example, assume a company employed 200 people and it eliminated 50 people so that it could continue to operate. Although 50 people were left jobless, 150 benefited by retaining their jobs.

Businesses are constantly faced with ethical dilemmas of various kinds. Should a lumber company cut down a forest if doing so would endanger a rare species of bird that nests there? Should oil drilling be permitted off a coast, thus destroying its natural beauty? Should a manager accept a request by a foreign official to arrange for his daughter's admission to an American university if the company wants to land a contract? Should a business hire a woman to win support from women's groups? How businesses handle these issues determines whether they are acting in an ethical manner. Notions of what is right or wrong change over time. Answers often are not clear-cut.

Because values also differ among nations, problems sometimes arise for firms involved in international business. Firms have to choose between the ethical practices of the foreign country and of their home country. For instance, it is an accepted business practice in Japan for employees to give expensive gifts to their bosses. Such behavior in the United States is generally discouraged. Should an American company behave in Japan as it does in the United States, or should it follow the Japanese practice? Answers to such questions are not readily apparent, and managers have to find ways to reconcile conflicting goals.

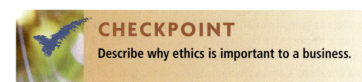

CHECKPOINT

Describe why ethics is important to a business.

Social Responsibility of Business

A question often raised is: What is business's responsibility to help solve society's problems? The answer is not simple, because the profit motive of a business often collides with what is good for society. Should businesses accept lower profit, for instance, in order to keep jobs in a declining community? In such cases, businesses must decide for themselves what is right and wrong.

The primary goal of business is to make a profit for the owners. Businesses cannot survive for long if their owners are not rewarded for their investment. Although profit plays a key role in our business system, businesses today also emphasize another business goal—social responsibility. **Social responsibility**

Focus On...

Ethics–The Wage Issue

Nike, Inc., based in Beaverton, Oregon, is one of the most famous names in sports shoes. Sports shoes of all kinds carrying the famous swoosh logo are sold throughout the world, often at prices above $100. But how much does it cost to make these shoes?

Nike does not manufacture any of its shoes. Instead, it has them made by private contractors in countries such as Indonesia and Vietnam. Nike provides design and quality specifications and places orders for millions of pairs of shoes. Indonesia and Vietnam are poor countries where there are lots of unemployed people, and government laws and regulations are weak and unenforced.

Various nongovernmental organizations have alleged that Nike's shoes are made under unacceptable working conditions. Workers as young as 14 working over 60 hours a week receive wages of about $1 a day. Safety and health standards are minimal. The cost of labor was estimated at less than 4 percent of the price that the consumer paid for a pair of shoes. Thus, shoes sold for $100 have a labor cost of less than $4. Even after paying the manufacturers and the distributors, Nike makes a profit of $15 on the pair.

Nike argued that its profits are comparable to those made by Reebok, Adidas, and others in the industry. It also claimed that the company had little control over the manufacturers, though Nike tried to ensure that these companies followed the employment laws of the respective countries with regard to minimum wages, hours of work, and the like.

Labor unions and human rights groups in the United States began a campaign to draw attention to the harsh conditions in which Nike's shoes were made. Pressure mounted on Nike's shareholders, bankers, retailers, and other stakeholders to force Nike to make changes in the working conditions at the foreign factories.

Nike reacted to the demand for change by establishing an office to monitor working conditions in its foreign factories. The critics demanded that independent monitoring groups in which they would be represented must be allowed to visit and inspect the factories abroad.

All this negative publicity led to sharp declines in sales and profits. Nike argued that it was incorrect to compare working conditions in the United States with those in less prosperous countries. The company pointed out that not too long ago, working conditions in the United States were also harsh, and only economic growth led to the enlightened work conditions prevalent today.

Think Critically

1. Suggest how Nike can successfully deal with the protests against it.
2. What is the motivation of the protestors against Nike? Why can't Nike ignore them?
3. Are Nike and its suppliers reacting in socially responsible ways? Why or why not?
4. Should one society force its work standards and wage rates on another? Why or why not?

refers to the duty of a business to contribute to the well-being of society. Because businesses depend on society for resources, opportunities, and rights, they have an obligation to the communities in which they operate.

Stakeholders are any individuals or groups that are affected by the firm's actions, such as owners, customers, suppliers, employees, creditors, government, and the public. Stakeholders expect a business to be responsible and responsive to their interests. Such responsibility may mean a variety of things. Examples include donating money to flood victims, sponsoring an exhibition on Hindu art at a local museum, providing college scholarships to needy students, training gang members in job-related skills, and setting up day-care centers for employees' children.

Stakeholders usually believe that a business has the resources to contribute to a community's well-being. Also, good deeds translate into favorable publicity for the business, which, in turn, means more sales and profits. The founders of Ben and Jerry's, the ice cream makers, for example, commit themselves to buying expensive milk from hormone-free Vermont dairy farms and giving 7 percent of pretax profits to charity. Such actions endear them to the residents of Vermont, where their operations are based.

Milton Friedman, a renowned economist, once said, "The business of business is business." People who follow his view believe that if a business uses some of its profits for social causes rather than using all of its profits to grow the business, the company will not remain very profitable. Thus, workers will get lower wages, customers will pay higher prices, and the owners will make less profit. Questions are also raised about the ability of a business to solve social problems. Does a manager know how to solve drug abuse? Should a business be responsible for promoting sporting events in the community? Are these not roles for the government or others to perform?

Despite these serious concerns, it is now widely recognized that business has an important responsibility to its stakeholders. Business has also realized that by getting involved socially, it advances its own interests. Enhancing goodwill in the community reduces government's desire to regulate the business.

Some businesses review their social programs regularly. The reviews show what the business is doing to fulfill its social responsibilities, its success in accomplishing its goals, and its plans for pursuing future activities.

The conduct of businesses is being increasingly and closely examined by various independent groups known as nongovernmental organizations (NGOs). Examples of such organizations are the American Civil Liberties Union and the Sierra Club. They specialize in particular issues, such as workplace discrimination or environmental protection. NGOs influence businesses through lobbying, publicity, and pressure tactics to alter their activities.

THE FUTURE

Given the fast pace of change in the world today, society and business will face different issues in the future. Although it is difficult to predict the future, current trends provide hints of what may be in store in the years to come.

Various economic and social data provide an in-depth picture of changes occurring in American society. The racial and ethnic mix of the labor force will continue to change. The Internet is

NETBookmark

Businesses are concerned about social responsibility. The organization, Business for Social Responsibility (BSR), helps companies demonstrate their respect for ethical values, people, communities, and the environment. Point your browser to www.thomsonedu.com/school/bpmxtra. Go to the BSR Issue Brief to view a list of corporate social responsibility issues. Choose two topics, summarize the major issues related to them, and list at least three reasons businesses should practice social responsibility. Write a short paragraph describing how you are personally affected by corporations for whom social responsibility is a priority.

www.thomsonedu.com/school/bpmxtra

dramatically altering how people communicate and businesses operate. Computer-related jobs are multiplying as entrepreneurs establish Internet companies to find new applications for this new technology.

Businesses are apt to become more and more involved in providing social services to the community that, in the past, have been provided by families, funded by the government, or purchased by individuals. The general public has become more conscious of environmental and human rights issues, and there is growing concern over balancing family and work life. Businesses have to ensure that their activities do not harm the natural environment and that they respect the individual rights of a rapidly diversifying workforce. As societal values change, each business will continue to shape and be shaped by the society in which it functions.

PHOTO: © GETTY IMAGES/PHOTODISC.

Wind power is considered a clean source of energy that does not add to environmental pollution. What are some other ways businesses can demonstrate social responsibility?

CHECKPOINT
List the reasons that a business needs to be concerned about social responsibility issues.

2.3 Assessment

UNDERSTAND MANAGEMENT CONCEPTS
Circle the best answer for each of the following questions.

1. Which of the following is *not* related to the concept of ethics?
   a. Ethics refers to standards of moral conduct.
   b. Ethical behavior is closely linked to personal values.
   c. Ethics always shows what is right and what is wrong.
   d. Ethics helps define what behavior is seen as right or wrong.

2. The duty of a business to contribute to the well-being of society is called
   a. business ethics
   b. social responsibility
   c. constituency analysis
   d. business responsibility

THINK CRITICALLY
Answer the following questions as completely as possible.

3. Because businesses are established for making profits, the only way to ensure that they behave ethically is to have strong laws that require them to do so. Do you agree with this statement? Justify your answer.

4. Explain how a business can ensure that its code of ethics will be effective.

Xtra! Study Tools
thomsonedu.com/school/bpmxtra

CHAPTER CONCEPTS

- The U.S. population has been growing largely because of immigration and because Americans are living longer. It is also becoming more diverse. The trend has been for people and businesses to locate in the southern part of the country.

- Changes in American society and its values affect how businesses function. Changes can be seen in the growing number of women in the workforce, the changing nature of the family, and rising job insecurity, stress, and violence. Poverty and discrimination persist. Businesses are becoming more environmentally conscious.

- Businesses are responding to employee needs by redesigning jobs, improving workplace health and safety, and providing flexible scheduling and family-friendly benefits.

- Ethical conduct in business requires doing more than the law pre-scribes. Businesses establish codes of ethics to identify right and wrong behavior for employees.

- The goal of business extends beyond merely making profits to being socially responsible to various stakeholders.

REVIEW TERMS AND CONCEPTS

Write the letter of the term that matches each definition. Some terms will not be used.

a. baby boom
b. baby bust
c. business ethics
d. code of ethics
e. comparable worth
f. ethics
g. Generation X
h. glass ceiling
i. labor force
j. labor participation rate
k. Net Generation
l. recycling
m. social responsibility
n. stakeholders
o. sticky floor syndrome
p. telecommute

1. High-birth-rate period between 1945 and 1965
2. Low-birth-rate period that followed the boomer period
3. Group that includes most people 16 or over who are available for work, whether employed or unemployed
4. Percentage of the labor force that is either employed or actively seeking employment
5. Invisible barrier to job advancement
6. Inability of workers to move up from low-level jobs
7. Paying workers equally for jobs with similar but not identical job requirements
8. To work from home or on the road, staying in contact with employer electronically
9. Duty of a business to contribute to the well-being of society
10. Standards of moral conduct that individuals and groups set for themselves, defining what behavior they value as right or wrong
11. Collection of principles and rules that define right and wrong conduct for an organization
12. Individuals or groups affected by a firm's actions, such as owners, customers, suppliers, employees, creditors, government, and the public

DETERMINE THE BEST ANSWER

13. The north central and northeastern states where the major manufacturing firms once dominated is called the
    a. Rust Belt
    b. Frost Belt
    c. Sun Belt
    d. Industrialized Belt

14. Workers born between 1977 and 1997 are called
    a. Baby boom
    b. Generation Y
    c. Generation X
    d. Net Generation

15. Which of the following is true of the U.S. labor participation rate?
    a. The labor participation rate force includes only those who are employed.
    b. The labor participation rate force does not include people actively seeking employment.
    c. The labor participation rate increased because more women have taken jobs outside the home.
    d. All of the above are true.

16. Businesses are reacting to a changing society by all of the following except
    a. job redesign
    b. increasing all worker's salaries
    c. improving health and safety
    d. putting in place family-friendly practices

17. The American Civil Liberties Union and the Sierra Club are examples of
    a. nongovernmental organizations (NGOs)
    b. quasi-governmental organizations (QGOs)
    c. legal-governmental organizations (LGOs)
    d. environmental-governmental organizations (EGOs)

18. Telecommuting means
    a. selling by telephone
    b. working via communication technology instead of showing up at an office
    c. selling over the Internet
    d. using an office as a telecommunications center

19. Stakeholders could include
    a. business owners
    b. customers
    c. creditors
    d. all of the above

20. By 2050, the Hispanic population in the United States will reach nearly ____ percent of the U.S. population.
    a. 15
    b. 20
    c. 25
    d. 30

APPLY WHAT YOU KNOW

21. Explain how the movement of people from cities to suburbs and from the Frost Belt to the Sun Belt has affected cities and businesses.
22. Describe the actions that the federal government has taken to protect the environment.
23. Describe why the age and ethnic makeup of the U.S. population is important to business.
24. List at least two examples of how values have changed in the United States in the past 20 years. Explain how these changes have affected businesses.
25. List at least two reasons why businesses should be socially responsible.

MAKE CONNECTIONS

26. **Research** Use your school library or the Internet to identify the differences in values between baby boomers, the X Generation, and the Net Generation. Relate these findings to changing business practices. Use examples from your own life.
27. **Math** Use the data from the period 2000–2050 to answer each of the following questions. (a) What is the percentage increase in population for the United States? (b) What is the percentage increase for each ethnic category? (c) Determine the ratio of each ethnic group to the total population in 2000. (d) Determine the ratio of each ethnic group to the total population in 2050.

Population in Millions	2000	2050
TOTAL	282	420
Caucasian (non-Hispanic)	190	210
African-American	36	60
Asian	11	33
Other races	7	14
Hispanic (of any race)	36	103

28. **Technology** Use presentation software such as PowerPoint to show how a variety of communication technology tools can be used to support telecommuting. Use the Internet to find content on how companies use these tools to support business operations.
29. **Speaking** Develop an argument for or against the concept of comparable worth. Include measuring levels of training and responsibility, comparing job value, and how to analyze special skills, physical strength, job dangers, responsibility, and education. Find someone in your class with the opposite view. Debate that person based on your analysis.
30. **Writing** List the CERES Principles. Use your library or the Internet to find articles that show how businesses are reacting to each of these principles. Explain the reasons that businesses are reacting positively or negatively to these principles.

CASE IN POINT

CASE 2-1: Corporate Generosity or Tax Deduction?

Greengrocers, a major food company in the United States, stores packaged foods such as vegetables, fruits, cereal, and meats in its warehouses. The quality of the food in the cans, bottles, and boxes declines over time. Therefore, an expiration date is stamped on each container, after which the product cannot be sold, even though the food is not spoiled and is still edible. Were it not for strict rules laid down by the government, the expiration date could easily be pushed to the future and the food would still be fit for human consumption.

Packages with expired dates are returned to Greengrocers, where they are destroyed. Recently an opportunity appeared for Greengrocers to use the expired food packages. A hurricane had devastated parts of Mexico, leaving people homeless and without food. Greengrocers decided to make a generous donation of free packaged food to the destitute Mexicans, and this was announced with great fanfare. The U.S. military transported the food on one of its relief flights. The donation was reported in the national media, and Greengrocers received favorable publicity as a socially responsible firm stepping in to lessen human misery in the highest tradition of American generosity.

The donated packages, of course, had expired dates. Mexico's laws on selling food products with expired dates were very weak and rarely enforced. Greengrocers' managers assumed that starving people would rather have food with expired dates than no food. In any case, the food was still edible. In addition, Greengrocers could claim a charitable-contribution tax deduction in the United States.

Once the relief flight arrived in Mexico, the donated food was turned over to a relief organization, Save the Children Fund, for distribution to the hungry. As several young American volunteers unpacked the boxes, they noticed that the packages had expired dates. A huge group of starving Mexicans was waiting for the packages and the correspondent of a television network was waiting to broadcast the event in the United States. What was broadcast instead was news about the expired dates on the donated food.

THINK CRITICALLY

1. Because Mexico has weak laws on food dates and the food was still edible, do you think Greengrocers acted in a socially responsible manner? Explain.
2. If you were the president of Greengrocers, how would you explain your conduct now that the details of the donation have been revealed?
3. Do you believe the American volunteers acted ethically when they made an issue of the expiration dates on the food?
4. Suggest some ways by which Greengrocers can discourage unethical conduct by its employees in the future.

CASE 2-2: Tobacco Rights?

Cigarettes are a lawful product in the United States. Many farmers grow tobacco, and big companies such as Philip Morris process the leaves into cigarettes. Thousands of people are employed in the industry, and local, state, and federal governments earn billions of dollars in taxes on the sale of tobacco products.

Although the Surgeon General of the United States has long required that cigarette packages carry a warning stating that smoking is injurious to health, it was only in the 1990s that a concerted campaign was mounted to discourage smoking and to punish tobacco companies. After denying it for decades, senior managers of the tobacco companies admitted that smoking was addictive and dangerous to human health. Lawsuits were filed against the company by state governments that claimed compensation for the extra medical costs that had to be incurred for treating people suffering from smoking-related illnesses. Individuals who had become ill from smoking sued the tobacco firms for seducing them into the habit through aggressive advertising. Groups such as flight attendants claimed that they were subjected to secondhand smoke from passengers and thus needed to be compensated for their suffering. In addition, the government drew up plans to ban advertising of tobacco products and ultimately to ban the product itself.

Faced with such opposition, the tobacco companies agreed to pay the government billions of dollars, reduce their active advertising of the product, and accept stringent laws on how the product would be described and distributed. Philip Morris recognized that the United States was no longer going to be a viable market for its cigarettes. The cost of doing business was only going to rise as individual Americans began filing lawsuits. The company instead turned its attention to countries in Asia, such as China, Thailand, and Turkey. In those countries, health concerns over smoking were not yet fully recognized, and the governments earned lots of money through taxing tobacco products. The quality of locally produced cigarettes was not high, and American cigarettes were highly valued. Through creative advertising, American cigarettes had acquired an image of success, glamour, and independence, all of which made a strong mark on young Asian consumers, a huge market. Philip Morris agreed to build cigarette factories in several foreign countries to create jobs, a move welcomed by their governments. Sales of Philip Morris in foreign countries rose sharply while they stagnated in the United States.

THINK CRITICALLY

1. Is the behavior of Philip Morris to aggressively sell cigarettes abroad socially responsible? Explain.
2. Should the foreign governments be as concerned over tobacco smoking as the American government is?
3. Should individual Americans sue tobacco companies because they smoke, although they have been warned through cigarette labels that smoking is harmful?
4. Should Philip Morris have disclosed to the public that cigarette smoking was addictive as soon as it found out?

SOCIAL RESPONSIBILITY

The way people in a community view a business can often determine whether it will be successful or not. A business owner must consider changes in population, income, attitudes, and values. In this project, you will study the social environment in which your business will operate and the importance of socially responsible and ethical operations to business success.

DATA COLLECTION

1. Collect newspaper and magazine articles or information from the Internet that describe social and environmental changes that could affect your business. Try to identify issues that have national/international implications as well as those that are currently important to your own community.

2. Interview five people of various ages and backgrounds. Ask them to describe their positive and negative feelings about fast-food businesses. Ask them the same questions about the health/fitness industry. Create a table comparing the positive and negative responses for each type of business.

3. Discuss the importance of business ethics with a businessperson. Ask the person to identify the areas of business operations where he or she believes ethics is most important.

4. Contact government agencies in your community to identify local recycling regulations that will affect your business and health laws your business must observe.

ANALYSIS

1. Using information from the Internet or business publications, try to describe the typical customers for health and fitness products. Develop charts that illustrate the information you gathered, including age, gender, education level, ethnicity/race, etc.

2. Develop at least four business operating procedures that show how you will operate in an ethical and socially responsible manner. Examples are use of resources, pollution, product quality, and employment practices. Compose a letter to the city council about these procedures. Explain how you will become involved with the city and how it will benefit from your presence.

3. Analyze the information collected from #2 of the Data Collection activities. What can you do in your business operation to take advantage of the positive factors and overcome the negative factors?

4. Some juice bars add supplements such as vitamins to their juices at an additional charge. These supplements may be unhealthy for some people, and the price charged is very high compared to their cost. Each of these is an ethical dilemma for a business owner. Select either the health dilemma or the pricing dilemma. Complete an analysis, describing both sides of the issue and deciding how you would respond as the business owner.

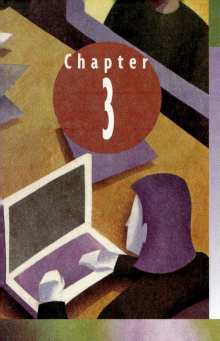

Economic Environment of Business

REALITY CHECK

Hard Work Pays Off

Juan Gonzales grew up in a small Mexican village. His parents were "dirt-poor shopkeepers," as he would often say, but Juan's dad was intent on going to America. And that's what the family did when Juan was 19. They moved to a large village in the state of New Mexico.

Upon arrival his parents bought a small neighborhood grocery store that had a large backyard. Juan entered a technical college where he learned about agricultural methods. One day after graduation his father said, "Join me in running the store, Juan. Maybe together we can expand with this growing neighborhood." Juan smiled and told his dad he would use the large backyard and his new knowledge to experiment with raising and selling vegetables. Within a year, customers from other neighborhoods were stopping by the Gonzaleses' store to buy Juan's fresh produce.

By the second year, the family decided to expand the store and move to a nearby shopping area. Juan's dad had already bought a farm to expand the popular vegetable department and to add a homegrown-fruit department as well. The store would now be called the Gonzales Fruit and Vegetable Market. Within a short time, the store was prospering. Like so many people before them, another family of motivated and hardworking immigrants had succeeded in a country known for its prosperous economic system. The Gonzales family had become an active part of the country's growing economy.

3.1 Economic Wants

Goals
- Describe economic concepts that apply to satisfying economic wants.
- Explain the role of capital formation in an economy.

Terms
- economics
- economic wants
- noneconomic wants
- utility
- producer
- factors of production
- natural resources
- labor
- human capital
- capital goods
- capital formation
- consumer goods and services

All societies face the problem of trying to satisfy the wants of their citizens for goods and services. Although all societies share this problem, different societies developed different systems for producing and using goods and services. The body of knowledge that relates to producing and using goods and services that satisfy human wants is called economics.

At the beginning of this chapter, you will study the concepts that are essential to understanding any economic system. You will then learn about the world's economic systems, along with economic-political systems. The chapter concludes with fundamentals of capitalism and factors related to economic growth.

Satisfying Our Economic Wants

Businesses help to make the economic system work by producing and distributing the particular goods and services that people want. A good place to begin the study of economics is with the two broad categories of wants found throughout an economic system: economic wants and noneconomic wants.

People have many wants. The economic system, however, operates on the basis of economic wants—the desire for scarce material goods and services. People want material goods, such as clothing, housing, and cars. They also want services, such as hair care, medical attention, and public transportation. Items such as these are scarce because no economic system has the resources to satisfy all the wants of all people for all material goods and services. People also have noneconomic wants. Noneconomic wants are desires for nonmaterial things that are not scarce, such as air, sunshine, friendship, and happiness.

The goods and services that people want have to be produced. Clothes must be made. Homes must be built. Personal services must be supplied. And as you learned in the opening scenario, the Gonzales family expects their customers to want fruit, vegetables, and other basic foods.

UTILITY

Utility is the ability of a good or a service to satisfy a want. In other words, a good or a service that has utility is a useful good or service. Something is not useful, however, unless it is available for use in the right form and place and at the right time. As a result, four common types of utility exist: form, place, time, and possession. Definitions of the four types of utility, with examples, appear in Figure 3-1.

Anyone who creates utility is a **producer**. Producers are entitled to a reward for the usefulness that they add to a good or service. Hairstylists are entitled to a reward for the usefulness of their services. The price you pay for a pen includes a reward for the manufacturer who made the pen, the shipping company that delivered it to the merchant, and the retailer who made it possible for you to buy the pen at the time you wanted it.

FACTORS OF PRODUCTION

In creating useful goods and services, a producer uses four basic resources. These resources, called **factors of production**, are land (natural resources), labor, capital goods, and entrepreneurship.

NATURAL RESOURCES The extent to which a country is able to produce goods and services is, in part, determined by the natural resources that its land provides. **Natural resources** are anything provided by nature that affects the productive ability of a country. The productive ability of the United States, for example, depends on its fertile soil, minerals, water and timber resources, and mild climate.

LABOR **Labor** is the human effort, either physical or mental, that goes into the production of goods and services. In today's world of technology and special equipment such as computers, physical effort is much less important than mental effort—knowing what tasks to complete and how to complete them. A part of labor is **human capital**, the accumulated knowledge and skills of human beings—the total value of each person's education and acquired skills. In a highly

---

FIGURE 3-1 Satisfying wants involves four common types of utility.

Types of Economic Utility

FORM UTILITY

Created by changes in the form or shape of a product to make it useful.
(Form utility usually applies only to goods and not to services.)
Example: Is the swimsuit you desire to buy available in a particular fabric and style?

PLACE UTILITY

Created by having a good or service at the place where it is needed or wanted.
Example: Is the swimsuit you desire available in a nearby store where it can be purchased?

TIME UTILITY

Created when a product or service is available when it is needed or wanted.
Example: Is the store open when you are ready to buy and use your swimsuit?

POSSESSION UTILITY

Created when ownership of a good or service is transferred from one person to another, but may also occur through renting and borrowing. Example: Is the swimsuit available at a price you can afford and are willing to pay?

technological world, the need for human capital has increased significantly. Juan's expertise at growing fruit and vegetables and his father's knowledge and skill needed to operate a store are examples of labor and human capital.

CAPITAL GOODS To produce goods that people want, producers need capital goods. **Capital goods** are buildings, tools, machines, and other equipment that are used to produce other goods but do not directly satisfy human wants. A robot on a car assembly line is an example of a capital good. The robot does not directly satisfy human wants. Instead, it helps make the cars that do satisfy human wants. Capital goods allow the production of goods in large quantities which, in turn, should decrease production costs and increase the productivity of labor.

ENTREPRENEURSHIP For the production of goods, more is needed than the mere availability of natural resources, labor, and capital goods. Someone, or some group, must take the risks involved in starting a business and plan and manage the production of the final product. Entrepreneurship, the fourth factor of production, brings together the other three factors—land (natural resources), labor, and capital. By starting and managing a business, Juan and his father are acting as entrepreneurs. You will learn more about the many aspects of management in Unit 4.

Because government provides many services that are essential to the operation of a business, economists often list it as a fifth factor of production. Some of the essential services provided by government are streets and highways, police and fire protection, and courts that settle disputes.

CHECKPOINT
What are the four basic resources used by a producer?

Capital Formation

The production of capital goods is called **capital formation**. Capital goods, such as buildings and equipment, are needed to produce consumer goods and services. The Ford truck that Juan uses to deliver farm products to the store is a capital good. Unlike capital goods, **consumer goods and services** are goods and services that directly satisfy people's economic wants. The foods that Juan's father sells customers are consumer goods.

A country is capable of producing a fixed quantity of goods and services at any one time. As a result, total production is divided between capital goods and consumer goods and services. When the production of consumer goods and services increases, the production of capital goods decreases. On the other hand, when the production of consumer goods and services decreases, the production of capital goods increases. New capital goods must be made—capital formation—in order to add to the total supply and to replace worn-out capital goods. Capital formation takes place, for example, when steel is used to produce the tools and machinery (capital goods) needed to make cars rather than to produce the cars themselves (consumer goods).

When productive resources are used for capital formation, it becomes possible to produce more consumer goods. For example, when robots and other tools and

Success *tip*
Many people are much happier working for themselves than they are working for others. Entrepreneurs do work for themselves, but successful entrepreneurs must know how to work with others. They must be able to form partnerships, work with employees, and work with customers. Entrepreneurs must develop strong interpersonal skills.

machinery are produced for making trucks, it is then possible to increase the production of trucks.

However, using steel, labor, and management to produce tools and machinery (capital goods) means that these same resources cannot also be used for automobiles (consumer goods). The immediate result is that consumers have fewer automobiles to buy. But, because the tools and machinery were made, consumers will have more automobiles to buy in the future. China and other developing countries are examples of nations that use a large portion of their productive resources in capital formation rather than in the production of consumer goods and services. Developing nations must take this first step before they can satisfy consumers with consumer products.

CHECKPOINT

Create a list of capital goods and a list of consumer goods.

3.1 Assessment

UNDERSTAND MANAGEMENT CONCEPTS

Circle the best answer for each of the following questions.

1. The body of knowledge that relates to producing and using goods and services that satisfy human wants is called
   a. needs analysis
   b. marketing
   c. economics
   d. none of the above
2. The ability of a good or a service to satisfy a want is called
   a. economizing wants
   b. utility
   c. production
   d. benefiting

THINK CRITICALLY

Answer the following questions as completely as possible.

3. What are the four most common types of utility?
4. What is the difference between capital goods and consumer goods?

Xtra!
Study Tools
thomsonedu.com/school/bpmxtra

3.2 Economic Systems

Goals
- Discuss three economic systems and three economic-political systems.
- Explain why a business considers the economic-political system of a country.

Terms
- economic system
- market economy
- command economy
- mixed economy
- privatization
- capitalism
- socialism
- communism

Remember that no country has enough resources to satisfy all the wants of all people for material goods and services. Because productive resources are scarce, difficult decisions must be made about how to use these limited resources. For example, somehow countries must decide whether to produce more capital goods and fewer consumer goods or more consumer goods and fewer capital goods.

Ethics *tip*

Economists play an important role in regulating the economy. They help identify companies who engage in monopolistic practices (limiting supply) or illegal pricing strategies to drive out competition. As economic watchdogs, they help ensure ethical behavior.

Economic Systems

All countries have an economic system. An **economic system** is an organized way for a country to decide how to use its productive resources; that is, to decide what, how, and for whom goods and services will be produced. While there are many countries in the world, all economies operate under some form of three basic economic systems, described below.

TYPES OF ECONOMIC SYSTEMS

The primary types of economic systems are a market economy, a command economy, and a mixed economy. All countries' economic systems have characteristics of these basic three types.

A **market economy** is an economic system in which individual buying decisions in the marketplace together determine what, how, and for whom goods and services will be produced. For example, if more consumers choose to buy whole-grain bread than white bread, their buying decisions will influence bread producers to use their productive resources to produce more whole-grain and less white bread. Thus, individual consumers, making their own decisions about what to buy, collectively determine how the society's productive resources will be used. In a market economy, individual citizens, rather than the government, own most of the factors of production, such as land and manufacturing facilities. The free-enterprise system found in the United States is the best example of a market economy.

A **command economy** is an economic system in which a central planning authority, under the control of the country's government, owns most of the factors of production and determines what, how, and for whom goods and services will be produced. Countries that adopt a command economy are often dictatorships. The government, rather than consumers, decides how the factors of production will be used. Forms of command economies exist in some Asian countries—North Korea, Cambodia, and Vietnam—and in other small countries, such as Cuba.

Each nation decides whether to have a market, command, or mixed economic system. These same nations may change economic systems from time to time. Can you name any countries that have changed their economic systems in recent years?

PHOTO: © GETTY IMAGES/PHOTODISC.

facts & figures

In general, communist countries that try to move toward capitalism face both political and economic problems in the short run, as Russia and China are now experiencing. The process of transition is difficult because the economic and social infrastructure needed for a market economy is not in place. For example, in the command economy of the Soviet Union, the government directed what was to be done and there essentially was no legal system governing contracts.

A **mixed economy** is an economic system that uses aspects of a market and a command economy to make decisions about what, how, and for whom goods and services will be produced. In a mixed economy, the national government makes production decisions for certain goods and services. For example, the post office, telephone system, schools, health care facilities, and public utilities are often owned and operated by governments.

No country has a pure market economy or command economy. All have mixed economies, although some have more elements of a market economy and others have more elements of a command economy. In the United States and Canada, for example, the government plays a smaller role in the economy than it does in the more command-oriented economies of Cuba and North Korea. Even countries of the former Soviet Union, once a predominantly command economy, now allow some privately owned businesses to operate freely and make their own economic decisions, such as what to offer for sale and at what prices. China and Iran do as well.

Today most countries are moving more toward market economies. For example, England, France, Sweden, Mexico, and Eastern European countries have restricted the number of goods and services owned and controlled by national governments. China also has been making major attempts to move more toward a market economy.

Privatization is the transfer of authority to provide a good or service from a government to individuals or privately owned businesses. Some governments of former Soviet countries have sold telephone and transportation services to private firms. Some states and cities in these countries have privatized by paying businesses to operate jails, collect trash, run cafeterias in government buildings, and perform data-processing activities. The governments' incentive is to reduce costs for taxpayers and to increase efficiency.

CHECKPOINT

Explain how a market economy differs from a command economy.

Types of Economic-Political Systems

Each country has an economic system and a political system. The political system nearly always determines the economic system. Because the two systems cannot be separated, we refer to them as an economic-political system.

The importance of the individual citizen has always been emphasized in the United States. Therefore, the United States developed an economic-political system that permits a great deal of individual freedom. History tells us that there is a relationship between political and economic freedom; that is, political freedom usually is found in countries where individuals and businesses have economic freedom. And political freedom is quite limited in countries that do not give people and organizations much economic freedom.

All economic-political systems are forms of three basic types: capitalism, socialism, and communism. As you read about these three economic-political systems, compare their features as shown in Figure 3-2.

FIGURE 3-2 Three main economic-political systems exist throughout the world.

Comparison of Economic-Political Systems

	CAPITALISM	SOCIALISM	COMMUNISM
	Market/ Mixed Economy	Mixed Economy	Command/ Mixed Economy
Who may own natural resources and capital goods?	Businesses and individuals	Government for some, but not all	Government for most
How are resources allocated?	By customers based on competition	By government for some and customers for others	By government only
To what extent does government attempt to control business decisions?	Limited	Extensive over the allocation of some resources, but little over distribution	Extensive
How are marketing decisions made?	By market conditions	By market conditions	By government
What one country is a good example of this economic system?	United States	Sweden	North Korea

CAPITALISM

The economic-political system in the United States is called capitalism, or the free-enterprise system, which operates in a democracy. Capitalism is an economic-political system in which private citizens are free to go into business for themselves, to produce whatever they choose to produce, and to distribute what they produce. Also included is the right to own property.

This strict definition of capitalism would have accurately described our economic system during much of the 19th century and the early part of the 20th century. In recent decades, however, government has assumed an important economic role in the United States. As the economy developed without controls by government, certain abuses took place. For example, some people began to interfere with the economic freedom of others. Some large businesses began to exploit small businesses. In addition, manufacturing firms did not take into account the cost of pollution. In essence, these costs were passed on to the public. For example, assume a firm produced a new type of pesticide and sold it to farmers and gardeners. Several years after some pesticide had washed into streams and lakes, it was found to kill fish and harm swimmers. Neither the producer nor the buyers of the pesticide were required to pay for damages. The public ultimately pays in the form of poor health and medical costs as well as in the inability to safely swim in lakes and other bodies of water. To protect the public and to correct such abuses, Congress passed laws, many of which require producers to avoid harm to the public or reduce the costs to the public of the producers' operations.

SOCIALISM

Socialism is an economic-political system in which the government controls the use of the country's factors of production. How scarce resources are used to satisfy the many wants of people is decided, in part, by the government.

Socialists do not agree as to how much of the productive resources government should own. The most extreme socialists want government to own all natural resources and capital goods. Middle-of-the-road socialists believe that planning production for the whole economy can be achieved if government owns certain key industries, but they also believe that other productive resources should be owned by individuals and businesses. As a result, socialism is often associated with mixed economies.

Socialism is generally disliked in the United States because it limits the right of the individual to own property for productive purposes. The right to own property, however, exists in socialistic economies in different degrees, depending upon the amount of government ownership and control. Socialism in its different forms exists in many countries, particularly in the Western European countries of Sweden and France.

COMMUNISM

Communism is extreme socialism, in which all or almost all of a nation's factors of production are owned by the government. Decisions regarding what to produce, how much to produce, and how to divide the results of production among the citizens are made by government agencies on the basis of a government plan. Government measures how well producers perform on the basis of volume of goods and services produced, without much regard for the quality of or demand for the goods or services. A command economy is most often practiced by communist countries.

Consumer goods are often in short supply in communist countries such as Cuba and North Korea, because the government channels a large proportion of the factors of production toward capital formation. Even Chinese leaders have recognized the shortcomings of the system when it comes to meeting the needs of consumers. As a result, they are making adjustments that introduce market economy principles. Two such adjustments are judging the performance of producers by the demand for their products and permitting consumer demand to influence production.

Workers in a communist system cannot move easily from one job to another. And managers of businesses do not decide what is to be produced. A communist country's central planning agency makes most such decisions. Capitalism relies, instead, on consumers and managers to make these decisions. People in a pure communist society do not own property. All economic decisions are made by government leaders. These leaders decide how scarce resources will be used. The members of a communist country have few of the economic freedoms that Americans believe are important.

CHECKPOINT

List three types of economic-political systems.

3.2 Assessment

UNDERSTAND MANAGEMENT CONCEPTS

Circle the best answer for each of the following questions.

1. An organized way for a country to decide how to use its productive resources is called a(n)
   a. economic system
   b. political system
   c. economic-political system
   d. political economy

2. Jax lives in a country where only individual buying decisions in the marketplace determine what, how, and for whom goods and services will be produced. Jax lives in a country that has primarily a
   a. market economy
   b. command economy
   c. socialist economy
   d. none of the above

THINK CRITICALLY

Answer the following questions as completely as possible.

3. Describe why most countries can be seen as having a mixed economy.

4. Describe the goals of privatizing government services.

Xtra!
Study Tools
thomsonedu.com/school/bpmxtra

3.3 Fundamentals of Capitalism

Goals
- Describe why private property is important to capitalism.
- Describe how prices are set in a capitalistic system.

Terms
- private property
- profit
- demand
- supply
- competition

Some economic-political systems either do not permit ownership of property (communism) or may impose limitations on ownership (socialism). One of the basic features of capitalism is the right to private property, a right reserved to the people by the Constitution. Other features include the right of each business to make a profit, to set its own prices, to compete, and to determine the wages paid to workers.

Private Property

The principle of **private property** is essential to our capitalistic system. Private property consists of items of value that individuals have the right to own, use, and sell. Thus, individuals can control productive resources. They can own land, hire labor, and own capital goods. They can use these resources to produce goods and services. Also, individuals own the products made from their use of land, labor, and capital goods. Thus, the company that produces furniture owns the furniture it makes. The furniture company may sell its furniture, and it owns the money received from the buyer. The Gonzales family owns its store, the farm it purchased, and the food it produces and buys before selling it. And the family is entitled to make and keep its profits.

PROFIT

In a capitalist system, the incentive as well as the reward for producing goods and services is **profit**, which is computed by subtracting the total costs of producing the products from the total received from customers who buy them. The company making furniture, for example, has costs for land, labor, capital goods, and materials. Profit is what the furniture company has left after subtracting these costs from the amount received from selling its furniture.

The profit earned by a business is often overestimated by society. The average profit is about 5 percent of total receipts while the remainder, 95 percent, represents costs. Consider a motel with yearly receipts of $500,000. If the profit amounts to 5 percent, then the owner earns $25,000; that is, $500,000 times 0.05. Costs for the year are 0.95 times $500,000, or $475,000. Some types of businesses have higher average profit percentages, but many have lower ones or even losses. Owners, of course, try to earn a profit percentage that is better than average.

One of the basic features of capitalism is the right to private property. How is property ownership handled in socialist and communist systems?

PHOTO: © GETTY IMAGES/PHOTODISC.

Being in business does not guarantee that a company will make a profit. Among other things, to be successful a company must produce goods or services that people want at a price they are willing to pay. Other fundamental features of capitalism covered next deal with competition and the distribution of income.

CHECKPOINT

Explain why private property is essential to a capitalistic system.

Price Setting

Demand for a product refers to the number of products that will be bought at a given time at a given price. Thus, demand is not the same as want. Wanting an expensive luxury car without having the money to buy one does not represent demand. Demand for a Mercedes Benz is represented by the people who want it, have the money to buy it, and are willing to spend the money for it.

There is a relationship between price and demand. With increased demand, prices generally rise in the short run. Later, when demand decreases, prices generally fall. For example, if a new large-screen TV suddenly becomes popular, its price may rise. However, when the TV is no longer in high demand, its price will likely drop.

business *note*

Microsoft Corporation recently announced an initiative to use a sell/lease strategy to put computers in the hands of poor people around the world. The system would work like pay-for-minutes cell phones. Individuals would buy a computer at a reduced price and then pay for usage over time. Microsoft has two goals with this strategy. One is to increase the overall sales of Microsoft software. The other goal is economic development. Putting computers into the hands of billions of people around the world can increase their education and productivity.

facts & figures

Economic math concepts may seem abstract, but they have very concrete uses in business decision making. The concept of supply and demand is very important in understanding economic events and developing business strategies. For example, in 2006 the price for oil and gasoline grew very high. This was due to shifts in both supply and demand. Businesses needed to decide future energy strategies based on projected changes in supply and demand. They needed to determine if prices would go up or go down.

The supply of a product also influences its price. **Supply** of a product refers to the number of like products that will be offered for sale at a particular time and at a certain price. If there is a current shortage in the supply of a product, its price will usually rise as consumers bid against one another to obtain the product. For example, if bad weather damages an apple crop and apples are in short supply, the price of apples will go up. When apples become more abundant, their price will go down. Thus, price changes are the result of changes in both the demand for and the supply of a product.

Generally, changes in prices determine what is produced and how much is produced in our economy. Price changes indicate to businesses what is profitable or not profitable to produce. If consumers want more sports shoes than are being produced, they will bid up the price of sports shoes. The increase in the price of the shoes makes it more profitable to make them and provides the incentive for manufacturers to increase the production of sports shoes. As the supply of the shoes increases to satisfy the demand for more shoes, the price of the shoes will fall. Because it is now less profitable to make sports shoes, manufacturers will decrease their production of them.

Prices, then, are determined by the forces of supply and demand; that is, prices are the result of the decisions of individual consumers to buy products and of individual producers to make and sell products. Therefore, consumers help decide what will be produced and how much will be produced.

Here is how supply and demand work in setting prices. Refer to Figure 3-3 as you study this example of a producer planning to sell a sweatshirt. In Figure 3-3, the market price for the sweatshirt, $30, is shown where the supply line crosses the demand line. The market price is the price at which the producer can meet costs

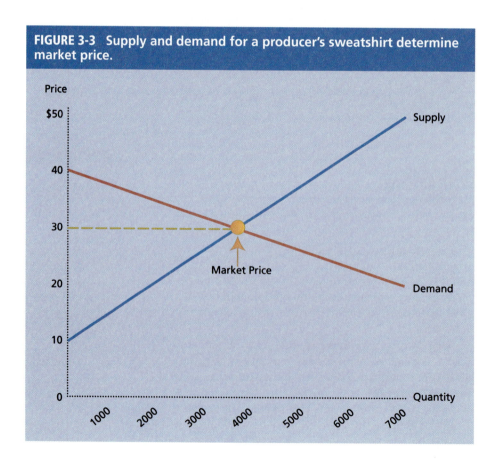

FIGURE 3-3 Supply and demand for a producer's sweatshirt determine market price.

PHOTO: © GETTY IMAGES/PHOTODISC.

Prices for many products and services are determined by the forces of supply and demand. What causes the price of gasoline to change from time to time?

and make a reasonable profit. It is also the price at which consumers will buy enough of the product for the producer to make a reasonable profit.

If demand drops, profit drops; but if demand increases, the producer's profits will increase. If the profit gets quite large, other producers will enter into production with similar sweatshirts, which will then increase the total supply and lower the price. If the supply and demand lines never cross, the producer will not make the goods, because not enough consumers will want the product at the offered price and the profit reward disappears. If Juan Gonzales grows a new type of apple but only a small number of people buy them, he will lose money and stop growing those apples.

COMPETITION

In our free-enterprise system, sellers try to make a profit and buyers try to buy quality goods at the lowest possible prices. This conflict of interest between buyers and sellers is settled to the benefit of society by competition. **Competition** is the rivalry among sellers for consumers' dollars.

Competition in a free-enterprise system benefits society in many ways. To attract customers away from other sellers, a business must improve the quality of its products, develop new products, and operate efficiently in order to keep its prices down. Thus, competition serves to ensure that consumers will get the quality products they want at fair prices. In addition to benefiting consumers, competition benefits the country because it tends to make all businesses use our scarce productive resources efficiently. If a firm does not operate efficiently, it will fail because customers will buy lower-priced or higher-quality products from a firm that is operating efficiently. Often these competing firms are from foreign countries. Competition in our economic system also provides the chance for people to go into business for themselves and to share in the profits being made by those already in business.

One aspect of competition is price competition. Price competition occurs when a firm takes business away from its competitors by lowering prices for identical goods. Today, however, more and more competition takes place in the form of nonprice competition. For example, a company attracts customers away from other sellers by providing products of better quality or by adding features to the product that competitors do not have. Or a company may attract customers away from competitors with unusual and colorful product packaging. Another company may conduct an extensive advertising campaign to convince the public that its product is better than all other brands. All these are effective devices used in nonprice competition.

Competition is the opposite of monopoly. Monopoly is the existence of only one seller of a product. With no competition, a monopolist can charge unreasonably high prices and make extraordinary profits. For example, if a seller does not have to compete with other sellers for consumer dollars, it can usually increase profit by raising the price. Consumers have no choice. If they want that product, they must pay whatever price the monopolist sets. As you will learn in Chapter 7, legislation exists that encourages competition and discourages monopolistic practices.

INCOME DISTRIBUTION

Not only must all countries decide how scarce productive resources are to be used, but they must also decide how the goods produced will be divided among the people in the society. In a free-enterprise economy, the share of goods produced that an individual receives is determined by the amount of money that person has to purchase goods and services.

People receive income—wages and salaries—by contributing their labor to the production of goods and services. People also receive income as interest on money that they lend to others, as rent for land or buildings that they own, and as profit if they are owners of businesses.

The amount of money an individual receives in wages or salary is determined by many factors, including personal traits and abilities. The same factors that

How do supply and demand affect the wages or salaries in the types of business you are most interested in?

PHOTO: © GETTY IMAGES/PHOTODISC.

determine the prices of goods are also important factors in determining wages and salaries; that is, the amount of wages paid for a particular kind of labor is affected by the supply of and demand for that kind of labor. The demand is low and the supply is high for unskilled workers. Thus, the price (income) of unskilled workers is low. On the other hand, the demand for brain surgeons is high in terms of the supply of brain surgeons and the services they provide; therefore, their price (income) is high.

CHECKPOINT

What special feature of a free-enterprise system helps keep the prices of goods and services down?

3.3 Assessment

UNDERSTAND MANAGEMENT CONCEPTS

Circle the best answer for each of the following questions.

1. Items of value that individuals have the right to own, use, and sell are known as
   a. public goods
   b. product utility
   c. private property
   d. all of the above
2. The number of products that will be bought at a given time at a given price is called
   a. supply
   b. demand
   c. price
   d. quantity

THINK CRITICALLY

Answer the following questions as completely as possible.

3. Explain how the overestimation of profits earned by a business can affect a society.
4. Explain how supply and demand help determine the price of goods and services.

Xtra! Study Tools
thomsonedu.com/school/bpmxtra

Focus On...

Global Perspectives–India's Changing Economy

India's population numbers around 1 billion, and about 40 percent are under 25 years of age. By the year 2015, about 55 percent will be in this same age group. Although the national average income per person is only $450, this youth group will shift the old India to a new India for themselves, their families, and their country. As a dominantly socialist country, India is moving toward capitalism as the young open new businesses and modify how business is conducted. How? The answer is the electronic age.

Computers and the Internet are already quickly modifying the culture of India. Unlike their parents, children are buying computers, cellular phones, and other electronic gear. They are mingling among the world's citizens through television and the Internet. New technological devices make it easy for them to communicate with relatives and friends and to chat with people from other lands. It is not uncommon for India's youth to buy cellular phones and charge fees to villagers without phones who wish to make calls, such as to distant family members. The money these entrepreneurs make often provides income for their families and allows them to stay closer to home rather than leave for one of the large, crowded cities. This helps to provide a better life for millions of village people. Most youth feel a strong pride in their country and are helping families improve their standard of living.

Computers are a primary tool enabling India's youth to become a powerful force in producing rapid economic advances. The youth attend computer schools and have a strong desire to start and run their own Internet-type firms. They also admire young people from other countries who have started their own computer companies, such as Bill Gates of Microsoft Corporation. They are profit motivated while at the same time respecting their cultural traditions. Much to the surprise of their elders, young women are also using computers, starting businesses, and shedding or modifying past cultural practices that are honored by their parents. For these reasons, many adults are both concerned about and proud of their children. India's youth are in the process of changing India's view of itself to the rest of the world.

Think Critically

1. If India has 1 billion people now, how many people are now under 40 years of age? If by the year 2015 the population is 1.2 billion, how many people will be under 25 years of age?
2. From your knowledge of economic-political systems, what key factors probably exist in India that make it currently a socialist country?
3. How will India's youth contribute to making the country more capitalistic than it currently is?
4. From the library or the Internet, find out more about the general nature of the country. Such information can be found in an up-to-date encyclopedia in print or online, such as at www.encarta.msn.com/.

3.4 | Managing the Economy

Goals
- Explain how economic growth can be promoted and measured.
- List basic economic problems that exist and state what government can do to correct the problems.

Terms
- economic growth
- consumer price index (CPI)
- recession
- inflation
- business cycles
- depression

The strength of a nation depends upon its economic growth. Economic growth is measured by an annual increase in the gross domestic product, increased employment opportunities, and the continuous development of new and improved goods and services. However, growth cannot always be at the most desired rate. As you will soon learn, when the economy grows too fast or too slow, businesses and consumers suffer. Of concern to everyone is the promotion and measurement of such growth along with the identification and control of growth problems.

Promoting Economic Growth

Economic growth occurs when a country's output exceeds its population growth. As a result, more goods and services are available for each person. Growth has occurred and must continue if a nation is to remain economically strong.

The following are basic ways to increase the production of goods and services in order to encourage economic growth:

1. Increase the number of people in the workforce.
2. Increase the productivity of the workforce by improving human capital through education and job training.
3. Increase the supply of capital goods, such as more tools and machines, in order to increase production and sales.
4. Improve technology by inventing new and better machines and better methods for producing goods and services.
5. Redesign work processes in factories and offices to improve efficiency.
6. Increase the sale of goods and services to foreign countries.
7. Decrease the purchase of goods and services from foreign countries.

For economic growth to occur, more is required than just increasing the production of goods and services. More goods and services must also be consumed. The incentive for producing goods and services in a free-enterprise economy is profit. If the goods and services produced are in demand and are profitable, business has the incentive to increase production.

Economic growth is basic to a healthy economy. Through such growth more and better products become available, such as a new drug that cures a disease, a battery that runs a small computer for months, and fuel-efficient cars. More and better services also become available, such as those provided by hospitals, travel agencies, and banks. But more important, economic growth is needed to provide jobs for those who wish to work.

facts & figures

The Great Depression of the 1930s resulted in tremendous economic difficulties around the world. In the United States, the prices of stock fell 40 percent; 9,000 banks went out of business; 9 million savings accounts were wiped out; 86,000 businesses failed; and wages were decreased by an average of 60 percent. The unemployment rate went from 9 percent to 25 percent—about 15 million jobless people.

MEASURING ECONOMIC GROWTH

To know whether the economy is growing at a desirable rate, statistics must be gathered. The federal government collects vast amounts of information and uses a variety of figures to keep track of the economy. The gross domestic product (GDP) that was discussed in Chapter 1 is an extremely valuable statistic. Another is the Consumer Price Index.

The **Consumer Price Index (CPI)** indicates what is happening in general to prices in the country. It is a measure of the average change in prices of consumer goods and services typically purchased by people living in urban areas. To calculate the CPI, the government tracks price changes for hundreds of items, including food, gasoline, housing, and even cellular phones. With the CPI, comparisons can be made in the cost of living from month to month or from year to year, as shown in Figure 3-4.

Some commonly used indicators for tracking the economy are shown in Figure 3-5. Government economists and business leaders examine the CPI, GDP, and other statistics each month to evaluate the condition of the economy. If the growth rate appears to be undesirable, the government can take corrective action.

CHECKPOINT

List the basic ways of encouraging economic growth.

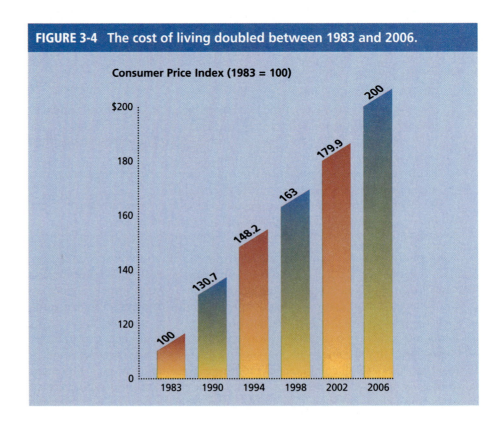

FIGURE 3-4 The cost of living doubled between 1983 and 2006.

Consumer Price Index (1983 = 100)

Year	CPI
1983	100
1990	130.7
1994	148.2
1998	163
2002	179.9
2006	200

FIGURE 3-5 The federal government issues many statistics each year to help determine whether the economy is growing or declining

A Sample of Major Economic Reports Released Regularly by the U.S. Government

GROSS DOMESTIC PRODUCT

Measures the total goods and services produced. Released quarterly by the Commerce Department.

CONSUMER PRICE INDEX

Measures inflation at the retail level. Released monthly by the Department of Labor.

INDEX OF LEADING ECONOMIC INDICATORS

Measures the economy's strength for the next six to nine months using a variety of forward-looking indicators. Released monthly by the Commerce Department.

EMPLOYMENT

Measures the jobless rate and the number of jobs available. Released monthly by the Department of Labor.

RETAIL SALES

Measures consumer spending. Released monthly by the Commerce Department.

PERSONAL INCOME CONSUMPTION

Measures growth in personal income and consumer spending. Released monthly by the Commerce Department.

Identifying Economic Problems

Problems occur with the economy when the growth rate jumps ahead or drops back too quickly. One problem that occurs is a recession, which is a decline in the GDP that continues for six months or more. A recession occurs when demand for the total goods and services available is less than the supply. Sales drop, production of goods and services declines, and unemployment occurs during recessions. In most recessions, the rate of increase in prices is reduced greatly, and in some cases prices may actually decline slightly.

Another problem arises when consumers want to buy goods and services that are not readily available. As revealed in the Consumer Price Index, this increased demand causes prices for existing goods and services to rise. Inflation is the rapid rise in prices caused by an inadequate supply of goods and services. In other words, total demand exceeds supply. Inflation results in a decline in the purchasing power of money; that is, a dollar does not buy as much as it did before inflation. Retired people and those with fixed incomes are financially hurt the most, because their incomes don't increase fast enough to keep up with rising prices. Therefore, their buying power decreases faster during inflation than does the buying power of workers who receive raises from their employers. The effect of inflation on the purchasing power of the dollar is shown in Figure 3-6 (see p. 72).

FIGURE 3-6 Purchasing power is inversely related to CPI. Inflation has reduced the purchasing power of a dollar over time.

Source: *Statistical Abstract of the United States, 2006*

What are some of the indicators that an economy may be heading for a recession?

CORRECTING ECONOMIC PROBLEMS

Most industrialized nations experience <mark>business cycles</mark>, a pattern of irregular but repeated expansion and contraction of the GDP. Business cycles, on average, last about five years and pass through four phases, as shown in Figure 3-7. These four phases—expansion, peak, contraction, and trough—can vary in length and in intensity, with many lasting only a few years. Some, however, can be severe. When statistics show that the economy may be about to enter a recessionary period (a contraction) or an inflationary period (an expansion), the government can take certain actions. Several specific devices used include controlling taxes, regulating government expenditures, and adjusting interest rates.

One way to control economic growth is to raise or lower taxes. Taxes are raised to slow growth and lowered to encourage growth. When taxes are raised, there is less money to spend, which discourages economic growth. When taxes are lowered, people and businesses have more money to spend, which encourages economic growth.

PHOTO: © GETTY IMAGES/PHOTODISC.

FIGURE 3-7 Business cycles are irregular in length and in severity.

Business Cycle Phases

PHASE	EXPLANATION	POPULAR NAME
Expansion		Low inflation
	Modest rise in GDP, profits, and employment	
Peak		Modest to runaway inflation
	Growth reaches its highest level, as do profit and employment	
Contraction		Modest inflation
	Growth begins to decline, as does employment	
Trough		No growth, recession, or depression
	Lowest point in the cycle, with increased unemployment	

Government expenditures also influence economic growth. The federal government operates by spending billions of dollars each year to pay salaries and to buy equipment. Government can increase its spending to stimulate a slow economy or reduce spending to slow economic growth.

In addition, economic growth is regulated through interest rates, the money paid to borrow money. Borrowing by businesses and consumers generates spending. Spending stimulates economic growth. When interest rates are lowered, businesses are encouraged to borrow. This stimulates business activity and, in turn, the economy. When interest rates are raised to discourage borrowing, a slowdown occurs.

Through interest rates, government spending, taxes, and other devices, the rate of economic growth can be controlled somewhat. Control, however, is usually kept to a minimum in a free-enterprise system. Furthermore, in a complex economic system the results of such controls are not always clearly visible in the short run. Economists do not always know exactly when control devices should be used, for how long they should be applied, or how effective they may be. Although the nature of controls can be debated, some control is needed to prevent a destructive runaway inflationary period or a **depression**—a long and severe drop in the

NETBookmark

Many industry trade organizations try to maintain demand for their products. They do this by creating advertising to influence consumer consumption and lobbying governments to influence trade policies. Point your browser to www.thomsonedu.com/school/bpmxtra. Visit the National Cattlemen's Beef Association Web site. Explain how cattlemen's industry groups help to maintain demand for beef. Consider the impact on both consumer demand and government actions. Explain how high demand affects the price of beef. Visit another product trade organization's Web site (such as that for milk, orange juice, or another common product). Explain what actions they are taking to increase the demand for their products.

www.thomsonedu.com/school/bpmxtra

GDP. Such conditions affect not only U.S. citizens but also the economic climate of foreign countries.

Because most nations engage in international trade and because of the impact of global competition on nations, a major recession or depression in one country usually impacts negatively on other countries. For example, during the first half of the 1990s the United States experienced a period of recession and slow growth. Japan, Germany, France, England, and other major nations also faced similar circumstances shortly thereafter. Economic aspects of international trade will be discussed in the next chapter.

CHECKPOINT

Describe the two problems that occur when the economic growth rate jumps ahead or drops back too quickly.

3.4 Assessment

UNDERSTAND MANAGEMENT CONCEPTS

Circle the best answer for each of the following questions.

1. Which of the following are basic ways to increase the production of goods and services in order to encourage economic growth?
   a. Increase the number of people in the workforce.
   b. Decrease the purchase of goods and services from foreign countries.
   c. Improve technology by inventing new and better machines.
   d. All are ways to increase the production of goods and services.

2. A(n) _____ occurs when demand for the total goods and services available is less than the supply.
   a. inflation
   b. recession
   c. depression
   d. business cycle

THINK CRITICALLY

Answer the following questions as completely as possible.

3. Explain the three problems that can occur within an economy when the growth rate is too fast or too slow.

4. Explain how an economic system can control its business cycles.

CHAPTER CONCEPTS

- To produce goods and services, businesses use land (natural resources), labor, capital goods, and entrepreneurship. Because a nation does not have enough resources to satisfy everyone's wants, it must decide what goods or services will be produced, how they will be produced, and who will get them.

- There are three basic economic systems. A market economy in a capitalistic society makes decisions through the forces of supply and demand. In a command economy, generally in a communist society, government makes these decisions. A mixed system has characteristics of both market and command economies.

- Capitalism is founded on basic principles: the right of individuals and businesses to own private property and produce goods and services; compete with other producers, set prices, and earn a profit; and buy whatever goods or services they like.

- In all political-economic systems, governments reserve the right to control unfair competition and to correct undesirable inflation and recession problems that occur in business cycles.

REVIEW TERMS AND CONCEPTS

Write the letter of the term that matches each definition. Some terms will not be used.

1. Economic-political system in which the government controls the use of the country's factors of production
2. Human effort, either physical or mental, that goes into the production of goods and services
3. Anything provided by nature that affects the productive ability of a country
4. Rapid rise in prices caused by an inadequate supply of goods and services
5. Transfer of authority to provide a good or service from a government to individuals or privately owned businesses
6. Items of value that individuals have the right to own, use, and sell
7. Decline in the GDP that continues for six months or more
8. Ability of a good or a service to satisfy a want
9. Number of like products that will be offered for sale at a particular time and at a certain price
10. Desire for scarce material goods and services
11. Pattern of irregular but repeated expansion and contraction of the GDP
12. Buildings, tools, machines, and other equipment that are used to produce other goods but do not directly satisfy human wants

a. business cycles
b. capital goods
c. capitalism
d. command economy
e. communism
f. demand
g. depression
h. economic wants
i. human capital
j. inflation
k. labor
l. mixed economy
m. natural resources
n. private property
o. privatization
p. recession
q. socialism
r. supply
s. utility

DETERMINE THE BEST ANSWER

13. The free-enterprise system, which operates in a democracy, is called
    a. capitalism
    b. communism
    c. socialism
    d. free market

14. The average change in prices of consumer goods and services typically purchased by people living in urban areas is known as the
    a. Capital Price Index
    b. Consumer Price Index
    c. National Price Index
    d. Product Price Index

15. When a country's output exceeds its population growth it will have
    a. inflation
    b. economic growth
    c. a recession
    d. none of the above

16. Factors of production include
    a. money only
    b. labor and capital goods only
    c. land (natural resources), labor, and capital goods only
    d. land (natural resources), labor, capital goods, and entrepreneurship

17. Which of the following is true about labor in today's world?
    a. Low-cost labor is the key to U.S. competitiveness.
    b. Physical effort is much less important than mental effort.
    c. Computers will be able to take the place of mental effort.
    d. All of the above are true.

18. The accumulated knowledge and skills of human beings and the total value of each person's education and acquired skills are called
    a. human capital
    b. human potential
    c. human knowledge
    d. human labor

19. An economic system that uses aspects of a market economy and a command economy to make decisions about what, how, and for whom goods and services will be produced is called a(n)
    a. average economy
    b. market economy
    c. mixed economy
    d. socialist economy

20. People have
    a. economic wants
    b. noneconomic wants
    c. both economic and noneconomic wants
    d. no wants

APPLY WHAT YOU KNOW

21. Describe how an economic want differs from a noneconomic want. Give an example of each.
22. Compare capitalism, socialism, and communism as to (a) how each allocates scarce resources among alternative wants and (b) the existence of private property.
23. Describe how form, place, and time utility apply to a small pizza business that just opened in your community.
24. Discuss why the following statement might be true: Economic decisions in a capitalist country are influenced by the federal government about 10 percent of the time; in a socialist country about 50 percent of the time; and in a communist country about 90 percent of the time.
25. Compare the three basic economic systems in terms of the economic opportunities available to businesses.

MAKE CONNECTIONS

26. **Research** Use your school library or the Internet to research the Great Depression. Identify the causes and the impact of the Great Depression on the economy of the United States. List the strategies that were used to move the U.S. economy out of the Great Depression.
27. **Math** Use the Consumer Price Index information provided in Figure 3-4 to determine the following.
    a. What was the percentage of increase between 1983 and 1998?
    b. What was the percentage of increase between 1998 and 2006?
    c. If the percentage of increase between 1983 and 2006 remains the same between 2006 and 2029, what will the CPI be in 2029?
28. **Technology** Use presentation software such as PowerPoint to show how a variety of technology tools are being used to increase labor productivity. Be specific with your examples.
29. **Speaking** Develop an argument in favor of or against one type of economic system outlined in the chapter. Relate your arguments to other points brought up in the chapter such as how economic wants are met, how utility is decided, how factors of production are distributed, and how capital is formed. Find someone in the class who has chosen a different economic system and debate the advantages and disadvantages of each system.
30. **Writing** Assume you are working for a politician who is running for office based on increasing economic growth in the United States. Write a speech indicating how the United States can obtain economic growth and what specifically the politician will do to create this growth.

CASE IN POINT

CASE 3-1: Using Information

Marsha and Carlos sat on a bench, looking at a newspaper. "Castro Experiments with Capitalism," one headline read, while another shouted, "Headwinds in China's Nudge to Market Economy." "Brazil's Inflation Out of Control," read still another. Lower on the page could be seen "CPI Inches Downward."

Marsha and Carlos read on. They were thinking about whether these stories had any bearing on their jobs and their lives. Finally, Carlos broke the silence.

Carlos: *Now I know why I never liked reading newspapers. The headlines don't make any sense—nothing in common. The same stuff appears on the Internet. They jump all over the place, and most of the news is bad. And half of it isn't understandable. Then we have to hear it again on TV and on the radio.*

Marsha: *I try to read some of the articles, but it's true many are unclear. For example, yesterday I saw "County Privatizes Trash Collection." The headlines aren't always clear, but fortunately things usually are explained in the stories. By reading each day, you learn more than you think you can, especially about economics.*

Carlos: *The sports pages are what I read. You get the "stats" like team won/lost records and learn about how much the superstars are paid in contracts. Some of them make as much in one year as you and I will make in a lifetime. You don't have to worry about inflation when you make $2 million.*

Marsha: *Today's headlines deal with economics and you're talking economics when you deal with how much people are paid. If you like "stats," you'll like looking at the economic indicators. You have a contract with your employer, Carlos. Someday when you have more knowledge and skills to sell, your "contracts" will get larger, too.*

Carlos: *Maybe I'll take this paper and read some of those headline details later . . . after I find out who won last night's big game between the Cowboys and the Bears. See you after work.*

THINK CRITICALLY

1. Is the headline that reads "CPI Inches Downward" good news or bad news? Explain your answer.
2. What did all the headlines have in common?
3. Explain to Marsha what the county did when it "privatized" the trash service.
4. Bring the business section of a newspaper to class. Determine what economic ideas presented in this chapter are directly or indirectly revealed in one or more of the headlines. If your instructor decides to divide the class into groups, pick the two best stories in your group that cover the most important chapter ideas.

CASE 3-2: The Fruits of Economic Progress

Mei-ling and Yi Cheng and their four children live on a farm in China located near the large city of Shanghai. Life on the farm today is unlike it was when they were younger. Less than 10 years ago, the family was quite poor and lived in a run-down small home with no plumbing. There were seldom good times. Raising enough food to eat and to sell barely made ends meet, and the economy was not at all like today's, with the GDP growing so rapidly.

Many people have moved to the city in order to earn more money and to learn new skills while working in new or growing businesses. Some of the factories are owned by foreign firms such as those based in Germany, Japan, and the United States. Yi travels to the city each day to work in one of the new plants, whereas Mei-ling runs the farm with her oldest son and other children when they are not in school. The family cannot afford to live in the city.

During the last few years, the Chengs have made improvements to their small home, adding indoor plumbing, a telephone, and a small television. Yi even has a cell phone that he uses with pride when bicycling the seven miles to and from work. The days are long, but life is getting easier. If things continue to improve, Yi may consider buying a motor scooter. The children want a computer but even a used one is an unaffordable luxury for now. The Chengs have learned that good times do not last forever. They must save for bad times, for the children's education, and for retirement. There is no social security system to depend upon when Yi retires. And if someone becomes ill or injured, the government can provide only limited help. Yi is also concerned that his foreign employer might leave China because of government regulations that are often unfair to foreign competitors. For now, the happy times continue for the Chengs, who consider themselves somewhat well-off for a rural family.

THINK CRITICALLY

1. How does the current life of the Chengs compare with that of the average American family? By American standards, would they be classified at the poverty level? Explain your answer.
2. Do the Chengs live more under a capitalistic or a communistic system? Explain your answer.
3. Using the library or the Internet, find out whether the Chinese people who live in large cities have a better quality of life than do people like the Chengs who live in rural areas. Report your findings to the class.
4. What conditions exist or could occur that would cause Yi's employer to leave China? Obtain information from your library or the Internet to make a report to the class.

project: MY BUSINESS, INC.

STUDY THE COMPETITION

As a new business owner, you must be aware of the type of competition the business will face and the strengths and weaknesses of that competition. Also, you must determine customer demand for the business's products. Competition affects the prices you can charge for your products. You will study these factors in this segment of your project.

DATA COLLECTION

1. Identify five businesses in your area that could be considered competitors for your juice bar. Review the information from your work in Chapter 1 to help you. Rate each business on the basis of variety of products, location, prices, service, and image. Use a 1–5 scale, with 1 indicating the most competitive and 5 the least competitive.
2. Identify five products that would typically be offered on the menus of juice bars. Visit businesses in your area and determine the highest and lowest prices being charged for each of the products you identified.
3. Interview 10 people to determine how price affects their purchase decisions. Ask the following questions and summarize the responses
   a. How much would you usually expect to pay for a freshly prepared frozen juice drink?
   b. How important is the price when you decide to purchase that drink?
   c. What factors would cause you to pay a higher-than-normal price for a fresh juice drink?

ANALYSIS

1. A business must be able to satisfy consumer needs in order to be successful. Describe how your new business will provide the four basic utilities discussed in the textbook: form, place, time, and possession.
2. Identify four specific ways you can reduce the level of competition or increase the customer demand for your products.
3. Analyze the data you collected in the interviews for Data Collection #3 above. How important do you think the prices of your products will be to the success of your business? What is the evidence to support your decision? What nonprice factors do you believe will be important in attracting and keeping customers?
4. Identify five products you plan to offer at your juice bar. The products may be five varieties of juice drinks or other food products such as muffins and bagels. Make initial pricing decisions for each of your products. (You may decide to change the prices later.) If you will serve different sizes of drinks, make sure to price each size. Justify why you selected those prices.

International Environment of Business

4.1 Importance of International Business

4.2 Forms of International Business

4.3 Theories of International Trade and Investment

REALITY CHECK

Not Made in America

Jake Applegate owned a fish bait and tackle shop in Ely in northern Minnesota, just outside a region famous for fly fishing. During the long summer season, anglers—professional and amateur—from all over the country stopped by Jake's shop to stock up on lures, baits, and other supplies en route to their favorite fishing spots. Jake carried a full line of fishing-related products. They were good-quality, American-made products. Sales were usually quite brisk. By late September, when he boarded up his business each year for the cold season, he usually had made enough to sustain himself and his family until April, when he would reopen.

This summer, Jake noticed that fewer tourists were stopping by his store. His sales were falling. It was not as if people had given up fishing. In fact, it was becoming more popular as more women took up the sport. Jake was very concerned.

Jake soon found out what was happening. A Wal-Mart department store had opened just outside Ely, and it carried a complete range of fishing gear including many new varieties of colorful and inexpensive lures. Checking out the prices, Jake found that they were all cheaper than comparable products that he carried. A close look at the packaging and boxes of the products told the story. In small print were the words "Made in Thailand."

4.1 The Importance of International Business

Goals
- Describe the nature, growth, and importance of international trade and investment.
- Explain the reasons for the growth of international business.

Terms
- international business
- Pacific Rim
- World Trade Organization (WTO)
- trading bloc
- European Union (EU)
- euro
- North American Free Trade Agreement (NAFTA)
- International Monetary Fund (IMF)
- World Bank

International business is not new. People around the world have been trading since the beginning of history. Phoenician and Greek merchants were sailing the seas to sell and buy products in Africa and Europe long before recorded history. In 1600, the British East India Company was formed in order to establish branches and trade with countries in Asia. As Europeans discovered sea routes around the world, trade flourished among the nations of Europe and countries such as China, India, and Indonesia. American colonial traders began operating in a similar way.

Similarly, people throughout the world were investing in businesses abroad. An early example of successful American investment abroad was a factory built in Scotland by the Singer Sewing Machine Company in 1868. By 1880, Singer had become a worldwide organization with several sales offices and factories in other countries. During the 18th and 19th centuries, a great economic expansion occurred in the United States. Largely financed by foreign money, businesses laid railway lines, opened mines to extract coal and iron ore, and built factories.

The Scope of International Business

International business typically means business activities that occur between two or more countries. Every country has its own laws and rules, its own currency, and its own traditions of doing business. When a restaurant in New Jersey buys lobsters from Maine, everyone understands the rules of business, because they are similar from state to state. When the restaurant buys salmon caught by Chilean fishermen, the rules of business are not as clear, because they differ from country to country.

Only since the end of World War II in 1945 has international business become a dominant aspect of economic life. Foreign trade has flourished. Companies have grown rapidly and operate on a global scale. Countries have become highly interdependent, so that events in one place have an impact in another place. Almost every business and individual is affected directly or indirectly by international business. As you saw in the opening vignette, although Jake was not directly involved in international business, his business was being hurt by the availability of cheaper products from Thailand.

EXTENT OF INTERNATIONAL TRADE

Look around and you will see names you are sure are foreign: Honda cars, Sony tapes, Benetton clothes, and Chanel perfume. But what about names such as Cadbury chocolates, Shell gasoline, 7-Eleven Stores, and Magnavox televisions? They are the brand names of products of foreign companies. See Figure 4-1 for a list of other common foreign brands. Also, think of familiar American companies such as McDonald's, General Motors, IBM, Coca-Cola, and Eastman Kodak. A growing portion of their total sales occurs in foreign countries.

As we move into the new millennium, it is clear that business activities are no longer confined to one country. Foreigners buy American products (computers, wheat, airplanes) and services (banking, insurance, data processing) just as Americans buy foreign products (petroleum, cars, clothes) and services (vacations, shipping, construction). American firms make many products in factories in foreign countries just as foreign companies make products in the United States. In a recent year, world trade in goods exceeded $10 trillion.

Most of the world's trade takes place among the developed countries of North America, Western Europe, and Japan. Over the past 30 years, countries on the western edge of the Pacific Ocean—referred to as the **Pacific Rim**—have emerged as big trading nations. These countries include China, South Korea, Taiwan, Hong Kong, and Singapore, as shown in Figure 4-2. A list of the major countries with which the United States trades is shown in Figure 4-3 (see p. 84).

Trade patterns have shifted from goods to services. Although goods remain dominant, service industries now represent more than one-fifth of international trade. When service industries emerged as an important segment of the American economy, more and more trade and investments occurred in businesses such as tourism, banking, accounting, advertising, and computer services.

Success *tip*

Most Americans have a very limited understanding of the factors related to international business. To be a successful international communicator, Americans must learn the history, culture, and language of the countries where they want to do business. Learning a foreign language is a good starting point. Even if you do not become fluent, people appreciate the effort you take to understand their language and culture.

FIGURE 4-1 Selected Products That Are Foreign-Owned

BRAND NAME	PRODUCT	COMPANY	COUNTRY
Acer	Computers	Acer	Taiwan
Adidas	Footwear	Adidas	Germany
Burger King	Fast food	Diageo	United Kingdom
Close-up	Toothpaste	Lever Brothers	United Kingdom
Michelin	Tires	Michelin	France
Novotel	Hotels	Accor	France
Nescafe	Coffee	Nestle	Switzerland
Panasonic	Television	Matsushita	Japan
Walkman	Personal stereo	Sony	Japan

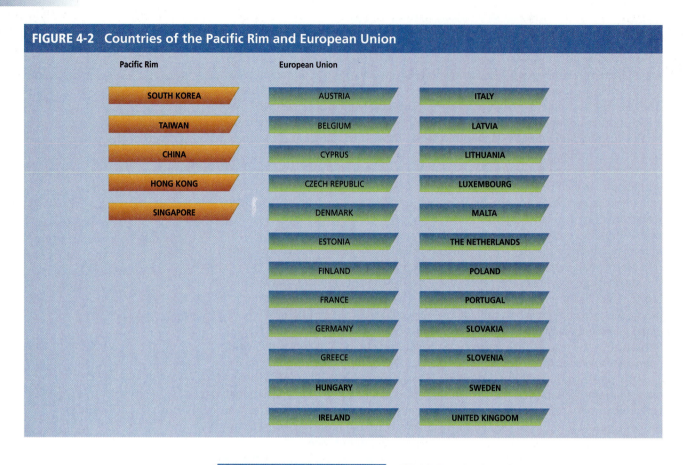

FIGURE 4-2 Countries of the Pacific Rim and European Union

Pacific Rim

SOUTH KOREA

TAIWAN

CHINA

HONG KONG

SINGAPORE

European Union

AUSTRIA	ITALY
BELGIUM	LATVIA
CYPRUS	LITHUANIA
CZECH REPUBLIC	LUXEMBOURG
DENMARK	MALTA
ESTONIA	THE NETHERLANDS
FINLAND	POLAND
FRANCE	PORTUGAL
GERMANY	SLOVAKIA
GREECE	SLOVENIA
HUNGARY	SWEDEN
IRELAND	UNITED KINGDOM

FIGURE 4-3 The Top Ten Countries with Which the U.S. Trades, 2005

CANADA

CHINA

MEXICO

JAPAN

GERMANY

UNITED KINGDOM

SOUTH KOREA

TAIWAN

FRANCE

MALAYSIA

Source: U.S. Census Bureau (www.census.gov/foreign-trade/)

TRADE, INVESTMENT, AND THE ECONOMY

As with trade, most investments are made within and by the world's most industrialized economies. Annual foreign investment by businesses in these countries exceeded $300 billion. In recent years, though, China has become a major recipient of foreign investment, mostly from Taiwan, Japan, and the United States. Foreign investment occurs when firms of one country build new plants and facilities or buy existing businesses in another country. An example of such investment would be the acquisition of Chrysler in the United States by Daimler-Benz of Germany in 1998.

International trade and investment are a big and growing part of the American economy. In a recent year, America sold over $1.3 trillion of its goods and services to foreign customers. Almost 10 percent of all jobs depend on foreign trade, and nearly 5 percent of workers are employed by foreign companies operating in the United States. Foreign firms have invested nearly $1.3 trillion in the United States. Total American investment abroad exceeds $860 billion. Figure 4-4 shows the top countries that have invested

FIGURE 4-4 Leading Investment Countries, 2004

Top Five Countries Investing in the United States	Top Five Foreign Countries for American Investors
UNITED KINGDOM	UNITED KINGDOM
JAPAN	THE NETHERLANDS
THE NETHERLANDS	SWITZERLAND
GERMANY	BERMUDA
FRANCE	JAPAN

in the United States and the top countries where American businesses have invested.

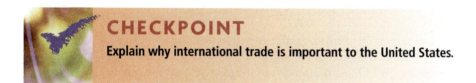

CHECKPOINT
Explain why international trade is important to the United States.

Reasons for Growth in International Business

Why would McDonald's want to open a restaurant in Beijing, or Nokia sell mobile telephones in the United States, or Volkswagen build its Beetles in Mexico? For that matter, why would Macy's buy the jeans it sells from a garment maker in Hong Kong? Firms enter international business for many good reasons.

The main reason is profit. Businesses may be able to earn more profit from selling abroad or may be able to charge higher prices abroad than at home, where competition could be more intense. When the cost of making goods is lower in foreign countries than at home, it becomes cost effective for companies to buy goods made abroad or even set up their own factories abroad. The potential for sales abroad, when combined with the size of the domestic market, increases the overall size of the market. Using mass-production techniques, production costs should drop and profits should rise.

In many cases, a company goes international in reaction to what other companies are doing or because of changes in the domestic market. If some firms are making large profits by selling abroad, other companies may be encouraged to do the same. When a large foreign market opens up, as in China in recent years, an American company may lose the market to firms from other countries if it does not act quickly.

Similarly, sales at home may be small, stagnant, or declining, whereas opportunities to sell abroad may be abundant. A company may have overproduced, and the only way to possibly dispose of its surplus goods profitably is to sell them abroad. It could also be that a company is physically close to foreign customers and markets. For example, Argentine firms can sell easily to Brazilian firms because they are neighbors.

Japanese officials want to launch a national campaign to establish English as Japan's second official language. Too few Japanese speak the language of the Internet and international finance—which is English. Some Japanese see this as a serious competitive disadvantage that undermines Japan's global influence, particularly in the areas of technology, commercial exploitation of the Internet, and finance, where English proficiency is critical.

Although international trade and investment have existed for centuries, they did not become major topics of study and interest until fairly recently. What are some reasons for this?

Several factors help firms engage in international business. One key factor is treaties on trade and investment signed by different countries. The **World Trade Organization (WTO)** is an international organization that creates and enforces the rules governing trade among countries. Trade agreements negotiated under the authority of the WTO have led to huge cuts in tariffs. These cuts have boosted exports and imports among the almost 150 member countries.

Development of trading blocs has also stimulated global trade and investment. A **trading bloc** is a group of two or more countries who agree to remove all restrictions between them on the sales of goods and services, while imposing barriers on trade with and investment from countries that are not part of the bloc.

There are many forms of trading blocs. The best example of an advanced form of trading bloc is the **European Union (EU)**. The EU currently has 25 members, as shown in Figure 4-2. Since it was formed in 1957 as the European Economic Community, the EU has gone beyond free trade among its members. It is trying to create a "United States of Europe," where there will also be free movement of capital and labor and where common economic and monetary policies will be followed. On January 1, 1999, 11 EU members took a major step toward integrating their economies by merging their national currencies into a single new currency called the **euro**. With a single currency, international firms can look at these European countries as a single market and do not have to worry about exchange rate changes.

In 1989, the United States signed a free-trade agreement with Canada. In 1992, Canada and the United States signed a similar agreement with Mexico, called the **North American Free Trade Agreement (NAFTA)**, which created the world's largest trading bloc by removing tariffs and other barriers to trade among the three nations. Many American firms have relocated to Mexico to take advantage of the lower costs of production in that country. Unlike the EU, under NAFTA there is no move yet to allow unrestricted movement of people among the three countries or to integrate the three economies with common monetary or economic policies.

International business is also facilitated by two major international institutions—the **International Monetary Fund (IMF)** and the **World Bank**. The IMF's main purpose is to help countries that are facing serious financial difficulties in paying for their imports or repaying loans. The World Bank provides low-cost, long-term loans to less-developed countries to develop basic industries and facilities, such as roads and electric power plants.

Another factor that has helped international business is the tremendous advances in communication and transportation. Telephone, fax, and the Internet have made it cheaper and quicker to obtain information from around the world and conduct business round the clock. The Internet and television broadcasts enable firms to advertise their products worldwide and create a global consumer culture. Faster and cheaper transportation has meant that firms can easily ship goods long distances. For example, thanks to air transport, tulips grown in the Netherlands are shipped daily to florists in New York City.

Since the early 1990s, the world has seen a move toward free-enterprise practices. Many governments have reduced their control over the economy. Several types of businesses that were strictly regulated by the government, such as telecommunications and airlines, have been opened up to competition. In many foreign countries, business enterprises owned by the government have been sold to private owners—both domestic and foreign. All these changes have opened up new investment and trading opportunities for foreign firms.

CHECKPOINT

Explain why there has been growth in international business.

4.1   Assessment

UNDERSTAND MANAGEMENT CONCEPTS

Circle the best answer for each of the following questions.

1. International business has become more dominant in the United States since
   a. 1900
   b. World War I
   c. World War II
   d. 2000
2. NAFTA includes
   a. the United States and the EU
   b. the United States and Canada
   c. the United States and Mexico
   d. the United States, Canada, and Mexico

THINK CRITICALLY

Answer the following questions as completely as possible.

3. List the countries where most international trade occurs.

4. Give four reasons why a firm may go into international business.

Xtra!
Study Tools
thomsonedu.com/school/bpmxtra

4.2 Forms of International Business

Goals

- Distinguish between the different forms through which international business is conducted.
- Describe the policies, rules, and laws that governments use to affect international trade and investment.

Terms

- exporting
- importing
- international licensing
- joint ventures
- wholly owned subsidiary
- strategic alliances
- multinational firm
- home country
- host country
- parent firm
- subsidiaries
- tariffs
- dumping
- quota
- nontariff barriers
- embargo
- sanctions
- exchange rate
- culture
- low-context culture
- high-context culture

Forms of International Business

International business takes place in many forms. Usually, when a firm decides to enter into international business, it starts by selling its products or services to buyers in another country. This is known as exporting. For example, Boeing makes airplanes in the United States and sells some of them to Qantas, an Australian airline. Importing refers to buying goods or services made in a foreign country. When Americans buy Darjeeling tea, they are buying goods imported from India. Exporting and importing are usually the simplest forms of international business. Both can be done with limited resources and relatively risk free.

International business also takes place through licensing. International licensing occurs when one company allows a company in another country to make and sell products according to certain specifications. Thus, when an American pharmaceutical company allows a German firm to make and sell in Germany a medicine the American company has invented, this is licensing. The American company receives a royalty from the German company for any medicines the latter sells. Licensing and its related concept, franchising, are relatively more costly and risky methods of expanding abroad, compared to exporting.

Firms may set up businesses in foreign countries by forming joint ventures with other companies. In joint ventures, two or more firms share the costs of doing business and also share the profits. When the firm sets up a business abroad on its own without any partners, it is known as a wholly owned subsidiary. These are more expensive to set up and also more risky should the business fail.

PHOTO: © GETTY IMAGES/PHOTODISC.

What factors make exporting and importing the simplest forms of international business?

In recent years, many competitors have entered into strategic alliances with each other. Under strategic alliances, firms agree to cooperate on certain aspects of business while remaining competitors on other aspects. Thus, because of the high cost of developing new medicines for curing cancer, two pharmaceutical companies may agree to share research information and costs while competing with each other in selling other medicines.

The expansion of international business has created multinational firms. A multinational firm is a firm that owns or controls production or service facilities in more than one country. The country in which the business has its headquarters is referred to as the home country. The foreign location where it has facilities is referred to as the host country. Company headquarters is called the parent firm; and the foreign branches, if registered as independent legal entities, are referred to as subsidiaries. Most of the world's largest businesses are multinational firms. However, many small firms, too, are multinational businesses.

Trade and investment in the international environment have some unique complications. Businesses must consider government policies toward foreign firms and products, the value of foreign currencies, and the contrast of cultures when doing business abroad.

facts & figures

The Japanese find it hard to answer a definite "no" to either a question or a statement. They signal that they "don't know" or "don't understand" by waving their own hand in front of their face, with the palm outward.

CHECKPOINT
List the different forms of international businesses.

Focus On...

Global Innovation–Business Via the Internet

When the Lee Hung Fat Garment Factory started 35 years ago, overseas orders usually came by messenger from one of the big Hong Kong trading houses. Today, customers send in specifications for denim jeans and leather jackets directly to a computer terminal on the desk of Mr. Eddy Wong Fun-Ming, the company's operations director. "What we do in one day used to take five weeks in the 1970s," says 39-year-old Mr. Wong.

This small Hong Kong company with annual sales of $40 million is using the Internet to completely change the way it does business. With the click of a mouse, Mr. Wong pulls up a customer's order on the screen. He can see all the details—from production at his factories in China and Bangladesh to shipping schedules to individual customers' accounts. So can many of his staff. Each order is simultaneously sent to any department involved in getting it filled.

Lee Hung Fat supplies apparel to about 60 companies in Europe. Many of these customers have gone online. So the decision to wire the company into the Internet was driven partly by customers wanting to do e-commerce, and partly by his own desire to cut costs.

Using the Internet to communicate has saved the company on phone bills. Before the company went online, fax and telephone calls to customers and factories overseas cost about $10,000 a month. With electronic mail, "you can have 50 messages to your buyer in a day and it doesn't really cost you anything," says Mr. Wong, who often checks his e-mails on the golf course using a mobile phone. He also applies over the Internet for required documents to ship his goods. Before, he had to send someone to the government office and apply for the export license in person.

The company saves money in other ways, too. Before, the company sent a mockup of a garment to buyers overseas by courier or by mail. Now, Mr. Wong holds the item in front of a camera mounted on his PC and flashes it over the Web. He can scan a picture of a sample and transmit that to the customers, who can play with the cloth pattern or the stitching and then zap back a new version. This means samples are approved three to four times faster. Even after paying for the costs of installing computers, Mr. Wong estimates he saves about 15 to 20 percent in costs.

Think Critically

1. How does the Internet help the Lee Hung Fat Garment Factory remain globally competitive?
2. Are there some aspects of the business that cannot be handled by the Internet?
3. What problems could the company encounter because of its heavy reliance on the Internet?

Government Policies

Because international business takes place between two or more countries, the policies, rules, and laws of more than one national government affect trade and investment. Although economists consider free trade desirable for a society, on occasion governments impose **tariffs**. These are taxes on foreign goods to protect domestic industries and to earn revenue. For instance, assume that the U.S. government sets a tariff of 10 percent on a pair of jeans made in Colombia, South America. If the jeans are valued at $30, the American customs department will collect a tax of $3 ($30 x 0.10), and the price per pair will rise to $33.

Governments also impose tariffs when a foreign supplier is guilty of "dumping" its products. **Dumping** refers to the practice of selling goods in a foreign market at a price that is below cost or below what it charges in its home country. When a company dumps, it is trying to win more customers by driving domestic producers out of the market. The government prevents dumping by setting tariffs that increase the price of goods being dumped. For example, if Brazilian firms tried dumping steel in the United States, a tariff might be levied to sufficiently raise the price of that steel to permit domestic producers to compete successfully.

Another way by which governments restrict the availability of foreign goods is to create quotas. A **quota** limits the quantity or value of units permitted to enter a country. For instance, the U.S. government may allow only 10,000 tons of salmon to enter the country annually from Chile, although much more salmon could be sold. Alternatively, the government could allow salmon worth up to $100 million into the United States from Chile annually. In either case, quotas limit the number or dollar value of foreign goods that can be sold in a country. Quotas are designed to protect the market share of domestic producers. However, both tariffs and quotas increase the price of foreign goods to consumers.

In addition to tariffs and quotas, it may be difficult to sell goods and services abroad because of **nontariff barriers**. These are nontax methods of discouraging trade. In many cases, such barriers do not target specific foreign companies or

PHOTO: © DIGITAL VISION.

Many of the clothes you buy are made in foreign countries. Do they generally cost more or less than similar clothes made in the United States? What factors affect the pricing of foreign-made clothing?

business *note*

Many international companies buy businesses in the United States. In 2006, a Dubai company, Dubai Ports World, purchased a British firm that operated six U.S. ocean ports. This led to an outcry from the U.S. public and politicians. U.S. protestors did not want a company from the Middle East to buy these U.S. assets. Dubai Ports World finally transferred ownership of the U.S. ports to a U.S. entity. Each year, the United States buys billions of dollars of oil from the Middle East. These actions could hurt the United States's image as a good country to invest in.

products, but have the practical effect of keeping them out. In other cases, barriers are deliberately created to protect domestic producers.

Almost all countries have nontariff barriers of one sort or another. For example, in the United States, steering wheels are on the left side of motor vehicles, whereas in Ireland, the steering wheel is on the right side. Thus, before an American company can sell cars in Ireland, it would have to make changes to the vehicle. Another example of nontariff barriers would be a public campaign to "Be American, Buy American." This is clearly designed to discourage the buying of foreign goods and services. Non-tariff barriers are difficult to remove because they are often part of a country's culture and tradition.

Governments may place restrictions on what goods and services can be exported or imported. The goals are again to protect domestic businesses, citizens, or cultures and to ensure national security. American firms need government licenses to sell high-technology or military products abroad. For political reasons, a government may bar companies from doing business with particular countries. Such a restriction is known as an embargo. For instance, the U.S. government has established an embargo that bars U.S. companies from conducting business with Cuba.

Sanctions are a milder form of embargo that bans specific business ties with a foreign country. For instance, it is illegal for an American company to sell nuclear technology to Pakistan, which tested atomic bombs in 1998.

Governments place restrictions on what domestic companies foreigners are allowed to buy or invest in. In the United States, foreign firms are not allowed to have a majority control of airlines or television stations. The government fears that allowing that to happen might endanger national security. In extreme cases, a government may seize foreign firms with or without compensation, if such businesses are thought to be harmful to the national interests.

CURRENCY VALUES

International business involves dealing with the money, or currency, of foreign countries. Currencies have different names, such as the dollar in the United States, peso in Mexico, and yen in Japan, but more important, they differ in value. This is a key difference between doing business domestically and doing business internationally. The exchange rate is the value of one country's currency expressed in the currency of another country. For example, one U.S. dollar might be worth nine Mexican pesos right now. If you were traveling to Mexico and wanted some Mexican money, you would receive nine pesos for every dollar you turned in to the bank at this exchange rate. The value of each currency in terms of another can change every minute, depending on many factors, such as the demand for a particular currency, interest rates, inflation rates, and government policies. Major newspapers and several Web sites publish exchange rates for most currencies.

Managers must closely watch exchange rates, as they affect profits and investment decisions in a big way. For example, assume the value of one American dollar is equal to 125 Japanese yen. A camera made in Japan for 12,500 yen would sell in the United States for $100 (12,500/125). If the exchange rate changes to

100 yen to the dollar, that same camera will now cost $125 (12,500/100). Thus, the Japanese camera becomes more expensive in the United States entirely because of exchange rate changes. To protect firms against adverse changes in the exchange rates, international business managers use many techniques.

CULTURAL DIFFERENCES

International business also requires understanding and coping with cultural values and traits in foreign countries that are different from those of the home country. Culture refers to the customs, beliefs, values, and patterns of behavior of the people of a country or group. It also includes language; religion; attitudes toward work, authority, and family; practices regarding courtship, etiquette, gestures, and joking; and manners and traditions. In many countries, especially large ones like India, Russia, and South Africa, numerous cultural differences exist within their own populations. Likewise, in the United States, there are cultural differences, such as among various racial and ethnic groups.

Some cultures may be more familiar to Americans, such as those of Canada and Great Britain. Others seem very unfamiliar to Americans, such as those of India and Thailand. Businesspeople who work in foreign countries need to be aware of cultural differences in order to be successful in their assignments. The greater the cultural gap, the more the businessperson will have to adjust.

Culture affects how people communicate in a country. In a **low-context culture** such as the United States, people communicate directly and explicitly. A

FIGURE 4-5 Australian and American English

AUSTRALIAN ENGLISH	AMERICAN ENGLISH
Arvo	Afternoon
Biscuit	Cookie
Bloke	Man
Brolly	Umbrella
Cozzie	Bathing suit (also bathers or swimmers)
Crook	Sick
Entree	The appetizer, not the main course
Fair dinkum	The real thing
Footpath	Sidewalk
Jumbuck	Sheep
Jumper	Sweater
Lollies	Candy
Mate	Friend
Nought	Zero
Sandshoes	Sneakers
Serviette	Table napkin
Sweets	Dessert
Ta	Thank you
Takeaway food	Food to go
Taxi rank	Cab stand
Yank	An American

person is expected to come to the point directly and not beat around the bush. An American manager might say, "Do this task immediately." The receiver of this message is not expected to read between the lines. In contrast, in a **high-context culture** such as Japan, communication tends to occur through nonverbal signs and indirect suggestions. Ambiguity and indirect suggestions are expected and highly valued. A person is not supposed to come right out and say it. A Japanese manager might say, "This task is very important, and your attention to it will be greatly appreciated." The difference between high- and low-context cultures can cause communication misunderstandings.

Although English has become the language of international business, its usage and terminology vary across the world. As Figure 4-5 suggests, even though Australians speak English, Americans may not recognize some of their terms and phrases.

CHECKPOINT

Describe the government policies that can be used to control international trade.

4.2 Assessment

UNDERSTAND MANAGEMENT CONCEPTS

Circle the best answer for each of the following questions.

1. When a company ships a product to a buyer in another country it is engaging in
   a. exporting
   b. importing
   c. international licensing
   d. a joint venture

2. Which of the following is *not* a barrier to free trade?
   a. tariffs
   b. dumping
   c. quota
   d. importing

THINK CRITICALLY

Answer the following questions as completely as possible.

3. What policies can a government adopt to protect domestic businesses from foreign competition?

4. How do changes in currency exchange rates affect international business?

Xtra!
Study Tools
thomsonedu.com/school/bpmxtra

4.3 Theories of International Trade Investment

Goals
- Explain two theories of international trade.
- Discuss the concepts of balance of trade and balance of payments.
- Consider career opportunities in international business and understand the factors related to being sent abroad on assignment.

Terms
- comparative advantage theory
- product life cycle theory
- balance of payments
- current account
- capital account

Theories of International Trade

In this section, you will learn about two well-known theories that explain why international trade and investment occur.

COMPARATIVE ADVANTAGE THEORY

The comparative advantage theory states that to gain a trade advantage, a country should specialize in products or services that it can provide more efficiently than can other countries. For instance, because of climate and soil conditions, Brazil is better able to grow coffee than India, whose soil and climate favor the growing of tea. Each country could gain by specializing—Brazil in coffee and India in tea—and then trading with each other.

What if one country can produce both coffee and tea at a lower cost than another country? The comparative advantage theory says that the focus should be on comparing the cost of producing both products in each country. For example, it is possible that India may be able to produce more tea than coffee for the same cost, whereas Brazil may find that it can produce coffee at a lower cost than it can produce wine. In such a case, Brazilians should specialize in producing and selling coffee to the Indians and buying tea from India. Similarly, the Indians should produce tea and sell some to the Brazilians to pay for the coffee they need. This theory explains why the United States produces computers, Saudi Arabia extracts oil from the earth, and Indonesia makes athletic shoes.

PRODUCT LIFE CYCLE THEORY

The product life cycle theory provides another explanation for trade and investment. In a later chapter, you will learn that a product or service goes through four stages: introduction, growth, maturity, and decline. Consider black-and-white televisions, for example. When they were first introduced in the 1940s and 1950s, they were the only televisions available. As more people in the country started buying TVs, their sales grew—the growth stage. When most households owned a TV, sales leveled off—the maturity stage. When color TVs appeared, the sales of black-and-white sets started falling—the decline stage.

How does the product life cycle theory relate to trade and investment? When sales begin to slow in a country (the mature stage), Company A that makes the product starts selling it to foreign countries where the product may be in the introductory or growth stage. However, selling abroad is expensive because of transportation, tariffs, quotas, and other nontariff barriers. Companies in the foreign country find it attractive to make and sell the product at lower prices. To counteract this action, Company A sets up a factory in the foreign country where it makes and sells the product. Company A may even sell some of the products back to the home country.

Many American companies move to foreign countries when sales at home start lagging. Examples are fast-food restaurants and soft-drink companies. Because of technological changes, the life cycle of new products is much shorter. New products are regularly introduced. Their sales grow, then flatten, and eventually decline. To prolong the life of the product, firms first ship their products abroad, and later build factories there.

CHECKPOINT

Explain the comparative advantage theory and product life cycle theory.

Balance of Trade

Goods and services sold abroad by American companies bring money into the United States. Money also comes from foreigners who buy American companies or set up new businesses in the United States or lend money to Americans. At the same time, money leaves the country when Americans buy foreign products, vacation abroad, invest in foreign businesses, or give aid to refugees in a troubled nation. National governments and international organizations such as the United Nations and WTO keep records of international transactions, and governments use these to develop economic policies.

All international transactions are recorded in an accounting statement called the **balance of payments**. The balance-of-payments statement has two parts: the current account and the capital account. The **current account** records the value of goods and services exported and those imported from foreigners, as well as other income and payments. The **capital account** records investment funds coming into and going out of a country. Investment funds include bank loans or deposits, purchase and sale of a business, and investing in a new business.

For several decades, the United States has had a consistent deficit on its current account. Figure 4-6 shows how the deficit has ballooned over time. The balance-of-payments deficit means that Americans have been buying more goods and services made abroad than they have been selling to foreigners. How long can a country continue to buy more than it sells? Not indefinitely, of

business *note*

How long can a country run a negative account balance? This is a question that many people have about the U.S. negative account balance. If the negative account balance were to continue for too long, foreign countries could lose confidence in the U.S. dollar, leading to higher interest rates for U.S. bonds. This not only increases the expense to the U.S. taxpayer but also can raise all other interest rates, slowing economic growth.

FIGURE 4-6   U.S. Balance of Trade (in billions of dollars)

	1980	1998	2000
1. Total exports of goods	224.3	670.2	807.5
2. Total exports of services	47.6	263.7	343.9
3. Other income from abroad (e.g., royalties)	72.6	258.3	379.5
4. TOTAL	344.5	1,192.2	1,530.9
5. Total imports of goods	249.8	917.2	1,472.9
6. Total imports of services	41.5	181.0	296.1
7. Other payments to foreigners	42.5	270.5	430.0
8. TOTAL	333.8	1,368.7	2,199.0
9. Balance on trade in merchandise (goods)	−25.5	−247.0	−665.4
10. Balance on trade in services	6.1	82.7	47.8
11. Net balance on trade (9+10)	−19.4	−164.3	−617.6
12. Current account balance (4-8)	10.7	−176.5	−668.1

Source: U.S. Department of Commerce Bureau of Economic Analysis, www.bea.gov

course. However, the United States has several advantages. Countries everywhere value its currency, the dollar, because the United States is a stable society, government policies are pro-business, and its economy is the world's largest and richest. Foreign banks and governments are willing to lend money to the United States to enable it to pay for the excess product it buys.

Not all countries are so fortunate. Countries with prolonged trade deficits may not be able to pay their bills or may have to limit international trade. In addition, their governments may have to place restrictions on the outward flow of money or on the activities of foreign businesses in their countries. At such times, they may obtain financial assistance and economic advice from the International Monetary Fund.

When deficits continue, it means that companies and individuals are demanding more foreign currency to buy the foreign goods. For instance, if Americans buy more Korean toys, the demand for the Korean currency—the won—goes up, because American toy companies will need won to pay the Koreans. When demand increases for won, more dollars are needed to buy won. Thus, the value of the dollar declines in relation to the won. In turn, Korean products become more expensive for Americans, whereas American products become less expensive for Koreans. Theoretically, at this stage, higher prices discourage the sale of Korean products in America, and lower prices encourage the sale of American products abroad. In this way, the deficits can be reduced and eventually eliminated.

Why has the United States usually had an advantage when it comes to the balance of trade?

PHOTO: © GETTY IMAGES/PHOTODISC.

To illustrate this process, consider IBM computers made in the United States and sold in Korea. Assuming an exchange rate of $1 = 1,000 won, a $1,200 computer would sell in Korea for 1,200,000 won (1,200 × 1,000). As more Koreans buy IBM computers, they will need more and more U.S. dollars to pay for the computers. This will increase the demand for dollars, and more won will be needed to buy a dollar. Thus, if $1 is now worth 1,200 won, the IBM computer will cost the Koreans 1,440,000 won (1,200 × 1,200).

With the computers costing more, Koreans will buy fewer of them and U.S. exports will decline. Contrast this situation with what happens to a Korean product—say, a Samsung mobile phone costing 120,000 won. The phone will sell in the United States initially for $120 (120,000/1,000). When the exchange rate becomes $1 = 1,200 won, the same phone will now cost Americans less: 120,000/1,200, or $100. This decline in price will lead Americans to buy more Samsung phones, which will lead to an increasing demand for won and raise the value of the won in terms of dollars. In turn, American goods will become less expensive to Koreans, and they will buy more American products. Thus, the trade deficits work out over the long run.

CHECKPOINT

Explain the difference between current and capital accounts.

Career Opportunities in International Business

The growth of international business has created many new types of jobs. In addition to those who work for foreign firms in the United States, over 150,000 Americans work abroad for American or foreign firms.

Many people work in various aspects of international business, such as exporting and importing, teaching and translating languages, administering trade laws, managing offices and operations in foreign countries, and in banking and insurance firms. Others work in international trade organizations such as the WTO and the IMF, or in federal and state government agencies. As countries become economically interdependent, more and more jobs will require a knowledge of international business.

Most international companies hire at the entry level, but usually they send workers abroad who are very skilled, mature, and experienced. Studies show that the average salary in foreign companies located in the United States is higher than for similar jobs in American companies. As firms gain experience in doing

NETBookmark

The world is becoming more competitive. Many countries produce more goods and services than the U.S. in specific product categories. Point your browser to www.thomsonedu.com/schoo/bpmxtra. Use the Nation Master's Menu system to view "Economy," then choose at least four product categories (world trade > exports > product) to determine which countries are the top 10 producers of each product. Determine where the United States places in these product categories. Investigate the background of three high producers and explain why they are able to produce at such a high level.

www.thomsonedu.com/school/bpmxtra

business globally, they employ more and more people from various backgrounds and countries. However, although working several years overseas may promote workers' careers in many companies, it may hurt their careers in others. Workers abroad lose close contact with people and developments in the parent firm.

Today, both businesses and government agencies recruit extensively for jobs that require skills useful for international business. These include not only knowledge of business but also foreign-language ability, familiarity with foreign countries, and being comfortable with and in a foreign culture. Many colleges and universities provide coursework and academic degrees in international business. Many offer programs that allow students to do part of their studies in a foreign country or even in a foreign company.

EMPLOYMENT OF INTERNATIONAL MANAGERS

Firms need managers who can work successfully in a wide variety of countries. Such managers adapt readily to other cultures and are competent, socially flexible, and receptive to new ideas. Managers benefit from knowing the foreign language and from having strong self-confidence, a motivation to live abroad, and a skill for innovative problem solving.

During the start-up phase of foreign operations, firms tend to rely on managers sent from headquarters. However, most managers are citizens of the host country where the business is situated. Occasionally, businesses hire citizens of other countries (neither the home nor the host countries) because they are exceptionally qualified or because host country managers are not available. Sending managers abroad is expensive, because companies must provide extra benefits (such as housing, airfare for families, and cost-of-living allowances). Managers sent to a country that is culturally different from their own may experience culture shock. Many firms provide cross-cultural training to managers before sending them abroad.

facts & figures

Americans vote with their dollars. In a free-market system, customers are free to buy whatever goods and services they want. For many Americans, this means buying foreign products that are perceived as cheaper and/or of higher quality. Americans will buy domestic products if they offer a greater value than imported products, or they can vote to pay more for domestic products.

PHOTO: © GETTY IMAGES/PHOTODISC.

Jobs in international business take many forms. What kinds of international careers appeal to you?

The support of the entire family is often necessary for the manager to succeed in the foreign location. With more and more spouses of managers having careers of their own, many firms are finding it difficult to persuade managers to take long-term transfers to a foreign location. Instead, they are using frequent short business trips, bringing in host-country managers to headquarters, and using teleconferencing and the Internet to manage their foreign operations.

CHECKPOINT

Describe the skills international managers need to be successful.

4.3 Assessment

UNDERSTAND MANAGEMENT CONCEPTS

Circle the best answer for each of the following questions.

1. The theory that a country should specialize in products or services that it can provide more efficiently than can other countries is called
   a. international specialization
   b. competitive advantage theory
   c. comparative advantage theory
   d. specialization theory

2. Which of the following is not part of the balance of payments?
   a. current account
   b. capital account
   c. economic surplus
   d. All are included as part of the balance of payments.

THINK CRITICALLY

Answer the following questions as completely as possible.

3. If a country regularly has a trade surplus, what will happen to its international business?

4. Explain the situations under which a multinational firm will use home-country, host-country, and third-country nationals in its foreign operations.

Xtra!
Study Tools
thomsonedu.com/school/bpmxtra

CHAPTER CONCEPTS

- Firms go into international business because of the potential for larger profits and limited opportunities in the home market. Removal of barriers to trade and investment, creation of trading blocs, and technological advances in communication and transportation have created a positive environment for conducting international business.

- International business occurs in various forms, such as exporting and importing, licensing, joint ventures, wholly owned subsidiaries, strategic alliances, and multinational firms.

- International business faces unique challenges, such as the need to work within the rules set by more than one government, currency exchange rates, and cultural differences.

- Two theories explain international trade and investments. The theory of comparative advantage explains why a particular country specializes in producing a particular product or service. The product life cycle theory explains how a product's life stage encourages international business.

- Data on trade and investment are used to set business and economic policies. The balance of trade between countries is evidence of a nation's financial strength or weakness.

REVIEW TERMS AND CONCEPTS

Write the letter of the term that matches each definition. Some terms will not be used.

1. Business activities that occur between two or more countries
2. Buying goods or services made in a foreign country
3. Business arrangement in which two or more firms share the costs of doing business and also share the profits
4. Type of business in which a firm sets up a business abroad on its own without any partners
5. Firm that owns or controls production or service facilities in more than one country
6. Foreign location where a firm has facilities
7. Value of one country's currency expressed in the currency of another
8. Taxes on foreign goods to protect domestic industries and to earn revenue
9. Nontax methods of discouraging trade
10. Government block preventing companies from doing business with particular countries
11. Selling goods in a foreign market at a price that is below cost or below what is charged in the home country
12. Record of investment funds coming into and going out of a country

a. capital account
b. dumping
c. embargo
d. exchange rate
e. home country
f. host country
g. importing
h. international business
i. joint venture
j. multinational firm
k. nontariff barrier
l. parent firm
m. tariffs
n. wholly owned subsidiary

DETERMINE THE BEST ANSWER

13. The Pacific Rim includes countries on the western edge of the Pacific Ocean such as
    a. South Korea
    b. Taiwan
    c. China
    d. all of the above

14. The arrangement in which one international company allows another international company in another country to make and sell products according to certain specifications is called
    a. international joint venture
    b. international licensing
    c. international franchise
    d. international partnership

15. Culture includes all of the following except
    a. laws
    b. customs
    c. beliefs
    d. values

16. A type of culture in which people communicate directly and explicitly, and a person is expected to come to the point directly and not beat around the bush is a/an
    a. direct culture
    b. explicit culture
    c. low-context culture
    d. high-context culture

17. The international organization that creates and enforces the rules governing trade among countries is the
    a. United Nations
    b. World Bank
    c. World Trade Organization
    d. International Monetary Fund

18. An agreement between two or more countries to remove all restrictions between them on the sales of goods and services, while imposing barriers on trade and investment from countries that are not part of it, creates a/an
    a. free-trade zone
    b. economic union
    c. trade agreement
    d. trading bloc

19. The way by which governments restrict the availability of foreign goods, limiting the quantity or value of units permitted to enter a country, is called
    a. quota
    b. sanction
    c. limitation
    d. restriction

APPLY WHAT YOU KNOW

20. Why is it easier for a firm to export instead of setting up a wholly owned foreign subsidiary?
21. Explain the purposes of the WTO, IMF, and World Bank.
22. How can a person from a low-context culture communicate with a person from a high-context culture and avoid misunderstandings?
23. If the value of the Canadian dollar continues to rise in relation to the American dollar, what can a Canadian exporter do to keep the price of the goods it sells in the U.S. market competitive?
24. Explain how it is possible for the United States to have a deficit in its current account year after year.

MAKE CONNECTIONS

25. **Math** The current accounts of the imaginary nation of Utopia for the past three years are given below in millions of dollars.

	Year 1	Year 2	Year 3
Exports of goods	$100	$120	$125
Imports of goods	$175	$195	$205
Exports of services	$80	$100	$150
Imports of services	$40	$60	$80
Other income from abroad	$30	$25	$40
Other payments abroad	$50	$70	$70

   Given the above information, answer the following questions: Does Utopia have a deficit or surplus in its current account in Year 1, Year 2, and Year 3? Calculate the balance on merchandise trade for Year 1, Year 2, and Year 3. If you were the president of an American company, would you set up a business in Utopia? Why or why not? Suggest ways by which Utopia can reduce its deficit or surplus.

26. **Technology** An Australian sheep farmer who sells much of his wool in the United States has seen the exchange rate for the Australian dollar (AUD) change from U.S. $1 = AUD $1.20 to U.S. $1 = AUD $1.45 over the past six months. Use spreadsheet software to answer the following questions, assuming the farmer sells 1,000 AUDs worth of wool:
   a. Will this change in currency rates help or hurt his sales in the United States?
   b. What may be some of the reasons for the change in the currency rates?
   c. Do American consumers gain or suffer with the change in the currency rates?

CASE IN POINT

CASE 4-1: Host-Country Politics

The premier of the Canadian province of Quebec announced that he was not ruling out the option of calling another referendum on whether Quebec should remain a part of Canada or become an independent country. Over the past 10 years, two such referenda have been held. In the last one, the pro-independence supporters lost by only 50,000 votes. Although these referenda have failed, the issues that led to them have not gone away.

Unlike the rest of Canada, the overwhelming majority of the residents of Quebec are of French ancestry. They fear that their cultural and linguistic identity is being swamped by the majority of Canadians, who are English-speaking. Many people in Quebec also feel more culturally tied to France than they do to the rest of Canada or the United States. The French speakers in Canada feel like a cultural and linguistic minority. Independence would allow them to protect and advance their culture and society.

White Goods, Inc., an American firm that has a microwave oven manufacturing factory outside Montreal, was nervous when it heard the statement from the Quebec premier. The talk of separation created a great deal of uncertainty. Many foreign firms were passing over Montreal and establishing offices in another major Canadian city, Toronto. Many Canadian firms, too, were moving out of Quebec or postponing new investments in their Quebec operations. White Goods wondered whether the NAFTA agreement would remain in effect in Quebec if it became a separate country. There was also concern about other issues, such as being able to sell goods made in Quebec in other parts of Canada, whether there would be a new currency, and what the exchange rates would be, if the political relationship with the United States would change, and many other matters.

The White Goods firm is doing well, with sales growing rapidly. It has to decide soon whether to expand the Montreal plant or build a new one elsewhere in the United States or Canada.

THINK CRITICALLY

1. What should White Goods do? Why?
2. If Quebec became an independent country, how might this event affect White Goods's operations in that country?
3. If White Goods decides not to expand its factory in Montreal, how will that affect the company's relations with the Quebec provincial government?
4. Why would the political uncertainty in Quebec hinder White Goods's ability to plan for the future?
5. Should White Goods get involved in Quebec politics and try to influence the outcome of the next referendum?

CASE 4-2: NAFTA's Impact on a Mexican Business

Despite intense lobbying by Mexican frozen-food companies against NAFTA, the Mexican government approved the treaty. Hidalgo Tortilla Company is a small firm based in Guadalajara, Mexico's second-largest city. It makes frozen taco and enchilada products for Mexico's rapidly growing middle class. The company was against the trade treaty, because it feared that American competitors would come to Mexico and drive smaller Mexican firms like itself out of business. American food companies, such as Sara Lee and Swanson, are very large and resourceful. They have huge modern factories with low production costs. Because the frozen-foods market is well developed in the United States, the American companies produce a wide range of products and use sophisticated marketing techniques.

Once NAFTA became a reality, Hidalgo began to prepare for competition in Mexico from American frozen-food companies. It was clear that Hidalgo could not go head-to-head in competition with larger and well-off American companies. However, the company's brand name is well known to Mexicans, and the company produces frozen food that appeals to the Mexican palate. There is a very large population of Mexicans in the American states just across the Mexican border.

Hidalgo Tortilla Company's management is exploring a number of options, such as focusing only on the Mexican market, using NAFTA to expand into the U.S. market, expanding into other Central and South American countries, or selling their current business to a large U.S.-based company.

THINK CRITICALLY

1. Does the fact that no tariffs and quotas will exist under NAFTA necessarily mean that American companies will be successful in Mexico? Explain.
2. Does NAFTA provide any opportunities for Hidalgo Tortilla Company to grow? Explain.
3. If Hidalgo proves to be a tough competitor to the American companies, what may the American companies do?
4. What should Hidalgo do to prepare itself for possible competition from American products?
5. How might cultural differences work to Hidalgo's competitive advantage?
6. How likely would it be for an American company to buy Hidalgo?
7. Explain how increased competition from American companies would help or hinder the competitiveness of Mexican businesses.

GOING INTERNATIONAL

New small businesses seldom consider the impact of international business on their operations, yet almost all businesses today operate in an international business environment. Many suppliers of products and services purchased by small businesses are international or are owned by businesses located in other countries. A foreign market becomes less foreign as you learn more about it. As a business owner, you need to study those markets in order to understand potential foreign business opportunities. A small business that carefully researches a foreign market can be just as successful in international markets as a large business.

DATA COLLECTION

1. Fresh fruits are often imported from other countries. Using the Internet or the library, locate information that identifies the major international suppliers of fruits to the United States. Prepare one or more pie charts that illustrate your findings.
2. Using the Internet or the library, collect information on recent trade agreements and legislation that deal with international business. Summarize what experts are predicting will be the effect of the agreements and laws on U.S. businesses.
3. If you have access to people who have lived in other countries, discuss the types of health and wellness businesses, including juice bars, they are familiar with in the country in which they lived. Identify similarities to and differences from the ways businesses operate in the United States.

ANALYSIS

1. Identify three ways that international trade by U.S. businesses can have a positive effect on small businesses and three ways it can have a negative effect on those businesses.
2. Identify several food products popular in other countries and cultures that you would consider adding to your product line in the juice bar. Remember that the products should fit the image of health and fitness.
3. Assume that you have operated your business for 15 years, and it has been very successful in the United States. You now have franchises in 30 states. You want to test the international market to see if the business will work in other countries. Identify at least two countries in which you would consider introducing your business and justify your choices. Base your justification on information you have collected from the Internet or the library about the countries you chose.

Career Cluster
Customs Inspector

Customs inspectors enforce laws governing imports and exports. Stationed in the United States and overseas at airports, seaports, and border crossing points, they examine, count, weigh, and measure cargoes entering and leaving the United States to determine whether the shipments are legal and how much duty must be paid. They determine whether people, ships, planes, and anything used to import or export cargo comply with all necessary regulations.

Employment Outlook

National security concerns and growing international trade are increasing the demand for customs inspectors, which is expected to rise 10 to 20 percent over the next 10 years. Customs inspecting is a federal job and less susceptible to economic conditions.

Job Titles

Customs and Border Protection Officer
Customs Agricultural Agent
Import Specialist
Compliance Inspector
Facility Operations Specialist
Intelligence Analyst

Needed Skills

- Must be a U.S. citizen and pass an extensive background investigation and medical examination.
- Must possess a bachelor's degree from an accredited college or university or possess three years of generalized experience.
- Must be willing to accept temporary or permanent assignments in a variety of geographical areas.

PHOTO: © DIGITAL VISION.

Working in Customs Services

Leopoldo began his career as a police officer in a small Texas town. After three years, he applied for a job as a customs inspector. His first assignment was on the U.S.–Mexico border, where he inspected cargo, baggage, people, cars, and trains entering the United States for contraband. This experience led to a new opportunity as an intelligence analyst. He will work with larger cases related to narcotics smuggling, money laundering, child pornography, and customs fraud. His goal is to move eventually into top management at the Customs Service.

Career Assessment

Why are customs agents important to international business? Why are they important to national security? What do you like and dislike about this career area?

Case Study

ILLEGALS EXPLOITED IN KATRINA CLEANUP

Hurricane Katrina devastated New Orleans and the Gulf Coast of Mississippi. Post-Katrina reconstruction in New Orleans has depended heavily upon illegal workers from Mexico who appear at dawn and wait to be picked up for 14-hour shifts of hauling debris, ripping out drywall, and nailing walls.

Before Hurricane Katrina, Louisiana had one of the smallest Hispanic populations in the country. Hispanics represented 2.5 percent of residents, compared with 12.5 percent nationally. Nearly 100,000 Hispanics moved to the Gulf Coast region after Katrina, lured by promises of plentiful work and high wages. Nearly one-fourth of the construction workers in New Orleans are illegal immigrants.

Since many of the workers rebuilding New Orleans are in the U.S. illegally, they are vulnerable to exploitation. They work in hazardous conditions without protective gear and earn much less than their legal counterparts. Documented workers in New Orleans are paid $16.50 per hour, while illegal immigrants are paid $10 per hour.

Workers from Mexico have responded to a national priority to rebuild the city while their rights to safety are being violated. Under federal labor laws, illegal immigrants are given the same health and safety protections as documented workers.

Fewer than one-third of illegal immigrants said that they understood the hazards of removing asbestos or mold, compared with more than 65 percent of documented laborers. Many immigrant workers are afraid to raise their concerns to employers for fear they will be deported to Mexico.

Protecting the border between the United States and Mexico has become a hot political topic. Numerous illegal immigrants are performing important work in construction, agriculture, food processing, and the reconstruction of areas devastated by Hurricane Katrina. Opinion polls indicate that Americans want the borders tightened to shut down the pipeline of illegal immigrants coming into the United States.

THINK CRITICALLY

1. Why are illegal workers likely candidates for rebuilding the areas devastated by Hurricane Katrina?
2. Why do workers from Mexico risk coming to the United States for employment?
3. What are two ethical issues involved with this case?
4. What types of jobs provide popular employment for illegal immigrants? Why?

Emerging Business Issues Team Event

This team event (two or three members) challenges FBLA members to develop and demonstrate research and presentation skills for an emerging business issue. Your research should help you develop affirmative and negative arguments for each topic.

- Citizenship for Illegal Immigrants Working in the U.S.
- Consumer Credit in the Economy
- Conducting Trade Throughout the World
- Tax Cuts in the Market Economy
- Investment in the Development of Alternative Fuel Products
- Making English the National Language in the United States
- Increasing Security at the Border of the U.S. and Mexico
- Raising the Minimum Wage in the U.S.

PERFORMANCE INDICATORS EVALUATED

- Understand the given emerging business issue.
- Present a relevant affirmative or negative argument for the topic.
- Conduct research to support your argument with relevant quality evidence.
- Demonstrate persuasive speaking and oral presentation skills.
- Involve all team members in the research and presentation.

For more detailed information about performance indicators, go to the FBLA Web site.

Fifteen minutes before your presentation time, you will draw to determine whether you will present an affirmative or negative argument for your emerging business issue. Each presentation may last no more than five minutes. Following each oral presentation, the judges have five minutes to ask questions. Each team should be prepared to defend its affirmative or negative argument. Any presentation that lasts more than five minutes will receive a five-point deduction.

THINK CRITICALLY

1. Why is it important to consider both sides of an issue before presenting your viewpoint?
2. Why is it important to list pros and cons for an issue when trying to sell your viewpoint?
3. Why is it important to determine the demographics of your audience before presenting a speech?

http://www.fbla-pbl.org/

Forms of Business Ownership and the Law

CHAPTERS

" Recent changes in the economy have stimulated increased interest in being one's own boss. The downsizing of large corporations has displaced millions of workers and managers. Many of these employees have taken the trauma of being laid off and turned it into a self-employment opportunity, frequently financed in large part by severance pay or an early retirement bonus. "

Stephen P. Robbins

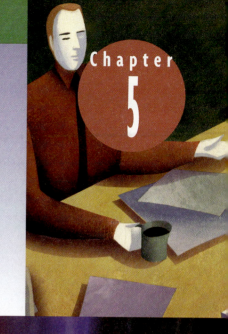

Proprietorships and Partnerships

5.1 Entrepreneurship

5.2 Proprietorship

5.3 Partnership

One Way to Start a Business

Nancy Watanabe wondered about the rest of her life as she sat in front of her computer. Was she too young to even consider starting her own business? Was the whole idea of opening a small computer rental business ridiculous for a 19-year-old? "My father would be proud if he knew my dream of investing the money I inherited to start a business," she thought to herself. "If only he were here to show me what to do. Fortunately, the library and the Internet have plenty of information on how to get started."

Nancy continued thinking to herself. "I've learned plenty during the last several weeks, reading and talking with my neighbor who runs the local Taco Bell fast-food business. Working as a cashier and computer salesperson in the local computer store while in high school also gave me experience. Yet, there's so much I don't know. I've never hired anyone or kept the books. But the idea is so exciting. Will people stop at . . . Nancy's Computer Rentals . . . for an extra computer during busy times or while they wait for their broken computer to be repaired?" Nancy turned back to her Web browser. "Did I just name my store?" she asked, smiling to herself.

Many people have dreamed about owning their own business. The idea may have crossed your mind, too. These dreams often start as simple ideas. Some dreamers with practical ideas do form businesses. That is how many well-known founders of large businesses got started. Hundreds of young entrepreneurs have started their own firms, including Dell Computer's Michael Dell, Microsoft's Bill Gates, and Amazon.com's Jeff Bezos.

Most businesses begin with one owner. But some firms start with two or more owners. One person, or a group of people, invests in a business with the hope of becoming successful owners. This chapter will examine the basic elements, advantages, and disadvantages of starting a business alone or with others.

5.1 Entrepreneurship

Goals
- Describe the characteristics of successful entrepreneurs.
- Discuss the responsibilities of owning your own business.

Terms
- business plan
- Small Business Administration (SBA)
- Small Business Development Centers (SBDCs)

Characteristics of Entrepreneurs

You learned earlier that an entrepreneur is a person who assumes the risk of starting, owning, and operating a business for the purpose of making a profit. Although individuals form businesses to earn a profit by providing consumers with a desired product or service, they often must invest months or even years of hard work before they earn a profit. About half of all new businesses end within the first five to six years. Businesses often fail for financial reasons, but many closings of young firms occur because the owners are not well suited to entrepreneurship. But although successful entrepreneurs are all uniquely different, they also have some common personal characteristics.

Some people would rather work for others, whereas other people prefer to work for themselves. Entrepreneurs who prefer self-employment enjoy the freedom and independence that come with being their own bosses and making their own decisions. Even when their businesses are not immediately successful, they do not give up. In fact, some entrepreneurs who are eventually successful often experience unsuccessful business start-ups. However, they learn from their mistakes and start over.

Entrepreneurs are self-starters who have plenty of energy and enjoy working on their own. They like to take charge of situations and usually work hard and for long periods in order to meet their goals. Entrepreneurs are also creative thinkers, often coming up with new ideas and new ways to solve problems. Most successful small-business owners like people, and people like them. As a result, they are often community leaders.

Prosperous entrepreneurs have other common characteristics. Generally, they obtain work experience in the types of businesses they launch. The person who starts a computer store, for example, has usually taken some computer courses and worked for a business that makes, sells, or services computers. In addition to having appropriate work experience, successful business owners are well informed about financial, marketing, and legal matters.

There is no magic age for starting a business. Teenagers, parents of teenagers, and retirees have all started successful firms. In recent years, increasing numbers of women, Asian-Americans, Hispanics, and African-Americans of all ages have opened their own firms. To start your own business, you need adequate funds, a general knowledge about business, some work experience, and a business opportunity.

One of the very first decisions a budding business owner must make is what legal form of ownership to adopt. The form of ownership selected depends on

facts & figures

The U.S. economy is dominated by family businesses. According to some estimates, as many as 90 percent of all businesses, including the majority of small- and medium-size companies, are owned by families.

several factors, such as the nature and size of the business, the capital needed, the tax laws, and the financial responsibility the owner is willing to assume. Two legal forms of business ownership—proprietorships and partnerships—are presented in this chapter. Also discussed in this chapter is the selection of a legal name for a business. But first, let's investigate the challenging responsibilities that entrepreneurs face.

CHECKPOINT

Explain why small businesses often fail.

Getting a Business Started

Starting a business entails many more responsibilities than simply being an employee does. Assume, for example, that you are employed as a delivery person. Your duties include making pickups and deliveries. After obtaining several years of valuable work experience, you decide to start your own delivery service. You need to create a plan and develop an awareness of your responsibilities as the owner of a business.

PREPARE A BUSINESS PLAN

Before starting a business, you need to prepare a **business plan**. A business plan is a written document that describes the nature of the business, its goals and objectives, and how they will be achieved. The business plan requires a great deal of careful thought. Most plans include the items shown in Figure 5-1 (see p. 114).

PHOTO: © GETTY IMAGES/PHOTODISC.

An entrepreneur assumes the risk of starting and operating a business for the purpose of making a profit. What are some personal characteristics of entrepreneurs?

FIGURE 5-1 Elements of a Business Plan

NATURE OF THE BUSINESS

Detailed description of products and/or services
Estimation of risk based on analysis of the industry
Size of business
Location of business
Background of entrepreneur(s)

GOALS AND OBJECTIVES

Basic results expected in the short and long run
Results expressed in terms of sales volume or profits

MARKETING PLAN

Customers and their demand for the product or service
Prices for the product or service
Comparison of product or service with competitors

FINANCIAL PLAN

Investment needed to start and maintain the business
Projected income, expenses, and profit
Cash start-up and cash flow needs

ORGANIZATIONAL PLAN

Legal form of ownership
Legal factors—licenses, leases, contracts
Organization chart
Job descriptions and employee skills needed
Physical facilities—buildings, equipment, tools

Developing a business plan will help you see more clearly the risks and responsibilities involved in starting a business, and will help you decide whether you really want to do it. Writing down your strategies for achieving your goals can give you confidence that your business can succeed. Your plan can also inspire the confidence of others with whom you will deal. Bankers, for instance, will ask to see your plan if you wish to borrow start-up funds. They will have greater assurance when they see how carefully you have considered potential problems and solutions before launching your new enterprise. Equally important will be your own conviction that your business will thrive. Too many people who enter business fail for one of three reasons: (1) they did not prepare a business plan, (2) their plan was unrealistic, or (3) they wrote the plan only because the lender, such as a bank, required it. To be successful, you need to start with a well-designed, realistic plan.

GOVERNMENT SUPPORT

The U.S. government has a strong support network to help entrepreneurs and small businesses. The Small Business Administration (SBA) is a government-supported agency that counsels, assists, and protects the interests of small businesses. It provides SBA loan guarantees to small businesses that have strong business plans or need help after disasters. The SBA also sponsors free consulting assistance through **Small Business Development Centers (SBDCs)**. Entrepreneurs who need help researching and writing business plans can use SBDC services.

ASSUME THE RESPONSIBILITIES OF BUSINESS OWNERSHIP

By developing a workable business plan, entrepreneurs become aware of their risks. As a result, they may be able to anticipate problems and take preventive action. The business plan also causes the aspiring business owner to become more realistic about the responsibilities of ownership.

As the owner of your new delivery service, you have duties that include not only pickups and deliveries but also many other responsibilities. Even if you run the business from your home, you will have added expenses for an office, a garage, a computer and printer, and communication devices such as a fax, cell phone, and answering machine. You must find customers, persuade those customers to pay a fair price for your services, and collect from those customers. Furthermore, you must assume responsibility for damage that may occur to your merchandise. You will have to pay fees for various licenses, taxes, insurance premiums, gasoline, van repairs, and other operating expenses. It may also be necessary to hire, train, and supervise employees.

Aspiring entrepreneurs should carefully consider the responsibilities of ownership before opening a business. These tasks are welcome challenges for some people, but may seem like overwhelming burdens to others. People who enjoy being leaders and making decisions find great satisfaction in owning a business. Ownership offers opportunities to make

NETBookmark

The SBA provides an extensive Web site to support small business. Point your browser to www.thomsonedu.com/school/bpmxtra. Create a list of the major areas of SBA support. Click on "Starting Your Business." Write a brief summary of the types of information provided. Describe how this information can help a small business be successful.

www.thomsonedu.com/school/bpmxtra

The most common form of business ownership is the proprietorship. What are some advantages and disadvantages of proprietorships?

PHOTO: © GETTY IMAGES/PHOTODISC.

one's own decisions and to experience other rewards. Some of these rewards will be identified in the section that follows.

INTRAPRENEURS

Entrepreneurship is not just a skill for new business start-ups. Most large companies realize that they must be innovative in order to compete against smaller start-up businesses. They look to hire individuals with entrepreneurial skills. These individuals act as intrapreneurs, or people who take on the responsibility of developing a new innovation in a larger company.

 CHECKPOINT
Describe the advantages of developing a business plan.

5.1 Assessment

UNDERSTAND MANAGEMENT CONCEPTS

Circle the best answer for each of the following questions.

1. Which of the following is *not* characteristic of entrepreneurs?
   a. They are self-starters.
   b. They like to make sure others do most of the work.
   c. They enjoy working on their own.
   d. They usually work hard and for long periods.

2. A business plan is a written document that
   a. describes the nature of the business
   b. describes the company's goals and objectives
   c. describes how goals and objectives will be achieved
   d. all of the above

THINK CRITICALLY

Answer the following questions as completely as possible.

3. Describe how the U.S. government supports small businesses.

4. Explain why a large business would want to have an employee with entrepreneurial skills.

thomsonedu.com/school/bpmxtra

5.2 Proprietorship

Goals
- Explain the advantages and disadvantages of proprietorships.
- Describe the types of businesses suited to being proprietorships.

Terms
- sole proprietorship
- proprietorship
- proprietor
- creditors

The Nature of Proprietorships

The most common form of business organization is the proprietorship, of which there are over 16 million in the United States. A business owned and managed by one person is known as a **sole proprietorship**, or **proprietorship**, and the owner-manager is the **proprietor**. In addition to owning and managing the business, the proprietor often performs the day-to-day tasks that make a business successful, with the help of hired employees. Under the proprietorship form of organization, the owner furnishes expertise, money, and management. For assuming these responsibilities, the owner is entitled to all profits earned by the business.

Provided that no debts are owed, a proprietor has full claim to the assets, or property owned by the business. If the proprietor has business debts, however, **creditors** (those to whom money is owed) have first claim against the assets. Figure 5-2 presents a simple financial statement of Jennifer York, who is the proprietor of a small retail grocery store and fruit market.

This simple financial statement, known as a *statement of financial position*, or *balance sheet*, shows that the assets of the business are valued at $218,400. Because York has *liabilities* (money owed by a business) amounting to $14,400, the balance sheet shows her capital as $204,000 ($218,400 minus $14,400). In accounting, the terms *capital*, *net worth*, and *equity* are interchangeable and are

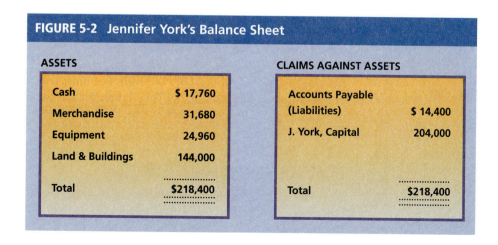

FIGURE 5-2 Jennifer York's Balance Sheet

ASSETS		CLAIMS AGAINST ASSETS	
Cash	$ 17,760	Accounts Payable (Liabilities)	$ 14,400
Merchandise	31,680	J. York, Capital	204,000
Equipment	24,960		
Land & Buildings	144,000		
Total	$218,400	Total	$218,400

defined as assets less liabilities. If there are profits, York gets the total amount. She must also absorb losses. Because she owns the land and the building, she does not have to pay rent, although she must pay the cost of maintenance and taxes for the property.

ADVANTAGES OF PROPRIETORSHIPS

The fact that almost three out of four businesses are proprietorships indicates that this form of organization has definite advantages. Can you list any of the advantages before reading further?

OWNER IS BOSS There is a great deal of pride and satisfaction in being one's own boss and being responsible only to oneself. The proprietor can be inventive and creative in working out ideas to make the business a success.

OWNER RECEIVES ALL PROFITS Very closely related to the first advantage is the fact that all the profits belong to the sole proprietor. As a result, the owner is more likely to work overtime and to think continually of how the business can operate more efficiently.

OWNER PERSONALLY KNOWS EMPLOYEES AND CUSTOMERS Because most proprietorships are small, the proprietor and the employees know one another personally. This relationship can lead to mutual understanding and a feeling of "family" as employer and employees work side by side in daily business activities. Sole proprietors often develop close relationships with their customers as well.

OWNER CAN ACT QUICKLY IN DECISION MAKING Sole proprietors can make decisions without consulting others, so they can act promptly when the need arises. If an unusual opportunity to buy merchandise or equipment arises, or if the owner wishes to change the location of the business or to sell on credit terms rather than on a cash basis, there are no dissenting partners to stop such action. Thus, the management of a proprietorship is flexible and can adjust rapidly to changing conditions.

OWNER IS FREE FROM RED TAPE A sole proprietor can usually begin or end business activities without legal formality. Sole proprietorships can be organized without a lot of legal documents or government red tape. In some types of businesses, however, such as restaurants, it is necessary to obtain a license before operations can begin.

PAY LESS INCOME TAX THAN A CORPORATION For most sole proprietorships, the income tax is less than for the corporation type of business, which is explained in the next chapter.

DISADVANTAGES OF PROPRIETORSHIPS

There are many advantages to owning your own business. However, there are also some disadvantages facing the sole proprietor.

business *note*

Entrepreneurs are the lifeblood of the U.S. economy. Many of the most successful businesses in the United States started in a home garage, including: Ford, Apple Computer, Mattel, Hewlett Packard, and Disney.

The risk of business start-up failure is very high. Not all business start-ups end up as failures. One study showed that about 30 percent of start-ups show a profit, about 30 percent break even, and 30 percent lose money. Businesses close because owners don't make enough money, they want to move on to new things, or they get tired. Real failures (loss of money) are most often due to lack of planning in business goals, marketing, management, and financing. Entrepreneurs can lower risk by researching and writing a strong business plan.

OWNER MAY LACK NECESSARY SKILLS AND ABILITIES Each person has special skills and abilities. One person may excel at selling. Another person may be more talented at purchasing goods or keeping records. A third person may be superior at supervising employees. All of these activities are important to the success of a business, but the proprietor is likely to be weak in one or more areas. No one can do everything well. It is therefore easy to understand why some proprietorships end in failure within a short time.

OWNER MAY LACK FUNDS Additional funds (capital) are often needed for emergencies. Financial assistance on a large scale may be difficult to obtain by a single owner. Therefore the expansion of the business may be slowed because of the owner's lack of capital.

OWNER BEARS ALL LOSSES Sole proprietors assume a great deal of risk. Although sole owners receive all the profits of the business, they also bear all the losses if the business fails. If the business fails and the owner is unable to pay the debts of the business, the creditors have a claim against the owner's personal assets, not just the assets of the business. The sole entrepreneur may therefore lose not only the money invested in the enterprise but also personal possessions, such as a car or home.

ILLNESS OR DEATH MAY CLOSE THE BUSINESS The continuing operation of a sole proprietorship depends on the longevity of the proprietor. If the owner becomes unable to work because of illness or dies, the business would have to close.

CHECKPOINT

List the advantages and disadvantages of being a sole proprietor.

Businesses Suited to Being Proprietorships

The kind of business that is primarily concerned with providing personal services is well suited to the proprietorship form of organization. Dentists, accountants, landscape gardeners, carpenters, painters, barbers, beauty salons, Web site developers, and computer *consultants* (experts) are examples of businesses frequently organized as proprietorships.

Another type of business that seems to be well suited to proprietorship is the type that sells merchandise or services on a small scale. Newspaper and magazine stands, roadside markets, fast-food and family restaurants, flower shops, gasoline stations, small grocery stores, fish markets, and many Web-based businesses that sell crafts, gourmet foods, or grocery delivery services are examples. In general, the type of business that can be operated suitably as a proprietorship is one that (1) is small enough to be managed by the proprietor or a few people hired by the proprietor and (2) does not require a large amount of capital.

PART-TIME PROPRIETORSHIPS

Not all proprietors run full-time businesses. Many people run part-time businesses out of an office or their home. The IRS found that more than 6 percent of individual taxpayers filed a Schedule C form (tax form for proprietorships) as sole proprietors in 2001. Up to a third of all proprietorships are part-time. Part-time proprietorships are especially appealing to stay-at-home parents.

CHECKPOINT
List the types of business that would be a good fit for a sole proprietor.

5.2 Assessment

UNDERSTAND MANAGEMENT CONCEPTS

Circle the best answer for each of the following questions.

1. Advantages of proprietorships include all of the following *except*
   a. owner is their own boss
   b. owner receives all the profits
   c. owner deals with limited red tape
   d. owner pays more taxes than corporations

2. Disadvantages of proprietorships include all of the following *except*
   a. owner is likely to have all of the skills needed for the business
   b. owner may lack funds
   c. owner bears all the losses
   d. owner may need to close the business in case of illness

THINK CRITICALLY

Answer the following questions as completely as possible.

3. Explain how a balance sheet is used to show owner equity.

4. Explain why a business that is small enough to be managed by one or a few people and does not require a large amount of capital would be good for a proprietorship.

Xtra!
Study Tools
thomsonedu.com/school/bpmxtra

5.3 | Partnership

Goals

- Explain advantages and disadvantages of partnerships.
- Describe the types of businesses suited to the partnership form of business.

Terms

- partnership
- limited partnership
- unlimited financial liability

The Nature of Partnerships

Jennifer York, who operates the proprietorship mentioned earlier, is faced with the problem of expanding her business. She has run the business successfully for over 10 years. She sees new opportunities in the community for increasing her business, but she does not wish to assume full responsibility for the undertaking. She realizes that the expansion of the business will entail considerable financial and managerial responsibilities. She also realizes that in order to expand, she needs additional capital, but she does not want to borrow the money. Because of these reasons, she has decided that it would be wise to change her business from a proprietorship to a **partnership**, a business owned by two or more people.

Robert Burton operates an adjoining bakery, where he bakes fresh bread and pastries daily. He has proven to be honest and to have considerable business ability. Combining the two businesses could result in more customers for both groceries and fresh baked goods. Customers who have been coming to the bake shop may become grocery customers also. And those who have been buying at the grocery and fruit market may become customers of bakery products. A discussion between York and Burton leads to a tentative agreement to form a partnership if a third person can be found who will invest enough cash to remodel both stores to form one large store and to purchase additional equipment. The financial statement for Burton's business is shown in Figure 5-3.

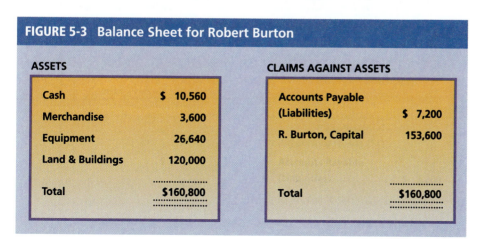

FIGURE 5-3 Balance Sheet for Robert Burton

ASSETS		CLAIMS AGAINST ASSETS	
Cash	$ 10,560	Accounts Payable (Liabilities)	$ 7,200
Merchandise	3,600	R. Burton, Capital	153,600
Equipment	26,640		
Land & Buildings	120,000		
Total	$160,800	Total	$160,800

The net worth of Burton's business is $153,600. In other words, after deducting the amount of his liabilities ($7,200) from the total value of his assets ($160,800), his business is worth $153,600. According to Jennifer York's balance sheet in Figure 5-2, her business is worth $204,000. In order to have an equal investment in the partnership, Burton must invest an additional $50,400 in cash.

They find Lu Chan, a person with accounting experience, who has $144,000 and is able to borrow the remaining $60,000 to become an equal partner. The partnership agreement, shown in Figure 5-4, is then written and signed by York, Burton, and Chan.

Once the partnership is formed, a statement of financial position (balance sheet) must be prepared. This statement shows the total assets, liabilities, and capital of the owners at the start of the business. The partnership's balance sheet is shown in Figure 5-5. Each asset category on the combined balance sheet (merchan-

FIGURE 5-4   A clearly written and understood partnership agreement can prevent problems later.

Partnership Agreement

This contract, made and entered into on the first day of June, 20-- by and between Jennifer L. York, of Buffalo, New York, party of the first part, Robert R. Burton, of Buffalo, New York, party of the second part, Lu Chan of Niagara Falls, New York, party of the third part:

Witnesseth: That the said parties have this day formed a partnership for the purpose of engaging in and conducting a retail grocery-fruit-meat market and bakery under the following stipulations, which are made a part of the contract:

First: The said partnership is to continue for a term of ten years from date hereof.

Second: The business shall be conducted under the firm name of Y, B, & C Fine Foods, at 4467 Goodson Street, Buffalo, New York.

Third: The investments are as follows: Jennifer L. York: Cash, $17,760; Merchandise, $31,680; Equipment, $24,960; Land and Buildings, $144,000; Total Assets, $218,400; less Accounts Payable, $14,400, equals Net Investment, $204,000. Robert R. Burton: Cash, $10,560; Merchandise, $3,600; Equipment, $26,640; Land and Buildings, $120,000; Total Assets, $160,800, less Accounts Payable, $7,200, equals Net Investment, $153,000. Lu Chan: Cash, $204,000.

Fourth: All profits or losses arising from said business are to be shared equally.

Fifth: Each partner is to devote his or her entire time and attention to the business and to engage in no other business enterprise without the written consent of the others.

Sixth: Each partner is to have a salary of $5,000 a month, the same to be withdrawn at such time as he or she may elect. No partner is to withdraw from the business an amount in excess of his or her salary without the written consent of the others.

Seventh: The duties of each partner are defined as follows: Jennifer L. York is to supervise the grocery-fruit-vegetable departments. Robert R. Burton is to supervise the bakery and meat departments. Lu Chan is to manage finances, inventory, and records.

Eighth: No partner is to become surety for anyone without the written consent of the others.

Ninth: In case of the death, incapacity, or withdrawal of one partner, the business is to be conducted for the remainder of the fiscal year by the surviving partners, the profits for the year allocated to the withdrawing partner to be determined by the ratio of the time he or she was a partner during the year to the whole year.

Tenth: In case of dissolution the assets are to be divided in the ratio of the capital invested at the time of dissolution.

In Witness Whereof, the parties aforesaid have hereunto set their hands and affixed their seals on the day and year above written.

In the presence of: . . . . (Seal)

. . . . (Seal)

. . . . (Seal)

FIGURE 5-5 Balance Sheet for York, Burton, and Chan at Start-up

ASSETS		CLAIMS AGAINST ASSETS	
Cash	$282,720	Accounts Payable (Liabilities)	$ 21,600
Merchandise	35,280	J. York, Capital	204,000
Equipment	51,600	R. Burton, Capital	204,000
Land & Buildings	264,000	L. Chan, Capital	204,000
Total	$633,600	Total	$633,600

dise, equipment, and land and buildings) as well as the accounts payable liability category is the totals of these categories from Burton's and York's businesses. The cash category combines the cash from both businesses plus Chan's cash investment of $204,000.

A key factor in the success of a partnership is that the partners must clearly agree upon each person's responsibilities. York, Burton, and Chan divide their duties: York supervises the grocery department, Burton supervises the bake shop and meat department, and Chan handles the finances, inventory, and records.

During the year the three partners combine the stores, remodel them, buy new equipment, and open for business. The financial statement at the end of the year, shown in Figure 5-6, shows the results of the new partnership.

Has the partnership had a successful year? Each partner has received a salary of $5,000 a month (according to the terms of the partnership agreement). In addition, the capital or net worth of each partner has increased from $204,000 to $221,700 as a result of profits made during the year. This increase in the total capital from $612,000 ($204,000 times 3) to $665,100 ($221,700 times 3) amounts to $53,100 and is an increase of nearly 8.7 percent. Chan, who borrowed some of the money for his investment, had to pay 7 percent interest to the lender. His investment in the partnership brought him a return that is more than the interest on his loan.

FIGURE 5-6 York, Burton, and Chan's Balance Sheet at Year's End

ASSETS		CLAIMS AGAINST ASSETS	
Cash	$ 240,000	Accounts Payable (Liabilities)	$ 74,900
Merchandise	60,000	J. York, Capital	221,700
Equipment	90,000	R. Burton, Capital	221,700
Land & Buildings	350,000	L. Chan, Capital	221,700
Total	$740,000	Total	$740,000

ADVANTAGES OF PARTNERSHIPS

Many businesses are organized as partnerships at the very beginning. There are nearly 1.6 million businesses operating as partnerships in the United States, which is a small number in comparison to sole proprietorships. Though most partnerships have only two or three partners, there is no limit set on the number of partners. Some businesses have as many as 10 or more partners. Some of the advantages of partnerships are discussed below.

SKILLS AND ABILITIES POOLED A partnership is likely to be operated more efficiently than a proprietorship, because a partnership can draw on the skills of two or more people instead of just one. One partner may have special sales ability; another may have an aptitude for buying the right kind, quality, and quantity of merchandise. One partner may propose a change in the business; another partner may be able to point out disadvantages in the plan and suggest changes that were not initially apparent. In a sole proprietorship, the single owner must have skills in all key business areas or be able to hire people with the needed skills for the business to succeed.

SOURCES OF CAPITAL INCREASED A new business needs capital to buy the equipment, inventory, and office space needed to get started. Often two or more people can supply more capital than one person can. When the business needs to expand, generally several partners can obtain the additional capital needed for the expansion more easily than one person can.

CREDIT POSITION IMPROVED The partnership usually has a better credit reputation than the sole proprietorship. This is often true because more than one owner is responsible for the ownership and management of the business.

CONTRIBUTION OF GOODWILL Each partner is likely to have a large personal following. Some people will be more likely to do business with the newly formed partnership because they know one of the owners. This is known as *goodwill*.

INCREASED CONCERN IN BUSINESS MANAGEMENT Each owner of the business will have a greater interest in the firm as a partner than as an employee. Much of this is due to the greater financial responsibility each person has as a partner.

LOWER TAX BURDEN THAN CORPORATIONS Partnerships usually have a tax advantage over corporations. You will learn more about this in Chapter 6. Partnerships prepare a federal income tax report but do not pay a tax on their profits, as do corporations. However, partners must pay a personal income tax on their individual share of the profit.

REDUCTION IN COMPETITION Two or more proprietors in the same line of business may become one organization by forming a partnership. This move may substantially decrease, or even eliminate, competition.

RETIREMENT FROM MANAGEMENT A sole proprietor may wish to retire. However, the proprietor may not want to close the business. In such a case, the owner may form a partnership and allow the new owner to manage the business.

OPERATING ECONOMIES It is often possible to operate more efficiently by combining two or more businesses. In such a case, certain operating expenses—such as advertising, supplies, equipment, fuel, and rent—can be reduced.

DISADVANTAGES OF PARTNERSHIPS

Although there are many advantages of
partnerships, there are also disadvantages, as described below.

UNLIMITED FINANCIAL LIABILITY According to
the law, each member of the partnership
has an unlimited financial liability for all
the debts of the business. If some of the
partners are unable to pay their share,
one partner may have to pay all the debts.

Suppose that the partnership of York,
Burton, and Chan failed and that after all
the business assets were changed into cash
and used to pay business debts, the partnership still owed creditors $18,000. Legally,
the partners must pay these debts from their
own personal savings or sell personal property, such as their car or house, to obtain the
cash to pay off the debts. In this case, each
partner should contribute $6,000 ($18,000
divided by 3) from their personal assets. But if, say, Burton and Chan did not have
the $6,000 in personal assets to pay their portions, York would be legally respon-
sible for using her personal savings and property to pay the entire $18,000.

PHOTO: © DIGITAL VISION.

*A partnership is a business
owned by two or more persons.
Why might a partnership be
operated more efficiently than
a proprietorship?*

DISAGREEMENT AMONG PARTNERS There is always the danger of disagreement among
partners. The majority of the partners may want to change the nature of the business but are unable to do so because one partner refuses. For example, a partnership may have been formed to conduct a retail business selling audio equipment.
After a while, the majority of the partners may think it wise to add cellular phones
to their line of merchandise. The change may benefit the business. However, as
long as one partner disagrees, the partnership cannot make the change. Furthermore, partners sometimes feel that they are not properly sharing in the management. This situation may cause disagreements that could hurt the business. Such a
condition can be partly prevented if the partnership agreement states the duties of
each partner.

EACH PARTNER BOUND BY CONTRACTS OF OTHERS Each partner is bound by the partnership contracts made by any partner if such contracts apply to the ordinary
operations of the business. If one partner commits to a contract in the name of
the partnership, all partners are legally bound by it, whether they think the contract is good for the business or not. Disagreements can eventually lead to partnership failure.

UNCERTAIN LIFE The life of a partnership is uncertain. Sometimes when partners
draw up a partnership contract, they specify a definite length of time, such as
10 years, for the existence of the business. Should one partner die, however, the
partnership ends. The deceased partner may have been the principal manager,
and as a result of his or her death, the business may suffer. The heirs of the deceased partner may demand an unfair price from the surviving partners for the
share of the deceased partner. Or the heirs may insist on ending the partnership
quickly to obtain the share belonging to the dead partner. In the latter case, the
assets that are sold may not bring a fair price; as a result, all the partners suffer

A limited partnership restricts the liability of a partner for the amount of the partner's investment. Why might a limited partnership be a useful form of business organization?

a loss. A partnership can carry insurance on the life of each partner to provide money to purchase the share of a partner who dies. Under the laws of most states, the bankruptcy of any partner or the admission of a new partner are other causes that may bring a sudden end to the partnership.

LIMITED SOURCES OF CAPITAL The contributions of the partners, the earnings of the business, and the money that can be borrowed limit the amount of funds that a partnership can obtain. It is difficult for a partnership to obtain enough capital to operate a large business unless each member of the partnership is wealthy or unless there are many partners. Too many partners, however, may cause inefficient operations.

UNSATISFACTORY DIVISION OF PROFITS Sometimes the partnership profits are not divided fairly according to the contributions of the individual partners. Partners should agree up front on how to divide profits according to the amount of labor, expertise, and capital each partner is expected to contribute. The partnership should then specify the agreed-upon division in the partnership agreement, such as 60 percent to one partner and 40 percent to another. If no provision is made in the agreement, the law requires an equal division of the profits. Then if, say, one partner contributes more time, expertise, or labor to the business than do the others, this partner may feel that he or she deserves more than an equal share of the profit.

DIFFICULTY IN WITHDRAWING FROM PARTNERSHIP If a partner wishes to sell his or her interest in the business, it may be difficult to do so. Even if a buyer is found, the buyer may not be acceptable to the other partners.

LIMITED PARTNERSHIPS

In an ordinary (general) partnership, each partner is personally liable for all the debts incurred by the partnership. The laws of some states, however, permit the formation of a **limited partnership**, which restricts the liability of a partner to the amount of the partner's investment. In a limited partnership, not all partners have unlimited financial liability for the partnership debts. However, at least one partner must be a general partner who has unlimited liability. In many states, the name of a limited partner may not be included in the firm name.

Under the Uniform Limited Partnership Act, the states have created similar regulations for controlling limited partnerships. For example, the law requires that a certificate of limited partnership be filed in a public office of record and that proper notice be given to each creditor with whom the limited partnership does business. If these requirements are not fulfilled, the limited partners have unlimited liability in the same manner as a general partner.

The limited partnership is a useful form of business organization in situations where one person wishes to invest in a business but does not have the time or interest to participate actively in its management. Any business that is formed as a proprietorship can usually be formed as a limited partnership.

CHECKPOINT

List the advantages and disadvantages of being in a partnership.

Businesses Suited to Being Partnership

The partnership form of organization is common among businesses that furnish more than one kind of product or service. Each partner usually looks after a specialized phase of the business. For example, car dealers often have sales and service departments. One partner may handle the sale of new cars, and another partner may be in charge of servicing and repairing cars. Still another partner could be in charge of used-car sales or of the accounting and financial side of the business. Similarly, if a business operates in more than one location, each partner can be in charge of a specific location. Businesses that operate longer than the usual eight hours a day, such as the retail food business advertised in Figure 5-7, find the partnership organization desirable. Each partner can be in charge for part of the day.

Partnerships are also common in the same types of businesses that are formed as proprietorships, particularly those that sell goods and services to consumers. It is especially popular among those offering professional services, such as lawyers, doctors, accountants, and financial consultants. Internet businesses have been formed as partnerships as well. Good faith, together with reasonable care in the exercise of management duties, is required of all partners in a business.

BUSINESS NAME

A proprietorship or a partnership may be conducted under the name or names of the owner or owners. In many states, the law prohibits the use of *and Company* or *& Co.* unless such identification indicates additional partners. For example, if there are only two partners, it is not permissible to use a firm name such as Jones, Smith & Co., because that name indicates at least three partners. The name or names included in the term "Company" must be identified by registration at a public recording office, usually the county clerk's office. Usually one can do business

FIGURE 5-7 An Advertisement Announcing the Opening of the Y, B, and C Partnership

under a trade or artificial name, such as The Superior Shoe Store or W-W Manufacturing Company. Likewise, proper registration is usually required so that creditors may know everyone who is responsible for the business. Operating under a trade name, therefore, does not reduce the owners' liability to creditors.

CHECKPOINT

List the types of businesses that would be a good fit for a partnership.

5.3   Assessment

UNDERSTAND MANAGEMENT CONCEPTS

Circle the best answer for each of the following questions.

1. Advantages of partnerships include all of the following *except*
   a. partners can pool skills and abilities
   b. partners provide greater amounts of capital
   c. partners have limited liability
   d. the business's credit is improved

2. Disadvantages of partnerships include all of the following *except*
   a. partnerships may reduce competition
   b. partners may disagree
   c. partners are bound by contracts of others
   d. partnerships have an uncertain life

THINK CRITICALLY

Answer the following questions as completely as possible.

3. Explain the advantages of being a limited partner in a company.

4. Describe the nature of businesses that are suited to being partnerships.

Focus On...

Partnerships–Ben and Jerry's Homemade, Inc.

On May 5, 1978, Ben Cohen and Jerry Greenfield formed an ice cream parlor partnership in a renovated gas station in Burlington, Vermont. The two former seventh-grade buddies used top-quality ingredients and were delighted by their early success.

The business grew rapidly, but they had early concerns about getting too large. When the business was small, they enjoyed working alongside employees while making and experimenting with new products and flavors. But as the business expanded, they began to grow apart from their employees and felt as if they were losing the excitement and enjoyment they had experienced during the start-up days. Job fulfillment clearly mattered more than profits.

They tried to resist further expansion but knew the business either had to grow or fade away. Jerry retired. Another entrepreneur, however, convinced Ben that he could serve employees and the public while continuing to expand. With a new focus, Jerry rejoined Ben. Together they modified the firm's goals to expand their product line and also improve the quality of life for their employees and all of society.

In August 2000, Ben & Jerry's was purchased by the international corporation Unilever. The Ben & Jerry partnership continues because they act as spokespersons for the company they started. The principles on which Ben and Jerry founded the company remain relevant today. Ben & Jerry's is still committed to its employees. The company has achieved national recognition for developing a proud and productive workforce.

The Ben & Jerry's company continues to make, distribute, and sell super-premium ice cream, sorbet, and yogurt to supermarkets, restaurants, and franchised and company outlets in highly populated states and 20 foreign countries.

One important thing has not changed: Ben & Jerry's company is still committed to social responsibility. The Ben & Jerry's foundation gives away over $1 million each year to charities and to social and environmental causes. Ben and Jerry—an unusual pair of innovative partners—created a unique style of doing business.

Think Critically

1. At the outset, was Ben and Jerry's business typical for a new enterprise? Give reasons for your answer.
2. Why did Ben and Jerry want their company to remain small?
3. If the lowest-paid employee earned $15,000 a year, what would the maximum salary be for the highest-paid manager under the 7-to-1 rule? Why might this manager be unhappy with this rule?
4. Determine what the company is doing today to fulfill its social obligations. Also find out about its new products, sales, and profits.

CHAPTER CONCEPTS

- Most small businesses begin with one or a few owners. Characteristics that help assure these entrepreneurs' success include the strong need to be boss, to make their own decisions, and to take reasonable risks. To aid their success, they must prepare a business plan.

- A sole proprietorship, or proprietorship, is a business owned and operated by one person. Many small retail and service businesses are single-owner firms because they are the easiest to start. Other advantages include the power to make all decisions, receive all profits, pay less in taxes than corporations, and know employees and customers personally.

- Proprietorships have a few disadvantages, such as lacking skills or knowledge needed to perform all key business tasks, lacking funds for expansion, surviving major financial losses, and closing should illness or death occur.

- A partnership is a business owned by two or more people. Key advantages over sole proprietorships are that multiple owners can contribute more skills and capital to start or expand, can obtain more credit from banks and other sources, are in a better position to compete, and need not close because of an owner's retirement.

- Partnerships have several disadvantages. Each partner has unlimited financial liability for all business debts and is responsible for contracts made by other partners. Other problems can arise when a partnership breaks up, decides how to divide profits, or lacks the capital needed to expand.

- Some partnerships have limited partners who do not participate in running a business and have limited liability. However, one or more members of a partnership must be an ordinary (general) partner with unlimited liability.

REVIEW TERMS AND CONCEPTS

a. business plan
b. creditors
c. intrapreneur
d. limited partnership
e. partnership
f. proprietor
g. proprietorship
h. Small Business Administration (SBA)
i. Small Business Development Centers (SBDC)
j. sole proprietorship
k. unlimited financial liability

Write the letter of the term that matches each definition. Some terms will not be used.

1. When each partner is personally liable for all the debts incurred by the partnership
2. Written document that describes the nature of the business, the company's goals and objectives, and how they will be achieved
3. Those who have first claim against a business's assets
4. Business owned by two or more people
5. Type of business in which a partner's liability is limited to the amount of his or her investment
6. Person who owns and manages the business and often performs the day-to-day tasks, with the help of hired employees
7. Business owned and managed by one person
8. Government-supported agency that counsels, assists, and protects the interests of small businesses

DETERMINE THE BEST ANSWER

9. A business owned and managed by one person is a
   a. proprietorship
   b. sole proprietorship
   c. limited partnership
   d. either a or b
10. The SBA sponsors free consulting help through
   a. Entrepreneurship Support Centers (ESCs)
   b. Small Business Development Centers (SBDCs)
   c. SBA Development Centers (SDCSs)
   d. all of the above
11. Part-time proprietorships are common because
   a. part-time proprietors do not need to pay taxes
   b. part-time proprietorships work well for stay-at-home parents
   c. part-time proprietors have limited liability
   d. part-time proprietors are more likely to make money
12. Limited partnerships are characterized by all of the following (in some states) *except*
   a. the limited partner has limited financial liability
   b. at least one partner must be a general partner who has unlimited liability
   c. the name of a limited partner may not be included in the firm name
   d. all of the above are characteristic of a limited partnership in some states

APPLY WHAT YOU KNOW

13. Explain how a good business plan will help someone successfully open a new business.
14. Describe what kinds of businesses are most suited to the proprietorship form of business ownership.
15. Explain the types of situations in which a limited partnership would be most useful.
16. Explain why it is necessary for proprietorships and partnerships to register their company names with local authorities.
17. Your friend follows your advice and writes a business plan to create a new business called Cookies to Go. She does not include a marketing plan and you mention it. She says, "Everyone likes cookies. My prices depend on how much it costs to make each type of cookie. And there isn't a cookie store within three blocks of where I plan to locate my business. How could I go wrong?" List questions that should be answered in the marketing plan that would make your friend give more thought to her decision.
18. You have been working part-time and summers at a local service station. You have performed just about every task from pumping gas to repairing cars and even handling some of the bookkeeping. Discuss how your responsibilities as an employee will change if you become the owner of the station.

19. A partner signs a partnership contract for television advertising while the other two partners are on vacation. Upon returning, the vacationing partners claim the partnership is not bound to the contract because both of them disapprove of television advertising. Is the partnership legally bound?

MAKE CONNECTIONS

20. **Research** Assume you are considering forming a small business in your state. Search for information that will help you decide whether to open a sole proprietorship or a partnership. Use your school or public library to obtain information for writing a report on business plans, legal advice, and general state assistance. Find information from a government Web site, such as the Small Business Administration, or from a magazine targeted to small businesses.

21. **Math** Alvares invested $80,000 and Navarro invested $60,000 in their partnership. They share profits and losses in proportion to their investments. How much should each receive of last year's $33,600 profit?

22. **Technology** Use computer spreadsheet software such as Excel to analyze the following information. Assume the balance sheet of Tran and Nizami's partnership appeared as follows when they closed the business:

Assets	
Cash	$18,000
Merchandise	40,000
Fixtures and Equipment	24,000
Land and Building	108,000
Total	(Use formula here)

Claims Against Assets	
Accounts Payable (Liabilities)	$10,000
N. S. Tran, Capital	90,000
A. J. Nizami, Capital	90,000
Total	(Use formula here)

When selling the assets, the partners sold the merchandise for $32,000, the fixtures and equipment for $18,000, and the land and building for $110,000. After paying their debts, what amount of the remaining cash should each partner receive? Show the formulas you used in your spreadsheet.

23. **Speaking** Choose a few sample businesses and develop an argument for or against starting these businesses as a sole proprietorship or a partnership. Outline the pros and cons of each business form. Make a recommendation for each of the business examples you have chosen. Compare your recommendations to those of other students in the class.

CASE IN POINT

CASE 5-1: Partnership Problems

Sharon Gillespie, John Jensen, and Laura Cho have been close friends for years. About two years ago they formed a partnership to build Web pages for small entrepreneurs who want to expand their businesses. Sharon, John, and Laura are experts at what they do. However, their partnership has not been very successful and is not growing. John is in charge of finding and dealing with customers and handling the necessary paperwork. Both Sharon and Laura build the Web pages for their customers.

Recently, John confided to Laura that he is getting many complaints about Sharon's treatment of customers. "That may be the major reason we aren't doing that well, but what can we do about it?" He continued, "Her customers don't often come back to us when they need to add new products or offer new services on their Web pages. Some have even jotted complaints about her on the bills I send them. Yesterday one customer said he'll take his business elsewhere if we don't replace her." The phone rang, and John excused himself to answer it.

After thinking about this for a while, Laura told John, "We have to get rid of her because she isn't going to change. If we want our business to survive and grow, let's ask her to leave. What else can we do?"

John paused and then said, "She owns one-third of our business. You can't fire a partner."

Laura asked, "Didn't our lawyer provide for this type of problem in our partnership agreement? Or maybe it's in our business plan."

"No, it's not in either place," John responded. "We have to work this out together."

THINK CRITICALLY

Your instructor may wish to place you into groups of three students each to answer the following questions and to report their answers to the class.

1. What conditions existed before the partnership was formed that gave rise to this problem?
2. How important are the skills and personalities of the partners to the formation of a successful partnership?
3. Can Sharon's attitude toward customers somehow be changed? If so, how?
4. What is the best solution for this problem? Carefully explain your answer.
5. Do you believe that John and Sharon would be better off trading jobs with each other?
6. How is this partnership situation different from that of student groups that attempt to solve other types of group problems?

CASE 5-2: To Partner or Not to Partner

John Willis, who is 27 and single, had just completed his fifth year of employment as a carpenter for a very small homebuilder. His boss, the sole owner of the company, is Tyrone Young. A few days ago, Tyrone asked John if he would like to become a partner, which he could do by contributing $70,000. In turn, John would receive 40 percent of all profits earned by the business. John had saved $30,000 and could borrow the balance from his grandmother at a low interest rate, but he would have to pay her back within 15 years.

John was undecided about becoming a partner. He liked the idea but he also knew there were risks and concerns. He decided to talk to Tyrone at lunch. Here is how the conversation went.

John: *I've been giving your offer a lot of thought, Tyrone. It's a tough decision, and I don't want to make the wrong one. So I'd like to chat with you about some of the problems involved in running a business.*

Tyrone: *Sure. I struggled with these issues about 15 years ago. When you own your own business, you're the boss. No one can tell you what to do or push you around. You can set up your own hours and make all the decisions. I enjoy the feeling of ownership.*

John: *I don't know if I'm ready to become part owner of a business. I'm still young and single, and I like working for you. I'm not sure I want all those responsibilities—getting customers, paying bills, and buying tools and lumber. You say you set your own hours, but I know you're already working when I arrive each morning, and you're still here when I leave in the evening. I know you spend some nights in the office, because I see the lights on when I drive by.*

Tyrone: *Well, I do put in many hours. That goes with the territory. But I don't mind all those hours because I like making decisions. And when you join me as a partner, we'll share the work.*

John: *Then I'll be working longer hours. Both of us could go to work for that big new contracting firm on the other side of town. Let them struggle with all the problems and decisions. Then we could work shorter hours and have more time to relax.*

THINK CRITICALLY

1. Does John have the personality to be a sole proprietor?
2. Do you think John is seriously ready to become a partner? Explain your answer.
3. If you were in John's position, how would you decide? Explain.
4. If John decides to accept Tyrone's offer, what action should be taken next?
5. Why would Tyrone offer to make John a partner?
6. Find information from the library or the Internet that might help John make a decision. One possible source is the Web site of the Small Business Administration.

PROPRIETORSHIP OR PARTNERSHIP?

New owners often start a business without carefully considering other possible forms of ownership. In this chapter, you will evaluate the advantages and disadvantages of the proprietorship and partnership forms of ownership for your new business.

DATA COLLECTION

1. Review copies of magazines written for entrepreneurs. Identify the current issues and problems faced by individual business owners as well as the successful operating procedures described in the magazines.
2. Identify a person who currently is or has been a partner in a business. Ask the person to describe the advantages and disadvantages of operating a business as a partnership from his or her viewpoint.
3. Go to the U.S. federal government Web site or your state government Web site to research the advantages and disadvantages for proprietorships and partnerships in your state. Develop a list of pros and cons for each legal form.
4. Using the Internet, if possible, find a sample copy or outline of a business plan. Speak with a banker or your business mentor about the importance of business plans for new businesses. Ask that person to describe the elements he or she feels are most important in a good business plan.

ANALYSIS

1. You have found a partner who wants to invest $6,000 and become involved in the operation of your business. You have already invested $12,000. Develop a simple partnership agreement for the business. After you have completed the agreement, ask your business mentor to review it with you.
2. Develop a chart that compares the proprietorship and partnership forms of business ownership for your business. Be certain to consider financial, personal, and management factors. When you have finished the analysis, decide whether you will remain a sole proprietor or form a partnership.
3. Develop an outline for a business plan for your new business. Begin to list the information that will go into each section of the plan. Identify the information you need to complete the business plan and the sources of that information. Continue to develop the business plan during the time you are working on this continuing project.
4. Given the business plan you developed above, outline the specific skills that are needed to make your business successful. Evaluate your skills and resources that you can bring to the business. Identify other skills or resources that a partner will need to bring in.

Corporate Forms of Business Ownership

6.1 Corporations

6.2 Close and Open Corporations

6.3 Specialized Types of Organizations

REALITY CHECK

Corporate Concept

Thanh Vu came to this country from Vietnam 10 years ago and earned a college business degree. After graduation he worked as a manager in a small firm, where he learned a great deal. But after five years, the job became less challenging. He wondered about opening his own business with the money he had saved, but that seemed too risky.

Surely there was some way to be an entrepreneur without having to assume so much responsibility alone or with a partner. The partnership idea sounded acceptable, but fear of lawsuits from creditors if he didn't do well haunted him. Yet his fear of unlimited liability did not stop him from thinking about starting a business.

On his way home from work one day, Thanh stopped to get his hair styled. He overheard two other customers talking about changing their small partnership to a corporation. One said, "We would pay higher taxes." The other responded, "But our financial liability would be less than in our partnership." Thanh listened intently but said nothing until after the first person replied, "But we can't expand our successful business unless we can raise more money."

By now Thanh could no longer restrain himself. "Excuse me for listening, but I have an idea. I'm a manager and have a degree in business; but more important, I'm looking for an opportunity to become a business owner."

The two men looked at each other and nodded. "Let's hear your idea," one said cautiously.

"There's a special type of corporation that permits you to be a corporation but allows you to pay taxes as if you were still a partnership," Thanh replied. "And if you're looking for another stockholder who can invest some money and help expand the business, I'd be very interested in talking with you."

After the introductions and handshakes, they scheduled a luncheon meeting for the next day.

6.1   Corporations

Goals

- Explain the basic structure of a corporation.
- Describe how a corporation is formed and organized.

Terms

- corporation
- charter (certificate of incorporation)
- stockholders (shareholders)
- shares
- dividends
- board of directors (directors, board)
- officers
- capital stock (stock)
- proxy

In Chapter 5, you learned about proprietorships and partnerships as legal forms of organizing a business. This chapter will deal with the features and formation of corporations. In addition, you will learn about special organizational structures: limited liability companies, joint ventures, virtual corporations, nonprofit corporations, and cooperatives. If you were to join the three people in the opening story at their luncheon meeting tomorrow, you would need to understand the contents of this chapter.

Corporate Structure

Corporations are towers on the business landscape. Although proprietorships are many in number, they are generally small in size. In comparison, corporations are few in number, but generally large in size. Because corporations tend to be large, they play a powerful role in this country and in others. For example, corporations employ millions of people and provide consumers with many of the goods and services they need and want. In a recent year, corporate sales of goods and services were more than 17 times greater than sales from proprietorships, and more than 16 times greater than sales from partnerships in the United States.

Not all corporations are large. Corporations such as Ford, IBM, and Wal-Mart are known to almost everyone, but many small corporations also exist. Small corporations are popular for reasons you will discover later in this chapter.

Because the corporation plays a vital role in business, we need to understand its basic features as well as its advantages and disadvantages. To gain knowledge of the basic features of the corporation, we can follow York, Burton, and Chan as they consider incorporating their fast-growing food store partnership, which they launched in the last chapter.

BASIC FEATURES

Elena Morales, a lawyer, helped York, Burton, and Chan prepare the partnership agreement under which they now operate. The partners asked Elena to describe a corporation to them. She stated that a corporation is a business owned by a group of people and authorized by the state in which it is located to act as though it were a single person, separate from its owners. To get permission to form a corporation, organizers must obtain a charter. A charter (often called

facts & figures

Business experts believe that in the 21st century, corporate boards will need one or more directors with expertise in these areas: telecommunications and technology, marketing, international markets, top-level finance, restructuring, entrepreneurial skills, and service industries.

a **certificate of incorporation**) is the official document through which a state grants the power to operate as a corporation.

A corporation is, in a sense, an artificial person created by the laws of the state. A corporation can make contracts, borrow money, own property, and sue or be sued in its own name. Any act performed for the corporation by an authorized person, such as an employee, is done in the name of the business. For example, the treasurer of a corporation has the power to borrow money for the business. An unauthorized employee, such as a receptionist who was hired to answer the phone and greet visitors, could not borrow money for the corporation.

Morales further explained the important parts played by three key types of people in corporations: (1) stockholders, (2) directors, and (3) officers.

STOCKHOLDERS **Stockholders** (often called **shareholders**) are the owners of a corporation. Ownership is divided into equal parts called **shares**. A person who buys one share becomes a stockholder. Therefore, thousands of people can own a corporation. Each stockholder receives a certificate from the corporation, which shows the number of shares owned. Stockholders have a number of basic rights, including the following:

1. To transfer ownership to others.
2. To vote for members of the ruling body of the corporation and on other special matters that may be brought before the stockholders.
3. To receive dividends. **Dividends** are profits that are distributed to stockholders on a per-share basis. The decision to distribute profits is made by the ruling body of the corporation.
4. To buy new shares of stock in proportion to one's present investment should the corporation issue more shares.
5. To share in the net proceeds (cash received from the sale of all assets less the payment of all debts) should the corporation go out of business.

A stockholder does not have the same financial responsibility as a partner; that is, there is no liability beyond the extent of the stockholder's ownership. If the corporation fails, a stockholder can lose only the money invested. Creditors cannot collect anything further from the stockholder.

A person can become a stockholder in any one of hundreds of major corporations. In which corporations would you be interested in owning stock?

PHOTO: © GETTY IMAGES/PHOTODISC.

DIRECTORS The **board of directors** (often shortened to **directors** or the **board**) is the ruling body of the corporation. Board members are elected by the stockholders. Directors develop plans and policies to guide the corporation as well as appoint officers to carry out the plans. If the corporation is performing successfully, its board is content to deal with policy issues and review the progress of the company. However, if the corporation's profits fall, or if it experiences other serious difficulties, the board often steps in and takes an active role in the operation of the business.

In large firms, boards generally consist of 10 to 25 directors. A few board members are top executives from within the corporation. The directors often are from outside the corporation and are usually executives from other businesses or people from nonprofit organizations, such as college professors. Often, directors are stockholders who hold many shares. But directors need not be stockholders. People who hold few or no shares are sometimes elected to the board because they have valuable knowledge needed by the board to make sound decisions. In some countries, such as Sweden, France, and China, one employee of the company is also a board member.

OFFICERS The officers of a corporation are the top executives who are hired to manage the business. The board of directors appoints them. The officers of a small corporation often consist of a president, a secretary, and a treasurer. In addition, large corporations may have vice presidents in charge of major areas, such as marketing, finance, and manufacturing. The titles of these officers are often shortened to letters. For example, the top officer is called a CEO (chief executive officer) and the head financial officer is the CFO (chief financial officer).

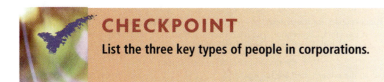

CHECKPOINT
List the three key types of people in corporations.

Formation of Corporations

Over several months, York, Burton, and Chan asked their attorney, Elena Morales, many questions. Only after careful thought did the partners decide to form a corporation. Morales told them that there were basically three steps involved. First, a series of decisions had to be made about how the corporation would be organized. Second, the proper legal forms had to be prepared and sent to the state office that handled such matters. And third, the state would review the incorporation papers and issue a charter if it approved.

PREPARING THE CERTIFICATE OF INCORPORATION

Each state has its own laws for forming corporations. No federal law exists. To incorporate a business, it is necessary in most states to file a certificate of incorporation with the appropriate state office. Morales prepared the certificate of incorporation for York, Burton, and Chan shown in Figure 6-1.

Notice the general type of information called for in the certificate of incorporation. In addition to the firm name, purpose, and capital stock, it requires information about the organizers.

NAMING THE BUSINESS A business is usually required by law to have a name that indicates clearly that a corporation has been formed. Words or abbreviations such as *Corporation, Corp., Incorporated,* or *Inc.* are used; see Figure 6-2 for examples. The organizers have decided to name their corporation York, Burton, and Chan, Inc.

STATING THE PURPOSE OF THE BUSINESS A certificate of incorporation requires a corporation to describe its purpose clearly. In Figure 6-1, Article 3 precisely states the purpose of the corporation: to operate a retail food business. It allows the corporation to expand into new food lines, but it does not allow the corporation to start nonfood operations. For major changes in purpose, a new request must be submitted and approved by the state.

INVESTING IN THE BUSINESS The certificate of incorporation could not be completed until York, Burton, and Chan decided how to invest their partnership holdings in the corporation. They agreed that the assets and debts of the partnership should be taken over by the corporation. They further agreed that

FIGURE 6-1 A certificate of incorporation includes information about the organizers of a corporation.

Certificate of Incorporation of

York, Burton, and Chan, Inc.

Pursuant to Article Two of the Stock Corporation Law.

State of New York
County of ....Cattaraugus.... } ss.

We, the undersigned, for the purpose of forming a Corporation pursuant to Article Two of the Stock Corporation Law of the State of New York, do hereby make, subscribe, acknowledge and file this certificate for that purpose as follows:

We, the undersigned, do hereby Certify

First.—That all the undersigned are full age, and ......all...... are citizens of the United States, and ......all...... residents of the State of New York.

Second.—That the name of said corporation is ...York,Burton,and Chan,Inc....

Third.—That the purpose for which said corporation is formed is .to operate a ..... retail food business...

Fourth.—That the amount of the Capital Stock of the said corporation is ....
One Million .... Dollars ($...1,000,000...)
to consist of ..Ten Thousand...(10,000)... shares of the par value of ....
One Hundred...................... dollars ($....100......) each.

Fifth.—That the office of said corporation is to be located in the .City....... of Buffalo........., County of ....Cattaraugus... and State of New York.

Sixth.—That the duration of said corporation is to be ...perpetual................

Seventh.—That the number of Directors of said corporation is .three..............

Eighth.—That the names and post office addresses of the Directors until the first annual meeting are as follows:

Jennifer L.York..1868 Buffalo Street,.Buffalo,.NY.14760-1436.............
Robert.R.Burton..1309 Main Street,.Buffalo,.NY.14760-1436...............
Lu.Chan..........4565 Erie Avenue,.Niagara Falls,.NY.14721-2348.........

Ninth.—That the names and post office addresses of the subscribers and the number of shares of stock which each agrees to take in said corporation are as follows:

Names	Post Office Addresses	No. of Shares
Jennifer L.York	1868 Buffalo Street	
	Buffalo, NY 14760-1436	2,217
Robert R.Burton	1309 Main Street	
	Buffalo, NY 14760-1436	2,217
Lu Chan	4565 Erie Avenue	
	Niagara Falls, NY 14721-2348	2,217

Tenth.—That the meetings of the Board of Directors shall be held only within the State of New York .....at Buffalo...

In Witness Whereof, we have made, subscribed, and executed this certificate ..in.... duplicate...... the ......tenth.... day of ...September.......... in the year ...Two.thousand...

Jennifer L. York
Robert R. Burton
Lu Chan

their capital (net worth or equity) of $221,700 each should be invested in the corporation. **Capital stock** (or simply **stock**) is the general term applied to the shares of ownership of a corporation.

Here is how the details were worked out. The organizers requested authorization from the state to issue $1,000,000 in capital stock, as shown in Figure 6-1.

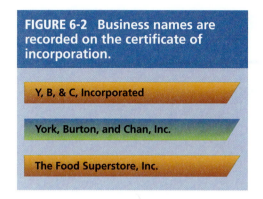

FIGURE 6-2 Business names are recorded on the certificate of incorporation.

Y, B, & C, Incorporated

York, Burton, and Chan, Inc.

The Food Superstore, Inc.

FIGURE 6-3 The Food Superstore, Inc.

York	2,217 shares x $100 / share =	$221,700
Burton	2,217 shares x $100 / share =	$221,700
Chan	2,217 shares x $100 / share =	$221,700
Total		$665,100

Shares were valued at $100 each at the time of incorporation. There were 10,000 shares in all ($1,000,000 divided by $100 equals 10,000). York, Burton, and Chan each agreed to purchase 2,217 shares, as shown in Figure 6-3.

The 3,349 unissued shares (the difference between the 10,000 authorized shares and the 6,651 shares bought by the organizers) can be sold at a later date to raise more funds to expand the business.

PAYING INCORPORATION COSTS Usually a new corporation must pay an organization tax, based on the amount of its capital stock. In addition, a new corporation usually pays a filing fee before the state will issue a charter entitling the business to operate as a corporation. In some states, the existence of the corporation begins when the application or certificate of incorporation has been filed with the Department of State.

OPERATING THE NEW CORPORATION

York, Burton, and Chan, Inc., received approval to operate as a corporation. They turned their attention next to getting the business started.

GETTING ORGANIZED One of the first steps in getting the new corporation under way is to prepare a balance sheet or statement of financial position. The new corporation's balance sheet is shown in Figure 6-4.

The ownership of the corporation is in the same hands as the ownership of the partnership was. The ownership of the corporation, however, is evidenced by the issued capital stock. The former partners each received a stock certificate indicating that each owns 2,217 shares of stock with a value of $100 a share.

The three stockholders own the business and elect themselves directors. The new directors select officers. York is appointed president; Burton, vice president; and Chan, secretary and treasurer. An organization chart of the new corporation is shown in Figure 6-5.

HANDLING VOTING RIGHTS The owners agreed that each owner will have 2,217 votes on matters arising in the meetings of the stockholders. Voting stockholders usually have one vote for each share owned. However, if Chan, for instance, sold 1,200 of his shares to Burton, Burton would own 3,417 shares, or more than 50 percent of the total 6,651 shares of stock that have been issued. Then Burton could control the corporation; that is, York and Chan would lose if Burton voted differently

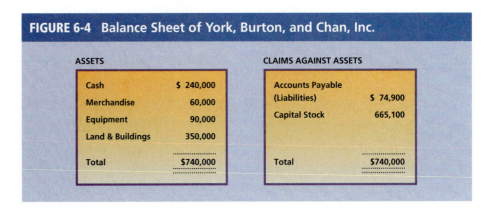

FIGURE 6-4 Balance Sheet of York, Burton, and Chan, Inc.

ASSETS		CLAIMS AGAINST ASSETS	
Cash	$ 240,000	Accounts Payable (Liabilities)	$ 74,900
Merchandise	60,000	Capital Stock	665,100
Equipment	90,000		
Land & Buildings	350,000		
Total	$740,000	Total	$740,000

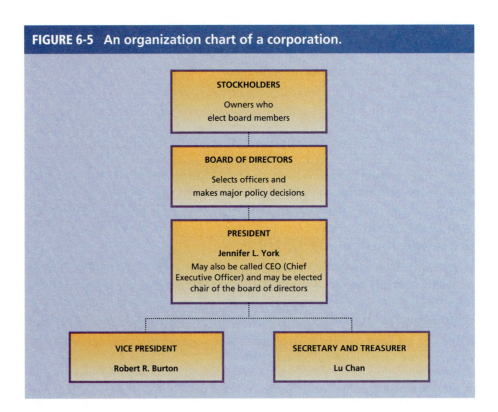

FIGURE 6-5 An organization chart of a corporation.

STOCKHOLDERS
Owners who elect board members

BOARD OF DIRECTORS
Selects officers and makes major policy decisions

PRESIDENT
Jennifer L. York
May also be called CEO (Chief Executive Officer) and may be elected chair of the board of directors

VICE PRESIDENT
Robert R. Burton

SECRETARY AND TREASURER
Lu Chan

from them on an important issue. Burton would have more votes than York and Chan together.

Their lawyer told the officers of the corporation that they must send each stockholder notices of all stockholders' meetings to be held. Even stockholders with just one share must receive notices of meetings. If stockholders cannot attend the meetings personally, they can be represented through a **proxy** that can be submitted by Internet, phone, or mail. A proxy is a written authorization for someone to vote on behalf of the person signing the proxy. It is common practice for a proxy form to be enclosed with the letter that announces a stockholders' meeting. One example of a proxy that a corporation might use is shown in Figure 6-6.

FIGURE 6-6 A proxy signed by a stockholder.

Brumway Eastmont Power Corporation – Proxy – Annual Meeting, Nov. 7, 20--

The undersigned hereby appoints Henry T. Brumleve III, Dean G.Rehme, D.A. Dromboski, and Donald F. Stark, and any of them, proxies of the undersigned, with power of substitution, to vote at the Annual Meeting of Stockholders of Brumway Eastmont Power Corporation, at Kenwood, Ohio, on November 7, 20--, at 11:00 a.m., and at any adjournments thereof.

(1) FOR ☒ or NOT FOR ☐ the election of a Board of Directors;

This Proxy is Solicited by Management

(2) FOR ☒ or AGAINST ☐ the proposal to increase the number of authorized shares of Common Stock; and

(3) for the transaction of any other business property brought before the meeting.

RAYMOND L COOKE
349 MIDPINES DRIVE
BUFFALO NY 14202-4449

Dated *October 25, 20--*

Raymond L. Cooke
....
Signature of Stockholder

If no preference is indicated, this proxy will be voted FOR items (1) & (2).

(Please give your full title when signing as attorney, trustee, executor, administrator, or guardian, etc.)

CHECKPOINT

List the three basic steps involved in setting up a corporation.

6.1 Assessment

UNDERSTAND MANAGEMENT CONCEPTS

Circle the best answer for each of the following questions.

1. Which of the following is *not* true for a corporation?
   a. A corporation is owned by one person or a group of people.
   b. Corporations are authorized by the state.
   c. A corporation acts as though it were a single person, separate from its owners.
   d. All of the above are true.

2. The ruling body in corporations is called
   a. stockholders
   b. directors
   c. officers
   d. all of the above

THINK CRITICALLY

Answer the following questions as completely as possible.

3. List the basic rights of stockholders.

4. Describe the steps a company must take to become a corporation.

Xtra!
Study Tools
thomsonedu.com/school/bpmxtra

Focus On...

Corporate Ethics–Trouble in the Boardroom

Experts agree that top management greatly influences the extent to which ethics are practiced in corporations by CEOs and boards of directors. Shareholders assume that their elected directors are ethical, but are they?

The relationships among shareholders, boards, and CEOs should be as harmonious as possible. In practice, however, CEOs sometimes manipulate boards. As a result, employees, retirees, customers, and shareholders often suffer.

For example, CEOs know that the boards who hire them can also fire them. As a result, CEOs want to build relationships with board members. CEOs in firms that are not doing well are often motivated to take defensive action. One such defense is to get elected chairperson of the board. In this way, CEOs set meeting agendas and thereby control topics that are discussed. CEOs can also recommend friends as nominees to the board for stockholders to elect via proxy statements. Through such actions, CEOs build loyal followers.

On the other hand, directors who are elected by stockholders and who are loyal to CEOs may be disloyal to the stockholders they represent. A condition like this creates problems.

For example, CEO salaries may be raised despite poor performance. A CEO's plans may be approved without adequate review. During tough competitive periods when a firm has difficulty making a profit, everyone is hurt. That's when employees get fired and stockholders lose money.

Employees get hurt in another way when employee pension funds are invested in corporations by the fund managers. Pension funds are pools of money set aside for employee retirement benefits. When corporations do poorly, managers of large pension funds try to see that changes are made within these companies. Changes made in recent years as the result of action taken by pension fund managers include these examples. First, boards now select more directors from outside firms who are more critical of poor CEO leadership. Second, more boards take greater care in selecting, evaluating, and paying CEOs.

Ethics in boardrooms have been improving gradually. Now good boards listen to stockholders and no longer permit CEOs to control them. Rather, good boards control CEOs. And good CEOs encourage frank discussions with their boards and stockholders.

Think Critically

1. What defensive actions have CEOs taken that might cause boards of directors to perform their jobs improperly?
2. What happens when boards and CEOs do not adequately represent stockholders?
3. Do you believe the ethics of corporations differ much from the ethics in nonprofit organizations, such as between the superintendent of a school system and the board of education? Explain your answer.
4. Using a library or the Internet, find a recent report that deals with a CEO being fired by a board. Determine the causes for dismissal.

6.2 Close and Open Corporations

Goals

- Distinguish between close and open corporations.
- Explain the major advantages of the corporate form of business.
- Explain the major disadvantages of the corporate form of business.

Terms

- close corporation (closely held corporation)
- open corporation (publicly owned corporation)
- prospectus

Close and Open Corporations

A close corporation (also called a closely held corporation) is one that does not offer its shares of stock for public sale. Just a few stockholders own it; some of them may help run the business in the same manner that partners operate a business. York, Burton, and Chan, Inc., is an example of a close corporation. The three former partners own all the stock and operate the business as well.

In most states, a close corporation does not need to make its financial activities known to the public. Its stock is not offered for general sale. It must, however, prepare reports for the state from which it obtained its charter. And it must, for tax purposes, prepare reports for all states in which it operates.

An open corporation (also called a publicly owned corporation) is one that offers its shares of stock for public sale. One way to announce the sale of common stock to the public is with an ad in the newspaper. The corporation must file a registration statement with the Securities and Exchange Commission (SEC) containing extensive details about the corporation and the proposed issue of stock. A condensed version of this registration statement, called a prospectus, must be furnished to each prospective buyer of newly offered stocks (or bonds). A prospectus is a formal summary of the chief features of the business and its stock offering. Prospective buyers can find information in the prospectus that will help them decide whether or not to buy stock in the corporation.

Open corporations often have a large number of stockholders, perhaps hundreds of thousands or more. Many of the stockholders in large corporations own only a few shares. But because of the great number of stockholders, such a corporation has a large amount of capital. When people buy stock, they are investing their capital (money) in the corporation. If the corporation fares well, stockholders will earn a return on their investment by receiving dividends and by selling their stock for more than they paid for it. If the corporation does not do well, stockholders may receive no dividends and may

business note

Before investing in a corporation, it is important to analyze the company's strategy and financial history. Expense and return ratios are used to evaluate companies over time and against competitors. Identify the skills you will need to be a good stock purchaser.

even have to sell their stock for less than they paid for it. If the corporation goes out of business, stockholders may lose their entire investment.

CHECKPOINT

Explain why a corporation would want to be open instead of close.

Advantages of Corporations

The corporation has a number of advantages as compared with the proprietorship and partnership. Four such advantages are discussed below.

AVAILABLE SOURCES OF CAPITAL

The corporation can obtain money from several sources. One of those sources is the sale of shares to stockholders. This special privilege helps to raise enough capital to run large-scale businesses. Because corporations are regulated closely, people usually invest more willingly than in proprietorships and partnerships. Also, corporations usually find borrowing large sums of money less of a problem than do proprietorships or partnerships.

LIMITED LIABILITY OF STOCKHOLDERS

Except in a few situations, the owners (stockholders) are not legally liable for the debts of the corporation beyond their investment in the shares purchased. Thus, people—whether they have only a few dollars to invest or thousands of dollars—can invest in a corporation without the possibility of incurring a liability beyond their original investment.

PERMANENCY OF EXISTENCE

The corporation is a more permanent type of organization than the proprietorship or the partnership. It can continue to operate indefinitely, or only as long as the term stated in the charter. The death or withdrawal of an owner (stockholder) does not affect its life.

EASE IN TRANSFERRING OWNERSHIP

It is easy to transfer ownership in a corporation. A stockholder may sell stock to another person and transfer the stock certificate, which represents ownership, to the new owner. When shares are transferred, the transfer of ownership is indicated in the records of the corporation. A new certificate is issued in the name of the new stockholder. Millions of shares are bought and sold every day.

CHECKPOINT

List the advantages of a corporation over a proprietorship or partnership.

Disadvantages of Corporations

Although there are several distinct advantages to the corporate form of ownership, there are also disadvantages. A discussion of some of the major disadvantages follows.

TAXATION

The corporation is usually subject to more taxes than are imposed on the proprietorship and the partnership. Some taxes that are unique to the corporation are a filing fee, which is payable on application for a charter; an organization tax, which is based on the amount of authorized capital stock; an annual state tax, based on the profits; and a federal income tax.

Another tax disadvantage for corporations is that profits distributed to stockholders as dividends are taxed twice. This double taxation occurs in two steps. The corporation first pays taxes on its profits as just described. Then it distributes some of these profits to shareholders as dividends, and the shareholders pay taxes on the dividends they receive. Most other industrialized countries do not permit double taxation on corporate profits. (Small close corporations with few stockholders may avoid double taxation by changing their form of ownership, which you will learn about later in this chapter.)

GOVERNMENT REGULATIONS AND REPORTS

A corporation cannot do business wherever it pleases. To form a corporation, an application for a charter must be submitted to the appropriate state official, usually the secretary of state. York, Burton, and Chan, Inc., has permission to conduct business only in the state of New York. Should it wish to conduct business in other states, each state will probably require the corporation to obtain a license and pay a fee to do business in that state. State incorporation fees are not very expensive. The attorney's fee accounts for the major costs of incorporating. Each state has different laws that govern the formation of corporations.

The regulation of corporations by states and by the federal government is extensive. A corporation must file special reports with the state from which it received its charter as well as with other states where it conducts business. The federal government requires firms whose stock is publicly traded to publish financial data. As a result, there is a greater need for detailed financial records and reports.

STOCKHOLDERS' RECORDS

Corporations that have many stockholders have added problems—and expenses—in communicating with stockholders and in handling stockholders' records. By law, stockholders must be informed of corporate matters, notified of meetings, and given the right to vote on important matters. Letters and reports must be sent to stockholders on a regular basis. In addition, each time a share of stock is bought or sold and whenever a dividend is paid, detailed records must be kept. Keeping records for the thousands of stockholders of General Electric, for example, is a time-consuming and costly task.

CHARTER RESTRICTIONS

A corporation is allowed to engage only in those activities that are stated in its charter. Should York, Burton, and Chan, Inc., wish to sell hardware, the organizers

Success *tip*

Money management is considered one of the top career fields of the future. Many people are interested in investing in companies to build their retirement income and maximize their future savings. To be a money manager, look at careers in business, accounting, and finance.

would have to go to the state to obtain a new charter or change the old one. As a partnership, they could have added the other line of merchandise without government approval.

CHECKPOINT

List the disadvantages of the corporate form of ownership.

Businesses Suited to Being Corporations

Even though the corporation has major disadvantages, a survey of business firms shows that almost every kind of business exists as a corporation, including Web-based firms. The corporate form of ownership is especially suited to the following types of businesses:

1. Businesses that require large amounts of capital, such as airlines and auto manufacturers. To start a 500-room hotel, for example, requires millions of dollars for buying land and for constructing and furnishing the hotel.
2. Businesses that may have uncertain futures, such as amusement parks, new magazines, and novelty goods. The publisher of a new magazine, for example, takes a great risk in assuming that the magazine will be popular enough to make a profit. Organizers of firms with uncertain futures do not wish to assume the added financial risks that fall upon a proprietor or a partner in case the business fails.

Each form of business organization has special advantages for owners of different types of businesses. Whereas the corporate form of organization is suited to firms that have uncertain futures or require large amounts of capital, the partnership is especially suited to small, growing business firms. The proprietorship, in comparison, has great appeal to the person who wants to run a small business.

CHECKPOINT

Identify the types of businesses that would benefit from a corporate form of ownership.

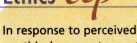

Ethics tip

In response to perceived unethical corporate practice, the U.S. government passed the Sarbanes-Oxley Act in 2002. Officers in public (or open) corporations now face much higher levels of responsibility and are held responsible for the ethical behavior of their corporations.

Is corporate ownership the best form of ownership for a theme park, given liability and transfer-of-ownership issues?

6.2 Assessment

UNDERSTAND MANAGEMENT CONCEPTS

Circle the best answer for each of the following questions.

1. A corporation that does not offer its stock to the public for sale is called a(n)
   a. close corporation
   b. open corporation
   c. private corporation
   d. none of the above

2. The advantages of a corporate form of ownership include all of the following *except*
   a. double taxation
   b. available sources of capital
   c. limited liability
   d. permanency of existence

THINK CRITICALLY

Answer the following questions as completely as possible.

3. List the major advantages of the corporate form of business.

4. List the major disadvantages of the corporate form of business.

Xtra!
Study Tools
thomsonedu.com/school/bpmxtra

PHOTO: © GETTY IMAGES/PHOTODISC.

6.3 | Specialized Types of Organizations

Goals

- Describe organizations that are specialized alliances between companies or individuals.
- Describe specialized forms of corporations formed for tax or non-profit reasons.

Terms

- joint venture
- virtual corporation
- cooperative
- limited liability company (LLC)
- Subchapter S corporations
- nonprofit corporation
- quasi-public corporation

Organizational Alliances

In addition to sole proprietorships, partnerships, and corporations, organizations can be legally formed as joint ventures, virtual corporations, cooperatives, limited liability companies, and nonprofit corporations. Joint ventures, virtual corporations, and cooperatives are specialized alliances between companies or individuals.

JOINT VENTURES

Sometimes businesses want to join forces in order to achieve an important objective. A **joint venture** is an agreement among two or more businesses to work together to provide a good or service. The legal formation of the business is not important. For example, a sole proprietorship and a corporation could agree to work together. Each partner in the joint venture is expected to bring management expertise and/or money to the venture. Many major corporations today have learned that alone they may not have all the expertise or capital they need.

An example of a joint venture is an agreement between two major contractors to connect two cities by building a tunnel for cars under a river. Neither company on its own may have the capital to build the tunnel, and each may lack special equipment or skills that the other firm has. By forming a joint venture, however, they can acquire the needed capital and expertise. There are thousands of joint ventures between and among many companies. Many Web-based companies rely extensively on joint ventures to build their businesses.

VIRTUAL CORPORATIONS

Because organizations must adapt quickly to compete effectively, a more fluid form of the joint venture, the virtual corporation, is evolving in the world of business. The **virtual corporation** is a network of companies that form alliances among themselves as needed to take advantage of fast-changing market conditions. Nike, the world's largest athletic shoe and sports apparel company, is a virtual corporation. Nike manufactures and markets its products worldwide. A large network of Asian companies purchase materials and manufacture shoes and other apparel products in countries such as China, Taiwan, Indonesia, and Korea. Then separate companies on all continents sell the shoes. In all, more than 500 companies worldwide participate in making and selling Nike products.

facts & figures

Joint ventures often include business partners from foreign countries. For example, Ford Motor Company produces cars in a joint venture with Mazda. Joint ventures help corporations expand into new markets, and companies in developing countries learn about doing business in a free-market economy.

Virtual corporations tend to be more temporary relationships than are joint ventures. Several companies within the network may team up to take advantage of a market opportunity. These same companies may also work with a different combination of partners within the network, depending on the expertise needed to take advantage of a particular market opportunity at that time.

An example of a virtual corporation is the following situation. Company A wishes to rush to market a new sophisticated computer but needs special parts that it does not produce. Company A learns that Company B produces one part and Company C produces another. Unfortunately, none of the three companies has customers who would likely have an interest in the new computer. After searching, the firms find that Company D sells computers to customers with special needs. Ultimately, all three companies agree to join with Company A to market the new computer. This virtual corporation, illustrated in Figure 6-7, makes it possible for all four companies to benefit when no one company could have made and marketed the new computer quickly on its own. Many companies involved in selling the goods of other firms, especially Web-based firms, are virtual corporations.

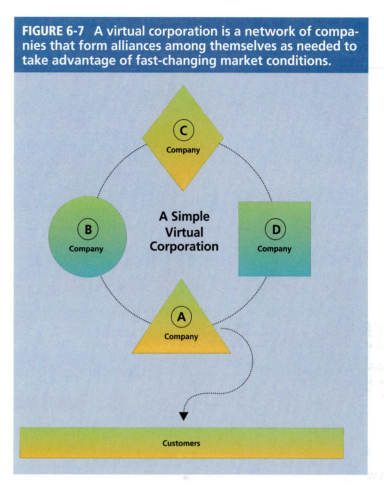

FIGURE 6-7 A virtual corporation is a network of companies that form alliances among themselves as needed to take advantage of fast-changing market conditions.

A Simple Virtual Corporation

C Company
B Company
D Company
A Company
Customers

COOPERATIVES

A **cooperative** is a business owned and operated by its user-members for the purpose of supplying themselves with goods and services. The members, who are much like stockholders in a corporation with the protection of limited liability, usually join a cooperative by buying shares of stock. The members elect a board of directors, which appoints officers to run the cooperative. Much like a corporation, a cooperative must also obtain a charter from the state in which it is organized in order to operate. Some types of cooperatives need authorization from the federal government.

The purpose of cooperatives is to provide their members with cost and profit advantages that they do not otherwise have. For example, a group of blueberry growers believes that individually they can save money and make more profit by forming a cooperative for the purpose of selling their berries. Once the business is organized and operating, the members (owners) sell their berries through the cooperative. The cooperative markets the berries. In turn, the growers earn more than if they tried to market the berries on their own. In addition, as owners they share in the profits of the business.

With almost 19 million businesses in the United States, cooperatives represent only a small percentage of all businesses. This small number, however, does not reduce their importance. Cooperatives are popular in agriculture for buying and selling crops. And many employees belong to credit unions, where they can invest and borrow money at low interest rates. Many insurance firms are formed as cooperatives. Apartment buildings are often formed as cooperatives as well.

Why would the corporate form of ownership be suited to a solar energy plant?

PHOTO: © GETTY IMAGES/PHOTODISC.

CHECKPOINT

List three types of organizations that are specialized alliances between companies or individuals.

Other Limited Liability Corporations

Small, growing partnerships are especially attracted to the **limited liability company (LLC)** form of corporation or **Subchapter S corporation**. The limited liability company is a special type of corporation allowed by states that is taxed as if it were a sole proprietorship or partnership. Two factors make LLCs popular. First, a major disadvantage of a partnership is its unlimited liability, whereas a major advantage of a corporation is its limited liability. Second, a major advantage of a partnership is its lower income tax rate, whereas a disadvantage of a corporation is a higher income tax rate than that paid by partnerships. Stockholders also have to pay personal income taxes on dividends distributed by a corporation (double taxation).

A Subchapter S is a special type of corporate tax status that offers liability protection but allows taxation like a partnership, avoiding double taxation. To qualify, a corporation elects to be taxed under the Subchapter S corporation regulations of the U.S. Internal Revenue Service (IRS). However, not all companies are eligible for Subchapter S status. A few important rules determine eligibility. First, the firm must have no more than 100 stockholders. Second, it must be a domestic corporation and not have any nonresident aliens as stockholders. Third, it must have only one class of stock. Finally, it must meet a list of other specific limitations specified by the IRS, such as not being a bank, insurance company, and so on. Large corporations and multinational firms do not meet these qualifications.

Limited liability corporations provide ideal solutions—lower taxes and limited liability. In addition, the profits from the corporation go directly to the stockholders, who then include the earnings on their individual income tax returns. Double taxation is avoided. York, Burton, and Chan, Inc., would qualify for this special tax advantage. An LLC also may be the solution to the dilemma that Thanh Vu and his two acquaintances faced at the start of this chapter.

NONPROFIT CORPORATIONS

Close and open corporations, as discussed earlier, are businesses that operate mainly to make a profit for their owners. A **nonprofit corporation**, on the other hand, is an organization that does not pay taxes and does not exist to make a profit. Organizations that manage cities or operate schools are examples of nonprofit corporations. Because a nonprofit corporation is not established as a profit-making enterprise, it does not pay dividends to shareholders. Otherwise, it operates much like a close or open corporation. The Rotary Club, private schools and universities, United Way, and most local hospitals are other examples of nonprofit organizations. Even Educational Testing Service, the company that develops the Scholastic Assessment Test (SAT), is a nonprofit organization.

In this country, nonprofit corporations provide nearly one third of the GDP. However, in most other countries, nonprofit corporations contribute much more to the GDP. The principles of business and management provided

NETBookmark

Virtual corporation outsourcing has become a significant ethical issue for firms. For example, companies like Nike have been accused of using foreign companies that employ child labor. Point your browser to www.thomsonedu.com/school/bpmxtra. Use a search engine to look up "Nike outsourcing." Evaluate some of these sites, then visit the site of the Nike Foundation. Explain how Nike is responding to international criticism.

www.thomsonedu.com/school/bpmxtra

PHOTO: © DIGITAL VISION.

Nonprofit organizations do not make a profit for distribution to stockholders. Can you name some examples of nonprofit organizations in your community?

in this text apply equally to managers who run profit-making as well as non-profit corporations.

QUASI-PUBLIC CORPORATIONS

A business that is important to society but lacks the profit potential to attract private investors is often operated by local, state, or federal government. Government financial support (called a subsidy) may also be required. This type of business is usually described as a **quasi-public corporation**. Government imposes regulatory controls over quasi-public corporations.

The Tennessee Valley Authority, a rural electrification program started in the 1930s by the federal government, was one of the first quasi-public corporations. The organizations that run interstate highways, such as the Massachusetts and Pennsylvania turnpike authorities, are state-owned quasi-public corporations. At the local level, examples of quasi-public organizations include water and sewer systems, parking garages, and civic and cultural facilities. The Los Angeles County Museum of Art is a government-owned cultural organization.

CHECKPOINT

List the main advantage of choosing an LLC or Subchapter S status.

6.3   Assessment

UNDERSTAND MANAGEMENT CONCEPTS

Circle the best answer for each of the following questions.

1. Organizations that are specialized alliances between companies or individuals include all of the following *except*
   a. joint ventures
   b. virtual corporations
   c. cooperatives
   d. LLCs
2. A corporation can have a special tax status by filing as a(n)
   a. LLC
   b. Subchapter S corporation
   c. nonprofit corporation
   d. all of the above

THINK CRITICALLY

Answer the following questions as completely as possible.

3. Explain the advantages of structuring a virtual corporation.
4. Explain why a company would elect to have an LLC or Subchapter S status.

Xtra!
Study Tools
thomsonedu.com/school/bpmxtra

CHAPTER CONCEPTS

- A corporation is a form of ownership preferred by large and growing firms. Corporations are more difficult to form than sole proprietorships or partnerships. A business must specify its purpose, identify its owners (stockholders), elect a board of directors, select officers, establish operating policies, and prepare a charter for approval by the state.

- The chief advantages of corporations are that liability is limited, more capital can be raised for growth, stock can be bought and sold more easily than ownership shares in partnerships, and the life of the corporation does not end when owners sell their shares.

- The chief disadvantages of corporations include higher tax rates, double taxation, and more extensive record keeping and government-required paperwork.

- Joint ventures are alliances formed among companies to produce a product or service that neither alone could provide efficiently. A virtual corporation is a type of joint venture in which a network of companies form temporary alliances among themselves as needed to take advantage of current market conditions. Cooperatives, such as credit unions, are businesses owned and operated by their user-members for the purpose of supplying themselves with goods and services.

- Limited liability companies (LLC) and Subchapter S corporations avoid double taxation and the unlimited-liability disadvantage of partnerships. Nonprofit corporations do not pay taxes and do not exist to make a profit. Quasi-public corporations are important to society but are government-run because they lack the profit potential to attract private investors.

REVIEW TERMS AND CONCEPTS

Write the letter of the term that matches each definition. Some terms will not be used.

1. State document granting corporate status
2. Ruling body of a corporation
3. Owners of a corporation
4. Written authorization to vote on behalf of a person
5. Formal summary of the chief features of the business and its stock offering
6. Agreement among two or more businesses to work together to provide a good or service
7. Organization that does not pay taxes and does not exist to make a profit
8. Corporation that offers its shares of stock for public sale
9. Corporation that does not offer stock for public sale
10. Profits that are distributed to stockholders on a per-share basis
11. Top executives who are hired to manage the business
12. Special type of corporation that is taxed as if it were a sole proprietorship or partnership

a. board of directors
b. charter
c. close corporation
d. cooperative
e. dividends
f. joint venture
g. limited liability company
h. nonprofit corporation
i. officers
j. open corporation
k. prospectus
l. proxy
m. stockholders
n. virtual corporation

DETERMINE THE BEST ANSWER

13. Ownership of a corporation is divided into parts called
    a. shares
    b. corporation parts
    c. memberships
    d. partnerships

14. Stockholders' basic rights include the right to
    a. transfer ownership
    b. vote for members of the board
    c. receive dividends
    d. all of the above

15. A business owned by a group of people and authorized by the state in which it is located to act as though it were a single person, separate from its owners, is called a
    a. corporation
    b. joint venture
    c. virtual company
    d. subcorporation

16. A business that is important to society but lacks the profit potential to attract private investors and is often operated by local, state, or federal government is called a
    a. not-for-profit corporation
    b. quasi-public corporation
    c. nano-public corporation
    d. Subchapter S corporation

17. A corporation must include in its name
    a. the purpose of the business
    b. the major owners' names
    c. the state in which the company was founded
    d. an indication that the company is a corporation

18. A network of companies that form alliances among themselves as needed to take advantage of fast-changing market conditions is a
    a. corporation
    b. joint venture
    c. virtual company
    d. subcorporation

19. If a corporation wants to enter into a different business, it
    a. must close and re-form
    b. can do this at any time
    c. must change its charter or file a new one
    d. must change its name

APPLY WHAT YOU KNOW

20. Explain why the five basic rights of stockholders are necessary in corporate forms of organizations.

21. Explain why a corporation can be viewed as an artificial person.

22. Compare the financial responsibility of owners of a corporation with that of owners of a partnership.

23. Explain how a joint venture could be valuable in a situation in which Corporation A has expertise in one area and Corporation B has expertise in another.

24. Discuss whether the Girl Scouts organization meets the qualifications for operating as a nonprofit corporation in light of the fact that it sells a large volume of cookies each year.

MAKE CONNECTIONS

25. **Math** The board of directors of Melby Company, Inc., decided to distribute $40,950 as dividends to shareholders who hold 27,300 shares of stock. What is the amount of the dividend to be distributed on each share? John Taylor owns 240 shares. What amount will he receive in dividends?

26. **Research** Alone or in teams (as specified by your instructor), search the library or the Web to gather information about the basic features of a cooperative. Then report to your class on how cooperatives differ from typical corporations in the way they operate and how investors share in the benefits. In particular, go to the USDA Rural Development site and find the publication "Co-ops 101" for additional information.

27. **Technology** George Fernandez purchased stock in the Elite Manufacturing Co., Inc., for $76 a share. Last year he received quarterly dividends of $1, $1, $1, and $0.80 on each share. Use spreadsheet software to answer the following questions.
    a. What were his total dividends for the year as a percentage of the price he paid for each share?
    b. Assume the stock price increases to $100, but the company pays the same dividend. Determine the new percentage return for the year.

28. **Speaking** Assume you are in a partnership. Prepare a speech that you will give to your partners to justify changing to a corporate form of ownership. Choose a specific corporate form and link it to your company goals. Justify your choice by addressing its advantages and disadvantages for your company.

CASE IN POINT

CASE 6-1: Pay for Performance

Takoda Koriyama, whose parents came from Japan, is interested in how corporations operate in Western countries, particularly the United States. In one of his business classes, he and two classmates—Marcus Jordan and Brianna Ashman—are assigned a team project to study the total pay of the chief executive officers (CEOs) of 10 companies. Takoda is the leader. Other class teams are assigned other firms. Their assignment is to determine the total pay that individual CEOs earn in American corporations in relation to how well their firms do for their stockholders.

All three members have gathered information. Before they can prepare a class report, they need to sort it all out. During their first meeting, the group shares information and creates the chart below that summarizes their main points. CEO total pay is shown in thousands of dollars.

Corporations	CEO Total Pay	Percent of Shareholder Return
Walt Disney	$ 594,892	56
Citigroup	491,976	146
General Electric	151,179	199
Occidental Petroleum	110,670	−11
H. J. Heinz	104,678	86
Immunex	2,437	663
Microsoft	1,696	532
Costco	1,483	373
Capital One	1,312	393
Berkshire Hathaway	842	118

Source: *Business Week, April 19, 1999*

THINK CRITICALLY

1. Which five company CEOs benefited their shareholders the most? Which five CEOs benefited their shareholders the least?
2. What general statement can you make to Takoda and his team about the fairness of pay for CEOs relative to their contributions to their corporations?
3. If you were just elected to serve as a board member of Citigroup, what would you recommend to other board members about the CEO's future pay? Provide a reason for your answer.
4. Which CEO would most deserve a raise in pay? Justify your answer.
5. Alone or in teams, as specified by your instructor, gather information about CEO pay from *Business Week, Fortune,* or other magazines in your library or from the Internet. Prepare a report for your class that answers the question: Are CEOs overpaid, underpaid, or paid what they are worth? Include any proposals you find on how to keep CEO pay fair and under control.

CASE 6-2: Stockholder Responsbility

Alicia Fuentes owns 15 shares of stock in the Shale Oil Company, a large corporation that deals with oil and gas products. Hugh Jones, a friend of Alicia's, owns 20 shares. Today they both received an invitation to attend the annual stockholders' meeting in Chicago, which neither can attend. They had this conversation over dinner at a local restaurant.

Alicia: *Since I can't attend the meeting, I'm going to sign the proxy card and answer "for" regarding the two proposals that are to be voted on. Of course, I don't know any of the board members who are up for election, but they must be OK. I wish they could distribute more dividends, though.*

Hugh: *You shouldn't just give your vote away to management, Alicia. You should elect one of the candidates to be an outside board member. That person could then shake things up a bit, get some changes made. You probably also don't know anything about the other item asking for approval to increase the number of shares of stock that can be sold.*

Alicia: *I don't have time to do homework on the company. Shale Oil Company always makes a profit; therefore, it deserves my vote.*

Hugh: *Too many stockholders don't do their homework on the company and not many go to the meetings. So management always has its own way. Why bother sending a proxy statement at all? I'm not going to waste time sending my proxy back.*

Alicia: *I'm still going to vote, Hugh. Besides, the company pays the postage.*

Hugh: *You're doing what everyone else does. Management always wins. But since you're going to vote, I will too. The difference is that I'm going to vote against the two items . . . no, on second thought, I'll just sign the proxy. That will really confuse them.*

THINK CRITICALLY

1. Whether they vote "for" or "against" the proposals listed on the proxy statement, how many votes can Alicia and Hugh cast?
2. If the proxy statement is like the one shown in Figure 6-6 and Hugh signs it but does not mark "for" or "against" the two proposals, how do you think the management will use the proxy?
3. If Hugh or Alicia wanted an important proposal to be made known and voted on by the stockholders, how could they achieve their goal?
4. How should Alicia and Hugh have received information about each of the proposals from management that would enable them to vote with adequate information?
5. What might an outside board member do that an inside member might not do?
6. Why do Alicia and Hugh need to worry about who is on the board at Shale Oil Company?

CORPORATE FORM

Corporations are another form of business ownership. In addition to financial advantages, there are other reasons to organize a new business as a corporation. In this segment of the project, you will study some of those reasons as well as the procedures necessary to form a corporation in your state.

DATA COLLECTION

1. Make a list of the advantages and disadvantages of the corporate form of ownership.
2. Write out the legal procedures you must follow in your state to organize a close corporation to operate your business. Obtain the information from a library, the Internet, or a government office.
3. Interview the owner of a small business that has been organized as a corporation. Ask the owner to identify the advantages and disadvantages of the corporate form of ownership for a small business.
4. Identify one other form of ownership that could be appropriate for your business other than a proprietorship, partnership, or close corporation. Locate a business that is organized using that ownership form and study its operations.

ANALYSIS

1. Most new small businesses are formed as proprietorships and partnerships rather than corporations. However, new corporations have a higher success rate than other types of business organizations. What might be some reasons for that higher success rate?
2. Assume that your business is successful and expands during the next five years. Identify specific situations that could occur during that five year period in which it would be beneficial to reorganize the business as a corporation. Collect and analyze the necessary legal documents. Consider changing financial needs, management activities, business operations, and your own personal needs.
3. Assume you are going to organize your juice bar as a corporation. Use the information from the Data Collection section above to determine if your business should be a corporation, and if so, what type.
4. Collect and review the documents needed to register your corporation with the state and complete the formation of the corporation.

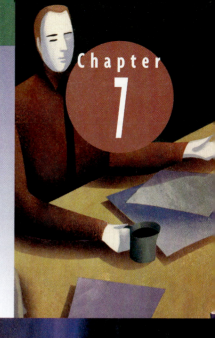

Legal Aspects of Business

REALITY CHECK

Legal Limits for a Taxi Business

Deion Banks, who owned a small taxi business in his hometown, was meeting for lunch with his lawyer, Laura Maddox. He needed to discuss several matters that had arisen during the past few weeks. While waiting for the server, Laura said, "You seem quite upset."

Deion sat back and replied, "I am, Laura. Here are the new tax forms that need to be filled out. And that's the easy part. Would you check with the town officials to see why they want to review my franchise before I buy another cab? Also, while you're at the Town Hall, see what you can do to prevent those officials from giving another taxi firm a license to operate. This town isn't big enough for two taxi companies. I'll get less business, and it will probably force down my fares. If there is a chance of going bankrupt, I should probably move my business across the river. The income tax rate in that state is much lower."

"Don't do anything drastic," said Laura. "Let me see what I can find out from our government officials. I'll get back to you in a few days with both your tax forms and the answers to your questions."

Deion Banks, like other business owners, must operate within the law. Laws that regulate business cover both products and services, and they govern general relationships of businesses with competitors, consumers, employees, and the public. Deion Banks's taxi business is no exception. He currently benefits from being the only taxi company in town, but he now feels threatened. The town may, indeed, allow someone else the right to open a competing firm. So what can Deion do?

7.1 | Regulations Maintaining Competition

Goals
- Explain how federal laws help regulate monopolies.
- Explain how federal laws help promote fair competition.

Terms
- monopoly
- natural monopoly
- price discrimination
- false advertising
- bankruptcy

In the following pages, you will learn how government encourages free enterprise by controlling monopolies and promoting competition. You will also learn how the government protects the general public as well as business. Like Deion, you will learn about taxes and how taxes influence business decisions.

Regulating Monopolies

Competition is the rivalry among companies for customers' dollars. Competition, however, does not always operate smoothly by itself. To provide for fair competition, government has passed laws and created regulations to enforce the laws. These laws and regulations grow out of a need to preserve competition, which is done, in part, by controlling monopolies and unfair business practices. Firms that cannot survive in a competitive atmosphere either go out of business or face bankruptcy.

CONTROLLING MONOPOLIES

A **monopoly** exists when only one company provides a product or service without competition from other companies. Without competitors, the one producer can control the supply and price of the product or service. By controlling the supply of an item, a single producer can set a price that will generate the greatest profit. In a monopoly situation, such as Deion Banks's taxi company, the prices are generally very high. Without competitors to lure customers away with lower prices, the monopolistic company can raise its price as high as it wants. If customers want the product or service, they have no choice but to pay the monopolist's price.

In actual practice, however, few monopolies exist, because of the effectiveness of competition. To illustrate, assume a business offers a new product that no other business does. The product suddenly becomes quite popular. The prospect of profits to be made entices other companies to enter the market to help meet the demand. A temporary monopoly will exist until those competitors can produce and sell similar products. Usually, through competitive pricing, the more efficient companies will attract the greatest number of purchasers, whereas the less efficient may struggle for survival or go out of business. Even if some competitors fail, however, a monopoly will not exist as long as there are at least two or more producers.

Deregulation of the telecommunications industry has helped benefit consumers through lower prices and improved phone services. Are cellular telephone prices deregulated?

PHOTO: © GETTY IMAGES/PHOTODISC.

NATURAL MONOPOLIES

In some situations, a **natural monopoly** may be better for consumers than competition because of the large cost involved in developing or supplying a product or service. These situations usually involve providing public services, such as public utilities, which have a fairly stable demand and which are costly to create.

A natural gas company, for example, must build hundreds of miles of pipeline along streets and roads in order to deliver gas to homes and industries to fuel furnaces and stoves. If two or three gas companies incurred these same costs to sell gas to a relatively fixed number of customers, the price of gas would be higher than if only one company existed. Also, installing and maintaining so many pipelines would create nuisance problems along crowded streets and highways. In these types of situations, the government grants a monopoly to one company, regulates the prices that the company can charge, and influences other company policies.

Until recently, the federal government had approved of closely regulated monopolies, such as the postal system, utility companies, railroads, and communication firms. However, the trend has shifted from allowing monopolies to weakening or eliminating them in order to encourage competition. No longer, for example, are passenger fares on commercial airlines regulated. As a result, fares have generally dropped. Even telephone service, the trucking industry, and railroads have been deregulated. Today utilities are undergoing deregulation. Firms such as Cingular and Sprint offer communication services at competitive prices and compete fiercely. The result overall has been that consumers pay lower prices and have more services from which to select.

business *note*

At one time the telecommunications (telephone) industry was viewed as a natural monopoly. American Telephone & Telegraph (AT&T) was given the public monopoly. In 1984, competitor lawsuits forced AT&T to be broken into seven Baby Bells. The rise of independent cellular phone companies has created enough competition to allow some Baby Bells to merge back into larger companies, even forming a new AT&T. How has the breakup of AT&T affected communication in the United States?

CHECKPOINT

Describe the reasons that society may want to allow a natural monopoly.

Promoting Fair Competition

One way to promote competition is to limit the number of monopolies created and controlled by government. Monopoly conditions can also arise when businesses compete too harshly or unfairly. A large, powerful business can lower its prices deliberately to drive out competitors, thereby discouraging competition. Thus, the federal government supports business practices that encourage competition and discourage monopolies. To achieve this goal, government has passed important laws and created agencies to enforce the laws.

SHERMAN ACT

The first major law promoting competition was the Sherman Antitrust Act of 1890. One of its primary purposes is to discourage monopolies by outlawing business agreements among competitors that might tend to promote monopolies.

For example, agreements among competitors to set selling prices on goods are unlawful. If three sellers met and agreed to set the same selling price on the same product each sold, they would all be violating the Sherman Act.

CLAYTON ACT

Like the Sherman Act, the Clayton Act of 1914 was aimed at discouraging monopolies. One part of the law forbids corporations from acquiring ownership rights in other corporations if the purpose is to create a monopoly or to discourage competition. Corporation A cannot, for example, buy more than half the ownership rights of its main competitor, Corporation B, if the aim is to severely reduce or eliminate competition.

Another section of the Clayton Act forbids business contracts that require customers to purchase certain goods in order to get other goods. For example, a business that produces computers cannot require a buyer also to purchase supplies, such as paper and software, in order to get a computer. Microsoft Corporation was charged with such a violation. Microsoft required computer makers that wanted to buy its dominant Windows operating system to also accept its Internet Explorer browser. The result of this action was to severely damage the sales of Netscape's Navigator browser, which was Microsoft's dominant competitor.

ROBINSON-PATMAN ACT

The Robinson-Patman Act of 1936 amended the portion of the Clayton Act dealing with the pricing of goods. The main purpose of the pricing provisions in both of these laws is to prevent price discrimination. For example, a seller cannot offer a price of $5 a unit to Buyer A and sell the same goods to Buyer B at $6 a unit. Different prices can be set, however, if the goods sold are different in quality or quantity. Buyer A is entitled to the $5 price if the quantity purchased is significantly greater or if the quality is lower. The same discounts must then be offered to all buyers purchasing the same quantity or quality as Buyer A.

WHEELER-LEA ACT

In 1938, the Wheeler-Lea Act was passed to strengthen earlier laws outlawing unfair methods of competition. This law made unfair or deceptive acts or practices, including false advertising, unlawful. False advertising is advertising that is misleading in some important way, including the failure to reveal facts about possible results from using the advertised products. Under the Wheeler-Lea Act, it is unlawful for an advertiser to circulate false advertising that can lead to the purchase of foods, drugs, medical devices, or cosmetics, or to participate in any other unfair methods of competition.

FEDERAL TRADE COMMISSION

The Federal Trade Commission (FTC) was created as the result of many businesses demanding protection from unfair methods of competition. The FTC administers most of the federal laws dealing with fair competition. Some of the unfair practices that the FTC protects businesses from are shown in Figure 7-1.

OTHER FEDERAL AGENCIES

In addition to the FTC, the federal government has created other agencies to administer laws that regulate specialized areas of business, such as transportation and communication. Figure 7-2 lists some of the more important agencies.

FIGURE 7-1 Types of Practices Prohibited by the Federal Trade Commission

1. Any act that restrains trade.
2. Any monopolies except those specifically authorized by law, such as public utilities.
3. Price fixing, such as agreements among competitors.
4. Agreements among competitors to divide territory, earnings, or profits.
5. Gaining control over the supply of any commodity in order to create an artificial scarcity.
6. False or misleading advertising.
7. Imitation of trademark or trade name.
8. Discrimination through prices or special deals.
9. Pretending to sell at a discount when there is no reduction in price.
10. Offering so-called free merchandise with a purchase when the price of the article sold has been raised to compensate for the free merchandise.
11. Misrepresentation about the quality, the composition, or the place of origin of a product.
12. Violation of one's guarantee of privacy of information on the Internet, including e-mail.

FIGURE 7-2 Laws promoting fair practices that benefit businesses and consumers are enforced by government agencies.

Some Federal Agencies That Regulate Business

AGENCY AND REGULATION

FEDERAL AVIATION ADMINISTRATION
Safety standards, airplane accidents, and take-offs and landings

FEDERAL COMMUNICATIONS COMMISSION
Radio, television, telephone, telegraph, cable, and satellite communications

FOOD AND DRUG ADMINISTRATION
Foods, drugs, medical devices, cosmetics, and veterinary products

NUCLEAR REGULATORY COMMISSION
Nuclear power plants

SECURITIES AND EXCHANGE COMMISSION
Stocks and bonds

In 2005, more than 39,000 U.S. businesses filed for bankruptcy. The state with the most business bankruptcy filings was California, with 4,236; the state with the least filings was Virginia, with 7.

PROVIDING BANKRUPTCY RELIEF

All firms face the risk of failure. The free-enterprise system permits unsuccessful businesses to file for bankruptcy as a means of protecting owners and others. **Bankruptcy** is a legal process that allows the selling of assets to pay off debts. Businesses as well as individuals can file for bankruptcy. If cash is not available to pay the debts after assets are sold, the law excuses the business or individual from paying the remaining unpaid debts. In such a case, all those to whom money is owed would very likely receive less than the full amount.

A bankruptcy judge can permit a company to survive bankruptcy proceedings if a survival plan can be developed that might enable the firm to recover. As a result, after starting bankruptcy proceedings, many firms do survive. However, bankruptcy carries serious consequences. The business will have a bad credit rating. A record of the unpaid debts will stay on file for 10 years, and the business may not file for bankruptcy again for eight years. As a result, the business will have difficulty obtaining credit.

CHECKPOINT

List the four federal acts that are designed to promote fair competition.

7.1 Assessment

UNDERSTAND MANAGEMENT CONCEPTS

Circle the best answer for each of the following questions.

1. A _____ exists when only one company provides a product or service without competition from other companies.
   a. oligopoly
   b. monopoly
   c. monogamy
   d. none of the above

2. The _____ protects businesses from unfair methods of competition.
   a. Federal Trade Commission (FTC)
   b. Federal Competition Commission (FCC)
   c. Federal Transportation Commission (FTC)
   d. Federal Monopoly Commission (FMC)

THINK CRITICALLY

Answer the following questions as completely as possible.

3. Explain why monopolies are bad for a society.

4. Describe how bankruptcy works for debtors and creditors.

7.2 Regulations Protecting Business and the Public

Goals
- Explain how patent, copyright, and trademark protection benefits business.
- Describe the ways in which government regulations protect consumers.
- Describe three methods used by state and local governments to regulate business.

Terms
- patent
- copyright
- trademark
- information liability
- cookies
- interstate commerce
- intrastate commerce
- licensing
- public franchise
- building codes
- zoning

In the previous section, you learned about regulations that help to make the economic system work by establishing rules of fair competition. In this section, you will learn about regulations that protect those who create goods and services and those who use them.

Intellectual Property

The federal government has passed laws to protect the rights of those who create uniquely different products and new ideas. Specifically, it grants intellectual property rights to inventors, authors, and creators of distinct symbols and names for goods and services (see Figure 7-3).

PATENTS

A **patent** is an agreement in which the federal government gives an inventor the sole right for 20 years to make, use, and sell an invention or a process. No one is permitted to copy or use the invention without permission. This protection is a reward for the time and money invested to create the new product. An inventor may allow others to make or use a product by giving them a license to do so.

In a sense, through the Patent and Trademark Office, the government gives the inventor a monopoly on newly invented products, designs, and processes. This temporary monopoly provides a profit incentive that encourages manufacturers to spend the huge amounts of money required to research and develop new ideas. Research departments have produced many inventions. For example, Apple, Sony and other companies have developed digital players that allow users to listen to music and view videos on display screens. Even synthetic tissue and altered vegetable plants are patentable. For example, insulin that diabetics need and a new rot-resistant tomato are products of biotechnology (biology plus technology) innovations.

New processes as well as new products can be patented, but process patenting can be undesirable at times. For example, Priceline.com, Inc., received a patent for its auction price-bidding system on the Internet. If other companies used this simple process, they would be violating the owner's patent rights. However, the process is so fundamental to many Internet practices that competitors believe the

Success tip

Are you an inventor? It is possible for individuals to patent their inventions. This does not gaurantee success, however. An invention must be backed by a market need and a good marketing plan; otherwise it is just one of thousands of patented products with no sales potential.

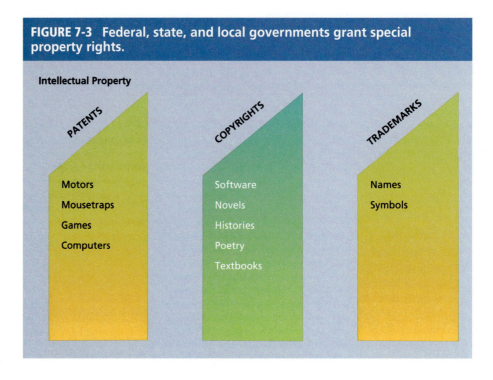

FIGURE 7-3 Federal, state, and local governments grant special property rights.

Intellectual Property

PATENTS
Motors
Mousetraps
Games
Computers

COPYRIGHTS
Software
Novels
Histories
Poetry
Textbooks

TRADEMARKS
Names
Symbols

patent is essentially unfair. Should doctors who develop a new method for healing people prohibit other doctors from using it or require them to pay a licensing fee? Occasionally, the Patent and Trademark Office revokes or denies patents that discourage desirable competition.

Unfortunately, stealing patents is an acceptable practice in some countries that do not honor the U.S. patent law. As a result, American firms lose millions of dollars. By tightening trade agreements with these countries, this great loss to American firms may begin to decline. On the other hand, patent laws differ worldwide. For example, Japan's patents promote technology sharing, whereas U.S. patents protect inventors.

What kinds of laws protect the duplication and distribution of computer software?

PHOTO: © GETTY IMAGES/PHOTODISC.

COPYRIGHTS

A **copyright** is similar to a patent in that the federal government gives an author the sole right to reproduce, publish, and sell literary or artistic work for the life of the author, typically, plus 70 years. No one may publish or reproduce copyrighted work without permission of the copyright owner. However, the law permits occasional photocopying of copyrighted material for fair use. Whereas a teacher could copy a magazine article to distribute to students, articles from the same magazine could not be copied and distributed weekly throughout the school year without obtaining permission.

Copyright laws also cover electronic methods for distributing creative work. Copyrights protect creators of CD games and music, video and audio tapes, and computer software programs, for example. Duplicating CDs, tapes, disks, and software programs for distribution to others is usually illegal. When an employee makes a personal copy of a computer software program for use on a home computer, the employee violates the copyright law. Furthermore, if a warning is not publicized that copying creative work such as a software program is illegal, the employer is also guilty.

Copyrights are regulated by the federal Copyright Office. Like a patent, a copyright is a special type of monopoly granted to authors, publishers, and other creators of original works. An example of a copyright notice appears on the back of the title page in the front of this book.

TRADEMARKS

Trademarks are like patents because they are special types of monopolies. A **trademark** is a distinguishing name, symbol, or special mark placed on a good or service that is legally reserved for the sole use of the owner. Many nationally known products have trademarks that most people recognize. Some trademarks are symbols, such as the Nike "swoosh" or the McDonald's "golden arches." Others are company or product names, such as the Sony "Walkman" or Nintendo's "Game Boy." Trademarks, like patents, are regulated by the Patent and Trademark Office.

Trademark rights may continue indefinitely, as long as the mark is neither abandoned by the trademark owner nor loses its significance in the marketplace as a trademark by becoming a generic term. For example, the generic terms *escalator, linoleum,* and *zipper* were once trademarks.

CHECKPOINT

Describe the three areas of intellectual property protection.

Regulations Protecting the Public

The federal government protects the legal rights of not only those who create new products and ideas but also those who consume goods and services. Two major goals of legislation are to ensure safe products for consumers and to prevent the misuse of information.

FOOD AND DRUGS

Products related to the human body are closely regulated. The Food and Drug Administration (FDA) administers the Federal Food, Drug, and Cosmetic Act and related laws. These laws prohibit the sale of impure, improperly labeled, falsely guaranteed, and unhealthful foods, drugs, and cosmetics. Producers of cosmetics, for example, must show that their products will not harm users. Should a product cause harm, the FDA may require the producer to stop its sale or to notify the public of its possible danger.

NONFOOD PRODUCTS

Legislative activity dealing with the safety of nonfood products has increased in recent years. Laws now require labels on many products if possible danger exists from product use. A health warning message, for example, must appear on cigarette packages. The FTC forbids the sale of tobacco and smokeless tobacco to those under 18 because research shows that the majority of those who smoke when young die prematurely of smoking-related diseases. Also, auto and highway safety laws exist to reduce death and injury.

The Consumer Product Safety Act sets safety standards on many items. When products already sold are found to have a dangerous defect, businesses are legally required to recall, repair, or stop selling the products. Dangerous toys, for example, have been removed from the market. And recalls have occurred with such products as cars and sport utility vehicles. A federal Warranty Act requires sellers to specify what they will or will not do if their product is defective. Many product liability laws also exist at the state level.

INFORMATION

Businesses need information. This need has resulted in the heavy use of computers to manage data. Vast amounts of information from many sources are collected, processed, stored, and distributed by computer, especially on the Internet. As a result, individuals and businesses need protection from the wrongful use of private information.

Stores check credit card balances, banks check credit ratings, hospitals store patients' health records electronically, and the government collects income tax data on all taxpayers. Incorrect information in any of these sensitive records could be very damaging to the individual. Also, only authorized people should have access to such highly personal information. Unauthorized use of personal information can result in *identity theft*.

Therefore, businesses that use computer information extensively must handle it carefully to protect the rights of individuals and organizations. Carelessly handled information can lead to <mark>information liability</mark>—the responsibility for physical or economic injury arising from incorrect data or wrongful use of data.

Information liability is similar to product liability. If a defective product injures someone, the injured party can sue the producer of the product. Similarly, if a person's credit rating suffers because an employee keys a Social Security number into a credit record incorrectly, the business is liable for creating the problem. Also, a company not directly involved in collecting or recording incorrect information may be held liable for distributing it. For instance, if a store gives an incorrect credit balance to a bank that results in the refusal for a loan, the bank is as liable as the store that provided the incorrect information.

Occasionally, someone tampers with computerized data. The Electronic Communications Privacy Act and related laws make it a crime for any unauthorized person to access a major computer system and view, use, or change data. The laws deal with the interception and disclosure of electronic communications, including e-mail privacy. Privacy laws help protect the public from the wrongful use or misuse of information.

A debate continues over the electronic collection of information over the Internet. Web sites can place small files called "cookies" on the computers of site visitors without their knowledge. <mark>Cookies</mark> are files of information about the user that some Web sites create and store on the user's own computer. These cookies can, among other things, track where users go on the Internet to gather information on interests and preferences for marketing purposes. Some people feel that such data gathering is an invasion of privacy. The companies argue that they are simply identifying what consumers want so they can better serve them.

facts & figures

In the 1990s, Disney's licensing business became a victim of its own success. The strategy during the first half of the 1990s was geared to hit films like *Beauty and the Beast, Aladdin,* and *The Lion King*. Licensees reached a peak of over 4,000, far too many to manage. Disney eventually cut the number of licensees in half. By having broader relationships with fewer licensees, Disney could build more effective new merchandise campaigns to strengthen established characters like Mickey Mouse and Winnie the Pooh.

CHECKPOINT

Describe three areas in which government protects consumers.

State and Local Regulations

The federal government regulates interstate commerce, and individual states regulate intrastate commerce. Interstate commerce is defined as business operations and transactions that cross state lines, such as products that are produced in one state and sold in other states. Intrastate commerce, on the other hand, is defined as business transacted within a state. Most small service firms are involved mainly in intrastate commerce, because they usually sell to customers located within the same state. Because most large companies are likely to be involved in both interstate and intrastate commerce, they are subject to state and federal regulations.

Moreover, each state has a constitution that allows it to create other governing units, such as cities, towns, and counties. These units also regulate business transacted within them. Large businesses especially are subject to local, state, and federal laws.

Many state and local laws are related to federal laws. Most states, for instance, have laws that promote competition, protect consumers and the environment, safeguard the public's health, and improve employment conditions. In addition, however, state and local governments regulate business by issuing licenses, franchises, and building codes, and by passing zoning regulations.

LICENSING

State and local governments have used licensing as a way to limit and control those who plan to enter certain types of businesses. To start a business that requires a license, the owner must file an application. If the government believes there is a sufficient number of these kinds of businesses, the application can be refused.

Business is regulated not only by the granting of licenses but also by regular inspections by government officials to see that the company is operated according to the law. If it is not being properly operated, it can lose its license. For example, government agents inspect a licensed restaurant from time to time for cleanliness. If the restaurant fails inspection, the government may withdraw its license, and the restaurant would have to close.

Licensing laws vary from place to place. In some cities, businesses of all types must obtain licenses, whereas in other communities only certain types need licenses. It is particularly common to license restaurants, beauty salons, health and fitness centers, barbershops, and other types of service firms that may affect the health of customers. In most states and in many cities, licensing laws regulate the sale of such items as liquor and tobacco.

Businesses may also license the use of property. For example, a computer software company may give a business a license to use and copy a software program in return for a fee. Likewise, for a fee a business may license another firm to make a product using its patented device. Even firm names can be licensed. For example, Walt Disney Productions licenses its animal characters for use on clothing and other products.

PUBLIC FRANCHISING

Another way for state and local governments to control business is through public franchises. A public franchise is a contract that permits a person or organization to use public property for private profit. No individual member of society,

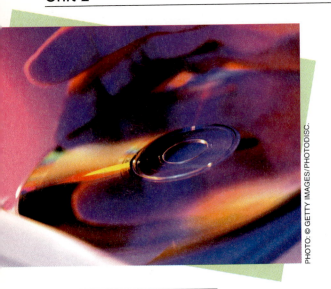

PHOTO: © GETTY IMAGES/PHOTODISC.

How could the concept of information liability affect the way in which a business handles computer information?

however, has a right to use public property for profit except through a special grant by society. Cities often grant public franchises to companies to operate bus lines, or to install electric power or cable for television. For example, as presented in the story that started this chapter, Deion has a franchise from his community to operate his taxi company.

BUILDING CODES AND ZONING

Local governments regulate business through **building codes**, which control the physical features of structures. Building codes may specify such things as the maximum height, minimum square feet of space, and the types of materials that can be used. Local governments also regulate the types of buildings and where they are built. **Zoning** regulations specify which land areas may be used for homes and which areas may be used for different types of businesses. A business must obey all local regulations relating to zoning and construction.

CHECKPOINT

List three ways that local governments regulate business.

7.2 Assessment

UNDERSTAND MANAGEMENT CONCEPTS

Circle the best answer for each of the following questions.

1. A _____ allows an inventor the sole right for 20 years to make, use, and sell an invention or a process.
   a. patent
   b. copyright
   c. trademark
   d. license

2. Business operations and transactions that cross state lines are called
   a. interstate commerce
   b. intrastate commerce
   c. multistate commerce
   d. national commerce

THINK CRITICALLY

Answer the following questions as completely as possible.

3. Describe how the federal government protects consumers of goods and services.

4. Describe how local governments regulate businesses.

Xtra!
Study Tools
thomsonedu.com/school/bpmxtra

Focus On...

Internet Ethics–Internet Advertising

The Internet is a popular place to browse for general information and to buy products or services. But as the Internet grows in popularity, buyers have become concerned about the privacy of their personal information and its possible misuse. Are buyers' fears justified?

DoubleClick, or DC, is a provider of advertising services to retailers who sell their wares to Internet shoppers. DC has more than 1,500 business customers, including Ford. DC's clients want to target their Internet advertising to the people most likely to buy their products. DC can identify, for example, which potential customers might buy Ford cars online. The main way to identify these buyers is through "cookies"—files stored on customers' computers. The cookies collect information on what customers buy and where they go on the Web, revealing their preferences and buying habits.

DC manages its clients' advertising. From the customer information it collects online, it selects the customers that best match a firm's target audience. DC uses this information to help its clients advertise effectively.

DC requires its business customers to collect information from customers when they make sales. DC itself claims not to collect personally identifiable information about people, such as names, addresses, and telephone numbers. It does collect non–personally identifiable information, such as whether people have responded to an advertisement and the type of computer system they use. The nonpersonal information is used to measure advertisement effectiveness for DC's business clients. Internet customers have a choice of whether to forbid, restrict, or deny the use of information stored in cookies. Clear notice must be given customers so that they can make that decision.

DoubleClick merged with Abacus Direct, a company with data on the catalog-buying habits of more than 80 million families, including names, addresses, and telephone numbers. This information permits DC's business clients to target these people with e-mail advertising. Some consumer groups have objected strongly, claiming that this is an invasion of privacy that should be stopped. The Federal Trade Commission initiated an investigation in 2000 but dropped the suit in 2001. Privacy questions are still an issue for online advertising.

Think Critically

1. Identify three people who have purchased an item on the Internet. Ask these people if they read the privacy policy before purchasing and if they know what a "cookie" is. Report your findings to the class.
2. Do the selling methods of Internet advertisers invade your privacy any more than do companies who mail you advertising or call you at home to try to sell you their products? Defend your answer.
3. A very young person is often not concerned about what information he or she provides to others on the Internet. How could an unethical business capture and use this information in a way that could harm the family?

7.3 Business Taxes

Goals
- Discuss the nature of taxes and the fairness of progressive, proportional, and regressive taxes.
- Identify and explain the most common types of taxes that affect business.

Terms
- proportional tax (flat tax)
- progressive tax
- regressive tax
- income tax
- sales tax
- excise tax
- property tax
- real property tax
- personal property tax
- assessed valuation

General Nature of Taxes

Although government uses many different ways to regulate business, no way is more important than taxes. The types and amounts of taxes influence business decisions that, in turn, can influence the total amount of business activity in a region and in the nation.

Both businesses and individuals pay many kinds of taxes to local, state, and federal governments. Taxes collected by the federal government account for about 56 percent of all taxes collected, while various state and local taxes account for the remaining 44 percent. Most corporations pay nearly one-half of their profits in various kinds of taxes.

Government levies taxes for different reasons. When government decides to levy a particular type of tax, it must consider fairness to taxpayers.

For what purposes do governments use taxes?

PHOTO: © GETTY IMAGES/PHOTODISC.

REASONS FOR TAXES

Governments levy taxes mainly to raise revenue (money) to fund new and ongoing programs. Governments also use taxes to regulate business activity.

Governments set revenue goals that must be reached in order to provide the various services desired by the public. Examples of these services range from law enforcement and road building to providing for the military defense of the country. It is costly for government to provide the many services the public wants. To pay for these services, therefore, it must collect taxes.

Governments also use taxes to control business activity. They can speed up economic growth by lowering taxes and slow it by raising taxes. The federal government also taxes certain foreign goods that enter this country in order to encourage consumers to purchase American-made rather than foreign-made products. State and local governments also control business activity through taxation. For example, they often set high taxes on alcoholic beverages and tobacco, in part to discourage customers from purchasing these products.

FAIRNESS OF TAXATION

It is difficult for government to find ways to levy taxes fairly and still raise sufficient amounts of money to meet government expenses. The question of fairness has caused many debates. One problem is determining who will, in fact, pay the tax. For example, a firm may have to pay taxes on the goods it manufactures. But, because the tax is part of the cost of producing the product, this cost may be passed on to the customer. Another problem of fairness is whether those with the most assets or most income should pay at a higher rate than those who own or earn the least. Government tries to solve the fairness problem by adopting a proportional, progressive, or regressive tax policy.

PROPORTIONAL TAXATION A **proportional tax**—sometimes called a **flat tax**—is one in which the tax rate remains the same regardless of the amount on which the tax is imposed. For example, in a given area the tax rate on real estate per $1,000 of property value is always the same, regardless of the amount of real estate the taxpayer owns. The total dollar amount of the tax paid by someone with a $400,000 home will differ from that paid by the person with a $175,000 home in the same area, but the rate of the tax is the same for both owners. A flat state tax of 6 percent on income is also proportional. Those with higher incomes pay more dollars than those with lower incomes. But the tax rate of 6 percent stays the same.

PROGRESSIVE TAXATION A **progressive tax** is a tax based on the ability to pay. The policy of progressive taxation is a part of many state and federal income tax systems. As income increases, the tax rate increases. As a result, a lower-income person is taxed at a lower rate than a higher-income person is. In fact, the Tax Foundation found that in a recent year, 5 percent of the taxpayers who pay the most taxes contributed over half of all the federal individual income taxes collected.

Some local and state governments have combined the policies of proportional and progressive taxes. For example, a state may apply a flat tax of 5 percent to incomes up to $20,000 and 6 percent to all incomes over $20,000.

The current federal tax law is a combination of progressive and proportional taxation policy. A 10 percent tax applies to taxable income up to $14,300 and a 15 percent tax applies to taxable income up to $58,100 for married couples filing joint returns. On taxable income from $58,100 and up to $117,250, the rate jumps to 25 percent and to 28 percent for incomes between $117,251 and $178,650. With still higher incomes, the rate jumps within brackets to 33 percent and 35 percent, respectively. For single taxpayers, the rate is 10 percent up to $7,150. On taxable income from $7,150 to $29,050, the tax rate is 15 percent. Tax rates continue to rise within brackets to 25 percent, 28 percent, 33 percent, and then 35 percent, respectively, for people with higher taxable incomes. Because people with higher incomes pay at a higher rate than those with lower incomes, most people consider the tax fair.

REGRESSIVE TAXATION The third type of tax policy is a **regressive tax**. With this type of tax, the actual tax rate decreases as the taxable amount increases. Although general sales taxes are often thought to be proportional, they are actually regressive, because people with lower incomes pay a larger proportion of their incomes in taxes than those with higher incomes. Suppose, for example, that Person A and Person B live in a state with a 6 percent general sales tax. As shown in Figure 7-4, Person A, with an annual take-home pay of $15,000, pays a 6 percent tax rate, whereas Person B, with an annual take-home pay of $45,000 pays only a 5.7 percent tax rate. Because the sales tax

Ethics tip

Is it okay not to pay your taxes? Legally you can avoid paying taxes by maximizing tax deductions. You cannot evade taxes by not reporting income. This is both unethical and illegal.

FIGURE 7-4 People with very high incomes often prefer regressive taxes.

	PERSON A	PERSON B
Take-Home Pay	$30,000	$100,000
State Sales Tax	6%	6%
Take-Home Pay Not Spent	0	$20,000
Take-Home Pay Spent	$30,000	$80,000
Tax Calculation	($30,000 x .06)	($80,000 x .06)
Tax	$1,800	$4,800
Tax Rate Calculation	($1,800/$30,000)	($12,400/$60,000)
Effective Tax Rate	6%	5%

applies to purchases rather than to income, the general sales tax is regressive. For a less regressive sales tax, some states exclude taxes on such purchases as food and clothing. These exclusions are usually items on which low-income families spend a high percentage of their income.

CHECKPOINT

Explain the three types of tax policies.

Types of Taxes

Taxation has become so complicated that the average businessperson spends a great deal of time filling out tax forms, computing taxes, and filing reports. In many businesses, various taxes reduce income by a large percentage. The three most common taxes affecting businesses and individuals are income taxes, sales

FIGURE 7-5 The Most Common Business Taxes

Assessments	Payroll taxes
Corporation taxes	Property tax — intangible property
Federal excise tax	Property tax — merchandise
Federal social security tax	Property tax — personal
Federal income tax	Property tax — real estate
Franchise tax	Sales tax
Gasoline tax	Severance tax
Licenses	State income tax
Local income tax	State unemployment tax
Motor truck licenses and taxes	State workers' insurance tax

taxes, and property taxes. Figure 7-5 gives examples of the types of taxes that a business operating in only one state may be required to pay.

INCOME TAX

The federal government and most state governments use the income tax to raise revenues. An **income tax** is a tax on the profits of businesses and the earnings of individuals. For individuals, the tax is based on salaries and other income earned after certain deductions. For businesses, an income tax usually applies to net profits (receipts less expenses).

The income tax is the largest source of revenue for the federal government. Individuals pay about 70 percent of the total federal income taxes collected, and businesses pay nearly all of the remaining 30 percent. Businesses share the cost of collecting individual income taxes. Every business is required to withhold income taxes from employees' earnings and turn them over to the government. Thus, business performs an important tax service for government. Individuals and businesses pay lower rates in the United States than in most other developed nations, as shown in Figure 7-6.

SALES TAX

A **sales tax** is a tax levied on the retail price of goods and services at the time they are sold. A general sales tax usually applies to all goods or services sold by retailers. However, when a sales tax applies only to selected goods or services, such as cigarettes and gasoline, it is called an **excise tax**.

Sales taxes are the main source of revenue for most states and some cities and counties. Although state governments do not all administer sales taxes in the same way, in most cases the retail business collects the tax from customers and turns this tax over to the state government. A business must be familiar with the sales tax law of the state in which it operates so that it can collect and report the tax properly.

From time to time, federal officials have considered charging a national sales tax. State officials, however, strongly oppose a national sales tax because the state tax is their primary source of revenue. The question as to how and whether to tax Internet sales is also under debate between the states and the federal government.

FIGURE 7-6 U.S. tax rates are relatively low in comparison to those of other nations.

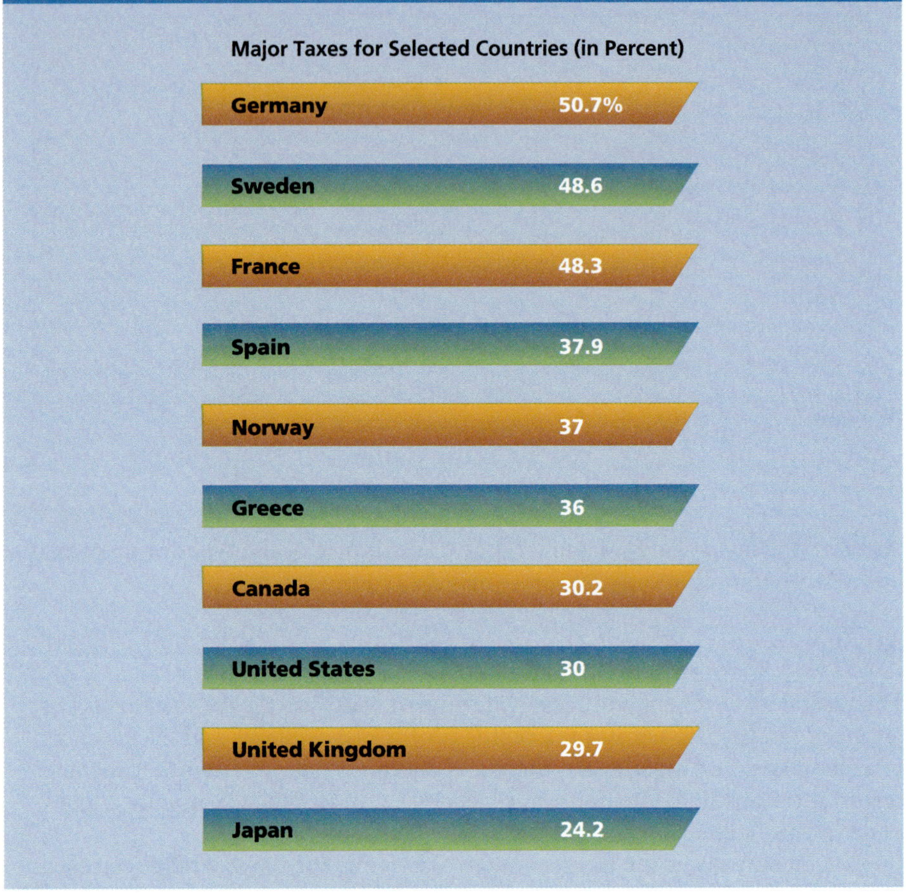

Major Taxes for Selected Countries (in Percent)

Country	Percent
Germany	50.7%
Sweden	48.6
France	48.3
Spain	37.9
Norway	37
Greece	36
Canada	30.2
United States	30
United Kingdom	29.7
Japan	24.2

Source: Organization for Economic Cooperation and Development (www.oecd.org), 2001.

Both see this source of taxes as highly attractive. Traditional retailers who pay sales taxes, however, believe it is unfair for Internet sales not to be taxed.

PROPERTY TAX

A **property tax** is a tax on material goods owned. Whereas the sales tax is the primary source of revenue for most state governments, the property tax is the main source of revenue for most local governments. There may be a real property tax and a personal property tax. A **real property tax** is a tax on real estate, which is land and buildings. A **personal property tax** is a tax on possessions that are movable, such as furniture, machinery, and equipment. Essentially, personal property is anything that is not real estate. In some states, there is a special property tax on raw materials used to make goods and on finished goods available for sale.

A tax on property—whether it is real property or personal property—is stated in terms of dollars per hundred of assessed valuation.

Assessed valuation is the value of property determined by tax officials. Thus, a tax rate of $2.80 per $100 on property with an assessed valuation of $180,000 is $5,040 ($180,000/100 = $1,800; $1,800 × $2.80 = $5,040).

EFFECT OF TAXES ON BUSINESS DECISIONS

Businesses consider taxes in many of their major decisions. Taxes may influence the accounting method a business selects to calculate profits and the method used to pay managers. Often, taxes are used as a basis for deciding where to locate a new business or whether to move a business from one location to another.

For example, assume that a producer of garden tools is trying to decide in which of two cities to build a new factory. City A is located in a state that has a low state income tax and low property taxes. City B is located in a state with no state income tax but high property taxes. After weighing all the factors, the producer decides to locate in City A. City A, which has both an income tax and a property tax, has been selected mainly because the total tax cost each year is less than in City B.

NETBookmark

The U.S. government's Internal Revenue Service (IRS) is charged with collecting taxes owed to the federal government. The IRS maintains a Web site to help ensure that individuals understand how to comply with complex tax rules. Point your browser to www.thomsonedu.com/school/bpmxtra. Click on the "site map" link. Identify the different information areas that the site supports. Choose an information area of interest to you. Explain how this site helps individuals and companies comply with tax regulations.

www.thomsonedu.com/school/bpmxtra

CHECKPOINT

Describe the three most common taxes levied on businesses and individuals.

7.3 Assessment

UNDERSTAND MANAGEMENT CONCEPTS

Circle the best answer for each of the following questions.

1. A tax based on a person's ability to pay is called a
   a. proportional tax
   b. flat tax
   c. progressive tax
   d. regressive tax
2. The largest source of revenue for the federal government is
   a. sales taxes
   b. income taxes
   c. import taxes
   d. property taxes

THINK CRITICALLY

Answer the following questions as completely as possible.

3. Describe the two ways governments use taxes.
4. Explain how taxes affect business decisions.

Xtra! Study Tools
thomsonedu.com/school/bpmxtra

CHAPTER CONCEPTS

- Federal, state, and local governments regulate business activities to protect citizens and businesses. The Federal Trade Commission administers federal laws that regulate commerce. Landmark laws such as the Sherman and Clayton Acts helped set the stage for defining fair competition. Other federal agencies regulate basic industries such as aviation, communications, and food and drugs.

- A downside of free enterprise is that some firms go bankrupt, but bankruptcy laws allow businesses to recover or to exit business operations fairly. The federal government protects individuals and firms from the theft or misuse of their inventions, publications, and other intellectual property by granting the owners patents, trademarks, or copyrights. Local and state governments also regulate business through licenses, zoning laws, and franchising regulations.

- Governments obtain revenues through taxes to pay for public services, such as police, schools, and other human services. The most common sources of revenue are income, sales, and property taxes.

- A progressive tax such as an income tax is based on one's ability to pay, and is higher for those who earn more than for those who earn less. A proportional tax such as a county's real estate tax stays the same regardless of a property's current value. A regressive tax, such as a sales tax, requires people who earn less to pay a greater portion of their income than do people who earn more. Arguments can be made for each of the three types of taxes.

REVIEW TERMS AND CONCEPTS

Write the letter of the term that matches each definition. Some terms will not be used.

a. assessed valuation
b. bankruptcy
c. excise tax
d. false advertising
e. information liability
f. interstate commerce
g. intrastate commerce
h. personal property tax
i. price discrimination
j. proportional tax (flat tax)
k. public franchise
l. sales tax
m. trademark
n. zoning

1. Setting different prices for different customers
2. Advertising that is misleading in some important way
3. Legal process that allows the selling of assets to pay off debts
4. Distinguishing name, symbol, or special mark placed on a good or service that is legally reserved for the sole use of the owner
5. Responsibility for physical or economic injury arising from incorrect data or wrongful use of data
6. Regulating which land areas may be used for homes and which may be used for different types of businesses
7. Tax rate that remains the same regardless of the income
8. Tax that applies only to selected goods or services, such as cigarettes and gasoline
9. Business transacted within a state
10. Tax levied on retail price of goods and services when they are sold
11. Tax on movable possessions
12. Value of property determined by tax officials

DETERMINE THE BEST ANSWER

13. A type of tax in which the actual tax rate decreases as the taxable amount increases is the
    a. proportional tax
    b. regressive tax
    c. progressive tax
    d. sales tax

14. An agreement in which the federal government gives an author the sole right to reproduce, publish, and sell literary or artistic work is called a
    a. patent
    b. copyright
    c. trademark
    d. license

15. A contract that permits a person or organization to use public property for private profit is called
    a. public franchise
    b. public license
    c. public patent
    d. none of the above

16. Which of the following are true for computer cookies?
    a. They are stored on the user's own computer.
    b. They can track where users go on the Internet.
    c. They can gather information on user interests and preferences for marketing purposes.
    d. All of the above are true.

17. A tax on real estate is called
    a. excise tax
    b. home tax
    c. property tax
    d. real property tax

18. State and local governments limit and control those who plan to enter certain types of businesses by issuing
    a. patents
    b. copyrights
    c. trademarks
    d. licenses

19. Which of the following are controlled by building codes?
    a. physical features
    b. maximum height
    c. types of materials that can be used
    d. all of the above

APPLY WHAT YOU KNOW

20. Discuss how a business that has a monopoly on a good or service can keep its prices unreasonably high.

21. Explain why it is necessary for the federal government to pass laws promoting fair competition.

22. Explain why state and local governments would want to regulate businesses.

23. Explain how it is possible for a business to continue operating even after it has filed for bankruptcy.

24. Explain how a computer software program might be both copyrighted and licensed.

MAKE CONNECTIONS

25. **Research** Use the library or the Internet to research the history of the Sherman Antitrust Act. Identify the unethical business practices that led to the passage of this law. Identify the most recent use of this act. Specify how the U.S. economy is stronger because of the Sherman Antitrust Act.

26. **Math** You live in a state that has the following tax schedule:

Taxable Income	Rate
$0–$6,999	no tax
7,000–14,999	5%
15,000–24,999	6%
25,000 and over	7%

Your state allows everyone $2,000 of exemptions from total income to arrive at taxable income. Your total income this year is only $12,000 because of work lost due to illness. Your friend's total income is $19,000.
a. What is your tax this year? What is your friend's tax?
b. What is the actual tax rate you and your friend paid this year based on your total incomes?

27. **Writing** You work for one of three manufacturers that sells nationally. You have heard that your company has discussed prices of a product that all three manufacturers sell but that has become unprofitable to each. These companies believe that it is foolish to sell at a loss. They all agree to raise prices, but they do not agree on how much each will charge. Write a memo outlining your feelings about this action. Refer to specific federal regulations as necessary.

CASE IN POINT

CASE 7-1: Pricing Competition

Hitesh Nazami owns and operates a hardware store in a community of 50,000 people. The nearest town is at least 25 miles away, but there are two competitors in the area, one of which is a new "big box" home store. All usually run weekly advertisements. Hitesh has noticed that the big-box store is selling many brand-name products at prices lower than he can buy them for from his suppliers. This has hurt Hitesh's overall sales.

Recently a customer Hitesh had never seen before came into the store to replace a broken tool. "I certainly hope you carry Weaver tools," the customer said. "The other stores in town, including that new big-box store, don't carry the Weaver brand."

"Sure, we carry Weaver," answered Hitesh. "It's one of my best lines."

The customer looked happy and relieved, and went to his truck to get the old tool he wanted to replace. While the customer was outside, Hitesh had a chance to think about what the customer had said. Now Hitesh knew why the Weaver brand was so popular in his store. He was happy that the big-box store didn't carry the Weaver brand. As a result, he decided to raise prices on Weaver tools by the next morning. Also, he could promote the fact that he was the only local supplier of Weaver tools in next week's advertisements. A smile crossed Hitesh's face as the customer returned.

"Here's the tool," said the customer. "I hope you can replace it. As you can see, it's quite different from the other brands."

"I can see that it's different," Hitesh responded. "You're lucky to get it at this low price. The price will be going up in the very near future."

THINK CRITICALLY

1. Is the big-box store practicing illegal price competition? Explain your answer. If it is, what federal act is it violating?
2. If the big-box store is not practicing illegal price competition, how can it sell at such low prices?
3. Does Hitesh have a monopoly on Weaver tools in his community?
4. If Hitesh raises his prices by very much, what might happen? What could the big-box store do?
5. Is raising the price suddenly (and for the reason given) an unfair business practice? Discuss your answer.
6. Could Hitesh advertise that he has an exclusive contract with Weaver even though he doesn't?

project: MY BUSINESS, INC.

PAYING TAXES AND MEETING REGULATIONS

Regulations and taxes harm businesspeople most often when they are not aware of them or do not understand them. In this chapter, you will study the effects of local, state, and federal laws on your business.

DATA COLLECTION

1. Identify the city/county office you will need to contact about local zoning regulations, licenses and permits, and taxes and fees.
2. Identify an information source (city booklet or Web site) on the legal procedures necessary to start a new business in your city or state.

ANALYSIS

1. Analyze the information you collected in the Data Collection section above. Outline the legal procedures you would have to follow and identify the permits and licenses you would need to start your juice bar. List the problems you might have in adhering to the legal requirements.
2. The legislature in your state has just increased the sales tax from 4 percent to 6 percent of total sales. This will cause you problems because of the way you have priced your products. In order to make prices easier to remember and to simplify making change, you priced your products as shown below to include the 4 percent tax. (Do not be concerned if these are not the same products or prices you have previously identified for your juice bar.)

Large one-variety juice/yogurt mix	$3.75
Small 3-juice combo	2.50
Vitamin/mineral supplement	.60
Turkey sandwich	5.25
Bagel with cream cheese	1.25
Nutrition bar	1.90

   It will be difficult to collect the additional 2 percent for sales tax and keep your pricing method. How will the sales tax increase affect your business? Evaluate several methods for dealing with the tax increase. Define your new pricing structure.
3. To reduce your start-up costs and to find a business location with a large number of potential customers, you have decided to rent a mobile cart in a large local mall in which to start your juice bar. Many fast-food business owners in your city are concerned that if mobile carts are allowed to operate, they will take business away from the other restaurants. They have approached the city council to pass a zoning regulation to prevent food from being sold from mobile carts, suggesting that it might be a health hazard. What actions can you and the owners of other similar businesses take to prevent the zoning law from being adopted by the city council? If the law is passed, how will it affect your business?

Career Cluster
Tax Accountant

Tax accountants work with businesses and individuals to reduce their taxes by developing strategies that maximize deductions and minimize taxable revenue. They also help develop investment strategies. Tax accountants must understand federal and state tax laws. Some work for federal and state tax agencies.

Employment Outlook

In 2004, there were about 1.2 million jobs for U.S. accountants and auditors. These are expected to increase significantly through the year 2014. This job expansion is linked to economic growth, changing financial laws and regulations, increased scrutiny of company finances due to accounting scandals, and congressional legislation designed to curb corporate accounting fraud.

Job Titles

Accounting Trainee
Junior Tax Accountant
Tax Accountant
Tax Accounting Manager
Chief Tax Accountant

Needed Skills

- Must possess a bachelor's degree in accounting from an accredited college or university.
- Should have an aptitude for mathematics and be able to analyze, compare, and interpret facts and figures quickly.
- Public accountants must pass the Certified Public Accounting (CPA) exam. Some employers may require a master's degree and a CPA license.

Working in an Accounting Firm

Ryan completed his bachelor's degree in accounting. As a student, he worked as a volunteer helping people fill out personal tax forms. After graduating, he started working for a medium-size accounting firm as a trainee. After passing the CPA exam, he worked for three years as a junior tax accountant. He was then promoted to tax accounting, supervising a team of accountants helping businesses develop tax strategies. Ryan hopes to become a tax accounting manager, then a chief tax accountant, and ultimately a partner in the firm.

Career Assessment

Why are tax accountants important to businesses and individuals? Why do they need years of training? What do you like and dislike about this career area?

PHOTO: © DIGITAL VISION.

Case Study

ENDANGERED CAREERS FOR AMERICAN ENTREPRENEURS

America's job outlook may be healthy, with many industries planning on growth in the coming years. But there are indicators that some occupations are becoming obsolete. Occupations facing decline include farmers and ranchers, stock clerks and order fillers, sewing machine operators, computer operators, secretaries, telemarketers, meter readers, parts salespeople, and telephone operators. These career fields are endangered as a result of technological advances and corporate changes. Nearly 155,000 jobs for farmers and ranchers are endangered due to consolidation of farms into fewer and larger corporate operations that are replacing small independent farms. The growing use of computers for inventory control and the installation of new, automated equipment are expected to replace the jobs of 115,000 stock clerks and order fillers. The growing volume of imports, greater use of offshore assembly, and increased productivity through new automation will contribute to the loss of 93,000 sewing machine operator jobs. Private delivery companies and electronic communications may replace 59,000 positions for mail clerks and mail-machine operators. Nearly 49,000 computer operator jobs are being replaced with the latest technology. Telemarketing jobs are losing steam due to the number of people choosing not to receive telemarketing calls and the greater use of blocking technology. Meter reader positions are being replaced with the latest technology. Electronic commerce ordering and reordering systems will automate the work of nearly 16,000 parts salespersons. Voice recognition systems will lead to a decline in the need for telephone operators.

Some of the hottest growth areas include elder care and pharmaceuticals for an aging baby boomer population. Entertainment products, the latest technological devices, and household appliances are also in high demand.

THINK CRITICALLY

1. Why should potential entrepreneurs pay attention to national trends for different occupational areas?
2. Why should the buying habits of baby boomers be considered when determining entrepreneurial ventures to pursue?
3. What entrepreneurship opportunities may be available to small farmers and ranchers?
4. How has international trade affected entrepreneurship opportunities in the United States?

Presentation Management Individual Event

You have been hired by the Small Business Administration to prepare an effective multimedia presentation that explains the four forms of business ownership: sole proprietorship, partnership, corporation, and franchise. The multimedia presentation should include details about starting each type of business, pros and cons for each form of business, investment requirements, liability for the owner(s), distribution of profits/losses, and examples of businesses in each category.

You will design a computer-generated multimedia presentation about different forms of business ownership. No VCR or laser disc may be used. The presentation content must be on the contestant's computer hard drive or on CD-ROM. Graphics, including charts, must be included in the presentation. National Business Professionals of America grants permission for the use of the logo and/or organization's name in the multimedia presentation. Students are responsible for securing a release form from any individual whose name, photograph, and/or other information is included in the presentation. No photographs, text, registered trademarks, or names may be used without permission. It is the policy of Business Professionals of America to comply with state and federal copyright laws. Although a work may be freely accessible on the Internet and contain no statement of copyright, copyright law provides that such works are protected. Projects will be disqualified for copyright violation and for not citing a source and/or receiving permission to use the material.

PERFORMANCE INDICATORS EVALUATED

- Demonstrate knowledge of multimedia software and components.
- Demonstrate effective oral communication skills.
- Apply technical skills to create a multimedia presentation that enhances the oral presentation.

For more detailed information about performance indicators, go to the BPA Web site.

THINK CRITICALLY

1. Why are more businesses counting on multimedia presentations for sales and other promotional purposes?
2. Why would a multimedia presentation about forms of business ownership be useful for the Small Business Administration?
3. Why should the multimedia presentation be easy for many individuals to use?

http://www.bpa.org/

Information and Communication Systems

CHAPTERS

> " Already, the Web work style is changing business processes at Microsoft and other companies. Replacing paper processes with collaborative digital processes has cut weeks out of our budgeting and other operational processes. Groups of people are using electronic tools to act together almost as fast as a single person could act, but with the insights of the entire team. Highly motivated teams are getting the benefit of everyone's thinking. With faster access to information about our sales, our partner activities, and most important, our customers, we are able to react faster to problems and opportunities. "

Bill Gates

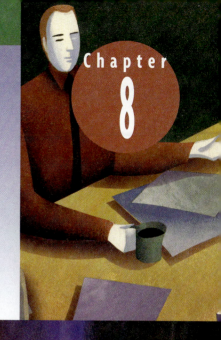

Technology and Information Management

8.1   Electronic Technology Fundamentals

8.2   Managing Technology

8.3   The Effects of Technology on Work and Workers

REALITY CHECK

Brave New Business World

After Mia Herrera rose, dressed, and hopped into her car, she used her voice-activated cell phone to call several customers who had e-mailed her late the previous evening. Before entering her favorite coffee shop, she reached into her pocket for her handheld computer and jotted a few brief messages that she then e-mailed to her regional sales manager.

After enjoying a hearty breakfast and returning to her car, Mia opened her briefcase and was soon dictating a message on her computer that was sent wirelessly via the Internet to her office assistant. Before starting the engine, she checked the car's global positioning system for the most direct but timesaving route to her new client.

At the next two stoplights, she read a few e-mails and found a favorite Web site to check yesterday's closing stock price for Egloff and Fox, Inc. Her first client that morning was the E&F purchasing manager. In the company's parking lot, Mia quickly reviewed E&F's background and database files from the small wireless computer she kept in her briefcase.

Now Mia felt ready to face the business day ahead.

8.1 | Electronic Technology Fundamentals

Goals

- Describe the basic elements of computers.
- Describe how the Internet provides information to users.

Terms

- knowledge workers
- data
- information
- computer
- hardware
- software
- personal digital assistant (PDA)
- operating system software
- application software
- Moore's Law
- Internet (Net)
- World Wide Web (WWW, Web)
- hyperlink
- modem
- Internet Service Provider (ISP)
- browser
- search engine

Through the ages, discoveries and inventions have had major impacts on society. No inventions in recent years have had a greater impact than the computer, Internet, World Wide Web, and wireless communications. These new tools have profoundly affected the personal work lives of Mia Herrera and millions of other workers. New technologies have made dizzying changes in the way we live and work, and the pace of change is not likely to slow in the years ahead.

The traditional business office that once operated with filing cabinets, typewriters, and secretaries was labor intensive when compared to today's electronic office. Simple business transactions that once took weeks of paper handling are now processed in minutes. Now workers create and store most documents electronically.

Whether an office is in a bank, factory, or day-care center, it must still collect, process, store, retrieve, and distribute data. The modern electronic office is an information center operated by **knowledge workers**—people who work with information. Clerks, supervisors, and managers at all levels are knowledge workers who handle data and information. **Data** are the original facts and figures that businesses generate. **Information** is data that have been processed in some meaningful way that is useful to decision makers.

In this chapter, you will learn how technology has changed the way businesses handle data and information. You will also learn how computers and the Internet affect organizations, people, and jobs. Finally, you will learn how information systems help managers make sound decisions by getting the right information in the right form at the right time to the right people.

Computer Technology

The current electronic revolution started with the creation of the computer over 50 years ago. More recently the Internet developed into a tool that people and businesses could use to communicate with each other. The computer and the Internet plus additional electronic devices set the stage for reconstructing how businesses operate.

COMPUTERS

A **computer** is a machine that processes and stores data according to instructions stored in it. The machine parts and anything attached to it are called **hardware**. The instructions that tell the computer what to do are called **software**.

As illustrated in Figure 8-1, computers have three basic elements: a way to enter data, a central processing unit to act on the data, and a way to output the results. Users can enter data through such devices as keyboards, voice-recognition systems, and scanners. The central processing unit receives and processes the data as directed by the software stored permanently or temporarily in the computer. Users can view data entered and processed on monitors or can print or store the data on disks, such as hard drives, floppy disks, CDs (compact discs), and DVDs (digital video discs).

PHOTO : © GETTY IMAGES/PHOTODISC.

How have new technologies changed the traditional business office?

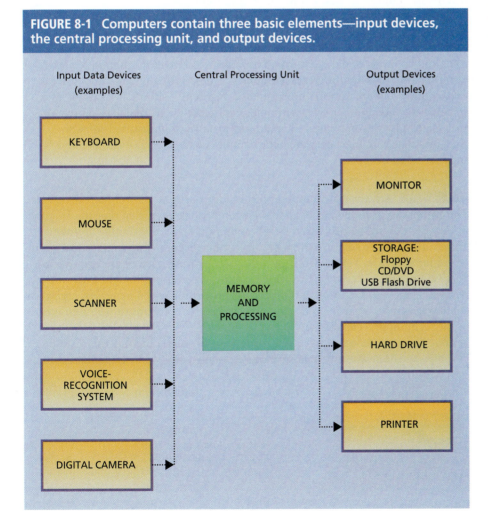

FIGURE 8-1 Computers contain three basic elements—input devices, the central processing unit, and output devices.

Input Data Devices (examples)

KEYBOARD

MOUSE

SCANNER

VOICE-RECOGNITION SYSTEM

DIGITAL CAMERA

Central Processing Unit

MEMORY AND PROCESSING

Output Devices (examples)

MONITOR

STORAGE:
Floppy
CD/DVD
USB Flash Drive

HARD DRIVE

PRINTER

facts & figures

In 2003, the Census Bureau surveyed the U.S. population to assess ownership and use of computers. Among the findings: More than 62 percent of American households had computers and 55 percent had Internet access. Eighty-six percent of children used a computer at home or at school. Over 70 percent of American adults used a computer at home, work, or school.

TYPES OF COMPUTERS Computers come in different sizes and serve different purposes. Companies use large computers (mainframes) to store and retrieve vast amounts of data for the entire company. Major divisions of the company may use medium-size computers. The typical office computer that most workers use is a desktop or personal computer (PC). Workers can carry smaller computers (laptops or notebooks), such as those used by Mia Herrera in the opening story, in briefcases and backpacks.

In addition to desktops and laptops, smaller handheld devices also serve specific purposes. A **personal digital assistant (PDA)** is a computer-like device that can be carried in a pocket and used, among other things, to send and receive messages wirelessly. PDAs may also be built into cell phones. PDAs usually contain a calculator, an address book, a notepad for keeping "to do" lists, and a fax modem. PDAs come with features to meet a variety of needs. Such devices will become standard voice-messaging equipment built into vehicles. Because wireless computing is rapidly developing, new products will continue to pour into the marketplace.

TYPES OF SOFTWARE All computers need two types software: operating system software and application software. **Operating system software** is a master control program that manages the computer's internal functions and file system. Operating system software directs and channels application software instructions and data for processing. Examples of operating system software include Microsoft Windows, Mac OS X, Unix, and Linux.

Application software refers to programs that perform specific tasks. The most common examples of application software are word processing for creating written documents, spreadsheets for performing calculations on rows and columns of data, databases for storing related information for later retrieval, and software for creating graphics. A description of common business application software appears in Figure 8-2. Figure 8-3 shows an example of a spreadsheet. Many other types of popular software are available to perform specialized tasks. Companies, for example, produce sophisticated software packages that help businesses manage complex tasks such as customer and supplier relationships.

MOORE'S LAW Advances in computer technology occur at an ever-increasing rate. The cofounder of Intel Corporation, Gordon Moore, predicted that the amount of data that could be processed by a computer chip would double about every 18 months. **Moore's Law**, as this prediction has become known, has proven to be rather accurate. Figure 8-4 shows this accelerating pace of change over the past two decades. According to Moore's Law, a computer bought only one to two years ago will be obsolete this year. As processing speed increases, high-tech companies are constantly producing new and better software to take advantage of the technology's capabilities.

But new technologies make old equipment obsolete. Buying and installing new equipment and software, as well as retraining employees, are costly business expenditures.

CHECKPOINT

Describe the three main parts of a computer.

FIGURE 8-2 Other Common Types of Software Application Programs

TYPE AND APPLICATION

ACCOUNTING

Maintain general and specific accounting records such as accounts receivable, accounts payable, and general ledger.

COMMUNICATIONS

Send and receive information from other computers, including fax, e-mail, and surfing the Web.

DESKTOP PUBLISHING

Create high-quality newsletters, brochures, manuals, advertising, and other special documents combining text, photographs, and graphics.

FORMS

Provide standard business forms such as invoices and purchase orders but allow for the modification of forms and the creation of entirely new forms.

GRAPHICS

Prepare diagrams, organization charts, line and bar graphs, pie charts, and other kinds of illustrations.

TRAINING

Teach employees about various topics, including how to use computers, how to supervise workers, and how to prepare a talk.

UTILITIES

Aid other software to work more effectively, such as providing a variety of type styles and font sizes, recovering lost files, and finding and correcting computer system errors.

FIGURE 8-3 Spreadsheets are used to prepare financial statements and other documents.

Cartright Corporation Comparative Income Statements

	Year 1	Year 2	Percent of Change
Sales	$58,000,000	$59,000,000	1.7
Cost of Goods Sold	30,000,000	32,000,000	6.7
Gross Profit on Sales	28,000,000	27,000,000	-3.6
Operating Expenses	12,000,000	11,000,000	-8.3
Administrative Expenses	10,000,000	9,000,000	-1.0
Net Profit Before Taxes	6,000,000	7,000,000	16.7

FIGURE 8-4 Microprocessors composed of chips on integrated circuits are constantly being developed by Intel Corporation and other firms to process data at faster speeds.

The Development of Microprocessors

MICROPROCESSOR	TRANSISTORS	TOP SPEED	YEAR
8086	29,000	10 Megahertz	1978
80386DX	275,000	16 Megahertz	1985
Pentium	1,200,000	25 Megahertz	1993
Pentium III	9,500,000	733 Megahertz	1999
64-bit Dual Processors	233,000,000	3 Gigahertz	2006

Source: Modified from Business Week, November 15, 1999; 2006 data retrieved from www.amd.com August 10, 2006.

facts & figures

Businesses involved in e-commerce are advised to have a privacy policy, post it on their Web site, and make it well known. Companies should: give notice about what personal information is collected and how it is used; give consumers the choice of whether and how their information can be used; establish adequate security measures to protect data; and allow consumers to access data about them so they can confirm its accuracy and make changes if necessary.

The Internet

Advances in computer technology invited the entrance of another electronic wonder—the Internet. The Internet, or Net, is a worldwide network of linked computers that allows users to transfer data and information from one computer to another anywhere in the world. People can use the Net to send e-mail, visit Web sites, and participate in discussion groups.

The Internet permits businesses to work together electronically and for employees to communicate with other employees at any distance. Even consumers can buy online from businesses or sell personal products. Two individuals with common interests can chat or join a discussion group, seek information from electronic libraries, or compare products. The Internet is also used as a substitute for phoning and to download music and update computer software. Internet uses are virtually unlimited.

WORLD WIDE WEB

Creation of the World Wide Web, WWW, or Web made the Internet accessible to the average person. Previously, the Internet allowed computer users to share only printed text and required sophisticated technical knowledge to use. Therefore, at first, researchers and the military were the main users. Now the Web permits text plus photographs, videos, and sound to be transmitted over the Net, all with just a minimal amount of computer savvy. This Internet access tool for the general public has enabled the Net to grow rapidly during the last decade. Now, for most of us, the Web is synonymous with the Internet.

The Web uses links, called hyperlinks, for navigating easily among its pages. A hyperlink is a Web page address embedded in a word, phrase, or graphic that, when clicked, transports users to that address. Web pages usually contain hyperlinks to other sites on the Web that contain information of interest to site visitors.

Hyperlinks often appear as colored, underscored words, but addresses can be embedded just about anywhere on the Web page. As you move your mouse pointer around a Web page, you will know when you encounter a hyperlink, because the pointer will turn to a hand with a pointing index finger.

Many companies, large and small, have Web sites. Their addresses usually contain the company name or initials. For example, the General Electric site address is http://www.ge.com. All addresses begin with "http://" for "hypertext transport protocol," which is a code that helps computers connect to each other on the Web. Your browser will assume that all addresses begin with this, so you need not type it. The next part of the address, www, stands for "World Wide Web." Many Web addresses begin this way, but not all. The company name or abbreviation usually appears next. The three letters at the end identify the type of organization. The ".com" following "ge" indicates a commercial or profit-making organization. A government office is ".gov," a school is ".edu," and a not-for-profit organization is ".org." Saying "dot.com" is a way advertisers and others may refer to Web sites in general.

The line under the GE Web address shown above indicates a hyperlink. If you were reading this page on the Internet and you wanted to visit GE's home page, you could immediately jump there by clicking the mouse on the hyperlink. You may want to know what products GE sells or what jobs are available. You could find out about GE's products by following hyperlinks on the company's site to different product pages.

Much business is transacted on the Internet. The use of the letter "e" before a name means "electronic." For example, "e-commerce" refers to businesses that buy and sell to other businesses as well as businesses that sell to consumers. "E-business" means businesses that buy and sell only to other businesses. Retailers that sell to customers on the Web are known as "e-tailers." Anyone who sends messages to others is using "e-mail." And "e-appliances" are consumer appliances, such as refrigerators and microwave ovens, that contain chips that allow people to use e-mail to obtain data such as cooking, freezing, and maintenance information that can be stored in the e-appliance. New "e" words are likely to evolve. You will learn more about e-commerce in Chapter 9.

PHOTO: © DIGITAL VISION.

The creation of the World Wide Web has made the Internet accessible to the average person. What effect has it had on the transaction of business?

USING THE INTERNET

To get onto the Internet, you need a **modem**, an electronic device inside or outside the computer that enables it to send data over phone lines or cable. You also need an **Internet Service Provider**, or **ISP**, a service that provides access to the Internet through its large computers. Examples of ISPs include AOL, NetZero, and many regional telephone companies or cable TV companies. ISPs usually charge a monthly fee.

To use the Web, you also need a **browser**. This is a program that permits you to navigate and view Web pages. Most computers come already equipped with a browser, or your ISP will provide one. The two most popular browsers are Microsoft Internet Explorer and Firefox.

Once you are on the Net, you can go directly to a Web address, or you may have to search for information. A **search engine** is a program that assists in locating information on the Net. After you type in one or more key words, the search engine will display a list of sites that contain information matching those key words. Some of these sites may have the information you want, but others may be way off target. A mouse click will take you to the Web sites that look promising. For example, assume you wish to buy a notebook computer. To use a search engine such as Google (www.google.com), key in "notebook computer" and wait for Google to provide a list of Web sites that you could visit.

CHECKPOINT

Explain the difference between the Internet and the World Wide Web.

8.1 Assessment

UNDERSTAND MANAGEMENT CONCEPTS

Circle the best answer for each of the following questions.

1. An individual who wishes to access the World Wide Web needs
   a. an ISP
   b. a browser
   c. a computing device
   d. all of the above

2. The original facts and figures that businesses generate are called
   a. data
   b. information
   c. figures
   d. information points

THINK CRITICALLY

Answer the following questions as completely as possible.

3. Describe the type of information that can be processed with a PDA.

4. Explain why Moore's Law is an important idea.

Xtra!
Study Tools
thomsonedu.com/school/bpmxtra

8.2 Managing Technology

Goals

- Describe the basic technology infrastructure used by businesses.
- Describe the information systems that managers use to aid in their decision making.

Terms

- chief information officer (CIO)
- telecommunications (data communications)
- local area network (LAN)
- file server (server)
- wide area network (WAN)
- intranet
- extranet
- firewall
- database
- information system
- management information system (MIS)
- decision support system (DSS)
- executive information system (EIS)

Managing Technology

As computers became a dominant force throughout the world, organizations had to manage the computer systems as well as the computer specialists. In major organizations, the top computer executive is the chief information officer, or CIO. The CIO reports to the CEO (chief executive officer). The CIO must possess not only knowledge about electronic equipment but also expert management skills.

CIOs must keep up with new technologies and know what types of equipment to purchase to meet an organization's specific needs. Because many workers use computers, keeping them trained and productive is equally important. CIOs make it possible for all people who need information to get it easily and quickly from anywhere it exists. CIOs also protect information from being improperly used or getting to people who should not have it.

DISTRIBUTING INFORMATION

Employees are constantly using their computers to record, process, send, store, and retrieve information. The company's computer system must make these tasks easy and fast to perform. Telecommunications (data communications) is the movement of information from one location to another electronically. The means used for this movement may be telephone lines, cable, or satellite. Telecommunications companies sell different systems for transmitting information within firms and to business partners and customers. Customers can even have training programs and sports events appear on a portion of their computer monitors, thanks to telecommunications providers.

Workers need an electronic means for sharing information. A local area network (LAN) is a network of linked computers that serves users in a single building or building complex. In a LAN, a computer that stores data and application software for all PC workstations is called a file server, or, more commonly, a server.

Firms with multiple locations have to send information to employees who are geographically dispersed. A **wide area network (WAN)** is a network of linked computers that covers a wide geographic area, such as a state or country. The LANs and the WANs and their servers are connected to a mainframe computer. The servers are also channels through which individual workers can use their computers to communicate with others inside and outside the organization.

INTRANETS AND EXTRANETS

An **intranet** is a private company network that allows employees to share resources no matter where they are located. An intranet works like the Internet. Users access information through a browser, navigate with hyperlinks, and send e-mail through the intranet. Usually the intranet even connects to the Internet, but it is sealed off from the general public to protect company information.

Intranets enable employees to accomplish many electronic tasks. Groups of employees working on the same project can discuss, share, plan, and implement ideas without having to leave their desks. These same employees can use company records stored electronically to aid in performing their tasks. Workers may use their computers to check employer-sponsored events, such as new training programs, or see choices of health care benefits and the balance in their retirement plan. The easy accessibility of information on an intranet reduces the time spent finding and thumbing through paper documents.

Another type of network that operates similarly to the Internet is an extranet. An **extranet** is a private network that companies use to share certain information with selected people outside the organization, such as suppliers and major customers. A supplier of raw materials for a manufacturer or merchandise for a national retailer, for instance, could serve the company better by tracking the company's daily inventory balance. When inventory gets low, the supplier could deliver its goods just when the company needs them. An extranet enables the supplier to see the company's inventory records without allowing access to other company data.

facts & figures

Computer scientists, computer engineers, and systems analysts are expected to be some of the fastest growing occupations through the year 2014. The increase will be driven by the rapid expansion in computer and data processing services and software development.

Why is information security such a critical issue? What are some ways in which information can be protected?

INFORMATION SECURITY

One of the major concerns of chief information officers is information security. The CIO must do whatever is necessary to make certain that hackers cannot steal, destroy, or alter information. The penalty for not controlling information may well be lawsuits by employees, customers, suppliers, and the public, as well as the loss of critical company records.

Organizations also may violate business ethics when they gather, and sometimes sell, information about people who use the Internet to browse or buy merchandise. Programs launched from Web sites can track your travels from Web site to Web site. Where you go frequently on the Web reveals your general interests and what you buy. After collecting this information, some firms may sell it to businesses that sell goods related to your interests. For example, if

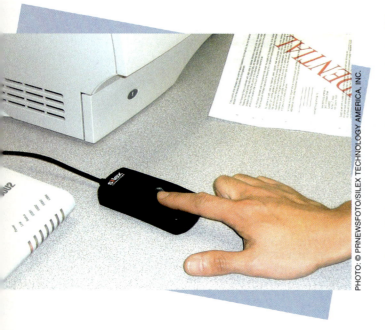

PHOTO: © PRNEWSFOTO/SILEX TECHNOLOGY AMERICA, INC.

Focus On...

Innovation–The Net's Booster Rocket–The Web

The purpose of the first crude Internet was as an emergency communication system for the military in case an enemy attack knocked out more conventional means of communication. Soon after this important goal was achieved, experts began using the slow, unreliable, and troublesome military Internet to share research findings. At the same time, improvements were being made, but the system's clumsiness and the need for technical knowledge limited its growth. However, the stage was set for the next breakthrough.

In 1989, Tim Berners-Lee, an English physicist who had been working at the European Particle Physics Laboratory, created the World Wide Web. This relatively unknown Web inventor developed a means for using the Internet to send more than just typed material to any computer in the world. What was needed was a global Internet-based hypermedia means for sharing global information. His new system permitted multimedia—graphics, videos, animations, and sounds— to be sent over the Internet. The Net's popularity grew by leaps and bounds as further refinements were made. The laboratory also created the first Web browser, leading to navigation through hyperlinks. The marriage of the Internet and the Web led to rapid global acceptance during the last decade of the 20th century.

Tim Berners-Lee believes the Web is a powerful force for social and economic change and that it has already modified how we conduct business, entertain ourselves, find information, and swap ideas. His goal is to keep the Web wide open and free to everyone, but he expects the Web will continue to alter our lives. He resisted efforts by major corporations to own and operate parts of the Web, because that would lead to charging user fees, which would not make it free. As the director of the World Wide Web Consortium, Berners-Lee discusses Web refinements with other consortium members worldwide. The group also oversees and recommends solutions to a variety of problems.

Tim Berners-Lee could easily have become very rich if he had personally built his own Web business or worked with a major computer firm to exploit it. He chooses to guide his creation to benefit humankind first and foremost. *Time* magazine named him one of the greatest geniuses of the 20th century. Yet he is not a household name like Albert Einstein. But unlike many other famous people before him, he has a Web site.

Think Critically

1. Why was the first Internet created? Why didn't the early version of the Internet catch on with everyone?
2. How did the addition of the WWW increase use of the Internet?
3. Do you think Tim Berners-Lee would be happier being the CEO of a highly successful firm making millions more than he is now as an employee in nonprofit organizations?
4. Using a library or the Internet, find out more about Tim Berners-Lee and write a report for the class.

NETBookmark

The World Wide Web is governed by an independent board called the W3C (Word Wide Web Consortium). Point your browser to www.thomsonedu.com/school/bpmxtra. Visit the W3C site and evaluate its current initiatives. Determine what the W3C is doing to allow the Web to continue to grow and meet people's needs around the world. Determine the background you would need to help the W3C move the Web forward into the future.

www.thomsonedu.com/school/bpmxtra

you frequently look at Web sites related to MP3 music or games, firms that sell these goods will contact you and try to sell you their products.

When you buy goods on the Net, you must provide basic information, such as name, address, telephone number, and e-mail address. Often Web sites store this information in your computer as a "cookie" file that the sites can retrieve when you visit again. This can be helpful when you buy from the business again. But the seller can also sell this personal information to other businesses without your knowledge.

The Federal Trade Commission and good business practice require that businesses notify buyers of their rights and how personal information will be used. However, some businesses may not properly inform buyers of their rights or continue to sell their confidential information. These actions are unethical and illegal in some states. Many computer users would buy on the Internet if they did not fear invasion of their privacy.

Companies must also take defensive strategies to protect electronic information. Such strategies often include requiring user passwords to access data, saving information as backup files, and scrambling information to make it unreadable to others.

Firms often use firewall systems to protect information from outsiders who try to break into their networks. A **firewall** uses special software that screens people who enter and/or exit a network by requesting specific information such as passwords. Passwords should change frequently. But even firewalls are not totally hacker-proof. Other systems are either available or being developed. For example, fingerprint scanning, voice verification, retina scanning, and other methods are being tested to safeguard organizational information.

CHECKPOINT

Describe the difference between an intranet and an extranet.

Information Systems

Organizations are experiencing an information explosion. New computerized methods can gather and store more information quicker than could traditional methods. As a result, many managers suffer from information overload, the existence of more data than anyone can attend to. Information overload leads to needless costs and inefficiencies as managers try to sort through all the available information to find what they really need to make decisions. Thus, organizations need effective means for managing information.

Employees generate business data constantly. They record sales transactions, collect customer information, and track inventory. When employees key such data into their computers, the data become part of the company's database. A **database** is a collection of data organized in a way that makes the data easy to find, update, and manage.

But a collection of data is not useful until it is processed into a form that decision makers can use. A computer system that processes data into meaningful information is called an **information system**. Three key types of information systems are management information systems, decision support systems, and executive information systems.

MANAGEMENT INFORMATION SYSTEM

A **management information system** (MIS) integrates data from various departments to make it available to help managers with day-to-day business operations. An MIS deals with specific and highly structured data. Different departments collect and process the data. Employees enter daily transactions into the system as they occur, such as when they prepare purchase orders and record sales. From this gathered and stored information, managers can request reports to help them make daily operating decisions. For example, a sales report can show a manager where sales are slow. From this information, the manager might decide to do a special promotion for customers in this area.

DECISION SUPPORT SYSTEM

A **decision support system** (DSS) helps managers consider alternatives in making specific decisions. For example, a DSS can help a manager determine the most efficient routes for the company's delivery trucks. The ability to analyze "what if?" scenarios is a key capability of a DSS. What if we continue our current strategy? Would that work? What if we try something else? What are the likely consequences of that action? The company's management information system provides much of the information for its decision support system.

PHOTO: © GETTY IMAGES/PHOTODISC.

How can different information systems be used to streamline the delivery of merchandise to customers?

EXECUTIVE INFORMATION SYSTEM

An **executive information system** (EIS) combines and summarizes ongoing transactions within the company to provide top-level executives with information needed to make decisions affecting the present and future goals and direction of an organization. Information used in executive information systems is gathered from the MIS and DSS. An EIS collects data from both internal and external sources to help executives make decisions. For example, executives might use the EIS to collect outside information that affects the company, such as information regarding competitors, the state of the economy, and government policies. With information from inside and outside the organization, top managers make long-term decisions that help a business survive and grow.

CHECKPOINT

Describe the three key types of information systems.

8.2 | Assessment

UNDERSTAND MANAGEMENT CONCEPTS

Circle the best answer for each of the following questions.

1. The movement of information from one location to another electronically is called
   a. a network
   b. the Internet
   c. telecommunication
   d. computer-based communication

2. A computer that stores data and application software for all PC workstations is called a
   a. mainframe
   b. server
   c. network
   d. local area network

THINK CRITICALLY

Answer the following questions as completely as possible.

3. Describe the advantages intranets offer to businesses.

4. Describe the advantages that information systems offer to businesses.

Xtra!
Study Tools
thomsonedu.com/school/bpmxtra

8.3   The Effects of Technology on Work and Workers

Goals
- Discuss types of problems that employees face in today's high-technology organizations.
- Describe technology's present and future impact on businesses.

Terms
- carpal tunnel syndrome (CTS)
- ergonomics

Technology and Workers

Computers, the Internet, and other forms of electronic technology have affected our lives as consumers and as workers. The work of employees has changed because of new technological devices and because firms have restructured the ways in which they operate. Over the last several decades, computers have changed the ways individuals perform work tasks, which in turn has caused anxieties in people about job security, about their ability to cope with new technology, and about electronic devices that may affect their health.

HEALTH PROBLEMS

Certain complaints arise among workers who spend most of their work time using computers and other automated equipment. Employees may complain about eye strain, cancer-causing radiation, backaches, and hand-muscle problems. Eye strain is likely to occur when computer operators view monitors (computer screens) for long periods. Usually, eye strain can be reduced or eliminated by adjusting light intensity on screens, shading screens from glare, wearing glare-reducing glasses, and taking work breaks every few hours. Sitting in uncomfortable chairs for long periods can cause back problems. Hand problems are often the result of improper keyboard or chair heights. Proper chair design with good back support helps, as do special exercise routines and breaks from being seated for long periods.

Employees may also be concerned about radiation. Many types of electronic equipment such as cell phones, televisions, and computers give off modest amounts of radiation. Some studies have shown that the amount of radiation is small and therefore does not affect health. However, other studies claim computer radiation is harmful. Pregnant women are especially concerned. Many businesses assign women to noncomputer jobs during pregnancy to avoid possible harm from radiation.

One type of injury that can occur from repetitive motion such as using a computer keyboard or playing video games is **carpal tunnel syndrome** (CTS). CTS occurs when the tunnel in a person's wrist becomes too narrow for the nerves and tendons that support the hands. This can result in a tingling or numbness in the hand. CTS can be prevented by proper posture when using a computer, using a wrist rest, and having an ergonomic keyboard. If someone gets CTS, they may need to use a wrist brace or have surgery.

The science of adapting equipment to the work and health needs of people is called **ergonomics**. Ergonomic experts study the relationships between people and

What health problems can occur when computers are used frequently? What steps can a business take to reduce such problems?

PHOTO: © GETTYIMAGES/PHOTODISC.

machines. For example, they work with engineers to design more comfortable chairs and produce lighting that reduces eye strain. In recent years, ergonomic experts have focused on making computer hardware, software, furniture, and lights adjustable, practical, and comfortable.

CHANGED JOBS

A major role of today's managers is to manage change. The rapid rate at which changes occur can be disruptive. To survive, businesses must be adaptable and employees must change to meet the needs of employers.

Nearly all jobs have been restructured, and new jobs are evolving. Large numbers of employees must use computers. In turn, job tasks once done manually, such as taking shorthand and using typewriters, are now done on computers. Bosses who key their own messages have greatly modified the role of the secretary. For example, most secretaries have had title changes, with many becoming administrative assistants who perform a variety of higher-level tasks. Many are assigned leadership roles, serve as project managers and members of work teams, and train employees on how to use electronic equipment. Similarly, other jobs have been greatly modified as workers are given far more responsibilities than during the precomputer age.

Often employees are retrained for new jobs, but others are let go. This downsizing action creates anxiety among workers. Many firms provide retraining, and others help employees find new jobs with other firms. Each new major technological change, however, creates employee anxiety. Managers must be ready to deal with this problem, because these employees may become less productive, leave, or create problems.

THE NEW JOB MARKET

Computerization has reduced the need for some skills and increased the need for others. Today's employees must have technical skills as well as interpersonal skills. For example, employees who work at computer help desks assist workers who have computer problems. Help desk employees must have "people skills," such as a friendly personality and a willingness to help others. They must also have a great deal of technical knowledge about computers and about solving software problems that employees encounter.

Other technically oriented jobs include programmer (one who creates and modifies software programs), network administrator, systems analyst (one who helps create, develop, and maintain MISs, DSSs, and EISs), software trainer, Web page designer, Webmaster (someone who manages and maintains a Web site), computer equipment salesperson, and computer repair person.

Telecommuters, as mentioned in Chapter 2, work at home using electronic equipment such as computers, scanners, and printers to complete their "at home" tasks. Still other individuals are entrepreneurs who start and run their own businesses from home using electronic equipment. Many of the popular Internet businesses were started from the homes of entrepreneurs.

business *note*

Advancement in computer technology may be ready to take a greater leap. New computers may have quad-processors, providing more than twice the fastest current computer speed. A new Internet2 is promising speeds of up to 100 gigabits per second, versus the 10 megabits most systems have today. Businesses will need to continue to change as these technologies allow for new means of obtaining and delivering information. Explain how these changes will affect your future career plans.

CHECKPOINT

Describe how technology has impacted the cost of producing goods and services.

The Future

Computer technology is now an indispensable part of business throughout the world. Businesses either move with the technology or fade away. Well-managed firms do not stand still. How much additional change will occur during the next 5 to 10 years? No one knows, because these are dynamic times. What is known, however, is that change is constant and is occurring at amazing speeds. Rapid change has been occurring in nearly every industry and in most countries. Slow-moving firms are attempting to catch up. Some of those are catching up by buying healthy firms or by creating joint ventures that will move them through the 21st century.

The world is in the middle of a major shift in how business is conducted. Just as cars, planes, television, telephones, and computers changed life during the last century, the Internet is changing life in this century. It is transforming how we work and live. It has increased the intensity of worldwide competition. No longer can major businesses in any nation think of their markets or competitors as being exclusively within their own boundaries.

The cost of producing goods and services in this electronic age has led to increased competition that has lowered prices. And computers and other electric marvels have cut paperwork, increased worker productivity, shed nonproductive tasks, and maximized business efficiency. Consumers have been the beneficiaries. Even the nature of how businesses are organized and operated has been permanently affected. Living in the Internet age, however, does not mean that all firms have closed their doors where customers might enter to see, touch, and even try before they purchase. You cannot go to a health club or a hairstylist on the Internet, but you can get advice there. You may prefer to go to the grocery store for the personal contact. But in this fast-paced world, you may prefer to buy your groceries on the Internet and have them delivered to you.

Many businesses will thrive by operating stores on Main Street and on the Internet. Like Mia Herrera in the opening story, we will have our personal digital assistants as we meet and talk with friends from our homes and cars, in restaurants, and at the mall.

CHECKPOINT

List the health problems someone can have from using computers.

8.3 Assessment

UNDERSTAND MANAGEMENT CONCEPTS

Circle the best answer for each of the following questions.

1. Which of the following can be seen as health problems for knowledge workers?
   a. eye strain
   b. backaches
   c. carpal tunnel syndrome
   d. all of the above

2. Which of the following is *not* true about ergonomics?
   a. Ergonomics studies the relationships between people and machines.
   b. Ergonomics engineers design systems that reduce strain.
   c. Ergonomics includes the use of lighting.
   d. All of the above are true.

THINK CRITICALLY

Answer the following questions as completely as possible.

3. Explain why managing change is important for today's managers.

4. Explain how technology is affecting workers' jobs.

Xtra!
Study Tools
thomsonedu.com/school/bpmxtra

CHAPTER CONCEPTS

- Computers come in all sizes, shapes, and configurations, and all need an operating system and application software to perform tasks.

- The Internet is a worldwide network of linked computers that permits users to share data and information over phone lines or cable. The development of the World Wide Web made the Internet accessible to the general public through Web browsers and hyperlink navigation.

- The chief information officer is accountable for managing all of an organization's electronic information and supporting systems that help employees make timely and informed decisions.

- Many businesses use information systems. A management information system (MIS) integrates data from many departments, helping managers make decisions. A decision support system (DSS) helps managers consider alternatives when making specific decisions. An executive information system (ESS) combines and summarizes ongoing transactions to help top-level managers make decisions affecting the future direction of the company.

- Computers have modified existing jobs and created new ones. Employees have been affected in various ways, including new job and skill requirements, layoff fears, and health factors.

REVIEW TERMS AND CONCEPTS

Write the letter of the term that matches each definition. Some terms will not be used.

1. Machine that processes and stores data according to instructions stored in it
2. Prediction that the amount of data that could be processed by a computer chip would double about every 18 months
3. Service that provides access to the Internet through its large computers
4. Network of linked computers that serves users in a single building or building complex
5. Data that have been processed in some meaningful way that is useful to decision makers
6. Instructions that tell the computer what to do
7. Top computer executive
8. Program that assists in locating information on the Net
9. Collection of data organized in a way that makes the data easy to find, update, and manage
10. Information system that integrates data from various departments to help managers with day-to-day business operations
11. Information system that helps managers consider alternatives in making specific decisions
12. Science of adapting equipment to the work and health needs of people

a. chief information officer (CIO)
b. computer
c. database
d. decision support system (DSS)
e. ergonomics
f. hyperlink
g. information
h. Internet Service Provider (ISP)
i. local area network (LAN)
j. management information system (MIS)
k. Moore's law
l. search engine
m. software
n. wide area network (WAN)

DETERMINE THE BEST ANSWER

13. Knowledge workers are
    a. people who work with information
    b. computer programmers only
    c. college professors only
    d. CIOs only

14. The parts of a computer and anything attached to it are called
    a. hardware
    b. software
    c. computer ware
    d. network equipment

15. Programs that perform specific tasks are known as
    a. application software
    b. operating system software
    c. network software
    d. program software

16. A worldwide network of linked computers that allows users to transfer data and information from one computer to another anywhere in the world is
    a. a wide area network
    b. the Internet
    c. a local area network
    d. all of the above

17. To share certain information with selected people outside a company, such as suppliers and major customers, the company would use a(n)
    a. intranet
    b. extranet
    c. Internet
    d. wide area network

18. A Web page address embedded in a word, phrase, or graphic that, when clicked, transports users to that address is a
    a. hyperlink
    b. Web link
    c. jumplink
    d. Web site

19. An information system that combines and summarizes ongoing transactions within the company to provide top-level executives with information needed to make decisions affecting the present and future goals and direction of an organization is a(n)
    a. information support system (ISS)
    b. decision support system (DSS)
    c. executive information system (EIS)
    d. management information system (MIS)

APPLY WHAT YOU KNOW

20. Describe how the basic parts of a computer work together to process information.
21. Describe how businesses have benefited from the efficiencies that have resulted from the use of electronic technology.
22. Explain how management information systems use data to help businesses operate.
23. Describe the characteristics that a chief information officer must possess in order to be successful.
24. Describe the techniques that are being tried to make sure that the wrong people do not gain access to information on a firm's computer system.

MAKE CONNECTIONS

25. **Math** Deborah and Kenneth Parks obtained prices from the following companies for a desktop computer system with a modem for their new business.

	Computer House	E-Z Electronics
Computer	$1,200	$1,000
Monitor	500	550
Printer	400	350
Software programs	850	950

   a. Which company has the best total price and by how much?
   b. If the lowest-priced item were purchased from each company, what would the total cost be? How much would each company be paid?

26. **Research** Using a library or the Internet, find information about a specific ergonomic problem related to working with electronic equipment, such as one related to radiation from computer equipment, uncomfortable chairs, or poorly designed desks. Prepare a report of your findings.

27. **Technology** Trina Jones is considering purchasing cellular phone PDAs for her employees. She wants to determine the yearly cost for each type of PDA. PDA 1 costs $300 and has a monthly charge of $65. PDA 2 costs $225 and has a monthly charge of $85. PDA 3 costs $100 and has a monthly charge of $105. Use spreadsheet software to answer the following questions.
   a. What would be the total annual cost for each PDA?
   b. Assume Trina's employees will use the PDAs for two years at the same monthly cost. Which PDA is the least expensive over two years?

28. **Writing** Join other students to write a report about any trouble group members have had with losing data and files from school or home computers on or off the Internet. Present the report to your class, specifying the problems and indicating the security steps that should be taken to prevent or reduce these problems.

CASE IN POINT

CASE 8-1: Technostress

Carmen Alonso and Maria Corsi were on their lunch break at work when a friend, Jan Bailey, joined them. As they conversed, each woman expressed her concerns about trying to juggle home life with work, raising a family, and spending time with others. "It's a crazy world," Jan said. "No wonder everyone tries to keep up by being glued to cell phones." Carmen was concerned that cell phones caused accidents. Maria added that she spent a lot of time at home ordering things from the Internet. "There's almost no time for the mall or to grocery shop, let alone to spend quality time with the children." At that point, Jan launched the heated conversation that follows:

Jan: *The world's gone overboard with all this electronic technology. Yes, we use phones and e-mail to chat with family and friends, but that's not the same as seeing people in person.*

Maria: *I think these gadgets are aids, not obstacles. How else could we both work if we couldn't stay in touch, even if it's not in person?*

Carmen: *Communication is too impersonal these days. Everyone's rushing to get things done. Few people stop to have an old-fashioned conversation. I wish we could turn the calendar back 25 years when people just sat around and chatted.*

Maria: *But you wouldn't have all the luxuries we have today. You'd be wasting time chatting. The Internet allows you to get so much more done. I'll bet my parents would have loved to have what we have.*

Carmen: *Mine refuse to learn new technology. They're very happy without the gadgets.*

Jan: *I agree with Carmen's parents. We have new problems, like worrying about someone stealing our personal records, destroying our files, and crashing our computers. Those can be expensive problems in terms of time, money, and invasion of privacy.*

THINK CRITICALLY

1. Do you tend to agree more with Jan, Mary Ann, or Carmen? Explain why. Which person most likes and which most dislikes today's technological lifestyle?
2. What electronic equipment, such as cell phones, computers, access to the Internet, scanners, digital cameras, or other devices, do you personally have readily available to you seven days a week?
3. Which one piece of electronic equipment is most valuable and which is least valuable to you? Explain why.
4. Use your library or the Internet to find information that deals with the topic of how electronic equipment contributes to the possible depersonalization of everyday life. Report the results to your class.

CASE 8-2: Technology-driven Job Redesign

Mei Shen and Jack Compton are employed at the Waterside Company, a small life insurance firm. Both Mei and Jack have been with the business for more than 10 years but are now quite upset by recent events. The office manager announced yesterday that all employees must attend several all-day training sessions on two coming changes. A new computer system is replacing the old one, and jobs are being restructured to improve processes that will lead to greater efficiency and productivity.

Unlike past practice, the new plan will have each person in the office doing all of the tasks now done separately. The training will prepare them to do everyone else's work, but all work will be done on the computer. To even the workload, all 10 standard insurance policies will be loaded in each computer, and employees and salespersons will be assigned specific customers on an alphabetic basis. When a salesperson calls with questions, the designated office worker can find the answers immediately. With the old system, answers might take as long as two weeks to get to customers.

The new computerized system has been installed but will not be used until the employees are all trained. They have just returned from the first day's training session. The following conversation takes place:

Jack: *I don't know about you, Mei, but this change is just like coming to an entirely new job. I don't know how all of this is going to work out.*

Mei: *We should have at least been told about this in advance, rather than have it come as a complete surprise. We could easily get a job at another insurance company. Maybe we should quit. The company isn't willing to give us more money to learn all the new procedures, new software, and new computers. With our experience, we shouldn't have any trouble finding a new job.*

Jack: *Hold on, Mei. We shouldn't be too hasty. We make good money here, but I agree that they should have told us about this so we could have been doing some reading and getting ourselves ready for the change. If the system works well, our jobs will be more secure. Most other insurance companies already operate the new way.*

Mei: *From what we learned today, we could certainly make the company sorry that they didn't get our opinions before deciding to change computers and our jobs.*

THINK CRITICALLY

1. Describe what mistake the Waterside Company management made in replacing the computer system.
2. In what ways could Mei make the company regret not involving the employees in the decision? Explain.
3. If the new computer system is to be successful, will it be because of restructuring the work, installing a new computer system, or both? Explain your answer.
4. If the new changes are successful, how will the salespeople and customers benefit?

project:

COMPUTER SYSTEMS ANALYSIS

As the owner of a new business, you will spend a great deal of time dealing with information. Poorly organized business records would make it hard for you to find and use the information you need. Use the following activities to review information management systems for small businesses and make decisions about how technology will benefit your business.

DATA COLLECTION

1. Interview the owner of a small business. Discuss the type of information management system used in that business. Identify (a) the type of records and information maintained, (b) whether or not the system is computer based, (c) who is responsible for information management, and (d) how the system could be improved.
2. Visit a computer systems retailer and discuss the hardware and software the retailer recommends for new small businesses. Collect information on system prices, capabilities, and ease of operation.
3. Visit an office furniture company in person or online and investigate ways to create an ergonomically healthy work environment for your employees.
4. Use the Internet to identify companies that offer information management services for businesses. Go to the companies' Web sites to determine the types of services offered and prices charged for those services.

ANALYSIS

1. Create a list of the types of information that your business will need. Identify the hardware and software that you will need to turn data into information useful to management. Describe the types of skills you or your employees will need to use and maintain both the hardware and the software that your company will be using.
2. The Internet can be a very valuable tool for small businesses. Identify and describe five specific types of information, accessible through the Internet, that can help you develop and manage your business. Then use an Internet search engine to identify one or more sites that supply each type of information you listed. Bookmark each location (use a storage device to store your bookmarks) so you can easily revisit the sites.
3. List three ways that e-commerce might have a negative effect on your business and three ways that you might use e-commerce to improve your new business.

E-Commerce

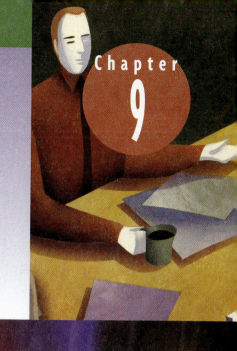

REALITY CHECK

The Case for Cyber Commerce

Turan Ozmat sat in the Chamber of Commerce meeting only half-listening to the presentation. The speaker was talking about the use of the Internet by businesses. She had just made the statement that any business without a presence on the Web would be at a competitive disadvantage in the next few years.

Turan thought of his photography studio and believed the speaker couldn't be talking about that type of business. His business required personal contact between the photographer and the customer. Customers wanted to be able to come into the studio and see the quality of the portraits and photos as well as the settings and backgrounds that Turan used. Whether people were scheduling a wedding, family portraits, or students' graduation photos, Turan believed that face-to-face meetings allowed him to understand the customer's needs and to develop the customer's trust and confidence. He didn't see how any of that could be possible with the Internet.

When Turan returned to his business that afternoon, he still was thinking about the speaker's comments. Even though he felt his business was different, he didn't want to miss an opportunity. He sat down at his computer, typed "photographer" into a search engine, and was amazed at the results. The search engine returned over 100,000 hits! Turan narrowed the search by typing in the name of his city. Immediately, three competitors' names popped on the screen. Turan decided he would spend the weekend exploring how other photography businesses were using the Internet.

213

9.1 Business and the Internet

Goals

- Describe the recent growth of the Internet.
- Discuss common business uses of the Internet other than e-commerce.

Terms

- e-commerce
- Internet domain
- Voice over Internet Protocol (VoIP)

People are sitting down at their computers in ever-increasing numbers to use the Internet. Sometimes it is hard to believe that the Internet has a relatively short history. It developed from the first efforts to link computers less than 50 years ago. The introduction of the personal computer in the late 1970s began to expand computer access onto business desktops and into homes. Today, through low-cost or free connections to the Internet, millions of people throughout the world can instantly access information and communicate with each other.

The Internet has become a very important business tool. **E-commerce** means doing business online. It includes the use of the Internet to buy and sell products as well as to exchange business-related information, such as transmitting purchase orders electronically or advertising online. E-commerce is now a multi-billion-dollar part of our economy.

The Internet has allowed many small businesses to compete with larger, established companies and to reach consumers all over the world. Currently less than 11 percent of all business sales are completed using the Internet, but that figure is growing rapidly. Businesses need to plan for e-commerce.

The Growth of the Internet

Since its infancy as a military and research tool in the 1950s, the Internet has grown impressively, as shown in Figure 9-1. Over 400 million Internet domain sites were online by January 2006. An **Internet domain** is a registered Web site, such as www.thomsonlearning.com. Millions more domains are being added each year. Since the invention of the World Wide Web in the late 1960s, access to the Internet has grown to an estimated 1 billion people around the world. More than 77 million homes in the United States had access to the Internet in 2005, up from just 13 million in 1995. The United States currently leads the world in Internet use, with approximately 20 percent of all users. China's Internet growth could put it ahead of the United States within a decade. Internet use is growing all over the world, as shown in Figure 9-2.

Business use of the Internet is increasing rapidly as well. Although there are many other business uses of the Internet, as we will discuss in the next section, an important measure of business Internet use is the sale of products and services. According to the U.S. Census Bureau, U.S. Internet sales to consumers in 2004 totaled $130 billion—$71 billion in retail sales and $59 billion in selected services. These seem like very large figures, until they are compared to business-

Ethics tip

Many young people think that downloading songs or movies from the Internet is not theft because they do not take it from a store. Digital products are intellectual property that are owned by a producer. Illegal downloads are the same as theft.

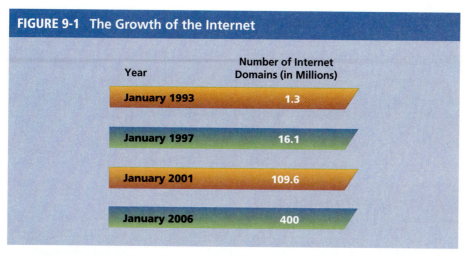

FIGURE 9-1 The Growth of the Internet

Year	Number of Internet Domains (in Millions)
January 1993	1.3
January 1997	16.1
January 2001	109.6
January 2006	400

Source: www.isc.org

E-commerce experts believe there is a tremendous amount of money to be made in online business-to-business selling. They cite the fact that selling to businesses is more cost-effective than to individual consumers; orders from businesses are, on average, higher in dollar value; and businesses order larger quantities of an item.

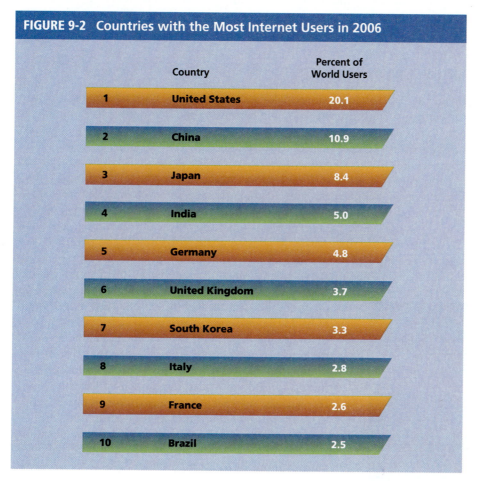

FIGURE 9-2 Countries with the Most Internet Users in 2006

	Country	Percent of World Users
1	United States	20.1
2	China	10.9
3	Japan	8.4
4	India	5.0
5	Germany	4.8
6	United Kingdom	3.7
7	South Korea	3.3
8	Italy	2.8
9	France	2.6
10	Brazil	2.5

Source: InternetWorldStats.com

to-business Internet sales in the same year. Business-to-business (B2B) sales totaled $1.95 trillion. Still, there is a great deal of room for growth in the Internet sale of products and services to consumers. The total sales to consumers represent less than 2.5 percent of all consumer purchases. Business-to-consumer sales in the United States are expected to reach $200 billion by 2010. Some experts say even that estimate is low.

CHECKPOINT

List six current Internet business statistics.

Business Uses of the Internet

In the opening scenario, Turan didn't believe the Internet was useful for his photography business. Like many of us, he was considering only the ways he could sell his products using the Web and not the many other uses of the Internet. The use of the Internet for selling products is important, but businesses can benefit from this new tool in many other ways. These uses include communications, information gathering, and improving business operations.

BUSINESS COMMUNICATIONS

Businesses use the Internet most for communication, both within and outside the company. Most internal communications on the Internet are transmitted via e-mail. But new tools are available to assist with communications, including **VoIP**, or **Voice over Internet Protocol** (using the Internet for telephone services), videophones, and software that allows several people to share application software and collaborate using text and graphics tools while sitting at their computers. Using the Internet, a company can post an employee newsletter online. This speeds the information to all employees while reducing mailing and distribution costs. Employees can quickly send reports, memos, and other information to coworkers.

For what purpose do businesses use the Internet most frequently?

Companies use the Internet to communicate with current and potential customers. The Internet has become an important way to provide information about the company and its products to customers. Remember in the chapter-opening story that when Turan was searching for information on photographers, he quickly located the Web sites of three of his local competitors. As customers try to find specific products and businesses, they are increasingly turning to the Internet. Even those who use telephone directories to identify businesses frequently want more information than is typically included in a directory advertisement. By using the Internet, a customer can often obtain product descriptions, determine the days and hours a business is open, and even print a map showing the location of the business. Today, if a business has not posted information about its location, products, and services on the Internet, it will likely miss some customers.

Businesses also communicate with each other via the Internet. Businesspeople send e-mail messages, exchange documents, and sell their company's products and services to other businesses. Common business-to-business services offered via the Internet include online training, financial planning and accounting, maintaining personnel records, and data processing.

PHOTO: © GETTY IMAGES/PHOTODISC.

INFORMATION GATHERING

A second business use of the Internet is for research. You have probably used the Internet to gather information for a project or report. Businesses also use the Internet to obtain information they need in order to make decisions. A great deal of information on the Internet is free and is provided by government agencies, colleges and universities, libraries, and even private businesses. Other information that businesses need can be purchased from companies specializing in research, from professional and trade associations, and from publishers. For example, Dun & Bradstreet provides specialized research reports, information, and publications for businesses.

Businesses can also gather information on current and prospective customers. When companies sell products, they often encourage purchasers to complete a product registration or warranty online. People who regularly use the Internet are more likely to complete a product registration if it is online than if they have to fill in a registration card by hand and mail it. The registration process allows the company to collect important information about the customer, including address, telephone number, and even an e-mail address. That information is valuable in future communications and promotional activities with customers. Also, the company can gather information on where the product was purchased, the price, reasons for purchasing the product, and other related products the consumer currently owns or plans to purchase.

Many Web sites include a place where prospective customers can request information, be placed on an e-mail or mailing list, or obtain answers to specific questions. That capability allows the company to develop a list of prospective customers and determine their specific interests. The information can be used for future communications and promotions.

Competitive information is easier to obtain using the Internet. A great deal of information is contained in many businesses' Web pages. It is relatively easy to learn about the competitors' products, prices, credit terms, distribution policies, and the types of customer services offered. Some Web sites provide information on product tests, offer comparisons and reviews of products, and even have places for consumers to discuss their experiences with a company and its products.

NETBookmark

The first large consumer e-commerce site was Amazon.com. This company pioneered a number of technologies and e-commerce design features. Point your browser to www.thomsonedu.com/school/bpmxtra. Visit Amazon.com. Evaluate how this site's design makes it easy for customers to find a product. Make a list of the features that Amazon.com uses to serve its customers. Explain how the company has been able to maintain its dominance in consumer e-commerce.

www.thomsonedu.com/school/bpmxtra

IMPROVING BUSINESS OPERATIONS

The Internet has become an important tool to improve business operations and control costs. Salespeople can log on to the company's Web site and determine whether a certain product is in inventory for delivery to a customer. When a product is sold, the order can immediately be entered into the computer from anywhere in the world to speed the processing and shipping of the order. A production manager can access the records of a transportation company to see when an expected shipment of raw materials will be delivered. An accountant in a branch office can download financial statements from the main computer to compare current financial performance with last year's information. Product designers from three countries can collaborate on a new design by examining a three-dimensional drawing online and making changes that each of them can see instantly.

Small businesses can benefit competitively from the use of the Internet due to the rapid exchange of information. For example, several small automotive parts retailers can consolidate their orders through an e-business wholesaler by submitting information on needed parts via the Internet. Then the wholesaler can place a very large order with the manufacturer and receive a significant price reduction for each of the retailers. This can be done almost instantly with online order processing. In addition to the lower costs, the needed parts get to the retailers quickly, rather than taking days and weeks under older purchasing methods.

The Internet has proven to be an important tool in reducing the cost of several business activities. A recent government report identified the following cost savings to businesses when customers used the Internet:

Ordering airline tickets	87% savings
Online banking	89% savings
Paying bills	67% savings
Distributing software	99% savings

CHECKPOINT

Describe the three main business uses for the Internet.

9.1   Assessment

UNDERSTAND MANAGEMENT CONCEPTS

Circle the best answer for each of the following questions.

1. How many people are online around the world?
   a. 600 million
   b. 1 billion
   c. 1.5 billion
   d. 3 billion

2. The Internet can improve business operations by facilitating
   a. logging on by salespeople to a company's Web site
   b. gathering information for research reports
   c. communicating with customers
   d. all of the above

THINK CRITICALLY

Answer the following questions as completely as possible.

3. Briefly describe the history of the Internet.

4. Describe how the Internet is changing business communication.

Xtra!
Study Tools
thomsonedu.com/school/bpmxtra

9.2 Stages of E-Commerce Development

Goals
- Describe the stages businesses commonly go through in developing an e-commerce business.
- Identify successful e-commerce businesses and strategies.

Terms
- dot-com business
- bricks-and-mortar businesses
- bricks-and-click businesses
- pixel
- banner ad

E-Commerce Development

A company that does almost all of its business activities through the Internet is often referred to as a **dot-com business**. The name "dot-com" comes from the end of a commercial business's Web address: *.com*. A number of dot-com companies have received a great deal of publicity (Amazon.com, eBay.com, iTunes.com), but most businesses use the Internet for only a portion of their activities. Businesses that conduct most of their business activities at a physical location rather than through the Internet are referred to as **bricks-and-mortar businesses**. The name "bricks-and-mortar" suggests that the company conducts most of its business in an actual building. Many traditional businesses are now using the Internet to support their bricks-and-mortar business. These businesses are called **bricks-and-click businesses**.

Businesses generally progress through three stages as they develop their e-commerce presence on the Internet: They begin by (1) offering information only, then progress to (2) interactive capabilities, and finally to (3) full integration of business transactions on the Web.

INFORMATION STAGE

Most existing businesses first begin using the Internet for e-commerce by developing a basic Web site. The site often is quite simple—only one or a very few pages. It provides basic information about the company that might typically be included in an advertisement or brochure. Customers can use the Web site when trying to locate information about where they can purchase specific products and to learn more about the company and its products. As the company gains more experience with the Internet, it will add additional information with *hyperlinks* (also called *links*) from the home page. The company might add complete product descriptions, information on payment methods, customer services, and even product manuals, updates, and procedures for obtaining product upgrades.

The limitation of the first stage of e-commerce development is that customers cannot use the Web site to interact with the business. They must still visit the business in person or use the telephone, mail, or other traditional methods to obtain information that is not on the Web site or to make a purchase.

Technology *tip*

INTERACTION STAGE

The second stage of e-commerce development is interaction. In addition to providing information, the site offers visitors the ability to interact with the company via the Web site. The first type of interaction is the use of e-mail. Site visitors click a link to bring up an e-mail form that they can use to request information, ask questions, or contact specific people in the company.

Beyond e-mail, companies can add a database that customers can search for specific information, such as choices of brands, product features, and services. They can check product availability, calculate product costs and shipping charges, and determine how long it will take to have an order delivered. There may even be three-dimensional photos, short video clips, or simple models of products for customers to examine.

It is possible with interactive e-commerce for customers to place orders using information from the Web site but not place the orders directly from the site. An order form may be included on the site along with a product catalog. Customers can complete, print, and then fax or mail the form to the company.

INTEGRATION STAGE

Companies that want to take full advantage of the Internet in their business move to full integration. With full integration, the entire customer transaction can be completed over the Internet. Customers can get necessary product, pricing, and shipping information. They can place an order and pay for it, track the shipment until the product is delivered, and obtain customer assistance following the sale—all using the Internet. Companies with integrated business activities do not have to be dot-com companies. Much of their business can still be accomplished through traditional methods. But customers have the option of conducting their business transactions with the company over the Internet if they choose.

What does it mean to have a fully integrated e-commerce presence on the Internet?

Consider how Turan Ozmat can begin to use the Internet in his photography business. Because competitors are already using the Internet, he should at least develop a Web page and advertise on the Web in order to make prospective customers aware of his business and the services he offers. He could include examples of his photos and portraits on the Web site. As Turan gains more experience with the Internet, he may find ways to build customer interaction into the site. Turan may choose not to have a fully integrated Web site, but he may be able to sell some types of products online, such as reprints of photos and related products such as frames and photo albums.

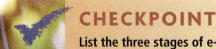

CHECKPOINT

List the three stages of e-commerce development.

PHOTO: © GETTY IMAGES/PHOTODISC.

Success with E-Commerce

Although e-commerce is still very young, it has already had a major impact on the way business is done. New types of businesses have appeared, offering products and services that did not exist prior to the Internet. Web design companies, Internet service providers (ISPs), and Web security businesses are some of these new types of businesses.

Focus On...

Tax Ethics–Tax Fairness and E-Commerce

Sales of products and services on the Internet have exceeded almost everyone's expectations. Although e-commerce sales of both consumer products and business products are a very small percentage of the total sales of goods and services in the United States, there is a mounting complaint from bricks-and-mortar retailers and from state and local government officials. The complaint: e-commerce companies are not currently required to collect sales taxes on the products they sell over the Internet, although some states require them to do so when they sell to customers within their home state.

Sales tax in most states is a small percentage of the cost of the purchase, usually 3 to 5 percent. So why should this tax matter to other businesses and to the government? Just look at the total amount of dollars spent on Internet purchases. When you take that figure and apply the sales tax rate, it amounts to millions of dollars. State governments are missing out on a source of revenue that would help them balance their budgets.

Bricks-and-mortar businesses say it is unfair competition. Sales tax increases the price of products to customers. Traditional businesses believe that if e-commerce businesses don't have to collect sales tax from customers, they can sell their products for less, gaining an unfair advantage. Traditional businesses feel that if they must collect and pay the tax, e-commerce companies should as well.

On the other hand, e-commerce businesses say that customers already pay taxes for access to the Internet. Telephone companies and Internet service providers that provide connection to the Internet are required to collect federal and state taxes on their services. E-commerce companies also suggest that eliminating the sales tax does not reduce the cost of products purchased online, because they charge shipping and handling costs that are much higher than the amount of the sales tax.

It would be very difficult for an Internet business to collect sales taxes imposed by each state and city. The tax rate would differ for each location and might change regularly. Each business would have to collect the correct amount of tax based on where the customer lives and then send the tax to the correct state or city.

Think Critically

1. Currently in many states, some products (such as food and newspapers) are not subjected to sales tax, and other products (such as automobiles and business equipment) have a lower sales tax rate. Do you agree that all businesses should be treated equally in the amount of taxes they are required to collect? Why or why not?
2. If e-businesses are required to collect sales taxes, what do you believe the effect will be on Internet sales? Justify your answer.
3. Use the Internet to find recent information on the status of taxation of e-commerce sales by the federal government as well as by your state and city.

Web-based business activities have resulted in many new kinds of jobs as well. Today, you can become a Webmaster or Web applications developer, which wasn't possible just a few years ago. A number of jobs are directly related to the development and management of Internet operations in companies. These include technology-related jobs such as programming, database management, and Web design. In many cases, a number of workers within a business maintain and expand the company's Web site.

Companies such as Dell Computer Corporation and Charles Schwab, an investment brokerage company, have emerged as industry leaders in their fields as a result of their moves into e-commerce. E-commerce companies such as Amazon.com, eBay.com, and Buy.com have taken advantage of these new types of business activities to dominate online consumer sales.

LEADING INTERNET BUSINESSES

As you learned earlier, consumers currently purchase billions of dollars' worth of products over the Internet each year. Customers are more likely to purchase certain types of products online than others. The top Internet retailers for 2005 are listed in Figure 9-3. As you can see, books, office supplies, computer hardware, and electronics are the most frequently purchased items.

A big change from previous lists of top Internet retailers is the growth of bricks-and-click businesses. These include Office Depot, Sears, and Wal-Mart. Other rapidly growing product categories for consumer purchases on the Internet are travel, investing, and services like education.

In business-to-business Internet sales, computers and electronics have the highest sales volume, as they do in consumer sales. The other top categories in business sales are utilities (electricity and gas), petroleum and chemicals, vehicles, office supplies, and shipping services.

INTERNET ADVERTISING

Another rapidly growing area of Internet sales is advertising. In 1998, businesses spent less than $2 billion to advertise their products and services on the Internet. By 2005, that number had grown to $12.5 billion. In 2005, the top Internet advertisers were Vonage (cell phone company), the University of Phoenix Online, Classmates.com, and Ameritrade. Some advertising costs are hidden, because many small Internet businesses use bartering to place their ads on another Web site. In return, they run advertisements for the cooperating businesses on their Web site. No money is exchanged between the companies to pay for the advertising.

You have probably noticed when you go online that the Internet is filled with advertisements. Because space on a Web page is limited, companies compete for the attention of Internet users. They try to place their advertisements on pages that prospective customers are most likely to visit. They also use creative advertising designs. Varied sizes, colors, and placements of advertisements encourage Internet users to stop and read the company's information. Advertisements now include moving text and graphics plus links to more detailed information.

The Internet Advertising Bureau has established standards for the size and appearance of Internet advertisements. Internet advertising is measured in pixels. A **pixel**, short for PIX (picture) Element, is one or more dots that

business note

You would never know it by looking at Google's search engine page, but Google is one of the Internet's top advertising revenue sites. Advertisers pay for placement based on the search terms used. So if you are interested in soccer shoes, your search will bring up sites that sell these shoes. These links are called AdWords. In addition, every time you click on the link, Google gets money for the click-through.

FIGURE 9-3 Top Internet Retailers in 2005

WEB SITE	TYPE OF BUSINESS	ESTIMATED 2005 SALES
Amazon.com	Books and other merchandise	$8.5 billion
Office Depot Inc.	Office supplies	3.8 billion
Staples Inc.	Office supplies	3.8 billion
Dell Inc.	Computer manufacturer	3.78 billion
HP Home and Home Office Store	Computer manufacturer	2.8 billion
OfficeMax Inc.	Office supplies	2.6 billion
Sears	General merchandise	2.2 billion
CDW Corp.	Computers and electronics	1.8 billion
SonyStyle.com	Electronics	1.6 billion
Newegg.com	Computers and electronics	1.3 billion
Best Buy Co.	Electronics	1.2 billion
Wal-Mart Stores Inc.	General merchandise	1.04 billion
J.C. Penney Co. Inc.	General merchandise	1.03 billion
QVC Inc.	General merchandise	1 billion
Apple Computer Inc.	Computers and electronics	900 million

Source: InternetRetailer.com

act as the smallest unit on a video display screen. Some of the common sizes of Internet banner ads are illustrated in Figure 9-4 (see p. 224). A **banner ad** is a Web advertising unit, like a placement ad in a newspaper.

MEETING CUSTOMER NEEDS

E-commerce is still a very new method of conducting business for both companies and consumers. Every year a larger percentage of businesses and consumers are willing to use the Internet to purchase online. Over one-half of the U.S. population has purchased online. Growing online retail sales competition is forcing business to use good online sales practices to ensure success.

Most people use the Internet for research and communication. If they are interested in purchasing products, consumers are more likely to use the Internet to gather information and compare alternatives before deciding to buy in a bricks-and-mortar store or buy online.

The primary reasons consumers report that they do not shop online are security concerns, difficulty in making purchases using the Internet, and a belief that

Career tip

In a business setting, e-mail should be used with care. Your managers and colleagues will use your messages to judge your on-the-job performance. Don't send messages just because you can. Use e-mail to provide a record of events, advise supervisors or peers on particular topics or procedures, direct others to do something specific, state company policy and explain procedures, pass on information, and promote goodwill.

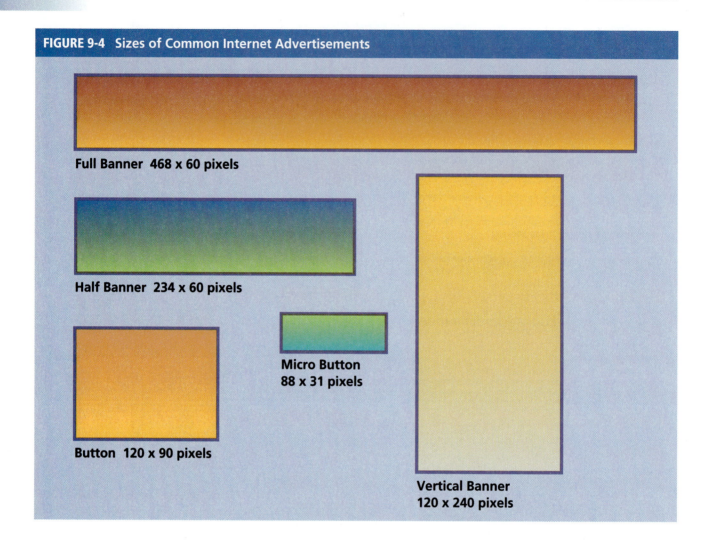

FIGURE 9-4   Sizes of Common Internet Advertisements

Full Banner 468 x 60 pixels

Half Banner 234 x 60 pixels

Micro Button
88 x 31 pixels

Button 120 x 90 pixels

Vertical Banner
120 x 240 pixels

they will receive poor customer service if there are problems with the order or the product. To be successful with e-commerce, businesses must create Web sites that move customers from gathering information to making a purchase. Customers must have confidence that the shopping experience will be positive and trouble free.

Online shoppers are often very loyal to specific businesses and brands. They usually prefer to shop at the same businesses and buy the same brands that they have traditionally purchased. However, they will switch to other businesses and brands if the online shopping experience is not satisfactory. Consumers list the following factors as important in maintaining their loyalty to an e-commerce business:

1. An understandable, easy-to-use Web site
2. Getting products quickly after ordering them
3. Familiar businesses and brand names
4. Useful and accurate information

On the other hand, the factors that cause customers to switch to another company for their online purchases are:

1. Out-of-date or limited information
2. Slow response time in answering questions, processing orders, and shipping merchandise

3. A Web site that is very slow or frequently does not work
4. Poor customer service

Advertising, careful pricing, and even online coupons are proving to be important in encouraging consumers to try online buying. Most important, however, is an inviting, easy-to-use Web site with effective customer service. If consumers have a bad experience with a company's online sales, it is very difficult to get them to come back. Consumers say that low prices and special offers will not influence them to use an online business again if they have had a bad shopping experience.

Because of the growth of the Internet and e-commerce, many organizations have begun to identify the best Web page designs and most effective online business sites. The Webby Awards were developed by the International Academy of Digital Arts and Sciences to recognize the best Web sites each year. This association presents awards in a large number of categories, including "commerce," which identifies the best business uses of the Web. Experts select one set of awards, and consumers vote on another set.

Technology *tip*

Sales copy on a business's Web site should be short and to the point. Paragraphs should be limited to fewer than 10 lines each. Use bulleted lists, indented paragraphs, bold or colored type, and other devices to break up copy.

CHECKPOINT

List four leading e-commerce companies and their business areas.

9.2 Assessment

UNDERSTAND MANAGEMENT CONCEPTS

Circle the best answer for each of the following questions.

1. The three stages of e-commerce development for the Internet include all of the following *except*
   a. offering information only
   b. progressing to interactive capabilities
   c. developing online videos
   d. integrating business transactions on the Web

2. Most people use the Internet for
   a. purchasing products
   b. research and communication
   c. online gambling
   d. playing interactive games

THINK CRITICALLY

Answer the following questions as completely as possible.

3. Describe the difference between a dot-com business and a bricks-and-mortar business.

4. Explain how a dot-com business can increase customer loyalty.

Xtra!
Study Tools
thomsonedu.com/school/bpmxtra

9.3 | Establishing an E-Commerce Business

Goals

- Outline the steps for starting a new e-commerce business.
- Describe the technology needed to run an e-commerce business.
- Describe promotional strategies for an e-commerce business.

Terms

- social networking
- Web-hosting service
- domain name
- electronic shopping carts

E-Commerce Business Planning

Developing an effective e-business requires careful planning. It is not easy to get people to buy from an online business, especially if it is a new business with which customers are not familiar. Large businesses invest millions of dollars in creating and managing their Internet operations. Small businesses can create attractive, professional-looking Web sites themselves for much less, using commercially available Web authoring software. Whether businesses create their sites themselves or hire professional Web designers to do it, they must still carefully plan the design and content of their site and update it regularly to keep customers coming back.

Three major tasks must be completed if you own a small business and want to establish an e-commerce Web site: business planning, technology development, and site promotion. Following these steps will help ensure the success of your site.

Business planning

1. Determine the purpose of your Web site.
2. Study your customers, their needs, and their Internet experience.
3. Plan your online business.

Technology development

4. Obtain a Web server and a domain name.
5. Develop order processing and customer service procedures.
6. Design the Web site.

Site promotion

7. Advertise your online business.
8. Open for business.

DETERMINE THE PURPOSE OF YOUR WEB SITE

You may want to have your entire business on the Internet or you may want to use it only to promote your bricks-and-mortar business and provide information to prospective customers. Some products and services are easier to sell over the Internet than others. Study the sites of similar businesses and talk to experts in e-commerce to determine whether to use the Internet for a limited set of business activities at first and progress gradually toward full integration, or limit the goals for your site to the informational or interactive stage.

STUDY YOUR CUSTOMERS

To develop an online business that your customers will use, you must first know who your customers are, what they want, and their interest in doing business online. You will want to know their experience with e-commerce and whether they use the Internet primarily for information or for shopping. What products do they typically buy online, and which are they more likely to buy from a bricks-and-mortar business? The ages of prospective customers are important as well. Younger consumers are often more comfortable using computers, whereas older shoppers may be reluctant to purchase online. You need to understand your customers in order to design a Web site that is inviting to them and gives them confidence to purchase from your business.

PHOTO: © GETTY IMAGES/PHOTODISC.

What are some reasons consumers might be loyal to particular e-commerce businesses?

A growing phenomenon on the Internet is the use of **social networking** sites such as Classmates.com and MySpace. These sites are virtual communities for people interested in sharing information about themselves with others. The sites were expected to earn more than $350 million in advertising revenue worldwide in 2006.

PLAN YOUR ONLINE BUSINESS

Based on your study, you will determine what products and services to offer through your online business and whether you will have an information-only, interactive, or integrated Web site. If your entire business is not going to be online, you must determine where and how the bricks-and-mortar part of your business will operate.

Another decision is whether you will handle all activities yourself or use other businesses to handle some of them. For example, most e-commerce businesses use shipping companies such as FedEx or UPS to ship their merchandise. Others use banks or other financial institutions to process credit card transactions and collect payment from customers.

CHECKPOINT
Describe the three main tasks of e-commerce business planning.

Technology Development

An Internet business relies on computer technology for operations. In Chapter 8, you learned about Web servers—computers that contain the software and store the data for networks. A Web server is the backbone of an e-commerce business. In addition to the server, the Internet site must be easily accessible to a number of customers at one time, at any time of the day. If customers cannot access your Web site whenever they want or if it has technical problems, they will not return to your online business.

OBTAIN A SERVER AND DOMAIN NAME

Because many new and small businesses do not have adequate computer or network technology or the necessary technical skills to build and manage a Web site, they use a Web-hosting service. A **Web-hosting service** is a private business that maintains the Web sites of individuals and organizations on its computers for a fee. The Web-hosting service often provides design services, the hardware and software needed to maintain Web sites, and the technical personnel to make sure the sites operate effectively.

To open your Web business, you will need an Internet address at which to locate your site. A **domain name** is a Web-site owner's unique name that identifies the site. Most Internet business addresses use the format www.*businessname*.com. Amazon.com is a domain name, but it has multiple Internet domains or server addresses (mirrored sites) to handle sales volume. Before you can use a domain name, you must register it with one of several companies that maintain and approve all domain names used throughout the world. Many possible domain names have already been registered, so you may not get your first choice. Also, individuals have registered many popular names and specific words related to products and services, hoping they can sell the domain name at a sizable profit to a business wanting to use that name.

DEVELOP ORDER PROCESSING AND PROCEDURES

If your business will process orders and collect payments online, you will need specialized software. Many companies offer software that enables the use of **electronic shopping carts**. These are specialized programs that keep track of shoppers' selections as they shop, provide an order form for them to complete, and submit the form to the company through the Internet.

Also, you will need a secure server to accept credit card payments while protecting your customers' personal data from theft. Your business will need a process to quickly check the customers' credit and approve credit card purchases. You will also want to offer customers the alternative of paying by check if they are not comfortable with using a credit card online.

After the order has been accepted, you will need a process for quickly and accurately filling the order and delivering it to the customer. Also, customers will expect you to accept returns, replace products damaged in shipment, and offer other services to make sure their shopping experience is positive.

DESIGN THE WEB SITE

This step in developing an online business may seem to be out of order. Many people want to design their Web pages as the first step. However, until you plan the business completely, you will not know what needs to go on your Web site. Remember, to be successful, Web sites must be attractive and easy to use. If customers cannot find the information they need, if the site takes a long time to load, or if ordering instructions are confusing, prospective customers will leave your site and go to a competitor's.

Web sites should use a basic design with easy-to-understand buttons and links. If customers can purchase products through the Web site, the shopping and ordering procedures should be very obvious and simple. Shoppers should be assured of security and customer service.

CHECKPOINT

Describe the three main steps in e-commerce technology development.

Site Promotion

As with any new business, prospective customers will not know your online business exists without advertising and promotion. Two steps will help you promote your online business.

ADVERTISE YOUR ONLINE BUSINESS

First, register your business with the major search engines, such as Google and Yahoo! Each search engine has an electronic means for collecting site addresses and categorizing them by key words, so that Web visitors can find them. However, you can make sure the search engines include your site under appropriate key words by registering it with them directly. You can find registration information at the search engines' sites.

It is important to place advertising for your business in other Internet locations where prospective customers are likely to search for information related to the products and services you sell. You may want to sponsor sites that are popular with the people you would like to attract to your business. Make sure your Web address is included in all materials your business distributes and in all advertising you do.

Why is designing a Web site not the first step in developing an online business?

ADVERTISE YOUR BUSINESS OFFLINE

The second step is to advertise and promote your e-commerce business offline. Although being on a search engine can be useful, it will not necessarily drive viewers to your Web site. Your business may be one of thousands in the search engine database. If your site doesn't make it to the first or second search page, it may never be viewed.

Your domain name should be placed on all company materials such as business cards, brochures, and correspondence. Traditional media can create an interest in your site. Then individuals may search for your company's name or go directly to the Web site.

OPEN FOR BUSINESS

After careful planning, you are now ready to open your Internet business. As with any business, you will have to maintain the Web site

PHOTO: © GETTY IMAGES/PHOTODISC.

and update it regularly. You will want to keep in contact with customers to make sure they are pleased with your site and with their purchasing experiences. Watch competitors to keep up-to-date with the products and services they are offering. Keep up with the latest technology and online business procedures to make sure your e-commerce business continues to be successful.

CHECKPOINT

Explain why it is important to advertise your online business offline.

9.3 Assessment

UNDERSTAND MANAGEMENT CONCEPTS

Circle the best answer for each of the following questions.

1. Establishing an e-commerce business requires
   a. business planning
   b. technology development
   c. site promotion
   d. all of the above

2. If a business cannot host its own e-commerce site, it could use a
   a. domain service
   b. Web-hosting service
   c. server company
   d. all of the above

THINK CRITICALLY

Answer the following questions as completely as possible.

3. Describe the basic elements of successful e-commerce site design.

4. Describe how a search engine can help promote a business.

Xtra!
Study Tools
thomsonedu.com/school/bpmxtra

CHAPTER CONCEPTS

- More than a billion people worldwide have access to the Internet, and 400 million Internet domains were registered by 2006. By 2004, online retail sales totaled over $130 billion and business-to-business online sales topped $1.95 trillion.

- Buying and selling merchandise is not the primary use of the Internet for either consumers or businesses. Consumers use the Internet to communicate and gather information. Businesses use the Internet to communicate, gather information about prospective customers and other businesses, and improve business operations.

- A small business must complete three major tasks to establish an e-commerce Web site: business planning, technology development, and site promotion.

- Online customers are loyal to businesses that have easy-to-use Web sites, provide shopping security, and offer efficient delivery and customer service. However, if customers have problems with an online business, they are likely to switch to a competitor or to a bricks-and-mortar business.

- Developing an e-commerce business requires business planning, technology development, and site promotion.

REVIEW TERMS AND CONCEPTS

Write the letter of the term that matches each definition.

1. Using the Internet to buy and sell online
2. Company that does almost all of its business activities over the Internet
3. Business that uses both a physical location and the Internet for sales
4. Web site owner's unique Internet name
5. One or more dots that act as the smallest unit on a video display screen
6. Any registered Web site
7. Business that conducts most of its business activities at a physical location rather than through the Internet
8. Private business that maintains the Web sites of individuals and organizations on its computers for a fee
9. Using the Internet for telephone services
10. Specialized programs that keep track of shoppers' selections, provide an order form for them to complete, and submit the form to the company over the Internet
11. Web advertising unit, like a placement ad in a newspaper
12. Virtual community in which people share information about themselves

a. banner ad
b. bricks-and-click business
c. bricks-and-mortar business
d. domain name
e. dot-com business
f. e-commerce
g. electronic shopping carts
h. Internet domain
i. pixel
j. social networking
k. Voice over Internet Protocol (VoIP)
l. Web-hosting service

DETERMINE THE BEST ANSWER

13. Online business sales account for ____ percent of total business sales.
    a. 11
    b. 21
    c. 30
    d. 50

14. By 2006, there were ____ Internet domains.
    a. 100 million
    b. 200 million
    c. 300 million
    d. 400 million

15. A Web-hosting service may provide
    a. Web site content
    b. free advertising
    c. software needed to maintain Web sites
    d. all of the above

16. Businesses use the Internet to communicate
    a. inside their companies
    b. outside their companies
    c. both inside and outside their companies
    d. only through e-mail

17. A company that does almost all of its business activities over the Internet is often referred to as a(n)
    a. online-only business
    b. dot-com business
    c. bricks-and-click business
    d. click-only business

18. A traditional business that uses the Internet to support its bricks-and-mortar business is called a(n)
    a. online/offline business (OOB)
    b. dual business
    c. bricks-and-click business
    d. click-and-visit business

19. A business that allows the entire customer transaction to be completed over the Internet is at the
    a. information stage
    b. interaction stage
    c. integration stage
    d. e-commerce stage

20. When researching customers, a business should consider
    a. what products they typically buy online
    b. their interest in doing business online
    c. their experience with e-commerce
    d. all of the above

APPLY WHAT YOU KNOW

21. Explain how the Internet makes it easier for small businesses to compete with larger businesses.
22. Explain why there are such large cost savings to businesses when they use the Internet to sell airline tickets, provide banking and bill-paying services, or distribute software.
23. Describe why a business would use the Internet only for information rather than for developing interaction or integration.
24. Explain why only a few Internet users go online to purchase products and services but many more go online to gather information and then purchase products from a local business.
25. On what types of Internet sites would you advertise to make prospective customers aware of your new e-commerce business that sells CDs and music videos?

MAKE CONNECTIONS

26. **Math** Internet usage varies according to individuals' ethnic and racial background. The following chart lists the number of people in each of the major ethnic/racial classifications in the United States and the percentage of that population that uses the Internet.

Racial/Ethnic Classification	U.S. Population (in millions)	% of Population Using the Internet
African-Americans	13.3	40%
Hispanic	10.1	32%
All U.S. ethnic minorities	29.8	39%
Caucasian/White	186.7	60%

a. Calculate the number of Internet users for each racial/ethnic classification listed. Then determine the total number of people in the U.S. population, the total number of Internet users in the U.S. population, and the average percentage of the total population using the Internet.

b. What are some possible reasons the usage rate of the Internet varies, based on a person's racial/ethnic classification?

27. **Research** Go online and find at least three examples of businesses for each stage of e-commerce development: information, interaction, and integration. If possible, print a copy of each company's home page. Using that home page, describe why the business fits the stage in which you classified it.

28. **Technology** Use Web page creation software or a word processor that creates HTML documents to create a personal Web page. Include hyperlinks to other Web sites. Explain how your Web page design addresses your communication goals.

CASE IN POINT

CASE 9-1: Online or Offline Shopping

Jillian, Dontae, and Toni were sitting in front of a computer, listening to music they had downloaded and looking at a Web site that identified the top e-tailers for the year.

Jillian: *I really like the idea of shopping on the Web. It seems like you get many more choices, probably lower prices, and it's so convenient.*

Dontae: *I'm not sure I'm convinced yet. Look at the names of some of the businesses on the list. I've never heard of many of them. Do you believe they're all legitimate?*

Toni: *I don't need to worry about stores to shop online for music. I found some sites that offer lots of music for free.*

Jillian: *Well, some of our favorite stores are on the list. Maybe we should start with buying from them. I'm not sure downloading from those sites is legal.*

Dontae: *But why not just go to the mall and buy from the stores? I'd get the products faster and not have to pay shipping charges. Besides, I don't want to enter my credit card number online, even if it says it's safe.*

Jillian: *But you hand your credit card to a person in every store when you make a purchase. They process it through a telephone line to get the amount approved. Isn't that the same thing?*

Toni: *If we use the free sites, they don't ask for credit cards.*

THINK CRITICALLY

1. Many people do not trust businesses that sell products online, especially if they are not familiar with the company's name. Yet they will walk into a new business in their city and shop with little concern. What causes the difference in people's views of online businesses versus traditional businesses?
2. Do you agree with Dontae that it is easier to shop in an actual store in a mall than from the same business online? Why or why not?
3. What is your opinion of Jillian's comparison between entering a credit card number online and handing the card to a clerk who checks it using a telephone line from the store to the credit card company?
4. What do you think of Toni's idea of downloading music for free? Do you think this is legal? How can Toni be sure that she is engaging in legal and ethical behavior when she uses the free-music site?

CASE 9-2: Stockholder

Jimmy Lai Chee-Ying is a Chinese entrepreneur who wanted to take on two commercial giants in Hong Kong. He started a new business called AdMart, which used the Internet as well as telephones and fax to take orders for grocery products. The orders were to be filled in eight warehouses located throughout the city and delivered in one of 220 vans to customers' homes. The giants he was challenging were two supermarket chains that controlled over 60 percent of the grocery business in Hong Kong.

Lai believed his business could be successful for two reasons. He offered a very limited selection of products. He carefully studied customer needs and sold only the products they bought frequently and in larger quantities, such as soda pop, juice, canned goods, and baby diapers. He also selected products that he could offer for prices as much as 40 percent lower than those of the big supermarkets. He also sold computers. Why? Every home needs a computer, and if consumers own a computer, they are more likely to purchase over the Internet.

Some business experts said he couldn't succeed. They thought that people wouldn't be willing to buy most of their groceries in a store and then order a few online. Others felt the larger stores would cut their prices and drive Lai out of business. But Jimmy Lai looked at it differently. All customers like to save money, and they like the convenience of home delivery. Lai thought that as he became more successful online, he could add more products. He felt that because the two chains were so large, they would hardly notice the trade lost to his new e-business.

THINK CRITICALLY

1. Do you believe it was a good idea for Jimmy Lai Chee-Ying to start a new business that competes with two very large businesses that control most of the grocery market in Hong Kong? Justify your answer.
2. Discuss the advantages and disadvantages of Lai's strategy of selling a very limited number of popular products. What do you think of his idea of selling computers?
3. Why is the new e-business able to sell products at much lower prices than the larger chains can? Do you believe the large businesses will drop their prices on the products Lai sells? Why or why not?
4. Identify another new Internet business that is competing with much larger traditional businesses. What is the business doing to encourage customers to switch from the larger business to the new e-business?
5. Use the Internet to research AdMart in Hong Kong. Report on the status of the AdMart venture. Identify what went right and what went wrong. Explain how this example could help other e-commerce entrepreneurs.

MY BUSINESS, INC.

CORPORATE FORM

E-commerce may allow new businesses to compete equally with larger, established businesses. Many businesses develop a simple Web site to provide information about the business, but others use the Internet more extensively. Some complete all of their business transactions online. Consider how you can use the Internet in your business.

DATA COLLECTION

1. Use the Internet to identify
   a. information sources that will be helpful in completing your planning
   b. examples of other beverage businesses that are using the Internet
   c. e-commerce businesses from which you could purchase products and services you will use in your business
2. Identify at least two Web-hosting companies that work with small businesses. Collect information on the services they provide and the costs of their services.
3. Conduct a short survey of 10 or more people who you believe would be prospective customers of your business.
   a. How regularly do they use the Internet, and how much time per week do they spend online?
   b. Do they purchase products online? How regularly and what types of products?
   c. What are their positive and negative feelings about e-commerce and making purchases online?

ANALYSIS

1. Prepare a chart that compares the advantages and disadvantages of e-commerce for your business. Based on the chart, make a decision about whether you will use the Internet for your business: (a) right away, (b) after your business has operated for a few years, or (c) probably not at all.
2. Outline the way you would use the Internet for your business if you used it for: (a) information, (b) interaction, and (c) integration.
3. Look at privacy statements on several Web sites. Then write one for your company. It should state the ethical guidelines you plan to follow in the collection and use of customer data and in e-mail communications.
4. Using three of the Internet advertisement formats shown in Figure 9-5, develop ads you would use to encourage consumers to visit your business's Web site. Then go to the Internet and identify three sites that accept advertising you believe would be good locations for your ads. List the URL address for each site and give a brief rationale for each choice.

Career Cluster
Webmaster

Webmasters are called the "guardians of cyberspace." They are the people who create, organize, and manage Web sites for schools, businesses, and governmental organizations. There are two kinds of Webmasters: those who focus on hardware, software, and communication protocols (such as "http"), and those who focus on the site's content. Webmasters spend their time in a highly technical environment that is constantly changing.

Employment Outlook

Employment in all computer-related fields is expected to grow faster than average. Almost all businesses in the United States are planning or have Web sites to develop and maintain.

Job Titles

System Administrator
Webmaster
Chief Information Officer (CIO)

PHOTO: © GETTY IMAGES/PHOTODISC.

Needed Skills

- Must have an associate's degree or certificate at a minimum.
- Must be self-motivated and detail-oriented.
- Must have strong writing skills.

- Must be familiar with the software tools used to create and maintain Web sites.
- Must be able to work with a wide variety of individuals, including computer programmers, managers, marketers, and customers.

Working as a Webmaster

Lucinda started working with a small advertising company after she received her graphic design degree from a local community college. Her job was to help the company design Web sites. She was soon hired as a Webmaster by a larger company, where she learned more about Web page creation software and HTML programming. She was also required to work with other computer engineers. Lucinda has been receiving offers to work for larger companies on more complicated Web sites.

Career Assessment

Why are Webmasters important to businesses? Why do they need to be trained in a number of different skill areas? What do you like and dislike about this career area?

REALITY CHECK

Many Ways to Communicate

Erica Komuro, one of many managers for an international book company, sat at her desk looking at the next day's schedule. In the morning, she would review the new organization chart for her department that would appear in the employees' manual. Later she would meet with two other managers and her boss to resolve a conflict. She dreaded the shouting match that was sure to occur between two people who never agreed on anything.

The afternoon would include interviewing a new employee and giving her best worker instructions on how to perform a new assignment. Then Erica would write a few business letters and e-mail messages. She also had to finish her computerized monthly report for the division manager, which would be sent over the local area network. If the morning meeting did not drag on, Erica might also have time to return phone calls that came in while she was dealing with a customer relations problem. Perhaps she could also squeeze in a call to Sabrina in accounting to learn more about a rumor regarding the sudden resignation of the vice president.

Just before leaving the office she flipped the calendar page ahead a few days. In large letters she saw: "Meet with Mr. Nozaki." She was not sure how to deal with the major problems this manager was having running the Tokyo office. At least she could recall a few Japanese words from earlier days when her family lived in Kyoto.

As she closed the office door, she smiled and waved to the evening cleaning person arriving for duty. On the way to her car she thought, "Tomorrow will be a busy day."

10.1 The Communication Process

Goals
- Describe the communication process and barriers to effective communication.
- Describe the various communication channels.

Terms
- communication
- feedback
- distraction
- distortion
- channel of communication
- nonverbal communication
- flame
- spam
- emoticons

Erica is a typical manager because much of her time is spent communicating—speaking, listening, writing, and reading. Managers communicate in person, by phone and fax, by e-mail, and by paper documents. They also communicate through other means, such as a smile, a frown, or a wave.

Communication is vital in running organizations. Communication provides a link between employees and customers and between employees and managers. In fact, it has been estimated that managers communicate more than two-thirds of each workday, as shown in Figure 10-1. In this chapter you will learn about the communication process, corporate communications, communication problems, and how good businesses and managers improve communication.

The Communication Model

Communication is the sharing of information, in which the receiver understands the meaning of the message in the way the sender intended. Communication includes more than passing along factual data. It includes sharing ideas, beliefs, and

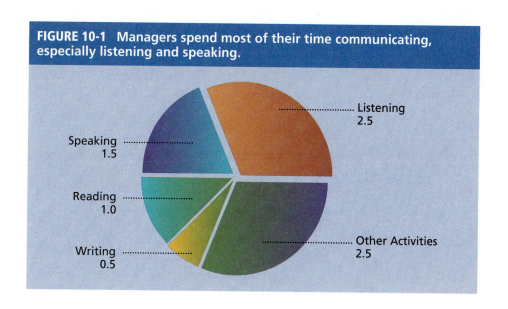

FIGURE 10-1 Managers spend most of their time communicating, especially listening and speaking.

Listening 2.5
Speaking 1.5
Reading 1.0
Writing 0.5
Other Activities 2.5

opinions. It is a *two-way process* between senders and receivers. The senders must put the information into clear words, and the receivers must try to understand the message as the senders intended. If the receivers do not fully understand the message or need more information, they should ask for clarification. Thus, feedback is critical to effective communication.

Feedback is a receiver's response to a sender's message. The response may be in the form of asking questions to clarify the meaning of a message. Or, receivers may restate the message in their own words, so that the senders can verify that the receivers understood the meaning as intended. The communication process and the role of feedback are illustrated in Figure 10-2.

Poor communication is one of the biggest problems managers face. Poor communication can lead to disagreements, faulty work, delayed performance, and industrial accidents. Two major barriers that interfere with communication are distractions and distortions.

DISTRACTIONS

Interruptions occur all too often while communicating. Anything that interferes with the sender's creating and delivering a message and the receiver's getting and interpreting a message is a **distraction**. Distractions are potential causes of communication problems. Two workers who whisper to each other during a meeting create a distraction that may cause a nearby worker to miss a point made by the manager. It may also cause the manager to forget to mention a point. Ringing phones, grammar errors in messages, and loud noises are other examples of barriers to communication.

Because distractions affect communication, some managers learn to work with various interruptions, whereas others try to keep interruptions to a minimum. For example, some managers place telephone calls or write messages during specific times of the day when interruptions are less likely to occur.

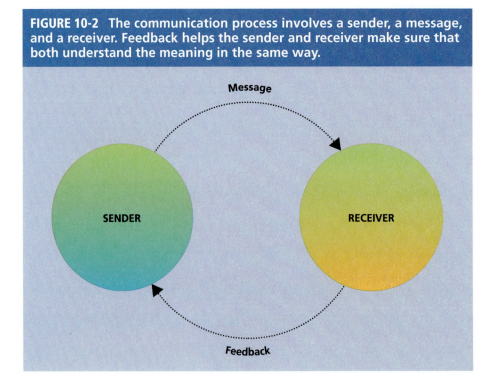

FIGURE 10-2 The communication process involves a sender, a message, and a receiver. Feedback helps the sender and receiver make sure that both understand the meaning in the same way.

PHOTO: © STOCKBYTE.

What kinds of distractions can occur during a business meeting? How can these barriers to communication be overcome?

DISTORTIONS

When senders create messages, they must select the information they want to include. They need not include every bit of data surrounding an idea, event, or situation. Senders select only the information they think the receivers need in order to understand the message. Depending on the information selected, though, the message can become distorted. **Distortion** refers to how people consciously or unconsciously change messages.

Distortion is usually not deliberate. People unconsciously pass along only information they feel others need. Often they leave out important data. Distortion may be deliberate, however, for self-enhancement or self-protection. For example, an employee may tell a supervisor about a machine breakdown but not admit that he or she did not oil the machine regularly. Or a manager may give an employee a very good rating because she likes him, even though the worker's performance may be only average.

Distortion can also occur because people often "hear" what they want to. We all bring our own perspectives to any situation. We filter messages we receive through our own system of beliefs and experience. Therefore, sometimes what we understand the sender to say was not at all what the sender meant. Receivers don't necessarily have to agree with the message, but they have a responsibility to use feedback to try to understand it as the sender intended.

CHECKPOINT

Describe the communication model and the factors that lead to poor communication.

Channels of Communication

A **channel of communication** is the means by which a message is conveyed. The three major channels are oral, written, and nonverbal.

ORAL COMMUNICATION

In the opening story, we learned that Erica's schedule for the next business day is nearly filled with oral communications. Speaking with employees, attending meetings, and receiving and making phone calls consume a great deal of a manager's time. Day-to-day communications require frequent contact with people on a one-to-one basis. That contact may be formal, as when Erica interviews a potential employee, or it may be informal, as when she chats with another employee about the company picnic. Giving employees oral instructions is an especially common and significant task. How well managers communicate determines in great part how high they rise on the management ladder.

WRITTEN COMMUNICATION

Written business communications take many forms. The most common are memos, e-mails, formal reports, and letters. Figure 10-3 lists some common uses of business letters. Other written communications include manuals, invoices, telephone message reminders, and notes. Written communications sent electronically include e-mails, faxes, and postings on electronic bulletin boards.

To communicate effectively in writing, senders should compose messages using precise, unambiguous words and proper grammar. The messages should also be

Ethics tip

Often employees receive non-work-related e-mail, such as jokes or product solicitations. These e-mails should not be forwarded to other employees. They are a distraction, and they can be tracked back to the sender.

FIGURE 10-3 Business letters serve many purposes.

Some Uses for Business Letters

- request credit from suppliers
- give and refuse credit to customers
- collect overdue accounts from customers
- request product catalogs from suppliers
- order merchandise from suppliers
- send information customers requested
- acknowledge and fill orders from customers
- ask for and make adjustments in customers' orders
- refuse adjustments in customers' orders
- persuade others to take action
- convince others about an idea
- sell goods and services
- congratulate others
- thank people for tasks performed
- request information about job applicants
- request interviews with job applicants
- hire or reject job applicants

concise. Long or unnecessary messages contribute to information overload. In turn, information overload slows decision making and becomes an obstacle to effective use of work time. Written messages may also include the use of psychology. For example, good news should appear early in a message, and bad news should appear later, after the explanation.

NONVERBAL COMMUNICATION

Delivering messages by means other than speaking or writing is called nonverbal communication. Flashing lights, stop signs, and sirens are examples of physical ways to communicate. Even colors, such as in traffic lights (green, yellow, and red), signal messages—go, caution, and stop. Nonverbal communication also appears in written documents in the form of charts, diagrams, and pictures. People also give nonverbal messages through their body movements. "Body language," as this is sometimes called, may appear as frowns, smiles, posture, hand or body movements, or the presence or absence of eye contact. Nonverbal messages convey meaning as much as verbal messages do.

PHOTO: © DIGITAL VISION.

Body language may get the message across better than the spoken word. What message is this businesswoman sending?

Managers should be aware of the nonverbal messages they convey to others and that others convey to them. These messages are often given unconsciously. Sometimes a nonverbal message confirms or contradicts a verbal message. For example, what impression would Erica get if the job applicant said, "I am extremely interested in the position," but came unprepared for the interview and wore jeans and a dirty T-shirt? If you were interviewing this person, which message would you believe—the verbal or nonverbal one? Actions often speak louder than words.

ELECTRONIC COMMUNICATION

Electronic communication can be verbal, written, or nonverbal. E-mail has changed written communication. Each day over 31 billion e-mail messages replace what otherwise would be paper correspondence. Evidence of the growth of e-mail is the great decline in messages previously sent through the U.S. Postal System. Electronic mail is popular because it lowers communication costs, minimizes paper handling, speeds communications and decision making, and improves office productivity. Because of its rapid growth and widespread use, businesses have adopted policies and practices that address e-mail use.

E-MAIL POLICIES Some businesses establish e-mail policies to protect the organization, business partners, employees, and customers. Typically such policies state that employees should use e-mail only for job-related matters, with occasional exceptions. In fact, businesses can track all inbound and outbound messages and read them if they want. Employees should not use e-mail for personal purposes, such as contacting friends outside the organization or participating in chat groups. In general, employee communications cannot be considered private, because all employee actions represent the firm. Companies like General Electric remind employees as they log on that most Internet and e-mail use should be solely for business tasks and all activity may be recorded and reviewed.

Also, e-mail should not be considered private, because outsiders can access it. For that reason, some organizations install software programs that automatically self-destruct messages after a designated time, limit the number of times a message can be opened and read, and prevent the forwarding of messages.

Protecting the company from lawsuits is too critical to be left to chance. Jokes, off-color stories, and flame messages reflect negatively on the company image. A **flame** is an electronic message that contains abusive, threatening, or offensive content that may violate company policy or public law. Abusive sexual language, for example, can lead to a sexual harassment lawsuit by offended employees. Abusers are subject to dismissal and firms may be sued for allowing harassment situations to develop.

E-MAIL PRACTICES E-mail volume can be quite heavy. Information overload is a common complaint of employees in information-intensive jobs. They need strategies for processing large amounts of mail efficiently. Different avenues are available for doing so. Important mail from superiors and coworkers deserves priority, but other need not be read at all, such as spam. **Spam** is unsolicited advertising that finds its way into e-mail boxes. Close to 40 percent of e-mail is considered spam. Most common e-mail programs allow users to sort incoming messages by sender, subject line, or whatever they specify. Thus, users can have all messages from the boss grouped together so they can give those top priority. Spam from unknown senders can be grouped together for quick disposal. Special spam filters are also used to move or remove suspected spam. Productive employees set aside certain times of the day to send or read e-mail, so that this task does not interfere with other priority tasks.

Writing and responding to e-mail deserve the same courtesy that other written mail deserves. Good business writing requires that messages have a meaningful subject line as well as a pleasant but businesslike tone that gets to the point quickly and ends graciously. Most messages should be short, but some may have attachments, such as tables, charts, or diagrams. Users often write e-mail messages hurriedly, and do not carefully craft them. Furthermore, employees may not realize that e-mail, like letters, are written documents that can be used for legal purposes.

A possible weakness of e-mail, as opposed to telephone or in-person conversations, is the lack of facial expressions and other gestures that show emotion. However, senders can express some common emotions through emoticons. **Emoticons** are facial expressions created with keyboard symbols and used to express feeling in an e-mail message. Figure 10-4 shows some common text-based emoticons. To see the expressions, look at the emoticons sideways. There are also graphical emoticons that allow individuals to use nonverbal communication to express emotions. Users should be careful not to overuse emoticons, especially in business correspondence. Too many emoticons can make the message seem unprofessional.

Every e-mail message should follow good writing guidelines. Writers should construct sentences properly, without spelling errors. They should not include gossip or nasty comments. Carelessly prepared messages reflect negatively on the writer and the organization.

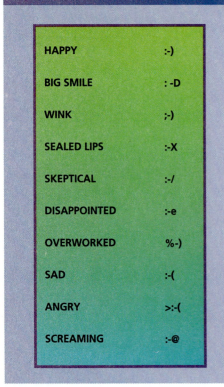

FIGURE 10-4 Emoticons provide e-mail users a way to convey feelings.

HAPPY	:-)
BIG SMILE	:-D
WINK	;-)
SEALED LIPS	:-X
SKEPTICAL	:-/
DISAPPOINTED	:-e
OVERWORKED	%-)
SAD	:-(
ANGRY	>:-(
SCREAMING	:-@

WIRELESS The use of cellular phones is growing to dominate electronic verbal communication. New cellular devices allow not only voice communication, but also short message service (SMS) or text messaging, the sending of images, and Internet access. In the first three months of 2006, 235 billion text messages were sent worldwide. It was expected that by 2007 there would be more than 1 billion wireless devices able to access the Internet. Cellular devices allow a business-person to use verbal, written, and nonverbal communication.

CHECKPOINT

List the three major channels of communication.

10.1 Assessment

UNDERSTAND MANAGEMENT CONCEPTS

Circle the best answer for each of the following questions.

1. The way people consciously or unconsciously change messages is called
   a. feedback
   b. distortion
   c. noise
   d. misunderstanding
2. What percentage of e-mail is considered spam?
   a. 10
   b. 20
   c. 30
   d. 40

THINK CRITICALLY

Answer the following questions as completely as possible.

3. Describe how the communication model works.
4. How can electronic communication be verbal, written, and nonverbal?

Xtra!
Study Tools
thomsonedu.com/school/bpmxtra

10.2 Corporate Communications

Goals

- Explain how corporate culture influences formal and informal communication networks.
- Describe how to conduct effective meetings.

Terms

- communication network
- formal communication networks
- informal communication networks
- grapevine
- nominal group technique (NGT)
- brainstorming

Each business has its own internal culture that influences the way formal and informal communications occur. In this section, you will learn how communication networks influence the communication process. You will also learn how to conduct effective meetings.

Corporate Culture

As you learned in Chapter 4, culture is shared values, beliefs, and behavior patterns of groups of people. The group may be a corporation, a nation, or any other organized group. An organization, such as a corporation, develops its own corporate culture or personality. Factors such as the type of business, the personalities of its leaders, and its operating procedures create this corporate culture, which its members understand.

The culture of a corporation influences the communication climate. Cultures differ widely among firms. Cultures may be very closed, very open, or somewhere in between. A closed culture is one that relies on top-down decision making and adheres to numerous rules and strict disciplining for violations of established procedures. Rigid rule making and authoritarian leadership can breed distrust and secrecy while discouraging creativity and decision making at lower levels. In such organizations, communications tend to be quite formal. Experts refer to this type of organization as having a closed communication system.

When trust and confidence prevail among employees, an organization is said to have an open communication system. This type of culture encourages creativity and problem solving at all levels and supports communication and information sharing. Trust, supportiveness, risk taking, and decision making influence whether an employee will like or dislike working for a company. In turn, these factors help determine how productive employees will be.

Most organizations have neither a fully open nor fully closed culture. Sometimes a business may change its culture. A comfortable culture for one person, however, may not be comfortable for another. Some employees prefer a culture with primarily an open communication system, whereas others prefer a culture with primarily a closed communication system. Employees often change jobs in search of an organization that has a set of beliefs, values, and practices suited to their needs.

COMMUNICATION NETWORKS

A **communication network** is the structure through which information flows in a business. Communication networks can be formal or informal.

FORMAL NETWORKS A **formal communication network** is the system of official channels that carry organizationally approved messages. These channels generally follow the reporting relationships in the firm. Formal communication flows upward, downward, and across the organization in a prescribed manner. Typically, certain information, such as budget allocations, flows downward from top-level managers to lower-level managers. Other information, such as requests for budget expenditures, flows from the bottom to the top of the organization.

Upward communication includes oral and written reports from lower-level to upper-level managers. Usually, upper-level managers rely on lower-level managers for information that deals with new or unusual problems, the quality of employee performance, and the way employees feel about their jobs and the company. Supervisors receive upward communication from their subordinates about such things as project status and suggestions for making a task more efficient.

Organizations with closed, rather than open, communications are less likely to benefit from upward communication. Upward communication is subject to distortion, especially in corporate cultures that are relatively closed. Supervisors, for example, might withhold or distort upward-flowing information when problems appear to reflect negatively on their performance. On the other hand, a supervisor might exaggerate information about successes. In a closed culture, employees often fear revealing negative information and avoid making honest criticisms.

Downward communication in organizations occurs mainly by memos, e-mails, reports, and manuals. To be effective, this information should be timely and clear. In organizations with closed communications, there is often no opportunity for feedback, because information does not flow upward easily. However, in open cultures, employees receive downward-flowing information at meetings and their feedback is welcome.

Lateral communication flows horizontally or across the organization. For example, the production manager in one plant might want to know what problems other production managers face. Perhaps common problems could be solved jointly. However, many organizations do not have easy and fast channels for such communications. In a business with an open corporate culture, lateral communications are more likely to exist. One communication expert has estimated that 80 percent of poor management decisions occur because of ineffective communications.

INFORMAL NETWORKS Like formal communication networks, informal networks exist in all organizations. **Informal communication networks** are the unofficial ways that employees share information in an organization. The most common informal networks include small informal groups and the grapevine. Informal networks rely heavily on interpersonal communications and e-mail.

A great deal of communicating occurs among small informal groups, especially among employees who get along well together. These employees may or may not have the same supervisors, but often they do. They share information about the organization, assist one another in solving work problems, and look after one another. Members may even support one another when conflicts arise with other employees. Most employees belong to a small informal group.

Managers should be aware of informal groups. Often informal groups have more influence than managers do over the behavior of individual workers. It is extremely important that informal groups support the efforts of the entire business. If they do not, informal groups can interfere with business goals and,

Career tip

Employees are most happy and productive when they work for a business culture that matches their personality. In which type of communication atmosphere do you think you would be most productive? Do you like open informal communication, or do you like more formal, rule-based communication? Identify the types of jobs that match your preferred communication style.

PHOTO: © GETTY IMAGES/PHOTODISC.

Office grapevines are the most common way employees communicate informally. What types of communication grapevines do you use?

in turn, hurt morale and decrease productivity. Managers often work closely with informal group leaders to obtain support and test new ideas.

An extensive amount of organizational communications occurs in an unofficial way through interpersonal relationships. Employees working side by side, for example, generally talk about their jobs and about personal matters. These conversations are normal and usually do not interfere with work. Employees also talk together on breaks, in the hall, or around the drinking fountain.

The informal transmission of information among workers is called the **grapevine**. In a grapevine, one person informally talks to another, and that second person talks to another, and so on. Informal messages travel quickly through the grapevine and can be distorted, because they are often based on unofficial, partial, or incorrect information. That is why grapevine messages are often labeled rumors. Very often, however, grapevines convey accurate messages. For example, when a formal memo announces that a manager has just retired for "health reasons," the grapevine may provide the actual reason. The manager may have been asked to quit but was given the opportunity to resign voluntarily. When Erica Komuro calls Sabrina in Accounting, she may also learn that the rumor about the vice president's resignation is true.

Generally, managers should not interfere with grapevines. Grapevines often fill the social needs of workers to communicate about their work lives. Only when a grapevine message is inaccurate and negatively affects company business should managers attempt to correct the situation.

CHECKPOINT

Describe the two types of communication networks.

Conducting Effective Meetings

Meetings are a common way for employees to share information, discuss problems, and make decisions. Managers often prefer meetings when open communication is needed to encourage discussion and feedback. Employees doing the hands-on work often have good ideas about how to improve their work quality and efficiency. However, meetings also have disadvantages. The chief disadvantage is the excessive time meetings take. Good managers overcome this weakness by careful planning and by following suggestions such as those shown in Figure 10-5.

A second major problem with meetings occurs because of differences among those who attend the meetings. For example, an outspoken person may tend

FIGURE 10-5 Suggestions for Running Effective Meetings

1. Have a good reason for calling a meeting.
2. Develop a specific agenda and stick to it.
3. Decide who should and who should not attend.
4. Schedule the meeting at a convenient time and place.
5. Start and stop the meeting on time.
6. Encourage communications by arranging the seating so that participants face one another.
7. Summarize the results at the end of the meeting.

to dominate, whereas a quiet person may say nothing. Neither situation is desirable. The person who leads the meeting should encourage but control discussions, so that the group hears and discusses all ideas. Two methods used to encourage group thinking and problem solving are the nominal group technique and brainstorming.

NOMINAL GROUP TECHNIQUE

The **nominal group technique** (**NGT**) is a group problem-solving method in which group members write down and evaluate ideas to be shared with the group. For example, assume a manager needs to solve a long-standing problem. The manager begins by stating the problem and then follows the steps described in Figure 10-6.

The NGT encourages each group member to think about the problem, and it gives the quiet person and the outspoken person an equal opportunity to be heard. Private voting encourages employees to choose the best solutions rather than spend time defending their own suggestions. This technique has proven very effective.

FIGURE 10-6 Steps in Using the Nominal Group Technique

1. Present the problem to be resolved to group members.
2. Distribute blank cards and, without discussion, ask members to write possible solutions by using a different card for each solution.
3. Read solutions from the cards and display for all to see.
4. Discuss each solution listed.
5. Distribute blank cards and ask members to write their three best solutions on separate cards.
6. Tabulate and display results.
7. Select the solution receiving the most agreement and present it to the group leader.

There is a formal set of rules for running meetings called Robert's Rules of Order. Point your browser to www.thomsonedu.com/school/bpmxtra. Visit sites that cover parliamentary procedure. Evaluate some of these sites and the rules they describe. Explain how Robert's Rules of Order can be helpful in running meetings.

www.thomsonedu.com/school/bpmxtra

BRAINSTORMING

Problems arise in business for which prior solutions do not exist or are no longer acceptable. One technique for handling such situations is brainstorming.

Brainstorming is a group discussion technique used to generate as many ideas as possible for solving a problem. A group leader presents a problem and asks group members to offer any solution that comes to mind. Even wild and imaginative ideas are encouraged. The group should make no attempt to judge any ideas as good or bad while brainstorming is under way. Only after participants have identified all possible solutions should they begin to judge the usefulness of each one. Often, an idea that appeared to be impractical or unusual when first presented may become the best solution to the problem. Brainstorming is frequently used to deal with problems that need especially creative solutions, such as when generating new product ideas and creating advertisements.

CHECKPOINT
Explain the two methods used to encourage group communication.

10.2 Assessment

UNDERSTAND MANAGEMENT CONCEPTS
Circle the best answer for each of the following questions.

1. The system of official channels that carry organizationally approved messages is called a(n)
   a. sanctioned communication network
   b. official communication network
   c. formal communication network
   d. informal communication network

2. A group problem-solving method in which group members write down and evaluate ideas to be shared with the group is the
   a. group idea technique
   b. nominal group technique
   c. brainstorming
   d. none of the above

THINK CRITICALLY
Answer the following questions as completely as possible.

3. Describe how corporate culture influences communication.

4. Explain how managers overcome common problems that occur in meetings.

Focus On...

Labeling Ethics–Communicating to Change Attitudes

Monsanto frequently ranks as one of America's 200 largest firms. Although the public may not recognize the name, many people are familiar with at least one product—NutraSweet. NutraSweet is Monsanto's brand of the sugar substitute aspartame often used in diet foods and drinks. At any grocery store, read the "contents" portion of labels on canned and packaged foods, and you will see how popular aspartame has become.

Aspartame received bad press in its early days and still does in spite of the fact that the Food and Drug Administration (FDA), American Diabetes Association, and other groups declared it safe for public consumption. Research by organizations other than Monsanto has also found it safe. Critics, however, think aspartame is not safe. Some think aspartame use may lead to headaches, blindness, cancer, and other problems, although these assertions are not supported by scientific evidence. Yet Monsanto continues to receive complaints in spite of its extensive communication efforts to convince the public otherwise.

Although American-made products must list sugar substitutes, some other countries do not have the same requirement. In Europe and Asia, for example, manufacturers are not required to list sugar substitutes. Simply listing "sweetener" is acceptable, whether it is sugar, aspartame, or something else. This practice arises for economic reasons. For example, aspartame is easier and cheaper to ship, is subjected to fewer trade barriers and tariffs, is easily available when there is a sugar shortage, and is cheaper when sugar prices are high.

Monsanto makes other controversial products that have also received public criticism. Those products involve biotechnology—the genetic altering of crops that we eat. Examples include modifying one or two genes in soybeans, potatoes, and corn to make them more resistant to insects and diseases. Although scientific experts find biotechnology acceptable, critics reject genetic altering and want it stopped or tightly controlled. With a growing population worldwide, how can farmers increase crop output and be more productive? Biotechnology can increase crop yields. Again, Monsanto has spent millions of dollars persuading the public that its new products, which are approved by the FDA and the American Dietetic Association, are not injurious to human health.

Think Critically

1. How does the public's resistance to Monsanto's NutraSweet differ from the resistance to its biotechnology products?
2. Is it unethical to exclude aspartame from the listed contents of prepared foods in other countries?
3. Would Americans find it acceptable if the contents of food and drink products simply listed "sweetener" rather than "sugar" or "aspartame"?
4. Investigate Monsanto's success with its public communication efforts. Obtain information from your library or visit Web sites such as www.monsanto.com. Present a report to your class.

10.3 Organizational Communication

Goals
- Describe different ways to resolve communication conflicts.
- Describe the problems that can occur with cross-cultural communication.
- Identify ways to improve communication in organizations.

Terms
- conflict
- avoidance strategy
- compromise strategy
- win/lose strategy

Managers deal with a variety of communication problems. Some problems that challenge the communication skills of managers involve resolving conflicts and handling cross-cultural communication effectively.

Communication Conflicts

At times, people disagree with each other. Most job-related disagreements are likely to be temporary and easy to settle. Disagreements become a concern to a business when they lead to conflict. **Conflict** is interference by one person with the achievement of another person's goals. Conflicts usually occur between two people, but they may also occur between an individual and a group or between groups. Because conflicts are sometimes an obstacle to job performance, managers must deal with conflicts.

DESIRABLE CONFLICT

A small amount of conflict is sometimes beneficial, because it may challenge employees and stimulate new ideas. For example, the advertising manager may decide to budget as little as possible to advertise a particular product, whereas the sales manager may have decided to try to boost sales for that particular product through increased advertising. At this point, conflict exists because the goals set by each manager differ. However, this type of conflict can lead to a healthy discussion of how much to spend on advertising and how best to advertise to produce the highest sales at the lowest advertising cost. The result can lead to the achievement of a goal that is best for the business.

When employees discuss and resolve their conflicting goals, the organization can benefit. However, when conflicting goals are not resolved, long-term problems often result. If the sales and advertising managers went ahead with their individual plans, money would be wasted and sales would be lost.

UNDESIRABLE CONFLICT

Whereas some conflict in organizations may be healthy, too much conflict can be harmful. Undesirable conflict results when the actions of any person or group interfere with the goals of the organization. In the preceding example, if the sales manager became resentful of the advertising manager and undermined the company's budget goals by deliberately spending more than the amount agreed upon for the product, undesirable conflict would result. Employees who dislike others and carry grudges often cause problems for an organization. Therefore, undesirable conflicts should be resolved as soon as possible.

RESOLVING CONFLICT

Conflicts can be resolved in various ways. Because every situation is different, managers must decide which type of strategy will best resolve each conflict.

AVOIDANCE STRATEGY One strategy for resolving conflict is to take a neutral position or to agree with another person's position even though it differs from your personal belief. This approach, known as the avoidance strategy, avoids the conflict. One manager may decide to accept the goal of another manager or avoid expressing an opposing opinion about the goal. When a conflict is relatively unimportant, the avoidance strategy may be the best approach. However, if a disagreement involves important issues, avoidance is not a good strategy. It can often lead to resentment.

COMPROMISE STRATEGY A second way to resolve conflict is through a compromise strategy. Everyone involved in a conflict agrees to a mutually acceptable solution. Often, a compromise grows out of a thorough discussion of the goals and the best way to achieve those goals. This strategy is better than avoidance because it

PHOTO: © GETTY IMAGES/PHOTODISC.

If handled properly, conflicts can be beneficial and productive. How do you handle conflict with another person?

PHOTO: © GETTY IMAGES/PHOTODISC.

Why is a compromise strategy generally the best solution to a conflict?

usually leads to a workable solution, as everyone involved personally contributes to the decision. Also, people are more likely to support a compromise solution that they have helped to develop.

WIN/LOSE STRATEGY The most dangerous approach to resolving conflict is a win/lose strategy. A **win/lose strategy** is one in which no one compromises, thereby resulting in one person winning and one losing. A win/lose strategy is never acceptable to everyone, although people often engage in such a strategy. Win/lose strategies interfere with the achievement of organizational goals because they often (1) take time and energy away from the main problems and issues, (2) delay decisions, (3) arouse anger that hurts human relationships, and (4) cause personal resentment, which can lead to other problems.

Because win/lose situations are destructive, managers should attempt to prevent them. Setting clear objectives that employees understand and agree on, stressing the need for cooperation in reaching objectives, and working for group decisions when special problems or disagreements arise are ways managers can avoid win/lose strategies.

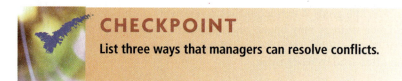

CHECKPOINT

List three ways that managers can resolve conflicts.

Cross-Cultural Communication Problems

What kinds of communication barriers might companies face when doing business abroad?

Cultures differ from country to country. A country's culture influences how its people communicate, just as corporate culture does within organizations. When doing business abroad, companies face communication barriers created by language, cultural, and nonverbal differences.

PHOTO: © DIGITAL VISION.

LANGUAGE DIFFERENCES

Few American managers speak a foreign language fluently. However, doing so does not solve all problems when someone is transferred to another country. The people of most nations realize that learning a new language is difficult. But they are more than willing to help foreigners learn. They are especially impressed when someone who does not know their language makes a noble effort to learn. Many corporations now provide intensive language training for managers assigned to foreign branches. Information on the social customs and education, legal, and political systems is included in the training.

Joint ventures between American and foreign firms often reveal language problems. A successful joint venture between Ford Motor Co. and the Japanese Mazda Motors Corp. provides an example of overcoming language difficulties. The president of Mazda estimated that 20 percent of the meaning of a conversation with Ford leaders was lost between him and the interpreters. Another 20 percent was lost between the interpreters and the Ford leaders. Working with only about two-thirds accuracy, the Mazda president tried extra hard to make sure his message was getting through. He strongly believes people should meet face-to-face and talk freely.

CULTURAL DIFFERENCES

People from other countries place different values on such things as family, status, and power. In India, for example, providing jobs for male family members in a business is more important than earning a profit. Humor differs worldwide, too. In addition, accepted practices in one country may be impolite elsewhere. For example, American businesspeople generally like to start and end meetings on time. In Japan and certain other countries, this practice would be considered rude rather than businesslike.

NONVERBAL DIFFERENCES

Great differences exist in the area of nonverbal communication, especially body language. For example, how close one stands when talking to someone else differs from country to country. For most conversations, Americans stand two to three feet apart, whereas Middle Eastern people stand much closer. Even colors have different meanings. In Western countries, black is often associated with death, but in Latin American countries, death is represented by white and purple. A handshake also varies from place to place. In Spain, it should last from five to seven shakes, but the French prefer one single shake.

Because differences exist among nations, executives prefer to conduct extremely important business transactions in a formal manner. Usually, that means greater use of written reports and expert translators. For oral translation services by phone, long-distance telephone firms such as AT&T provide an 800 number to assist callers. However, for day-to-day international operations, managers must learn to understand the cultural and communication practices of other nations.

business *note*

There are numerous ways that individuals communicate nonverbally in international settings. Often business meetings are held during a meal. In China, this often will require that a business manager knows meal etiquette. This can include where to sit and how to eat with chopsticks. You should try each type of food. You should know how to make drinking toasts, how one should dress for dinner, when to start negotiating, and how to bring a meal to a close. These cultural norms will differ between countries. Choose a country you would like to visit. Research that country's business meal etiquette. Lay out a plan for how you will behave during the meal. Practice these techniques with your family or friends to be sure you can handle these important cultural norms.

facts & figures

Listening is considered both a sign of politeness and a valuable skill in business negotiations in Japan. Japanese often think North Americans need to listen more attentively, not talk as much, and certainly not interrupt when someone else is speaking.

CHECKPOINT

Describe three types of communication barriers managers may encounter doing business abroad.

New managers often spend time listening to as many employee points of view as possible before making corporate changes. What kinds of questions would you ask employees before making such changes?

PHOTO: © GETTY IMAGES/PHOTODISC.

Improving Organizational Communication

Good managers are usually good communicators. Some ways to improve communication are discussed in this section.

ENCOURAGE TWO-WAY COMMUNICATION

Small businesses provide for plenty of two-way communication between owners and employees. As companies get larger, however, a shift to one-way communication often occurs for efficiency purposes. When this happens, however, problems arise because valuable feedback from employees and customers is reduced. Good managers develop plans to obtain feedback even when they are extremely busy. Some managers, however, discourage two-way communication because they feel uncomfortable with it and because it is time-consuming. For example, one boss in a firm fired an employee by e-mail, even though the employee's office was right next door. Organizations that encourage managers to consciously engage in two-way communication are often more successful than those that do not.

LISTEN ACTIVELY

Two-way communication assures feedback. Effective listening results in effective feedback. Frequently, employees have questions and encounter problems on the job. They need to talk to someone who listens carefully. Hearing and listening are not the same. Most people can hear when someone speaks, but they may not pay attention to the message. Listening involves hearing and understanding. Good listeners make every effort to practice the rules of good listening shown in Figure 10-7 to make certain that they receive the messages accurately.

FIGURE 10-7   Ten Rules for Good Listening

Rule and Reason Behind the Rule

1. Stop talking!

You cannot listen if you are talking.

2. Put the talker at ease.

Help a person feel free to talk; create a permissive environment.

3. Show a talker that you want to listen.

Look and act interested; listen to understand, not to oppose.

4. Remove distractions.

Don't doodle, tap, or shuffle papers; shut the door if necessary to acheive quiet.

5. Empathize with talkers.

Try to see the other person's point of view.

6. Be patient.

Allow plenty of time; do not interrupt; do not start for the door or walk away.

7. Hold your temper.

An angry person takes the wrong meaning from words.

8. Go easy on argument and criticism.

These put people on the defensive and may cause them to "clam up" or become angry. Do not argue—even if you win, you lose.

9. Ask questions.

This encourages a talker and shows that you are listening. It helps to develop points further.

10. Stop talking!

This is first and last, because all other guides depend on it. You cannot do an effective listening job while you are talking. Remember that:
- Nature gave people two ears but only one tongue, which is a gentle hint that they should listen more than they talk.
- Listening requires two ears, one for meaning and one for feeling.
- Decision makers who do not listen have less information for making sound decisions.

FACILITATE UPWARD COMMUNICATION

In large organizations, upward communication is sometimes neglected. Managers may not want to hear complaints or deal with suggestions because they require time. To make certain that upward communications occur, some businesses ask managers to use specific techniques.

One technique is called "management by walking around." Managers leave their offices from time to time and make trips through the working areas. While doing this, they chat with employees about various problems and conditions.

Another practice is for managers to encourage employees to meet with them when they have concerns. To control the time this "open door policy" takes, some managers restrict the practice to one hour per week, when employees can make appointments. Suggestion boxes have been used for many years and have great value in encouraging communication.

No technique is better than regular meetings with employees. Some firms select a certain number of employees from different departments and organizational levels to meet with top managers on a regular basis. The manager informs them about important company matters and invites questions and ideas. Studies have shown that employees who are informed about their companies have stronger positive feelings than those who are not. The top-level managers benefit by getting feedback from people throughout the company.

SELECT COMMUNICATION CHANNELS CAREFULLY

When managers want to communicate with others, they should carefully select an appropriate communication channel. Generally, when a manager must reprimand an employee or settle a dispute, the oral communication channel is best. The oral channel is most effective for explaining the reason for the reprimand or for working out an acceptable solution to a dispute.

The written communication channel is best when managers want to communicate information requiring future action or information of a more general nature, such as a new policy or a revised operating procedure. Such matters should be put in writing for later reference. Managers should follow up on information provided in writing, because it serves as a reminder that the information is important and it provides an opportunity for the receiver to ask questions. E-mail is a good way to follow up because it is fast, easy, and provides immediate feedback. E-mail is not a good substitute for oral communication in situations that call for face-to-face discussion.

In some situations, two channels of communication work best—first oral and then written. Managers should use both channels when they want to (1) give an

Communication channels should support communication goals. Why is it good practice to follow an oral communication, such as a commendation for a job well done, with a written one?

PHOTO: © BLEND IMAGES.

immediate order, (2) announce a new policy, (3) contact a supervisor about work problems, or (4) compliment an employee for excellent work. In most of these situations, the information is best delivered orally on a one-to-one basis, which personalizes it and allows for immediate feedback. The written channel then allows for reinforcement and creates a record of the event.

CHECKPOINT

List the three strategies managers can use to improve two-way communication.

10.3   Assessment

UNDERSTAND MANAGEMENT CONCEPTS

Circle the best answer for each of the following questions.

1. The most dangerous approach to conflict resolution is
   a. avoidance
   b. compromise
   c. win/lose
   d. lose/lose

2. The most effective technique a manager can use to improve organizational communication is
   a. regular memos
   b. daily reports
   c. regular meetings with employees
   d. monthly employee evaluations

THINK CRITICALLY

Answer the following questions as completely as possible.

3. Describe how managers can resolve communication conflicts in a company.

4. Explain how a company can overcome cross-cultural communication problems.

Xtra!
Study Tools
thomsonedu.com/school/bpmxtra

CHAPTER CONCEPTS

- Communication is a two-way process that involves creating, sending, receiving, and interpreting messages. The three main channels of communication are oral, written, and nonverbal. Two barriers to effective communication are distractions and distortions.

- Corporate culture involves the shared values, beliefs, and behavior of an organization. Cultures may be (1) entirely open, with extensive interactive communication among all organization members, (2) entirely closed with dominantly downward communication, or (3) a combination of open and closed communication systems.

- Communications in organizations follow both formal and informal networks. Formal communication networks are official company channels, such as between managers and their employees. Informal networks are communications among informal groups.

- Managers must deal with problems that challenge their communication skills, such as conflicts and communication across cultures. They must also learn to run meetings effectively with techniques such as the nominal group technique and brainstorming.

- Good managers are generally good communicators. They listen effectively, facilitate upward communications, and choose the appropriate communication channels for their messages.

REVIEW TERMS AND CONCEPTS

Write the letter of the term that matches each definition. Some terms will not be used.

a. channel of communication
b. communication
c. communication network
d. compromise strategy
e. conflict
f. distortion
g. distraction
h. emoticons
i. feedback
j. flame
k. formal communication network
l. grapevine
m. informal communication networks
n. nominal group technique (NGT)

1. Sharing of information in which the receiver understands the message in the way the sender intended
2. A receiver's response to a sender's message
3. The way people consciously or unconsciously change messages
4. The means by which a message is conveyed
5. Electronic message that contains abusive, threatening, or offensive content that may violate company policy or public law
6. Facial expressions created with keyboard symbols or graphics and used to express feeling in an e-mail message
7. Structure through which information flows in a business
8. System of official channels that carry organizationally approved messages
9. Unofficial ways employees share information in an organization
10. Group problem-solving method in which members write down and evaluate ideas to be shared with the group
11. Interference by one person with the achievement of another person's goals
12. Way to resolve conflict in which everyone involved agrees to a mutually acceptable solution

DETERMINE THE BEST ANSWER

13. Anything that interferes with the sender's creating and delivering a message and the receiver's getting and interpreting a message is
    a. a distraction
    b. a distortion
    c. a barrier
    d. feedback

14. Unsolicited advertising that finds its way into e-mail boxes is called
    a. flame
    b. spam
    c. solicitation
    d. e-mail ad

15. Which of the following is *not* an example of nonverbal communication?
    a. flashing lights, stop signs, and sirens
    b. colors, such as in traffic lights
    c. charts, diagrams, and pictures
    d. All are examples of nonverbal communication.

16. The informal transmission of information among workers can take place via
    a. project status reports
    b. e-mails
    c. memos
    d. none of the above

17. Which of the following statements about conflict are true?
    a. All conflict should be avoided.
    b. A little conflict is sometimes beneficial.
    c. Win/lose strategies are most often used by managers.
    d. Managers should not compromise or they lose authority.

18. A strategy used to resolve conflict in which you take a neutral position or agree with another person's position even though it differs from your personal belief is called
    a. avoidance
    b. compromise
    c. conflict neutral
    d. win/lose

19. A group discussion technique used to generate as many ideas as possible for solving a problem is known as
    a. idea storming
    b. nominal groupthink
    c. creative thinking
    d. brainstorming

APPLY WHAT YOU KNOW

20. Explain how a grammar error in a memo might be considered a distraction and thus a barrier to communication.
21. A manager was enjoying giving a talk about business to a group of young people. An audience member asked the manager whether he believed in open communication. The manager looked uncomfortable with the question, snapped a fast "yes," and quickly asked, "Any other questions?" Compare the oral and nonverbal messages the manager was sending.
22. Distortion is not always unconsciously done. Explain why employees may consciously distort information. Do you think such behavior is ethical?
23. Discuss what strategy you would use to help resolve a conflict situation between two employees who always disagree on how a task should be handled.
24. Describe how busy managers can encourage effective listening.

MAKE CONNECTIONS

25. **Math** LaToya put the following idea in her company's suggestion box: "Rather than hire a new full-time worker at $15 per hour to handle our increased business, hire two half-time workers at $10 per hour. Then, if business slows later, we can cut back to one half-time worker or no workers."
    a. As the manager, write LaToya a note saying that her suggestion has been accepted and she will earn 20 percent of one year's savings for the idea.
    b. Assume one year has gone by and that one half-time employee worked 860 hours and the second worked 600 hours. A full-time employee would have worked 2,000 hours. How much will LaToya receive for her suggestion?
26. **Research** Use your school library or the Internet to research the topic of nonverbal communication. Find pictures in magazines that show examples of nonverbal communication. Show these images to members of your class. See if they can identify the nonverbal message. Ask them to explain why they are making these judgments.
27. **Technology** Keep track of your various types of communication during a school day. Use the charting feature in a software package to develop a pie chart like the one in Figure 10-1. Divide the pie according to the percentage of time you spend each school day (a) listening, (b) speaking, (c) reading, and (d) writing. Compare your communication times to those of a typical manager, as shown in Figure 10-1.
28. **Speaking** Divide into small groups. For this project, you may interact with your group only by e-mail. Brainstorm a list of e-mail do's and don'ts appropriate for a workplace setting. Using your group's ideas, compose an e-mail policy for your workplace. Present your group's policy to your class.

CASE IN POINT

CASE 10-1: Company E-Mail

Lauren Lemaster works at the headquarters of a major Internet corporation that has offices in five countries. The company has a strict set of rules regarding the use of e-mail. Hackers often try to break into the operating system to damage it, and that naturally hurts business.

The CEO sends all newly hired employees the following message: "Be careful what you say to others, especially when sending e-mail to other employees. A year ago a hacker learned that we were planning to buy another business that would increase the value of the company. He took the idea to a competitor, so we lost 'big' on that failed operation. For reasons like this, we require that you sign the attached oath. The oath states that if an employee is responsible in any way for inside information getting to the outside, that employee will be released immediately."

Without further thought, Lauren signed the oath, but that was two years ago. Yesterday on her lunch hour, Lauren sent a secret e-mail message to her best friend, Douglas, who likes to buy stock in Internet companies when they do something new and exciting. Lauren's message said: "Douglas, I learned that my company has its eye on Dawson and Donaldson, Inc. Keep it to yourself. Hopefully this will repay the favor you did to help me get this job. Trash this message after reading it. Lauren."

Douglas bought stock in the company and shared the message with several friends, who also bought stock. Then he destroyed the message. Within 24 hours, the stock price for Dawson and Donaldson doubled. However, Lauren's boss called her in and fired her on the spot for violating company policy.

THINK CRITICALLY

1. Was the company's Internet policy too severe? Why or why not? Because Lauren wrote the e-mail on her lunch hour, is she actually in violation of company policy?
2. How did the company find out about Lauren's e-mail message?
3. Does Lauren have any privacy rights that would enable her to sue the company for the loss of her job? Explain.
4. If Douglas e-mailed four friends and they each e-mailed four friends and this happened two more times, how many people heard of the potential purchase as a result of Lauren's action?
5. Was Lauren as unethical as Douglas was? What responsibility does Douglas bear for Lauren's plight?
6. How would the 10 rules for good listening apply when Lauren and Douglas meet to discuss what happened?

CASE 10-2: Changing Corporate Culture

As a former regional manager for Graphix International, Seth McClaren was promoted and transferred to the Philadelphia headquarters several years ago. A close friend, Josh Berry, manages the company's regional office in Atlanta. Seth called Josh and invited him to dinner to discuss concerns about changes going on in the company. After dinner the following conversation occurred:

Seth: *Tomorrow's a big meeting. The new president and the two new vice presidents will be there to explain the new reporting procedures.*

Josh: *Was something wrong with the old method? It worked fine for my office. We do the reports according to the rules. We hear from headquarters only when something isn't done right.*

Seth: *The new managers are different. They like meetings and lots of contact with employees. They even stop by my office every few weeks to chat. They seem friendly . . . even invited me to stop by their offices. Nothing like the former managers! You never saw them and never heard from them unless something went wrong. Then they'd send threatening memos.*

Josh: *Is that why most of the regional managers kept clear of headquarters? The person I replaced warned me not to break any of the rules. "Just keep your nose clean," she said. "If you don't bother them, they won't bother you."*

Seth: *That's the main reason the board of directors changed the top managers. The new managers expect good work, but they also seem to want the employees and managers to discuss problems. They even want us to suggest solutions. Imagine that! Some of us aren't sure whether to trust them yet. We're afraid if we make one mistake, we'll be fired.*

Josh: *They seem to be practicing what they preach, Seth. The Houston regional manager stuck her neck out and made a suggestion, and a vice president flew down to talk with her. The grapevine said he made a real big thing over the idea. Her picture is in the newsletter that just came out. The newsletter has plenty of information about her suggestion.*

Seth: *The way these new people operate . . . it's different. I'm not sure I like it. The new monthly report even has a place in it where you can state complaints and make suggestions. They're going to get an earful when the next month's forms are returned. That's no way to run a business.*

Josh: *Let's give them a chance, Seth. At least they're willing to listen, which is more than you could say about the departed managers.*

THINK CRITICALLY

1. Did the corporate culture change between the old and new top management? Explain.
2. What evidence is there that the new top management will encourage or discourage upward communication?
3. Did the new vice president use more than one channel of communication? If so, how?
4. Did the old or the new top managers place more stress on two-way communication? Explain.
5. Will Seth be as comfortable as Josh with the new managers? Explain your answer.

PLANNING ORGANIZATIONAL COMMUNICATION

As a small-business owner, you will be responsible for making sure communications flow smoothly within your business and with others outside your business. Unclear or poor communication can be very damaging to a new business as you work with employees, customers, other businesspeople, and the public. You need to plan communication carefully and use effective communication whenever you interact with others.

DATA COLLECTION

1. Using newspapers, business magazines, and Internet news services, identify situations in which businesses faced problems resulting from poor communication. Make a list of the types of communication problems you identify, using the following categories: communication problems with (a) employees, (b) customers, (c) other businesspeople, (d) the public, (e) other.

2. Advertising is one method of communicating with customers. However, advertisements often do not communicate the same message to everyone. Locate three ads for small businesses, preferably businesses similar to your juice bar business. Show the ads to five different people. Record their answers to the following questions:
   a. What is the most important message you receive from each of these ads?
   b. In general, do you believe the ad is effective or ineffective?
   c. As a result of the ad, would you be more or less likely to be a customer of the business? Why?

3. As a small-business owner, you are concerned that meetings with your employees be as effective as possible. Use library or Internet resources to research the topic of rules of order or parliamentary procedure in meetings. How can you apply these rules to your business?

ANALYSIS

1. Compose a letter that you would send to local health clubs and recreation centers. In the letter, request that your juice bar be identified as the "exclusive source for juice drinks" for their facility. Make sure the letter is persuasive and offers some value or benefit to the businesses you will contact.

2. You have been asked by the local organization of retailers to make a brief presentation at their monthly luncheon meeting about your new business. Using presentation software, prepare a five-minute presentation that describes the business, your business plan, and some of the challenges you believe you will face. Give your presentation to the class. Be prepared to defend your business plan. If possible, ask a local retailer to attend and ask questions of the presenters.

Case Study

PAYING CELEBRITIES FOR COMMERCIALS ON MULTIPLE MEDIA

Celebrities have been used in commercials for decades to sell products and services ranging from new automobiles to the latest health care for seniors. Prior to the use of numerous new forms of technology for advertising, the celebrities appeared on television commercials and in print advertisements, receiving a negotiated salary or royalty for their work. Most celebrities are paid for the number of times their commercial is aired or the number of times an advertisement that includes their likeness is used in magazines and newspapers.

The digital world of advertising has opened the issue of how actors should get compensated for their work. The ad industry and talent representatives agree that the old model formed in the 1950s does not work in today's diversified media landscape, in which advertisements are spread across cell phones, MP3 players, and video-on-demand. Representatives from the advertising industry and Hollywood are working on a new model for compensation in a digital world. Consultants have been asked by all negotiating parties to submit proposals that will address how actors in commercials will be paid when the spots appear on multiple media.

The ultimate goal of negotiations is to create a system of fair compensation for celebrities who promote products and services through numerous media channels.

THINK CRITICALLY

1. How has the increased use of technology affected the sales potential for products and services?
2. Why should celebrities be eligible for higher compensation when their advertisements are being relayed through many technological avenues?
3. What is your opinion of basing a celebrity's pay on the dollar amount of sales generated through the different avenues of advertisement, including the latest technology?
4. Give five examples of products or services that are promoted by celebrities. Why are these individuals good choices for promoting those particular products and services?

E-Commerce Management Team Decision-Making Event

Your management team will consist of two members. In addition to taking a multiple-choice exam for e-commerce, you must develop a solution for the following case study. You have 30 minutes to prepare your presentation using a laptop computer, if you wish. Your team is allowed 10 minutes to present your information to the judges, who will have five minutes to ask questions.

The Pottery Stop has successfully operated for five years, selling pottery and garden art along a busy highway in Texas. The mild climate allows the business to remain open the entire year. Customers from all over the United States are pleasantly surprised by the unique variety and quality of pottery available. The shop customizes orders and will ship merchandise throughout the United States for an additional shipping-and-handling fee. This feature is attractive to travelers who do not have room in their vehicles to haul pottery or travelers who will be flying back home.

The Pottery Stop is now ready to expand by selling over the Internet. You must develop a strategy to implement this new source of sales. You must decide what information to include on the Web site. Describe the kinds of pictures you will use and why. List the acceptable forms of payment and explain how credit card information will be secure. Describe how you will advertise the Web site at the store.

PERFORMANCE INDICATORS EVALUATED

- Understand the economics of expanding business through e-commerce.
- Explain the importance of increasing distribution channels for goods and services.
- Describe the links available on a successful Web site for e-commerce.
- Describe promotional materials that will be distributed at the store to inform customers about buying merchandise online.

For more detailed information about performance indicators, go to the DECA Web site.

THINK CRITICALLY

1. Why are businesses choosing to sell merchandise online?
2. Why are some consumers hesitant about purchasing merchandise online?
3. Why should the Pottery Stop collect data about customers who purchase online and at the store?

http://www.deca.org/

Management Responsibilities

CHAPTERS

" Business is now so complex and difficult, the survival of firms so hazardous in an environment increasingly unpredictable, competitive, and fraught with danger, that their continued existence depends on the day-to-day mobilization of every ounce of intelligence. "

Konosuke Matsushita

Management Functions and Decision Making

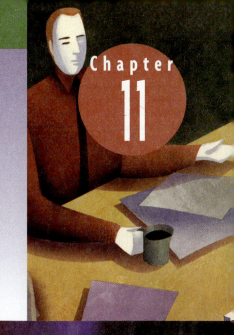

REALITY CHECK

Do I Want to be a Manager?

Erik Berman has worked for Freeden Web Technologies for five years. It was his first job since graduating from the local community college with a degree in computer network systems. He enjoys his work as a network specialist, a position he has held for over two years now. The company recognized his ability, and he has moved up rapidly from his first job as networking assistant to his current position.

Erik is facing an important career decision. At the end of his last six-month performance evaluation conference, his manager told him that the supervisor who has responsibility for Erik's work team and three other teams would be promoted in three weeks. The manager wants Erik to consider applying for the supervisor's position.

The opportunity to move into a management position is exciting. The job would provide a higher salary and status as a manager. At the same time, Erik isn't sure he has the skills or the interest in being a supervisor. It seems to him that supervisors are constantly dealing with employee complaints or with the concerns of their own bosses. He is used to working a lot of hours when big projects have to be completed. However, he knows that the company's supervisors work many extra hours each week to get all of their own work done while solving the problems that seem to come up regularly.

Erik really enjoys his current work in network systems, and he knows that he won't do as much of that work as a supervisor. Yet, he isn't sure if he wants to do technical computer work for the rest of his career. He also knows that he likes working with and helping to train the new employees who are assigned to his work group. He really feels good when he sees them performing well and being recognized for their excellent work. His biggest concern, however, is that he really doesn't know very much about the supervisor's job, and he's concerned that he won't succeed. He already knows he's a good network specialist. Freeden does not provide any specific training for prospective supervisors, and Erik's only preparation was a management course he completed while attending the community college.

11.1 The Role and Work of Managers

Goals
- Define management and the functions all managers complete.
- Differentiate the work of several levels of management.

Terms
- management
- planning
- organizing
- implementing
- controlling
- manager
- supervisor
- executive
- mid-manager

Erik's experience is similar to that of many employees. For people who want to become managers, their first management position will often be that of supervisor. However, they may not know very much about the work of managers. If they have worked for effective managers, it may appear that the job is quite easy. On the other hand, employees may have had experiences with poor managers who make their own jobs difficult and cause problems for their subordinates.

Moving into Management

Many employees believe they would like to be managers and often think they can do a better job than the managers for whom they work. However, when presented with the decision of whether to move into management, they may find that decision difficult to make. If they like the work they do, moving into management will mean they can no longer expect to spend much time doing that work. Will they enjoy a management job as much? If they have been successful in their current job, a move into management can be very risky. What if they are not successful in the management position? It is not likely they will be able to move back into their previous jobs, and, indeed, they may be fired if they do not succeed as a manager.

Understanding management and the work of managers will make it easier for employees to choose a management career. If the company helps employees move into management with training programs, there will be less risk and a greater opportunity for employees to be successful. Some companies are now allowing employees an opportunity to work in a beginning management position for a short time before making a permanent decision. If they find the job is not what they expected or if the company decides these new managers are not performing at the level required, they can reach an agreement to move the employees back into the same type of job they held before.

THE CHANGING NATURE OF MANAGEMENT

Managers make things happen in business. From the original idea for a business, through accumulating and determining the best ways to use the resources needed to operate the business, to managing people, managers are responsible for the success or failure of the company. The decisions managers make determine what a company will do and how well it will perform.

Managers make up only a very small percentage of all employees in a company. Employees are responsible for completing the day-to-day work of businesses. There are often several levels of managers in an organization. Some managers will be directly responsible for the operation of a part of the business and the work of the employees who complete those operations. Even those managers will usually not be active in that work.

Higher-level managers are not directly involved in day-to-day operations. Instead, they will spend their time planning, problem solving, and making decisions about how to make the business more successful. Because most managers do not perform the same type of work that most employees do, employees often do not recognize the contributions that managers make to the business or the difficult work they do. The daily work of managers is quite different from the work employees do. Yet both types of work are necessary for the business to succeed. Managers must understand and appreciate the work of employees. Employees will be more motivated to cooperate with managers if they understand what managers do and why management is important to business success.

The nature of management and employee relations has changed a great deal in the past 20 years. In the past, many managers exerted a great deal of authority and control, expected employees to follow orders without question, and shared little information about the company with employees. Employees and managers did not always share the same views and attitudes about the company and the work that needed to be done. Relationships between managers and employees were very formal and sometimes antagonistic.

Modern managers work more closely with employees, keep employees informed about company performance and upcoming changes, and involve them in important decision making. Employees have greater responsibilities in many companies, and employee teams now complete some work previously done by managers. Businesses in which managers and employees have respect for each other, communicate effectively, and work well together are usually more successful than older-style businesses.

PHOTO: © DIGITAL VISION.

Employees perform the important day-to-day work of a business. In what ways can they work with managers to ensure the business's success?

MANAGEMENT ACTIVITIES

Because there are so many types of managers, it is difficult to identify exactly what managers do. However, there are a number of activities that all managers must perform no matter what the type or size of the company or in what part of the business they work. The president of a large international corporation made up of several companies and thousands of employees is a manager, but so is the owner of a small service business with one location and only a few employees. The people who are responsible for human resources departments and for purchasing departments, for a company's salespeople, or for its information management activities are all managers. So are supervisors of people working on an assembly line, in a warehouse, or at data-entry terminals. Though each of these jobs involves many unique activities, each is also concerned with management.

Teamwork *tip*

Today, businesses expect employees to be able to work effectively in teams. Depending on your assignment, you may need to be an effective leader on some projects and a good follower on others. Find opportunities in and out of school to build your team skills.

Management is the process of accomplishing the goals of an organization through the effective use of people and other resources. As you learned earlier, those resources include money, buildings, equipment, and materials. The primary work of all managers can be grouped within four functions: (1) planning, (2) organizing, (3) implementing, and (4) controlling.

Planning involves analyzing information and making decisions about what needs to be done. **Organizing** is concerned with determining how plans can be accomplished most effectively and arranging resources to complete work. A manager is **implementing** when carrying out the plans and helping employees to work effectively, and is **controlling** when evaluating results to determine if the company's objectives have been accomplished as planned.

Operating any business is a very complex process. Even managers of small businesses must make product, marketing, personnel, and finance decisions every day. If managers are not well prepared to operate the business, problems will soon develop. The manager who knows how to plan, organize, implement, and control is prepared to make the decisions needed to operate a business successfully.

CHECKPOINT

What are the four functions all managers complete?

The Work of Managers

All managers perform the same four broad functions as a part of their jobs, but the specific activities they perform and the amount of time they spend on each function will be quite different. The functions of management may even seem to describe work activities of some employees who are not classified as managers.

MANAGERS AND NONMANAGEMENT EMPLOYEES

Many employees of a business complete activities that could be considered management activities. They might plan and organize their work or decide how to organize materials to complete work efficiently. An experienced employee may be given the responsibility to be the leader on a group project, and the group members may help the manager evaluate the project when it has been completed. The increasing use of teams in organizations is providing employees many more opportunities to participate in activities that previously have been the domain of managers.

In each of these examples, the employee is getting valuable experience. That experience will help the employee to understand the work of managers and to prepare for possible promotion to a management position. If the company in the earlier example had used these types of experiences to develop employees, Erik might have had a better idea of what it would be like to be a supervisor. Giving those types of responsibilities to employees can also be an effective motivating technique. However, even though employees perform some work that is similar to managers' responsibilities, the employees are not managers. There are important differences in the nature of managers' work and that of nonmanagerial employees.

LEVELS OF MANAGEMENT

A **manager** completes all four management functions on a regular basis and has authority over other jobs and people. In each of the situations above, where employees were completing what seemed to be management functions, they were doing those tasks infrequently, were not completing all of the management functions, or were completing them for their job only. Seldom do nonmanagement employees have authority over other employees for more than a short period of time.

There is typically more than one level of management in most companies. Large companies may have five or six management classifications. However, today many companies are attempting to reduce the number of levels of management, making each level of management and each manager's work more important.

A manager whose main job is to direct the work of nonmanagement employees is called a supervisor. **Supervisors** are typically the first (or beginning) level of management in a company and often have many nonmanagerial activities to perform as well. An **executive** is a top-level manager who spends almost all of his or her time on management functions and decisions that affect the entire company. Executives have other managers reporting to them. Between executives and supervisors in larger organizations, there will be one or more levels of mid-managers.

A **mid-manager** completes all of the management functions, but spends most of the time on one or two management functions such as planning or controlling, or is responsible for a specific part of the company's operations. Figure 11-1 shows how the time spent on management functions changes for different levels of managers in a business.

You can see from the figure that as a manager moves up in the organization, responsibilities change. Supervisors work most directly with employees

NET Bookmark

As businesses and industries grow and decline, employment opportunities change. As you think about your own future, you should use information to help you make a career decision. The U.S. Bureau of Labor Statistics publishes estimates of job growth. Point your browser to www.thomsonedu.com/school/bpmxtra. Review the estimates of job opportunities in major occupational areas from 1994 to 2014. Select three industries that offer jobs that may be of interest to you. Compare the projected job growth by total number of jobs and percentage increase. Prepare a bar graph that illustrates your findings. In addition to job growth, what other types of information are important to you as you make career plans?

www.thomsonedu.com/school/bpmxtra

FIGURE 11-1 The amount of time spent on each function depends on the level of management.

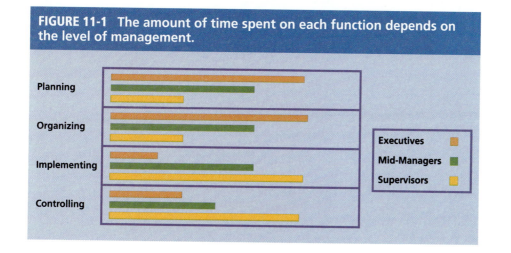

Planning
Organizing
Implementing
Controlling

Executives
Mid-Managers
Supervisors

and are involved primarily in ensuring that the day-to-day work of the business is completed. Therefore, they devote most of their management time to implementing. Executives work with other managers and are responsible for the long-term direction of the business. They spend most of their time on planning and organizing.

CHECKPOINT

How is a supervisor's work different from the work of mid-managers and executives?

11.1 | Assessment

UNDERSTAND MANAGEMENT CONCEPTS

Circle the best answer for each of the following questions.

1. Which of the following is *not* one of the four functions of management?
   a. planning
   b. budgeting
   c. implementing
   d. controlling

2. The level of management that devotes the greatest amount of time to planning is
   a. supervisors
   b. mid-managers
   c. executives
   d. All levels spend equal amounts of time on planning.

THINK CRITICALLY

Answer the following questions as completely as possible.

3. What can employees do both on and off the job to prepare themselves to be effective managers?

4. Why are businesses reducing the number and levels of managers?

11.2 Effective Supervision

Goals
- Identify the responsibilities of supervisors.
- Describe the day-to-day management activities of supervisors.
- Discuss ways that businesses can improve the skills of supervisors.

Terms
- subordinate
- performance review
- work schedules
- work coach

Supervisors are critical to the success of a business. They work directly with employees and are responsible for translating the company's plan into action. One of their most important tasks is to create a work environment that motivates employees to do their best. They must also make sure all of the work assigned to their area of responsibility is completed on time and that it meets established standards of quality.

The Supervisor's Job

Supervisors are often promoted into management in the same part of the business where they work. Remember from the beginning of the chapter that Erik was a network specialist for Freeden. Usually, supervisors are selected from among the most experienced and most skilled employees in an area. However, they will probably have little or no management training.

As first-level managers, supervisors are responsible for the day-to-day activities of the company's employees. They need to understand and work with both employees and management. They serve as the communications link between management and nonmanagement employees. Supervisors must implement the decisions of management. At the same time, they must solve employee problems and present employee concerns to management.

The job of supervisor will be quite different from the work they had been doing. They may not have the level of confidence or immediately have the same success they were used to as experienced employees. They often need to develop different working relationships with employees than they are used to. In the past, the employees they worked with were their coworkers. Now employees are their subordinates. A **subordinate** is subject to the authority and control of another person. Supervisors must command respect from the employees who report to them but in a way that encourages employees to do their best. Moving from the role of coworker to the role of boss is not an easy change. Many supervisors fail due to their inability to make that change.

The effectiveness of a supervisor's job is determined by three factors: (1) the quality of the work of the supervised employees, (2) the efficient use of the company's resources, and (3) the satisfaction of the supervisor's employees. If the employees are not doing the work well, management will not be pleased with the supervisor's performance. If they are not using resources efficiently,

facts & figures

In a recent year, the Bureau of Labor Statistics reported that just under 6.5 million Americans worked as managers, earning an average annual salary of $83,400. This compares to the average earnings of $36,520 for all employees.

a company may not be able to make a profit. And if the employees are not happy with their work, they will not perform their jobs well for long and may decide to leave the company.

RESPONSIBILITIES OF SUPERVISORS

You learned earlier that supervisors often divide their time between management activities and other work. They are responsible for implementing the plans developed by the company's executives. Supervisors must use the plans to determine what needs to be done and who will be assigned to complete the needed work. Then they must explain the work plans and assignments to their employees. Finally, they need to be able to motivate employees to perform effectively on a day-to-day basis.

One supervisor's job may be very different from another's, especially from those of supervisors in other departments and companies. Employees have different levels of education, training, and experience. Some supervisors manage experienced employees, whereas others work with new employees. In spite of the differences in their jobs, supervisors still have a common set of responsibilities in all companies.

COMMUNICATE THE GOALS AND DIRECTIONS OF MANAGEMENT TO EMPLOYEES
In order for employees to complete work effectively, they must understand what needs to be done and why. Supervisors must be able to communicate effectively with employees. Good supervisors can show employees the importance of the company's goals and help them see how they can accomplish their own goals by helping the company to be successful. They must use language and actions that are understandable and meaningful.

EXPLAIN EMPLOYEE CONCERNS AND IDEAS TO MANAGEMENT
Employees want to feel that they are a part of the company and that management considers their ideas and opinions. Therefore, supervisors must take the time to talk with the people they supervise in order to find out their concerns and ideas. Then they must communicate those concerns and ideas to management and follow up to find out what action was taken. Employees like to work for a supervisor who is interested in them and their ideas. They will work hard for a company that is concerned about them, involves employees in planning and decision making, and takes their ideas and suggestions seriously.

EVALUATE AND IMPROVE EMPLOYEE PERFORMANCE
Supervisors get work done through individual employees and work teams. They need to be sure that each employee is performing as effectively as possible. Supervisors regularly conduct performance reviews on each employee. A **performance review** is a procedure that evaluates the work and accomplishment of an employee and provides feedback on that performance.

Regular formal and informal performance reviews can reveal the employee's strengths and weaknesses. Supervisors must be both positive and objective when they complete employee evaluations. Good supervisors discuss these evaluations with their employees in ways that contribute to effective understanding, not conflict. They provide rewards and recognition for employees who perform well. They also provide help for employees who are not performing well, so that their skills can be improved. This help might be in the form of advice and coaching, or it might involve additional training. When serious problems occur, supervisors may be required to discipline employees or even recommend termination.

Keeping the best employees may be the wisest decision an organization can make. Lack of recognition is a common reason employees give for leaving a company. Secondary reasons include low wages, lack of opportunities, outdated skills, and lack of creative input.

ENCOURAGE EMPLOYEES TO DO THEIR BEST WORK How employees feel about their jobs affects their performance. If they are unsure about what they are doing or if the work environment is one of constant conflict, employees will not be able to perform well. Supervisors need to create a pleasant atmosphere in which employees can enjoy their work and do a good job. Employees want to feel accepted and comfortable. They want to know that they can get help if they have problems. They want others to realize that what they do is important and that they will be recognized for good work.

PHOTO: © GETTY IMAGES/PHOTODISC.

USE RESOURCES EFFICIENTLY Companies won't operate long if they are unable to make a profit. An important part of earning a profit is controlling the costs of the business. Because supervisors are responsible for the day-to-day activities of a business, they have a great deal of control over whether a company makes a profit or a loss. Good supervisors continually look for ways to operate more efficiently and to use resources more effectively. They seek advice from employees and make suggestions to managers on how activities can be improved and costs can be controlled.

Supervisors are sometimes called the most important managers in a business. Do you agree or disagree with that statement? Why?

CHECKPOINT
List the responsibilities that are common to all supervisors.

Managing Day-to-Day Activities

Supervisors are essential to a business, because they are responsible for the work of employees in the business. Each employee gets direction from a supervisor, and the supervisor is responsible for the work of each employee. Supervisors must be able to manage their own work effectively as well as the work of the employees for whom they are responsible. Supervisors are responsible for planning, organizing, implementing, and controlling the daily work of their units. Several management activities are important for day-to-day management. Those activities and some common tools used to complete those activities are shown in Figure 11-2 (see p. 278).

SCHEDULING WORK

Supervisors complete daily planning through the use of work schedules. Work schedules identify the tasks to be done, employees assigned to the work, and the time frame for completion of each task. Supervisors may be responsible for both full-time and part-time employees. The business may operate 7 days a week and 24 hours a day. Supervisors will have to decide what days of the week employees will work and which projects each person will complete. If they schedule too few people, the work will not get done. If they schedule too many employees, costs will increase. Projects may be assigned to individuals or to groups. The people

FIGURE 11-2 Common Tools Used by Supervisors for Day-to-Day Management

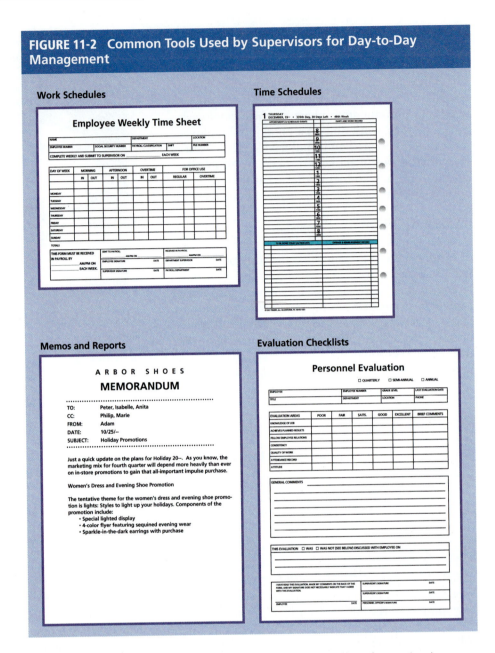

assigned must have the skills to complete the work as well as the motivation to do it and must work well together if they are part of a work team.

Time management is an important management skill for supervisors. A great deal of work must be done in a short time. Supervisors must be able to determine the work to be done, set priorities for the most important work, and ensure that it is completed properly and on time. They must not only use their time effectively, but also help their employees determine how to use their time most effectively each day.

COMMUNICATING WITH EMPLOYEES

Supervisors communicate every day with their employees. Though much of the communication between supervisors and employees is oral, they communicate in writing as well. Supervisors and employees today often communicate using technology such as e-mail and other computer communications.

Whether oral or written, communications must be specific and clear. Supervisors need to plan the content of their communications and determine the best method, place, and time to communicate the information. Supervisors should follow up on communications and ask for feedback to make sure the receivers understood the messages. Listening is an important communication skill for supervisors.

CONTROLLING QUALITY

The final daily management skill for supervisors is quality control. In some companies, employees spend a great deal of time correcting errors and redoing work that was not done well the first time. Supervisors can reduce those problems by planning work carefully, developing quality standards, and regularly checking the quality of the work being done. Also, supervisors can help employees recognize the importance of quality work, so the employees will take responsibility for reducing errors and controlling costs.

CHECKPOINT

What are some common tools used by supervisors and how does each help with day-to-day management responsibilities?

Improving Supervisory Skills

One of the most difficult problems facing new supervisors is to accept the fact that they must spend less time on nonmanagerial activities and more time on management functions. Because supervisors are usually skilled employees, they often want to continue to do the work they were doing before being promoted. At times, they may think that their employees are not doing the job as well as it can be done. Therefore, new supervisors are often tempted to step in and do the job themselves.

If a supervisor spends a little time helping an employee improve his or her work procedures, the employee will usually value the supervisor's support. However, if the supervisor steps in and takes over the employee's task, the employee will resent that action. Both the quality and quantity of the employee's work will suffer and the supervisor will have less time for important management work. Supervisors must rely on their employees to get the work done, so they can concentrate on management activities and use the talents of the people with whom they work.

Today, more companies help supervisors develop and improve their management skills. Many companies provide formal training programs for new supervisors. Employees moving into supervisor positions might, for instance, participate in management classes full-time for a few weeks and then continue training through a series of meetings and short training sessions during their first weeks and months in the new job. Or, they

business *note*

Managers are expected to read a large number of business reports that provide important information. Often reports are long and complex. To help managers recognize, understand, and remember the important information in a report, an executive summary is placed at the beginning. An *executive summary* is a concise overview of the full report. It highlights each major section and summarizes key information.

By reading the executive summary, managers understand what the report is about and what they will learn from it. They can read the full report faster and with greater understanding. They can also use the executive summary as a way to remember the important information at a later date without having to read the entire report again.

might study training materials, such as books and audio or videotapes, for several months after they begin their supervisory duties.

Other companies help supervisors develop their skills by paying for them to attend management classes at a nearby college or sending them to management development programs offered by companies specializing in training and development. A newer method of helping supervisors is to provide an experienced supervisor or another manager to serve as a work coach for the new supervisor. A work coach is an experienced manager who meets regularly with a new manager to provide feedback and advice.

If companies do not provide training, the new supervisor needs to develop management skills individually by enrolling in classes, attending meetings, reading management books and magazines, participating in professional associations for managers, and other similar activities. There are now computer-based training programs as well as training via the Internet to help supervisors continue their development. Talking with and observing the work of experienced supervisors is another way to improve management skills.

CHECKPOINT

How does a work coach help a new supervisor?

11.2 Assessment

UNDERSTAND MANAGEMENT CONCEPTS

Circle the best answer for each of the following questions.

1. As first-level managers, supervisors are responsible for
   a. developing company plans
   b. designing new products and services
   c. day-to-day operations of the business
   d. All are correct.

2. Which of the following is *not* found in a work schedule?
   a. a list of tasks to be completed
   b. the employees assigned to complete work tasks
   c. the time required to complete work tasks
   d. the way the work tasks will be evaluated

THINK CRITICALLY

Answer the following questions as completely as possible.

3. What are some ways that supervisors can increase the motivation and satisfaction of their employees?

4. Because supervisors are typically among the most experienced and effective employees, why are additional training and education so important?

Xtra!
Study Tools
thomsonedu.com/school/bpmxtra

Focus On...

Management Innovation—Total Quality Management

For much of the last century, the approach to business management did not change. Managers believed the best way to be successful was to operate the business as efficiently as possible. To achieve that goal, managers tried to get more and more work out of employees, make as few changes in products as possible, and find ways to reduce costs, often at the expense of quality.

Dr. W. Edwards Deming developed 14 guiding principles for managers that taught them to view their management role in a different way. He suggested that a long-term commitment to quality, customer satisfaction, and employee morale would lead to success. His process was called Total Quality Management (TQM).

- TQM emphasizes increasing quality and developing an effective organization.
- TQM is concerned with customer satisfaction and employee motivation.
- TQM relies on leadership and cooperation versus the traditional management focus on closely supervising employee behavior.
- TQM businesses constantly look for new and improved ways to complete their work to increase effectiveness and quality.
- TQM encourages teamwork and employee involvement in decision making.
- TQM businesses view employees as valuable contributors to success and use training to improve employee effectiveness and motivation.

A set of tools has been developed to help businesses implement Total Quality Management. A few examples of the tools are:

Flow charts. These identify each step in a procedure and how the steps are related to each other. They can be used to compare how work is being done to how it is supposed to be done in order to reduce errors.

Cause-and-effect analysis. Employee and management teams brainstorm about problems to find solutions. They develop a diagram that lists problems and possible causes and link them together until they discover and agree on the basic problem. Then they can develop solutions.

Scatter diagrams. Data from two different factors are visually plotted on a chart and analyzed to discover relationships. For example, the number of employee absences over a six-month period is compared to the number of product defects to see if the use of temporary employees is related to a reduction in product quality.

Today, quality, customer satisfaction, teamwork, and process improvement are making a difference in business competitiveness.

Think Critically

1. Why do many managers find it so difficult to change from traditional approaches to TQM?
2. Many schools are now implementing TQM and teaching students to use its tools. What types of procedures in schools could benefit from TQM?
3. If a school was facing a problem with students being tardy for classes, how could the school use one of the TQM tools to help solve that problem?

11.3 Managing with Information

Goals
- Explain how management information systems and business research help managers with planning and controlling activities.
- Identify the four steps in the problem-solving process and how the process supports decision making.

Terms
- what-if decisions
- problem
- symptom

Using Management Information

To do a good job of planning, organizing, implementing, and controlling, managers must have a great deal of information available. They need records on production and sales, personnel, expenses, and profit or loss to make decisions. Data must be collected, organized, and made available to managers so they can make decisions quickly and efficiently.

Even in very small businesses, managers cannot remember all of the information needed to make decisions. In large companies with many managers and hundreds of employees, it is impossible to operate without a systematic way to gather information for managers to use in decision making.

MANAGEMENT INFORMATION SYSTEMS

Management information systems were described in detail earlier in the book. Every company needs such a system as an important management tool. Computers help managers develop effective plans and also control business operations.

Planning involves making choices. Plans should be based on information from past experience as well as anticipated changes. With an effective management information system, managers can use information to make what-if decisions. **What-if decisions** explore the consequences of specific choices using computer software. A sales manager may ask, "*What if* we increased sales by 5 percent?" An analysis of the records of past costs and sales using specially designed computer software will show the manager whether the additional sales will generate more profit or not. An operations manager may ask, "*What if* we replaced our old fleet of trucks with new, more fuel-efficient models?" Again, the computer analysis will provide the needed information to determine whether the purchase would be cost-effective.

Managers can also use information systems to reduce the amount of time spent on controlling activities. If managers took the time to review all of the information collected on business operations, they would have little time for other activities. Computers can be used to monitor the performance of activities in a company. If activities are performed as planned and standards are met, no management attention is needed. Managers should become involved only when activities do not occur as planned or results do not meet standards. When managers want to evaluate performance, they can quickly access data from the management information system related to that performance. The data can be used to compare performance to previously established standards or to the performance of a similar group or a previous time period.

BUSINESS RESEARCH

Managers must be careful not to make decisions without sufficient information about the problem or possible solutions. When they need more information to make a good decision, they may need to conduct research. Research is conducted to gather new information not yet included in the management information system. The results of business research can be added to the management information system and then used for future decisions.

PHOTO: © CORBIS.

Business research is conducted in many areas. Wherever and whenever managers need information to make decisions and the needed information is not available, business research should be considered.

Marketing research and product development research are two common areas. A marketing manager may want to determine why certain groups of customers are purchasing a product whereas others are not. A proposed new product should not be developed unless research shows that the product can be produced at a profit and that customers are likely to purchase it.

Managers have much more information available today than ever before. How can too much information actually decrease a manager's effectiveness?

Human resources studies are conducted on such topics as the supply and demand of labor, employee motivation, and training techniques. Financial executives need the results of research that deals with borrowing and investing money. Those managers also need research results regarding economic factors, such as the expected economic performance of specific companies or of the industry in which a company operates. The research described as well as other types of research helps executives make important decisions relative to the growth and development of their companies.

Much of the needed business research is done by the business itself. Most large companies have research departments that plan and complete studies related to the specific problems of the company. But because research departments are expensive to maintain, small companies must depend to a considerable degree on professional research organizations.

Research centers and faculty members in universities conduct studies that are often helpful to businesses. Various divisions of the federal government undertake extensive research, and much of this information is available to and useful for business. Trade and professional associations conduct research studies that are useful to the particular industries they serve. Companies may also employ research organizations or individual consultants to gather and analyze information to solve problems or improve decision making.

CHECKPOINT

In addition to conducting their own research, what other sources of business research are available to companies?

Decision Making

In the process of planning, organizing, implementing, and controlling, managers encounter problems that require them to make decisions. Top-level managers make some of the decisions, such as new products to be developed or new markets that the business will enter. Mid-managers make other decisions that may result in new ways of organizing work, the use of new technology, or improved procedures for completing work. First-level managers, such as department heads and supervisors, make decisions about the daily operations of their units. It is important to the overall success of any business that the decisions be made as carefully as possible at every level of management.

PROBLEMS AND DECISION MAKING

Generally, a problem is a difficult situation requiring a solution. Problems usually do not have single solutions. Instead, they have a series of possible solutions. There may be several good solutions, but there may also be several poor solutions. For example, the problem may be to find the most effective and efficient method to ship products from a manufacturing plant in Texas to customers in Montreal, Canada. Possible solutions are to ship by airplane, ship, train, or truck. Depending on the circumstances, any one of the shipping methods could be the best or the worst solution. To find the best solution, managers should follow a systematic approach to solving problems. That procedure is outlined in Figure 11-3.

STEPS IN PROBLEM SOLVING

Most problems can be analyzed by completing a series of steps. You may have learned this problem-solving process already in other classes, such as a science class. The procedure works as well in business as it does in scientific problem

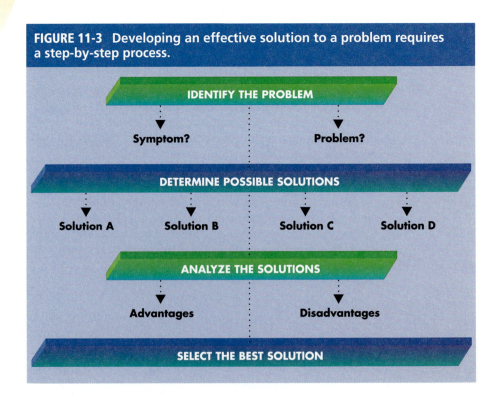

FIGURE 11-3 Developing an effective solution to a problem requires a step-by-step process.

IDENTIFY THE PROBLEM

Symptom? Problem?

DETERMINE POSSIBLE SOLUTIONS

Solution A Solution B Solution C Solution D

ANALYZE THE SOLUTIONS

Advantages Disadvantages

SELECT THE BEST SOLUTION

solving. The four steps in problem solving are (1) identify the problem, (2) list possible solutions, (3) carefully analyze the possible solutions, and (4) select the best solution using the results of the analysis.

IDENTIFY THE PROBLEM Before a manager can make a decision to solve a problem, the problem must first be located and identified. Often, a manager may not even be aware that a problem exists. For example, employees may be unhappy about a coworker. The manager may not know about the problem unless employees communicate this concern or it begins to affect their work.

A manager must also be careful not to identify a symptom as the problem. A **symptom** is a sign or indication of something that appears to be the problem. When a patient complains of a headache, the headache may be a symptom. The problem could be high blood pressure, a cold, or another illness. Falling sales of a line of appliances for a retailer is a symptom. The problem could be ineffective advertising, a bad product location in the store, untrained salespeople, quality problems in the products, poor service, and so on. Therefore, it will be difficult to change the symptom until the problem can be correctly identified and corrected.

What are some reasons that sales are declining? Are fewer customers entering the business? Are customers shopping but not buying? Are customers buying but then returning the products because they are not performing as expected? Or are customers now beginning to use the Internet to purchase products rather than buying from the store? Managers can often identify the problem by asking questions and gathering information. They can use the symptom to gather information that can isolate the problem.

Sometimes managers are unaware that problems exist until it is too late. They need to review plans and performance regularly to determine if operations are proceeding as planned. When any evidence appears that suggests a problem, they should study the evidence carefully rather than ignore it. It is better to review symptoms and determine that there is no problem than to wait until problems are so big that they are difficult to correct.

Good managers follow a clear problem-solving process to handle various kinds of problems that arise in any business. What is your problem-solving style?

LIST POSSIBLE SOLUTIONS Once they identify a problem, managers should begin to list all possible solutions. For example, if the problem is ineffective advertising, they should list all possible ways to change the advertising. The list might include more informative advertisements, a change in the advertising media used, the frequency and timing of advertising, as well as many other possibilities. Every problem has at least two possible solutions, and managers should not overlook any reasonable solution at this point in the problem-solving process.

There are many ways to identify possible solutions. Brainstorming is one method of developing a long list for later analysis. Managers should review solutions that have been used in the past or that were considered for solving related problems. Discussing the problems with other managers or with outside experts helps to identify solutions. Reading and studying can keep managers aware of new types of solutions. Many managers recognize that employees and customers are sources of possible solutions.

PHOTO: © DIGITAL VISION.

ANALYZE THE SOLUTIONS The third step in problem solving is to analyze the solutions. Managers do this by studying each possible solution separately, comparing the solutions, and reducing the number of solutions to the best two or three. To study each solution thoroughly and objectively, managers may need information from business records, trade associations, libraries, consultants, government sources, or the Internet. The use of management information systems and business research is an important part of this step.

After collecting all of the necessary information, managers should examine the strengths and weaknesses of each solution one by one. Then they should compare solutions and classify them in some way, such as extremely desirable, somewhat desirable, and least desirable. Some solutions may be too costly or impractical, whereas others may be inexpensive or very practical. For example, in a list of solutions comparing advertising media the business is considering, managers may find that the cost of television advertising is more than is available in the budget, whereas newspaper advertising is affordable. Managers need to compare the solutions on how effectively they will solve the problem, not just the symptom. After all the analyses have been completed, only two or three solutions may appear to effectively solve the problem.

For very important decisions, managers may want to conduct an experiment to test one or more solutions. A likely solution is often tested in one part of the organization to see how it works. The results are then compared with those from other tests to determine which was more effective in solving the problem before using it throughout the business. Managers then analyze the results of the experiment to eliminate some solutions and to identify those that seem to be effective.

SELECT THE BEST SOLUTION The last step in problem solving is to make the final decision from among the remaining solutions. Some problems have to be solved quickly, but for very important decisions, managers take several days or more before selecting the solution. Only after careful thought do they make the final decision and put it into action. For certain problems, managers may be able to make the decision and implement the solution. For others, managers may need to seek the approval or cooperation of other managers first.

After selecting a solution, the managers must determine the best way to implement it and who will be part of the implementation. As implementation proceeds, the managers must gather information to determine if the solution is solving the problem or if they need additional efforts or even another solution.

The problem is not solved just because the solution has been selected and implemented. The managers will want to carefully study the results and be prepared to make changes if the problem is not corrected. Once again, management information systems will be very helpful in monitoring the implementation of the solution and the results. Studying and evaluating the results of solutions to problems is a part of the controlling function for managers.

MAKING THE RIGHT CAREER CHOICE

At the beginning of the chapter, Erik Berman was trying to decide if he wanted to move into management as a supervisor. He knows that most of his time will be spent on management activities—planning, organizing, implementing, and controlling. As a supervisor, he will be the link between the employees he supervises and the company's management. Because of his work with computers, he may be familiar with management information systems, but he will have to become skilled at using information to make decisions. He needs to follow a careful decision-making process to identify and solve problems. If Erik finds that type of work challenging and interesting and is willing to develop the needed skills, he can become an effective supervisor for Freeden.

CHECKPOINT
List the four steps in problem solving.

11.3 Assessment

UNDERSTAND MANAGEMENT CONCEPTS

Circle the best answer for each of the following questions.

1. When managers use a management information system, no management action is needed if
   a. activities are performed as planned and standards are met
   b. all employee performance reviews are completed on schedule
   c. there are no changes in the organization
   d. None of the answers is correct.

2. Which of the following is *not* a step in the problem-solving process?
   a. Identify the symptoms.
   b. List possible solutions.
   c. Select the best solution.
   d. All are steps in the problem-solving process.

THINK CRITICALLY

Answer the following questions as completely as possible.

3. Why should managers ask what-if questions when developing plans?

4. How might a business benefit if employees are trained in the decision-making process and encouraged to use that process in their work?

Xtra!
Study Tools
thomsonedu.com/school/bpmxtra

CHAPTER CONCEPTS

- A manager performs four management functions on a regular basis—planning, organizing, implementing, and controlling—and has authority over other jobs and people.

- As first-level managers, supervisors are responsible for the day-to-day activities of the company's employees. One of their most important tasks is to create a work environment that motivates employees to do their best. They also serve as a communications link between employees and management.

- Every company needs a management information system to help managers reduce the amount of time they spend on controlling activities. Data must be collected, organized, and made available to managers so they can make decisions quickly and efficiently.

- Effective problem solving involves identifying the problem, listing possible solutions, analyzing the possible solutions, and selecting the best solution based on the results of the analysis.

REVIEW TERMS AND CONCEPTS

Write the letter of the term that matches each definition. Some terms will not be used.

a. controlling
b. executive
c. implementing
d. management
e. manager
f. mid-manager
g. organizing
h. performance review
i. planning
j. problem
k. subordinate
l. supervisor
m. symptom
n. what-if decisions
o. work coach
p. work schedules

1. Process of accomplishing the goals of an organization through the effective use of people and other resources
2. Procedure that evaluates the work and accomplishments of an employee and provides feedback on that performance
3. Person who performs all four management functions on a regular basis and has authority over other jobs and people
4. Evaluating results to determine if the company's objectives have been accomplished as planned
5. Determining how plans can be accomplished most effectively and arranging resources to complete work
6. Person who performs all management functions but spends most of the time on one or two management functions or is responsible for a specific part of the company's operations
7. Difficult situation requiring a solution
8. Experienced manager who meets regularly with a new manager to provide feedback and advice
9. Involves analyzing information and making decisions about what needs to be done
10. Carrying out plans and helping employees to work effectively
11. Subject to the authority and control of another person
12. Sign or indication of something that appears to be a problem

DETERMINE THE BEST ANSWER

13. Which of the following statements about the role of managers is true?
    a. Managers make up the greatest percentage of employees in a business.
    b. Managers are responsible for completing the day-to-day work of a business.
    c. There are only two levels of management in most businesses.
    d. Managers are responsible for the success or failure of the company.
14. The first level of management in a company is typically
    a. executives
    b. supervisors
    c. mid-managers
    d. work coaches
15. Which of the following is *not* one of the factors that determines the effectiveness of a supervisor's job?
    a. the quality of work of the supervised employees
    b. the efficient use of the company's resources
    c. increases in the company's total profits
    d. the satisfaction of the supervisor's employees
16. An appropriate way to improve the quality of work accomplished in a supervisor's work area is for the supervisor to
    a. spend a short amount of time helping an employee improve their work procedures
    b. step in and take over the work of an employee who is not performing correctly
    c. schedule more employees than are required to complete the work
    d. all of the above
17. New information not yet included in a management information system can be gathered by
    a. conducting research
    b. asking what-if questions
    c. reviewing company records
    d. asking employees
18. The first step in the problem-solving procedure is to
    a. conduct research
    b. identify possible symptoms
    c. analyze several solutions
    d. locate and identify the problem

APPLY WHAT YOU KNOW

19. List the advantages and disadvantages that Erik Berman should consider when deciding whether to apply for the supervisor's position at Freeden Web Technologies.
20. How could an employee perform all four of the management functions and still not be a manager?

21. Why would large companies need mid-managers who spend most of their time on one management function, such as controlling?

22. What are some reasons the best employee in a job may not make the best supervisor for other people in that job?

23. Why are most supervisors required to divide their time between supervisory responsibilities and other work?

24. Of the five areas of responsibility of supervisors, which do you believe is the most important to the success of the company, and why?

25. What are some ways that supervisors can help employees manage their time better?

26. What skills do supervisors and other managers need in order to manage business information effectively?

MAKE CONNECTIONS

27. **Math** During one month, three managers recorded the number of hours they spent on each of the four management functions. Ms. Perez spent 42 hours on planning activities, 26 on organizing activities, 83 on implementing activities, and 57 on controlling activities. Mr. Patton used 65 hours on planning, 24 hours on organizing, 36 hours on implementing, and 59 hours on controlling. Ms. Matsumi spent 18 hours planning, 40 hours organizing, 60 hours implementing, and 74 hours controlling. For each manager, determine the total hours worked during the month and the percentage of time devoted to each management function. Then determine the total percentage of time spent by the three managers on each of the functions. Develop a chart to illustrate the results. What conclusions would you draw from the information in the chart?

28. **Writing** Keep a record of how you spend your time for two days. Record your activities every half hour. Then review how you used your time. Identify the times when you believe you were using time effectively and the times you were not. Prepare written recommendations on how you could more effectively manage your time in the future.

29. **Critical Thinking** A list of symptoms of business problems follows. For each symptom, write a question that could be used to help identify the actual problem.
    a. The number of products returned by customers has increased greatly in the last six months for an e-commerce company.
    b. Three employees who have worked for the company less than a month quit without giving notice.
    c. Advertising costs have increased by 10 percent this year.
    d. The number of customers who have overdue credit accounts has doubled in the past six months.
    e. Employees have been given the authority to stop the assembly line anytime they notice a defective product. Since that decision was made, work stoppages have increased by four per week.

CASE IN POINT

CASE 11-1: What Makes an Effective Manager?

Amber and Travis are considering careers in business and have hopes of becoming managers someday. Both hold part-time jobs and have seen a number of managers at their work. Amber was even selected to fill in for a short time as the shift supervisor for her work team when the full-time supervisor was on vacation. That gave her a closer view of some of the work managers do and how their job is different from that of employees. Amber shared her experiences with Travis, which led to a discussion of their views of a manager's work.

Travis: *A manager's job is really very easy if the company hires good employees. All a manager has to do is make sure the work gets done.*

Amber: *Do you really think it's that easy? First, I don't think companies can always find employees who can do the work well. Also, a manager's job involves much more than working with employees.*

Travis: *I think a manager just has to be a good communicator. If a manager can explain clearly what needs to be done, good employees will take it from there.*

Amber: *But what about all of the things that can go wrong in a company that a manager can't plan for? Equipment can break down, new employees may not be well trained, or a big order may require everyone to work overtime.*

Travis: *I read that companies spend a large amount of their training budgets on management development. If you ask me, either you're a good manager or you aren't. I don't think taking classes on how to manage will do much good if you aren't the right type of person.*

Amber: *I might have agreed with you a few years ago, but today it seems that management is much more complicated. In fact, I believe that the problems each manager faces are so different it would be difficult to develop training programs that would benefit all of the managers in a company.*

THINK CRITICALLY

1. Analyze the views of Amber and Travis toward management. With what do you agree or disagree?
2. Do you believe that managers spend most of their time working with employees? Justify your answer.
3. What characteristics are common to all managers' jobs? What are the types of things that would be quite different from one manager's job to another?
4. If you were responsible for developing a training program for managers, what would you include?

CASE 11-2: Meeting the Standard

A'yanna Lyons is the manager of the accounting department for the Hemmerle Supply Company, an office supplies wholesaler. As the manager, she is responsible for all of the work completed by the employees in the accounting department, including its quality and quantity. A'yanna was proud of the work her employees did. They had a high level of motivation and always seemed to do their best to complete the work assigned to them. The entire department seemed committed to being an asset for the company. Therefore she was surprised by feedback she received on a work issue that affected her department.

Hemmerle had recently established a new standard that invoices would be prepared, printed, and mailed to customers within 24 hours of receiving the order. Although the new standard presented a big challenge to the accounting department, A'yanna had worked with her teams to do their part to meet the standard. By reorganizing the way they did their work and using a new computer tracking system for each order, the department was able to complete the invoice process within half a day from the time they received the information from the shipping department.

After the new procedures were in place, A'yanna had carefully checked the work of her department. Although there had been a few times when an employee absence or a problem with the new computer software had slowed the work, the department was meeting its standard of processing invoices in half a day 93 percent of the time. However, in the first productivity report she received that tracked the company's progress in meeting the 24-hour standard, A'yanna learned that 25 percent of the invoices were being mailed three days after the order was received. Upon checking further, she discovered that her department did not always receive the necessary information from the shipping department on schedule and that the mail room was having trouble meeting its deadline to ship out on the same day all mail received before noon.

THINK CRITICALLY

1. What are some possible problems in this situation? Identify problems that could be occurring in the accounting department as well as in other departments of the company.
2. List the symptoms of the problems. Explain why you believe the things you listed are symptoms rather than problems.
3. What are some alternative solutions?
4. How would you suggest that A'yanna proceed in this situation?
5. How can a management information system contribute to resolving this situation?

project: MY BUSINESS, INC.

PREPARING FOR THE MANAGEMENT FUNCTION

The failure rate for new small businesses is fairly high. Many people start a business without considering the difficulty of the process, the time required to manage a business, and the costs of starting a new business and operating it until it can become profitable. One of the major reasons for failure is that the owner does not practice effective management skills. Many new business owners have never been managers or have managed a specialized part of another business. They have not had the experience of being responsible for all aspects of managing. Few new business owners have undertaken any type of management training to prepare themselves for their new role.

To increase the chances of success for your new business, you need to prepare yourself for your new role as owner and manager. Through your study of management, you are now aware of all of the functions that top managers and executives perform. You know that you will have to devote much of your time to management activities in order to complete all the major management functions. In addition, you must be prepared to identify and solve problems before they negatively affect the business.

DATA COLLECTION

1. Survey five managers of small businesses. Ask them to identify the types of activities they commonly perform during the day and estimate the amount of time they spend on each activity during the typical day. Use your own judgment to classify the activities within the four management functions. You may also need a category for non-management activities. Prepare a chart to illustrate your findings on how small-business managers spend their time.
2. Identify two problems you expect to face in operating your business. Complete the steps in problem solving to develop an appropriate solution. As you analyze possible solutions, identify several sources of useful information, including business research.

ANALYSIS

1. Develop a chart with four headings: Planning, Organizing, Implementing, and Controlling. Under each heading, list the activities you will need to complete to manage your juice bar effectively.
2. Under the list of activities developed above, estimate (a) how much time you will need to devote to each activity and (b) when you will need to complete each activity during a typical month. Then develop a sample monthly calendar on which you schedule management activities.
3. For each problem identified in the data collection section above, select the solution you believe is likely to be most effective. Then develop a written set of procedures to follow to accomplish each solution and prevent the problem from occurring.

Career Cluster
Administrative Services Management

Administrative services managers are responsible for all the support services needed to maintain a company's operations: secretarial and clerical services; mail, telephone, and electronic communications services; operating supplies procurement and management; conference and meeting planning; employee travel; printing and reproduction; records management; and security services.

Employment Outlook

Administrative services careers will grow at an average rate over the next 10 years. The greatest demand will be in service industries, government, and health care. Demand for managers with special knowledge of security and safety issues and facilities management will increase.

Job Titles

Facilities, Office, Property, Operations, or Support Services Manager
Procurement Specialist

Needed Skills

- Must be analytical, detail-oriented, flexible, with good communication skills.
- In small businesses, may need only a high school degree and significant work experience. In large organizations and at higher levels, need at least a bachelor's degree, often in a specialized area such as information management, office technology, human resources, or accounting. For most positions, advanced computer and technology skills are increasingly important.

Working in Administrative Services

As executive vice president for administrative services, Janeen ensures that every department in the company has the support services it needs. She has just met with an architect who is designing an addition to the offices. She must make sure the building meets the requirements for communications and computer technologies and has adequate space for all the necessary administrative support activities. She is now on her way to meet with the CEO to discuss new information security procedures that will protect employee and customer data stored in the company's computers. She was called into work late last night to deal with a burst water line that flooded the first floor. She had to negotiate a contract for temporary work space and arrange for materials to be shipped overnight.

PHOTO: © GETTY IMAGES/PHOTODISC.

Career Assessment

Why is administrative services management important to the success of a business? What do you like and dislike about the career area?

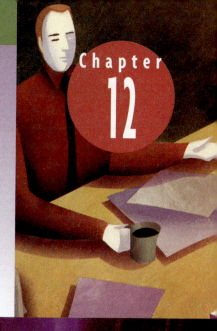

The Manager as Leader

REALITY CHECK

Is Politics a Popularity Contest?

Brittany and Foster walked to the bus stop to return home after attending a political debate. Because the election for the city's mayor and council members was only three weeks away, their government and economics class decided to attend the debate and then discuss the candidates the next day in class. Each student was asked to identify the characteristics they believed were most important for the office of mayor and be prepared to discuss each candidate using those characteristics.

Brittany: *Our city is growing rapidly and has a lot of problems. We need a mayor who's a problem solver and willing to make tough decisions. I don't know if any of the candidates showed me they were willing to do that.*

Foster: *I think as politicians they want people to like them. They all seem to be effective communicators but don't want to say anything that will upset voters. Do you really think they can do what has to be done for the city without making some people upset with them?*

Brittany: *Running a city is just like managing a large company. If you're a good manager and the business is successful, people will be satisfied.*

Foster: *I'm not sure. Being mayor of a city and manager of a large business may be similar in some ways. But a manager can make decisions that are best for the business and still have dissatisfied employees and customers. I don't think a mayor can risk upsetting voters even if a decision seems to be best for the city's future.*

Brittany: *I think we both agree that it's not easy to lead a large organization, whether it's a city or a business. It's hard to decide what the most important characteristics of an effective manager or mayor should be.*

12.1 The Importance of Leadership

Goals

- Recognize the importance of leadership and human relations.
- Identify important leadership characteristics and types of power.
- Describe four types of power available to leaders.

Terms

- leader
- leadership
- human relations
- power
- position power
- reward power
- expert power
- identity power

The Importance of Leadership

Anyone who holds a responsible position in an organization must have a number of qualities to meet his or her responsibilities successfully. One of the key qualities for a manager at any level is effective leadership. If you plan a career in business, you need to develop your leadership skills.

Many years ago, managers were totally responsible for all decisions in a business. The goal of management was to get the work of the business done. Therefore, managers just told employees what to do and expected them to do it.

WHAT IS LEADERSHIP?

Today, we recognize that management is not that simple. To get work done effectively, employees must understand why the work is important and must want to do the work. Employees want to be an important part of the business and want managers to value their ideas as well as their work. A manager who earns the respect and cooperation of employees to effectively accomplish the work of the organization is known as a **leader**.

Leadership is the ability to influence individuals and groups to cooperatively achieve organizational goals. Leaders have excellent human relations skills. **Human relations** refers to how well people get along with each other when working together. A group of people who respect each other and work well together will likely do better work than groups characterized by negative feelings, misunderstandings, hostility, and a lack of respect for each other. In a negative group atmosphere, individuals—and often the entire group—will do things that interfere with the group's success rather than contributing to it. You can probably think of groups that do not work well together. How do the members treat each other? How do they spend their time when the group is together? Usually it is not enjoyable to be part of a group with poor human relations.

DEVELOPING AS A LEADER

A manager can contribute to effective or ineffective human relations. All managers have a responsibility for getting work done through others, so relationships are important. Not every manager is currently an effective leader, but

Teamwork *tip*

If you want your team to be successful, the team will need both an effective leader and cooperative and supportive team members. Many of the traits of leaders are needed by team members as well.

leadership skills can be developed. Because leadership is so important in business, most management training programs today emphasize leadership and effective human relations.

CHECKPOINT

Why do leaders need human relations skills?

Leadership Characteristics

Although managers have many responsibilities, one of the most important is creating an atmosphere that encourages employees to do their best work to make the business successful. Individual employees, however, have their own goals and needs. Employees will be most productive when the work meets their needs as well as those of the company. Managers must work to satisfy important needs of each employee while also meeting the goals of the business. Success in this task requires leadership.

Because leadership has been shown to be directly related to the success of an organization, it is important that managers possess certain leadership characteristics. Leaders help employees get work done correctly and willingly. A poor manager may be able to get employees to perform the necessary tasks, but the work may be done poorly and inefficiently. A good manager, on the other hand, creates a work environment in which employees enjoy their work and want to do a good job.

In the past several years, many leaders have been studied to identify the characteristics that make them successful. The common characteristics that effective leaders possess are shown in Figure 12-1. Having those characteristics does not ensure that a person will be a good manager. Leaders must also understand the work to be done, and the business in which they work must be well organized. In addition, as you learned in the last chapter, managers must be able to plan, organize, implement, and control work.

PHOTO: © DIGITAL VISION.

Think of someone you know in a leadership position. What makes that person effective? How could his or her leadership style be improved?

FIGURE 12-1 Effective leaders possess most of these characteristics.

Basic Leadership Traits

INTELLIGENCE

A certain amount of intelligence is needed to direct others. Leaders use their intelligence to study, learn, and improve their management skills. They also help the people they work with to learn and develop new skills. Leaders must use their intelligence effectively.

JUDGMENT

Leaders must make many decisions. They consider all facts carefully; apply knowledge, experience, and new information; and use good judgment.

OBJECTIVITY

Leaders must be able to look at all sides of a problem and not make biased judgments or statements. They gather information and do not rush into actions before considering the possible results. They value individual differences, not stereotypes or first impressions.

INITIATIVE

Leaders have ambition and persistence in reaching goals. They are self-starters who plan what they want to do and then do it. They have drive and are highly motivated. They encourage others to take actions and make decisions when appropriate.

DEPENDABILITY

Those who lead are consistent in their actions, and others can rely on them. They do not make promises that cannot be fulfilled. When they make a commitment, they follow through, and expect others to do the same. The people they work with can count on leaders to help them.

COOPERATION

Leaders understand the importance of other people and enjoy being with them. Thus, they work well with others. They understand that people working together can accomplish more than the same people working alone. They work to develop cooperative relations.

HONESTY

Leaders are honest and have high standards of personal integrity. They are ethical in decisions and their treatment of others.

COURAGE

Leaders possess the courage to make unpopular decisions and try new approaches in solving problems. They are willing to take risks to support others.

CONFIDENCE

Leaders have a great deal of self-confidence. They attempt to make the best decisions possible and trust their own judgment. They respect others and expect quality work.

STABILITY

Leaders are not highly emotional. You can depend on their reactions. They can help others to solve problems and reduce conflicts.

UNDERSTANDING

Leaders recognize that the feelings and ideas of others are important. They try to understand the people they work with. They encourage others to share their ideas, experiences, and opinions and show that each person is a valuable member of the organization.

Leadership characteristics are personal qualities rather than specific ways that managers behave. Each company, each job, and each situation is different. Leadership characteristics prepare managers to be flexible and adjust to changes. Two managers who possess the same leadership qualities will probably respond in different ways to specific situations but will be able to work well with people to get the necessary work accomplished.

CHECKPOINT

How do leadership characteristics help managers do their work?

Influencing People

Managers influence people to accomplish the work of the organization. However, there are both negative and positive ways to influence others. Just because managers can get others to do what they want does not mean that the managers are effective leaders.

MANAGEMENT POWER

Managers can influence employees because of their power. **Power** is the ability to control behavior. There are several ways that managers obtain power. The type of power will determine how employees respond to managers. Four types of power available to managers and the source of each type are summarized in Figure 12-2.

Position power comes from the position the manager holds in the organization. If a manager is an employee's boss, the manager has the power to give directions and expect the employee to complete that work. If the manager does not directly supervise the employee, the manager's directions are more requests than orders. The manager does not have the position power to tell that employee what to do.

Reward power is power based on the ability to control rewards and punishments. If a manager can determine who receives new equipment, preferred work schedules, or pay increases, or can penalize people for poor work or inappropriate performance, employees are likely to respond to that manager's requests.

FIGURE 12-2 Managers use power to influence the behavior of employees.

TYPE OF POWER	RESULTS FROM
Position	The manager's position in the organization
Reward	The manager's control of rewards/punishments
Expert	The manager's knowledge and skill
Identity	The employee's perception of the manager

Employees are willing to work hard when they are satisfied with their jobs. Do employees as well as managers have a responsibility for increasing job satisfaction?

PHOTO: © DIGITAL VISION.

Expert power is power given to people because of their superior knowledge about the work. When workers are unsure of how to perform a task or need information to solve a problem, they may turn to an expert. That person will be able to influence behavior because of the knowledge and skill he or she has.

Identity power is power given to people because others identify with and want to be accepted by them. If an employee respects a manager and wants positive recognition from that person, the employee will likely do what the manager requests. Experienced or well-liked employees often have identity power. Those people can influence the work of others in the organization.

USING POWER EFFECTIVELY

An analysis of the types of power shows that managers can influence their employees because of position or because of the rewards and punishments they control. However, those types of power are not related to leadership characteristics. Employees do not grant those types of power to managers. Position and reward power come from the manager's position in the company. If a manager has only position and reward power, employees may do the requested work but may not do it willingly or well.

However, expert and identity power come from employees, not position in the company. Employees grant these kinds of power to managers they consider worthy of it. If employees consider the manager to be an expert, they will seek the manager's advice and help. If employees want the approval or positive recognition of the manager, they will work cooperatively and support the requests of the manager. Both expert and identity power are related to effective leadership characteristics.

Sometimes people other than managers have power in an organization. Other employees can influence people's behavior because they can control rewards and punishments, they are considered experts, or other employees identify with them and want their approval. If those powerful employees support the work of the organization, they can have a positive influence on other employees. On the other hand, employees with power can be disruptive if their needs and goals differ from those of the organization. Employees may choose to be influenced by those people rather than by their managers.

CHECKPOINT

Which types of power are related to effective leadership characteristics?

NETBookmark

Who are the greatest business leaders in U.S. history? Two Harvard business professors surveyed 7,000 executives to answer that question. The people who made the final list had to have changed the American way of life in some significant way. Point your browser to www.thomsonedu.com/school/bpmxtra. Review the list of the top 50 business leaders identified through the survey and select one. Use the Internet to learn more about that person and prepare a one-page summary about his or her unique contributions. Based on your research, would you agree the person is one of the greatest business leaders in U.S. history?

www.thomsonedu.com/school/bpmxtra

12.1 Assessment

UNDERSTAND MANAGEMENT CONCEPTS

Determine the best answer for each of the following questions.

1. Leadership ability is important to managers because
   a. a manager without leadership skills has no way to influence employee behavior
   b. businesses will not hire a manager without leadership skills
   c. leadership helps managers satisfy employees' needs while also meeting the goals of the business
   d. all of the above

2. Power given to people because of their superior knowledge about the work is
   a. identify power
   b. expert power
   c. reward power
   d. position power

THINK CRITICALLY

Answer the following questions as completely as possible.

3. Why are leadership characteristics important for employees to develop as well as for managers?

4. How can the inappropriate use of power by managers have a negative effect on employees? How might it negatively affect the business?

Xtra! Study Tools
thomsonedu.com/school/bpmxtra

12.2 Developing Leadership Skills

Goals
- Discuss why businesses value leadership skills of managers and employees.
- Identify and define five important human relations skills.

Terms
- self-understanding
- team building

Leadership in Business

For the most part, people are not "born" leaders. Through training and personal development, individuals can improve their leadership qualities. People can learn to be dependable, to take initiative, to cooperate with others, and so on. Training and experience can improve a manager's judgment in making business decisions. Most people can become effective leaders with preparation and practice.

Managers are not the only people in an organization who need leadership skills. Many businesses are using employee teams to plan work and make decisions. The team may include a manager, although many do not. Even when a manager is a part of the team, the leader of the group will not always be the manager. As the team completes various projects, individual team members may assume leadership for specific activities. If the team is well organized, the leaders will have expert and identity power to get individual projects completed. The entire team may be given position and reward power that they can use to manage team activities and to achieve the team goals.

Today, companies frequently evaluate applicants' leadership abilities before hiring them. Companies often prefer to hire workers who have already developed many leadership characteristics and have had leadership experience. Training programs for employees emphasize team building and leadership development. Some companies allow employees to volunteer for leadership training, whereas others expect everyone to be involved. Companies recognize that employees with leadership skills can make valuable contributions to a business's success. It is important to take advantage of leadership development opportunities whenever they occur.

CHECKPOINT

What are ways that businesses develop the leadership skills of employees?

Human Relations

Managers are continually in contact with employees, other managers, customers, and others who have interest in the work of the business. Because of these contacts, managers need human relations skills. They must be able to work well with others both inside and outside the business and help employees work well together.

Human relations involve several skills. Those skills may be just as important to the success of a business as the ability to make decisions or operate a complicated piece of equipment. Important human relations skills are (1) self-understanding, (2) understanding of others, (3) communication, (4) team building, and (5) developing job satisfaction.

SELF-UNDERSTANDING

In order to work well with others, managers must have self-understanding. **Self-understanding** involves an awareness of your attitudes and opinions, your leadership style, your decision-making style, and your relationships with other people.

Employees look to managers for information and direction. They want managers to be able to make decisions, solve problems, and communicate expectations. If managers understand themselves and what other people expect of them, they can decide on the best way to work with people and the leadership style to use. They can use the understanding of their strengths, weaknesses, and how others perceive them to improve their skills as managers.

UNDERSTANDING OTHERS

Every individual is different. Each person has a different background as well as different attitudes, skills, and needs. A manager cannot treat everyone the same way. Some people want a great deal of support and regular communication from their supervisor; others do not. Some employees want managers to consult them when making important decisions, whereas others do not care to be involved in decision making. Some people work harder when praised; others expect managers to tell them when their work needs improvement.

Managers need to know the best way to work with each employee. They need to be able to satisfy individual workers' needs and, at the same time, accomplish the goals of the company. The leader who works hard to get to know each person and his or her needs will be a better manager.

COMMUNICATION

In Chapter 10, you learned the importance of communication in business. Managers spend much of their time communicating. When communication breakdowns occur, human relations problems will likely develop.

Managers must understand what information needs to be communicated and what methods to use. They need to know when too much communication is occurring and when there is not enough. Managers must have skill in using official communications channels and in understanding informal channels.

Managers do not just provide information, although they must be skilled in both written and oral communications. Listening is an important communication skill as well. By listening to employee concerns, managers can identify problems, determine needs, and respond to them more effectively.

Many human relations problems occur when managers fail to recognize the unique qualities and differences among employees. Should all employees be treated the same by a manager? Why or why not?

PHOTO: © GETTY IMAGES/PHOTODISC.

business *note*

Most workforces today are very diverse in terms of age, gender, education, race, nationality, and culture. Effective interaction and communication in a diverse environment can occur if you:

- are aware that your background may cause you to misunderstand others and that they might misinterpret your actions or statements.
- get to know people you work with. Socialize with and work to involve everyone. Treat everyone and their work with respect and high expectations.
- communicate with others in ways that they understand and make them most comfortable.
- encourage open dialogue about diversity issues. Don't hide or ignore them.
- avoid offensive actions and language and don't tolerate them from anyone.
- learn more about others' cultures and backgrounds through reading, travel, and attending cultural events.

The language used in communications is very important. Managers must communicate with employees in language they can understand and through their communication channels. When employees have concerns or are involved in planning and decision making, managers must convey their information to upper management.

TEAM BUILDING

People need to feel that they are a part of a team, that they are important, and that they can count on other team members for help. Team building means getting people to believe in the goals of the company and work well together to accomplish them. Teams that take responsibility for work and pride in the results reduce the amount of time managers must spend monitoring the team's work.

DEVELOPING JOB SATISFACTION

Most people who work at a job for a reasonable length of time are not totally satisfied or dissatisfied with their jobs. However, some people enjoy their work much more than others. An employee's feelings about work may be very different from one day to the next. There are many reasons for these differences. Job satisfaction can be influenced by factors such as the personal characteristics of employees and managers, individual needs, the people with whom the employees work, and the actual work itself.

Managers must be aware of the differences among their employees to help them maintain a high level of job satisfaction. For example, when two people with different backgrounds, values, and needs must work together, they may have trouble relating to each other. Managers must consider those differences when making job assignments to keep personal differences from interfering with the work. Managers may offer training and development opportunities to improve the human relations skills of employees to decrease the number of job problems.

People should be carefully matched with the kind of work they perform, because personal characteristics can affect job performance. A shy person, or one who enjoys working alone, might perform better as a computer data entry operator than as a salesperson. A person who does not pay close attention to details may not be an effective quality inspector on a production line. Human resources departments often test new employees or those seeking a promotion in order to match people with appropriate jobs. Whenever possible, managers should match the job tasks with the needs and interests of the employees and watch people when they begin new tasks to identify possible problems.

CHECKPOINT

What are five important human relations skills?

PHOTO: © GETTY IMAGES/PHOTODISC.

A satisfied employee is a more productive employee. How can employees be matched to the jobs they perform?

12.2 Assessment

UNDERSTAND MANAGEMENT CONCEPTS

Determine the best answer for each of the following questions.

1. Which of the following statements about leadership is true?
   a. For the most part, effective leaders are "born" with many leadership skills.
   b. Businesses prefer to develop the leadership skills of employees rather than hire people with those skills.
   c. The leader of a work team is usually the employees' manager.
   d. With proper training, most people can become effective leaders.
2. Getting people to believe in the goals of the company and work well together to accomplish them is called
   a. human relations
   b. team building
   c. management
   d. leadership

THINK CRITICALLY

Answer the following questions as completely as possible.

3. How would you demonstrate to a prospective employer that you have already developed some important leadership skills?
4. Which of the human relations skills do you believe are most important for a manager in working with employees? Justify your choice.

Xtra!
Study Tools
thomsonedu.com/school/bpmxtra

LIVERPOOL
JOHN MOORES UNIVERSITY
AVRIL ROBARTS LRC
TITHEBARN STREET
LIVERPOOL L2 2ER
TEL. 0151 231 4022

12.3 Leadership Styles

Goals
- Describe three views of employees that affect the amount of management supervision.
- Differentiate among three leadership styles.

Terms
- leadership style
- autocratic leader
- democratic leader
- open leader
- situational leader

Management Views of Employees

All management jobs include the same basic functions, but the way individual managers deal with employees may be very different. Managers' attitudes about people and work affect the way they do their jobs and treat the people they supervise. Good managers adjust their management style to the characteristics of the people they supervise and to the situation.

CLOSE MANAGEMENT

Some managers believe employees will not perform their work well unless they are closely managed. This attitude results from a feeling that employees are not very interested or motivated and work only because they get paid. With this attitude, managers are likely to assume that employees will not work any harder than necessary and will try to avoid responsibility. These managers expect that they will have to find ways to force employees to put forth the effort necessary for the organization to achieve its goals. They do not assume that employees will take individual initiative or be concerned about the quality of their work. Managers with these beliefs closely supervise and control employees and make all important decisions. They are likely to use rewards and penalties regularly to try to influence worker performance. They spend much of their time in close supervision of employees rather than on other management responsibilities.

LIMITED MANAGEMENT

Managers who believe employees generally enjoy their work relate to people in a very different way. These managers believe that the job meets many of the employees' personal needs. Employees who enjoy their work are motivated to do a good job. With this set of beliefs, managers assume that employees like personal responsibility and will take the initiative to solve problems, help others, and perform quality work. Employees with those characteristics do not need close supervision and control.

Managers with this set of beliefs ask people for their ideas on how to perform the work. They allow employees a great deal of control over their own work and do not apply immediate punishments or rewards. These managers spend more time on other management activities and less on close employee supervision.

Focus On...

Ethics–Costs Versus Jobs

EndCore is a packaging manufacturer. The third unit produces cardboard boxes. EndCore led the industry in total box sales for 20 years. However, during the past five years, it fell to fifth place in sales. Competing businesses had improved the quality of their products and were able to undercut EndCore in product prices.

EndCore employees were trained for specific production jobs that had changed little over time. Because of the declining performance, EndCore management decided it had to cut costs and improve sales. They decided to involve employees in the process, hoping that would help employees to accept any changes that needed to be made. The company made a commitment to the new approach and the teams were formed and trained for their new roles.

Now the unit three team had to find ways to reduce production costs. The team developed several methods to change the way work was done, and boxes were assembled for a cost savings of about 4 percent. This left the company's costs just slightly higher than those of competitors.

Then the team learned of a new automatic glue machine that was coming on the market. EndCore always hand-glued its boxes because the quality of the seals was much better. Gluing was a major part of the process, involving more than 15 percent of the employees. The new machine completely automated the gluing process and increased the speed with which boxes could be assembled. It had a 98 percent reliability rating—equal to that of the hand-gluing method. The cost of the machines was just under $1 million. However, the cost would be recovered in three years because production could be increased by 5 percent, with a reduction in labor costs of 12 percent. Using the gluing machines would put EndCore's costs below the competitor's by more than 2 percent.

The employee team had found a way to make the company competitive. But implementing it would mean at least 30 employees would lose their jobs.

Think Critically

1. What are advantages and disadvantages of the two solutions identified by the employee team from management's viewpoint and from employees' viewpoint?
2. What responsibility does the employee team have to management and to other employees in making a recommendation?
3. What recommendation do you believe the employee team should make? Why?

facts & figures

The management style of many women is well suited for the team-oriented leadership of today's businesses. Women tend to emphasize communications and positive work relationships. Those skills work well when managing a diverse workforce and motivating others through the use of influence rather than authority. Nevertheless, women hold about one-third of management positions and under 10 percent of executive positions.

FLEXIBLE MANAGEMENT

Studies have found that neither of these management views is correct for all employees and all jobs. Although many managers tend to favor one view over the other, managers who adjust their approach as circumstances change are likely to be more effective. For example, if there is some work that employees strongly dislike, closer supervision may be required. When employees are doing work they enjoy, managers may not need to supervise as closely. Flexibility in managers' views of employees permits flexibility in their treatment. Employees tend to prefer managers who are flexible enough to increase or decrease the amount of supervision as needed.

Managers can influence whether employees like or dislike their work. Newly hired employees are usually excited about the work and want to do a good job. Only if they decide that the work is not something they enjoy or they believe their manager does not trust them will they require additional management attention. However, new employees may be nervous and unsure of some of their job assignments. They will feel better if their supervisor is available to provide help and feedback on good performance.

Experienced employees who have demonstrated they can perform their jobs well will be upset if they receive very close supervision. They will believe their manager doesn't have confidence in them or is expecting them to make errors or work too slowly. Employees who have demonstrated they can perform their work well will have a positive view of their manager when they see their manager's trust.

If the employees do not seem to enjoy the work they are doing, managers can do some things to change their attitudes. Managers can work with the employees to determine the reasons for their feelings and to find out what they like and dislike about that type of work. The managers can find opportunities to involve employees, encourage and respect their ideas, and give them opportunities to do more of the type of work they enjoy. In that way, managers may begin to change employees' attitudes and gradually reduce the amount of supervision and control required.

CHECKPOINT

What are the views of employees that lead to close management and to limited management?

Leadership Styles

The general way a manager treats and supervises employees is called **leadership style**. It includes the way a manager gives directions, handles problems, and makes decisions. Leadership style is influenced by many factors, including the manager's preparation, experience, and beliefs about whether employees like or dislike work, and each manager has a slightly different style from all other managers. However, leadership styles fall into three general categories: autocratic, democratic, and open leadership.

AUTOCRATIC LEADERSHIP

The **autocratic leader** is one who gives direct, clear, and precise orders with detailed instructions as to what, when, and how work is to be done. With an autocratic leader, employees usually do not make decisions about the work they perform. When questions or problems arise, employees look to the manager to handle them. The autocratic manager seldom consults with employees about what should be done or the decisions to be made.

Efficiency is one of the reasons for using the autocratic style. The employees are supposed to do the work exactly the way the manager says—no surprises. Employees generally know what the manager expects. If they are in doubt about what to do or how to do it, they consult the manager. The autocratic leader believes that managers are in the best position to determine how to achieve the goals of the organization. They also assume that workers cannot or do not want to make decisions about their work.

Some workers prefer leaders with autocratic styles, but many do not. A major disadvantage of the autocratic style is that it discourages employees from thinking about better ways of doing their work. As a result, some employees become bored. This type of leadership may lead to employee dissatisfaction and a decline in their work performance. Human relations problems arise, especially between managers and employees, when managers use an autocratic leadership style extensively. Finally, the autocratic style does not prepare employees for leadership opportunities or promotion, because they do not gain experience in decision making or problem solving.

The autocratic style is effective in some situations. For example, it is often the best style to use in emergencies. Getting out a large rush order, for example, may not allow time for a supervisor to discuss the necessary procedures with employees. It is much more efficient for a supervisor to give specific orders and expect a rapid response. Managers may also need to use an autocratic style with temporary employees, such as part-time workers hired for short periods of time. The effective leader is one who knows when a situation calls for an autocratic style of leadership and uses it only until that situation is over.

DEMOCRATIC LEADERSHIP

The **democratic leader** is one who encourages workers to share in making decisions about their work and work-related problems. When using the democratic style, managers communicate openly with employees and discuss problems and solutions with them rather than merely announcing decisions. The manager may still make the final decision, but only after discussing possible solutions with employees and seeking their advice. Even when a decision is not involved, the democratic manager provides workers with assistance or encouragement and offers reasons about why certain work changes must occur. The principal characteristic of the democratic style, however, is that it encourages employees to participate in planning work, solving work problems, and making decisions.

Many people say they prefer a manager who uses a democratic style of leadership. Involvement in planning and decision making helps employees feel like active members of a team striving to reach common goals, rather than just workers putting in their time. They are more likely to carry out plans and decisions that they helped to create. Employees

Can you think of a business situation in which an autocratic leader may be more effective than a democratic or open leader? Explain why.

PHOTO: © DIGITAL VISION.

Technology *tip*

Employee activities that used to require close supervision can now be monitored with technology. Managers can use computers to access reports on each employee's work, including the time spent on various tasks and the amount and quality of production.

who see that managers have confidence in them are often highly motivated and, as a result, need not be as closely supervised.

As good as the democratic style may sound, however, it has limitations. Not all people like to participate in decisions. Some prefer to just do the work for which they were hired. Also, planning and discussing problems is time consuming. Furthermore, many jobs are fairly routine, with little opportunity for sharing in decision making. Employees will certainly be upset if managers ask them to help make only unimportant decisions or if they don't see management carefully considering their ideas.

The democratic leadership style is effective in many situations, especially when employees are committed to their jobs and want more responsibility. It is also effective with experienced, well-trained workers. When special problems arise and the manager wants as many helpful ideas as possible, the democratic style is effective.

OPEN LEADERSHIP

The **open leader** gives little or no direction to employees. Employees are expected to understand the work that needs to be done, and methods, details, and decisions are left to individual employees or teams. Employees are generally allowed to do their work with little management overview or involvement. Only when problems occur or major changes are implemented will the manager take a leadership role. Generally, employees concentrate on specific tasks and are not involved in the tasks of others.

The open style works best with experienced workers and in businesses where few major changes occur. If people have their own specialized jobs and are experts at them, the manager might use this style of leadership. If people work in many different locations, such as salespeople or home-based employees, the open style may work well. Managers will not be able to closely control employees' work because of their location, and getting together to make decisions may not be feasible.

Managers should be careful when using the open style of leadership with inexperienced employees or employees who are not used to making their own decisions. When employees are not confident in their abilities or do not trust that managers will let them make their own decisions, they are likely to be ineffective with the open style. When effective teamwork is required without training in team responsibilities, the open style can lead to confusion and lack of direction. Open leadership should be used very carefully and only after ensuring that employees are prepared for it and comfortable with the individual responsibility.

SITUATIONAL LEADERSHIP

We have seen in our discussion that effective management is very difficult. It requires understanding of the four management functions, development of leadership characteristics, and skill in selecting and using the most appropriate management style. The most effective managers use situational leadership. A **situational leader** understands employees and job requirements and matches his or her actions and decisions to the circumstances. For example, if a situational leader forms a team of experienced employees to work on a task, the leader will use an open style. If the team were composed of new employees, the leader might be more involved and provide greater direction, using a more democratic or even autocratic style.

Employees have different expectations of managers and want to work for an effective manager who understands them and their needs. Figure 12-3 lists the qualities most employees would like to see in their managers.

FIGURE 12-3 Employees prefer managers who demonstrate these leadership qualities.

Employees prefer a manager who:

1. Encourages employee participation and suggestions.
2. Keeps employees informed and shares employee ideas with upper management.
3. Works to build and maintain morale.
4. Is available to employees and easy to talk to.
5. Supports employee training and development.
6. Communicates effectively with employees.
7. Is considerate of the ideas and feelings of others.
8. Makes changes when needed rather than relying on past practices.
9. Supports employees who are doing their best even when mistakes are made.
10. Shows appreciation and provides recognition for good work.

CHECKPOINT

Under what circumstances could an autocratic leadership style be used effectively?

12.3 Assessment

UNDERSTAND MANAGEMENT CONCEPTS

Determine the best answer for each of the following questions.

1. Managers who use close management believe that
   a. employees generally enjoy their work
   b. experienced employees are able to perform their jobs well
   c. employees work only because they get paid
   d. none of the above
2. Of the four leadership styles, the one that most employees prefer is
   a. autocratic
   b. democratic
   c. open
   d. situational

THINK CRITICALLY

Answer the following questions as completely as possible.

3. Do you believe younger workers generally prefer a different leadership style from their supervisor than do older employees? Why or why not?
4. As a supervisor, which leadership style would work best for you?

Xtra!
Study Tools
thomsonedu.com/school/bpmxtra

12.4 Dealing with Employee Problems

Goals

- Recognize when and how to deal with the personal problems of employees.
- Discuss why work rules are needed in organizations.

- Describe how managers should respond to employee rules violations.

Term

- work rules

Sometimes employees face personal problems that affect their work. In most cases, the employee is able to resolve the problem, and the manager doesn't have to take any action. At other times, a manager just needs to be sympathetic by listening to employees and showing an understanding of their situation. These situations occur infrequently, such as when an employee has an ill child or is late to work because of a transportation problem. Many businesses develop procedures that allow employees to deal with those types of problems.

Handling Difficult Personal Problems

Managers are increasingly confronted with some personal problems of employees that are more serious. Problems such as drug or alcohol abuse, conflicts in personal relationships, or serious financial difficulties may result in employees being unable to perform their jobs well. Some of the personal problems have effects beyond the individual employee and begin to affect the performance and morale of coworkers. In those situations, managers must do more than give the employee an opportunity to resolve the personal issues.

Managers need to be aware of employees who are having difficulty on the job and try to determine the reasons for it. Then they need to work with the employee to get the necessary help to resolve the problem even if it is a personal issue.

Most managers are not trained to solve difficult personal problems, and they should not attempt to do so. But they should not ignore the problems either. Many businesses offer professional counseling and other services to help employees with personal problems. Managers need to make employees aware of those services and the importance of solving personal problems before they affect job performance. Managers should encourage employees to use the services available in the company when the problem first occurs. Then the manager should support the employee's decision to seek help. That usually means treating the problem confidentially and providing some accommodation for the employee's schedule while he or she works to solve the problem.

CHECKPOINT

What should managers do when confronting a difficult personal problem of an employee?

Applying Work Rules

One difficult management responsibility is dealing with employees who violate work rules. Work rules are regulations created to maintain an effective working environment in a business. Employees must meet certain expectations if a business is to operate effectively. Those expectations might deal with hours of work, care of equipment, worker safety, and relationships among employees and between employees and management.

Many companies have developed work rules that apply to all employees. Other companies have unique sets of rules for workers in different divisions or for employees with different job classifications. For businesses with negotiated agreements between the business and a labor union, the union contract specifies most work rules and the procedures for handling violations. Procedures sometimes include an oral warning for the first violation, a written warning entered into the personnel file for the second violation, a short suspension, and finally termination if the problem continues. Penalties are usually more severe for serious violations of work rules. Also, there are normally protections for employees in the procedures that include hearings, appeals of penalties, and union representation.

If a business does not have a formal set of work rules, each manager needs to develop procedures and policies that tell employees what the manager expects of them and how the manager will resolve problems if they occur. If managers do not communicate expectations to employees and do not handle problems in a reasonable and equitable way, they soon lose the respect of the employees. Managers who involve employees in developing rules and procedures usually find greater support for those rules and fewer problems when penalties need to be applied for rules violations. Guidelines for managers to follow in enforcing work rules are listed in Figure 12-4 (see p. 314).

CHECKPOINT
What are work rules and why are those rules needed?

Responding to Rules Violations

It is not easy for new managers to handle difficult employee situations, especially if they must reprimand or punish an employee. Managers do not want employees to dislike them or perceive their actions negatively. However, it is important that managers deal with those situations in a direct way rather than postponing or ignoring them. The result of not dealing with an obvious rule violation or other employee problem is that employees will not have clear expectations and will not know whether the manager intends to enforce the rules or not. Often if a manager ignores a problem created by an employee, the manager will remember the situation and wait for the employee to make another mistake. If that happens, even for a minor problem, the memory of the earlier problem will cause the manager to overreact to the new situation and confront the employee for both problems.

FIGURE 12-4 Managers must be objective, fair, and consistent when enforcing established work rules.

Management Guidelines for Enforcing Work Rules

1. Explain work rules and provide written copies of the rules to all employees.
2. Acquaint employees with penalties for work rule violations and make sure they understand the penalties as well as when and how they will be applied.
3. Investigate any violation thoroughly before taking action.
4. Consider any special circumstances before determining the violation and the penalty.
5. Act as soon as possible after investigating a violation and deciding on the action to be taken.
6. Inform the employee who violated a work rule of the rule that was violated, the penalty that will be applied, and the reason for the penalty.
7. Treat similar violations consistently.
8. Punish in private and praise in public.
9. Encourage employees to follow work rules by rewarding those who consistently follow the rules.

facts & figures

Recent studies have shown that rates of illicit drug and heavy alcohol use were higher among workers age 18–25 than among older workers, and higher among males than females. Rates were also higher among white non-Hispanics than among black non-Hispanics or Hispanics. In addition, rates were higher among those with less than a high school education than among those with a high school diploma or more education.

Reacting immediately, objectively, and firmly to rules violations is sometimes referred to as the "hot stove principle." We may remember as small children that if we touched a hot stove we got immediate feedback in the form of a burn and probably an immediate reprimand from an adult. Because of that feedback, we learned not to touch the hot stove again. In the same way, if an employee gets an immediate reprimand from a manager for a violation of the rules, the employee will pay more careful attention to the rules in the future.

Effective leaders handle many types of work-related problems confidently. Successful leaders understand human behavior and apply good management and human relations principles in working with people. They also continue to study and learn to improve their management skills. When conflicts and problems occur, leaders work to solve them before they create larger problems. They understand that they must help employees satisfy their own needs while also accomplishing the goals of the business.

CHECKPOINT

Why should managers apply the "hot stove principle" when responding to difficult employee situations?

An effective manager must be concerned about human relations within the work group. What should a manager do when it appears that a conflict is developing between two employees?

PHOTO: © GETTY IMAGES/PHOTODISC.

12.4 Assessment

UNDERSTAND MANAGEMENT CONCEPTS

Determine the best answer for each of the following questions.

1. When confronted with an employee's personal problem that affects the employee's work or that of other employees, the manager should
   a. allow the employee to work through the problem alone
   b. help the employee identify services offered by the business that will help solve the problem
   c. spend as much time as needed counseling the employee
   d. begin termination proceedings on the employee

2. Appropriate procedures for handling violations of work rules would include all of the following except
   a. providing a verbal warning for the first infraction
   b. ignoring minor violations and responding to major violations
   c. putting a written reprimand in the employee's file
   d. giving the employee a short suspension

THINK CRITICALLY

Answer the following questions as completely as possible.

3. Why should employee participation in a company's counseling program or other services to help with personal problems remain confidential?

4. Do you believe employees should be involved in establishing work rules? In developing penalties for violations of work rules? Justify your decisions.

Xtra! Study Tools
thomsonedu.com/school/bpmxtra

thomsonedu.com/school/bpmxtra

CHAPTER CONCEPTS

- One of the key qualities for managers at any level is effective leadership. Leaders have excellent human relations skills. Employees are most productive when work meets their needs as well as those of the company. Managers must work to satisfy important needs of each employee while also meeting the goals of the business. Four types of power available to managers are position power, reward power, expert power, and identity power.

- Important human relations skills are self-understanding, understanding others, communication, team building, and developing job satisfaction.

- The general way a manager treats and supervises employees is called leadership style. Leadership styles fall into three general categories: autocratic, democratic, and open leadership.

- Work rules are regulations created to maintain an effective working environment in a business. Employees must meet certain expectations if a business is to operate effectively. Effective leaders handle many types of work-related problems confidently. When conflicts and problems occur, leaders work to solve them before they create larger problems.

REVIEW TERMS AND CONCEPTS

Write the letter of the term that matches each definition. Some terms will not be used.

a. autocratic leader
b. democratic leader
c. expert power
d. human relations
e. identity power
f. leader
g. leadership
h. leadership style
i. open leader
j. position
k. power
l. reward power
m. self-understanding
n. situational leader
o. team building
p. work rules

1. The ability to control behavior
2. The general way a manager treats and supervises employees
3. Manager who gives little or no direction to employees
4. Power based on the ability to control rewards and punishments
5. Regulations created to maintain an effective working environment in a business
6. Power given to people because of their superior knowledge about the work
7. Manager who understands employees and job requirements and matches his or her actions and decisions to the circumstances
8. Manager who encourages workers to share in making decisions about their work and work-related problems
9. Manager who earns the respect and cooperation of employees to effectively accomplish the work of the organization
10. Getting people to believe in the goals of the company and work well together to accomplish them
11. How well people get along with each other when working together
12. Power given to people because others identify with and want to be accepted by them

DETERMINE THE BEST ANSWER

13. An employee who understands a particular work procedure very well and uses that information to help other employees has
    a. position power
    b. reward power
    c. expert power
    d. identity power

14. Which type of power is not related to leadership characteristics?
    a. expert
    b. position
    c. identity
    d. none of the above

15. Which of the following statements about leadership in business is *not* true?
    a. Leadership qualities can be improved through training and personal development.
    b. Employees as well as managers need leadership skills.
    c. Even when a manager is a part of a work group, the leader of the group will not always be the manager.
    d. All of the answers are true.

16. An effective work team has all of the following characteristics except
    a. the manager monitors the work of the team closely
    b. employees feel that they are a part of the team
    c. an employee can count on other team members for help
    d. All of the answers are correct.

17. A manager who believes that employees are not very interested or motivated by their work will use
    a. close management
    b. limited management
    c. flexible management
    d. democratic management

18. A manager who discusses possible solutions with employees and seeks their advice before making a decision is a
    a. democratic leader
    b. autocratic leader
    c. open leader
    d. situational leader

APPLY WHAT YOU KNOW

19. Based on the Business Reality scenario at the beginning of the chapter, do you believe the executive of a large company and the mayor of a large city need the same leadership characteristics? Why or why not?

20. How is effective human relations related to effective leadership?

21. Using Figure 12-1, select the five most important leadership characteristics you believe are needed by business managers. Justify your choices.
22. Provide several examples of a manager using power inappropriately. Now provide other examples of how a manager uses power appropriately.
23. During the recruitment and selection process, how can businesses identify new employees that are likely to be effective leaders?
24. Why must managers have self-understanding before they can effectively understand their employees?

MAKE CONNECTIONS

25. **Creativity** Form a team of at least three classmates or join a team assigned by your teacher. Select one of the five human relations skills discussed in the chapter or use the skill assigned to you by your teacher. Think of a situation that could occur in a business that demonstrates the effective or ineffective use of that skill. Then prepare a short script of dialogue between a manager and one or more employees that illustrates the situation. Your script should contain at least four statements by each of the participants. Prepare to role-play the situation for your classmates using the script. Students from other teams should attempt to determine which human relations skill you are demonstrating and whether the role-play demonstrates a positive or negative example of the skill.
26. **Technology** Identify someone you believe is a good manager. Interview the person to determine his or her beliefs about (a) the use of power by a manager, (b) whether people need close or limited supervision, and (c) leadership style. Using a computer, prepare three or more charts that list the major points on these topics from the textbook and compare these points with the viewpoints of the manager you interviewed. Share your findings in an oral report with your class, using a computer graphics presentation program if possible.
27. **Teamwork** With a group of your class members, brainstorm things supervisors can do to increase the job satisfaction of workers. Identify the things that would have a direct cost to the business and those that could be provided with no real cost to the business. Compare the list developed by your group with those of other groups in your class. Try to reach agreement among the groups on the top five factors that your class feels would work for teenage employees. Then see if you can agree on five factors that the class believes would be most effective for employees over 30 years of age. Discuss reasons for any differences between the two lists.
28. **Writing** Compare the list of management guidelines for enforcing work rules in Figure 12-4 with the procedures used by administrators and teachers to enforce the rules in your school. Develop a one-page report that compares the similarities and differences and explains in your view why those similarities and differences exist.

CASE IN POINT

CASE 12-1: Supervising a New Work Group

Rita Meyers had been a supervisor of five research specialists in her company's marketing department for nearly two years. She had been promoted to the position after working as an employee in marketing for eight years. At the time of her promotion, she had more experience than the specialists she supervised. She had even helped train three of them when they were first hired by the company. The workers thought a great deal of Rita. In fact, many of them said she was the best supervisor they had ever had.

Rita's manager, Jesse Suarez, was most impressed with the good relations among the employees and with the excellent work Rita's department did. Mr. Suarez was so impressed he decided to help Rita advance into middle management in the near future. He felt that supervising a larger work team would be an important step in Rita's development. There was an opening for a supervisor of 10 data entry specialists in the accounting department. Even though Rita had not worked in accounting, she did have experience with computer systems and data entry as part of her marketing work. Jesse thought she would be perfect in the new job and would enjoy working with a new group of employees.

After only two months, however, Jesse received several complaints from the employees Rita was supervising in the accounting department. It seemed that her relationships with the new group were not as positive as with the employees in the marketing department. Also the work output had declined steadily since she had taken over as supervisor.

"What's happening, Rita?" Jesse asked when they met to discuss the problem. "Why isn't it working out? You're the same person who was so effective in the marketing department. What has changed?"

Rita responded, "I don't know. In the marketing department, I always discussed problems with the workers, and as a group we worked out solutions acceptable to everyone. Those employees wanted to be involved. In accounting, no one wants to discuss problems and solutions. They say they don't have time to meet as a group. They say solving problems is what a supervisor is for. You know that's not my style. I like to spend time with employees, help them, and get them to feel like a team. I don't feel I should make decisions on important problems without at least talking with them."

THINK CRITICALLY

1. Is it possible that a person might be an effective leader in one situation but not in another? Explain.
2. What type of leadership style does Rita practice?
3. What do you recommend that Jesse and Rita do to improve the situation in the accounting department?
4. If you could have talked to Rita before she moved from marketing to accounting, what recommendations would you have made to help her avoid the problem she encountered?

CASE 12-2: Enforcing Company Policies

Mikayla Fletcher was very upset because she had just suspended one of the employees she supervised, Dylan Holcomb. Although he was a good worker, he had begun to develop a problem with coming to work on time. Once and sometimes twice a week, he was 5 to 10 minutes late. Although he was usually not very late, the tardiness was frequent and caused hard feelings among Dylan's coworkers. They often had to wait for him to show up before they could continue with an important project.

The company had a policy on employee tardiness: a half-hour of pay was deducted for any part of 15 minutes the employee was late. If the employee was late more than 30 minutes, a verbal warning was given the first time, a written warning was given the second time, and the employee would be suspended for one week without pay the third time.

Dylan didn't seem to mind losing the money when he was late, and he had never been tardy to the point Mikayla had to issue a warning. However, because it was a continuing issue, Mikayla decided to talk with him informally about the problem. Dylan didn't seem overly concerned and simply said he would try to do better. Following the conversation, he had been on time for several weeks. Then, two weeks ago, he was 35 minutes late one day. Last Thursday he was late by 50 minutes. Following company policy, Mikayla gave him both a verbal and written warning.

Yesterday the city was hit by a heavy snowstorm. Because roads in the area were very slippery early in the morning, the company decided that employees who were late would not be penalized. Mikayla was surprised when Dylan showed up on time. He said he had used his new four-wheel-drive vehicle and had fun driving to work through the snow.

Today Mikayla was furious when Dylan walked in 40 minutes late. She confronted him and told him he was suspended. Dylan accused Mikayla of being unfair. He said the battery on his new vehicle had failed; otherwise, he would have been on time. Besides, the company hadn't penalized employees for tardiness yesterday when he had been on time. Because of that, he didn't feel he should be penalized today.

THINK CRITICALLY

1. What are the advantages and disadvantages of a policy such as the one described in the case?
2. Do you believe Mikayla should have suspended Dylan under the circumstances? Why or why not?
3. Do you believe Dylan was justified in his claim that Mikayla was being unfair? Support your answer.
4. What do you think Mikayla should do after Dylan returns from his suspension?

YOUR LEADERSHIP STYLE

If your business is successful, it will likely grow either by adding more employees to the current location or by opening additional locations. When you are the sole employee of a business, your primary responsibilities will be as a manager. However, as you add employees, you will take on the role of leader as well as manager. With more locations and more employees, leadership responsibilities become more complex and more important. You will need to earn the respect, confidence, and support of employees so they will want to do a good job. All employees will recognize you as their manager, although they may not view you as an effective leader unless you understand leadership and develop effective leadership skills.

Some new business owners have a difficult time developing and enforcing work rules. They didn't need rules when they were the sole employee or when the first few employees were hired. Many new managers believe that most employees want to do a good job. They try to avoid conflicts and don't want to have to reprimand or fire employees. They see work rules as difficult to develop and enforce and believe they build a wall between the business owner and the employees.

The activities below focus on analyzing your leadership style and preparing for your role as leader. You will prepare a plan to increase your leadership skills. You will also consider an initial set of work rules that you can use as you expand your business.

DATA COLLECTION

1. Write down brief descriptions of each leadership style. Give them to family members, teachers, or close friends. Ask them to identify the description that best expresses the way you work with people. Summarize their responses. Do you have a clear-cut leadership style?
2. Contact the owner or manager of a restaurant or fast-food business. Ask to review the company's employee handbook. Identify the work rules. Discuss the rules with the owner or manager to determine how effective the rules are in helping the person manage the business.

ANALYSIS

1. Using the information you collected on your leadership style in the Data Collection section above, do you agree or disagree with the responses of others? If you disagree, why do you believe others' view of your style differs from your own view? Develop a written statement of what you can do during this school year to increase your leadership skills. What leadership or career development activities are available through your local career and technical student organization or other school or community organization?
2. Develop at least 5 work rules for your business. Consider attendance and absences, relationships with others, safety, care of equipment, and other employee responsibilities.

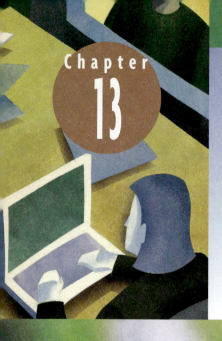

Planning and Organizing

13.1 The Planning Function

13.2 Using Planning Tools

13.3 The Organizing Function

13.4 Developing Effective Organizations

REALITY CHECK

Not So Fast!

Eldron Huntley was excited after attending a seminar titled "Moving Your Business to the Internet." He felt he had discovered a whole new idea for expanding his 10-year-old catering business.

People told Eldron that he offered menu items they could not find anywhere else. In addition, they could always count on the quality and great taste of the meals. Customers who had moved from the area frequently called his business to purchase their favorite meals. Eldron had been looking for ways to serve those customers and others like them.

At the seminar Eldron attended, the speaker explained the growth of Internet commerce and suggested that any business with a successful product should consider using the Internet to expand its market. That was just the idea Eldron was looking for. Most of his out-of-town business currently came from the word-of-mouth recommendations of satisfied customers. The Internet provided a way to affordably get his business name and menu to people all over the country.

Eldron estimated it would take about $80,000 for the computer hardware and software for reliable Internet service; an additional $200,000 to expand his food preparation and shipping facilities; and probably $50,000 to pay the expenses of additional personnel for several months until adequate sales were generated to meet the payroll costs. He anticipated the new business would ultimately result in a nice profit. He scheduled a meeting with his banker to request a loan for the expansion.

The banker was not quite as excited as Eldron. She explained, "Everyone seems to want to use the Internet for their business. I agree it has a lot of potential, but there are no guarantees you'll be successful. Before I can loan you the money you want, I'll need to see a business plan that demonstrates how you'll repay the loan. Who will be your customers and competitors? How much will each customer buy and what will they be willing to pay? Will this new business affect your ability to serve your current customers? What will it cost to ship the food to customers so that it arrives in perfect condition? When do you expect the new part of your business to start making a profit?" Eldron recognized that the answers to those questions were important but had not thought about preparing a written plan.

13.1 | The Planning Function

Goals
- Recognize the importance of planning to business success.
- Differentiate between strategic and operational planning.

Terms
- strategic planning
- operational planning
- SWOT analysis
- mission statement
- vision

Why Plan?

New businesses are started every day, and existing businesses regularly look for opportunities to expand. At the same time, many new and existing businesses fail. Most often that failure can be blamed to a large extent on a failure to adequately plan. Owners and managers who can effectively plan for a business's future are much more likely to be successful than those who concentrate only on day-to-day operations. Planning is a specific management activity and needs to be done carefully. Managers need to know how to plan and how to use some specific planning tools and procedures.

THE VALUE OF A BUSINESS PLAN

Eldron's banker reminded him that he had to plan carefully in order to make the best decisions about starting and managing his Internet business. Poor planning could result in huge losses and the possible failure of his existing business. However, the correct decision could result in a much larger business, higher profits, and a great deal of personal satisfaction.

In Chapter 5, you learned that a *business plan* is a written description of the nature of the business, its goals and objectives, and how they will be achieved. Review the elements of a business plan listed in Figure 5-1 on page 114. Planning how to achieve objectives includes analyzing the opportunities and risks the business faces. The business plan is an important tool for any business that is planning a major change. It includes a detailed financial analysis showing the potential profitability that should result from the planned operations.

Business plans may be brief and simple for a new small business. On the other hand, written plans for a large, existing business may be very long and complex. Large multinational businesses generally have more than one business plan. Each part of the business develops its own plan to guide its operations. However, all of the plans must work toward the same overall objectives. The top corporate executives and planning specialists work with all parts of the business to coordinate planning and to approve each unit's plans.

If Eldron Huntley develops an effective business plan, he will have long-range goals and directions for the business as well as specific plans for operations, marketing, financial management, and human resource decisions. The plan will address the new Internet business activities but also provide plans for the continuing operation of the existing business. As a result of completing the business plan, Eldron will have given much more thought to both the new and current business activities. He will have a greater understanding of what will be required to make both parts successful. His banker will have the information needed to determine if granting the requested loan is a wise business decision. The business plan will give the banker greater confidence that Eldron has carefully considered the new opportunity and knows what needs to be done to add it to his business. The banker is much more likely to make a positive decision about the loan when there is a carefully developed written plan.

THE IMPORTANCE OF PLANNING

Not all managers are responsible for preparing a business plan. However, all managers are involved in planning in some way. Their decisions may be bigger or smaller than Eldron Huntley's. Some managers make complex, expensive decisions, such as whether to build a new $20 million factory or expand operations into another country. Other managers develop very short-term plans, such as an employee work schedule for the next week.

Planning is probably the most important management activity. It sets the direction for the business and establishes specific goals. Plans serve as guides for making decisions. Managers also use their plans to determine whether the business is making progress. Planning also helps managers communicate with each other and with their employees and coordinate the activities of the business. Careful planning encourages managers to be more specific and objective in their decisions.

Planning in a large business is somewhat like assembling a jigsaw puzzle. Each piece must mesh with the others around it in order to assemble the entire puzzle. One missing or broken piece affects the look of the entire puzzle. Large businesses require a great deal of coordination to avoid problems, conflicts, and missed opportunities. Shared planning allows managers from various parts of the business to understand how their work affects other parts of the business. They are also able to recognize when coordinated efforts are needed. Each part of the organization's plan must "fit together" for a successful business.

PHOTO: © GETTY IMAGES/PHOTODISC.

Managers are involved in planning as specific as approving a vacation schedule or as broad as acquiring a new factory. How do you think the procedures used for planning would be different in each of those situations?

CHECKPOINT

How is planning in a large organization similar to assembling a jigsaw puzzle?

Levels of Planning

Managers plan on two levels—strategic planning and operational planning. **Strategic planning** is long-term and provides broad goals and direction for the entire business. **Operational planning** is short-term and identifies specific activities for each area of the business.

STRATEGIC PLANNING

Many important changes in a business require planning over a long period of time. Developing and producing a new product line can take more than a year. Building a new factory in another country may require several years for planning and construction.

When Eldron Huntley prepares his business plan, he will be involved in strategic planning. The banker was telling him that he should not make the decision to expand his business quickly without carefully considering how to do it. Managers need a great deal of information to determine if a particular decision will be profitable. Strategic planning provides the needed information and procedures for making effective decisions about the direction and goals of a business. Figure 13-1 describes the steps in strategic planning.

The external and internal analyses (steps 1 and 2 of Figure 13-1) are often referred to as SWOT analysis. **SWOT analysis** is the examination of the organization's internal *Strengths* and *Weaknesses* as well as the *Opportunities* and *Threats* from its external environment. *Internal factors* are all of those things within a business that managers can influence and control to help accomplish business plans. *External factors* are those things operating outside of the business that managers cannot control but that may influence the success of business plans.

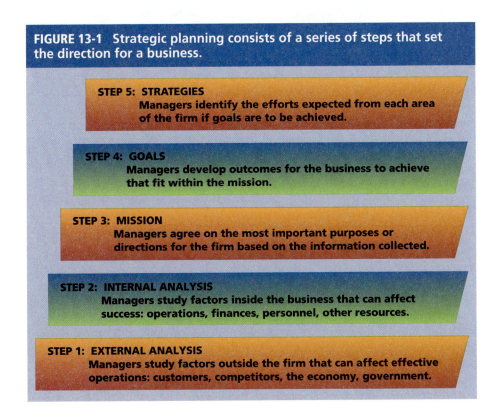

FIGURE 13-1 Strategic planning consists of a series of steps that set the direction for a business.

STEP 5: STRATEGIES
Managers identify the efforts expected from each area of the firm if goals are to be achieved.

STEP 4: GOALS
Managers develop outcomes for the business to achieve that fit within the mission.

STEP 3: MISSION
Managers agree on the most important purposes or directions for the firm based on the information collected.

STEP 2: INTERNAL ANALYSIS
Managers study factors inside the business that can affect success: operations, finances, personnel, other resources.

STEP 1: EXTERNAL ANALYSIS
Managers study factors outside the firm that can affect effective operations: customers, competitors, the economy, government.

Technology *tip*

In step 1 of the analysis, managers identify any opportunities for expanding and improving the business and any threats the company faces from competition, changes in the economy, new laws and regulations, technology improvements, and other factors outside the company. For example, Eldron Huntley identified an opportunity when he noticed that customers from outside his operating area wanted to have his meals shipped to them. The seminar helped him recognize that new Internet technology provided a low-cost way to reach those customers.

In step 2, managers evaluate the organization's own capabilities and weaknesses. A company has successful products, experienced employees, financial resources, and well-organized operations. On the other hand, it may be experiencing operational or financial problems, or may have outdated facilities and equipment or limited access to new employees. All of those factors can contribute to the success or failure of business plans. Eldron Huntley identified his company's strengths as the unique menu items and dependable quality and taste. His banker questioned whether Eldron currently had the capability to distribute his quality products to a large number of customers across the country. Managers want to build on the company's strengths and reduce its weaknesses whenever possible.

In step 3, managers describe and agree on the business's mission. A **mission statement** is a short, specific statement of the business's purpose and direction. The mission flows out of a broad, lasting, and often inspirational **vision** of the company's reason for existing. For example, Huntley's vision statement for his company might be "to become a leading provider of memorable meals to celebrate life's special occasions." His mission statement, then, might be "to prepare high-quality meals at reasonable prices to satisfy the tastes of our customers when and where they want them." Steps 4 and 5 then use the planning information and the mission to set specific goals for the company and descriptions of activities and resources needed to achieve the goals. We will study the process of establishing goals and strategies in the next lesson.

The top executives in a business are responsible for strategic planning. A careful and objective process is followed to prepare the strategic plan. The executives use information collected from lower-level managers, from the company's employees and operations, and from other sources. Large companies may have a special planning and research department to collect and analyze information and to develop proposals for executives to consider. Smaller companies may hire research firms or consultants to help with strategic planning. New and small businesses may be able to obtain planning assistance from state and federal government agencies such as the Small Business Administration and economic development offices or from the business departments of area colleges and universities.

OPERATIONAL PLANNING

A good strategic plan tells managers where the business is going. The managers must then take action to move the business toward those goals. Operational planning determines how work will be done, who will do it, and what resources will be needed to get the work done in a specific area of the business.

Operational plans in a factory could include developing department budgets, planning inventory levels and purchases of raw materials, setting production levels for each month, and preparing employee work schedules. Operational planning in a marketing department might include the development of promotional plans, identifying training needed by salespeople, deciding how to support retailers who will handle the product, and selecting pricing methods. A great deal of the operational planning in a business is the responsibility of middle-level managers and supervisors and even some experienced employees.

Operational plans are based on the business's strategic plan and are developed after the strategic plan is completed. Operational plans determine what resources will be required and how they will be used. Therefore, operational planning influences the amount and type of equipment and supplies needed, the number of employees and the training they require, work schedules, payroll, operating budgets, and many other factors. Operational plans direct the day-to-day activities of a business and largely determine whether the strategic plan of the business will be successful or not. The tools and procedures for completing operational planning are discussed in the next lesson.

CHECKPOINT
What is the difference between strategic and operational planning?

13.1 Assessment

UNDERSTAND MANAGEMENT CONCEPTS

Determine the best answer for each of the following questions.

1. Planning provides all of the following benefits to a company *except*
   a. encouraging managers to be more specific and objective in their decisions
   b. helping managers to determine whether the business is making progress
   c. ensuring a business will be successful and profitable
   d. Planning provides all these benefits.

2. The internal and external analysis completed by businesses as a part of planning is often referred to as
   a. PERT
   b. SWOT
   c. ABCD
   d. KISS

THINK CRITICALLY

Answer the following questions as completely as possible.

3. Why should top executives in a company be responsible for strategic planning but involve lower-level managers and employees in the planning process?

4. How can a clear and meaningful vision and mission statement help increase employee motivation and enthusiasm for a business plan?

Xtra!
Study Tools
thomsonedu.com/school/bpmxtra

13.2 Using Planning Tools

Goals
- Identify the characteristics of effective goals.
- Describe several planning tools and how they are used.

Terms
- goal
- schedule
- standard
- policies
- procedure

Establishing Direction

It has been said that you will never know when you have arrived if you don't know where you are going. Goals provide that direction for a business. A **goal** is a specific statement of a result the business expects to achieve. All types and sizes of businesses and all parts of a business need to develop goals.

Goals keep the business focused on where it wants to be in the future and the results it expects to accomplish. Managers and employees may overreact to short-term problems or the actions of competitors if goals are not clearly stated and communicated. Managers in large companies may take actions that conflict with those of other managers if they are not aware of goals. Here are several characteristics of effective goals:

1. *Goals must be specific and meaningful.* The goal "to make a profit" is vague. However, the goal "to increase sales by $25,000 in the next six months" is much more specific. Goals should relate to the activities and operations of the business so that employees see how their work relates to the goals.

   Managers must be careful in setting goals and must consider such factors as (1) the general economic conditions facing the business, (2) past sales and profits, (3) the demand for products and services, (4) the reactions of current and prospective customers, (5) the resources of the business, (6) the actions of competitors, and (7) any other factors that can influence the achievement of the goals.

2. *Goals must be achievable.* It is important that goals move the company forward, but they must also be realistic. It is not useful to set a goal "to increase unit sales by 5 percent" if the company does not have the capability of manufacturing that many more units. If telemarketing salespeople are already completing many more calls each day than the industry average, it may not be realistic to set a higher goal for completing calls without increasing the number of salespeople.

3. *Goals should be clearly communicated.* Company and departmental goals should be communicated to all employees, because they will be responsible for accomplishing those goals. Communicating the company's goals will help employees understand that they are part of a team effort working together for a common purpose. Usually, they will work harder to achieve goals they understand.

4. *Goals should be consistent with each other and with overall company goals.* Each department within a business has its own specific goals, but the goals must be coordinated with those of other departments. Assume, for example, that the sales manager sets a goal of increasing sales in a specific area of the country. The advertising manager, however, sets a goal of reducing expenditures in the same area to use the money for a new-product introduction that will occur in another part of the country. If advertising is needed to support the sales efforts, the managers have conflicting goals. Managers must work together so that their goals will complement each other and support the overall company goals.

CHECKPOINT

Identify the four characteristics of effective goals.

Planning Tools

All managers must develop skills in planning. There are a number of tools that can help in developing effective plans: budgets, schedules, standards, policies, procedures, and research.

BUDGETS

The most widely used planning tool is the budget. A *budget* is a specific financial plan. Financial budgets assist managers in determining the best way to use available money to reach goals. As a part of Eldron Huntley's business plan, his banker will require him to develop a budget for the new Internet business. This budget will help both Eldron and the banker see how much money he will need as well as if and when the new part of the business can be profitable. When department managers complete operational planning, they will prepare budgets for their departments. In addition to the financial budget, the managers often prepare budgets for personnel expenses, production costs, advertising, inventories of materials and supplies, and many others. You will learn more about budgets in Chapter 15.

SCHEDULES

Just as budgets help in financial planning, schedules are valuable in planning for the most effective use of time. For most business purposes, a schedule is a time plan for reaching objectives. Schedules identify the tasks to be completed by a department or individual and the approximate time required to complete each task. A supervisor may develop a schedule to organize the work done by each employee for a day or a week

business *note*

E-mail is now a common and well-accepted method of business communication. However, it must be used carefully and professionally. Bad habits developed when sending personal e-mail and instant messages are usually not acceptable in business situations. Writing clear, concise e-mail messages becomes easier with practice. Consider the following guidelines:

- Restrict your message to one main idea. This will help ensure the recipient understands it.
- Compose a short, clear subject line that reflects the main idea.
- Use tables or visual aids, if appropriate. With most e-mail systems, supporting information can be included as attachments to the main message.
- Use headings in long messages, to guide the reader.
- Number items in a list so the reader will easily recognize each point and can respond to a specific item if required.
- Proofread your message, because errors and typos interfere with clear communication. Misunderstandings and bad feelings can occur if e-mail messages are not carefully planned and written.

FIGURE 13-2 Schedules are important planning tools. A work schedule is one example.

WORK SCHEDULE FOR JULY 23		SPECIAL ORDER DEPARTMENT	
Employee	Order 532	Order 533	Order 534
Shenker, M.	X		
Duffy, P.		X	
Gaston, S.			X
Robinson, J.			X
Kingston, C.		X	

(see Figure 13-2). Production managers use schedules to plan the completion and shipment of orders. Salespeople use schedules to plan their sales calls efficiently, and advertising people use schedules to make sure the ads appear at the correct time and in the proper media. Office managers need to schedule the preparation and printing of mailings and reports to make sure they are completed on time.

STANDARDS

Another planning tool for managers is the use of standards. A **standard** is a specific measure against which something is judged. Businesses set quality standards for the products and services they produce. Managers then compare the products against the standards to judge whether or not the quality is acceptable. Companies also set standards for the amount of time that tasks should take. For example, a fast-food restaurant may set a standard that customers will receive their food within three minutes of placing their orders. If managers see that customers are getting their food five minutes after ordering, then the service time is not meeting company standards and is therefore not acceptable. Companies may also set standards for the number of defective products allowed on an assembly line or the number of calls a salesperson must make during a day.

Managers are responsible for setting realistic standards and for using those standards to judge performance. They also must know when to revise outdated standards. In Chapter 14, you will learn how standards are used to control work as well as to plan.

POLICIES

As part of planning, managers frequently establish policies. **Policies** are guidelines used in making decisions regarding specific, recurring situations. A policy is often a general rule to be followed by the entire business or by specific departments. Remember the discussion of work rules in Chapter 12? Work rules are examples of business policies.

A broad policy may state that the performance of each employee must be evaluated at least twice a year using the company's performance review procedures. Because of that policy, even an employee who has been with the company for 10 years must be evaluated. Policies help to reduce misunderstandings and encourage consistent decisions for similar conditions by all managers and employees.

PROCEDURES

A **procedure** is a list of steps to be followed for performing certain work. In order to implement the policy described in the previous paragraph, the company must develop specific performance review procedures. For routine tasks, procedures improve business efficiency and are of special help to employees who are learning a new job. The procedure shown in Figure 13-3 would be a great help to a new employee in the catalog order department of the Johnson Company. Experienced employees can help managers design new procedures and improve old ones.

RESEARCH

To do a good job of planning, managers need a great deal of information. To develop budgets, they need to know how money was spent in past years, what certain tasks will cost, and how competitors are spending their money. Managers can improve schedules if they know how long certain jobs take to complete. They

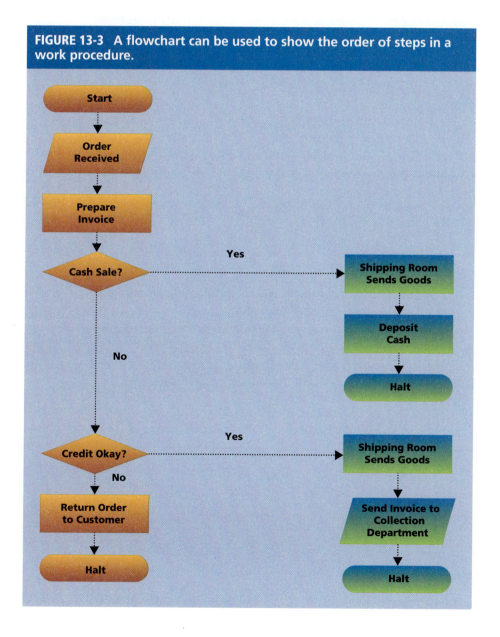

FIGURE 13-3 A flowchart can be used to show the order of steps in a work procedure.

can establish better standards and procedures by analyzing carefully collected information on the way jobs are performed. Research is done to collect data for managers and to provide the information needed to improve their planning decisions.

CHECKPOINT
What is the difference between a policy and a standard?

13.2 Assessment

UNDERSTAND MANAGEMENT CONCEPTS

Determine the best answer for each of the following questions.

1. The goal "to increase the average productivity of all work teams by 3 percent within six months" is an example of which characteristic of an effective goal?
   a. specific and meaningful
   b. achievable
   c. clearly communicated
   d. consistent with each other

2. Guidelines used in making decisions regarding specific, recurring situations are called
   a. standards
   b. policies
   c. procedures
   d. goals

THINK CRITICALLY

Answer the following questions as completely as possible.

3. How does the use of effective goals increase the chances that business plans will be successful? Discuss each of the characteristics of an effective goal.

4. How can businesses use information from competitors and customers when establishing quality standards for their products and services?

Xtra!
Study Tools
thomsonedu.com/school/bpmxtra

13.3 The Organizing Function

Goals
- Describe factors that managers should consider when organizing work.
- Discuss how the characteristics of good organization contribute to a more effective work environment.

Terms
- organization chart
- responsibility
- authority
- accountability
- unity of command
- span of control

Organizing Work

Before a plan can be put into operation, the company must be organized to carry out the plan and perform work effectively. In Chapter 11, you learned that *organizing* is concerned with determining how plans can be accomplished most effectively and arranging resources to complete work. More specifically, it involves arranging resources and relationships between departments and employees and defining the responsibility each has for accomplishing work. For example, when the plan is to start manufacturing a new product, managers must determine who is involved in accomplishing each part of the job. Making a new product would probably involve these departments: research, manufacturing, human resources, marketing and sales, finance, and information technology. Department managers would then determine the responsibilities of the people within their departments.

THE ROLE OF ORGANIZATION CHARTS

An organization chart is a drawing that shows the structure of an organization, major job classifications, and the reporting relationships among the organization's personnel. Figure 13-4 (see p. 334) is an example of an organization chart for a retail business. The purposes of the organization chart are to (1) show the major work units that make up the business, (2) allow employees to identify which unit they are affiliated with, how it relates to other units, and to whom they are accountable, and (3) identify lines of authority and formal communication within the organization.

Large organizations usually provide new employees information through an employee handbook or on the company's Web site that explains the organization of the business and shows an organization chart. By understanding an organization chart, employees have some idea of where and how they fit into the company, how the organization works, and possible promotion opportunities. As changes occur in an organization through reorganization of work or when major operating units are bought and sold, the company's organization chart can become outdated. To be a useful management and communication tool, the chart should be revised when changes occur in the organizational structure.

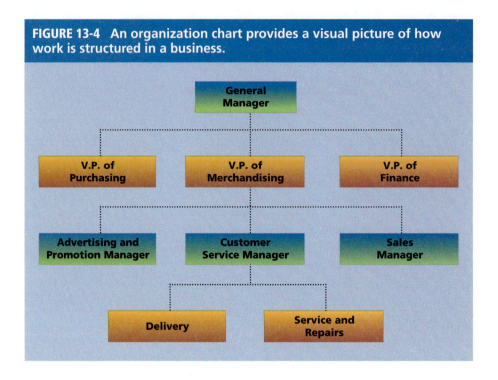

FIGURE 13-4 An organization chart provides a visual picture of how work is structured in a business.

THE PROCESS OF ORGANIZING WORK

The manager of a new business has the complicated task of organizing the entire structure of the business. A manager for an ongoing business cannot ignore the organization function either. The organization may need to change, for example, when goals are revised or when the business expands. Using the example from the beginning of the chapter, if Eldron Huntley is successful in developing the new Internet business, he will have a very different organization than before the expansion. It is not likely that the current organizational structure and employees will be able to accommodate all of the new activities and the extra workload. He will need to carefully organize the business to perform the new activities efficiently while still maintaining the existing business activities. If he does not pay attention to the organization of the work, the business may not be able to adjust to the changes.

Whether the focus is on a new or existing department, division, or firm, the process of organizing involves three elements: (1) the division of work, (2) the facilities and working conditions, and (3) the employees.

DIVISION OF WORK In establishing an organization structure, the total work to be done must be divided into units, such as departments. The first consideration is the grouping of activities into broad, natural divisions, such as buying and selling or production, marketing, and administration. For small businesses, only two or three divisions may be needed to separate the work into manageable units. For large businesses with many employees and activities, the major divisions will need to be divided several times into departments or work units of reasonable size. Departments should be organized around meaningful and related work, work should flow smoothly within and among departments, and employees should be assigned to the units where they have expertise to complete that work.

Major divisions of work vary with the type of industry and business. A small retailer will usually organize around the major activities of purchasing and selling. Manufacturing will have purchasing, production, and marketing. Most businesses have departments or work units for administration, information management, and human resources. For effective management and control, even small businesses benefit from organizing work into related and manageable units.

As a business grows, the number of major divisions will increase or existing divisions will be reorganized. When the small retailer expands, the basic selling division may be subdivided. A larger marketing division may be established and subdivided into advertising and promotion, personal selling, and customer service. Determining how to divide work into efficient units is based on (1) the type of work to be done in each unit and (2) the amount of work to be done. The organization charts shown in Figures 13-5, 13-6, and 13-7 (see p. 336) point out how a business may grow from a one-person enterprise into a partnership with specialized duties, then expand as additional employees are hired and assigned specialized duties including supervision and management.

A small business needs good organization just as much as a large organization. Management problems often begin to occur in a small business when employees are added but work responsibilities and relationships are not clear. Making organizing decisions as a small business expands may not at first result in a formal organization chart. However, the business's work should be carefully examined and assigned to specific employees. If there is not an organization chart, the work responsibilities, the relationships among employees, and their authority should be made clear to everyone.

For example, the owner of a retail business that sells and services home appliances hires two employees, A and B. The owner is responsible for management of the business and is involved in both selling and service as time permits. Employee A is given responsibility for appliance sales and is the contact with the businesses from which the company purchases appliances. Employee A is also in charge of the business when the owner is absent. Employee B is responsible for appliance service and repair and has the authority to make decisions related to customer relationships after the customer has purchased a product from the business. These organizational decisions clearly identify the work to be done by and the relationships among the people involved. The example illustrates how even very small organizations can develop an effective organizational structure and manage work.

FACILITIES AND WORKING CONDITIONS While divisions of work are being established, the physical aspects of organizing must also be considered. These aspects include providing the necessary equipment and materials for employees to be able to complete their work, and arranging the layout of the facilities so that all work flows smoothly and provides the best working conditions possible.

Work should move through the business as efficiently as possible. Employees should not have to waste time, and the work of one group should not delay the work of others. A mechanic repairing an automobile, for example, should have ready access to the needed tools and parts close to the work area. If special parts are needed, a system to quickly order and obtain the parts should be in place so the repairs are not delayed. Most auto repair companies have computer systems that can quickly locate auto parts from area suppliers and an express pickup and delivery service to immediately obtain the needed parts. When a customer comes in for service, an expert service writer will consult with the customer to identify problems and write a service order that identifies the work needed, the time and personnel required to perform the repairs, and the parts and supplies required. If the items are not in stock in the repair facility, an emergency order will be placed and quickly filled.

Physical working conditions also have an effect on the morale of workers. Job satisfaction is influenced by lighting, temperature, ventilation, and cleanliness of the work areas, as well as the quality and maintenance of tools and equipment. Even facilities outside the work area should be carefully planned, such as convenient and safe parking facilities and easy access to cafeterias and break rooms.

facts & figures

Employees gain satisfaction from having a say in what affects their careers. One expert suggests asking these questions to determine how much power employees have in an organization: What kind of access do they have to decision makers? How does the organization encourage employee participation? What systems are in place to act on employee suggestions? Do employees feel they can try new things and take risks?

FIGURE 13-5 The owner of a small proprietorship might perform all of the work.

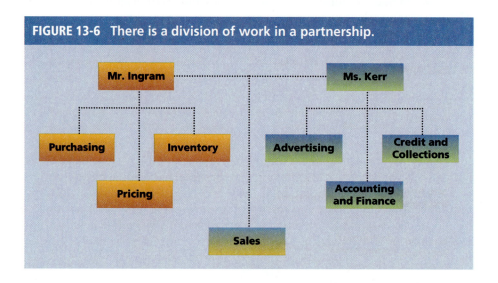

FIGURE 13-6 There is a division of work in a partnership.

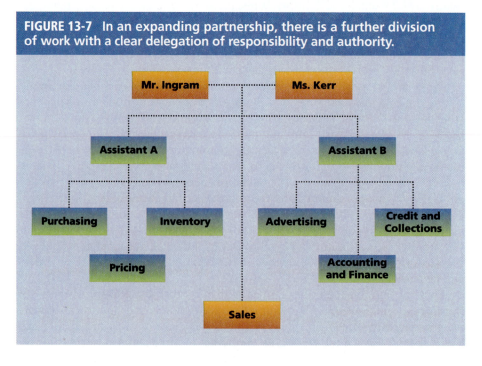

FIGURE 13-7 In an expanding partnership, there is a further division of work with a clear delegation of responsibility and authority.

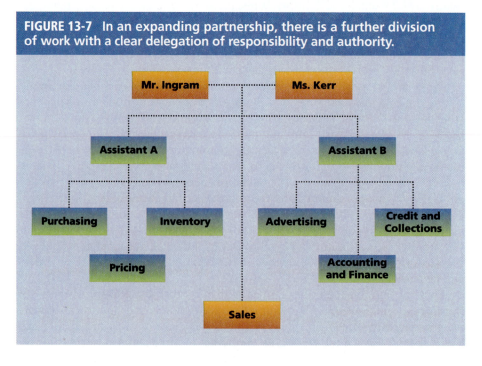

EMPLOYEES Dividing the work into manageable units and providing adequate equipment and facilities must be done with employees in mind. In fact, organizing involves establishing good relationships among the employees, the work to be performed, and the facilities needed, so that productivity will be high. In part, organization is a successful matching of the employee and the employee's materials and work. Employees should be matched to work that they are prepared to do. That means that they have the necessary preparation and skill to complete the assigned tasks. If employees are members of work teams, the total skills of the team should match the work requirements.

In addition, employees should be assigned to work that they enjoy. If employees are dissatisfied with their work assignment, problems with the quality and quantity of their work will result. Although not all work is enjoyable, managers should look for opportunities to make the best work assignments possible, to spread less desirable assignments among employees so a few people do not have to spend all of their time doing that work, and to work closely with employees to establish a positive working environment.

CHECKPOINT

What are the three elements that should be considered when organizing work?

Characteristics of Good Organization

When one person operates a business, there is little need for an organization chart—that person performs all the work. The need for organization increases when two or more people work together. When people engage in any kind of cooperative activity, whether as members of an athletic team or as construction workers building a house, they can accomplish better results if the overall task is planned and organized. In that way, each person knows what is expected and how they are expected to work together to accomplish the necessary work. Several characteristics of good organization apply to the management of work.

RESPONSIBILITY AND AUTHORITY

Responsibility is the obligation to do an assigned task. In a good organization, the assigned tasks are clearly identified so all employees know exactly the work for which they are responsible. **Authority** is the right to make decisions about assigned work and to make assignments to others concerning that work. Authority is delegated from the top of the organization to others at lower levels.

One of the greatest mistakes in business is to assign responsibilities to employees without giving them sufficient authority to carry out those responsibilities. Consider the situation of an employee at an auto rental counter. The employee is responsible for providing a car to a customer standing at the counter who has a reservation, but the type of car requested is currently unavailable. The employee must have the authority to rent another car that will meet the customer's needs or the customer will be very upset. Each employee and each manager should know specifically (1) the description and duties of each job, (2) what authority accompanies the job, (3) the manager in charge, (4) who reports to the manager, and (5) what is considered satisfactory performance.

A growing practice in many organizations today is employee empowerment. As you learned earlier, empowerment is the authority given to individual employees to make decisions and solve problems they encounter on their jobs with the resources available to them. Empowered employees need to be well trained and be effective decision makers and problem solvers. They need to understand the effects of their decisions on the business, other employees, and customers. Empowered employees have the confidence that their managers will support the decisions they make. Some companies are reluctant to empower their employees, believing that managers will lose control of the organization. However, experience has shown that empowerment increases employee morale, produces more satisfied customers and fewer reported problems, and increases work efficiency.

Unless employees know their specific responsibilities, duties, and authority, they are likely to be unsure about the work they are to do. Furthermore, conflicts may arise due to misunderstandings about what needs to be done and who makes decisions about work assignments and satisfactory performance. When employees understand responsibility and authority, overlapping duties can be eliminated easily. Effective organization is helpful in eliminating conflicts between individuals and departments and in increasing cooperation and collaboration.

ACCOUNTABILITY

Accountability is the obligation to accept responsibility for the outcomes of assigned tasks. When any manager assigns responsibility and delegates authority to an employee, the manager does not give away the responsibility for ensuring that the work is completed and for evaluating the quality of that employee's performance. Although the manager is ultimately responsible for the work, the employee is accountable to the manager for performing the assigned work properly, including the quality, quantity, and completion time. The manager, in turn, is accountable to his or her boss for the outcomes of all work done in the unit. Figure 13-8 shows how the owner of a small rental business might assign

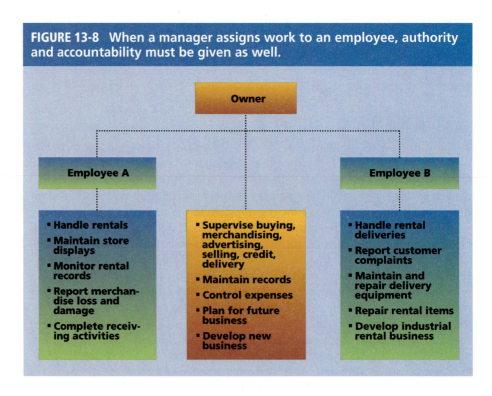

FIGURE 13-8 When a manager assigns work to an employee, authority and accountability must be given as well.

Owner

Employee A

- Handle rentals
- Maintain store displays
- Monitor rental records
- Report merchandise loss and damage
- Complete receiving activities

- Supervise buying, merchandising, advertising, selling, credit, delivery
- Maintain records
- Control expenses
- Plan for future business
- Develop new business

Employee B

- Handle rental deliveries
- Report customer complaints
- Maintain and repair delivery equipment
- Repair rental items
- Develop industrial rental business

responsibilities and delegate authority to two employees. Use the figure to identify the accountability of each person for the work of the organization.

Managers evaluate employees' work by comparing the work to established goals and work standards. For the assigned work, each employee is accountable for achieving the quality and quantity defined by the goals and standards. Managers need to communicate the goals and expected standards when assigning work and then use those same goals and standards when evaluating the employee's work.

UNITY OF COMMAND

An important principle of good organization is unity of command. **Unity of command** means that no employee reports to more than one supervisor at a time or for a particular task. Confusion and poor work relations result when a person has work assigned by and is accountable to more than one supervisor. The person may not know which assignment to perform first or may receive conflicting instructions regarding the same work assignment. With the increasing use of teams, problems with unity of command are more likely to occur. Teams and their supervisors must practice the same careful organization of work as when more traditional structures are used. Teams need clear assignments of responsibility and authority for their tasks, and all team members need to be aware of who is in charge of each activity. Ultimately the entire team and its supervisor are responsible for the results produced. A team member cannot shift the blame to someone else or fail to undertake a share of the workload if that organizational structure is to work successfully.

SPAN OF CONTROL

Span of control is the number of employees that any one manager supervises directly. Organizations must establish a reasonable span of control for each manager. The manager who supervises too many people is overworked and unable to perform all duties effectively. On the other hand, valuable time is wasted if a manager has too few people to supervise. That manager may supervise each person too closely or spend too much time in nonmanagement work. In general, the span of control is larger at the lower levels of an organization than at the

PHOTO: © GETTY IMAGES/PHOTODISC.

How can a business define what is a reasonable span of control for a manager?

higher levels. For example, the head nurse in charge of a floor unit in a hospital may supervise 15 or more employees, whereas only three vice presidents report to the chief executive of the hospital.

Companies that use work teams and encourage employees to be more involved in planning and decision making have found that they can increase the span of control. Well-trained and motivated employees do not require as much direct supervision as those who must rely on managers for direction. These companies have been able to reduce the numbers of managers required or have been able to increase the size of their workforces without hiring additional managers.

CHECKPOINT

What is likely to happen if employees are assigned responsibility for work tasks but are not given the needed authority?

13.3 Assessment

UNDERSTAND MANAGEMENT CONCEPTS

Determine the best answer for each of the following questions.

1. A well-designed organizational chart shows all of the following *except*
   a. the major work units that make up the business
   b. which unit each employee is affiliated with, how it relates to other units, and to whom employees are accountable
   c. lines of authority and formal communication within the organization
   d. the primary groups of customers to whom the business sells its products

2. The number of employees that any one manager supervises directly is the
   a. span of control
   b. unity of command
   c. division of work
   d. assignment of responsibility and authority

THINK CRITICALLY

Answer the following questions as completely as possible.

3. Do you believe that a large business will operate more efficiently and effectively with more or fewer organizational units? Justify your answer.

4. If you were a supervisor, what would you do to make sure each employee is aware of his or her responsibilities and authority? What could you do to make your employees feel empowered to make decisions and solve problems associated with their work?

Xtra!
Study Tools
thomsonedu.com/school/bpmxtra

Focus On...

Management Innovation–Putting Employees First

What kind of company would put employees first and customers second? Non-managerial employees are considered more important than managers. That is the innovative view of Vineet Nayar, president of HCL Technologies. HCL is located near New Delhi, India. The company employs 30,000 people in the competitive information technology outsourcing business.

Employee empowerment comes first with Nayar. He is a strong believer that effective teamwork and motivated employees build a great company. He trusts employees so much that management evaluation is put in their hands. Every employee rates not only his or her own boss but any three other managers in the company. Employees fill out an 18-item questionnaire and the results are posted online where all employees and managers can review them.

Another innovation in employee empowerment is the employee "ticket." Whenever employees see a problem or want managers to take some action, they can immediately fill out an electronic form. The issue can be as simple as a problem with the menu in the cafeteria or as major as a product defect the employee has identified. The "ticket" is immediately routed to a manager who becomes responsible for the solution. And when is the solution satisfactory? Not until the employee who filed the original form is satisfied.

A public question-and-answer space is provided on the company's intranet, where any employee can post a question and receive a reply from management. Again, all questions and answers can be reviewed by every employee. Over 400 questions are posted each month. Managers are actually rewarded by the number of employee tickets and questions submitted—the more the better. HCL managers receive regular training in how to be effective in an empowered work environment. Key courses are negotiation skills and expectation management—how to meet the expectations of employees.

The results of the company's employee empowerment program have been outstanding. Employee retention rates have doubled in an industry where highly skilled employees change jobs regularly to increase their pay. At the same time, sales, profits, and the company's stock price are climbing. "I want to be the company that gives superior service to my employees compared to everybody else," Nayar says. He wants anyone who leaves HCL to end up frustrated in their new job because of their loss of empowerment.

Think Critically

1. Do you agree or disagree with Vineet Nayar's management philosophy? Why?
2. Would you like to work as a manager in that type of company? Why or why not?
3. How do you believe customers feel about Nayar's views that employees are first and customers are second?

13.4 Developing Effective Organizations

Goals
- Describe the strengths and weaknesses of four types of organizational structures.
- Make recommendations for improving business organization.

Terms
- line organization
- line-and-staff organization
- matrix organization
- team organization
- self-directed work teams
- centralized organization
- decentralized organization
- flattened organization

Types of Organizational Structures

A business's organizational structure identifies the relationships among departments and personnel and indicates the lines of communication and decision making. Two principal types of organizational structures are (1) line and (2) line-and-staff organizations. Two newer structures in companies today are matrix and team organizations.

LINE ORGANIZATION

In a **line organization**, all authority and responsibility can be traced in a direct line from the top executive down to the lowest employee level in the organization. A line organization is shown in Figure 13-9 (sales is the only area for which the complete organization is shown). The lines joining the individual boxes indicate the lines of authority. The lines show, for example, that the president has authority over the sales manager, the sales manager has authority over the assistant sales manager, the assistant sales manager has authority over the branch managers, and the branch managers have authority over the sales representatives. In addition, the lines describe how formal communications are expected to flow up and down the organization.

In a line organization, the president has direct control over all units of the business, but responsibility, authority, and accountability are passed along from one person to another, down to the lowest level. Under this form of organization, each person is responsible to only one manager, who, in turn, is responsible to someone else. This type of organization can be very efficient, because new plans and ideas can be put into effect immediately in one area of the business without involvement from other areas. However, it often leads to many layers of management and isolation or lack of communication between departments and divisions. There is no direct way that managers of different departments not in the same line of authority can communicate and work together.

LINE-AND-STAFF ORGANIZATION

Large and complex businesses need a great deal of expertise to operate well. Managers have greater difficulty mastering the knowledge and skills they need

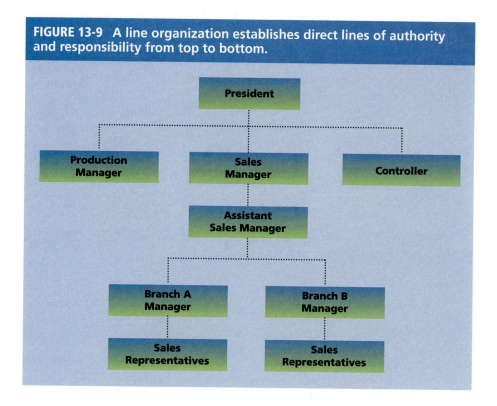

FIGURE 13-9 A line organization establishes direct lines of authority and responsibility from top to bottom.

in all of their areas of responsibility. In the line-and-staff organization, managers have direct control over the units and employees they supervise but have access to staff specialists for assistance. Specifically, the line-and-staff organization adds staff specialists to a line organization. It is designed to solve the problem of complexity and still retain the advantages of direct and definite lines of authority. Staff specialists give advice and assistance to line personnel. Staff personnel have no authority over line personnel; that is, staff personnel cannot require anyone in the line organization to perform any task. They are there to help with specialized jobs. Thus, line personnel are still responsible to only one supervisor.

The line-and-staff organization in Figure 13-10 (see p. 344) is like the line organization in Figure 13-9 except for the addition of the advertising specialist and the marketing research specialist. Their responsibility is to give specialized advice and assistance to the sales organization of the business. This relationship is indicated in the organization chart by broken lines. Other examples of staff positions in some organizations are legal, information management, strategic planning, and human resources specialists.

MATRIX ORGANIZATION

A newer, more flexible structure is the matrix organization, sometimes called a *project organization*. A matrix organization organizes employees into temporary work teams to complete specific projects. Employees report to a project manager with authority and responsibility for the project. When a new project must be done, employees with the needed skills are assigned to work on the project team. They work for that manager until the project is finished. Then they are assigned to a new project and another project manager. Work assignments and relationships in a matrix organization are clear but temporary.

In the matrix organization, there is no permanent organizational structure in which an employee continues to report to the same manager and works in only

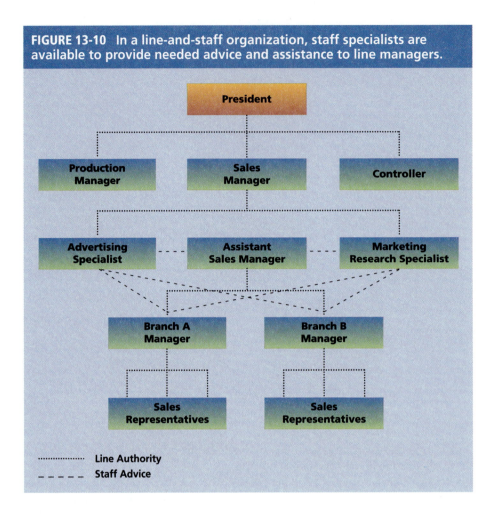

FIGURE 13-10 In a line-and-staff organization, staff specialists are available to provide needed advice and assistance to line managers.

one functional area. It is difficult to develop an organizational chart for this type of organization because it changes regularly. Typically, the company prepares an organization chart for each project, so that employees know the current project structure and the management and employee relationships. The company prepares a new chart when that project ends and a new one begins.

The matrix organization is used successfully in research firms, advertising agencies, and construction companies, but it is being considered by other types of businesses as well because it provides flexibility and allows for rapid change. This structure uses the specific skills of managers and employees as effectively as possible by bringing together people with the right skills for each project. When employees are given new project assignments, managers must be careful to define authority and responsibility so as not to violate unity of command.

TEAM ORGANIZATION

The newest type of organization structure is known as team organization. A **team organization** divides employees into permanent work teams. The teams have responsibility and authority for important business activities with limited management control over their daily work. Teams often have team leaders who are likely to be experienced employees rather than managers. Team

Teamwork *tip*

Most teams go through stages before coming together as an effective unit to achieve organizational goals. It is not easy to move from the individual actions required in traditional organizations to effective teamwork. Like good sports teams, organizations must provide team training and give teams time to practice and improve.

leaders replace the traditional position of supervisor and act as facilitators more than as traditional managers. Team leaders help their teams identify problems and work with them to solve the problems as a group. Team members report to the team leader, and the team leader makes some management decisions for the team. A full-time manager is responsible for several teams and meets with team leaders for planning, progress reports, and problem solving.

Sometimes teams are organized without a permanently designated team leader. These are **self-directed work teams,** in which team members together are responsible for the work assigned to the team. Self-directed work teams have a manager to whom they can turn with unusual or very difficult problems, but most of the time they work together to establish goals and to plan and organize their work. Often members take turns as team leader or facilitator. A self-directed team has full authority over planning, performing, and evaluating its work. For ideas and assistance, the team may talk to other teams or draw on the support of specialists available to work with all teams in the organization. In addition, the team is expected to talk to suppliers and customers from inside or outside the business to get their input and feedback.

In self-directed work teams, the team decides who will do which types of work and how they will do it. Each worker must be able to perform the tasks of most other team members to cover for absent members or additional workloads. Team members hire, train, and even fire new team members, evaluate individual and team performance, and handle most of the traditional management tasks. The role of the manager is to serve as the team's consultant and to concentrate on higher-level management tasks. Some differences between self-directed work teams and traditional work teams are shown in Figure 13-11 (see p. 346).

Effective work teams, whether self-directed or not, have been shown to increase productivity and improve quality. Individual team members work hard to support their team and make sure the team meets its goals. Companies that have developed effective team structures have a better record of keeping customers happy, reducing absenteeism, reducing turnover, and keeping motivation high.

Teams require certain ingredients for success. Managers must support the idea and assist the teams as needed. Team members must become competent in three areas:

1. Technical job skills
2. Interpersonal skills, such as writing, speaking, discussing, and negotiating
3. Administrative skills, such as leading meetings, thinking analytically, and maintaining records

PHOTO: © DIGITAL VISION.

What are some advantages of team organization to employees and to management?

NETBookmark

Employee satisfaction must be an important concern of every manager. Dissatisfied employees are likely to leave if another job becomes available. They will also be less productive than those who like their work. The Conference Board recently reported the results of a nationwide employee satisfaction survey. Point your browser to www.thomsonedu.com/school/bpmxtra. Read the article that summarizes the findings from their survey. What information surprises you the most and what results match your expectations? If you were the top executive of a company, how would you use this information to improve employee satisfaction in your company? Develop three recommendations that you would make to the managers who report to you.

www.thomsonedu.com/school/bpmxtra

FIGURE 13-11 Self-directed work teams have more authority and responsibility for their work than do traditional teams.

	Traditional WORK TEAM	Self-Directed WORK TEAM
Work Categories	Many narrow tasks	One or two broad tasks
Worker Authority	Team leader controls all tasks done daily	Team controls tasks through group decisions
Rewards	Based on type of job, on individual worker performance, and on seniority	Based on team performance plus breadth of skills of individual team members

Teams need top-management support as well as skills in these three areas to do well. New teams must have both time and support to be able to mature to their full potential.

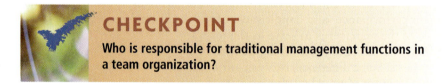

CHECKPOINT

Who is responsible for traditional management functions in a team organization?

Improving Business Organization

Traditionally, businesses have used **centralized organization**, in which a few top managers do all major planning and decision making. Studies of the effect of business organization on quality and productivity have discovered that centralized organizations cause problems in some companies. Large companies often develop very complex centralized organizational structures. Those structures may cause communication problems and the need for many policies and rules to control the organization. Individual managers and employees then begin to feel like unimportant parts of the business. They get frustrated when rules keep them from doing things they consider important or when it takes a long time to get decisions made.

To overcome these types of problems, companies are moving to **decentralized organization**. In this structure, a very large business is divided into smaller operating units, and unit managers have almost total responsibility and authority for the operation of their units. In many ways, the units operate as if they were independent companies. For example, a large computer manufacturer could be decentralized into work units by categories of products (mainframes, personal computers, accessory equipment) or by types of customers (industrial, government, international).

Another major type of reorganization occurring in businesses today is known as *flattening*. A <mark>flattened organization</mark> is one with fewer levels of management than traditional structures. To achieve a flattened organization, the remaining managers and employees assume many of the responsibilities previously assigned to other levels of management. A flattened organization should have improved communication, because information has to flow through fewer levels. There should also be more coordination and cooperation because there is less specialization within the organization. As competition increases and customers expect businesses to improve quality and service, the organization of a business becomes very important. A complex organizational structure that requires a great deal of time for making decisions and for communicating information will not be as competitive as one that is more flexible and responsive.

CHECKPOINT

How can business organization be made more effective?

13.4 Assessment

UNDERSTAND MANAGEMENT CONCEPTS

Determine the best answer for each of the following questions.

1. If managers in large organizations have difficulty mastering the knowledge and skills they need in all of their areas of responsibility, which type of organizational structure would be most helpful?
   a. line
   b. line-and-staff
   c. matrix
   d. team

2. For work teams to be successful in an organization, team members must become competent in all of the following areas *except*
   a. technical job skills
   b. interpersonal skills
   c. administrative skills
   d. All of the skills are required.

THINK CRITICALLY

Answer the following questions as completely as possible.

3. Why does the line organizational structure often create problems in sharing information and communicating among employees and managers from different parts of the organization?

4. Flattened organizations provide benefits in improved communications, coordination, and cooperation. Why does that occur? What problems do you believe might result from the flattened organization structure?

Xtra!
Study Tools
thomsonedu.com/school/bpmxtra

CHAPTER CONCEPTS

- Managers who plan for a business's future are likely to be more successful than those who work on day-to-day operations. Planning sets the direction for the business and establishes specific goals. Plans are guides for making decisions. Strategic plans tell where the business is going. Operational plans determine how work will be done, who will do it, and what resources will be needed to get the work done.

- Goals keep a business focused on where it wants to go and the results to be accomplished. Tools that can help develop effective plans include budgets, schedules, standards, policies, procedures, and research.

- Companies must be organized to carry out plans and complete work effectively. The process of organizing involves three elements: division of work, facilities and working conditions, and employees. Characteristics of good organizations include responsibility and authority, accountability, unity of command, and span of control.

- The type of organizational structure identifies the relationships among departments and personnel as well as lines of communication and decision making. Types of organizational structures are line, line-and-staff, matrix, and team organizations. Recently, traditional organizations have been decentralized and flattened.

REVIEW TERMS AND CONCEPTS

Write the letter of the term that matches each definition. Some terms will not be used.

a. accountability
b. centralized organization
c. flattened organization
d. goal
e. line organization
f. matrix organization
g. mission statement
h. organization chart
i. policies
j. procedure
k. self-directed work teams
l. span of control
m. standard
n. team organization
o. vision

1. Organization with fewer levels of management than traditional structures
2. Organization in which employees are organized into temporary work teams to complete specific projects
3. List of steps to be followed for performing certain work
4. Specific statement of a result the business expects to achieve
5. Specific statement of a business's purpose and direction
6. Specific measure against which something is judged
7. Organization in which team members together are responsible for the work assigned to the team
8. Obligation to accept responsibility for the outcomes of assigned tasks
9. Drawing showing the structure of an organization, major job classifications, and reporting relationships
10. Number of employees that any one manager supervises directly
11. Guidelines used in making decisions regarding specific, recurring situations
12. Company's reason for existing
13. Organization in which all authority and responsibility can be traced in a direct line from the top executive down to the lowest employee level

DETERMINE THE BEST ANSWER

14. Strategic planning in an organization is followed by
    a. operational planning
    b. organizational planning
    c. hiring and training employees
    d. None of the answers is correct.
15. Which of the following is *not* a characteristic of an effective goal?
    a. Goals must be specific and meaningful.
    b. Goals must be achievable.
    c. Goals must be clearly communicated.
    d. Each goal must focus on one company activity.
16. Businesses measure the quality of products and services by comparing them against
    a. procedures
    b. standards
    c. policies
    d. goals
17. The span of control at the top of an organization is usually _____ at the lower levels.
    a. greater than
    b. about the same as
    c. smaller than
    d. There is no span of control at the top of an organization.
18. The most efficient organizational structure is a
    a. line organization
    b. line-and-staff organization
    c. team organization
    d. decentralized organization

APPLY WHAT YOU KNOW

19. Based on the Reality Check scenario at the beginning of the chapter, identify one example of strategic planning and one example of operational planning that you believe Eldron Huntley should complete.
20. It is recommended that a new business develop a business plan. Do you believe large, well-established businesses need a business plan as well? Why or why not?
21. What is the difference between a business strength and a business opportunity? For a business in your community, provide an example of a strength of the business and an opportunity for the business.
22. Write a list of procedures that another person can follow to copy a computer file from the hard drive to a removable storage device. The procedures should be complete and in the order they need to be performed.
23. Do you believe employees prefer to work in organizations where they have very specialized work that they do over and over, or in organizations where they have a broader set of responsibilities and work changes regularly? Justify your answer.

24. What is the difference between responsibility and authority? Provide examples of each from your role as a family member and your role as a student.

25. Compare the line organization with the matrix organization in terms of how it affects the work, relationships, and communication of managers and employees.

MAKE CONNECTIONS

26. **Communication** Review the information from the beginning of the chapter about Eldron Huntley's idea to expand his catering business using the Internet. Write two goals that Mr. Huntley could set for the business—one that should be achieved in three months and one that should be achieved by the end of the first year. Write the goals to include the four characteristics of an effective goal.

27. **Visual Arts** Your class decides to hold a student recognition and parent appreciation event at the end of the school year. All students will participate in planning and managing the event. A matrix organization structure will be used. Identify the major divisions of work that need to be completed for a successful event. Using a computer drawing program, design an organization chart you believe will be most effective for getting the work done. Assign each student in your class to a particular role in the organization chart. Be prepared to discuss your decisions with other students.

28. **Technology** Use the Internet to locate an example of a business use of each of the planning tools identified in the chapter: budget, schedule, standard, policy, procedure, and research. Construct a 3×6 table. In the first column, identify the planning tool. In the second column, briefly describe its use. In the third column, identify how the use of the tool supports business planning.

29. **Research** Use a library or the Internet to locate three articles from business magazines on the effects of flattening (reducing the levels of management) on businesses and their employees. Take notes on the articles as you read. Then prepare a one-page analysis of your research, presenting the advantages and disadvantages of the use of downsizing.

30. **Mathematics** Research is an important tool businesses use for strategic planning. On average, businesses spend about 3.5 percent of sales on research activities each year. In a recent year, the top businesses worldwide in terms of research expenditures were Microsoft, Ford, and Pfizer. Microsoft invested $7.8 billion on research with sales of $36.8 billion. Ford's investment was $7.6 billion for research with $164 billion in sales. Pfizer's research budget was $7.1 billion and sales were $45.2 billion. Calculate the percentage of annual sales each company invested in research. Determine the percentage of sales invested in research by all three companies combined. Compare it with the average of all businesses.

CASE IN POINT

CASE 13-1: Solving Planning Conflicts

The ToyTime Company makes and sells a line of popular children's toys. In six months, retail stores will begin buying the company's products in large quantities in preparation for the holiday shopping season. Every year, ToyTime introduces one or two new toys designed to attract the attention and interest of children and their parents and get them into the stores at holiday time. Then they design in-store displays and promotions of the company's toys that have been popular for many years, bringing in a high volume of sales of both new and traditional toys.

Jacob Marks, the marketing manager, has recently reviewed the results of research on this year's newest toy. The toy received the most positive customer response of any toy they have introduced in the past five years. Based on that research, Mr. Marks is confident that sales will be 15 percent higher this year than last. As a result of these estimates, he plans to implement an advertising blitz to introduce the new toy. Several additional salespeople have been hired to work with retail stores to make sure both the national chains and independent retailers are prepared with adequate inventory for the upcoming holiday sales period.

At the same time Jacob Marks has been working on the expanded marketing efforts, Janice McConklin, the production manager, has been running into problems. She has had difficulty getting an adequate supply of one of the key raw materials from the firm's only supplier. Production levels for the new toy have been 20 percent below plans during the last two months. It would be possible for Ms. McConklin to devote additional production time to increasing the inventory of the company's traditional products. However, she was not aware of the recent marketing research or marketing plans. The production plans, developed three months ago, were to keep inventory levels of those toys just slightly above last year's level. In discussions with the raw-materials supplier, it appears that the supply problem may be solved in two weeks. If so, she might be able to meet the production goals for the new toys but product deliveries will be two weeks later than usual to retailers. She knows that retailers like to have the new toys early, but there is little she can do about it right now.

THINK CRITICALLY

1. What management problems are apparent in the ToyTime Company? Why have these problems occurred? Are the reasons related more to planning issues or to organizing issues in the company?
2. What is likely to happen to the company this year and in future years if the problem is not resolved quickly?
3. Using the management tools discussed in the chapter, give examples of how each could be used to help solve the company's problems.
4. What would you recommend right now that can help resolve the problems being faced by ToyTime? What should they do to avoid the same type of problem in the future?

CASE 13-2: Reorganizing a Business

Hector Fuego had just been hired by the board of directors to become the new CEO of You Build, Inc. You Build is a 50-year-old building supply company that operates in the southwestern United States. The company has a very successful history and has seen expansion to 50 stores in 23 cities. However, in the past three years, operations have been much less successful because the largest retailer in the industry, Home Warehouse, began to expand into the areas served by You Build. Home Warehouse built larger stores in very convenient locations with a broader set of products and low prices. It was clear the Home Warehouse was threatening the success of You Build. The board of directors made it clear to Mr. Fuego as they discussed their expectations with him that his most important priority was to find ways to meet the competition and maintain the success of You Build, Inc.

Because of its history, You Build had developed a very traditional line organizational structure. All strategic planning and major decisions were made by the CEO and a team of three vice presidents. There were two more levels of management at the corporate level; four regional offices with managers who reported to the corporate level; a management team in every city that had three or more stores; and a store management team. Most of the managers had many years of experience with You Build and had worked their way up through the system. Mr. Fuego believed most of the managers were very good at their jobs and worked hard to make the company successful. However, it seemed that the current organizational structure made decision making very slow, and the many employees at the store level who worked with customers had little input into store operations. He learned that the previous CEO had little contact with managers or employees of individual stores.

Hector Fuego wanted to change the organizational structure of You Build, Inc. He believed the business would be more effective if the organization was flattened and the line organization was replaced with a team organization. The executives would set an example by forming a team to do corporate-level planning, advised by regional teams of experienced employees and store managers. City management positions would be eliminated, and each store would develop teams of employees to make decisions for the store's departments. He knew the change would not be easy because the company had used the traditional organizational structure for 50 years.

THINK CRITICALLY

1. What are the advantages and disadvantages of the change in organizational structure Hector Fuego is planning?
2. How do you believe You Build's managers will feel about the change? How do you believe the employees will feel?
3. What steps do you recommend that Mr. Fuego follow to prepare managers for the change? What should he do to prepare employees for their new role in the organization?

PLANNING AND ORGANIZING YOUR BUSINESS

As you prepare to become a new business owner, you will spend the majority of your time on planning and organizing activities. If you recognize the importance of planning to the success of a new business, you will be willing to devote the necessary time to it. Starting with a business plan, you must develop goals, budgets, schedules, policies, and procedures. As you add employees, you will have to make decisions on how to organize and divide work so that it will be completed effectively. In the project activities for this chapter, you will plan and organize your business.

DATA COLLECTION

1. Meet with your business mentor and discuss the importance of planning and the types of planning tools he or she uses.
2. Go to several company or organization Web sites and read their vision and mission statements. Note several points you would like to include in your own company's vision and mission statements.
3. Using the Internet or your library, find and read several articles on ways that businesses are reorganizing work for more effective operations. Summarize the key points from those articles that you believe are useful to small businesses.
4. Locate several examples of organization charts for small businesses. Look for common elements and unique features. Consider how you can use the information in planning an organizational structure for your business that will support planned business growth.

ANALYSIS

1. Divide a sheet of paper or word-processing document into two columns. Label one column "Strategic Planning" and the other "Operational Planning." In each column, list as many areas of planning as you can that must be completed for your business.
2. Write a brief vision statement that reflects your vision of your company's reason for existing. Then write a mission statement that gives your company purpose and direction.
3. For each of the planning tools discussed in this chapter, identify how and when you will use the tool in your business. Prepare a one-month planning schedule in which you list when you will use each tool.
4. Assume you have hired two full-time and four part-time employees to help you operate your business. Consider the operations and activities that must be completed and prepare an organizational chart in which you list job titles and duties for each employee. Identify whether the organizational structure is line, line-and-staff, or some other type. Why do you believe that structure will be most effective?

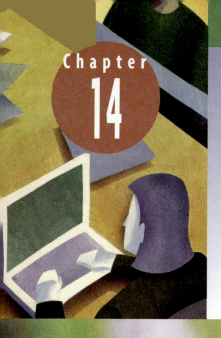

Implementing and Controlling

REALITY CHECK

Losing Control

Jasmine Marsh had been hired as the manager of the new telemarketing department of an office supply company. The department was fully automated with computerized telephone and order-processing systems. A strategy was developed to sell office supplies through catalogs and telephone sales. Jasmine was given a large budget to retrain current employees and to hire and train new employees for telephone sales. A catalog was prepared and mailed to all businesses in the city. Follow-up telephone calls were made, introducing the service and promoting the company's delivery guarantee. The promise was that any order placed by 10 p.m. would be delivered by 10 a.m. the next day.

Things got off to a good start. There was a real excitement among the employees when they made the sales calls to introduce the new service, and orders began to come in. However, the rapidly expanding sales volume was putting pressure on Jasmine's department. After the first month of operations, it was clear that a growing number of problems were leading to employee dissatisfaction and a high turnover rate. Experienced employees, especially those who had worked for the company before the change, were quitting or asking for transfers because of the pressure they were facing on the job.

Jasmine knew that her department was essential to the success of the company. If the department was not able to maintain and increase the level of sales and process orders efficiently, the new business strategy would fail. As the manager, she needed to figure out ways to solve the growing number of problems.

14.1 The Implementing Function

Goals
- Recognize problems that can occur when plans are implemented.
- Identify important implementing activities performed by managers.

Terms
- motivation
- work team
- process improvement

As you learned in Chapter 11, implementing involves carrying out the plans and helping employees to work effectively. The controlling function involves evaluating results to determine if the company's objectives have been accomplished as planned. The majority of managers, especially supervisors and middle-level managers, spend a great deal of their time on implementing and controlling activities. In this chapter, you will learn about these two important management activities.

The Challenge of Implementing

Implementing involves guiding employee work toward achieving the company's goals. For example, a manager may communicate important goals to an employee team, provide leadership to help them determine how to complete the necessary work, and make sure that rewards and recognition are provided to everyone involved when their work achieves the goals.

You will remember from the scenario at the beginning of the chapter that Jasmine had many activities for which she was responsible in the new department. She was spending a great deal of time implementing the company's plans. Jasmine discovered what many experienced managers have learned. Plans are not effective unless they are implemented well. Changing conditions in a business create problems in the way work is accomplished. Here is what Jasmine learned about the implementing function as she continued to study the problems she was facing as a manager.

At the beginning, employees seemed to enjoy using the new computer equipment and making calls to customers. Jasmine had an excellent training budget and three months to prepare employees for their new work. The preparation time and training made them comfortable with their new work. The careful planning to mail the catalogs to customers and make follow-up calls resulted in immediate orders. Employees were pleased with their initial success. Customers liked the service promise and the service-oriented approach of the telemarketers. But as Jasmine looked back, that was where the problems started.

The first problem occurred when Jasmine established sales quotas for each employee. With sales growing rapidly, she didn't think it would be difficult for most employees to make their quotas. Jasmine believed the quotas would encourage everyone to emphasize selling rather than just waiting for customers to call in orders from the catalog. However, some people easily exceeded their sales quotas whereas others seldom reached theirs. Several employees complained that the

PHOTO: © GETTY IMAGES/PHOTODISC.

Supervisors must be able to implement the plans that have been developed. What types of information are available in business plans to help supervisors direct employees?

quotas emphasized selling too much and didn't allow them adequate time to answer customers' questions and solve their problems.

The department began to experience some computer difficulties. When a high volume of calls came in, the computers would slow down. Employees would have to wait to get information on their screens, and occasionally all of the information entered would be lost before the order could be processed. Also, Jasmine was learning that when sales volume was high, the company sometimes was not able to meet its goal of overnight delivery. Although Jasmine had been able to hire more sales employees, the delivery department was still operating with the same number of employees as in the past. As a result, the telemarketing employees were starting to receive customer complaints that they were not prepared to handle.

While Jasmine was struggling with the computer problems and the sales quota issue, she was also facing the growing employee turnover problem. Even though she was hiring and training new employees, it seemed there were never enough employees to replace those who left and to handle the growing amount of business. To get new employees on the job faster, training time was reduced. That seemed to result in more errors in the orders processed. Veteran employees were being asked to work overtime to meet the demand and to help inexperienced telemarketers. That created even more employee dissatisfaction. Jasmine couldn't believe that a plan that seemed so good and had initially been successful could result in so many problems.

CHECKPOINT

Identify several types of changes that can occur in an organization that can create problems in accomplishing plans.

Implementing Activities

To implement successfully, managers must complete a number of activities designed to channel employee efforts in the right direction to achieve the goals. These activities include effective communications, motivating employees, developing effective work teams, and operations management.

EFFECTIVE COMMUNICATIONS

Communication is an essential part of implementing work in a business. Managers must be able to communicate plans and directions, gather feedback from employees, and identify and resolve communication problems. Both personal and organizational communications are important. Because so many forms of communications media exist in organizations today, managing communications technology is an important responsibility.

Communication is much more than telling employees what to do. In fact, if employees believe managers are being too directive, they will likely be dissatisfied and not work as hard or effectively as they could. An important communication skill for managers is to listen to employees and involve them in deciding how work should be done. A manager should use both formal and informal communications. Encouraging employees to contribute their ideas and involving them in deciding the best way to do the work will help gain their commitment to achieving the goals.

EMPLOYEE MOTIVATION

Motivation is a set of factors that influence an individual's actions toward accomplishing a goal. Employees may be motivated to achieve company goals, or they may be motivated to pursue other goals that do not benefit the company. Managers don't actually "motivate" employees, but they can use rewards and punishments to encourage employees to motivate themselves toward pursuing company objectives. A key to motivation is to know what employees value and give them those things for achieving company goals. A reward is not motivating unless it is something the employee values. The reward need not be money. People also value things like praise, respect, an interesting job assignment, or extra time off.

Motivation comes from influences both inside and outside the individual. *Internal motivation* arises from a person's beliefs, feelings, and attitudes that influence the person's actions. For example, many workers are motivated to do a good job because they get an internal sense of satisfaction from a job well done. *External motivation* comes from rewards and punishments supplied by other people. For example, doing a good job may result in a pay increase, coworkers' admiration, or praise from the boss.

Sometimes internal factors have the most influence on behavior. If an employee believes that the work is boring, she will not be motivated to do a good job. At other times, external factors have the strongest influence on performance. An employee who values praise would likely be motivated to greater performance when he sees his name posted on the bulletin board as "employee of the week." Simply repainting the work area can serve as a motivating reward for employees who value a pleasant work environment.

All people have their own needs, and they will choose to do things that satisfy their needs and avoid doing things that don't. Managers can influence employee performance by understanding individual needs and providing rewards that satisfy those needs when employees accomplish work goals. Psychologists have studied behavior to try to understand what motivates people to do what they do. Several theories of motivation will be reviewed in the next lesson.

WORK TEAMS

Seldom do people complete all of their work alone. Most people are part of a work group and rely on cooperation from others to perform their work. It has been said that groups can accomplish more than the same number of people working independently. Managers need to be able to develop effective work teams. A **work team** is a group of individuals who cooperate to achieve a common goal.

Effective work teams have several characteristics, as shown in Figure 14-1. First, the members of the group understand and support its purpose. They clearly understand the activities to be completed, know which activities they must perform, and have the knowledge and skills necessary to complete them. Group members are committed to meeting the expectations of others in the group and helping the group succeed. Finally, group members communicate well with each other and work to resolve problems within the group.

Just because several people work together does not guarantee that they will be an effective work team. In fact, there are many reasons why they may not be an effective team. They may not know each other well or trust each other. They may

Success tip

Managers can motivate employees with their actions more effectively than with monetary rewards. Provide lots of encouragement, don't harshly criticize one-time errors, add fun and variety to routine work, offer leadership opportunities, allow employee input and choice when possible, and encourage social interaction as part of the job.

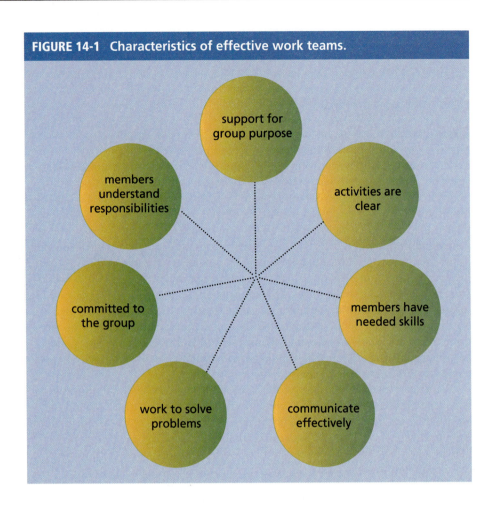

FIGURE 14-1 Characteristics of effective work teams.

(circles: support for group purpose; activities are clear; members have needed skills; communicate effectively; work to solve problems; committed to the group; members understand responsibilities)

have biases or stereotypes about other group members. They may not be prepared to cooperate in completing a task or know how to make effective team decisions.

Managers can play an important role in developing team effectiveness. To develop effective teams, they must understand the characteristics that make groups effective, help to organize the team and develop needed team skills, create a work environment that supports teamwork, and help the group resolve problems when they occur.

OPERATIONS MANAGEMENT

Operations are the major ongoing activities of a business. When completing the implementing function, managers are ensuring that employees are performing business activities as planned. Several activities are part of operations management. Facilities, equipment, materials, and supplies must be available and in good operating condition so employees can perform their work. Employees must have the knowledge and skills to do their work. Managers must make sure that employees complete their tasks on schedule, and work to resolve problems that could interfere with the successful completion of the job. Refer back to the beginning of the chapter and try to identify the operations issues that Jasmine was facing.

Effective planning and organizing are important parts of operations management. Planning helps employees know what to do. In the same way, well-organized work space and procedures for completing work tasks help operations run smoothly. If problems occur in the operations of a business, managers should examine the planning and organizing of the work.

Managers must be prepared to implement the activities assigned to their area of responsibility. Some activities are common to most management areas. For example, most managers must hire new employees, monitor work schedules, and communicate policies and procedures. However, most departments are organized to perform specialized operations. The manager of the marketing department may be responsible for advertising and sales. The information systems manager must ensure that computer systems are operational, the company's Internet sites are up-to-date, and software is problem-free. Managers need to understand the unique work of their departments in order to help employees complete that work.

In the past several years, organizations have paid a great deal of attention to improving the way work is done. Due to increasing competition, companies must operate efficiently to keep costs low so that they can compete successfully. Customers are demanding improved quality, so the company must produce products free of defects. The efforts to increase the effectiveness and efficiency of specific business operations are known as **process improvement**.

CHECKPOINT

List four activities managers must perform as part of the implementing function.

14.1 Assessment

UNDERSTAND MANAGEMENT CONCEPTS

Determine the best answer for each of the following questions.

1. An example of an internal motivation factor is
   a. praise from your boss
   b. a pay increase
   c. personal satisfaction
   d. the admiration of coworkers

2. The efforts to increase the effectiveness and efficiency of specific business operations are known as
   a. organizational change
   b. team effectiveness
   c. the implementing function of management
   d. process improvement

THINK CRITICALLY

Answer the following questions as completely as possible.

3. What are some reasons that managers with well-developed plans may still have problems when implementing those plans?

4. Why do some employees work well in teams and others do not?

Xtra!
Study Tools
thomsonedu.com/school/bpmxtra

14.2 | Motivation and Change Management

Goals

- Describe the main points of three theories of motivation.
- Identify the steps managers should follow when implementing change.

Terms

- achievement need
- affiliation need
- power need
- hygiene factors
- motivators

Motivation Theories

Think of the days when you are excited to get up and go to school or work. You enjoy the day and work hard. Time seems to move faster than usual. Compare that to the days when it is impossible to get up and you dread going to work or school. The day seems to go on forever, and you don't seem to be able to get anything done.

In the same way, you probably can identify teachers, coaches, or businesspeople for whom you enjoy working and who seem to be able to encourage your best work. You also know others whom you would prefer to avoid and for whom it is a struggle to perform well. What causes the differences?

You learned earlier that internal and external factors motivate people to act in certain ways. Psychologists have developed theories about what factors motivate people to behave as they do. Figure 14-2 summarizes these theories. Managers can influence employees to behave in ways that help achieve company goals by influencing these motivational factors.

MASLOW'S HIERARCHY OF NEEDS

Abraham Maslow described motivation in terms of a hierarchy of needs. The lowest level is physiological needs, followed by security, social, esteem, and self-actualization needs. *Physiological needs* are things required to sustain life, such as food and shelter. *Security needs* involve making sure you and those you care about are safe and free from harm. *Social needs* include the need to belong, to interact with others, to have friends, and to love and be loved. The need for *esteem* includes the need for recognition and respect from others. Finally, *self-actualization* is the need to grow emotionally and intellectually, to be creative, and to achieve your full potential.

According to the theory, people seek to satisfy these needs in order, from lowest to highest. Not until they fulfill the lowest needs on the hierarchy will the next level of needs motivate their behavior. For example, starving people will be more motivated to find food than to be concerned about friendships. But once people have satisfied their physiological and security needs, then the need for social interaction will motivate their behavior. Applying Maslow's hierarchy, managers can influence employee behavior by recognizing the levels of the hierarchy that are motivating an employee's behavior and then try to use things such as job assignments, praise and support, and financial rewards to meet those needs.

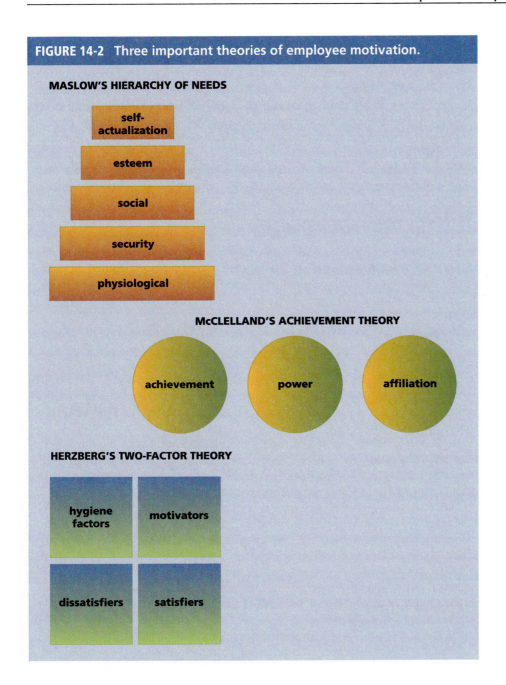

FIGURE 14-2 Three important theories of employee motivation.

MASLOW'S HIERARCHY OF NEEDS

- self-actualization
- esteem
- social
- security
- physiological

McCLELLAND'S ACHIEVEMENT THEORY

- achievement
- power
- affiliation

HERZBERG'S TWO-FACTOR THEORY

- hygiene factors
- motivators
- dissatisfiers
- satisfiers

MCCLELLAND'S ACHIEVEMENT MOTIVATION

Whereas Maslow's theory is based on a set of needs common to all people, David McClelland believed that people are influenced most strongly by one of three specific needs: the need for achievement, the need for affiliation, and the need for power.

McClelland suggested that people with a high **achievement need** take personal responsibility for their own work, set personal goals, and want immediate feedback on their work. People with a strong **affiliation need** are concerned about their relationships with others and work to get along well and fit in with a group. Finally, those with a strong **power need** want to influence and control others and to be responsible for a group's activities. You can probably think of people who fit into each of these three need classifications.

A survey of 350 human resources executives reported that the retention of employees was a very serious issue in their companies. Retention of employees younger than 30 was particularly difficult. Companies with programs to retain employees said that educational and lifestyle incentives were more effective than monetary compensation. Technical training, support for career advancement, and flexible work arrangements were viewed as valuable benefits by that employee group.

Managers who believe in McClelland's theory recognize that various jobs provide greater or fewer opportunities for achievement, affiliation, or power. Managers working with individuals with a high achievement need should provide opportunities for them to make decisions and control their own work. When managers see a high affiliation need in their employees, they should assign them to group projects and teams. These employees will respond well if socializing opportunities are built into the work environment. Finally, people with a high need for power will work best when given the opportunity to be project leaders or to be involved in planning and decision making. McClelland's theory suggests that the strength of the three needs can be changed over time with careful development.

HERZBERG'S TWO-FACTOR THEORY

A third important motivation theory was developed by Frederick Herzberg. He conducted studies of employees to identify what satisfied and dissatisfied them in their work. His research resulted in the identification of two distinct groups of factors related to motivation. Therefore his theory is known as the *two-factor theory*.

Herzberg called one group hygiene factors. **Hygiene factors** are job factors that dissatisfy when absent but do not contribute to satisfaction when they are present. Examples of hygiene factors are the amount of pay and fringe benefits, working conditions, rules, and the amount and type of supervision. For example, a good company-sponsored health care plan will not motivate employees to do a better job. But the lack of a good health plan could cause employees to be dissatisfied with their jobs.

Herzberg called the second group motivators. **Motivators** are factors that increase job satisfaction. The people whom Herzberg studied were motivated by factors such as challenging work, recognition, achievement, accomplishment, increased responsibility, and personal development.

The interesting part of Herzberg's theory is that the two types of factors and their results are separate from each other. In other words, hygiene factors can create dissatisfaction but cannot improve satisfaction. For example, people can be dissatisfied with the level of their pay and fringe benefits, but pay increases will not increase satisfaction very much or for any length of time. So, providing hygiene factors, such as pay increases and better working conditions, will only prevent employees from being dissatisfied. It will not motivate employees to perform at a higher level.

On the other hand, motivators increase satisfaction. To stimulate workers to higher achievement, managers should provide motivators such as opportunities for interesting work, greater individual control and responsibility, and recognition for good work.

Managers are often surprised by Herzberg's studies. It is easy to believe that a pay increase will motivate employees to perform better. However, people are often dissatisfied when they compare their pay to that of others, or they believe they are worth more than they are currently being paid. Factors such as fair pay, flexible work hours, and good fringe benefits can keep people from being dissatisfied but seldom are the major reason people are motivated to perform well.

CHECKPOINT

Why should managers understand motivation theories?

Managing Change

The only thing that seems certain in business today is change. Reengineering, downsizing, mergers, and many other organizational changes affect workers and their jobs.

People are not always comfortable with change. Consider changes you have experienced. Examples could include moving, changing schools, relationships with family or friends, or an important decision you may be facing. How did you react to that change? When it appears that things will be different, those affected by the change are likely to be very concerned.

When people's jobs are threatened, when they are uncertain about how a change will affect them, or when they do not trust those responsible for planning the change, they will probably resist the change. They are likely to resist most when change occurs suddenly, when they are not prepared, or when they don't understand the reasons for the change.

To implement organizational change, managers must work to overcome that resistance and to make change as comfortable as possible for the employees affected. Careful planning that involves the people affected will make the transition smoother, and employees will be more likely to support the change. The steps in an effective change process are shown in Figure 14-3.

PLANNING

Managers must be careful not to move too rapidly to make changes. They must be certain that change is needed and that the organization will be better off as a result of the change. Then they should follow a careful procedure to gather information, identify and study alternatives, and determine the consequences of change. A well-considered plan will help to assure the best results and will give confidence to those most affected by the change.

COMMUNICATING

Sometimes managers believe it is best not to say anything to employees about possible changes until a final decision has been made and they are ready to take action. They believe that early information will create confusion and misunderstanding.

FIGURE 14-3 Steps in successfully implementing change.

1. Carefully plan for the change.

2. Communicate with people, so that change does not surprise them.

3. Involve people, so they feel a part of the change.

4. Educate people, so they understand the change.

5. Support people in their efforts to change.

Change occurs regularly in business today. What are some examples of recent changes that have occurred in businesses in your community?

PHOTO: PR NEWSWIRE HONDA PRECISION PARTS OF GEORGIA.

People who study the change process recognize that it is almost impossible to conceal information about pending changes. Based on informal communication and limited information, rumors and misinformation will spread. If people are surprised by a change or feel they have been misled, the result is usually more damaging to the organization than the result of early, direct communications from management.

Managers who have previously established open communications with employees are in the best position to communicate with them about possible changes. Because change occurs frequently in business, employees who are used to regular communications with their managers will not be surprised by information about potential changes, even if the changes may appear to be negative. Open, two-way communications between managers and employees are part of an effective change process.

INVOLVING

It is frequently said that people support what they create. Managers must recognize that employees can be a good source of ideas for effective solutions and how to make changes. Most effective change processes involve the people who will be affected in gathering information, considering alternatives, and testing solutions. It is usually not possible to involve everyone in all parts of the change process or to use a majority vote to decide on a change. However, employees will be more supportive when they know their voices will be heard and that they have input into plans that result in change.

Managers need to respect and seek the input of employees. Sometimes managers say they want employees' ideas but then ignore their input. That will frustrate employees and make them reluctant to participate in the future. Managers must make it clear that not every idea contributed by an employee can be implemented but will be carefully considered in the planning process.

EDUCATING

Change in business does not just happen. New products, new technology, or redesigned jobs require people to prepare. Usually, that means information and training. As plans for change develop, managers must determine who will be affected and what new knowledge and skills those employees will need. Then managers should implement information meetings and training programs to prepare employees for the required changes.

Many companies have had to reduce the number of employees through downsizing. That type of change is very difficult for managers to implement and employees to accept. Some companies try to help the people who will no longer have jobs by offering training for other positions available in the company or to develop skills that will help them get jobs with another company.

SUPPORTING

How willing are you to make a change if you are uncertain of the result? When people believe they will receive support from their organization, they are more willing to accept changes. All changes involve some amount of risk, and organizations cannot guarantee success. However, managers need to assure employees that there is support available to help them adjust to the change.

The support can take many forms, such as allowing employees time to adjust to change. Managers may provide more feedback on employee performance and be less critical of mistakes early in the process. Counseling, training, and additional information are other methods of support.

Sometimes changes have negative effects on employees that cannot be avoided. Employees may have to be terminated or undergo major job changes that can require reductions in pay, different working conditions, and so forth. Support is especially needed under those circumstances. Employees who lose their jobs need time to adjust. Companies may provide full or partial salary for several weeks or months while the people affected try to find new jobs. The companies may look for other positions in the organization and help employees retrain or relocate. They can also give preference to those employees when new positions open. Many companies now provide personal and career counseling, help with job-seeking skills, and even pay for employment services for employees who are terminated due to change.

CHECKPOINT

What steps should managers follow to help employees understand and adjust to a major change?

Implementing change includes supporting employees who are affected by the change. What are the different ways employers can provide this support?

PHOTO: © GETTY IMAGES/PHOTODISC.

14.2 Assessment

UNDERSTAND MANAGEMENT CONCEPTS

Determine the best answer for each of the following questions.

1. The motivation theory that people are influenced most strongly by one of three specific needs—achievement, affiliation, or power—was developed by
   a. Maslow
   b. McClelland
   c. Pavlov
   d. Herzberg

2. Which of the following is *not* an effective way for a manager to implement change?
   a. Do not move too rapidly to implement change.
   b. Don't say anything to employees until a final decision has been made.
   c. Ask employees for ideas on effective solutions and procedures.
   d. Be less critical of mistakes made by employees while changes are being made.

THINK CRITICALLY

Answer the following questions as completely as possible.

3. Do you agree or disagree that increases in pay and other financial benefits are not good motivators for most employees? Explain your answer.

4. How do you believe a manager should involve employees in planning for a change that will result in some of the employees losing their jobs?

Xtra!
Study Tools
thomsonedu.com/school/bpmxtra

Focus On...

Teamwork–Changing the Face of Manufacturing

You can't make a mistake when building airplane engines. The jet engines produced by the General Electric Aircraft Engines plant in Durham, North Carolina, have over 10,000 parts. When completely assembled, they weigh more than eight tons. Yet a bolt not tightened, a tool left inside the engine, or a safety procedure not followed can cost hundreds of lives.

Approximately 200 people assemble the huge engines. But there is only one boss, the plant manager, and one instruction to guide the work of the plant—the date each engine needs to be finished. Beyond that instruction, employees make every decision about how the work will be completed. They hold a record for delivering every engine ordered on schedule for over three years. During that time, they were able to reduce the cost of producing the engine by nearly one-third.

How does this GE plant achieve its amazing record with only one manager? Here are some unique characteristics of the organization:

- Employees are organized into nine teams that make almost all decisions. Everyone is on a team, and team meetings are scheduled when all employees are available.
- There are three pay levels for employees, based on skill levels. As employees increase their skills, they can advance into a higher pay level.
- There is no time clock. If someone has a doctor's appointment or needs to go to their child's school activities, they work with team members to be able to leave.
- Everyone learns how to do many of the assembly tasks so they can help each other.
- Teams are responsible for hiring new team members. They do the interviewing, and they have to agree on the right person.
- Teams solve problems and often come up with unique but simple solutions.

The team environment in Durham works. The plant has the lowest turnover rate and lowest production costs of any of General Electric's engine assembly plants. Its unique organization demonstrates that when employees are given the chance to work together to manage their work, they do it better than anyone could have imagined.

Think Critically

1. How do you believe the pay plan affects employee motivation? What are the advantages and disadvantages of that plan?
2. Discuss reasons why the team problem-solving process seems to result in unique but effective solutions. Are there reasons a solution developed by employees is likely to be more successful than if the same solution was developed by a manager without the input of employees?

14.3 The Controlling Function

Goals
- List the three basic steps in the controlling function.
- Identify and describe four types of standards.

Terms
- quantity standard
- quality standard
- variance

Understanding Controlling

"Employee absences have increased by 3 percent this year."

"Maintenance costs are down an average of $150 per vehicle."

"Salespeople in the southern district have increased new customer orders by 12.3 percent in a three-year period."

"An average of 16 additional employees per month are enrolling in the company's wellness program."

"The adjustments to the welding robot's computer program have reduced the variations in the seam to 0.0004 mm."

These statements provide very valuable information to managers. With the proper information, managers can tell how well activities are being performed. Reviewing performance is one part of the fourth management function—controlling. Managers must be able to determine if performance meets expectations. If problems are occurring, managers need problem-solving skills to develop good solutions. In the last two lessons of this chapter, you will study the controlling function of management.

MANAGEMENT AS A CONTINUOUS PROCESS

As you have learned, all managers perform four management functions. Planning involves setting goals and directions for the business. Organizing deals with obtaining and arranging resources so the goals can be met. Implementing is the responsibility for carrying out the work of the organization. Controlling is determining whether goals are being met and what actions to take if performance falls short of the goals.

Although each of the functions includes a specific set of activities, they are all related. Planning improves if there is an effective organization to provide information to managers. Without effective planning, it is difficult to decide how to organize a business and what resources are needed. Implementation is impossible without plans and difficult with a poorly designed organization. Controlling cannot be completed unless the company has specific goals and plans. Figure 14-4 shows that management is a continuous process and that each function supports the others. Controlling is the final function and provides the information needed to improve the management process and business operations.

THE STEPS IN CONTROLLING

Controlling involves three basic steps: (1) establishing standards for each of the company's goals, (2) measuring and comparing performance against the established standards to see if performance met the goals, and (3) taking corrective action when performance falls short of the standards.

Consider the following example. A business has a goal to manufacture and deliver to a customer 1,000 made-to-order blankets by a specific date. The standard is to produce 25 blankets each day for 40 consecutive days. During the first 10 days, only 200 blankets are produced, or an average of 20 blankets a day. Because production is 50 blankets below the standard—250 blankets in 10 days—the managers must take action to increase production during the remaining 30 days. The corrective action may include scheduling overtime work or assigning more workers to the task. Even as they take action, the managers should carefully study the manufacturing process to see why the standard that was originally set could not be met.

As another example, the manager of a shoe store wants to make sure that new styles of shoes sell rapidly. The standard is to sell 30 percent of all shoes in a new style within one month. If the store sells only 20 percent, the manager must take corrective action. The manager may choose to increase the advertising for the shoes, give salespeople a higher commission for selling that style, or mark down the price to sell more. The manager will also want to use this information when planning purchases in the future.

In each example, the managers had to set a standard based on the work to be accomplished. Then they compared performance against the standard to see if the company's goals could be met. Finally, if performance was not meeting the standard, the managers had to determine how to correct the problem. Note that in both examples the managers did not wait very long to begin measuring performance. Controlling activities should be completed before the problem is too big or too expensive to correct.

FIGURE 14-4 The four functions of management are directly related.

controlling

planning

organizing

implementing

CHECKPOINT

What are the three basic steps in controlling?

Setting Standards

Managers establish standards in the planning stage. They need to set high but achievable standards. Managers can determine reasonable standards by studying the job, using their past experience, gathering industry information, and asking for input from experienced workers. The standards become the means for judging success and for applying controls.

TYPES OF STANDARDS

The standards used to control business operations depend on the type of business, the size of the business, and the activities being controlled. The major types of standards are quantity, quality, time, and cost standards.

QUANTITY STANDARDS A **quantity standard** establishes the expected amount of work to be completed. Quantity standards take different forms, depending on the tasks. Production managers may specify the minimum number of units to be produced each hour, day, or month by individual workers or groups of workers. Sales managers may establish the number of prospective customers that sales representatives must contact daily or weekly. A manager of administrative services may establish a minimum number of forms to be completed or number of lines of information to be keyed in an hour by information-processing personnel. The quotas Jasmine established for her employees in the telemarketing department described at the beginning of the chapter are examples of quantity standards.

QUALITY STANDARDS Quantity standards alone are often not enough to judge an employee, a product, or a service. A fast worker, for example, can be very careless, or a slow worker can be extremely careful. Thus, the quality of the work performed is often just as important as the quantity produced. A **quality standard** describes expected consistency in production or performance.

Perfection—having no errors—may be the only acceptable standard for some products and services. An automobile battery that does not work cannot be sold. An invoice with pricing errors cannot be sent to a customer. An accountant cannot calculate a client's taxes incorrectly. Perfection is the standard, but it may not always be practical or cost-effective to develop procedures to check every finished product. On an assembly line where thousands of products are produced every hour, sampling a few products each hour may be enough to identify when quality problems occur so corrective action can be taken.

TIME STANDARDS Time standards are closely related to quantity and quality standards. Most business activities can be measured by time. The amount of time it takes to complete an activity has an effect on costs, the quantity of work completed, and often on the quality of the work. Time standards are more important to some businesses than to others. Building contractors, bakeries, and newspaper publishers normally have very strict time schedules. If they do not meet the schedules, they suffer an immediate financial loss. If a building is not completed on time, the builder usually must pay a financial penalty. A baker who does not have doughnuts and bagels ready for the breakfast rush will lose a major portion of the day's sales. A day-old newspaper has almost no value to the reader. Other businesses may not see the immediate financial loss, but failure to maintain time standards will result in fewer products being produced, poor coordination of activities between departments, or other problems.

COST STANDARDS An important measure of the success or failure of a firm is financial profit or loss. Profit equals sales income (called "revenue") minus costs. Therefore, managers can increase profits by either (1) increasing sales revenue or (2) decreasing costs. Not all managers or employees are directly connected with work that increases sales. However, most employees and managers do influence costs. Wasting material or taking more time than necessary to perform a task adds to the cost of doing business. Increased costs, without a proportionate increase in sales dollars, decrease profit. Businesses must be cost-conscious at all times.

Generally, businesses pay more attention to cost controls than to any other type of control. The control devices used, as a result, are numerous. One of the main purposes of the accounting department is to provide detailed cost information. This is why the head of an accounting department is often called a *controller*. Most managers, however, act as cost controllers in some way. Increasingly, employee work teams and individual employees are assigned responsibility for cost controls.

The most widely used controlling device is the budget. Like schedules and standards, budgets are also planning devices. When a budget is prepared, it is a planning device; after that, it is a controlling device. Actual cost information is collected and compared with budgeted amounts. These comparisons permit judgments about the success of planning efforts and provide clues for making changes that will help the company reach its financial goals. Again, managers should not wait too long to check on costs. They can take corrective action if they identify budget problems early. If they wait too long, the needed changes may cause serious problems.

business note

Effective controlling requires that managers study a large amount of numerical data, determine its meaning, and make good decisions based on that information. An important business skill is understanding data presented in a number of forms—tables, graphs, charts, and even unorganized or "raw" data. Often simple statistics are used to summarize data, such as percentages, averages, and comparisons. Managers need to understand how to review data to make sure the information is complete, unbiased, and objective. They must make sure the reports provide all the information needed to understand the situation being studied. What experience have you had in reading and interpreting data? Have you had any coursework in statistics?

MEASURING AND COMPARING PERFORMANCE

Standards become the basis for determining effective performance. Managers gather information on all parts of business operations for which they are responsible. They compare that information against the standards to determine if performance is meeting the standards. A variance is a difference between current performance and the standard. A variance can be positive (performance exceeds standard) or negative (performance falls short of standard). Whenever a variance exists, managers must identify the reasons for the difference.

Actual performance exceeding the standard may seem to be an ideal situation that requires no corrective action. However, it is important to understand why the higher-than-expected performance occurred so that it can be repeated. Or, perhaps the positive performance in one area of the business is having a negative effect on another area. In addition, managers should review the process for developing standards to see why they set the standard lower than the performance that could actually be achieved.

The greatest concern occurs when performance is lower than the standard. That means that the company will probably not be able to perform at the expected level. It also says that there are problems between planning and implementing activities. Managers not only need to take corrective action as soon as possible to improve performance but must review procedures carefully to avoid the same problem in the future. Managers must be careful in the way they communicate the problem to employees and how they take corrective action. If employees believe the manager is blaming them for the poor performance, they may not be motivated to help solve the problem. On the other hand, if employees do not recognize the seriousness of the problem, they will continue the past level of performance, which will not result in improvement.

Monitoring all activities for which managers are responsible can take a great deal of time. Managers can use information systems to reduce the amount of time spent on controlling. Computers can monitor performance and compare it to the standard. When the computer identifies a variance, it prepares a variance report for the manager. Through the use of computer monitoring and variance reports, managers can identify problems quickly.

CHECKPOINT

Provide an example of each of the four types of standards.

14.3   Assessment

UNDERSTAND MANAGEMENT CONCEPTS

Determine the best answer for each of the following questions.

1. The final step managers take in the controlling process is
   a. establishing performance standards for company goals
   b. measuring performance using established standards
   c. establishing new goals
   d. taking corrective action when standards are not met

2. Consistency in products and performance is measured with a
   a. quantity standard
   b. quality standard
   c. time standard
   d. cost standard

THINK CRITICALLY

Answer the following questions as completely as possible.

3. Do you believe managers should perform each of the management functions in order? Why or why not?

4. Which type of standard do you believe is most important to improving the overall effectiveness of a business? Justify your choice.

Xtra!
Study Tools
thomsonedu.com/school/bpmxtra

14.4 Gathering and Using Performance Information

Goals
- Describe three corrective actions managers can take as part of controlling performance.
- Discuss several important areas of cost control in businesses.

Terms
- just-in-time (JIT) inventory controls

Taking Corrective Action

When managers discover that performance is not meeting standards, they can take three possible actions:

1. Take steps to improve performance.
2. Change policies and procedures.
3. Revise the standard.

If managers have planned carefully, they should be reluctant to change standards. In the blanket-manufacturing business discussed earlier, managers should know from past experience whether producing 25 blankets a day is reasonable. Only under unusual circumstances (major equipment breakdown, problems with suppliers, employee strikes, etc.) would the blanket managers reduce the standard. However, failure to meet the goal of 1,000 blankets by the specified date will not please the customer and may result in a loss of sales.

Most often, managers need to improve performance of activities when standards are not being met. This usually means making sure that the work is well organized, that supplies and materials are available when needed, that equipment is in good working order, and that employees are well trained and motivated.

Occasionally, standards are not met because activities cannot be accomplished as planned, or policies and procedures are not appropriate. This is likely to happen when a business begins a new procedure, starts to use new equipment, or has other major changes. In this situation, managers may need to change the policies or procedures that are not working in order to meet the standards. Process improvement discussed earlier usually results in policy or procedure changes.

Finally, when the managers have explored all possibilities to improve performance and it still does not meet the standards, they need to evaluate the standards themselves. Planning is usually not exact. Conditions can change between the time plans and standards are developed and the time activities are performed. Managers cannot expect that all standards will be appropriate. Managers like to raise standards when they believe workers can achieve higher performance. It is difficult to make the decision to reduce standards, but that may be necessary from time to time. If a group of new employees is doing the task, performance standards may need to be reduced until the employees have had the necessary training and opportunity to perfect their skills.

When new planning procedures are used or new activities are implemented, planning is less likely to be accurate. Standards developed in those situations should be studied more carefully than the standards for ongoing activities or standards that have been developed in the same way for a long period of time.

Standards should be revised when it is clear they will not accurately reflect performance and attempts to improve performance have been unsuccessful. When standards are changed, the new standards and the reasons for the changes should be clearly communicated to the employees affected. Also, the procedures for setting standards should be revised so that standards developed in the future are more accurate.

CHECKPOINT

Why should managers be reluctant to change standards even when performance does not meet those standards?

Controlling Costs

All managers need to watch constantly for ways to reduce costs. Excessive costs reduce the company's profit. There are several areas in a business where managers can anticipate cost problems and develop ways to reduce costs. They are inventory, credit, theft, and employee health and safety.

INVENTORY Manufacturers need to produce enough of each product to fill the orders they receive. They need enough raw materials to produce those products. Wholesalers and retailers must maintain inventories to meet their customers' needs. In all types of businesses, if inventories are too low, sales will be lost. If inventories are too high, costs of storage and handling will increase. There may be products in inventory that are never used or sold. In that situation, the company loses all of the money invested in those products.

Inventory control requires managers to walk a fine line. They must maintain sufficient inventory to meet their production and sales needs yet not so much that it is too costly to handle and store. They must select products to purchase that can be sold quickly at a profit. They must purchase products at the right time and in the correct quantities to minimize the company's inventory cost.

Many companies now use just-in-time (JIT) inventory controls. JIT is a method of inventory control in which the company maintains very small inventories and obtains materials just in time for use. To set up a JIT system, managers carefully study production time, sales activity, and purchasing requirements to determine the lowest possible inventory levels. They then place orders for materials so that they arrive just as they are needed for production or to fill sales orders. Production levels are set so the company has only enough products to fill orders as they are received. Effective inventory control methods can be very complicated. JIT inventory management requires the close support and cooperation of a company's suppliers as well as the companies providing transportation services to resupply inventories.

Inventory control is a kind of balancing act. What factors need to be in place for just-in-time inventory controls to be successful?

PHOTO: © GETTY IMAGES/PHOTODISC.

CREDIT Most businesses must be able to extend credit to customers. Businesses also use credit when buying products from suppliers. If the company extends credit to customers who do not pay their bills, the company loses money. Also, businesses that use credit too often when making purchases spend a great deal of money on interest payments. Those payments add to the total cost of the product and reduce profits.

Businesses must develop credit policies to reduce the amount of losses from credit sales. They must check customers' credit history carefully before offering them credit. They must develop billing and collection procedures that will collect most accounts on time. The age of an account is the number of days that payment is past due. Managers need to watch the age of each credit account. The longer an account goes unpaid, the greater the chance that the company will never collect the full payment.

Companies should buy on credit when they will lose money if they don't make the purchase. If a production schedule cannot be maintained without the credit purchase and if the price that can be charged for the sale of the product is high enough to cover the added cost, the credit purchase should be made. Companies may also need credit to purchase expensive equipment or large orders of products and materials. But managers responsible for purchasing must control the amount of money the company owes to other businesses. It is easy to make too many purchases on credit. When this happens, the interest charges are very high, and the company may not have enough money to pay all of its debts on time.

Managers must be sure bills are paid on time to protect the credit reputation of the business. If the supplier offers a discount for paying cash, managers should check to see if the company will benefit from taking advantage of the discount. Before using credit, managers should study the credit terms to see what the final cost will be. Credit can be a good business tool if used carefully but can harm the business if not controlled.

THEFT Businesses can lose a great deal of money if products are stolen. Thefts can occur in many parts of a business and can be done by employees as well as by customers and others. Businesses can lose cash, merchandise, supplies, and other resources due to theft. By establishing theft controls, businesses usually are able to reduce losses.

The theft of merchandise from warehouses and stores is a major business concern. Retail stores are the hardest hit by such losses. Retailers lose billions of dollars annually due to crime, much of which is from theft of merchandise. Shoplifting by customers and employees equals 6 percent or more of total sales each year for the typical retailer. Much of the loss occurs during the end-of-year holiday shopping season when stores are crowded and part-time workers are employed, but it is an ongoing and serious problem throughout the year.

Many stores, warehouses, and trucks are burglarized during the night or when merchandise is being transported. Security guards or special equipment are frequently used to reduce the chances of such thefts. Many companies carry insurance against losses, but with high loss rates the cost of insurance is very expensive.

A rapidly growing area of concern to businesses and consumers alike is computer and Internet fraud. Business data and personal information are held in large and small computer files. Financial records and personal identity information are moved back and forth via the Internet. Data are exchanged online as part of many business transactions. Businesses increasingly contract with specialized companies to handle activities such as order processing, customer billing, accounting, and personnel management. Businesses must carefully plan and review all procedures for gathering, storing, and exchanging data to ensure the highest level of security and to prevent data and identity theft.

Employee theft costs employers over $1 billion a week and is a major cause of small-business bankruptcies. It is estimated that 3 out of every 10 employees engage in some theft and that 95 percent of all businesses have an ongoing employee theft problem. Businesses employ security specialists, review cash handling and inventory procedures, use security cameras and other monitoring devices, and prosecute employees guilty of theft.

Businesses and individual computer users must apply security measures to protect data and personal information. Have you ever experienced identity theft?

PHOTO: © GETTY IMAGES/PHOTODISC.

HEALTH AND SAFETY Even when employees are absent from work because of sickness or injury, the company must continue to operate. Other employees must be available to fill in for the absent employee or the work will go undone. Usually, the salary of both the absent employee and the substitute employee must be paid. A share of health insurance costs and other benefits are often paid by the company as well. Studies estimate that the annual costs to many businesses of employee absence and health care now exceed 20 percent of the salary paid to each employee. An employee paid at the rate of $7.00 per hour requires an additional $1.40 each hour to pay those costs. A person earning $35,000 will add $7,000 or more to the costs of the business just for health expenses and employee absences.

The increasing cost of health insurance is causing many businesses to increase the percentage of premiums paid by employees and to drop their insurance coverage of part-time employees. Companies are working with insurance companies to find lower-cost insurance alternatives that may reduce benefits for employees. Many companies offer no health insurance benefits at all. The cost of health insurance is one of the major issues facing business managers and employees today.

Many businesses have found that costs that result from health and safety problems can be reduced if managed carefully. These companies provide safety training for all employees. Work areas and equipment are inspected regularly to make sure they operate correctly and safely. Employees are provided information on ways to improve their health. Investments in fitness centers and exercise programs have resulted in lower costs for the business due to fewer medical claims and reduced employee absences.

CHECKPOINT

Describe several ways that managers can reduce costs in the business by paying attention to areas where costs are often high.

14.4 Assessment

UNDERSTAND MANAGEMENT CONCEPTS

Determine the best answer for each of the following questions.

1. Which of the following is *not* one of the actions managers should take if they discover that performance is not meeting standards?
   a. Take steps to improve performance.
   b. Change policies and procedures.
   c. Revise the standard.
   d. Each of the actions is appropriate.

2. The best credit policy for a company is to
   a. never make purchases on credit
   b. charge very high interest rates to customers to increase profits
   c. only buy on credit when it will lose money if the purchase isn't made
   d. pay for credit purchases well before payment is due

THINK CRITICALLY

Answer the following questions as completely as possible.

3. Explain the meaning of the statement "Planning is usually not exact" as it applies to evaluating performance and standards.

4. What recommendations would you make to a business to increase computer and Internet security for the business and its customers?

Xtra!
Study Tools
thomsonedu.com/school/bpmxtra

CHAPTER CONCEPTS

- Implementing involves communicating effectively, motivating employees to do their best work, developing work teams, and managing company operations.

- People choose to do things that will satisfy their needs and avoid things that don't. Managers influence performance by providing rewards when employees accomplish work goals. Theories of motivation developed by Maslow, McClelland, and Herzberg describe factors that influence employee behavior.

- Change is common in organizations and managers need to help employees accept change. The steps in an effective change process are planning, communicating, involving, educating, and supporting.

- Controlling ensures that company operations meet expectations. Controlling steps are: establishing standards for goals, measuring and comparing performance against standards, and taking corrective action when performance falls short of standards. Common types of standards are quantity, quality, time, and cost standards.

- To help the company make a profit, managers must control costs. Areas commonly monitored for cost control are inventory, credit, theft, and employee health and safety.

REVIEW TERMS AND CONCEPTS

Write the letter of the term that matches each definition. Some terms will not be used.

a. achievement need
b. affiliation need
c. hygiene factors
d. just-in-time (JIT) inventory controls
e. motivation
f. motivators
g. power need
h. process improvement
i. quality standard
j. quantity standard
k. variance
l. work team

1. Group of individuals who cooperate to achieve a common goal
2. Wanting to influence and control others and be responsible for a group's activities
3. Difference between current performance and the standard
4. Standard that describes expected consistency in production or performance
5. Job factors that dissatisfy when absent but do not contribute to satisfaction when they are present
6. Set of factors that influence an individual's actions toward accomplishing a goal
7. System in which the company maintains very small inventories and obtains materials just in time for use
8. Taking personal responsibility for work, setting personal goals, and wanting immediate feedback on work
9. Standard that establishes the expected amount of work to be completed
10. Efforts to increase the effectiveness and efficiency of specific business operations

DETERMINE THE BEST ANSWER

11. Effective work teams have all of the following characteristics *except*
    a. all members understand and support the group's purpose
    b. the team does not need to have a group leader
    c. members work to resolve problems in the group
    d. All are characteristics of effective groups.
12. The person who described motivation in terms of a hierarchy of needs was
    a. Maslow
    b. Herzberg
    c. McClelland
    d. Jacobs
13. It is frequently said that people support what they
    a. choose to
    b. are paid for
    c. create
    d. have been told to support
14. The first step in the controlling process is
    a. establishing standards for each of the company's goals
    b. communicating with employees about the importance of controlling
    c. taking corrective action when performance falls short of standards
    d. organizing employees into work groups
15. Which of the following is not a way managers can increase profits?
    a. Increase sales revenues.
    b. Decrease costs.
    c. Add more employees.
    d. All are correct.
16. A production manager who specifies the minimum number of units to be produced each hour, day, or month is establishing a
    a. variance
    b. time standard
    c. quality standard
    d. quantity standard

APPLY WHAT YOU KNOW

17. Based on the Reality Check scenario at the beginning of the chapter, do you believe most of the problems were the result of poor planning or poor implementation? Justify your answer.
18. Why are businesses paying much more attention to developing effective work teams today than in the past?
19. What differences in implementation and controlling activities, if any, would there be for a manager of a small business and a manager in a large business?
20. What should a manager do if it is clear that many employees will view a planned change negatively?

21. What are some examples of business activities where perfection is the only acceptable standard for performance?
22. Should managers delegate controlling activities to employees and employee teams? Why or why not?

MAKE CONNECTIONS

23. **Teamwork** Form a team with three or four other students in your class to analyze motivation theories. As a team, develop a list of at least 15 things you believe motivate employees to perform well. After completing the list, prepare diagrams using a computer graphics program or on separate sheets of paper that illustrate each of the three motivation theories discussed in the chapter. Then add your team's motivating items in the appropriate locations on each of the three illustrations. Present your diagrams to the other teams and provide reasons for your decisions about the motivating items and the theories.

24. **Mathematics** The following chart shows several items from a company's budget. Column 1 shows the categories for which a budget amount has been determined. The budgeted amounts are shown in Column 2 and the actual amounts are shown in Column 3. Complete the chart by calculating the variance between the budgeted and actual amounts (Column 4) and the percentage increase or decrease (Column 5).

Budget Category	Budget	Actual	Variance	% + or −
Sales	$680,000	$720,000		
Merchandise returns	11,000	12,500		
Cost of goods	229,400	240,000		
Operating expenses	52,000	46,500		
Administrative costs	34,000	31,500		
Marketing expenses	306,000	350,500		
Net profit	47,600	39,000		

25. **Writing** Choose one of the following statements that best represents your beliefs. Write a one-page paper defending the statement and suggesting why the other statement is not correct in your opinion.
    a. The best way to develop management skills is to work for a company for several years and observe successful managers doing their work. You can't learn management from a book.
    b. Management in the 21st century is very different from management in the past. The best managers take classes to study management activities and motivation theories rather than relying on experience.

26. **Research** Gather information on the Internet about the growing problem of identity theft. Use a computer and presentation software to identify steps consumers can take to protect their personal information.

that runs on personal computers has replaced most manual systems. However, standardized accounting forms and records systems for manual recordkeeping can be obtained at office supply stores.

Many small firms rely primarily on their cash register to gather most of the information needed for their financial records. In addition to printing receipts for customers, cash registers maintain printed tapes of the details of each sales transaction. This information can be used to enter data into the business's accounting records. However, cash registers record only information on customer sales, which is an incomplete record of the financial transactions of the business. Records also have to be maintained of all purchases and payments as well as any income received that is not recorded in the cash register.

LARGE-SCALE RECORD SYSTEMS Today most large firms and many small ones use accounting software programs to record, process, and store information. A desktop computer is adequate for most small companies, but larger firms need more complex systems that can process huge amounts of data quickly and accurately. Large corporations employ many bookkeepers and accountants. Some prefer to hire outside firms to perform some of their required financial record keeping.

Outsourcing is hiring an outside firm to perform specialized tasks for a business. A business outsources because the firm that is hired has specialized expertise that the business needs. Buying these expert services may be less expensive than creating a new department in the business. An example of outsourcing for financial services is contracting with a data-processing center. A **data-processing center** is a specialized business that provides a full set of computerized financial records to other businesses for a fee. A business transmits financial data to the data-processing center, which processes the data and prepares records and reports that the business needs. Usually the center stores and maintains financial records for the business. Many firms use a data-processing center to outsource selected tasks, such as preparing bills for customers, keeping track of inventory, and preparing payroll records and checks. Banks and data-processing firms like ADP and EDS are popular for outsourcing. Data can be transmitted over the Internet and reports returned overnight, even when the data-processing centers are located in other countries.

Large companies require large and complex automated systems for keeping records. Accounting departments usually maintain these records, although the initial recording of transactions occurs throughout the organization. An accounting department is commonly divided into several sections. Each section is typically responsible for handling one or more phases of accounting, such as cash records, receipt and payment records, depreciation records, and tax and payroll records.

Most large stores with many branches use sophisticated cash registers connected to computers. Such a register is called a *point-of-sale terminal.* When cashiers use bar code scanners to record sales, for example, each item sold is subtracted from the inventory recorded in the computer. The computer calculates when the store needs to reorder merchandise (based on predetermined inventory needs) and provides other valuable information for management. With point-of-sale terminals, scanners electronically read product codes stamped on merchandise, thereby speeding the checkout

Technology allows companies to have their data processing done by companies that may be located in countries thousands of miles away.

PHOTO: © CREATAS IMAGES.

service for customers and reducing manual paperwork and labor costs for the store. Products and their costs can actually be tracked continually from the point of production through the entire distribution process until the products are sold.

CHECKPOINT
Identify several reasons businesses need to maintain financial records.

Types of Financial Records

Financial records in all types of businesses have similar characteristics. A few of the most common records kept by all businesses are discussed next.

CASH RECORDS

Cash is constantly coming into a business from customers and other sources, and cash must go out of the business to pay for things purchased. Regardless of how financial records are maintained, businesses follow similar procedures in accounting for cash. Figure 15-1 lists several suggestions for the safe handling of cash.

CREDIT RECORDS

All businesses must deal with money that they receive as a result of the sale of goods or services to customers. Because most businesses sell on credit, they keep records showing what each customer owes and pays. This record is called an **accounts receivable record**. When a credit sale is made, the salesperson completes an order, which is submitted to the accounting department. The accounting department enters the sale into the accounts receivable record and sends an invoice of the sale to the customer that identifies the payment terms and dates. When payments are made by the customer, the payments are recorded in the business records.

Businesses must also keep records showing money they owe and payments they make for all credit purchases. This kind of record is an **accounts payable record**. Each time a credit purchase is made, that purchase and its terms are recorded in the accounts payable record. When payments are made to the creditor, they are also recorded so the company has an accurate record of what they owe on each account.

DEPRECIATION RECORDS

An **asset** is anything of value owned. Businesses need to have a variety of assets, such as buildings, vehicles, equipment, and inventory, for use in their normal operations.

FIGURE 15-1 Safe and Accurate Handling of Cash in a Business

1. A *petty cash fund*, a supply of cash maintained in a business for small emergency payments, should be kept in a safe place with a responsible person. A written record of additions and withdrawals to the fund should be maintained.

2. A specific policy and procedures should be followed if small cash withdrawals from a cash register are allowed. A written form must be completed, signed by the person making the withdrawal, and placed in the register.

3. Cash registers should have a daily change fund of a specific amount to start each day's operations. A procedure to collect, count, and verify cash register receipts should be followed on a regular schedule at least daily. Any overages or shortages should be accounted for each time the cash balance is verified. Two or more people should work together to collect and verify cash register receipts.

4. All cash receipts should be counted, recorded, and immediately deposited in a bank. Do not keep large cash balances in the business. Make deposits in a bank frequently, several times a day if necessary.

5. Endorse all checks when received for deposit either with a cash register imprint or a rubber stamp.

6. All payments except petty cash amounts should be made by check or credit card so a written record is maintained.

7. Pay salaries by check or direct deposit, not cash.

8. Audit all cash receipts, payments, and deposits regularly and compare them with financial records. Reconcile bank statements as soon as they are received. Business records and bank records must be in balance. Any discrepancies must be resolved immediately.

Businesses need to plan for the replacement of expensive equipment that will lose their value over a number of years.

The value of an asset decreases through use over time. This gradual loss of an asset's value due to age and wear is called **depreciation**. For example, a Jiffy Lube franchise owner buys a computerized diagnostic tool that costs $16,000. The owner knows from experience that at the end of five years the equipment will not be worth any more than $1,000. The owner estimates, therefore, that the equipment will wear out or depreciate at the average rate of $3,000 a year:

$$\$16,000 - \$1,000 = \$15,000 \text{ value lost}$$
$$\$15,000/5 \text{ years} = \$3,000 \text{ depreciation per year}$$

When the diagnostic equipment loses its usefulness, it must be replaced. Therefore, depreciation represents a cost to the business.

Fixed assets are expensive assets of a business that are expected to last and be used for a long time. Buildings, land, and expensive equipment are common examples of fixed assets. Except for land, fixed assets depreciate over time. A business records the value of fixed assets on its books when it purchases them. They become part of the property the business owns. As the assets wear out or become less valuable, the business is allowed by law to charge the loss in value each year as an operating expense.

PHOTO: © BANANASTOCK.

Property may also decrease in value because of *obsolescence*. That is, even though the asset is still usable, it becomes out-of-date or inadequate for a particular purpose. An older computer, for example, may not have the capacity to run new software or manage the number of transactions as a business grows. Even though the computer still functions, it is obsolete and no longer as valuable to the business. Therefore, obsolescence is a form of depreciation.

The financial loss due to depreciation is very real, although it usually cannot be computed with great accuracy. Therefore, the Internal Revenue Service (IRS) provides rules and procedures that businesses must follow in calculating depreciation. Businesses need to maintain depreciation records and use them in their planning so they have money available to replace assets when they wear out.

SPECIAL ASSET RECORDS

Financial statements list assets and their values, but they do not provide detailed information about these assets. As a result, a business must keep special records. For example, a business should maintain a precise record of insurance policies, showing such details as type of policy, the company from which it was purchased, amount, premium, purchase and expiration dates, and the amount to be charged each month as insurance expense. A business also maintains detailed special records for all fixed assets, such as trucks and forklifts. These records provide such information as asset description, date of purchase, cost, monthly depreciation expense, and asset book value. *Asset book value* is the original cost less accumulated depreciation. In the Jiffy Lube example above, the equipment depreciates at a rate of $3,000 per year. At the end of the second year, the $16,000 equipment will have an asset book value of $10,000:

$3,000 depreciation $\times$ 2 years = $6,000 accumulated depreciation
$16,000 − $6,000 = $10,000 asset book value at the end of year 2

TAX AND PAYROLL RECORDS

Federal and state income tax laws require every business to keep satisfactory records in order to report its income and expenses, file required forms, and calculate and pay all required taxes. The law requires employers to withhold a certain percentage of each employee's wages for federal income tax purposes. It must do the same for Social Security, Medicare, and Medicaid. Other payments that employers must make to federal and state governments are for business taxes and government-sponsored unemployment compensation insurance.

For business planning as well as for tax purposes, businesses must keep detailed payroll records for each employee: hours worked, wage or salary rate, regular and overtime wages paid, and all types of deductions and withholding made from the employees' wages. Companies also record the value of benefits paid for each employee such as health insurance, paid vacation, and retirement benefits.

Each employee must fill out a W-4 form that provides information on the number of family members and exemptions. Using this information and a table furnished by the Internal Revenue Service, the employer determines the amount to withhold from the employee's paycheck. Employers submit payments of these withholdings to the IRS. Most companies use a computerized payroll system to maintain personnel records, to calculate payroll, and to process payments for each employee. Payroll information for an employee generated with QuickBooks® software is shown in Figure 15-2.

FIGURE 15-2 A Basic Payroll Record for One Employee

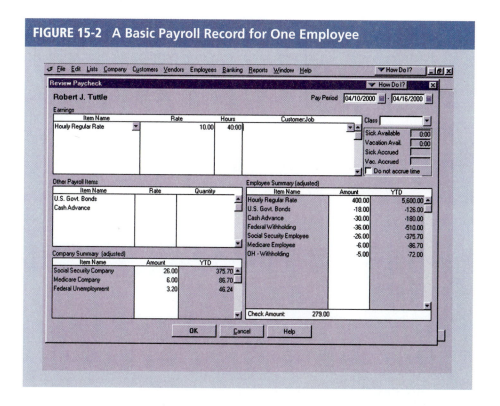

PROTECTING BUSINESS RECORDS

All financial records of a business, including personal information about customers and employees, must be maintained and retained for many years. Information must be secure from theft and misuse and also should be protected from hazards of nature such as fire, floods, hurricanes, and earthquakes. Also, the growing threat of terrorism offers other types of threats to businesses. Every business, therefore, should have secure areas such as vaults and safe rooms for records and secure areas for computer equipment and data storage. Fireproof and secure filing cabinets and other types of storage devices are also needed for maintaining important and frequently used documents. Methods to provide access to authorized people must be developed while keeping the information from those who are not authorized to access it.

Important documents such as mortgages, deeds, leases, contracts, and other critical but infrequently used documents may be better placed in bank safe deposit boxes or other secure locations if there is no adequate protection in the business. Companies protect their computer records by using such precautions as firewalls and passwords to keep out intruders. Most large organizations have security personnel or consultants who regularly review computer systems and

Vital business records must be specially protected to keep them from being damaged or destroyed.

PHOTO: © GETTY IMAGES/PHOTODISC.

look for attempts to "hack" or illegally access information from the computer systems. Companies should also store backup copies of electronic records in a secure off-site location. Service companies rent storage space on their computers or in their climate-controlled data warehouses for safe record archiving and protection.

CHECKPOINT

Describe five types of records a business should maintain.

15.1 Assessment

UNDERSTAND MANAGEMENT CONCEPTS

Determine the best answer for each of the following questions.

1. Which of the following is *not* a reason businesses need to maintain financial records?
   a. to determine the kinds and values of assets
   b. to track the financial progress of the business
   c. to prepare financial forms and reports required by the government
   d. to provide financial information to competitors

2. Expensive assets of a business that are expected to last and be used for a long time are known as
   a. fixed assets
   b. depreciated assets
   c. obsolete assets
   d. stable assets

THINK CRITICALLY

Answer the following questions as completely as possible.

3. Even if a business owner hires people to maintain financial records, why should he or she understand the procedures they use?

4. Describe several examples of ways that the financial records of a company can be harmed or damaged. For each example, how is the business harmed? How are others harmed? How can the company prevent the harm or damage?

Xtra!
Study Tools
thomsonedu.com/school/bpmxtra

15.2 Budgets and Budgeting

Goals

- Describe the uses of several types of business budgets.
- Discuss the reasons managers prepare more than one budget estimate.

Terms

- budget
- start-up budget
- operating budget
- capital budget
- sales budget

Business Budgets

Budgeting is critical to financial success. Studies of differences between successful and unsuccessful new businesses consistently find that businesses that carefully develop and follow budgets increase their chances of survival and success. The budgeting practices of successful businesses are (1) maintaining a complete and up-to-date set of financial records, (2) having financial records audited or checked by an experienced accountant, (3) keeping accurate records of business inventory and assets, and (4) using financial budgets as planning and management tools.

IMPORTANCE OF BUDGETS

A new company's business plan should include financial budgets for the first year of operations and more general financial projections for the next year or two. Unfortunately, many small businesses do not maintain a written budget for long even if one was developed as part of the business plan. Worse, a large number of business owners and managers report they don't have confidence in their ability to plan and use financial budgets.

A **budget** is a written financial plan for business operations developed for a specific period of time. Budgets are often developed for six months or a year but can cover a longer or shorter time period depending on the type of budget and the nature of the business. Budgets project and offer detail on the business's estimated revenue and expenses over the time period. Based on these estimates, businesses can set financial goals. They then use the budget to develop operating plans for that time period. By comparing actual results with financial goals and budget details throughout the year, managers can control operations and keep expenses in line with income. A realistic budget can prevent overspending and be used to plan for needed income, including the possibility of borrowed funds.

TYPES OF BUDGETS

Actual budgeting procedures depend on the type of business. For a small business, the process is mostly one of budgeting start-up costs, sales, expenses, purchases, and cash. Large businesses have a number of specialized budgets that predict the financial performance of departments and divisions of the company as well as specialized operations such as research and development, information technology, human resources, production, marketing, distribution and logistics, and many others.

In large businesses, the final overall budget for a business is made up of several specific budgets, such as the sales, merchandising, advertising, cash, capital, and operating budgets. Most specialized budgets are based on sales and income projections. However, in some types of businesses, either the production capacity or the financial capacity of the business or the unit for which the budget is being prepared must be determined first. Sales and all other estimates are then based on the amount that can be produced or the available financial resources for the time period.

START-UP BUDGET The **start-up budget** projects income and expenses from the beginning of a new business until it becomes profitable. A start-up budget is usually prepared in large and established businesses whenever a new venture is being planned, such as the introduction of a new product, expansion into a new market, or the development of a new type of business operation. Business start-ups usually require large expenditures for equipment, inventory, salaries, and operating expenses. Income will not be realized for some time while expenses grow. Even when the new company begins to sell products and services, the income will not be adequate to cover the initial expenses. A start-up budget will identify the start-up costs, initial operating expenses, types and sources of financing, and projected income for the time period of the budget.

OPERATING BUDGET An **operating budget** is a plan showing projected sales, costs, expenses, and profits for the ongoing operations of a business. It projects operating income and expenses for the entire business or for a specific part of the business for an identified time period such as three months, six months, or a year. The operating budget may also be called an income statement budget because it uses the same financial categories as the company's income statement. By subtracting its total projected costs and expenses from projected income, a business can estimate the profitability of its operations.

CASH BUDGET During normal operations, companies receive cash from sales and from borrowing and make cash payments for purchases and loan payments. The **cash budget** is an estimate of the flow of cash into and out of the business over a specified time period. Companies need a cash budget to make certain that enough cash will be available at the right times to meet payments as they come due. Cash comes into the company from two primary sources: (1) cash receipts and/or (2) borrowing. When companies borrow money, they must eventually pay it back. Therefore, the cash budget shows borrowed money as cash flowing in and repayments as cash flowing out when each payment is due.

Figure 15-3 shows a cash budget for a small business. Cash budgets are important for all companies, no matter how large or successful they are. A company can be highly profitable yet not have enough cash on hand at the right times to pay its bills. This situation could cause the company to borrow unnecessarily.

CAPITAL BUDGET Every business must plan for the costs of buildings, equipment, and other expensive purchases needed for its operations. Over the years, it must also budget to replace worn-out or obsolete fixed assets. For instance, if a company owns its own trucks and vans for distributing products, each will need to be replaced after a certain number of miles or years. A growing business plans for expansion by budgeting for the costs of new equipment, additions to buildings, and other major investments.

A **capital budget** is a financial plan for replacing fixed assets or acquiring new ones. Capital budgeting is important because acquiring assets ties up large sums of money for long periods of time. A wrong decision can be costly. For example, a decision to buy three new trucks that have a projected life of eight years involves

Technology *tip*

Both large and small companies can now use Internet-based financial programs rather than maintain financial software on a company computer. With online programs, authorized employees, suppliers, customers, and others needing access to specific financial information from the company can log on anytime from any computer in the world to input, retrieve, or work with company records. Of course the company must ensure that online records are secure and protected.

FIGURE 15-3   A Cash Budget

Cash Budget—for Three Months Ending March 31, 20--

	JANUARY	FEBRUARY	MARCH
NET SALES	$ 80,000	$ 80,000	$ 80,000
Beginning cash balance	33,500	4,000	7,000
Collections from customers	70,000	70,000	80,000
Total cash available	$103,500	$74,000	$87,000
Payments			
Accounts to be paid	45,000	45,000	60,000
Labor	9,500	12,000	16,000
Salaries and administrative expense	7,000	7,000	7,000
Sales expense	15,000	15,000	15,000
Other operating expenses	13,000	18,000	24,000
Purchase of fixed assets		10,000	10,000
Repayment of bank loan	10,000		
Total cash payments	$ 99,500	$107,000	$132,000
Expected cash shortage		33,000	45,000
Bank loans needed		40,000	50,000
Ending cash balance	4,000	7,000	5,000
End-of-month situation:			
Materials purchased	$ 45,000	$ 60,000	$ 80,000
Accounts receivable	150,000	160,000	170,000
Accounts payable	45,000	60,000	80,000
Bank loans		40,000	90,000

a large expenditure. The manager must plan well in advance if the money is to be available when the trucks are needed. Assume that the company buys the trucks based on a forecast that future sales will justify their need. However, if sales do not increase as expected, profits will be lower as a result of the added costs related to the purchase.

SALES BUDGET   The **sales budget** is a forecast of the sales revenue a company expects to receive in a month, a quarter (three months), or a year. Estimated sales are usually projected for sales territories, types of customers (government, industrial, consumer), sales representatives, geographic areas, or product categories. Sales managers responsible for the various categories (territories, customers, products) make independent estimates for the sales and expenses of their unit. The top sales manager uses those estimates to prepare a final sales budget. Sometimes managers prepare sales estimates with the idea of developing quotas or goals for sales representatives and territories. These estimates provide a goal for the sales department as well as a basis for preparing related budgets such as merchandising, advertising, or cash and operating budgets.

Figure 15-4 shows sales estimates determined in two different ways for the same company. Because the two sets of estimated figures are not the same, someone must combine them into one satisfactory estimate that the sales department can follow.

FIGURE 15-4 Two Ways of Forecasting Sales

Budget Based on Analysis of Sales Representatives

SALES REPRESENTATIVE	YEAR 1 SALES (ACTUAL)	YEAR 2 SALES (ESTIMATE)
T. A. Nader	$ 356,720	$ 380,000
H. E. Loch	348,380	360,000
C. D. Heidel	471,240	440,000
J. H. Sharmon	442,940	440,000
C. F. Powell	426,980	440,000
J. G. Dunbar	408,360	400,000
Total	$2,454,620	$2,460,000

Budget Based on Analysis of Products

PRODUCT	YEAR 1 SALES (ACTUAL)	YEAR 2 SALES (ESTIMATE)
Washers	$ 642,840	$ 680,000
Dryers	202,320	200,000
Ranges	189,260	180,000
Lamps	209,360	200,000
Refrigerators	1,210,840	1,300,000
Total	$2,454,620	$2,560,000

Numerous factors influence sales estimates. The specific operating and management factors of each company play an important part. Although one company may enjoy a high sales volume, another—at the same time and under the same conditions—may suffer a decline in sales. Economic conditions are often important in planning sales. If a good harvest and favorable prices for crops are anticipated in a certain area, a company that sells farm machinery should have good sales prospects in that area. A retail store in that same area might not anticipate the same increase in sales if agricultural customers make up a small percentage of their business. A major competitor entering a market for the first time may have a significant effect on established but smaller businesses. These are examples of some of the influences that should guide a manager in making sales estimates.

CHECKPOINT

Why is it important for a business to prepare a cash budget and a capital budget?

Administering the Budget

Because a budget is an estimate of what might happen, it usually cannot be followed exactly. Staying close to the amount budgeted is desirable. However, for various reasons beyond the control of managers, actual income and expenses may vary from the budgeted amounts. For that reason, managers often prepare three budget estimates. The first estimate assumes that sales will be less than expected. The second estimate considers what most likely will occur. And the third estimate assumes sales will be better than expected.

The second estimate—the one most likely to occur—is followed unless anticipated conditions change. If sales are less than expected, the business can shift immediately to the first (lower) set of budget figures. Should sales be better than expected, the business can shift to the third (higher) set of budget figures. Having more than one budget estimate allows for realistic flexibility during budget planning. It also forces managers to consider what might happen under favorable and unfavorable conditions and to be better prepared for rapid changes.

Whether a business is large or small or uses one or more budgets, managers must regularly use the budget to monitor ongoing operations and control expenses. That monitoring activity determines whether the business is on, under, or over budget. If expenditures exceed budgeted amounts, managers want to quickly understand why so they can make necessary changes. Some adjustments may be easy, whereas others may not even be possible. For example, labor costs might exceed budget estimates for the planned level of production because a number of new employees have been added who are not as productive as experienced employees. Additional training for those employees might help improve productivity, reducing the labor costs required to meet production goals during the rest of the budget period. However, if labor costs are higher than the budget because of an unanticipated increase in the minimum wage paid to a number of employees, little can be done to lower those costs in the short run.

If a comparison of actual operating performance with the budget estimates reveals that the business will not make the expected profit or will have a loss, the manager must review the expenses to determine what can be done to reduce them. Some expenses may be easier to reduce in the short run than others. However, cutting some expenses may lead to longer-term profitability problems. For example, if a manager tries to reduce costs in the short run by not purchasing new inventory, those costs will need to be increased in the future to replace the inventory or sales will be lost. Cutting the number of employees to save on labor costs may put too much pressure on the remaining employees. Their productivity may go down or some may quit, leading to increased costs to replace them.

The use of budgets and a budgeting system cannot guarantee the success of a business, but these management devices can help reduce losses or increase profits. The entire budgeting process is valuable in planning and controlling operations. But whether a business is a success or not can be determined only after the budget time periods have passed. Comparing budgets with actual operating conditions provides a basis for making timely and knowledgeable management decisions, which, in turn, leads to more accurate budgets and more profitable operations in the future.

CHECKPOINT

How do managers benefit from developing three different budget estimates for the same time period?

15.2 Assessment

UNDERSTAND MANAGEMENT CONCEPTS

Determine the best answer for each of the following questions.

1. A financial plan for replacing fixed assets or acquiring new ones is known as a(n)
   a. start-up budget
   b. capital budget
   c. operating budget
   d. cash budget

2. If a manager sees that actual expenses are exceeding budgeted amounts, he or she should immediately
   a. do nothing and see if things change
   b. discard the old budget and develop a new one
   c. review expenses to see what can be done to reduce them
   d. increase the prices of products to improve sales

THINK CRITICALLY

Answer the following questions as completely as possible.

3. How can the owner of a new business develop an accurate start-up budget when the business has not yet begun to operate?

4. Do you believe managers should involve their employees in developing financial budgets? Should they share budget information with employees? Why or why not?

15.3 Financial Reports

Goals

- Describe the information contained in a balance sheet statement and the importance of that information to a business.
- Explain how an income statement is different from a balance sheet and the value of the income statement to a business.

Terms

- financial statements
- balance sheet
- liabilities
- capital
- accounting equation
- income statement

Business activity is in large part measured in terms of money. The amount of money a business earns, its level of profitability, and the return received by owners and others who are involved in financing the business are important measures of its success. Because of the importance of the financial performance and financial condition of businesses, every business must (1) keep thorough and accurate records, (2) prepare important financial reports regularly, (3) interpret the financial information in the reports, and (4) make decisions that will have a positive influence on future financial results.

Financial statements are reports that summarize financial data over a period of time, such as a month, three months, half a year, or a full year. The two financial reports businesses use most are the *balance sheet* and the *income statement*. Each provides a specific view of the financial condition and financial performance of a business. Each is necessary to determining whether a business is being well managed or not.

Financial reports have many uses in business. Executives use them as a means to run an efficient, profitable business. Suppliers, lenders, employee unions, government agencies, and owners also use financial reports when making business decisions. Figure 15-5 (see p. 402) lists some reasons why various users need the financial information available in financial reports.

The Balance Sheet

A **balance sheet**, or *statement of financial position*, is a financial statement that reports a business's assets, liabilities, and capital on a specific date. As you learned in the last lesson, *assets* are anything of value owned, such as cash and buildings. **Liabilities** are claims against assets. In other words, liabilities are the business's debts. And **capital** (also called *net worth, owner's equity*, or *stockholders' equity*) is the value of the owners' investment in the business after subtracting liabilities from assets.

A balance sheet has two sides. Assets are listed and totaled on the left. Liabilities and capital are listed and totaled on the right. The two halves must always balance—thus the name. That is, the total of all assets must equal the total of all liabilities plus capital. In fact, the basic **accounting equation** is expressed as:

$$\text{Assets} = \text{Liabilities} + \text{Capital}$$

FIGURE 15-5 The financial reports of a business meet the information needs of several groups.

USER	NEEDS FINANCIAL DATA TO...
Manager	make day-to-day decisions. review past results. plan for the future.
Owner	decide whether to increase or decrease ownership investment. decide whether to continue business operations.
Supplier	decide whether to extend credit. decide how much credit to extend.
Lender	decide whether to lend a business money. decide on the terms of a loan to a business (amount, time period, and interest rate).
Union	determine fair increases in wages, salaries, and fringe benefits.
Government	arrive at fair tax rates. detect fraudulent practices.

Each balance sheet has a heading that includes the name of the business, the title "Balance Sheet," and the date. The information in the balance sheet presents a picture of the business's financial position on the date in the heading. Balance sheets are prepared at least once a year.

KINDS OF FINANCIAL DATA

An example of a balance sheet for a jewelry store, the Crown Corporation, is shown in Figure 15-6. On December 31, the accountants for the Crown Corporation prepared a balance sheet. The value of every asset the business owns is listed under Assets. As shown in the figure, Crown's total assets are $536,000. The company's debts—items purchased on credit and the mortgage still owed on the land and building—are listed under Liabilities, which total $136,000. The accountants subtracted total liabilities from total assets to calculate Crown's capital, $400,000.

Crown purchases jewelry from a manufacturer and then resells it to customers. Until the jewelry is sold, it is listed as an asset called merchandise inventory. *Merchandise inventory* is the value of goods purchased to sell to customers at a profit.

Crown Corporation sells merchandise on a cash or credit basis. For credit sales, the company allows customers to pay in 30, 60, or 90 days or use a credit card.

FIGURE 15-6 The balance sheet shows the financial position of a company on a given date.

Crown Corporation
Balance Sheet
December 31, 20--

ASSETS		LIABILITIES AND CAPITAL	
Cash	$ 24,000	Liabilities:	
Accounts Receivable	8,000	Accounts Payable	$ 32,000
Merchandise Inventory	64,000	Mortgage Payable	104,000
Equipment	80,000	Total Liabilities	$136,000
Land and Building	360,000	Capital:	
		Stockholders' Net Worth	400,000
Total Assets	$536,000	Total Liabilities and Capital	$536,000

The amount customers owe the business is an asset called *accounts receivable*. It is an asset because the business has a legal right to obtain cash for the goods sold and can sue customers who do not pay. The store will eventually collect cash from the customers.

The *accounts payable* item under Liabilities on the balance sheet is the amount the company owes for purchases it made on credit. In this example, the store bought jewelry worth $32,000 on credit from a manufacturer. Until the company pays the bill, the amount remains on the balance sheet as a liability, or debt.

VALUE OF BALANCE SHEET INFORMATION

The balance sheet for the Crown Corporation provides a great deal of useful data. It lists specific types and amounts of assets and liabilities. The balance sheet also shows that the business owns assets of $536,000, owes $136,000, and is worth $400,000 on December 31. The total figures on the balance sheet agree with the basic accounting formula as follows:

$$\text{Assets} = \text{Liabilities} + \text{Capital}$$
$$\$536,000 = \$136,000 + \$400,000$$

A careful look at the specific items reveals other valuable information. For example, Crown cannot now pay the $32,000 that it owes under accounts payable because it has only $24,000 in cash available. Ideally, the company will make enough cash sales and will collect cash from some of those customers listed under accounts receivable soon enough to pay its bills when due. Even though the money owed under accounts payable is not likely to become due all at once, the company could possibly have trouble meeting other day-to-day expenses. The company would be in trouble if a sudden emergency arose that called for a large amount of cash.

Crown may use its balance sheet to compare financial results with prior time periods or with other companies. Because companies prepare a yearly balance sheet, the business can review its financial progress by comparing this year's results with last year's. It may find, for example, that the amount of capital increased over

facts & figures

Corporations whose stock is publicly traded are required to provide an annual report to stockholders and to file financial information with the Securities and Exchange Commission. The reports include financial statements, including an end-of-year balance sheet. You can review the annual report of most corporations on their Web sites.

last year without an increase in liabilities. If Crown wished to do so, it could also compare some information on its balance sheet with that of other businesses of similar size and kind. Published information is available from several sources, such as trade associations. With comparative figures, the business can make judgments about its success and perhaps even find ways to improve its financial picture in the future.

CHECKPOINT

How does the term *balance sheet* reflect the organization of information in the financial statement?

The Income Statement

The **income statement**, or *profit and loss statement*, is a financial statement that reports information about a company's revenues and expenses for a specific period. Income statements are usually prepared monthly, quarterly, or semiannually. An annual income statement is also needed. Income statements have three major parts:

1. Revenue—income earned for the period, such as from the sale of goods and services
2. Expenses—all costs incurred in operating the business, such as the cost of materials used to manufacture the company's products
3. Profit or loss—the difference between total revenue and total expenses

When revenue is greater than expenses, the company has earned a profit. When expenses are greater than revenue, the company has incurred a loss. The income statement shows the financial performance (profit or loss) that occurs over a period of time. The balance sheet, on the other hand, shows the financial condition of a business at a particular point in time. Both types of financial statements serve useful but different purposes. An example of an income statement is shown in Figure 15-7. The period covered for the Crown Corporation is one year, as shown in the heading.

KINDS OF FINANCIAL DATA

The revenue for the Crown Corporation comes from one source—the sale of jewelry. Total revenue for the year was $800,000. If the company earned other income, such as from the repair of jewelry, the income from this source would be listed separately under Revenue.

To earn revenue, a retail business purchases merchandise from suppliers and sells it to customers at a profit. The amount the retailer pays the supplier for the merchandise it buys and sells is called *cost of goods sold*. In a manufacturing business, the cost of goods sold would include the amount the company paid for raw materials and parts to make its products.

Generally, the cost of goods sold is a rather large deduction from revenue. To make the cost of goods sold easy to identify on the income statement, it is listed separately from other deductions. *Gross profit* is the amount remaining after subtracting the cost of goods sold from revenue. *Net profit* is the amount remaining after subtracting all expenses from revenue, except taxes. Gross profit for the

Today, most well-run factories and retail stores do an excellent job of managing inventories of raw materials and finished goods. Managers know that being caught with excessive inventory costs money for storage and ties up money that might be better used elsewhere in the business. However, inadequate inventory results in reduced production and lost sales.

FIGURE 15-7 The income statement describes a business's profit or loss during a specified time period.

Crown Corporation
Income Statement
For the Year Ending December 31, 20--

Revenue from Sales	$800,000	
Cost of Goods Sold	440,000	
Gross Profit		$360,000
Operating Expenses		
Salaries and Wages	$160,000	
Advertising and Promotion	48,000	
Depreciation	32,000	
Utilities	20,000	
Supplies Used	12,000	
Other	8,000	
Total Operating Expenses		280,000
Net Profit (before Taxes)		$ 80,000

Crown Corporation is $360,000, which is calculated by subtracting the cost of goods sold ($440,000) from sales revenue ($800,000).

Expenses needed to operate the business during the year are listed next on the income statement. *Operating expenses* are all expenses not directly associated with creating or buying merchandise the business sells. For example, businesses spend money on advertising, supplies, and maintenance. For Crown Corporation, operating expenses total $280,000. On the income statement, operating expenses are subtracted from gross profit, $360,000, to arrive at the net profit or "bottom line," $80,000.

The net result of the business activity reported in the form of revenue, cost of goods sold, expenses, and profit on the income statement appears in one form or another on the balance sheet. For the Crown Corporation, the net profit of $80,000 will be added to its assets (left side of the balance sheet) and capital (right side of the balance sheet). Thus, the two sides of the balance sheet will still balance.

VALUE OF INCOME STATEMENT INFORMATION

The manager of Crown Corporation, and others who review the income statement, can learn a great deal about the business. Specifically, the total deductions from the $800,000 in revenue are $720,000, which consists of cost of goods sold ($440,000) and operating expenses ($280,000). The manager can also see that the net profit before taxes—$80,000—is a rather small part of the total revenue. Both of these observations might warn of a possible problem with high costs relative to income.

The Crown Corporation can improve its financial controlling and budget planning by doing an item-by-item analysis of the income statement, such as that shown in the first two columns of numbers in Figure 15-8 (see p. 406). Each expenditure

FIGURE 15-8 Budgets can be prepared and compared to actual performance from an income statement.

Crown Corporation
Budgeted Income Statement
for 12 Months Ending December 31, 20--

INCOME, EXPENSE, AND PROFIT	AMOUNTS FOR PAST 12 MONTHS	PERCENTAGE OF SALES	AMOUNTS BUDGETED FOR NEXT 12 MONTHS	ESTIMATED PERCENTAGE OF SALES
Sales	$800,000	100.0%	$960,000	100.0%
Cost of Goods Sold	440,000	55.0	528,000	55.0
Gross Profit	360,000	45.0	432,000	45.0
Operating Expenses				
Salaries and Wages	160,000	20.0	182,400	19.0
Advertising/Promotion	48,000	6.0	58,560	6.1
Depreciation	32,000	4.0	32,000	3.3
Utilities	20,000	2.5	28,800	3.0
Supplies Used	12,000	1.5	14,400	1.5
Other Expenses	8,000	1.0	9,600	1.0
Total Operating Expenses	280,000	35.0	325,760	33.9
Net Profit	80,000	10.0	106,240	11.1

can be calculated as a percentage of total sales. Managers can then compare the percentages with similar figures from prior months and years to reveal trends.

For instance, the first and largest operating expense is $160,000 for salaries and wages. When $160,000 is divided by total sales, $800,000, and the answer is changed to a percentage, the result is 20 percent. If last year the total wages and salaries expense amounted to only 18 percent of sales, the business would know that this expense had increased in relation to total sales. If possible, the company can try to correct this 2 percent increase for the next year by trying to increase sales, raise prices, or get by with fewer employees. The same type of calculation and analysis can be made for each of the remaining expenses on the income statement. In addition, managers can determine the percentages of gross profit and net profit in relation to sales. Based on that analysis, budgets can be prepared for the next 12 months, as shown in the last two columns of Figure 15-8.

CHECKPOINT
How are profit and loss calculated on an income statement?

Businesses must keep a variety of financial records, budgets, and statements. What kinds of personal financial records do you keep?

PHOTO: © GETTY IMAGES/PHOTODISC.

15.3 Assessment

UNDERSTAND MANAGEMENT CONCEPTS

Determine the best answer for each of the following questions.

1. The basic accounting equation is
   a. income − expenses = profit or loss
   b. liabilities = assets + capital
   c. assets = liabilities + capital
   d. income = profit or loss − expenses

2. The information from the income statement needed to calculate gross profit does not include
   a. revenue
   b. cost of goods sold
   c. operating expenses
   d. All are needed to calculate gross profit.

THINK CRITICALLY

Answer the following questions as completely as possible.

3. Why is the balance sheet an important financial statement for potential investors in a company to review?

4. Why is it important to study a company's financial performance over a period of time and its financial condition on a specific date?

Xtra!
Study Tools
thomsonedu.com/school/bpmxtra

Focus On...

Ethics–Cost Cutting at any Cost

The Sunbeam Corporation had been experiencing financial difficulties before the board of directors hired CEO Al Dunlap to fix the company. Sunbeam was a well-known manufacturer of household appliances. Soon after Mr. Dunlap came on board, Sunbeam's stock started to climb. Within seven months, he had saved the company $225 million by such actions as firing 12,000 employees, closing 16 of 26 factories, and disposing of unwanted products and facilities.

Employees learned early why others had nicknamed him "Chainsaw Al." The firm's culture changed quickly. Before Dunlap's arrival, the firm was in trouble, with few new products, weakening sales, and declining profits. His arrival seemed to signal a quick turnaround in the company's financial performance. The stockholders and investors were happy.

But soon after the major cost-reduction steps were completed, sales and profits again began to decline. The new CEO required all product managers to show increased sales. He suggested practices, many unethical, that would make it appear as if sales were rising and expenses were falling. Dunlap eliminated the information technology department by outsourcing it. As part of that change the computer system was replaced and no backup files were created. Not only did that make it nearly impossible to determine the accuracy of records but it created additional work as all records had to be manually reentered into the new computer system. Chaos prevailed. While the reduced number of employees manually prepared inventory records and invoices, they also had to handle hundreds of calls from upset customers and suppliers.

Dunlap pressured employees relentlessly to produce more. Morale dipped. Budget goals were unrealistic. To make it appear as though goals were being met without creating cash flow problems, some managers were forced to postpone paying bills and suppliers were asked to accept only partial payment to keep costs down temporarily. Unrealistic credit terms were extended to large retailers to obtain enough orders to meet sales goals. Large discounts were given to customers to encourage them to buy well in advance so as to make Sunbeam's income statement look good. These undesirable business practices led to high inventory levels, while accounts receivable and payable both rose and cash flow weakened. Sales were recorded for the current year that under accounting rules should have been postponed to the next year. Profit margins got thinner. The firm was in deep trouble.

The board of directors met and agreed it had made a serious error in hiring Al Dunlap. He was fired. The firm reorganized, but it couldn't recover and fell into bankruptcy. Even though Sunbeam eventually emerged from bankruptcy, its image had dropped among investors, suppliers, and customers. It has now become a subsidiary of a large international firm, Jarden Corporation.

Think Critically

1. Why do you believe Mr. Dunlap had early success and yet the financial fortunes of the company quickly turned around?
2. Why were Mr. Dunlap and company managers willing to use illegal and unethical practices to try to improve the financial position of Sunbeam?
3. If you were on the board of directors, what questions would you ask Al Dunlap about his beliefs and values before you hired him?

15.4 Analyzing Financial Data

Goals
- Describe several types of financial analysis that help in the understanding of a business's financial condition.
- Identify where business owners and managers can turn to get help with understanding and using financial information.

Terms
- cash flow
- working capital
- certified public accountant (CPA)
- consultant

Using Financial Information

Managers use financial statements as well as other financial information to understand the financial health of a business. Others are also concerned about the business's financial health. That includes current and prospective investors; creditors, including banks and suppliers who may make loans and offer credit to the business; government officials involved in taxation and oversight of business practices; and customers. They want to know such things as whether the cash flow and working capital are sufficient to pay the company's bills. They also analyze ratios calculated from financial statements to identify where any financial problems lie.

Financial statements must be prepared in a way that provides a clear and understandable picture of the financial health of an organization. The people who are affected by the financial condition of the business need to have access to the financial information and be able to analyze the information to draw conclusions about its financial health.

CASH FLOW

Cash flow is the movement of cash into and out of a business. Money comes in immediately as a result of the sale of goods and services for cash and later from customers who buy on credit. Money goes out to pay for various costs and operating expenses. Because money does not always flow in at the same rate that it flows out, managers need to carefully plan for the flow of cash.

Regardless of the size of a business, cash is both a short-term and a long-term concern. Businesses must have cash on hand to pay bills when they are due and to plan ahead for large cash payments, such as the purchase of equipment or the launching of a new product.

Figure 15-9 (see p. 410) illustrates cash flowing in and out of a retail piano store through the part of the year when cash shortages and overages are likely to occur. The bulk of the company's sales occur during the December holiday season. Although the company sells some pianos for cash, it sells most on credit.

FIGURE 15-9 Cash flow changes in most businesses from month to month. Businesses must plan to deal with cash shortages and excesses.

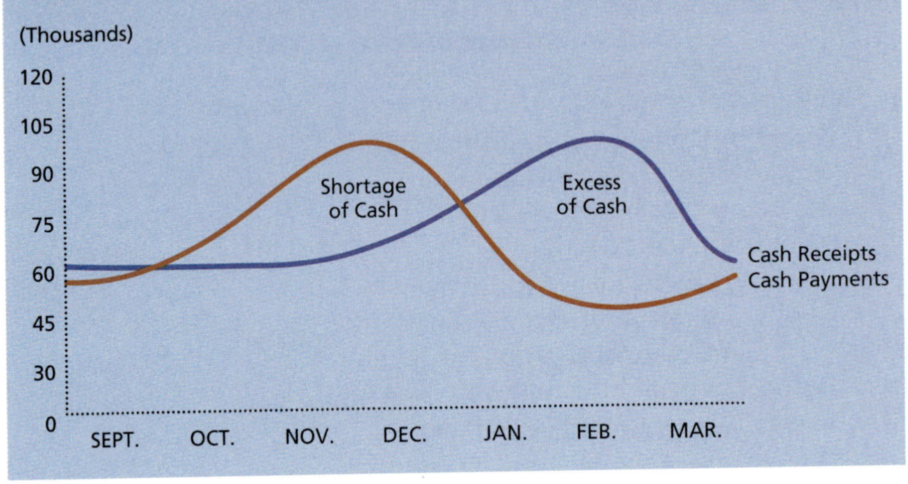

That means that even during the month of high sales, not a great deal of cash is generated. The need for cash is greatest during September, October, and November when the company buys its inventory of pianos to sell. It needs large sums of cash to pay for the pianos, for sales promotions such as advertising, and for regular operating expenses. The cash flowing out of the company from October through December is greater than the cash flowing in.

Larger amounts of cash start to flow in during December from customers who pay cash for their purchases. Credit customers who purchased in December, however, will make cash payments in January, February, and March. During these three months, the flow of cash coming into the business will be greater than the cash going out. From this information, managers can plan for short-term borrowing during times of cash shortage. They can also plan when to make any needed large purchases, so that their payments will be due when they have cash available to pay them.

WORKING CAPITAL

Working capital is the difference between current assets and current liabilities. The word *current* refers to assets and liabilities that are expected to be exchanged for cash within one year or less, such as accounts receivable and payable. For example, companies expect most customers to pay for their credit purchases within a year. Therefore, accounts receivable are current assets. Similarly, companies expect to pay for their credit purchases in accounts payable within a year, so accounts payable are current liabilities.

When current assets are much larger than current liabilities, businesses are better able to pay current liabilities. The amount of working capital is one indicator that a business can pay its short-term debts. Businesses with large amounts of working capital usually find it easier to borrow money, because lenders feel assured that these businesses will have the means to repay their loans. The working-capital analysis for the Crown Corporation is shown in Figure 15-10. Notice that the numbers used in the analysis are the current assets and current liabilities drawn from the company's balance sheet shown in Figure 15-6.

Teamwork *tip*

Teams that rely on technology to do most of their work must be careful in the ways they communicate with each other. Many people are uncomfortable relying on technology to communicate rather than meeting face-to-face. They feel that seeing people's faces, gestures, and body language brings more meaning to their words. New technologies that combine audio, video, text, and visuals help reduce that anxiety.

FINANCIAL RATIOS

Managers use ratios to examine different areas of the business for possible financial problems. Figure 15-11 describes some important ratios and their uses. The data for these ratios come from Crown Corporation's financial statements: Figure 15-6 (balance sheet), Figure 15-7 (income statement), and Figure 15-10 (working capital). Financial ratios for current financial statements can be compared with the same ratios from prior periods, with ratios from other firms, and with other types of ratios. Organizations such as Dun & Bradstreet publish a standard list of average ratios for various types of businesses. Companies can use those published ratios to compare with their own ratios to get a sense of how they are doing in relation to other companies in their industry.

Lenders use ratios to decide whether a company is a good loan risk. Managers use ratios to identify possible problems needing corrective action. For example, if

FIGURE 15-10 Working capital can be calculated using information on current assets and current liabilities from the balance sheet.

Crown Corporation
Working Capital
December 31, 20--

Current Assets:		
Cash	$24,000	
Accounts Receivable	8,000	
Merchandise Inventory	64,000	$96,000
Current Liabilities:		
Accounts Payable		32,000
Total Working Capital		$64,000

FIGURE 15-11 Financial ratios are an important tool for management decision making and investment decisions.

Frequently Used Financial Ratios

RATIO	CALCULATION	CROWN CORPORATION*	PURPOSE
Return on Sales	Net Profit / Sales	80,000 / 800,000 = .10	Shows how profitable a firm was for a specified period of time.
Inventory Turnover	Cost of Goods Sold / Ave. Mdse. Inventory	440,000 / 64,000 = 6.88	Shows whether the average monthly inventory might be too large or small.
Current Ratio	Current Assets / Current Liabilities	96,000 / 32,000 = 3.0	Shows whether a firm can meet its current debts comfortably.
Return on Owners' Equity	Net Profit / Owners' Equity	80,000 / 400,000 = .20	Shows whether the owners are making a fair return on their investment.
Return on Investment	Net Profit / Total Assets	80,000 / 536,000 = .149	Shows rate of return on the total money invested by owners and others in a firm.

* See Fig. 15-6, 15-7, and 15-10 for sources of figures for calculations.

the company's return on investment is below average for its industry, then managers know that they may have to increase profits to attract new investors. If the company's current ratio keeps decreasing each period, then its liabilities are growing faster than its assets. This indicates that the company may be getting into debt trouble.

CHECKPOINT

Why should managers monitor a business's working capital and cash flow?

Sources of Financial Information

If a business needs general advice or special help with a financial problem, it hires an expert. Types of experts available to businesses are accountants, bankers, consultants, and the federal government.

ACCOUNTANTS

Accountants establish systems for collecting, sorting, and summarizing all types of financial data. They prepare and explain in detail the many figures found on financial statements. Accountants also help managers interpret financial data and make suggestions for handling various financial aspects of a business. Large firms have full-time accountants, whereas small firms usually hire accountants on a part-time basis. A firm may hire a **certified public accountant**, or **CPA**, a person who has met a state's education, experience, and examination requirements in accounting. Corporations that sell stock to the public must hire CPAs to approve their yearly financial records.

BANKERS

Bankers also assist businesses with financial decisions. Bankers are well informed about the financial condition of businesses, and they also provide advice on how and where to get loans. Because bankers frequently work with businesses, they are aware of businesses' problems and needs. In the opening story, Clark knew he would need to ask his banker for help and advice to maintain his loan with the bank.

CONSULTANTS

A **consultant** is an expert whom companies hire to help them solve problems within a specific area of expertise. Consultants are not employees. They are outside experts with specialized knowledge.

A financial consultant is valuable to people thinking about starting a business and to managers facing challenges in existing businesses. Professors of accounting, finance, and management from colleges or universities often serve as consultants. Large and small consulting firms sell their services to other businesses. Some specialize in a particular area such as financial services; others offer expertise in a broad set of business issues.

GOVERNMENT

Many state and federal government agencies provide financial information and other resources for businesses. Probably the best known is the Small Business Administration (SBA). The SBA is an agency of the federal government that provides information, advice, and assistance in obtaining credit and other financial support for small businesses. Regional offices in every state offer expertise and access to a range of technical and managerial information for small-business owners and people considering starting a new business. Other federal agencies offering resources and assistance as well as regulations related to the financial performance of businesses are the Department of Commerce and the Department of the Treasury.

CHECKPOINT

Identify four types of experts who can provide advice and help on businesses' financial problems.

15.4 Assessment

UNDERSTAND MANAGEMENT CONCEPTS

Determine the best answer for each of the following questions.

1. The amount of working capital available to a business is determined by
   a. subtracting total liabilities from total assets
   b. adding current assets and current liabilities
   c. adding total assets and total liabilities
   d. subtracting current liabilities from current assets

2. An example of an important financial ratio is
   a. current ratio
   b. past ratio
   c. future ratio
   d. all of the above

THINK CRITICALLY

Answer the following questions as completely as possible.

3. What benefits might managers obtain from comparing the financial performance ratios of their company with the same ratios from competitors' companies? How might the comparisons be misleading?

4. Some businesspeople suggest that consultants should not be used in a business because they aren't familiar with the specific operations of the company. Do you agree or disagree? Justify your opinion.

Xtra!
Study Tools
thomsonedu.com/school/bpmxtra

thomsonedu.com/school/bpmxtra

CHAPTER CONCEPTS

- All businesses, large and small, must keep records to identify sources of income and receipts; identify expenses paid or owed to others; determine the kinds and values of assets; prepare financial statements, forms, and reports; track financial progress; and plan future direction.

- Financial records in all types of businesses have similar characteristics. A few of the most common records are cash, credit, depreciation, and special asset, tax, and payroll records.

- Actual budgeting procedures depend on the type of business. However, most businesses develop the following types of budgets: operating, cash, capital, sales, and other specialized types of budgets. New businesses develop a start-up budget to help with financial decisions until the business becomes profitable.

- Because of the importance of financial performance and financial condition, every business must keep thorough and accurate records, prepare financial reports, interpret the financial information, and make decisions that will influence future financial results. Two important financial statements are the balance sheet and the income statement.

- Financial statements must provide a clear picture of the financial health of an organization. The people who are affected by the business's financial condition must have access to the financial information and be able to analyze it to draw conclusions about the business's financial health.

REVIEW TERMS AND CONCEPTS

Write the letter of the term that matches each definition. Some terms will not be used.

a. accounting equation
b. accounts payable record
c. accounts receivable record
d. asset
e. balance sheet
f. budget
g. capital
h. cash flow
i. depreciation
j. financial records
k. financial statements
l. fixed assets
m. income statement
n. liabilities
o. start-up budget
p. working capital

1. Anything of value owned
2. Written financial plan for business operations developed for a specific period of time
3. Financial statement that reports a business's assets, liabilities, and capital on a specific date
4. Organized summaries of a business's financial information and activities
5. Value of the owners' investment in the business after subtracting liabilities from assets
6. Movement of cash into and out of a business
7. Financial statement that reports information about a company's revenues and expenses for a specific period
8. Records showing money a business owes and payments it makes for all credit purchases
9. Claims against assets
10. Gradual loss of an asset's value due to age and wear
11. Difference between current assets and current liabilities
12. Reports that summarize financial data over a period of time

DETERMINE THE BEST ANSWER

13. Manual record-keeping systems have been replaced in most businesses by
    a. accountants
    b. simple checkbook systems
    c. computers running accounting software programs
    d. cash register tapes
14. Studies of differences between successful and unsuccessful new businesses find that successful businesses use
    a. consultants
    b. computers
    c. budgets
    d. none of the above
15. The two financial statements most used by businesses are
    a. cash flow and capital assets record
    b. tax and personnel records
    c. income statement and balance sheet
    d. accounts receivable and accounts payable records
16. An agency of the federal government that provides information, advice, and assistance in obtaining credit and other financial support for small businesses is the
    a. SBA
    b. FDA
    c. FCC
    d. EEOC

APPLY WHAT YOU KNOW

17. Based on the Reality Check scenario at the beginning of the chapter, explain the meaning of the following statement by Clark's banker: "Either your current assets are too low or your current liabilities are too high. If you want us to continue your loan, you have to improve your working capital."
18. Can a piece of equipment such as a computer both depreciate and become obsolete? Explain.
19. Why will an operating budget likely be more accurate if the company's sales budget is prepared in advance and used as information for the operating budget?
20. Why is a budget an important tool for managers to use when evaluating current performance?
21. Discuss the accuracy of this statement: "The balance sheet tells you whether you made a profit or a loss for the year."
22. A net loss of $5,000 appears on an income statement. How would this loss affect the capital section of the balance sheet?
23. If the average return on sales for all jewelry stores is 7 percent, how would you judge the success of the Crown Corporation based on the financial information presented in lesson 15.3?

MAKE CONNECTIONS

24. **Math** As the budget director, you presented the following realistic yearly expense budget to your boss. After studying the figures, she asks you to prepare a flexible set of budget estimates because certain conditions might cause a 15 percent increase in sales, whereas certain other conditions might cause a 5 percent decrease in sales. The amounts budgeted for rent and insurance will not change under any circumstances.

Sales salaries	$300,000
Office salaries	60,000
Supplies	80,000
Advertising	48,000
Rent	36,000
Insurance	8,000

Prepare a new flexible budget showing three columns of figures: 5 percent Decrease, Expected, and 15 percent Increase.

25. **Communications** You have been hired as a financial consultant by the Crown Corporation to analyze the financial statements shown in the chapter. Calculate three financial ratios that you believe offer a realistic picture of the company's financial health. Prepare three computer slides and use them for a three-minute presentation to Crown's managers on what the information means to them.

26. **Technology** Use a computer spreadsheet to prepare an end-of-year balance sheet for the Starboard Corporation, using the following information and the format shown in lesson 15-3.

Cash	$5,000
Accounts receivable	8,000
Merchandise inventory	15,000
Land and buildings	120,000
Accounts payable	12,000
Mortgage payable	90,000
Stockholders' net worth	46,000

27. **Math** Use the following financial information from the Waterwing Company to calculate: (a) inventory turnover, (b) current ratio, (c) return on owners' equity, and (d) return on investment.

Revenue from sales	$600,000
Cost of goods sold	320,000
Net profit	25,000
Current assets	36,000
Total assets	200,000
Current liabilities	15,000
Owners' equity	50,000
Average inventory	20,000

CASE IN POINT

CASE 15-1: The Value of Budgeting

Karen Kline and Joe Kim are both junior accountants in a manufacturing firm. The head accountant, Brooke Shenker, has asked Karen to prepare the sales budget for next month's annual budget meeting. Brooke asked Joe to construct the cash budget. Neither was happy about the request, though neither complained directly to the head accountant. Karen did, however, let her feelings be known to Joe.

Karen: *We spend weeks developing these budgets and all the budget committee does is argue for two days and change our estimates. It makes me wonder why they ask for our figures in the first place.*

Joe: *I agree. What's worse is that the company never comes in on target with the budget. The collections on customer accounts never match the budgeted amounts, and it makes me look bad because it throws the cash budget off. Last year they projected sales to be $350,000 for the first quarter, and they were only $335,000.*

Karen: *Maybe if they would ask us to come to the meeting and explain how we develop the budgets it would save them time and discussion.*

Joe: *Last year they argued for three days and look what happened. They were so far off budget that I heard Brooke say a child could have done a better job forecasting. Budgeting this way is a waste of time.*

Karen: *I'll start on the sales budget tomorrow, but if I were smart my vacation would begin then, too!*

THINK CRITICALLY

1. If Karen and Joe prepared budget figures, why is it necessary for management to discuss them?
2. How serious is the variance between forecasted and actual sales? Do you agree with Joe that when budgeted amounts and actual figures do not agree, the budgeting process is not worthwhile? Explain.
3. How do you believe the company's budgeting process could be improved?

CASE 15-2: The Value of a New Business

Anneika Lafferty and her friend Bernie Williams started an Internet business 15 months ago selling affordable musical instruments for beginners. They named it A&B Musical Instruments. Because they live near each other, Bernie keeps the inventory in his garage and Anneika has the computer system, phones, and office space in her home. Business has not done as well as they expected, but they are still optimistic. They have learned from their mistakes and realize that their products are not as popular as expected. They would like to sell the business and create a different type of online business. A larger Internet music company wants to buy them but the $50,000 offered is not nearly what Anneika and Bernie expected, based on the company's potential. They quickly reject the offer. The offer is based on last year's balance sheet, shown below, and the income statement, which showed $175,000 in sales and $110,000 in expenses. Many of the expenditures were to get the business started.

A & B Musical Instruments
Balance Sheet
December 31, 20—

Assets		Liabilities and Capital	
Cash	$9,000	Liabilities:	
Accounts Receivable	8,000	Accounts Payable	$31,000
Inventory	37,000		
Equipment	25,000	Total Liabilities	31,000
		Capital:	
		A. Lafferty	24,000
		B. Williams	24,000
		Total Liabilities &	
Total Assets	$79,000	Capital	$79,000

THINK CRITICALLY

1. On what basis did the potential buyer probably make the $50,000 offer? What did the buyer learn from the sellers' rejection?
2. How might the working capital, current ratio, and return on sales have affected the offering price? Prepare the necessary calculations before answering.
3. Assume you wish to buy the company. What additional information would you want to gather from the sellers?

CASE 15-3: Can Consultants Help?

For several years, Delia and Lorenzo Garcia have been making leather items such as belts, purses, and wallets in their home as a hobby. They have sold many items to friends and neighbors. Because Lorenzo has just lost his regular job, he and Delia have decided to go into business full-time making leather craft items. The items will be sold at fairs, festivals, and flea markets and hopefully later to retailers. They will need a large amount of money, some of which they have saved, to expand to a full-time business. Both agree that they know a great deal about how to make leather items but very little about financial and other business decisions. Delia believes they should hire a consultant before they do anything else. Lorenzo, on the other hand, believes they should go to a bank to obtain the money they need to start the business. He thinks that they can hire an accountant after they have gotten the business started. He does not believe the consultant will know enough about the leather business to give advice. "Besides," he adds, "consultants are too expensive."

THINK CRITICALLY

1. Do you agree with Delia or with Lorenzo about whether they need a consultant? Explain.
2. How could a consultant help them? How might the bank help them?
3. Could the Small Business Administration be of help? How?

COMPLETING INITIAL FINANCIAL PLANNING

As a new business owner, you must be able to assess the financial needs of your business realistically. You will need this information to obtain financing and make operating decisions. Businesspeople need a complete set of financial records to make management decisions. This is very important for new businesses, as financial resources are usually limited. As you complete this part of the project, you will review the financial records needed for your business and the sources of record-keeping assistance available. You will use the information to make initial financial decisions and develop financial statements to serve as initial estimates of the financial condition of your new business.

DATA COLLECTION

1. Interview an accountant or review small-business management materials. Use the interview or materials review to determine the types of financial records you will need for your business. Develop a list of all of the records you believe you will need to maintain as the business owner.
2. Obtain a copy of a small-business financial planning software package for use on a desktop computer. Examine each of the forms and records included with the package and determine the type of information the business would need to acquire in order to complete each of the forms and records.
3. Locate a source of sample financial information for small retail businesses (especially fast-food or specialty-food businesses). You should be able to find average figures for balance sheets and income statements as well as average financial ratios. The Internet and most libraries are good places to begin your search.

ANALYSIS

1. Develop a detailed set of procedures to be followed in your business for the safe handling of cash. Be certain to consider all situations in which cash will be handled.
2. Prepare a sample cash budget for your business. The budget should cover the first three months of business operations.
3. Prepare a beginning estimated balance sheet for your new business. It should show the planned financial position of your business for its first day of operation.
4. Prepare an estimated income statement for the first three months of the operation of your business. Be realistic in your estimates. You may not show a profit.

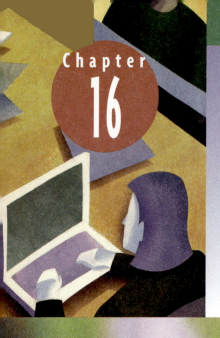

Financing a Business

16.1 Types of Business Capital

16.2 Raising Capital Through Stock Sales

16.3 Short- and Long-Term Debt Financing

REALITY CHECK

Show Me the Money!

The Video Shoppe opened for business in a popular mall a few years ago. Eva Diaz, its owner, used her entire savings to launch "The Shoppe," as she called it. After losing money the first year, she nearly closed down. But through hard work and creative marketing, Eva has made The Shoppe quite successful. Furthermore, she has left all the profits in the business except for a modest amount of cash for personal living expenses.

Today, Caleb Wegman, her accountant and friend, was in the back room balancing the books. As Caleb finished his work, Eva excitedly asked, "Can I open another shop with my current earnings? There's a new shopping center opening near the college and I think my type of business would be very successful there."

Caleb's shocked response came quickly. "No. Your earnings are good, but your balance sheet needs more muscle. I would encourage you to go slow and build the financial strength of this store before you consider opening in another location."

"But, Caleb, my business sense tells me I could open another store and apply what I have learned starting this location to make profits quickly. Don't tell me no. Tell me how. And let's not think of opening one shop. My idea is to have a chain of shops within the next three or four years."

Caleb, somewhat startled by Eva's bold plan, was momentarily speechless. "But have you thought about how you would finance that type of growth?" he asked.

"I was hoping that, working together, we could come up with some ideas," Eva replied. "For starters, I have an aunt who might be able to lend me some money. Maybe my brother would like to invest in the business."

"Your family might help some," Caleb interrupted, "but your plans would require 'big' dollars. Right now I have to go see my next client. Between now and when I return next week, if you still believe it is a good idea to plan for that amount of quick growth, think about whether you are willing to look for investors with the type of money you will need. You are making a big decision that will really affect your future as a business owner."

After Caleb left, Eva sat wondering how she could raise the money to expand her business. "Strike now while the market is hot," was the thought that stayed in her mind as three customers walked in.

16.1 Types of Business Capital

Goals
- Explain three methods of financing a business.
- Describe the differences in equity financing based on the ownership structure of a business.

Terms
- equity capital
- retained earnings
- debt capital

Eva faces the same problem most successful business owners face—how to get financial backing. On a balance sheet, capital is a business's assets minus its liabilities. Capital also refers to the money required to start or expand a business. Businesses need capital to acquire assets.

Capital comes from many sources. Owners can provide it from their own savings. They can also obtain capital by borrowing, by buying business necessities on credit, or by making profits and leaving those profits in the business. Business executives and business owners need to be familiar with various methods for raising capital and understand important considerations when deciding on sources of capital.

Methods of Obtaining Capital

Business owners have several options for obtaining the capital they need to start and operate their business. One way is to contribute their own money to the business. Business owners' personal contributions to the business are called equity capital or *owner capital*. This capital may come from personal funds, such as from accumulated savings, or from funds the owners borrow using their homes or other personal property as security for the loan. As shown in Figure 16-1 (see p. 422), small businesses rely heavily on equity capital. Eva Diaz can consider such sources for expanding The Video Shoppe. However, because she has already opened one store and has not taken profits from it, it is not likely she has a great deal of money to use as equity capital. If Eva wants to use equity capital to finance expansion, she will likely have to attract other investors willing to use their money in return for partial ownership of the business.

A second way to obtain capital is through retained earnings. Retained earnings are the profits that the owners do not take out of the business but instead save for use by the business. Retained earnings are a type of equity capital, because profits belong to the owners of the business. As Eva's business becomes profitable, she may be able to accumulate retained earnings and use those for business expansion in the future.

A third way of financing a business is through debt capital, or *creditor capital*—money that others loan to a business. Banks and other types of lending institutions usually will not lend money to a business unless the equity capital exceeds the debt capital. As a result, businesses in financial difficulty often have

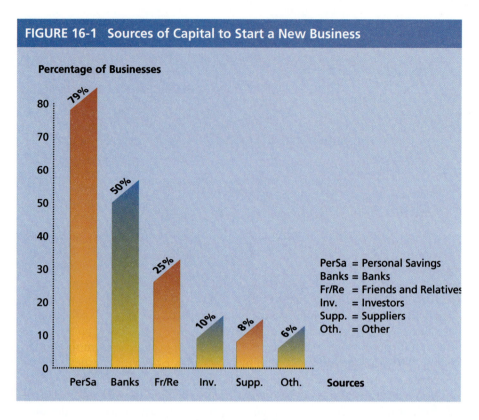

FIGURE 16-1   Sources of Capital to Start a New Business

Percentage of Businesses

PerSa = Personal Savings
Banks = Banks
Fr/Re = Friends and Relatives
Inv. = Investors
Supp. = Suppliers
Oth. = Other

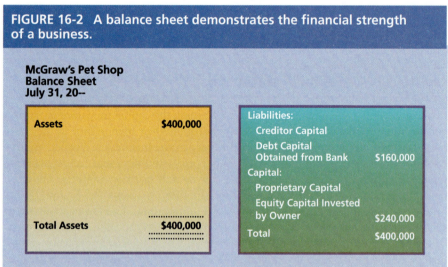

FIGURE 16-2   A balance sheet demonstrates the financial strength of a business.

McGraw's Pet Shop
Balance Sheet
July 31, 20--

Assets	$400,000
Total Assets	$400,000

Liabilities:	
Creditor Capital	
Debt Capital Obtained from Bank	$160,000
Capital:	
Proprietary Capital	
Equity Capital Invested by Owner	$240,000
Total	$400,000

trouble getting debt capital. McGraw's Pet Shop, as shown in Figure 16-2, might be able to get an additional loan from the bank because its liabilities, or debt, are much less than its equity capital. However, if its liabilities were $240,000 and its equity capital were $160,000, the Pet Shop probably would not get the loan.

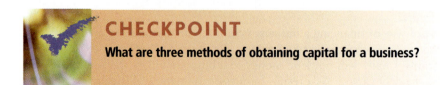

CHECKPOINT

What are three methods of obtaining capital for a business?

Obtaining Equity Capital

Acquiring equity capital is approached differently depending on the business's ownership structure. Because equity capital is money invested by the owner, the type of ownership structure determines who can provide the equity capital and how it is obtained and invested in the business.

SOLE PROPRIETORSHIPS

Sole proprietors must rely on their personal assets for capital if they want to retain ownership of the company. If owners are wealthy or the needed amount is small, they can invest more of their own money in the business. If they do not have available cash, they will have to sell personal assets to raise the money. Other options are to mortgage personal property such as a home or obtain a personal loan using the collateral of owned assets such as automobiles, insurance policies, or other property. Of course, when those funds are invested in the business by the sole proprietor, they are at risk and can be lost if the business is not successful. In addition, other personal assets that were not invested in the business can be lost if the business fails.

If the sole proprietor cannot provide additional financing for the business and chooses to use equity capital, alternative sources will have to be considered. When others provide equity capital, the form of business ownership will need to change. The sole owner of a business can obtain additional funds by (1) forming a partnership and requiring the new partner to invest money in the business, or (2) forming a corporation and bringing in additional equity and owners by selling stock.

PARTNERSHIPS

When a business expands by creating a partnership, the partner is not required to invest money. A partner may be brought into a business because of his or her business expertise rather than the need for additional capital. However, partners usually invest their personal resources in the business to balance the amount of

In a recent year, 16,183,715 people were involved as owners of 1,758,627 business partnerships. Most partnerships are found in finance, insurance, and real estate, followed by service businesses.

When successful entrepreneurs want to expand their businesses, they often face the problem of raising large sums of capital. Other than family and friends, where can a small business obtain money to expand or open additional stores?

PHOTO: © GETTY IMAGES/PHOTODISC.

NETBookmark

Financial managers, business executives, institutional and individual investors, and government policy makers need to keep up-to-date on national and international financial data. Investment opportunities, interest rates, exchange rates for foreign currencies, and the strength of various financial institutions are important factors in making financial decisions. The Federal Reserve Board is a government organization made up of economists and other financial experts. The Board is responsible for running the central bank system in the United States and setting monetary policy. It collects and reports a variety of financial data. Point your browser to www.thomsonedu.com/school/bpmxtra. Review the types of financial information available from the Federal Reserve Board site. Select one link for consumer financial information and one for business financial information. Study the information and describe how each type of information would be useful to business executives making decisions about whether to increase the amount of capital in their businesses.

www.thomsonedu.com/school/bpmxtra

money each owner has in the business and to spread the financial risk among the owners.

When a sole proprietorship is reorganized into a partnership, a formal partnership agreement must be created that identifies the financial contributions of each partner and how business profits will be shared. As with the sole proprietor, a new business partner will need to use personal finances to provide the required equity capital. Those resources can be personal savings, income from the sale of assets, or personal loans and mortgages. And just as in the sole proprietorship, the money invested by each partner as well as any other personal assets that were not invested are at risk if the business fails. If the assets of one partner are not adequate to cover the debts of a business, assets from other partners can be taken.

When a sole proprietorship expands ownership by forming a partnership, the owner gives up individual control over management and decision-making. If Eva Diaz decides to expand her Video Shoppe by forming a partnership, she will share ownership and management with her new partners.

CORPORATIONS

The third way to raise equity capital is by forming a corporation and bringing in additional owners through the sale of stock. The use of a corporate structure for a small business may be an effective way to raise equity capital because the amount of money that an individual needs to invest is usually much smaller than if a partnership is formed. Also, stockholders are not involved in the day-to-day management of the business. Therefore the person who was the original owner may be able to continue as the primary manager of the business.

Investors in corporations are protected financially; they can lose the money they have invested only if the business fails. This might be viewed as an advantage to Eva Diaz because she will be a stockholder based on her investment in the business, and any losses will be limited to that amount. Currently, as a sole proprietor, all of the money she has invested in the business and all her personal assets are at risk in the event the business fails.

Stockholders who invest in a business expect that the business will use their investment effectively and that they will make money. Stockholders earn money on their investments through dividends paid from profits earned by the business or through the sale of their stock at a profit. Depending on whether a corporation is organized as a public corporation or a close corporation, stockholders have more or less flexibility in the sale of stock and input into the direction of the business. If Eva Diaz decides she wants to expand the number of video stores very rapidly, she may need to choose to reorganize as a corporation. If the prospects for her business are good, she may be able to attract a number of investors who will purchase stock, giving her the needed capital.

There are advantages and disadvantages to each form of ownership in terms of the amount of equity capital that can be raised, the risk to the owners, and the role of investors in managing the business. To raise equity capital, therefore, a business owner must estimate whether it will be more advantageous to remain a sole owner or to form a partnership or a corporation. Eva Diaz must deal with this question if she wishes to expand her Video Shoppe.

CHECKPOINT

How is equity capital obtained in each of the three types of business ownership?

16.1   Assessment

UNDERSTAND MANAGEMENT CONCEPTS

Determine the best answer for each of the following questions.

1. Business owners' personal contributions to the business are called
   a. assets
   b. equity capital
   c. debt capital
   d. stock

2. Which form of business ownership provides the greatest protection of the owner's personal assets in case of business failure?
   a. sole proprietorship
   b. partnership
   c. corporation
   d. None of the ownership forms provides protection of an owner's personal assets.

THINK CRITICALLY

Answer the following questions as completely as possible.

3. Why would an owner of a business want to use equity financing rather than debt financing to raise money for a business?

4. What information would you want from a business before you decided to invest your money as a new partner? As a new stockholder?

Xtra!
Study Tools
thomsonedu.com/school/bpmxtra

16.2 Raising Capital Through Stock Sales

Goals

- Differentiate between common and preferred stock.
- Describe factors that affect the value of a company's stock.

Terms

- common stock
- par value
- market value
- preferred stock
- book value

Types of Stock

By far the greatest amount of equity investment in U.S. businesses comes from the sale of stock. The most recent figures from the Census Bureau show the total value of stock in all U.S. corporations that filed tax returns is $4.2 trillion. Over 25 million households own individual shares of stock, and more than double that number, 53 million households, have investments such as mutual funds and retirement plans that include stocks. Corporations use several types of equity and debt financing to raise money, but about 44 percent of the total equity in the average corporation is made up of stocks.

Stockholders are the owners of corporations but their ownership rights and responsibilities vary based on the type of stock they hold. Two kinds of stock are issued by corporations, common stock and preferred stock.

COMMON STOCK

Common stock is stock that gives holders the right to participate in managing the business by voting on basic issues at the corporation's annual meeting and by electing the board of directors. Holders of common stock receive one vote per share of stock owned. As owners they also can share in the corporation's profits. When the corporation makes a profit, some or all of that profit may be paid back to stockholders as dividends. The corporation's board of directors makes the decision about whether holders of common stock will receive a dividend or not and the amount of that dividend per share of stock.

The board of directors decides on the number of shares of common stock that will be issued by the corporation. If they decide to issue new shares, they assign a value to those shares, known as **par value**. The par value is somewhat arbitrary in that it may not be the price that stockholders pay for the shares. If stockholders believe the company is a good investment, they may pay more than par value. The price at which stock is actually bought and sold is its **market value**. The price of stock goes up and down based on the financial performance of the company and general economic conditions. Investors purchase stocks with the expectation that the company's financial performance will be strong, dividends will be paid, and the stock price will increase. They hope to sell the stock in the future for a much greater value than they paid for it.

Common stockholders have the right to purchase any new stock issued before it is offered for sale on the open market. That right protects the interests of the current stockholders. Otherwise it would be possible for management of the corporation to take control away from the current stockholders by issuing and buying a large amount of new stock.

PREFERRED STOCK

Preferred stock is stock that gives holders first claim on corporate dividends if a company earns a profit. In addition, in the event a business fails, preferred stockholders have priority over common stockholders on any remaining assets after creditors have been paid. However, preferred stockholders typically have no voting rights. Preferred stock carries a guaranteed fixed dividend. A corporation must use its earnings first to pay its debts. Then any remaining profits must go first to preferred stockholders. Preferred stockholders receive their guaranteed dividend before common stockholders get anything. If any profits remain, the corporation can then pay dividends to common stockholders.

For example, suppose that a corporation issues $100,000 of 7 percent preferred stock and $100,000 of common stock. Further assume that profits for the year are $10,000. The preferred stockholders would receive 7 percent of $100,000, or $7,000. Only $3,000 would be left for the holders of common stock. Their return on $100,000 would yield only 3 percent ($3,000/$100,000). Even that return is not guaranteed because the board of directors may choose not to declare a dividend for common stockholders.

A special class of preferred stock is *cumulative preferred stock*. If there is no profit in a particular year, the guarantee remains in place for cumulative preferred stockholders, so the dividend will have to be made up in future years when the company is profitable again.

Preferred stockholders have priority over common stockholders with regard to not only dividends but also assets. For instance, if the corporation ceases operations, its assets belong to its owners, the stockholders. The assets are first distributed to preferred stockholders. Any remaining assets go to common stockholders.

What would happen if a corporation with $500,000 of outstanding common stock and $500,000 of outstanding preferred stock ceased operating? Assume that after selling all of the assets for cash and after paying all of its creditors, $800,000 in cash remains. The sum of $500,000 (the par value of the preferred stock) must be paid to the preferred stockholders, because their stock has asset priority. As a result, the common stockholders would receive only $300,000, which is 60 percent of the full value of their stock ($300,000/$500,000). If no stock had been issued as preferred, all stockholders would share equally in the $800,000.

CHECKPOINT

What right do common stockholders have that preferred stockholders do not?

The Value of Stock

The original sale of stock provides the equity that a company needs to operate the business. It is used to finance long- and short-term assets and pay operating expenses. Even though the value of stock may increase or decrease after the original sale, that change in value is not directly reflected in the resources the company has available to finance operations. The change in the price of a company's stock is important to stockholders when they buy and sell the stock, so the company's management wants to maximize the value of its stock to make the company attractive to investors. If a corporation wants to increase its capital, it must issue additional stock or keep profits for use in the company rather than using those profits to pay stockholder dividends.

ISSUING STOCK

If an existing corporation needs additional equity and decides to raise it through the sale of stock, that decision will need to be approved by the board of directors. Common stockholders will have the first right to purchase the stock. Stockholders will be concerned about the effect of the sale of new stock on the price of their current shares. Having more shares of a company available usually results in a lower stock price.

Corporations must determine the kind of stock to issue. The certificate of incorporation states whether all authorized stock is common stock or whether part is common and part preferred. Corporations cannot issue other stock unless they receive authorization from the state in which they are chartered.

It is usually a good practice to issue only common stock when starting a business. That provides more flexibility to the board of directors in the way they use any profits earned in the first years of the company. Even if the new corporation earns profits right away, it is often wise to use those profits to expand the business, rather than distribute the profits as dividends. Although a corporation often pays dividends to holders of common stock, it is not required to do so. When the corporation issues preferred stock, however, it is obligated to pay the specified dividend from its profits. If it issues only common stock initially and later wants to expand, it may then issue preferred stock to encourage others to invest in the business. Investors may be attracted to a company whose stock price is not expected to increase if they can be assured of a regular dividend.

VALUING A COMPANY'S STOCK

The par value or market value of stock does not reflect the stockholder's equity in the company. A company's stock shows a par value of $5, for example, but may have a current market value of over $100, depending on how well the company has performed financially. The real value of stock to stockholders is not the par value but the amount buyers are willing to pay for it.

In the same way, the value of a share of stock to the company is not its par value or its market value. The value of stock to the company relates to the financial health of the company, which is measured by the stock's book value. The **book value** of a share of stock is calculated by dividing the corporation's net worth (assets minus liabilities) by the total number of shares outstanding. Thus, if the corporation's net worth is $75,000,000 and the number of shares of stock outstanding is 1,000,000, the book value of each share is $75 ($75,000,000/1,000,000), regardless of the stock's par value or market value. The lower the net worth of a company, the lower the book value of its stock. If the net worth is high, meaning the value of assets is much greater than the value of liabilities, the book value of the stock will also be high. Book value is an important tool when making judgments about the worth of a business. It is used as one measure to determine the value of a business that is about to be sold. It can be useful in a comparison of businesses by potential investors. Book value may also be used, in part, to esti-

Corporations obtain capital by selling stock. Where would you go to buy a share of stock?

mate the amount of money to distribute to shareholders when a corporation is dissolved.

RETAINED EARNINGS

Normally, a good policy for a firm is not to distribute all of its profits. It is better to hold some of its profits in reserve for use in the business through retained earnings. If the corporation distributes all of its profits as dividends to stockholders, it may later need to borrow money to carry on its operations. As illustrated in Figure 16-3, corporations usually distribute some of their profits as dividends and keep some in the business as retained earnings. In addition, if the corporation earns no profit during a particular period, it can use retained earnings to pay dividends for that period. If the corporation pays out all of its profits to stockholders, it has no retained earnings to fall back on during tough times.

A business that retains some of its earnings to reinvest in the business is "plowing back" earnings. A business plows back earnings for some or all of the following reasons:

1. Replacement of buildings and equipment as the result of depreciation (wearing out)
2. Replacement of equipment as a result of obsolescence (being out-of-date)
3. Addition of new facilities for expanding the business
4. The availability of cash to serve as financial protection during periods of low sales and profits, such as recessions and tough competitive times

Even when the business is not making a profit, it should have financial plans to replace assets that decrease in value because of depreciation or obsolescence. For instance, a car rental company starts operations with all new cars. If the owners of the business do not develop an asset replacement fund through retained earnings and instead distribute all profits as dividends, funds will not be available to buy new cars when the present ones wear out.

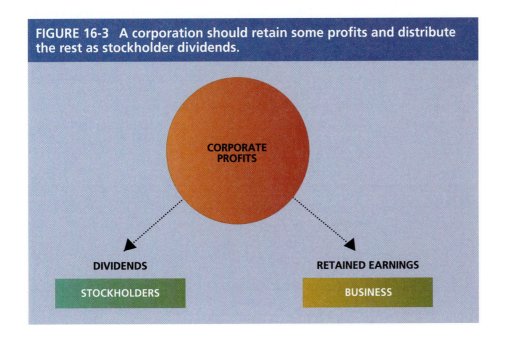

FIGURE 16-3 A corporation should retain some profits and distribute the rest as stockholder dividends.

Retained earnings are not kept in the form of cash only. Retained earnings may be tied up in such current assets as inventories and accounts receivable, which are later converted to cash. Any unused earnings should be invested in short- or long-term securities that earn interest for the company. Because retained earnings are a part of owner's equity, the earnings can be used for investment purposes and future expansion.

CHECKPOINT

How is the book value of stock determined?

16.2 Assessment

UNDERSTAND MANAGEMENT CONCEPTS

Determine the best answer for each of the following questions.

1. Which of the following statements about preferred stock owner-ship is true?
   a. Preferred stock owners are given one vote per share on corpo-rate matters.
   b. Preferred stock owners cannot lose the amount of their invest-ment if the business fails.
   c. Preferred stock owners receive a guaranteed dividend from the company's profits.
   d. All of the statements are true.

2. The _____ value of a share of stock is calculated by dividing the cor-poration's net worth by the total number of shares outstanding.
   a. book
   b. par
   c. market
   d. selling

THINK CRITICALLY

Answer the following questions as completely as possible.

3. If you had a choice of becoming a preferred or common stock-holder in a new small corporation, which would you choose? Explain your choice.

4. The board of directors of a corporation of which you are a stock-holder consistently votes to put 60 percent of profits in retained earnings and distributes only 40 percent to stockholders as divi-dends. The business is always profitable and you have received a small dividend each year. Do you agree or dis-agree with the board's policy? Justify your answer.

Focus On...

Business Innovation—Taking UPS Public

For most Americans, the brown UPS vans driven by people in brown uniforms delivering packages to businesses and consumers are a common sight. United Parcel Service also flies brown airplanes to make deliveries in many other countries. Since 1927, much of the company's equity had been held by the original owners and by those who participated in the firm's popular employee stock option plan. UPS has been a financially healthy company with plenty of assets and retained earnings. With its sound financial position and growth strategy, it competes with its archrival, Federal Express. So why did it decide to change its investment strategy and offer stock to the public?

In 1999, UPS launched an IPO (initial public offering) that at the time was the largest in Wall Street history. Its purpose was not the same as that of the typical fast-growing firm that wants additional equity capital to gain money for expansion. The real reason it sold the stock was to benefit its current owners, including its current employees and retirees. UPS believed the stock's value would increase with public trading and the cash raised could be used to buy back stock from current owners if they chose to sell. Up to this time, the firm has been a closely held corporation, not a publicly held corporation. A closely held corporation cannot sell its shares to the public.

The IPO raised what was then a record-setting $5.27 billion through 109.4 million shares of new stock. The IPO now permits the public and UPS employees as well as retirees and other investors to buy and sell UPS stock conveniently. In fact, soon after the IPO was completed, the firm offered to buy the stock from its shareholders at a price higher than the market price. All shareholders—insiders and outsiders—were pleased.

Think Critically

1. Assume you considered buying some of the new UPS stock. Do you think the price would be more than, less than, or the same as the price employees had to pay before the IPO? Why?
2. If you were retired or nearing retirement at UPS, how would you benefit from both the IPO and the firm's offer to buy stock from its shareholders? If you were an investor but not a present or past employee, how would you benefit from UPS's actions?
3. Using your library or the Internet, decide whether today you would prefer to become an owner of stock in UPS or Federal Express.

16.3 | Short- and Long-Term Debt Financing

Goals
- Differentiate between short-term and long-term debt.
- Explain the factors that businesses should consider when choosing debt financing.
- Describe several sources from which businesses can obtain additional capital.

Terms
- short-term debt
- line of credit
- promissory note
- trade credit
- long-term debt
- term loan
- lease
- bond
- investment bank
- stock option
- venture capital

Debt Capital

Businesses often borrow capital to expand the business, purchase or construct new facilities, purchase equipment, pay operating expenses, or replenish inventory. Much of this capital is made available from the savings of individuals. Millions of people deposit their savings in banks and other financial institutions that lend these funds to businesses. Because a business can borrow money for just a few days or for many years, debt capital is classified as either short-term or long-term.

SHORT-TERM DEBT CAPITAL

Short-term debt must be repaid with interest within a year, and often in 30, 60, or 90 days. Short-term debt capital is usually obtained from a bank or other lending institution but may be obtained from other businesses as well.

OBTAINING FUNDS FROM BANKS Before lending, banks want to be fairly certain that the borrowers will repay their loans. The business will need to supply adequate financial information, and the bank will usually obtain a financial report on the business from a company such as Dun & Bradstreet. If it is satisfied with the information and considers the business a good credit risk, the bank will grant a loan for a specific amount and a set time period. To allow the business flexibility to choose when to use the borrowed money, the bank may approve a line of credit. A **line of credit** is the authorization to borrow up to a maximum amount for a specified period of time. For example, a business may be allowed a line of credit up to $150,000 for a year. Whenever it needs to borrow, it may do so up to the $150,000 limit. Should the business borrow $50,000, it could still borrow an additional $100,000 during the year.

Another form of debt equity similar to an open line of credit is a business credit card, often used by small businesses. The credit card is issued by the bank with a set credit limit. The card can be used to finance purchases as long as the limit is not exceeded. Both the open line of credit and the credit card carry an interest rate that is usually lower than similar interest rates charged to consumers for short-term loans and personal credit cards. Normally, businesses have to pay the interest due on the loan monthly and may have a specific payment schedule for the principal as well.

When a business wants to borrow money from a lending institution, whether the business has a line of credit or not, it must sign a promissory note. A **promissory note** (see Figure 16-4) is an unconditional written promise to pay to the lender a certain sum of money at a particular time or on demand.

If the bank has some doubt about the ability of the firm to repay a loan, it may require the business to pledge its accounts receivable, inventory, or some other asset of significant value as security for the loan. If the loan is not repaid, the bank can claim the property pledged as security and sell it to obtain the value of the unpaid loan.

OBTAINING FUNDS FROM OTHER SOURCES A business may have access to other sources of short-term capital, depending on the type of business it is. Investment businesses and insurance companies often provide business financing. Federal agencies such as the Small Business Administration (SBA) can assist business owners in locating financing sources and may actually help guarantee repayment of a percentage of the loans to obtain a lower interest rate. Some states, counties, and cities offer loans at favorable rates to encourage businesses to locate in a particular area or to encourage businesses not to leave.

Trade credit is a common form of short-term financing for businesses. **Trade credit** is obtained by buying goods and services that do not require immediate payment. Vendors often provide trade credit as an incentive for a business to purchase their products and services. Trade credit is usually extended for a period of 30 to 60 days interest free. As an incentive for early payment, the vendor may offer a cash discount of 1 or 2 percent of the total sale if the bill is paid quickly, such as within 10 days. Terms of trade credit are often shown on the invoice in a form such as 2/10, net 30. Those terms mean that the purchaser can receive a 2 percent discount if the bill is paid within 10 days of the invoice date. Otherwise the bill must be paid in full within 30 days.

A *factor* is a firm that specializes in lending money to businesses based on the business's accounts receivable. The usual practice, however, is that the factor purchases the company's accounts receivable at a discount and then collects the full amount when customers pay their bills. In a similar manner, a *sales finance*

FIGURE 16-4 A Simple Promissory Note

DUE August 10, 20--.   NO 528

$ 5000.00   MUNCIE, IND., May 10, 20 --

Three months ------------------------ after date, we, or either of us, promise to pay

to the order of J.J. McKissick --

Five Thousand and 00/100 --. DOLLARS

With attorney's fees, negotiable and payable at INDUSTRIAL TRUST & SAVINGS BANK OF MUNCIE, IND.,for value received, without relief from valuation or appraisment laws. The drawers and endorsers severally waive presentation for payment, protest, notice of protest and notice of non payment of this note with 8 percent interest after date, and nine percent interest after maturity until paid.

1145 South High

---

business note

Every business manager and investor must know how to read stock tables. Following a stock is an important way to understand the financial picture of a company. Business managers can see how investors view the company as stock is bought and sold. Investors can make decisions whether to buy, hold, or sell a stock based on its performance.

Stock quotes appear in the financial section of newspapers and on financial Web sites. Reading and understanding a stock table is easy if you understand the abbreviations used. Here is an example.

52-Week Hi	52.75
Lo	40.93
Stock	Bnk of Amer
Sym	BAC
Div	2.2
Yld. %	4.36
PE	12.6
Vol. 100s	117,412
Hi	51.51
Lo	51
Close	51.4
Net Chg	−0.12

52-week Hi and Lo — The highest and lowest price at which the stock was traded over the previous 52-week period.
Stock (Sym) — The stock name, often abbreviated, and the stock symbol used for that stock.
Div — Dividend/distribution rate. Unless noted in a footnote, this reflects the annual dividend.
Yield % — The dividends paid to stockholders as a percentage of the stock's price.
PE — The price-to-earnings ratio, the per-share earnings divided by the closing price.
Vol 100s — Sales volume, expressed with two zeros missing. 283 means 28,300 shares traded that day.
Close — The last price the stock traded at that day, which is not necessarily the price the stock will open at the next day.
Net Chg — The net change in price calculated from the previous day's close.

company purchases installment sales contracts at a discount from businesses that need cash or that do not care to handle credit and collections. A sales finance company may also lend money to a business and use the business's installment contracts as security for the loan.

LONG-TERM DEBT CAPITAL

Long-term debt is capital borrowed for longer than a year. A business usually obtains such debt capital by issuing long-term notes and bonds.

TERM LOANS A **term loan** is medium- or long-term financing used for operating funds or the purchase or improvement of fixed assets. Term loans, or *long-term notes*, are written for periods of 1 to 15 years or longer. They are a significant source of capital for most businesses. Because term loans extend for a long period, lending institutions require the principal and interest to be repaid on a regular basis over the life of the note.

Long-term notes are one method used to finance the purchase of expensive equipment. Rather than borrow large sums of money, however, a company may prefer to lease the equipment. A **lease** is a contract that allows the use of an asset for a fee paid on a schedule, such as monthly. The lease may be obtained from the equipment manufacturer, a finance company that handles that type of leasing, or a bank. Leasing is a practical substitute for long-term financing, especially if capital is difficult to obtain. The maintenance of the equipment and the costs of insuring it are usually not included in the lease agreement. When businesses lease buildings and equipment, they know exactly what the monthly payment will be and how long the lease will last. They do not have to obtain the large amount of financing that would be needed to purchase the buildings or equipment.

BONDS A **bond** is a long-term debt instrument sold by the business to investors. It contains a long-term written promise by the business to pay the bondholder a definite sum of money at a specified time. The business receives the amount of the bond when it is initially sold. It must then pay the bondholder the amount borrowed—called the *principal* or *par value*—at the bond's maturity or due date. Bonds also include an agreement to pay interest at a specified rate at certain intervals.

Bonds are debt equity and do not represent a share of ownership in a corporation. Rather, they are debts the corporation owes to bondholders. People buy bonds as investments, as they do stocks. But bondholders are creditors, not owners, so they have a priority claim against the earnings of a corporation. Bondholders must be paid before stockholders are paid their share of the earnings. Because bonds are negotiable financial instruments, they can be bought and sold by investors. Based on the interest rate of the bond, economic factors, and the financial health of the company, the value of the bond may rise and fall during the time it is traded.

There are two general types of bonds: debenture and mortgage bonds. *Debentures* are unsecured bonds. No specific assets are pledged as security. Debentures are backed by the financial strength and credit history of the corporation that issues them. Public corporations, such as city, state, and federal governments, usually issue debentures when they need to borrow money. Reputable, successful corporations generally find it relatively easy to sell debentures. However, relatively unknown or financially weak firms usually find it easier to attract investors with secured bonds. *Mortgage bonds* are bonds secured by specific long-term assets of the issuer. Property often used as security includes real estate, equipment, and stocks and bonds held in other companies. If the company does not pay the principal and interest when due, creditors can force the company to sell the pledged property to recover the amount of the outstanding debt. Often, however, property cannot be sold for the amount of the loan. In some cases, a bond contract may have a provision that allows bondholders to claim assets other than the assets originally used as security.

Businesses issue debentures and mortgage bonds when they need funds for an extended period. Special features may be attached to these bonds to attract investors. For example, a mortgage bond may have a convertible feature to make it appealing to bond buyers. A *convertible bond* permits a bondholder to exchange bonds for a prescribed number of shares of common stock.

CHECKPOINT

List several sources of short-term and long-term financing available to businesses.

Obtaining Capital

Companies consider three important factors when deciding how to get the capital they need: (1) the original cost of obtaining the capital, (2) the interest rate, and (3) the power that the contributors of capital will have to influence business operations.

COST OF CAPITAL

It can be costly for a business to obtain capital by selling bonds, long-term notes, and new stock issues. For example, to launch a new bond issue, the business must file forms, obtain approval from government authorities, make agreements, print bonds, find buyers, and keep careful records. These costs are usually so high that only large or highly successful firms even consider obtaining capital by issuing new stocks or bonds. It is far less costly to obtain capital from a simple mortgage or a note.

INTEREST RATES

As suggested in Figure 16-5 (see p. 436), interest rates can fluctuate monthly, weekly, or even daily. Borrowing when rates are low costs less than borrowing

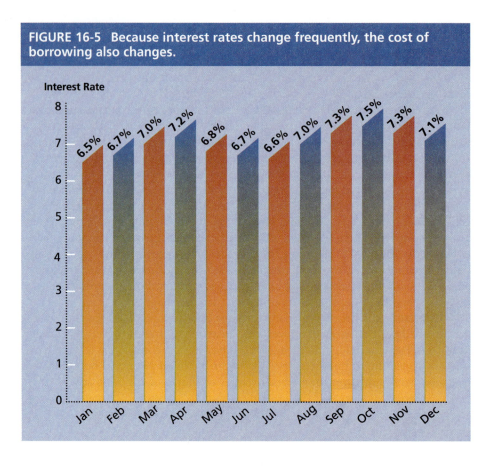

FIGURE 16-5 Because interest rates change frequently, the cost of borrowing also changes.

Interest Rate

Jan 6.5% Feb 6.7% Mar 7.0% Apr 7.2% May 6.8% Jun 6.7% Jul 6.6% Aug 7.0% Sep 7.3% Oct 7.5% Nov 7.3% Dec 7.1%

when rates are high. If a business needs money when interest rates are high, it will usually borrow for a short time with the hope that rates will drop. If rates drop, it can then issue long-term obligations, such as bonds, and use a portion of the capital obtained to pay off short-term obligations. In this way, a company has to pay high interest rates for only a short time. In following this plan, however, a business exposes itself to possible difficulty in obtaining funds when short-term obligations become due, and to the possibility that interest rates may rise even higher.

INFLUENCE OF CAPITAL CONTRIBUTORS

If short-term creditors contribute capital, they usually have no control over the management and operations of the business. If the obligations are not paid, creditors can take legal action to recover the amount due. Otherwise, owners of the business are relatively unrestricted by short-term creditors.

If the company obtains capital from mortgage bonds, however, the holders usually have a lien (claim) on at least part of the assets of the company. This lien may impose limitations on the use of the identified assets, and the agreement under which the mortgage bonds were issued may limit the use of the income of the company.

If new stockholders or new partners contribute equity capital, they gain a voice in the management of the business. In most states, stock can be issued that does not include voting rights, but that stock may be difficult to sell. Of course, if existing stockholders or partners provide the additional funds, the control of the company will not be affected as long as the existing stockholders contribute in proportion to past holdings.

facts & figures

Bonds are usually traded on an agreement between a buyer and seller. There is no central exchange market such as is used to buy and sell stocks.

Bond trading is usually done through bond dealers who work at the bond trading desks of major investment companies. The major bond investors are financial institutions, pension funds, mutual funds, and governments.

If the company increases the number of shares of stock by selling new shares, it must share earnings with a greater number of shareholders. For example, when the number of shareholders increases from 2,000 to 2,500, the distribution of $130,000 in dividends changes from $65 per share ($130,000/2,000) to $52 per share ($130,000/2,500). The original owners may not wish to give up any of their profits or voice in management unless it is profitable to do so. An increase in shareholders would need to be offset by an increase in earnings.

CHECKPOINT

What can a business do to obtain capital when faced with high interest rates?

Sources of Outside Capital

When a business decides to obtain capital, it must find sources willing to provide the financing. Some common sources of capital are shown in Figure 16-6. The particular source a business selects depends, in part, on such factors as the amount of capital needed and the risk involved. Companies with a poor perfor-

---

FIGURE 16-6 There are many sources of capital that should be considered by businesses.

Sources of Capital

1. Banks and related financial firms (the most popular source of outside capital)
2. Small loan companies (firms that lend money to individuals and businesses that may involve more risk than other lenders might accept)
3. Venture capital firms (companies that lend large sums of money to promising new or growing businesses)
4. Commercial credit companies (companies that lend money on current assets, such as accounts receivable and notes receivable)
5. Sales finance companies (used primarily when installment sales are involved; these firms purchase installment sales contracts)
6. Insurance companies (portions of funds collected from policyholders may be loaned to firms)
7. Individual investors and investment groups
8. Pension funds (retirement funds collected from employees may be loaned to firms)
9. Investment banking organizations (firms that specialize in selling new security issues to the public)
10. Equipment manufacturers (firms that do not actually lend money, but will sell needed equipment on an extended-time payment plan)

mance record find it hard to sell stocks or bonds to potential investors. A newly formed company has similar difficulties in securing a loan. Many banks avoid doing business with these types of organizations because of the added risk. When they do agree to provide financing, interest rates and other requirements are much higher than for successful, established firms.

INVESTMENT BANKS

Many commercial banks do not generally become involved in helping large corporations raise capital by selling stocks and bonds. For these services, a corporation may turn to an **investment bank**—an organization that helps a business raise large sums of capital through the sales of stocks and bonds. Investment banks are also known as *underwriters*. Investment banks can assist a rapidly growing, privately held company through an initial public offering (IPO). An IPO is the first time that a company sells stock to the public. Investment banks provide a variety of financial and investment services for their clients regarding large capital projects.

The process of selling securities is simple but expensive. Assume a corporation wishes to raise $50 million by selling bonds. It first finds a willing investment bank. The bank offers advice, buys the bonds at a price below the expected market value, then sells the bonds to the investing public through its marketing channels. The bank's profit would be the difference between what it paid the corporation for the bonds and the selling price it receives from the bond purchasers.

STOCK OPTIONS

Some corporations may wish to sell only a small number of additional shares of stock. In that case, a corporation can handle the sale itself. It can make the sale of additional shares attractive to current stockholders by offering stock options. A **stock option** is a right granted by a corporation that allows current stockholders to buy additional shares when issued at a fixed price for a specific period of time. These options give current stockholders the opportunity to buy enough stock to maintain the same percentage of ownership in the company as they had before the new stock was issued. Often the stock option is offered at a lower price to attract more funds to the corporation without the additional expense of

Venture capitalists provide large sums of money to people who want to start new companies. What do you think would most influence a venture capitalist's loan decision?

PHOTO: © GETTY IMAGES/PHOTODISC.

selling through an investment banker. If stockholders do not wish to take advantage of their stock rights, they can sell their options to others within a stated period at a small gain. Employers sometimes offer employees stock options as part of an employee stock ownership plan (ESOP).

VENTURE CAPITAL

Venture capital is financing obtained from an investor or investment group that lends large sums of money to promising new or expanding small companies. Venture capitalists often ask for a percentage of ownership rights in the company in return for the investment. These investors expect some of the businesses to fail, but they accept the risks in the expectation that others will be successful enough to more than offset losses. They demand a carefully developed business plan that shows a high potential for success. Venture capitalists, many of whom are former entrepreneurs, have helped many small firms become large successful firms.

CHECKPOINT

What do venture capitalists require of businesses before they provide financing?

16.3 Assessment

UNDERSTAND MANAGEMENT CONCEPTS

Determine the best answer for each of the following questions.

1. A short-term form of finance obtained by buying goods and services that do not require immediate payment is
   a. a line of credit
   b. trade credit
   c. a term loan
   d. a promissory note

2. An organization that helps a business raise large amounts of capital through the issue of bonds or stocks is a(n)
   a. commercial bank
   b. stock exchange
   c. venture capital firm
   d. investment bank

THINK CRITICALLY

Answer the following questions as completely as possible.

3. Why would a business choose to use a line of credit rather than obtain a loan and receive all of the money at that time?

4. If you were an entrepreneur with a successful new business, would you prefer to obtain financing for expansion from a venture capital firm or from selling stock through an IPO?
   Explain your choice.

Xtra!
Study Tools
thomsonedu.com/school/bpmxtra

Xtra! Quiz Prep

CHAPTER CONCEPTS

- Businesses can obtain capital in three ways: selling ownership shares in the company (equity or owner capital), keeping profits in the company (retained earnings), and borrowing money from others (debt capital). Equity capital is the investment owners have in a business. When equity financing is used to raise capital, owners give up some ownership rights regarding decision making and sharing of profits.

- For corporations, common and preferred stock are shares of ownership. Retained earnings are profits that have not been distributed to stockholders but may be used to help firms through times when profits or cash flow are low and to fund expansion and improvement plans.

- Debt capital consists of either short- or long-term loans, such as notes and bonds, which must be paid back with interest to the lenders. Types of debt financing include loans obtained through banks, business credit cards, open lines of credit, and using factors. Debt financing creates a legal obligation to pay back the lenders, usually on a fixed schedule.

- Large sums of outside capital can be obtained through initial public offerings (IPOs) and from venture capitalists. Firms desiring rapid growth often use these sources. Large firms hire investment bankers with special expertise to assist in obtaining those types of capital.

REVIEW TERMS AND CONCEPTS

Write the letter of the term that matches each definition. Some terms will not be used.

a. bond
b. book value
c. common stock
d. debt capital
e. equity capital
f. investment bank
g. lease
h. line of credit
i. long-term debt
j. market value
k. par value
l. preferred stock
m. promissory note
n. retained earnings
o. short-term debt
p. stock option
q. term loan
r. trade credit
s. venture capital

1. Business owners' personal contributions to the business
2. Price at which stock is actually bought and sold
3. Short-term form of financing obtained by buying goods and services that do not require immediate payment
4. Contract that allows the use of an asset for a fee paid on a schedule, such as monthly
5. Financing obtained from an investor or investment group that lends large sums of money to promising new or expanding small companies
6. Medium-term or long-term financing used for operating funds or the purchase or improvement of fixed assets
7. Stock that gives holders first claim on corporate dividends if a company earns a profit
8. Profits that the owners do not take out of the business but instead save for use by the business
9. Debt that must be repaid with interest within a year
10. Organization that helps a business raise large sums of capital through the sales of stocks and bonds
11. Right granted by a corporation that allows current stockholders to buy additional shares when issued at a fixed price for a specific period of time
12. Figure calculated by dividing the corporation's net worth by the total number of shares outstanding

DETERMINE THE BEST ANSWER

13. An example of equity capital is
    a. personal savings of a current owner invested in the business
    b. money contributed by a new partner
    c. retained earnings
    d. all of the above
14. An advantage an entrepreneur gains by forming a corporation to raise capital is
    a. it does not increase the number of owners
    b. the entrepreneur's personal assets have greater protection
    c. the entrepreneur still retains all profits earned
    d. none of the above
15. The number of shares of stock to be issued by a corporation is determined by
    a. common stockholders
    b. preferred stockholders
    c. company executives
    d. the board of directors
16. The best policy regarding the use of profits for a corporation is to
    a. avoid making a profit so no dividends have to be distributed
    b. distribute all profits as dividends to increase stockholder satisfaction
    c. distribute some profits as dividends and keep some profits as retained earnings
    d. keep all profits as retained earnings to build the value of the company quickly
17. A form of debt equity similar to an open line of credit is
    a. venture capital
    b. a business credit card
    c. trade credit
    d. a lease
18. Another name for *investment bank* is
    a. underwriter
    b. commercial bank
    c. factor
    d. venture capitalist

APPLY WHAT YOU KNOW

19. Based on the Reality Check scenario at the beginning of the chapter, do you believe Eva Diaz should immediately expand her business? Why or why not? If she does expand, what type of financing do you believe would be best for her? Justify your answer.
20. Why might an individual with enough money to start a new business consider forming a corporation rather than a sole proprietorship?

21. Why would a corporation's preferred stock probably cost more per share than its common stock?

22. When might a business lease, rather than purchase, equipment? What reasons other than the cost of the lease versus the cost of purchasing the equipment would justify the decision to lease?

23. How can venture capitalists make a profit even when they often invest in firms that eventually fail?

MAKE CONNECTIONS

24. **Research** The New York Stock Exchange is the largest stock exchange in the world and dates back to the late 1700s. It has been an important part of the economic growth of businesses in the United States and has contributed to the economic success of many individual investors. Use the Internet to study the history and growth of the NYSE. Prepare several computer slides that highlight important events and information in the history of the Exchange.

25. **Technology** Think carefully about the advantages and disadvantages of the three forms of business ownership (sole proprietorship, partnership, corporation) in raising equity capital. Use a word-processing program to prepare a table that summarizes your analysis. Then write a three-paragraph report that describes the circumstances under which each of the forms of ownership would benefit in raising equity capital.

26. **Economics** Use the Internet to gather information on current interest rates. Identify the highest and lowest rates you can find for each of the following:

    a. 30-year fixed rate mortgage
    b. APR for a personal credit card
    c. 6-month Certificate of Deposit
    d. 48-month new-car loan
    e. a federal student loan for college
    f. the federal prime lending rate

    Prepare a chart to illustrate your findings. Compare your findings with those of other students.

27. **Oral Communication** You are the chairman of the board of directors of a corporation with a long and successful history. Stock prices have been stable and a regular dividend has been paid each year for the past 10 years. The board has decided that the business needs to invest money to upgrade facilities and equipment. They believe the best choice is to retain all profits for the next three years and not pay a dividend. Interest rates are high, so borrowing the money would be expensive. The board does not want to issue new stock and dilute the value of current stock. Prepare a three-minute speech you will deliver to stockholders at the annual meeting justifying the decision. You know many stockholders will be upset that they won't receive the expected dividends.

CASE IN POINT

CASE 16-1: Is Debt the Best Way?

The Kyle Camping Company is located between a major state park and a national park in New York State's Adirondack Mountains. The business sells camping equipment and supplies from May through September to vacationers as well as to local people who enjoy mountain camping and fishing. Kyle Owens, the sole proprietor, started the business five years ago after graduating from college. Kyle is an avid outdoorsman and the business allows him to work with people and products he enjoys. Kyle was very busy for the first several years, with little personal time to enjoy the outdoors. However, the business has experienced success that has allowed him to add two full-time and five part-time employees. Over the last two years, sales have doubled and profits have increased by 25 percent. He has been able to pay back a loan from his parents that he used to start the business and has saved $75,000 from the business's profits.

Kyle now wishes to expand into a year-round business to take advantage of the winter hunting and ice fishing. In addition, he believes he can serve the many local boat owners. To do that he would need to expand the size of his store, add a dock on the lake behind the store, and expand his inventory. He also wants to create an Internet site through which he can sell his merchandise and provide area information that could attract more tourists and visitors to his business.

Kyle is interested only in debt financing because he wants to remain the sole owner and manager of his business. He is willing to consider equity financing only as a last resort. A small community 5 miles away has a commercial bank with which he has had good relations since starting his business five years ago. His credit rating is acceptable but not great; it is marred by several late loan payments during the first two years of business. Kyle does have good relationships with several of his suppliers, who have approved trade credit on some of his purchases.

Kyle has calculated that he will need to find $75,000 to add a dock and additional inventory this year and $30,000 additional capital next year to carry out all of his plans. He does have a concern that sales during the winter season may be slow at the beginning, making it difficult for him to make loan payments during those months.

THINK CRITICALLY

1. If you were the local bank's loan officer, what financial and nonfinancial information would you request from Kyle in order to make a good decision? Based on the information available in the case, would you recommend financing Kyle's needs through loans? Why or why not?
2. Other than a loan from the local bank, what other types of debt financing might Kyle consider, given his financial situation and his plans?
3. Why might Kyle wish to consider equity financing rather than debt financing? What are two types of equity financing he could use? What would be advantages and disadvantages of each?

CASE 16-2: Taking Stock of Investments

Reika Mori is a member of a four-person carpool. Morning conversations on the way to work often deal with what people did the night before. Reika started the discussion today because she had attended an information session the previous evening on investments. Here is the conversation that occurred among the carpool members.

Lou: *I've always thought about investing but really don't want to get in over my head. I have heard of people who made a fortune but also know that you can easily lose all your money as well. Did you learn anything that can help me, Reika?*

Reika: *I learned that there are all kinds of stocks and bonds and even other types of investments. There's something to meet everyone's needs. But at this point it's still quite confusing. I'm going to have to learn a lot more before I would feel comfortable giving you advice.*

Pablo: *My brother is an investment banker, and he told me that bonds might be a good choice to consider when I'm first starting out. He said choosing the right bonds really takes most of the risk out of investments. Did you hear anything like that at the seminar?*

Reika: *Not really. The speaker spent nearly all the time talking about stocks. Maybe next week's lecture will cover bonds.*

Brenda: *My uncle gave Larry and me some stock for a wedding gift five years ago. We have considered selling even though we get a regular dividend check every three months. It's not a lot of income, but it gives us some spending money. We wonder if we would make more if we sold the stock and put the money in the bank to earn interest.*

Reika: *Brenda, I did learn how to read stock tables at the seminar. Let's have lunch today. I'll get a copy of the newspaper and we can determine how much you would make if you sold the stock and how well the company's stock is doing. You might be better off keeping the stock because the market is doing pretty well right now. The increase in the stock price could be much more than you can make by putting the money in a savings account. Can you have lunch with me today? I did learn something about mortgage bonds that might be helpful.*

THINK CRITICALLY

1. Do you agree with Pablo's brother that bonds are less risky than other investments? Why or why not?
2. What information can Reika obtain from a stock table that will help Brenda understand what to do with the stock she owns? What additional information would you recommend they review in order to decide which investment choice is best for Brenda and her husband?
3. If you were in the carpool, what would you say to Lou to make him less fearful of investing some of his money?

A very important step in financial planning for a new business is determining the amount of capital needed and the sources of that capital. Most new businesses fail because they do not have adequate capital to operate the business until it becomes profitable. You have already estimated your financial needs in the Chapter 15 activities. Now you need to develop a plan to obtain the capital.

Your plans should consider both immediate and long-term needs, the type of ownership structure you currently have and whether you want to retain or change the form, and whether you believe it will be possible to obtain equity capital, debt capital, or a combination of both. If you choose equity capital, how will it affect your role as owner and manager? Will your business benefit in ways other than having additional capital? If you choose debt capital, how will you be certain your business will be able to repay the debt when it becomes due? What will happen to your business if you are unable to meet the debt payments? What are other possible consequences of your decision for the business?

DATA COLLECTION

1. Identify three sources of long-term financing for your business. For each source, determine the (a) amount of capital available, (b) interest rate, (c) amount and type of security needed, and (d) procedures for obtaining financing.
2. Identify three sources of short-term financing for your business. For each source, determine (a) what the financing can be used for in your business, (b) what the terms of financing would be, and (c) what information would need to be provided to obtain the financing.
3. Ask several small-business owners how they obtained the initial financing for their businesses. Have them identify problems they have faced in financing continuing operations and any expansions.

ANALYSIS

1. Based on the amount of capital you will need to start your business and operate it for six months, determine:
   a. the amount of money you can personally invest
   b. the capital available from family and friends, and how you can obtain and repay it
   c. sources for the remaining capital needs, interest rates, and procedures for obtaining the capital
2. Develop a written request for funds that can be presented to prospective investors. It must contain enough specific information to encourage them to invest money in your business. Develop the request on a computer so it has a professional look when printed. Provide supporting data, including the appropriate financial information and graphs or charts showing the source and amount of each type of capital.

Financial Services

REALITY CHECK

What Should We Do with the Money?

Among his many duties, Andrew Jones manages the finances for the rapidly growing Kilgore Kitchens, a distributor of all types of kitchen gadgets. During the morning break, he planned to discuss the large balance in Kilgore's checking account with Julie Vernon, the company's bookkeeper. As they entered the nearby deli, Julie expressed her frustration in balancing this month's checking account. Julie said, "Andrew, we run most of the business's financial transactions through the checking account. I spend days trying to keep track of all of the money coming in from our customers and all the bills we are paying. We need to find a way to get more efficient with the way we use our money or we will never know whether we are making a profit or not."

"You know, Julie," Andrew commented, "we are a successful and growing business. When we were younger we had to worry about having enough money to pay our bills, but over time we have built up a lot of cash. We should start thinking about how much money we really need in the checking account and what to do with the excess amount of cash we've managed to build up in that account. That is money not working for us."

"I agree, Andrew," Julie said. "We make almost no money in a regular checking account. And I don't see any upcoming heavy payment drains. Why don't we divide the excess between some good short-term and long-term investments?"

Andrew paused and then remarked, "But we need answers to some questions first. Where can we put the money and earn the most on it? Is one bank any different from another? What investment opportunities exist for short and long time periods? Can we make several investments and still have enough cash to pay our bills during the year?"

"Andrew, let's work together on this," Julie replied. "Can you find time by lunch tomorrow to do some financial shopping? Then we can sort out our information and be ready to make a decision."

"Sounds like the right move to make, Julie. I know you have to go to our bank to make deposits this afternoon. Why don't you talk with them about the options they can provide? I'm going to spend some time on the Internet gathering information on other investment choices."

Julie nodded her approval. "See you at lunch tomorrow. This could be just what the business needs."

17.1 Financial Institutions

Goals
- Identify several types of banks and how they are regulated.
- Discuss the similarities and differences among nonbanking financial institutions and banks.

Terms
- bank
- demand deposit
- time deposits
- commercial loan
- consumer loan
- nonbank
- Federal Reserve System
- Federal Deposit Insurance Corporation (FDIC)

Banks and Banking

All businesses rely on the services of financial institutions. A business like Kilgore Kitchens must deposit cash, make payments, invest excess funds, and borrow money. Knowledge of the available types of financial institutions and the services they provide help managers like Andrew and Julie operate businesses efficiently and use their financial resources wisely.

Financial institutions handle transactions that deal primarily with money and securities. Banks provide many of these services, and other financial institutions provide investment services that banks traditionally did not. However, each year it is getting more and more difficult to distinguish among the services provided by various financial institutions. Nonbank financial institutions have rapidly expanded the services they offer, competing directly with banks in areas such as checking and savings accounts. The deregulation of banking has made it possible for banks to offer a variety of new investment products and other financial services. Computer technology and the Internet have allowed consumers to conduct many financial transactions online and have contributed much to changing how the world conducts its financial affairs.

BANKS AND NONBANKS

Banks are financial institutions that historically have been closely regulated by the government to make sure financial services are widely available and that financial resources of individuals and businesses are protected. In order to operate, a bank must receive a charter. A *bank charter* authorizes the operation of a bank following the regulations established by the state or federal government.

To be recognized as a **bank**, a financial institution must accept demand deposits, make consumer and commercial loans, and buy and sell currency and government securities. A **demand deposit** is money put into a financial institution that the depositors can withdraw at any time without penalty. A checking account is an example of a demand deposit account. **Time deposits** (also known as *certificates of deposit* or *CDs*) are made for a specified period of time and cannot be withdrawn early without some financial penalty. A **commercial loan** is a loan made to a business, whereas a **consumer loan** is a loan made to an individual for personal use.

If the primary purpose of an institution is to offer financial products and services other than deposits and loans, it is classified as a **nonbank** financial institution. Although nonbank financial institutions initially developed to offer financial products such as insurance and investments, they have increasingly begun to offer services traditionally reserved for banks. As you will discover, the distinction between banks and nonbanks is fading fast.

TYPES OF BANKS

Banks are often known as *deposit institutions* because their customers deposit excess funds for the purpose of earning interest on the deposits. Depending on the type of institution, deposits are accepted from individual consumers, businesses, and local, state, and national governments. The banks use those deposits to make loans to customers who need additional financial resources for short or long periods of time. Those customers pay interest to the bank for the use of the funds. The bank accepts the risk that the loan may not be repaid. They take steps to reduce the risk by carefully evaluating loan customers and spreading the risk across a large number of loans.

There are three major types of banks, based on the customers served and the types of deposits and loans offered. The three types are described in Figure 17-1.

COMMERCIAL BANKS Commercial banks as a group are the largest and most important type of deposit institution. They are sometimes referred to as the "department store" of banks because of the broad range of services they offer and the many types of customers they serve. Commercial banks have assets of more than $8 trillion, made up of loans to businesses, government, and consumers, private and public securities, cash, and real estate. They hold deposits from customers of more than $6 trillion. Commercial banks provide most short-term loans to consumers. Nearly 10 percent of their loans are consumer loans. They also make a large number of loans to businesses to finance operations as well as commercial real estate loans. Commercial banks provide checking and savings accounts for both consumers and businesses. Ten percent of consumer deposits are demand deposits, and nearly 60 percent are various types of time deposits.

FIGURE 17-1 Three Major Types of Banks

The Three Major Types of Banks

Type	Description	Number of U.S. institutions (2004)
Commercial Banks	Full-service financial institutions that serve all types of customers with a variety of deposit accounts and lending services.	7,630
Savings Institutions	Financial institutions that emphasize loans for residential mortgages; include savings and loan associations and mutual savings banks.	1,345
Credit Unions	Nonprofit associations whose services are restricted to members who generally have a common relationship, such as employees of a large business, members of an employee association such as a union, or employees affiliated with a government unit (state employees, teachers); offer deposit services and loans to members.	8,695

Due to competition, deregulation, and consolidation, the number of commercial banks has declined dramatically since their peak in the mid-1980s. At that time, there were nearly 15,000 commercial banks. Figure 17-1 shows that the number had declined by nearly 50 percent by 2004. Despite that decline, consumers still have ready access to commercial banks. The total number of branch offices has increased in that same time from 41,000 to nearly 70,000. The 10 largest U.S. commercial banks are listed in Figure 17-2.

FIGURE 17-2 The size of banks has grown as large banks buy smaller banks.

The Ten Largest U.S. Banks (2006)

1. Bank of America, Charlotte, NC
2. JPMorgan Chase Bank, Columbus, OH
3. Citibank, New York, NY
4. Wachovia, Charlotte, NC
5. Wells Fargo Bank, Sioux Falls, SD
6. US Bank, Cincinnati, OH
7. SunTrust Banks, Atlanta, GA
8. HSBC Bank USA, Wilmington, DE
9. State Street, Boston, MA
10. KeyBank, Cleveland, OH

SAVINGS INSTITUTIONS Savings institutions developed as local or neighborhood locations to promote thrift and savings. They encouraged community members to deposit their earnings and other funds and in return offered loans to borrowers needing funds. There are two common types of savings institutions—savings and loans and mutual savings banks.

Mutual savings banks began in the early 1800s and are owned by their customers. Rather than buying shares as in a corporation, ownership is based on establishing a relationship with the bank as a depositor or borrower. The profits are divided and distributed in proportion to the amount of deposits of each owner. Customers who borrow funds from mutual savings banks do not have to be depositors or "owners." Both short- and long-term loans are made for a variety of purposes, but a large percentage of the loans are made within the community for long-term needs such as financing home mortgages.

Savings and loan associations served a similar purpose as mutual savings banks. They were often started by pooling the small savings of a large number of people and in turn lending that money back to their members for the purpose of building housing. Often the original savings and loan associations were dissolved when the building needs of members were met. Savings and loans were formed either as closely held corporations where members bought shares or as mutual companies where ownership was based on the value of deposits. Today, most savings and loans have expanded their purpose and no longer require membership to use their services. However, they still emphasize loans for real estate mortgages. Because of their limited size and services compared to many commercial banks, they often pay a slightly higher interest rate on deposits and charge lower mortgage rates.

Together, mutual savings banks and savings and loan associations have assets of about $1.6 trillion, made up mostly of loans and leases. They hold customer deposits of just under $1 trillion, over 90 percent of which is in time deposits.

CREDIT UNIONS Credit unions are not-for-profit financial organizations owned and managed by their members. Rather than making a profit, credit unions provide financial benefits to members such as higher interest rates on deposits and lower rates on loans. They also emphasize more personal service than many other financial institutions. Credit unions provide both demand and time deposits and emphasize shorter-term consumer loans such as personal loans, auto loans, and home loans of three to five years. Although there are large credit unions, many credit unions serve a very small number of customers who have a common relationship such as employment, an organizational affiliation, or location. You must be a member to use the services of a credit union. Today nearly 85 million people in the United States are credit union members. Credit unions

PHOTO: © GETTY IMAGES/PHOTODISC.

hold assets of nearly $680 billion, including loans valued at over $450 billion. Because credit union members are owners, their savings make up most of the owner's equity of the organizations. Total member savings are just over $577 billion.

REGULATING BANKS

Banks operate in an environment of high risk. Customers who deposit funds with banks risk that the bank will not have adequate funds to pay the interest or return the money when the customer requests its return. When banks make loans to customers, they risk that the customer will be unable to repay the loan with interest according to the terms of the loan. Of course customers should be careful to deposit money with banks that have the financial strength and history to protect deposits. Banks carefully review loan applicants and their applications to determine if they are creditworthy. However, there are many examples of bank failures that resulted in large financial losses to businesses and individuals. The bank failures of the early 1900s and again during the Great Depression in the 1930s were so dramatic in terms of the number of people affected and the size of their financial losses that the federal government increased its regulation of banks and banking.

Competition among financial institutions has grown as the services offered become more similar. Can you name three financial institutions in your community from which you might obtain financial services?

THE FEDERAL RESERVE SYSTEM The Federal Reserve System (Fed) is the central bank of the United States. It was developed to regulate banking and manage the economy through control of the money supply. Approved by Congress in 1913, the Fed is made up of a chairman and a board of governors appointed by the president of the United States. The chairman and board members are financial and economic experts who establish the interest rates at which member banks can borrow money. These rates in turn affect the rates on many of the loans and deposits made by consumers and businesses.

Most commercial banks and savings banks are members of the Fed system and must meet its requirements and regulations, which affect the types of loans they can make, the amount of assets that can be loaned, and the security requirements for loans. Banks are required to keep a percentage of their assets in reserve, with some deposited in one of the 12 Federal Reserve district banks.

Federal Reserve district banks are not traditional banks that serve businesses and consumers. They are government banks representing the U.S. Treasury. They offer services to U.S. commercial banks, credit unions, and savings and loans, so they are often called "bankers' banks."

THE FDIC In 1933, consumers lost confidence in banks and tried to withdraw all of their money at nearly the same time. Banks had not kept enough money in reserve to make the payments. As a result, more than 4,000 U.S. banks closed, with losses averaging nearly $1,000,000 each. Those losses were actually suffered by the banks' customers, who could not withdraw their deposits. Although many of those funds were ultimately recovered and nearly 80 percent was repaid to consumers, Congress wanted to avoid another "rush" on the banks in the future. It established the Federal Deposit Insurance Corporation (FDIC), a federal agency that insures deposits in banks and savings institutions up to approximately $100,000 per depositor account. Retirement accounts are insured up to $250,000. Since its creation in 1934, no insured deposits have been lost by customers of failed members of the FDIC.

The FDIC charges member banks premiums for the cost of insurance. The corporation also closely regulates banks to make sure they have adequate capital. If a bank becomes undercapitalized (having a risky loan volume in relation to assets), the FDIC can force the bank to take corrective action, including a change in management. It can even force the bank to close if the problems are not corrected. Only bank deposits are insured. Many banks now offer a variety of other financial products, but these are not covered by the FDIC insurance.

NCUSIF Credit unions are not members of the FDIC. However, credit unions that are members of the National Credit Union Association (NCUA) have a similar federal insurance plan. The National Credit Union Share Insurance Fund (NCUSIF) has offered protection for member deposits since 1970.

CHECKPOINT
Identify and briefly describe the three main types of banks.

Nonbank Financial Institutions

Nonbank financial institutions have grown rapidly because of the many valuable financial services they offer. Many customers value being able to obtain many of their financial services through one organization. An important reason for the growth of nonbank institutions is that they convinced lawmakers to reduce the restrictions on the traditional banking services they could offer, such as demand and time deposits. Based on those changes, traditional banks asked for the capability to offer a broader range of financial services, such as investments and insurance, that they previously could not legally offer. The resulting competition has led to an emerging group of full-service financial institutions, consolidation of businesses in the industry, and many new forms of products and customer services.

TYPES OF NONBANKS

Nonbanks exist in many forms. Stock brokerage firms, for example, not only buy and sell stocks and bonds but also offer checking privileges and even credit card services. The stock brokerage firm of Merrill Lynch, for example, also provides mortgages, insurance policies, and credit card services for customers. On the other hand, banks are now allowed to sell stocks and bonds if they wish. Insurance companies and business pension funds are also nonbank financial institutions that offer long-term loans in large amounts to eligible businesses. Nonbanks also include investment companies such as mortgage, insurance, and finance businesses as well as investment firms. Fierce competition for banking and other financial services has benefited consumers through better and more abundant financial products and services at lower cost.

FINANCE COMPANIES A finance company specializes in providing installment loans and leases to consumers and businesses. Unlike banks, it does not accept deposits

Career tip

According to the *Ocupational Outlook Handbook*, employment in the securities and financial investments industry is expected to grow 15.8 percent by 2014. That high growth rate reflects the increased number of baby boomers in their peak savings years and moving into retirement. It also recognizes the jobs that will be created in international finance in response to the globalization of the securities markets.

but obtains funds to make loans by issuing securities. A finance company often works with retailers selling expensive consumer products or vendors selling equipment to business clients. The products are sold on credit and the finance company approves and owns the credit account. Many finance companies such as CIT Group and American General are independent companies specializing in financial services. Some large manufacturers have a financial division that operates as a finance company, such as Lexus Financial Services and John Deere Credit.

INSURANCE COMPANIES Insurance companies collect premiums on a variety of insurance products and invest the premiums in securities, real estate, and other low- to moderate-risk investments to earn money. In that role, they provide both business and consumer loans. In addition to selling insurance, most insurance companies offer a number of savings and investment products.

PENSION FUNDS Many companies offer their employees retirement benefits. Those benefits are often invested in pension funds. Some pension funds are owned and managed by the employer or by an employee union. However, most are managed by an independent company or by a division of a larger financial services firm. Both employer and employee make regular contributions to the pension fund throughout the employee's working career. Those contributions are invested by the pension fund in stocks, bonds, real estate, and government securities. When the employee retires, money is returned from the fund as a lump-sum payment or as a regular series of payments over a period of years.

MUTUAL FUNDS A mutual fund is a company that pools the resources of a large number of investors and uses that money to make a variety of investments. Depending on the type of mutual fund, the investments may be in stocks, bonds, government securities, or other financial instruments. Some mutual funds focus their investments in particular industries or types of securities, whereas others look for a more balanced set of investments.

Investors purchase shares in the mutual fund. The price of shares increases or decreases based on the performance of the investments. Many mutual funds charge a small administrative fee for their services. The number of mutual funds and the value of their assets have grown dramatically as people rely on the expertise of fund administrators to increase the value of their investments.

Mutual funds carry varying levels of risk. How can investors assess the level of risk they can comfortably handle?

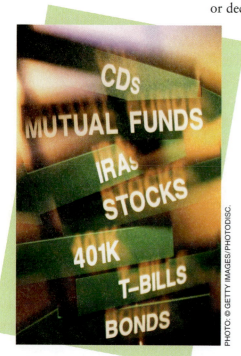

PHOTO: © GETTY IMAGES/PHOTODISC.

SECURITIES AND INVESTMENT FIRMS Securities and investment firms provide a variety of expert financial services for clients. Many serve as *brokers*, buying and selling securities, stocks, and bonds for their clients. Another service is underwriting new stock or bond issues. As an *underwriter*, the company purchases new securities from a company and then resells them to investors. It can also be a *dealer*, locating and purchasing securities with the intent of reselling them at a profit.

FINANCIAL SERVICES COMPANIES Large companies that have been a part of the financial services industry have seen the value of offering customers a full range of financial products and services. They often buy companies that offer specialized services such as credit cards, installment credit, or insurance and combine them under the management of one corporation. They serve both business clients and individual consumers with savings and investment plans, loans and credit choices, fund management, and financial counseling. Companies such as American Express, ING, Merrill Lynch, and Barclays operate worldwide and manage trillions of dollars in client assets. Financial services companies have seen the blending of traditional banking and nonbanking products and services. Large banks now sell insurance, securities, and other investments and provide financial counseling. Nonbank companies accept deposits, make loans, and provide check-writing services.

CHECKPOINT

Identify several nonbank financial institutions and describe the main products and services each offers.

17.1 Assessment

UNDERSTAND MANAGEMENT CONCEPTS

Determine the best answer for each of the following questions.

1. Which of these types of banks is organized as a nonprofit business?
   a. commercial bank
   b. mutual savings bank
   c. savings and loan organization
   d. credit union

2. A company that pools the resources of a large number of investors and uses that money to make a variety of investments is a
   a. finance company
   b. mutual fund
   c. insurance company
   d. savings and loan

THINK CRITICALLY

Answer the following questions as completely as possible.

3. What are the benefits to a bank of offering a variety of financial services rather than specializing in traditional banking services? What are the problems that might be encountered?

4. Do you think there is still a need for smaller and more specialized financial services businesses? What will they need to do to compete with large, full-service companies?

Xtra!
Study Tools
thomsonedu.com/school/bpmxtra

17.2 Common Financial Services

Goals

- Describe the value and uses of checking accounts and loans.
- Discuss the ways in which technology is changing banking services.

Terms

- check
- endorsement
- unsecured loan
- secured loan
- prime rate
- fixed interest rate
- variable interest rate
- electronic funds transfer (EFT)
- direct deposit
- automatic teller machine (ATM)

Common Banking Services

In spite of the changes that have occurred in the financial world, financial services have improved greatly in recent decades. Today, the majority of banking institutions provide a host of services. Historically, the most complete line of banking services designed for individual consumers and small businesses was offered by commercial banks. Those services included a number of types of savings and checking accounts and various types and lengths of commercial and consumer loans. Many banks offer financial services such as accounting and tax preparation, financial planning, and financial advice, and even rent safe deposit boxes in which customers can secure valuables.

Now, as specialized banks and nonbanks become more competitive with commercial banks, they are offering the traditional bank services that their customers demand. At the same time, commercial banks are adding more and more nonbank financial services to respond to the competition, attract new customers, and increase their revenues. Two of the most common banking services are checking accounts and loans. Nearly all businesses and many consumers regularly use these services.

CHECKING ACCOUNTS

Checking accounts enable depositors to write checks rather than pay bills in cash. A check is a written order requiring the financial institution to pay previously deposited money to a third party on demand. Businesses use checks to pay for purchases that are inexpensive or moderately expensive and are not financed with a loan, such as office equipment, supplies, and inventory. They also use checks to pay regular expenses such as payroll, utilities, and taxes. Many customers use checks to pay for purchases from businesses. When customers pay by check, the business must take precautions, such as requesting identification or using a check authorization system, to make sure the check is not stolen or forged.

To cash or deposit a check, the person to whom the check is written—the *payee*—must endorse the check. An endorsement is the payee's signature on the back of the check. A properly written check and three types of endorsements are shown in Figures 17-3 and 17-4.

FIGURE 17-3 The Proper Way to Write a Check

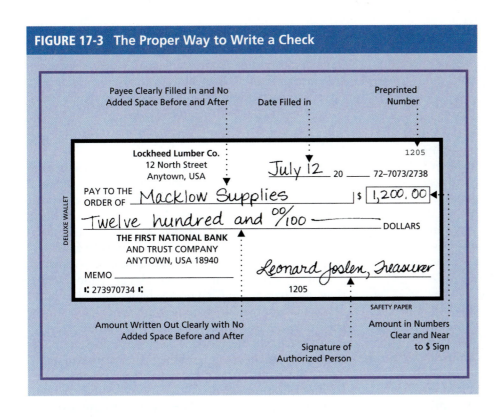

Payee Clearly Filled in and No Added Space Before and After

Date Filled in

Preprinted Number

Amount Written Out Clearly with No Added Space Before and After

Signature of Authorized Person

Amount in Numbers Clear and Near to $ Sign

FIGURE 17-4 When would you use each of these endorsements?

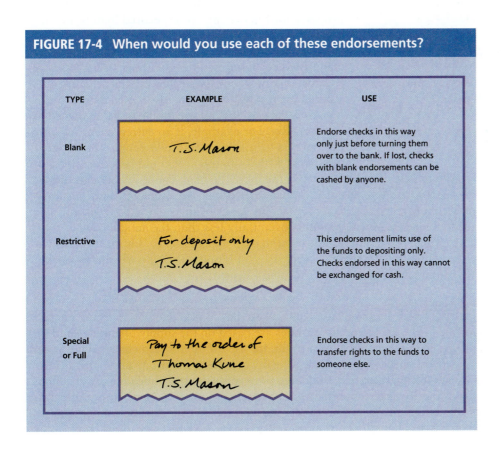

TYPE	EXAMPLE	USE
Blank	T.S. Mason	Endorse checks in this way only just before turning them over to the bank. If lost, checks with blank endorsements can be cashed by anyone.
Restrictive	For deposit only T.S. Mason	This endorsement limits use of the funds to depositing only. Checks endorsed in this way cannot be exchanged for cash.
Special or Full	Pay to the order of Thomas Kine T.S. Mason	Endorse checks in this way to transfer rights to the funds to someone else.

business *note*

When you take out a consumer loan, the payments are calculated by adding the interest to be paid over the term of the loan to the principal amount and then dividing the total by the number of months over which the money will be repaid. The result is your monthly payment. But what happens if you pay off the loan early? You do not owe all of the interest that was originally calculated. A relatively simple way to estimate the amount of interest you should receive back is known as the "Rule of 78." The percentage is calculated by dividing the sum of the integer numbers (digits) starting from 1 up to the number of payments remaining by the sum of the digits starting from 1 up to the total number of payments specified in the original loan contract. For example, if a five-month loan is paid off by the end of the second month (i.e., there are three payments remaining), the percentage of the interest that the lender would rebate is (1 + 2 + 3) / (1 + 2 + 3 + 4 + 5) = (6 / 15), or 40 percent. The name "Rule of 78" derives from the fact that 78 is the sum of the digits from 1 to 12 and, therefore, is the denominator in calculating interest rebate percentages for all 12-payment loans.

Banks send customers a monthly statement showing their deposits, checks that payees have cashed, ATM transactions, and bank service fees. Customers should compare the bank statement to their own record of deposits and checks written and reconcile any differences.

LOANS

Banks make many business and consumer loans. Before making a loan, the bank requires the prospective borrower to clearly state the purpose of the loan and provide financial evidence that the loan can be repaid. Most business loans provided by banks are for short time periods, often a year or less. A business may need funds to cover operating expenses at certain times, such as when it needs new equipment or when sales are temporarily slow. As discussed in Chapter 16, banks may offer businesses that are reliable customers a *line of credit*, which gives the business a maximum amount it can borrow over a specified time period. The business does not borrow on the line of credit until the money is needed, but it does not need approval as long as the maximum loan amount is not exceeded.

Collateral is property a borrower pledges to assure repayment of a loan. If the borrower does not repay the loan, the lender has the right to use the pledged property for repayment. An **unsecured loan** is a loan that is not backed by collateral. Usually only successful, long-standing business customers can obtain unsecured loans. For new businesses, those without strong financial records, and most consumer loans, banks require a secured loan. A **secured loan**, also called a *collateral loan*, is a loan backed by something of value owned by the borrower. For example, if an entrepreneur owned a fleet of cars for the business's salespeople and wanted to borrow $100,000, the fleet could be acceptable collateral. In case of failure to repay the loan, the bank could sell enough of the cars in the fleet to collect the money loaned. Businesses may pledge inventory or accounts receivable to secure smaller loans or lines of credit. Typically a secured loan is for an amount substantially less than the actual value of the collateral. The bank does not want to own the collateral. If it must take ownership of the collateral in the event the loan is not repaid, it will want to quickly sell the collateral and recover the money loaned.

INTEREST RATES Banks earn income when they loan money by charging interest for the life of the loan. Interest rates are based on the supply of and demand for money at any given time. As a result, the rate of interest can change daily, based on general business conditions. The lowest rate is the **prime rate**, which is the rate at which large banks lend large sums to the best-qualified borrowers. Small loans and loans to less-qualified customers are made at rates higher than the prime rate. Borrowers and lenders must establish a specific repayment plan so that the deal benefits both parties. Borrowers may be forced into bankruptcy and the lenders may be hurt financially when loans are not repaid. To help prevent losses, repaying a loan at intervals is safer than paying one lump sum at the end of the time period. Borrowers can then include the monthly payments in their budget plan.

Rates may be set for the full term of the loan or they may change during the loan period at predetermined times or based on specified conditions. An interest rate that does not change throughout the life of the loan is a **fixed interest rate**. Interest rates that can change are variable rates. A **variable interest rate** can increase or decline based on the factors used to adjust the rates. Often variable interest rates are based on changes in the prime rate or in the price of government securities. Variable interest rates are usually cheaper at the beginning of a loan but may become more expensive over the full term if economic conditions and government policies tighten the money supply.

Over 70 percent of all U.S. employees receive their paychecks through direct deposit, with a 97 percent satisfaction rate. Fifty-four percent of households have at least one monthly payment—such as for a mortgage, auto loan, or utility bill—paid directly to the company by their bank without having to write a check.

CHECKPOINT

Why do banks usually require collateral when loaning money to businesses and consumers?

Technology and Financial Services

Remarkable changes have occurred in banking over the last decade, thanks to the rapid development of computers and other forms of electronic technology. Much of the work once done by clerks, such as processing checks, recording deposits and withdrawals, and keeping customer accounts up to date, is now done electronically. **Electronic funds transfer** (EFT), transferring money by computer rather than by check, has enabled financial institutions to provide faster, improved services. For example, EFT transactions reduce the need for checks. Direct deposits, automatic teller machine transactions, and Internet banking are three common uses of EFTs. The use of debit cards is another form of EFT and will be discussed in the next chapter.

DIRECT DEPOSIT

A **direct deposit** is the electronic transfer of a paycheck directly from the employer's bank account into the employee's bank account. The use of direct-deposit banking has increased in popularity. Employees who select this service receive immediate use of their earnings. They no longer have to wait in line to cash checks or make deposits. For each pay period, the employer must provide the employee with a record listing gross pay and all deductions. The Social Security Administration and the Internal Revenue Service both prefer that individuals receiving checks from them use direct deposit. In this way, checks do not get lost or stolen. Direct deposit is also used for the direct electronic transfer of other payments from one bank to another.

AUTOMATIC TELLER MACHINES

An **automatic teller machine** (ATM) is a computer terminal that enables bank customers to deposit, withdraw, or transfer funds by using a bank-provided plastic card. ATMs are located at banks and other convenient places, such as

PHOTO: © GETTY IMAGES/PHOTODISC.

Why have automatic teller machines become so popular with consumers?

grocery stores, airports, and malls. ATMs are now common throughout the world and can be used to obtain foreign currency quickly and easily.

In addition to attracting more customers with ATMs, banks lower their operating costs by reducing the need for human tellers and increase income from service fees each time a customer withdraws cash. Furthermore, banks with ATMs need fewer branch offices to serve their customers.

Financial institutions try to reduce ATM-related crime by locating ATMs in well-lighted areas. Most have hidden cameras that may help police identify thieves. Along with crime, ATM customers are concerned about high withdrawal fees and having to pay an additional fee when withdrawing funds from another bank's ATM. For example, if your bank's ATM fee to withdraw $50 is $1.50, and you withdraw the money from a competitor's ATM that charges $2.50, you would pay $4 to obtain $50. Many customers object to paying both banks a high fee. But with so much banking competition, ATM fees are another means for banks to pay some of the costs of providing customer services.

ELECTRONIC BANKING

Electronic banking speeds business activities and serves customers more conveniently. Through computers, modems, and the Internet, banking without leaving the office or home has become common. Electronic banking makes it possible to obtain loans, pay bills, and transfer funds from one bank account to another. Of course, most banks charge fees for these services.

The Internet is a new way for banks and nonbanks to survive. Many have Web sites publicizing their services. Customers can search the Internet for the best interest rates for loans, best savings account rates, and best checking account terms. Loan and credit card applications can be processed and approved quickly online. Internet banks have several advantages over traditional banks. Not only can they perform most of the same services traditional banks offer, but they can also do it at lower cost. An Internet bank does not need large, expensive downtown buildings with numerous branches from which to conduct business. It can operate from a single, low-rent building 24 hours a day, seven days a week, to reach worldwide customers. Banking operations centers may actually be located in other countries. For many customers, online banking can satisfy most day-to-day banking needs. Breaking old banking habits, however, may not be easy to do for many people.

One study found that a single banking transaction costs a traditional bank $1.07, whereas an Internet bank's cost is 2 cents for the same transaction. That cost difference is one reason many large banks are quickly adding Internet-banking departments.

CHECKPOINT

How does the use of technology reduce the costs of providing financial services?

NETBookmark

The Federal Deposit Insurance Corporation (FDIC) is best known as the federal insurer of bank deposits for consumers and businesses. The FDIC makes sure the banks and savings and loans through which it insures deposits meet high standards for financial strength and stability. It is also a great source of information on how to be an effective banking consumer and protect your identity, personal information, and financial resources. Point your browser to www.thomsonedu.com/school/bpmxtra. Review the categories of consumer information and select one of interest to you. Create a poster that highlights the facts and consumer tips you learn.

www.thomsonedu.com/school/bpmxtra

17.2   Assessment

UNDERSTAND MANAGEMENT CONCEPTS

Determine the best answer for each of the following questions.

1. Transferring money by computer rather than by check is known as
   a.   automated cash transfer (ACT)
   b.   computerized money movement (CMM)
   c.   electronic funds transfer (EFT)
   d.   automated transfer machine (ATM)

2. Internet banks can operate at a lower cost than traditional banks because
   a.   they do not have to meet the same government regulations
   b.   they serve more customers than even the largest traditional banks
   c.   they locate their offices in other countries with lower labor costs
   d.   they need fewer and less expensive buildings

THINK CRITICALLY

Answer the following questions as completely as possible.

3. What are some reasons many bank customers refuse to use ATMs and want banks to increase access to bank tellers? If you were a bank executive, how would you respond to those customers?

4. Do you believe that as banks and nonbanks add services such as direct deposit and ATMs they should drop the traditional high-cost services that the technology replaces? Why or why not?

Xtra!
Study Tools
thomsonedu.com/school/bpmxtra

Focus On...

Business Innovation–Banks Team with Telecoms

Today many banks view the world as their market, and competitive barriers are fast disappearing in the Internet age. Bankers in Europe, for example, are now buying, merging, or partnering with major banks in other countries within the European Union and beyond. Some are also partnering with companies not typically considered a part of banking. For example, Spain's Banco Bilbao Vizcaya Argentaria (BBVA) developed an e-commerce partnership with the giant telecommunication company Telefónica. The stock value of both firms zoomed upward. BBVA is a major financial player in Europe and Latin America whose global leadership has been recognized by top financial publications. In 2000, it was chosen World's Best Bank *(Forbes)* and Best Bank in Spain *(The Banker)*. In 2001, it was named Best Bank in Latin America *(Forbes)* and Best European Bank *(Lafferty)*. It is now expanding into the United States. In 2005, BBVA acquired Texas-based Laredo National Bank. In 2006, it acquired Texas National Bancshares and State National Bancshares to become the fourth-largest bank in Texas.

Why would a bank and a telephone company team up to play in the world market? Cell phones with Internet access are becoming a primary means for consumers to gain instant access to business information and services. They may also become a primary means of delivering banking services. The phone companies possess both cable lines and excellent computer systems. Banks provide banking services and the telephone companies deliver the services electronically to worldwide customers.

Other banks are seeking telephone company partners. Germany's Deutsche Bank, for example, is becoming an all-Europe e-commerce bank by linking with mobile-telephone provider Mannesmann. The Bank of Scotland and England's Halifax Bank have both teamed with the telecommunications company BT Cellnet. It is expected that the worldwide competition in banking e-commerce will grow more intense, with more and bigger players every year.

Think Critically

1. If you owned stock in Citigroup, a large U.S. bank, and it signed an agreement with a foreign cell phone company to compete with European banks, would you sell your stock, take a wait-and-see attitude, or buy more stock? Why?
2. What might go wrong with these joint international banking and telephone deals, especially if telephone companies know little about the banking business and banks don't know the telephone business?

17.3   Investing and Investments

Goals

- Identify the characteristics of various investment instruments.
- Describe how investment decisions can be made to meet financial goals.

Terms

- investment
- savings account
- savings bond
- certificate of deposit (CD)
- money market account
- mutual fund
- Treasury instruments
- stock index

Investment Instruments

Individuals, families, businesses, and other organizations need adequate financial resources to meet their needs. Money can be obtained in two ways—earnings resulting from the work of individuals or the operation of businesses, and earnings from investments. An **investment** is the use of money to make more money. When individuals or businesses have cash that is not immediately needed, it can be invested.

There are many investment options available, whether the money to be invested is a small or large amount and whether it is available for a short or long time period. Some types of investments carry greater risks than others. Some provide greater returns or earnings than others. To make wise investment decisions, business managers and individual investors need to know about the types of investment instruments and how to choose among them to meet their investment goals.

Most investments are made using the services of financial institutions. Those institutions are constantly seeking new and better ways to serve customers. They offer a wide variety of financial instruments from which customers can select those that best fit their investment needs. Figure 17-5 identifies several of the most common financial instruments.

INTEREST-BEARING CHECKING ACCOUNTS A checking account is a demand deposit through which investors can safely maintain money in a financial institution yet access it at any time through writing a check or making an electronic withdrawal. Many checking accounts pay a very low interest rate if the account balance is kept

FIGURE 17-5 Investors can choose from a variety of financial instruments to meet their investment goals.

Interest-Bearing Checking Accounts	Treasury Bills
Regular Savings Accounts	Treasury Notes
Savings Bonds	Treasury Bonds
Certificates of Deposit (CDs)	Corporate Stocks
Money Market Funds	Corporate Bonds
Mutual Funds	

above a certain minimum amount. If a balance falls below the minimum, the bank may charge a service fee or eliminate the interest. Investors with small sums of money find interest-bearing checking accounts a convenient way to save while having easy access to the funds to pay expenses. Because checking accounts are not primarily designed as savings instruments, however, they serve an investment purpose only to a limited extent. If interest is paid, the interest earned is relatively small in comparison to most other investments, including savings accounts.

SAVINGS ACCOUNTS A **savings account** is also a time deposit account that allows customers to make deposits, earn interest, and make withdrawals at any time without financial penalties. Customers can deposit small amounts, but the interest rates are usually lower than those on other investment instruments. The bank may charge a service fee if the amount on deposit falls below the minimum balance required. Interest rates may increase if the amount placed in savings is relatively high. However, the interest rate is still quite low compared to those on other investment choices. Savings accounts are often used to make regular deposits with the goal of increasing the value of the account over time. Investors try to meet their longer-term savings goals by not withdrawing money from the savings account for immediate needs.

SAVINGS BONDS **Savings bonds** are non-negotiable securities sold by the U.S. Treasury in small denominations to individual investors. They can be purchased in denominations from $25 to $30,000. Savings bonds earn interest for up to 30 years. However, they can be redeemed at any time after six months. A penalty of three months of earned interest is charged if the bonds are redeemed within the first five years.

There are currently two series of savings bonds. *Series EE bonds* pay a fixed interest rate, and the interest is paid when the bond is redeemed. *Series I bonds* pay interest in two components: a basic fixed-rate established when the bond is purchased, then an adjustment to that rate made each year based on the rate of inflation.

Savings bonds can be purchased from any bank or through a payroll deduction plan at work. They can also be purchased online through the U.S. Department of Treasury. Unlike other Treasury instruments, ownership of savings bonds cannot be transferred. State and local income taxes do not have to be paid on the interest earned.

CERTIFICATES OF DEPOSIT A **certificate of deposit** (CD) is a time deposit account that requires a specified minimum deposit for a fixed period at a fixed interest rate. Banks offer CDs for $500 or more and for periods ranging from three months to five years. Typically, the longer the term of the CD, the higher the interest rate earned. For example, the interest rate on a six-month CD is normally less than on a two-year CD. Although CDs usually pay a higher rate of interest than do savings accounts without restrictions, a CD cannot be withdrawn before its stated time without penalty—a substantial loss of earned interest.

Interest is paid regularly on a CD, and the interest can be withdrawn as it is earned. If the interest is not withdrawn, it is added to the value of the CD and earns additional interest during the remaining term. CDs are negotiable instruments, so if money is needed the CD can be sold to an investor (often the bank that issues the CD). However, the sale will be at a lower value than the current value of the CD and interest earned, unless interest rates have increased significantly.

MONEY MARKET ACCOUNTS A **money market account** is a type of savings account in which the deposits are invested by the financial institution in short-term, government-backed securities. The interest rate on the account is not fixed. It goes up and down as interest rates in the economy change. Financial institutions often grant check-writing privileges on money market accounts but may require a minimum amount for the checks. The number of checks written during a given time period, such as a month, may be limited as well.

Unlike CDs, there is no minimum time the money must remain in the money market account. Depositors can withdraw their money at any time. Also, initial deposits may be as low as $500. Investors often put funds in money market accounts when they will need the money soon or when they want to earn some interest while waiting for a more profitable investment opportunity. Because government-backed securities are not very risky, the interest paid on money market accounts is generally lower than for other stock or bond investment options. However, money market accounts generally pay slightly higher interest than does a typical savings account.

MUTUAL FUNDS A mutual fund pools the money of many investors primarily for the purchase of stocks and bonds. Many investors believe they do not have the time or expertise to select individual stocks and bonds and prefer to purchase shares in mutual funds. A mutual fund company develops one or more funds and makes the decisions about the types of investments for each one. Professional fund managers and their staffs carefully evaluate and select a variety of securities in which to invest the fund's money.

Mutual fund investors can choose from among many types of funds, depending on their investment goals. A growth fund, for example, focuses on stocks that show potential for rapid growth in the fund's value. Some investment companies specialize in small, medium, or large companies or in companies from specific industries such as technology or pharmaceuticals. Some funds invest primarily in international stocks, and others balance their investments across types, sizes, and locations of businesses.

Risk is a major consideration in selecting mutual funds. There is no guarantee that the total investment will not be lost if wise investment decisions are not made by fund managers or if there is a serious economic downturn. Some funds reduce the level of risk by investing in bonds and relatively safe real estate investments. Those funds aim to generate a steady income for investors who do not expect the rapid growth in their investments that more risky funds might produce.

Most mutual funds require a larger minimum investment than the investment choices already discussed, often $1,000 or more. Also, investors may need to document that they have adequate financial resources to risk in the mutual fund investment. Investors can easily transfer money from one fund to another, but there may be administrative charges for those changes as well as for general fund management. Whenever sales are made that result in profits on the initial investment, the investor should consider the tax consequences for those earnings. The return earned in mutual funds has the potential to be quite high but is accompanied by a much higher risk of loss.

TREASURY INSTRUMENTS The U.S. government borrows money from investors by selling bills, notes, and bonds backed by the Treasury. Treasury instruments are securities issued by the U.S. government. They are used to finance the costs of running the government when income from taxes is not available or when costs exceed the revenues collected. Treasury instruments are considered one of the safest of all short-term investments because they are backed by the U.S. government, which has the resources to meet interest payments on the securities as they become due.

The instruments differ in the term of investment and the interest rates paid. Treasury instruments are sold at auctions where prospective purchasers bid based on the interest rate they are willing to accept. The securities are sold at the lowest available interest rates.

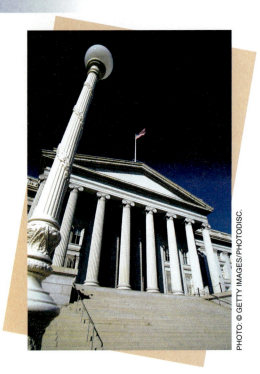

PHOTO: © GETTY IMAGES/PHOTODISC.

What kinds of investment instruments are backed by the U.S. Treasury Department?

Businesses and individual investors with large sums of money frequently invest in Treasury securities because they are practically risk free and are easy to buy and sell. All Treasury securities are very liquid, meaning they are easily traded even though they may not mature for several years. Because the interest rates on securities fluctuate based on demand and economic conditions, investors are willing to purchase securities owned by other investors, usually at a discounted price, with the hope of making a profit.

A *Treasury bill*, or *T-bill*, is a short-term security that pays the lowest interest rates of the various Treasury instruments. T-bills are sold in $1,000 multiples, but investors can purchase multiple amounts up to a total of $5 million. The bills mature in 4, 13, or 26 weeks. Treasury bills are normally purchased from the government by financial institutions, including banks, brokers, and dealers. They then resell the T-bills to individual and business investors. T-bills are purchased at a discount based on the interest rate of the security. For example, a $1,000 bill may cost $960. When it matures, the owner is paid the full $1,000. The $40 difference reflects a 4 percent interest rate.

A *Treasury note* is a medium-length security that is available in $1,000 multiples and matures in 2, 3, 5, or 10 years. Treasury notes are fixed-rate securities, meaning the interest rate remains the same throughout the term of the note. Interest is paid every six months. When the note is initially purchased, the investor may pay a premium or discount from the face value of the note. That increase or decrease in price reflects the demand for the notes and the value investors believe the note will have at its maturity.

A *Treasury bond* is the longest-term U.S. government security. As with the other securities, the bonds can be purchased in $1,000 multiples. The bonds do not mature for a long time, usually 20 or 30 years. Investors can purchase up to $5 million of bonds at an auction. Treasury bonds are auctioned infrequently by the government. Sometimes not all of the available bonds are sold at the original auction, and the government may later hold a reissue auction to sell the remaining amount. As with other securities, bonds can be purchased from other investors during their term through a bond dealer or securities trader.

CHECKPOINT
Describe several low-risk and high-risk investment choices.

Making Investment Choices

Inexperienced investors frequently give too little thought to determining their investment goals before selecting a specific investment. They may even put all their funds into one investment. To make good choices, investors must set their investment goals based on the amount of liquidity, safety, and growth that is right for them.

INVESTMENT GOALS

Liquidity refers to the ease of turning an investment into cash without significant loss. For example, checking accounts are very liquid. Depositors can withdraw their deposit as cash whenever they want without penalty. Certificates of deposit are less liquid. If depositors withdraw their money from a CD before the end of its term, they have to pay a penalty, which may be substantial. If a small company, such as Kilgore Kitchens in the opening scenario, needs cash regularly, it should choose more liquid investments. Kilgore's owners might choose to invest in money market accounts rather than mutual funds so they can get cash when they need it with a low risk of financial loss. On the other hand, an established, profitable firm may have a steady source of cash from its operations. Instead of needing cash soon, it may need to replace costly equipment in five years, so it may choose to invest in less liquid but more profitable investments. Treasury notes and bills might be appropriate choices for this firm. The different objectives of these two firms will determine, in part, the investments they select.

A second investment goal is the degree of safety desired. In general, riskier investments have higher earning potential than do less risky investments. However, with those choices, investors are more likely to lose all or part of their investment. Some investors want maximum safety—they do not want to risk losing any of their money. To achieve a high degree of safety, they will likely have to accept smaller earnings on the investment. Investment in savings accounts, money market accounts, and government securities should appeal to them because of the low risk. Other investors like to take some risks for the opportunity to earn more money. These investors might prefer to buy stock in a rapidly growing corporation, in a developing country, or in a new Internet firm.

The third investment goal involves the trade-off between investment growth and a stable income from the investment. Investors who do not need a steady income from their investments and are willing to invest for long periods of time will choose to invest in growth-oriented corporations. They hope to see their investments grow at a faster rate than inflation. Investors who want to count on a regular income might choose to invest in stocks or mutual funds with a history of paying high dividends.

Most experienced investors also suggest another rule that pertains to safety: "Don't put all your eggs in one basket." Investors should *diversify*, that is, spread their risk by placing money in different categories of investments, never in one alone. For example, a diversified investment plan might put one-third of available investment money into bonds, one-third into stocks, and one-third into money market accounts. To follow this rule further, not all investments in bonds should be in one company, nor should all stock investments be in one corporation. Diversification greatly reduces the risk factor.

INVESTMENT TRADING

Buyers and sellers trade all types of securities through special financial markets. The securities are typically bought and sold through the services of securities and investment organizations. For help in making investments, individuals and businesses often consult investment advisers, brokers, or dealers. Investors ask their brokers to buy or sell certain securities. The brokers then process the requests through the appropriate financial market that connects buyers and sellers.

Corporations that want to sell their stock to investors must be listed on a stock exchange. Although there are a number of such exchanges, the two largest are the New York Stock Exchange and the National Association of Securities Dealers' NASDAQ exchange. Technology firms, such as Microsoft, Intel, and Cisco Systems, are listed on NASDAQ, which is the nation's first electronic stock market. The much older New York Stock Exchange (NYSE) trades on Wall Street, with floor traders buying and selling securities face-to-face with other traders on the floor of

Just as the United States has the Dow Jones, NASDAQ, and Standard & Poor's stock indexes, other countries maintain indexes to reflect the performance of key stocks important to their economies. Some examples are the Bovespa in Brazil, Hang Seng in Hong Kong, Nikkei 225 in Japan, DAX in Germany, FTSE 100 in the United Kingdom, and TA-100 in Israel.

What activities take place in a stock exchange?

PHOTO: © GETTY IMAGES/PHOTODISC.

the exchange. The NYSE attracts more traditional companies. Most stock exchanges handle stocks, bonds, and other types of investments. Mergers and partnerships among stock exchanges continue to evolve as electronic trading grows worldwide.

A **stock index** is a kind of average of the prices of selected stocks considered to be representative of a certain class of stocks or of the economy in general. Investors watch the movement of the indexes to get a sense of stock market trends for those types of stocks and for the overall growth of the economy. The most well-known indexes in the United States are the Dow Jones Industrial Average Index, the NASDAQ Market Index, and Standard & Poor's 500 Index. When compared over time, each index provides investors with a picture of what is happening in this nation's and the world's financial markets. An index trend of rising share prices may influence investors to buy more shares, and a downward trend may prompt them to sell some shares. Unfortunately, predicting when the market will reach its low and high points is nearly impossible, even for the most skilled investors.

CHECKPOINT

Identify three important goals that can guide investment decisions.

17.3 | Assessment

UNDERSTAND MANAGEMENT CONCEPTS

Determine the best answer for each of the following questions.

1. Treasury instruments are considered low-risk investments because they
   a. are issued in very small denominations
   b. cannot be traded
   c. are backed by the U.S. government
   d. none of the above

2. When money is spread among many types of investments, the investor has
   a. increased the risk
   b. emphasized growth
   c. reduced the initial cost
   d. diversified the investments

THINK CRITICALLY

Answer the following questions as completely as possible.

3. If you had $10,000 to invest, what would you consider the most important factors in choosing among the various investment instruments?

4. Why should investors watch the performance of stock indexes over an extended period of time rather than reacting to daily increases or decreases?

Xtra!
Study Tools
thomsonedu.com/school/bpmxtra

CHAPTER CONCEPTS

- Financial institutions handle transactions that deal primarily with money and securities. Banks provide many of the needed services, and other financial institutions provide investment services that banks traditionally did not. Deregulation has made it possible for banks to offer a variety of new investment products and other financial services.

- Banks accept demand deposits, make loans, and buy and sell currency and government securities. There are three major types of bank: commercial banks, savings institutions, and credit unions. Nonbanks offer financial products and services other than deposits and loans.

- The Federal Reserve System is the central bank of the United States. It regulates banking and controls the money supply. The FDIC is a federal agency that insures deposits in banks and savings institutions.

- Most banking institutions provide a host of services, the most common being checking accounts and business and consumer loans. Many banking transactions can be done electronically through direct deposits, ATMs (automated teller machines), and Internet banking.

- There are many investment options available: savings bonds, certificates of deposit, money market accounts, mutual funds, and securities backed by the U.S. government (Treasury bills, notes, and bonds).

- Investors must clarify their investment goals in regard to liquidity, safety, and growth before making investment choices. Actual investments may be made through banks, nonbanks, and brokers.

REVIEW TERMS AND CONCEPTS

Write the letter of the term that matches each definition. Some terms will not be used.

1. The use of money to make more money
2. Federal agency that insures deposits in banks and savings institutions
3. Electronic transfer of a paycheck directly from the employer's bank account into the employee's bank account
4. Non-negotiable securities sold by the U.S. treasury in small denominations to individual investors
5. Loan backed by something of value owned by the borrower
6. Loan made to an individual for personal use
7. Rate at which large banks lend large sums to the best-qualified borrowers
8. Securities issued by the U.S. government
9. Written order requiring the financial institution to pay previously deposited money to a third party on demand
10. Interest rate that can increase or decline based on the factors used to adjust the rates
11. Institution whose primary purpose is to offer financial products and services other than deposits and loans
12. Central bank of the United States

a. check
b. commercial loan
c. consumer loan
d. direct deposit
e. FDIC
f. Federal Reserve System
g. fixed interest rate
h. investment
i. mutual fund
j. nonbank
k. prime rate
l. savings bond
m. secured loan
n. Treasury instruments
o. unsecured loan
p. variable interest rate

DETERMINE THE BEST ANSWER

13. In order to be considered a bank, a financial institution must do all of the following *except*
    a. accept deposits
    b. make loans
    c. buy and sell currency and government securities
    d. Banks must do all of those things.

14. Which of the following is classified as a bank rather than a nonbank?
    a. securities and investment firms
    b. savings and loan organization
    c. financial services company
    d. none of the above

15. Before making a loan, banks require that the prospective borrower
    a. make a substantial deposit in the bank
    b. provide collateral even if the loan is very small with low risk
    c. provide financial evidence to show that the loan can be repaid
    d. show that all of the business's cash has been used

16. Which of the following cannot be accomplished through direct deposit?
    a. receiving a Social Security payment
    b. accepting a tax refund from the IRS
    c. providing wage and salary payments to all employees in a business
    d. All can be accomplished through direct deposit.

17. Which type of investment instrument would usually pay the lowest interest rate?
    a. checking account
    b. CD
    c. money market account
    d. Treasury bill

18. The savings instrument issued by the federal government that can be purchased in the smallest denominations is the
    a. savings bond
    b. Treasury bill
    c. Treasury note
    d. Treasury bond

19. Of the savings instruments listed, the one with the highest risk is the
    a. savings account
    b. money market fund
    c. mutual fund
    d. Treasury bill

20. "Don't put all your eggs in one basket" is investment advice related most directly to
    a. liquidity
    b. safety
    c. growth versus a stable income
    d. diversity

APPLY WHAT YOU KNOW

21. Based on the Reality Check scenario at the beginning of the chapter, what should be the investment goals of Kilgore Kitchens? What are three investments you would recommend to Andrew and Julie?

22. Why would a business choose to use a bank rather than a nonbank as its primary financial institution? Why might it choose a nonbank?

23. What effects have changes in laws and increases in competition among financial institutions had on consumers?

24. What effect does the prime rate have on those who apply for bank loans?

25. How has the Internet improved banking services? What problems have resulted from its increased use?

26. What are the advantages and disadvantages of certificates of deposit over savings accounts?

27. Why would individuals and businesses want to purchase Treasury securities for terms as long as 20 or 30 years? What risks, if any, are they taking when purchasing those very long-term investments?

28. If you had to pick one financial goal today to guide your financial planning, what would it be? Why? How do you think your goals may need to change in 15 years? What will be your top goal at that time?

MAKE CONNECTIONS

29. **Research** Use the Internet to check the current interest rates offered by (a) a local bank, (b) a credit union, (c) an Internet bank, and (d) a large financial services organization. Determine the rates for a checking account, a 12-month CD of $10,000, a money market account, a 30-year mortgage, and a 48-month auto loan. Prepare a table that compares the interest rates from all of the financial institutions.

30. **Law and Politics** You are an intern for Melinda Jones, a local bank vice president who is concerned about the changing competition the bank is facing. She asks you to use the Internet to investigate the current status of federal banking regulations and their effect on banking. Conduct the research and prepare a one-page memo to Ms. Jones discussing significant developments within the past five years and any proposed changes.

31. **Visual Communications** Track the value of the Dow Jones Industrial Average, NASDAQ Market Index, and Standard & Poor's 500 Index for one week. Prepare graphs that illustrate and compare the performance of the three indexes.

32. **Oral Communications** Assume you are an investment adviser. One of your clients is a 35-year-old single female employed by a fast-growing firm and making $60,000 a year. She wants her current savings of $25,000 to be 80 percent liquid, with the balance in short-term bonds. Pair with a classmate and role-play a conversation in which you advise her on the advantages and disadvantages of her financial plan.

CASE IN POINT

CASE 17-1: What's Wrong with Savings?

Jun Wang, owner of a delicatessen in a shopping center, often chats outside his business with Cassidy Hall, who owns the bakery next door. One weekday morning just after they opened their businesses, Jun mentioned that he had just returned from his bank to deposit money. He told Cassidy that as a recent immigrant, he was not that familiar with the American financial system. But he had decided it was important to save money from his business and had opened a savings account in the local bank down the street.

Cassidy wanted to help, so she asked Jun if he had a lot of money in the savings account and if he was investing his profits in other ways. Jun said he had a regular practice of putting 10 percent of his profits in the account each month and was getting concerned that perhaps he should start an account with another bank because the sum was getting quite large. The rest of the conversation follows.

Cassidy: *You're losing money you could otherwise be earning, Jun, by putting that much of your savings in a savings account.*

Jun: *What do you mean? I've always believed that a savings account in a bank was the best place to save money. Now you tell me I'm losing money? I've never lost any money, and each month I earn interest.*

Cassidy: *It certainly is a way to save money, but the interest you're making right now is at least 2½ percent less than what you could make by putting that money in other types of accounts. If I were you, I would be looking at CDs and T-bills. At least put some of your money in a money market account. There are several types of businesses in our community other than banks that offer savings opportunities.*

Jun: *Wait. I don't understand these words you are using. But I do know that I don't want to lose my hard-earned profits in any risky investments.*

Cassidy: *There is a good financial adviser right here in our shopping center. I meet with her quite frequently, and she has taught me a lot about saving and investments. If you want, I can introduce you to her.*

THINK CRITICALLY

1. Is it likely that Jun could invest his money in other savings instruments at his savings bank? Is it likely that the bank could meet all of his financial needs as his business grows? Why or why not?
2. Are T-bills and CDs considered risky investments? Explain your answer in a way that a novice investor like Jun might understand.
3. How much more could Jun earn if he withdrew the $100,000 he has in his savings account and invested it instead in Treasury notes earning 2½ percent more interest? What problems might that create for his finances?

CASE 17-2: Financing Business Expansion

Doria Russell had just sold a half-acre lot on one side of her prosperous tile and wallpaper shop. She decided to sell it because she needs the money to enlarge the store as part of her business expansion plan. Currently she sells window treatments including shades, curtains, drapes, and other accessories in addition to floor and decorative tile and wallpaper. She wants to add an interior-decorating center with some small model rooms to display her products as they would appear in homes. She needs the remaining empty lot to enlarge her current building and to expand the parking lot.

Doria estimates she will need $500,000 to reach her growth goal, but not all at once. She needs time to find and hire an architect, obtain a building permit, and start construction. Once the building is enlarged, she will then order inventory items, hire a part-time decorator and an additional installer, and plan a promotional campaign. Each step will take time, and overlooked tasks might require additional time and money.

Doria received $200,000 for the half-acre lot she sold and will use this money as the major source of initial financing. Her business currently has $40,000 in a savings account and $80,000 in a mutual fund. She does not want to use any of her personal savings to finance the business's new venture. Because she has some time before she needs money for the project, her plan is to invest her current funds in such a way that cash will be available when needed, but she will also earn as much as possible on the investments until the expansion is completed. Doria believes the total plan will take from 18 to 36 months to complete once it starts 6 months from now.

Doria is willing to take some financial risk but cannot really afford to lose any of the money she has accumulated to finance the project. She accepts the possibility that she might need a short-term loan once or twice if major costs arise at the same time, but she will resort to loans only if necessary.

THINK CRITICALLY

1. What is the total amount of money Doria has available to invest?
2. As Doria's investment adviser, suggest an overall financial plan that includes a timeline for investing available funds that will enable her to reach her goals. Provide reasons for your investment advice.
3. If Doria needs a short-term loan, what type of loan would you recommend she seek and from what type of financial institution? Justify your recommendation.
4. Assume a year has passed and that Doria's plan is on schedule, but she needs a $75,000 loan. Find out where she can get a six-month loan at the lowest interest rate. Compare your best loan terms with those of others in your class.

SELECTING FINANCIAL SERVICES

A good working relationship with a financial institution is important for a small business. Income received through cash, checks, and credit cards must be invested and protected, because they can be important sources of interest income. You must select the correct types of accounts and manage them carefully, so that your account balance is neither too large nor too small to meet your business's financial needs. You may need short-term loans to solve cash-flow problems. Other banking services may help you make the best financial decisions for your business.

DATA COLLECTION

1. Identify at least two bank and two nonbank financial institutions in your community that offer services for individuals and businesses. Gather information on the types of accounts and services each offers. If possible, identify the interest rates they offer on checking and savings accounts as well as the interest rates they charge for common types of loans. Prepare a chart comparing the information you collected on each of the businesses.
2. Use the Internet to identify:
   a. Financial institutions that offer banking services via the Internet.
   b. Sources of financial information for small-business owners, such as information on loans, interest rates, and investments.

ANALYSIS

1. Assume you will need a four-year loan of $15,000 to start your business. You estimate that you will need a $2,000 line of credit for the first year of operation. Of the financial institutions you studied in Data Collection #1 above, which one would you go to for the necessary financing? Justify your answer. What do you feel the greatest personal obstacles will be in obtaining a line of credit for your new business? Why?
2. Obtain a loan application form from a local bank or an Internet bank and fill in the necessary information as if you were requesting the $2,000 line of credit.
3. Answer the following questions:
   a. What type of financial institution will you use for regular business activities? Why?
   b. What type of checking account will you open?
   c. What minimum and maximum balances will you attempt to maintain in the checking account? What will you do with any excess funds beyond the maximum checking account balance?
   d. What will you do with your deposits of daily receipts? When will you do it?
   e. In what ways can you use technology to access and use financial services? What type of electronic equipment will you need? What risks do you see in using the Internet for financial transactions?

Credit and Insurance

Chapter

18

REALITY CHECK

Setbacks for Sandra

Sandra Gilbert started her jewelry business six months ago on a cash-only basis. She reasoned that her large inventory took up much of her capital as well as the time needed to manage it. "Credit card companies charge new small businesses too much. Besides, because my jewelry is quite expensive, most customers won't use credit cards for their purchases. If I use my own credit system, customers will have to fill out a long application that will then take a few days to get approved. Customers won't want to wait several days to take their purchase home. I think they would rather pay cash. If they have the money, they can get cash from their bank to pay. If they don't have the money, I don't want them as customers."

Contrary to her expectations, her business did not pick up very fast. Because of the slow sales, she was unable to make a profit. Many customers stopped in to look at her jewelry and always made positive comments about both the designs and the prices. But they would invariably say they would think about it and then never return to make the purchase. By word of mouth, she learned that some customers were not returning because competitors accepted credit cards or offered credit terms. She decided she had made a mistake. She quickly approached her bank about setting up a credit service for her business, even though it cost more money than she wanted to spend. To pay for it she had to raise her prices.

The credit program seemed to be working. Her sales increased, and she was making a small profit. Sandra was just beginning to feel good about the future of the business when she was faced with an even more serious problem. An employee left a storage area unlocked. Several custom pieces of jewelry she had just finished to fill customer orders were missing. She had purchased an insurance policy that protected her merchandise against fire damage and burglary, but the policy didn't cover this type of loss. Without adequate coverage, she would have to pay the cost of the missing jewelry and would have to redo the orders. She wasn't sure the customers would wait for the orders or that she could afford the losses.

18.1 Credit Principles and Practices

Goals
- Describe three types of credit plans used by businesses.
- Identify several types of financial transaction cards and the main uses of each type.

Terms
- merchant account provider
- installment credit
- revolving credit
- co-branded credit cards
- affinity credit cards
- debit card
- smart card

Determining Business Credit Needs

When establishing a system for credit sales, businesses need to understand various types of credit plans, the relationship with a credit card company or bank, the kinds of credit cards available, and guidelines for establishing general credit policies. They must also be familiar with sources of credit information, credit laws, and basic practices for managing customers who do not pay on time. Businesses offer credit if they believe it will increase sales and profits while satisfying customer needs. Consumers approach credit from the point of view of convenience, and they buy from businesses that satisfy that need.

ACCEPTING MAJOR CREDIT CARDS

Businesses that wish to start selling on credit have several choices of credit systems. They can (1) choose to work with a major credit card company, (2) offer their own store credit, or (3) use credit plans developed by banks and finance companies.

ESTABLISHING A CREDIT CARD ACCEPTANCE SYSTEM Starting an operation to accept credit cards involves a series of actions. The most common approach is to establish a relationship with a major credit card company such as Visa, MasterCard, or American Express. Most small and medium-size businesses do not work directly with the company but instead develop an agreement with a bank that represents one or more major credit card companies or with a merchant account provider. A **merchant account provider** is a private company that acts as an intermediary between businesses and one or more credit card companies to establish and maintain credit services. Using a bank or merchant account provider makes it easier and faster to begin accepting credit cards. It also allows the business to accept several major credit cards while dealing with only one intermediary rather than developing agreements with each of the credit card companies.

To be approved to accept credit cards, a business is screened to make sure it is financially strong enough to offer credit and has effective operating procedures in place to process and approve credit purchases. The bank, merchant account provider, or credit card company will need information on the business's operations and history. It will need credit reports and financial statements to determine if the business is a good credit risk. Companies that provide credit card services to businesses must be cautious because too many businesses fail to handle credit operations well. Having a successful relationship already established with a bank will speed the process of being approved to accept credit cards.

Once the application has been approved and a relationship established with one or more credit card companies, the business must then obtain credit card–processing equipment. Most businesses use electronic processing and approval systems that are built into point-of-sale terminals or cash registers. A few businesses, especially those that are part-time or mobile, still use a small nonelectronic device. The salesperson places the customer's credit card in the device and mechanically imprints the card information on a paper credit sales slip. The customer signs the sales slip and keeps a copy. The business delivers a copy of every sales slip to the business that handles its credit sales, usually its bank. The bank then forwards the slips to the credit card company. This process may take a week or more to complete, even if the business processes its credit sales every day. Upon receipt of the sales slips and approval of the credit sales, the credit card company informs the bank, and the bank credits the business's account. Often the business is required to call the credit card company to verify the acceptability of a customer's payment before completing the sale.

PHOTO: © DIGITAL VISION.

Why might a consumer prefer to pay with a credit card rather than with cash?

Computerized credit card systems are now the accepted way to process credit transactions and are much more efficient and accurate. The customer's credit card is swiped through an electronic device that records the sale and prints a sales slip for the customer's signature. Some signatures are recorded on an electronic pad at the sales terminal. The bank and credit card company receive the credit sales information electronically at the same time. The electronic system also checks to make certain the customer's card was not stolen and the sale is within the customer's credit limit. A quick authorization decision is received on the computer terminal. For security purposes, many businesses require their salespeople to compare the signature on the credit card with the signature written by the customer on the credit receipt.

Credit card sales can also be made over the telephone and via the Internet. Procedures for those sales are developed by each credit card company and must be followed carefully to make sure the information is correct and the purchase is authorized. Internet credit card sales are made on secure Web sites (https://) to keep the customer's personal information, including the credit card account number, secure.

Once a business makes a credit sale, the credit card company electronically notifies the bank, which credits the payment to the business's account. The credit card company collects the payment from the customer through monthly billing. If the customer returns the merchandise, a similar process occurs, and the bank deducts the amount from the business account and returns it to the credit card company.

DEALING WITH THE BANK AND CREDIT CARD COMPANY When considering a credit card operation for a business, it pays to shop around. Credit card company and bank agreements are not all the same. Business owners should compare the requirements established by the company to make certain they are acceptable and establish procedures for employees to follow that will ensure those requirements are met.

Equally important is the fee business owners must pay for credit sales. The bank and the credit card company both provide a service for which they receive a fee, generally between 2.5 and 5.5 percent of credit sales. The rate usually depends on the total monthly credit sales and the average size of each sale. The greater your sales volume, the lower the rate will be.

Technology *tip*

Credit card security is becoming more important, especially with the growing number of online credit card transactions. Credit cards now contain a security code, called a card verification value (CVV), embedded on the magnetic strip to ensure the card is not counterfeit. A three- or four-digit CVV is also imprinted on the card and is usually required to verify the account when the card is used for online purchases.

You may also be charged fees if the number of errors your business makes on credit sales exceeds a reasonable limit. For example, if your salespeople are careless and do not obtain customer information as required or process the same sale twice, you have created unnecessary work for the bank and credit card company and also will upset customers when they learn of the errors. You will also pay a fee if you accept expired credit cards too often or have frequent customer disputes or a high volume of returned merchandise. Some businesses believe they can be lax with credit card transactions because it is not their own credit system. Such an attitude can be costly.

CREATING A PRIVATE CREDIT CARD SYSTEM

Some large regional and national businesses, especially retail and service businesses, develop their own private credit card systems using the name of the business—Sears, Target, Home Depot. They may accept only that private card. However, customers are increasingly expecting them to accept other major credit cards as well. Running its own credit system requires that a business establish a credit department to perform the tasks that a bank and credit card company would do. A credit manager, credit analysts, and clerks would have to be hired to solicit credit card applications, check applicants' creditworthiness, and issue cards. Then they must manage the credit accounts, including recording credit sales, sending out monthly statements, and collecting unpaid accounts.

The major advantage of a store credit card is the opportunity to advertise and offer special promotions to cardholders. Customers who regularly use a private card are usually quite loyal to that business. A major disadvantage is the cost and inconvenience of operating a credit system. Only a very large and efficient system would be less expensive than the fees charged by major credit card companies. Many customers do not want to have to carry a separate credit card for each business where they shop. Some customers sign up for a private credit card to receive a one-time discount or as part of a promotion and then seldom use it. The large majority of consumers prefer cards they can use in Boston, Bombay, or Beijing.

CONSUMER CREDIT PLANS

In addition to or instead of accepting credit cards, businesses may offer customers other types of credit plans. For sizable purchases, businesses often offer **installment credit**. Under this plan, customers agree to make a stated number of payments over a fixed period of time and at a specified interest rate. Consumers buy cars, furniture, and major home electronics and appliances using installment credit. For example, if you bought a car on an installment plan, you would pay a fixed monthly amount for perhaps five years until you have paid off the loan and gain full title to the car.

Some businesses operate their own installment credit system. However, unless they are very large and have the financial resources to make multiyear loans to consumers, they offer the credit through a finance company. The business takes the customer application and sends it to the finance company for approval. If the credit is approved, the finance company pays the selling company the selling price of the merchandise less a discount for the cost of the credit service. Then the finance company collects the installment payments from the customer.

The most popular type of installment credit is **revolving credit**, which combines the features of a store credit card and installment credit. With revolving credit customers can make credit purchases at any time up to a specified dollar limit. Under most revolving plans, customers may pay off the full amount by the end of the billing period without a finance charge. Customers who do not choose to pay in full have the option of making partial payments each month.

The minimum amount of a partial payment depends on the amount of the unpaid balance in the account. A finance charge, stated as an interest rate, is added each month to the unpaid amount. Usually revolving credit plans carry a high interest rate on unpaid balances. Credit card systems are a type of revolving credit. Figure 18-1 shows an example of a revolving credit plan agreement.

FIGURE 18-1 Revolving credit for a department store may be provided by a financial institution such as a bank.

Credit Card Bank of Philadelphia
Key Terms of Agreement

This application is for residents of AK, AL, AR, AZ, CA, CO, DC, DE, FL, GA, HI, IA, ID, IL, IN, KS, LA MD, ME, MI, MN, MO, MS, MT, NC, ND, NE, NJ, NM, NV, NY, OH, OK, OR, RI, SC, SD, TN, TX, UT, WA, WI, WV, WY. If you live in another state, please call 1-800-555-0000 for a credit application.

Annual Percentage Rate (APR for Purchases)	Minimum Finance Charge
Standard Accounts – 21% Starter Accounts – 23.9% All Accounts – Delinquency Rate – 24.99%*	50¢

Grace Period for the Repayment of the Balance for Purchases – 25 days if no previous balance or full payment is made; otherwise, none.

Method of Computing the Balance for Purchases – Average Daily Balance (including New Purchases)

Late Payment Fee - $25 ($15 in IA). If your New Balance is less than $50, the Late Payment Fee is $10.

*Finance Charge – Delinquency Rate** – The Delinquency Rate will apply if the required minimum payment is past due twice in any six consecutive billing periods. Once in effect, if you are not late with any required minimum payment for six consecutive billing periods, the rate will return to the higher of the rate applicable to your Account before the Delinquency Rate was imposed or 21%.

The information about the costs of the card described above is accurate as of November 2000. This information may have changed after that date. To find out what may have changed, write us at P.O. Box 25, Philadelphia, PA 17054.

By signing this application, I ask that Credit Card Bank of Philadelphia ("you") issue me a credit card. I understand that if I qualify for a credit card, you may open an account for me depending on my credit worthiness as determined by you. I affirm that the information I have submitted is complete and truthful and that my account will be used only for personal, family, and household purposes. I authorize you to make inquiries you consider necessary (including requesting reports from consumer reporting agencies and other sources) in evaluating my application, and subsequently, for purposes of reviewing, maintaining or collecting my account. Upon my request, you will advise me of the name and address of each consumer reporting agency from which you obtained a report. I also understand that the credit card agreement will govern my account, the terms of which are hereby incorporated by reference into and made a part of this application and that my signature on this application represents my signature on the Agreement. I understand that there is no agreement between us until you approve my application, and that if approved, our Agreement will be deemed to have been made in Pennsylvania. I understand that I may apply for my own Account regardless of my marital status. I ALSO UNDERSTAND THAT THE AGREEMENT CONTAINS AN ARBITRATION PROVISION WHICH MAY SUBSTANTIALLY LIMIT MY RIGHTS IN THE EVENT OF A DISPUTE, INCLUDING MY RIGHT TO LITIGATE IN COURT OR HAVE A JURY TRIAL, DISCOVERY AND APPEAL RIGHTS, AND THE RIGHT TO PARTICIPATE AS A REPRESENTATIVE OR MEMBER OF A CLASS ACTION. I MAY REQUEST THE CODE OF PROCEDURE, RULES AND FORMS OF THE ARBITRATION ASSOCIATION I SELECT BY CALLING THE TOLL-FREE NUMBERS LISTED IN THE AGREEMENT.

Information About You and Your Account – I acknowledge that the terms of the agreement and the applicable law provide that certain information about me or my account may be shared with third parties. By requesting a credit card, I am agreeing to this sharing of information, subject to my right described in the Agreement to be excluded from certain formation sharing, and from certain marketing lists. In addition, I agree that you may provide information from this application to Dawn's Department Store (and its affiliates) to enable Dawn's Department Store to create its customer records for me, and in connection with the offering or products and services to me, among other purposes.

Types of Financial Transaction Cards

Consumers often view credit cards as plastic money. Over the years, purchases with "plastic" have grown steadily. Most people have two or more credit cards. The major credit card firms compete intensely in most industrialized nations. Newer types of "plastic" have been developed for financial transactions, and more and more brands of credit cards are offering an increasing number of features to attract customers.

BANK AND NONBANK CREDIT CARDS

Banks and nonbanks provide credit cards. For consumers, bank cards do not differ much from nonbank cards. Visa and MasterCard are bank cards in that their ownership is made up of banks. You can obtain a bank credit card under the MasterCard or Visa brand from many local banks. Examples of nonbank cards are American Express and Discover. American Express is a large financial services company that provides credit through a variety of cards that use the American Express name. Discover is actually a credit card system owned by Morgan Stanley, an international investment bank. Nonbank credit cards are obtained from the company by filling out and mailing an application, applying online through the company's Web site, or completing an application at cooperating businesses.

Most bank and nonbank credit card companies have different cards for different types of customers. For example, American Express offers cards with a range of services. The blue, green, gold, platinum, and optima cards meet the needs of different consumers and businesses. So-called "prestige cards," such as the platinum card, often charge higher fees for added services but can be free of annual fees for customers with excellent credit.

Credit cards are often co-branded. **Co-branded credit cards** are cosponsored by two companies and have benefits and rewards designed specifically for their joint customers. For example, the American Express Delta SkyMiles Card is a co-branded credit card for people who travel frequently on Delta Airlines that offers cardholders travel discounts and other travel-related benefits.

Another type of credit card that builds on consumer loyalties is an affinity card. **Affinity credit cards** are associated with specific organizations and offered to people affiliated with those organizations. An affinity credit card is cosponsored by the organization it is associated with, and the organization receives a percentage of the sales or profits generated by the card. Many universities offer affinity credit cards to their alumni. People who use affinity credit cards generally do so to help support an organization or cause they care about.

DEBIT CARDS

Debit cards resemble credit cards in appearance but are very different. A credit card is like a short-term loan, whereas a debit card is more like cash or a check. A **debit card** immediately transfers funds electronically from the customer's checking account to the business's account when a purchase is made. With a debit card, customers can also withdraw cash from their checking or savings accounts through ATMs and pay bills by phone or computer. Usually the same system, a card scanner, is used to process debit cards as credit cards. However, with debit cards, customers may have to enter a personal identification number (PIN) before the transaction can be processed.

A debit card saves retailers the trouble of sending sales slips to the bank, and the bank doesn't have to bill and collect from customers. The bank, however, sends monthly summaries of transactions to retailers and customers. The bank charges fees, of course, for debit card services.

The use of debit cards and credit cards reduces the amount of cash and the number of checks handled in the economy. Customers benefit from debit cards by not having to carry large amounts of cash or a checkbook. People who cannot obtain credit cards may be able to carry a debit card because it reflects money already deposited in a bank. A debit card is riskier than a credit card, however, because the money transfer is immediate. There is less legal protection for consumers using debit cards than for those using credit cards. With credit cards, customers who pay their bill at the end of the month are actually receiving a "free" loan of that money for a short time. Debit card charges are withdrawn immediately from the account, so no money is loaned.

Prepaid calling cards are a type of debit card. They have become very popular in an age of increased travel and fewer public pay telephones that accept cash. Calling cards carry relatively low per-minute costs and can be replenished online using a credit card or simply discarded when empty.

American Express and other companies sell prepaid debit cards that can be used in place of traveler's checks or as a ready source of funds for shoppers. Parents may buy a card with a relatively small prepaid amount for their children to use at summer camp, on school trips, or even in college. The card can be used to pay for a variety of low-cost goods and services, such as school supplies, snacks, and laundry machines.

Gift cards issued by many stores are also examples of prepaid debit cards. The price of these cards includes a profit margin for the retailers that sell them. Customers who buy them do not need to carry as much cash, but they have no protection against lost or stolen cards and the value of some prepaid cards expires after a certain date.

Smart cards have the potential for a wide range of applications. Can you name some ways in which a smart card could be useful to you?

SMART CARDS A **smart card** is a plastic card with an embedded microprocessor that can store and process a large amount of information. The microprocessor has a reader "pad" on the surface that replaces the magnetic strip used on credit and debit cards. Smart cards are used extensively in Europe but are just beginning to be used by consumers in the United States. In Germany, every citizen has a smart card containing his or her health records. Swedish citizens use smart cards to vote. Currently smart cards are used by businesses for computer security, in cable and satellite television receivers, and in cell phones.

The information on smart cards can be tailored to specific purposes, and it can be changed and updated. For example, financial institutions can offer a smart card that serves as a credit, debit, and ATM card. Health care professionals can record and update medical information on each patient's smart card. Commuters can use smart cards on city buses, subways, trains, or even to pay tolls on toll roads. University students can use them for student identification,

PHOTO: © THINKSTOCK IMAGES.

food service, library book checkout, parking meters, copy machines, and campus computer labs.

Smart cards hold up to 80 times more data than cards with magnetic strips, and their storage capacity is increasing rapidly. They have the potential to replace debit, credit, and ATM cards for several reasons. First, because a smart card provides up-to-the-minute account balances after every transaction, it can reduce bad debts. Second, because lost or stolen cards cannot be used without personalized verification, the cards can reduce fraud. Uses for smart cards are expected to expand in the future, including online security protection for purchases made on the Internet.

CHECKPOINT

How are debit cards and smart cards different from credit cards?

18.1 Assessment

UNDERSTAND MANAGEMENT CONCEPTS

Determine the best answer for each of the following questions.

1. Which of the following is *not* one of the ways a business can begin accepting major credit cards?
   a. Seek authorization directly from the credit card company.
   b. Work with a merchant account provider to be able to accept several different cards.
   c. Establish a credit account with a bank that represents a major credit card company.
   d. All these methods can be used.

2. A credit card associated with a specific organization and offered to people affiliated with that organizations is a(n) _____ card.
   a. co-branded
   b. affinity
   c. private
   d. smart

THINK CRITICALLY

Answer the following questions as completely as possible.

3. Why would a major retailer want to offer its own private credit card, with the expense of a credit department, and also accept major credit cards?

4. Why will smart cards likely replace other types of financial services cards such as credit and debit cards? What problems, if any, do you see with the widespread use of smart cards?

Xtra!
Study Tools
thomsonedu.com/school/bpmxtra

18.2 Managing Credit

Goals
- Identify the information on which decisions about credit applications is based and how that information is obtained.
- Describe the steps in collecting unpaid accounts.

Terms
- creditworthiness
- character
- capacity
- capital
- conditions
- credit agency
- aging of accounts

Determining Credit Standing

A business must have a policy and a system for approving credit for customers. **Creditworthiness** is a measure of a person's ability and willingness to repay a loan. Two methods commonly used to check applicants' creditworthiness are (1) the four Cs of credit and (2) the point system.

THE FOUR CS OF CREDIT

To determine the creditworthiness of people or organizations, businesses gather information as part of the credit application process. They then apply the "four Cs" of credit to analyze the information: character, capacity, capital, and conditions. A review of each factor helps to determine the answers to two important questions about the applicant's creditworthiness: (1) Can the customer pay? and (2) Will the customer pay?

Character is a measure of a person's sense of financial responsibility or personal belief in the obligation to pay debts. It includes honesty, integrity, and attitude toward indebtedness. Credit-granting businesses check an applicant's credit reputation, payment habits, and job stability to judge the person's character. The applicant who is always late in making payments or who frequently changes jobs will not likely be approved for credit. Credit references are frequently requested to determine how others view the applicant.

Capacity is a measure of earning power and reflects the person's potential to pay, based on current income and other financial obligations. To judge capacity for consumer credit, businesses look at the credit applicant's employment history, income level, and number and amount of debts. For business credit, they carefully examine the business's financial performance and financial statements.

Capital, the third C, is a measure of the credit applicant's current financial worth or ability to pay based on assets. For an individual, "capital" means assets such as savings, a car, or a home. For a business, "capital" means a healthy balance sheet—far more assets than liabilities. Capital is especially important if people lose their jobs or when businesses suffer losses or poor cash flow. With adequate capital, individuals or businesses can still pay for credit purchases. Creditors can also ask that assets be pledged as collateral for loans.

Conditions, the last of the four Cs of credit, is an assessment of the economic environment, such as the economic health of a community or the nation and the extent of business competition. The local economy, for example, may be depressed. As a result, many people would be unemployed. Inflation, rising taxes, and recessions also affect a business's willingness to grant credit.

As part of evaluating the four Cs of credit, businesses often use a point system. They assign points to each of the four C factors. Credit applicants provide information about these factors by answering questions on credit applications. Answers are assigned a specific number of points. To receive credit, an applicant must earn a predetermined score. Some factors that are rated and assigned points include the type of job, the length of time the applicant has held the job, and the applicant's income, savings, and total debts. The higher the person's income, for example, the higher the number of points assigned. No points are assigned if the applicant's income is too small to cover loan payments.

Credit experts agree that the best single measure of creditworthiness is the applicant's past credit-paying record. For that reason alone, credit applicants need to build and maintain excellent credit records.

SOURCES OF CREDIT INFORMATION

After selecting a method for making decisions about credit applicants, businesses must collect information about them. They can obtain much of the information directly from the applicants and from credit agencies.

APPLICANTS Banks, credit card companies, consumer credit firms, and businesses that operate their own credit departments obtain information directly from applicants who complete credit application forms. A simple form used by a retail store is shown in Figure 18-2. The application requests basic information such as name, address, phone number, date of birth, Social Security number, bank accounts, and employer's name and phone number. After the retailer reviews the credit application, it either rejects the application, obtains more information from other sources, or approves the applicant for a limited amount of credit. If the customer demonstrates responsible use of that credit, the business will gradually increase the credit limit.

CREDIT AGENCIES Most businesses want more information than they can gather through a credit application. One of the best sources is a credit agency. A credit agency is a clearinghouse for information on the creditworthiness of individuals or businesses. In general, there are two types of credit agencies—those that provide credit information about individual consumers and another that provides credit information about businesses. Private credit agencies, or bureaus, regularly collect data from businesses and publish confidential reports for their subscribers, who are usually retailers. Although there are hundreds of credit agencies, most are associated with the top three national credit-reporting firms: Experian, Equifax, and TransUnion. Each national agency maintains vast amounts of computerized data about millions of customers. A business subscriber to one of the agencies can get information quickly for making credit decisions, often through direct computer access to credit reports. The credit agency provides a summary report of the individual's credit and financial history and a credit score.

Businesses that sell on credit to other businesses need different types of credit information than do retailers that sell to consumers. An important source of information on the credit standing of retailers, wholesalers, and manufacturers is Dun & Bradstreet (D&B). As a service to subscribers, D&B regularly publishes and sells credit ratings and financial analysis reports. Those reports are used to make a number of decisions about prospective business relationships as well as about granting credit.

FIGURE 18-2 To apply for credit, you must complete an application form.

DAWN'S DEPARTMENT STORE CREDIT APPLICATION
APPLICANT INFORMATION

A married applicant may apply for a separate account.　　PLEASE PRINT IN BLUE OR BLACK INK

Your First Name	Middle Initial	Last Name	Social Security Number
Laura	B.	Cooper	000-00-000

Street Address	City	State	ZIP
1400 Walnut Street	Philadelphia	PA	17054

Years at Address	Number of Dependent Children	Home Phone with Area Code	Business Phone with Area Code	Date/Birth
Yrs. 2　Mos. 3	2	215-555-2337	215-555-6870	5/8/72

Do You	Own	Rent	Own Mobile Home	Live with Parents	Other	Monthly Rent/Mortgage
	☐	☑	☐	☐	☐	$850.00

Monthly Income – Total from All Sources *	Employer	Years on Job	Occupation
$4,200	Wanamaker's	Yrs. 2　Mos. 6	Assistant Buyer

*You need not furnish alimony, child support, or separate maintenance income information if you do not want us to consider it in evaluating your application. Include co-applicant income if applicable.

CREDIT INFORMATION

Checking/Savings	Checking	Savings	Bank Loan	MasterCard/Visa	Discover	AMX/Diners	Dept. Store	Other
☑	☐	☑	☐	☑	☐	☐	☑	

CO-APPLICANT ☐　Also Responsible For Account　　AUTHORIZED BUYER ☐　Allows Person to Purchase on Account　　SPOUSE Yes ☐　No ☐

Name (First, Middle Initial, last)	Occupation	Business Phone With Area Code	Years on Job Yrs.　Mos.

NOTICE TO APPLICANT(S): A) Do not sign before you read the agreement or if the agreement contains any blank spaces. B) You are entitled to a completely filled in copy of the agreement. C) You may at any time pay off the full unpaid balance under the agreement without incurring any additional charge.

SIGNATURE	Date	CO-APPLICANT SIGNATURE	Date of Birth (Co-App)
Laura B. Cooper	11/17/00		

CREDIT INSURANCE ENROLLMENT AREA – OPTIONAL

☐　YES　I wish to protect my Dawn's Department Store Account with Credit Insurance for the cost as Described on the enclosed insert. I understand the insurance is not required.

APPLICANT (SIGN TO ENROLL)　　Date of Birth
_____　　_____

SPOUSE'S NAME　　Date of Birth
_____　　_____

☑　NO　Do not enroll me for Credit Insurance at this time.

In signing the enrollment form above, I authorize that the premiums due for the insurance coverage enrolled for be changed to my Dawn's Department Store credit card account. I agree to pay such amounts in full when billed.

For Store Use:

Picture I.D. Type (Store Call-In Apps Only)	Account Number	Date Approved/Disapproved

FEDERAL AND STATE CREDIT LAWS

Credit is governed to a great extent by state and federal laws. The main provisions of four federal laws that relate directly to credit appear in Figure 18-3 (see p. 484).

All 50 states also have laws that regulate credit transactions. The legal profession created the Uniform Commercial Code and the Uniform Commercial Credit Code to deal with matters not covered by federal legislation. Both national codes have been adopted by most states. These model laws cover credit conditions relating to credit terms and installment sales contracts. Because of

FIGURE 18-3 To use credit effectively, both businesses and consumers must understand credit laws.

EQUAL CREDIT OPPORTUNITY ACT

This law makes it illegal to deny credit because of age, sex, marital status, race, national origin, religion, or public assistance. It requires businesses to notify credit card applicants of their application status within 30 days and give a reason for rejection, if requested.

TRUTH-IN-LENDING LAW

This law requires businesses to reveal on forms and statements the dollar costs of obtaining credit. Businesses must show the finance charge on statements as annual percentage rates (APR), to make comparing rates easier. If a credit card is lost or stolen and used by an unauthorized person, the card owner's loss is limited to $50. If a business advertises credit terms, it must include all information that a buyer might need to compare similar terms with competitors (down payment and number, amounts, and dates of payments).

FAIR CREDIT REPORTING ACT

This law gives cardholders the right to see their credit agency reports and to correct errors.

FAIR DEBT COLLECTION PRACTICES ACT

This law forbids debt collectors to use abusive, deceptive, or unfair collection methods. Under most state laws, if an account has not been paid within a specified number of years, collection efforts may not legally continue.

the abundance of laws, businesses often hire attorneys who are experts on state and federal credit law to review and approve credit policies, procedures, and forms.

CHECKPOINT
What are the four Cs of credit?

Collection Policies and Procedures

Any business that extends credit to customers is concerned about losses from uncollectible accounts. Some firms have practically no bad-debt losses. Others have very high losses that reduce their financial capabilities in other parts of the business. Surveys show that the losses from uncollected debts can easily run 2 to 4 percent of net sales, even for well-managed businesses. Poor management of credit procedures can increase losses to 7 to 10 percent of sales, which exceeds the profit margins of many businesses. Even with good credit management, if economic conditions are poor, bad-debt losses increase, putting even more pressure on businesses. Effective credit policies and collection procedures can reduce losses and make credit services a valuable element of the business.

COLLECTION PROCEDURES

Once a business establishes a credit system, it must decide how to collect money owed by customers. This is an important function, because it affects the health of the firm. Managers try to meet two objectives when establishing collection procedures: (1) collect the amount due and (2) retain the goodwill of the customer.

Most credit customers pay their bills, but some will always be a few days late. Communicating and enforcing a policy that interest is added to the customer's account for every day the payment is late will encourage prompt payment. The usual collection procedures include sending a statement at the end of the billing period, followed by reminders at 15-day intervals if the bill is not paid. Businesses often use letters and duplicate copies of invoices with printed stickers on them to remind customers that their accounts are overdue. Those are followed by telephone calls to discuss the reason for late payment and to negotiate an alternative payment plan. All collection steps should be done professionally, with the goal of retaining the customer if payment is made. After 60 to 90 days, if it appears that the customer is not going to send payment or agree to a payment plan, the final collection step is usually either to turn the account over to a collection agency or to bring legal proceedings against the customer. With installment credit, the business may have to repossess the merchandise that was sold on credit. These actions are a last resort but must be taken unless the amount due is so small it is not worth the cost of those actions.

During the collection process, businesses should try to find out why customers are not paying their overdue accounts. Most people are honest and plan to pay. Besides, it is better for the business to get paid late than not at all. Therefore, it is important to learn why an account is overdue and work out a revised payment schedule that the customer can meet.

Part of the reason for overdue accounts may be that the business extends too much credit too easily. Overextension of credit is as much the seller's fault as it is the buyer's. Too often, businesses issue credit cards to unqualified applicants who sometimes get carried away by their new purchasing power. When they fall behind in their payments, some get new credit cards to pay off overdue balances on other cards. But more cards only get the customers into further debt trouble. Young people are often poor credit risks because they are inexperienced in managing money. Older people also experience credit difficulties when they lose their jobs, are involved in an accident or a lawsuit, or continue to add small amounts of debt without considering the overall amount they owe.

Collecting bad accounts is time-consuming and costly. It is always better to spend the time developing effective credit policies and screening credit applicants before credit is extended than having to work to collect accounts that are not paid.

CHECKPOINT
What is the last step in the collection process?

Analyzing Credit Sales

It is important for every business to watch its accounts receivable (the debts or money owed to the business), so that the total does not grow out of proportion to the amount of credit sales. For example, if credit sales are not increasing but accounts receivable are gradually growing larger each month, then the company is not collecting payments from customers quickly enough. Soon, the company may not have enough cash to pay its own bills. Before accounts receivable get too large, the company must take action to collect accounts more efficiently.

The total accounts receivable may not show the true picture. For instance, an analysis may show that most of the overdue accounts are only 30 or 60 days overdue, with only a few 90 days or more overdue. In this situation, the problem lies with just a few customers. The company can take aggressive action toward those customers and may not have to change overall collection policies. On the other hand, if an analysis of the accounts receivable record shows that most of the late accounts are 90 days or more overdue, the collection problem is more pervasive. In this case, the company may have to take stronger action to determine the reason so many customers are not paying their accounts.

One common method of studying accounts receivable is referred to as **aging of accounts**, a process in which customers' account balances are analyzed in categories based on the number of days each customer's balance has remained unpaid. The form in Figure 18-4 is an example of aging of accounts.

In the example, the amounts owed by the Adams-Jones Company and the Artwell Company are not overdue. However, Brown and Brown owes $82.23, which has been due for more than 60 days but less than 90 days; $120, which has been due for more than 30 days but less than 60 days; and $157.50, which has been due less than 30 days. The $228.18 owed by Custer Stores has been due more than 60 days but less than 90 days. And the amount due from A. Davis, Inc., has been due more than 90 days. The form enables the manager to see clearly the status of all accounts receivable and to plan any necessary corrective action.

Another method of measuring the efficiency of collections is to compute the percentage of delinquent accounts in relation to the total outstanding accounts. For example, if 10 percent of the accounts in January are delinquent, 15 percent are delinquent in February, and 20 percent are delinquent in March, this indicates an unfavorable trend. One recent study revealed that if accounts are not paid within 3 months, the chance of collecting is 73 percent; after 12 months, it is less than 30 percent.

FIGURE 18-4 The status of each account is apparent through aging of accounts.

ANALYSIS OF ACCOUNTS RECEIVABLE

DATE January 2, 20--

NAME AND ADDRESS	1 TO 30 DAYS	31 TO 60 DAYS	61 TO 90 DAYS	OVER 90 DAYS	TOTAL	EXPLANATION
Adams-Jones Company Cincinnati, Ohio...	$705.00				$705.00	
Artwell Company, Chicago, Illinois..	$1279.53				$1279.53	
Brown and Brown, Gary, Indiana......	$157.50	$120.00	$82.23		$359.73	They wrote "will clear up account this month."
A. Davis, Inc. Detroit, Michigan..				$525.00	$525.00	Account in hands of attorney.
Custer Stores, Granville, Ohio....			$228.18		$228.18	Now on COD basis.

By carefully analyzing credit sales, a business can learn which policies and procedures are most effective for increasing total sales while keeping uncollectible account losses to a minimum so that net profits will increase. When bad debts increase, a firm's cash flow, profits, and credit reputation decline.

CHECKPOINT
How do businesses benefit from aging of accounts?

18.2 Assessment

UNDERSTAND MANAGEMENT CONCEPTS

Determine the best answer for each of the following questions.

1. A measure of earning power that reflects the person's potential to pay, based on current income and other financial obligations, is
   a. character
   b. capacity
   c. capital
   d. conditions

2. Which of the following should *not* be an objective of a company's collection procedure?
   a. converting credit customers to cash customers
   b. collecting the amount due
   c. maintaining the goodwill of customers
   d. All are appropriate objectives.

THINK CRITICALLY

Answer the following questions as completely as possible.

3. What do you believe is evidence of a person's character that would make him or her a good credit customer? A poor credit customer?

4. What can a business do before a customer's account becomes overdue to encourage timely payments?

Xtra!
Study Tools
thomsonedu.com/school/bpmxtra

Focus On...

Ethics–Improved Credit Ratings Don't Always Help

Jonathan Allan worked as a computer specialist. He and his wife, Anita, used the same bank credit card. For two years, they always paid the balance of their monthly credit statements on time. But six months ago, Jonathan lost his job because a larger firm purchased his employer's firm.

To get by, Jonathan used the credit card but was often not able to pay on time and finally missed payments for two consecutive months. The credit card firm reported his recent poor record to the national credit agencies. As a result, he now had a low credit score and was unable to get any new credit at all.

Jonathan finally found another job that paid almost as well as his previous one. He wanted to restore his credit record, so both he and Anita worked hard to save money. Within a few months, they had paid off their credit card debts. But unknown to Jonathan and Anita, the credit card firm deliberately did not report this positive information to the credit agencies. When Anita decided she wanted to obtain a new credit card being offered through one of her favorite stores, now that the family financial picture was much better, she was shocked when the credit application was rejected.

Jonathan and Anita are not alone in facing this dilemma. A study reported by Experian, one of the three largest credit bureaus, found that one in four credit consumers do not always get as good a credit rating as they actually deserve. Some of the largest credit-issuing firms have withheld information about customers who improve their credit performance. They don't want that information to reach their competitors. As competitors search for new customers, they tend to avoid people like Jonathan and Anita with poor ratings to focus on people with good ratings. In Anita's case, her credit card firm is preventing her from qualifying for credit with a competitor. If competitors had the updated information showing the higher credit score, they would likely issue a credit card and the original company could lose a current customer.

Competition for credit customers has caused the practice of not reporting updated information to credit bureaus to increase in recent years. In spite of warnings issued by bank regulators and complaints from consumer groups, not all companies have changed their practices. Credit card issuers seem to be ignoring the warnings. The association of credit card firms is trying to resolve this problem rather than have the federal government take action to stop it. However, it is not easy to get businesses to change practices that they believe give them a competitive advantage.

Think Critically

1. Why should consumers regularly ask for copies of their credit reports from companies such as Equifax, Experian, or TransUnion, especially before a major credit transaction or after resolving a credit problem?
2. Assume you are the CEO of a credit card company that refuses to withhold positive credit information, as your competitors are doing. How would your action help and hurt your company?
3. Do you believe the credit card companies will stop their unethical practice voluntarily? Explain why or why not. If they don't, how should the practice be changed?

18.3 Insurance Principles

Goals

- Discuss several ways that businesses can attempt to reduce risks.
- Define important insurance terms.
- Describe several noninsurable risks facing businesses and how managers can respond to each.

Terms

- insurance
- insurance rate
- actuaries
- insurable interest
- deductible

Insurance and Risk Reduction

If you have $5 in your pocket, there is a risk that you might lose it. Although you might not want to lose the money, its loss would not be a serious problem. However, if you own a $300 bicycle, you may not be able to afford to replace it if it is stolen. You may choose to buy insurance to protect against the larger loss.

WHEN BUSINESSES NEED INSURANCE

If you own a business, you face uncontrollable events that could result in financial loss. A fire could destroy your building. Someone might steal your property or money. A customer or employee could get hurt at the business and sue you. Or an important employee could quit or even die, leaving a gap in the skills needed to run the business. Some events could be minor (like a broken window) and so have little effect on the business. However, a major loss could result in the failure of the business. Consider the problem faced by Sandra Gilbert and her new jewelry business, discussed in the opening scenario. Because she didn't have the proper type of insurance, she lost thousands of dollars of inventory and had no way of recovering the cost. Many small businesses do not have the resources to survive a loss of that size.

Businesses face risks every day. Managers must determine the types of risk the business is likely to face and find ways to reduce or eliminate the risk. If an important risk cannot be eliminated or reduced, the business may purchase insurance to protect against a loss that would result in its failure. Insurance is a risk management tool that limits financial loss from uncontrollable events in exchange for regular payments. As Figure 18-5 (see p. 490) demonstrates, business losses can be very expensive.

MANAGING TO REDUCE RISK

Just as you would not buy insurance to protect against the loss of a $5 bill, businesses do not insure against every possible financial loss. As a normal part of operations, businesses experience losses due to operational problems. Planning can anticipate those problems and prevent them from harming the business so much that it cannot continue to operate. Most businesses expect a certain amount of shoplifting and employee theft. Rather than insuring against that loss, they take

FIGURE 18-5 Estimates of Annual Losses from Major Business Risks

- One-third of all small business failures result from significant business theft.

- Companies spend up to $10 million per year protecting against copyright losses.

- Companies lose $15-25 billion to employee theft each year.

- The average company loses $1.3 million each year to credit card fraud.

- Bad checks written by customers cost businesses an estimated $5 billion per year.

- The average cost to settle a liability claim brought against a company is $1 million.

Under federal law, if a company fails to maintain accurate business records and safeguard those records, the company may be held liable. A recent European study found that each incidence of lost data costs a business an average of $2,615. The total in one year to European businesses was estimated at $4.5 billion.

steps to improve security. For example, if Sandra Gilbert had lost one inexpensive piece of jewelry, she might have been able to make up for the loss through additional sales. However, now that a large loss has occurred, Sandra probably wishes she had done more to emphasize and implement security procedures with her employees.

Businesses can also lose money if employees do not show up for work. An absent employee's work will not be completed unless the company takes some action to get the work done. Because large businesses expect a number of employees to be absent on any given day, they may have part-time workers available on short notice or have a contract with a temporary employment agency to provide replacements. Some businesses may actually employ more people than necessary because of the expected absentee rates. Managers should watch absentee rates carefully and keep them as low as possible through policies, incentives, and penalties.

In most manufacturing processes, small amounts of materials are lost or damaged. To make sure that losses do not interfere with production, a company should keep a larger quantity of those materials on hand to ensure an adequate supply to complete production. Planning, training, and controls for production processes should also reduce the amount of material loss in the manufacturing process.

Many businesses, such as banks, investment firms, and insurance companies, base their operations on records. The records are so valuable that the businesses could not operate if the records were damaged or destroyed. In this case, insurance is not adequate protection. The businesses must rely on the safety and security of their records. They store them in well-protected, secure areas. They also keep duplicate records in a separate location, often in another city.

Another way businesses attempt to protect their vital operations is with a disaster plan. Businesses anticipate the types of disasters that could occur, the protection required, and ways to respond. Each department in the company regularly practices the disaster plan. For example, a manager may be asked without warning to assume that an electrical problem has shut down all computers in a department. The department must recover and operate again as quickly as possible by following the procedures developed in the disaster plan.

In each of the cases described, the company is gathering information, making plans, and in some cases spending a small amount of money to prevent large losses. This may be a better strategy for the company than purchasing insurance for those losses, but it does not replace the need for insurance.

CHECKPOINT

In what ways can managers anticipate and reduce the effects of risks to their business without insurance?

Basic Insurance Concepts

Even with effective management, companies must purchase insurance to cover many types of risks. Figure 18-6 defines some basic insurance terms.

It is difficult for one business to predict specific losses or the amount of those losses. However, many businesses face the same types of perils. Based on records kept over many years, insurance companies can estimate that a certain number of businesses will have fires each year and a percentage of merchandise will be shoplifted from retail businesses. By grouping the loss records of a very large number of businesses, insurance companies can estimate the probability of a certain type of loss and the amount of the loss. For example, using historical records of fire losses over many years, insurance companies estimate the probable amount of fire damage that 10,000 businesses will suffer during a year. The actual amount of loss in a specific year might be different from the estimate, but over a number of years the estimates prove to be very accurate.

Insurance companies insure only against losses that are reasonably predictable. Because they cannot know which specific business will suffer a loss, they spread the cost of the predicted losses across many businesses by selling many policies. Each policyholder pays a regular premium to the insurance company to insure against a specific type of loss. A premium is a small amount of money that pays for protection against a larger possible loss.

Insurance companies use the funds collected from policyholders in somewhat the same way that banks use deposits: They make investments that earn an income. They then use the income to cover losses suffered by insured companies. To make a profit, the insurance company must earn more from premiums and investments than it pays out in claims to policyholders.

Sometimes insurance companies lose money because they do not make wise investments or because policyholders have many more losses than the company anticipated. For example, in a recent year, several large natural disasters (hurricanes, floods, and fires) occurred in several parts of the United States at about the same time. Because of the number of disasters and the large amount of property in each area that was damaged or destroyed, insurance companies had to pay out a much higher amount than they expected. Some small insurance companies failed, and larger companies raised their rates to recover their losses.

INSURANCE RATES

An insurance rate is the amount an insurance company charges a policyholder for a certain amount of insurance. For example, a business may pay $60 a year for each $10,000 of property insured against fire loss. Rates vary according to the risk involved. For instance, if a particular type of business, such as convenience stores, experiences a large number of robberies, theft insurance rates are likely to be higher for that type of business than for, say, printing companies, which have

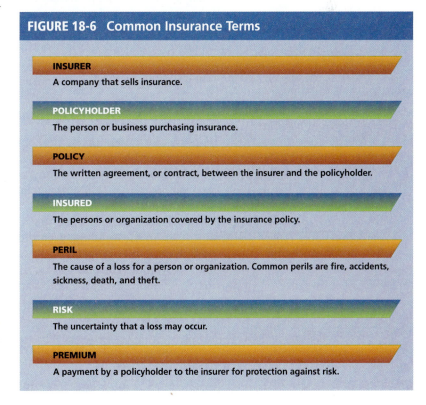

FIGURE 18-6 Common Insurance Terms

INSURER
A company that sells insurance.

POLICYHOLDER
The person or business purchasing insurance.

POLICY
The written agreement, or contract, between the insurer and the policyholder.

INSURED
The persons or organization covered by the insurance policy.

PERIL
The cause of a loss for a person or organization. Common perils are fire, accidents, sickness, death, and theft.

RISK
The uncertainty that a loss may occur.

PREMIUM
A payment by a policyholder to the insurer for protection against risk.

a lower rate of robberies. If fire protection is poor in a particular city or the building codes do not require fire walls or sprinkler systems in buildings, the fire insurance rates will be high in that city.

Calculating insurance rates is a very scientific process performed by people known as actuaries. **Actuaries** review records of losses, determine the number of people or organizations to be insured, then use statistics to calculate the rates insurance companies must charge to be able to cover the cost of losses and make a reasonable profit. Insurance companies compete with each other for business, so they must set their rates carefully. If rates are set too high, potential customers will purchase from a company with lower rates. However, if rates are set too low, the insurance company may sell many policies but be unable to pay for the losses that occur among its policyholders. Insurance companies are very careful in setting insurance rates and rely on skilled and experienced people to determine possible losses, total amounts of premiums to be collected, and returns on investments. In many cases, states have departments that review rates charged by insurance companies to make sure those rates are fair to the purchasers.

Regardless of the basic rates set by an insurance company, the rate for a specific policyholder may be lower or higher than the basic rate, depending on certain circumstances. For example, a new building that has an automatic sprinkler system and is located where there is good fire protection can be insured at a lower rate than an older building that does not have a sprinkler system and is located where there is poor fire protection. In many states, automobile rates vary from the basic rate depending on the driver's age and accident record and the brand, model, and age of the car.

CANCELLATION OF INSURANCE

An insurance policy contains information about how the contract may be terminated. Most property or liability insurance contracts may be canceled by the insurer or may not be renewed when they expire if the insurer believes the risk has increased. If the insurer cancels the insurance, it must give enough notice to policyholders to allow them to find another insurer. Most states have passed laws that do not allow companies to arbitrarily cancel insurance without a good reason. Many states allow companies and individuals whose insurance has been canceled to purchase insurance from a special state-sponsored fund, although often at a very high rate.

INSURABLE INTEREST IN PROPERTY

To insure any kind of property, the policyholder must have an insurable interest in it. An **insurable interest** is generally defined as the possible financial loss that the policyholder will suffer if the property is damaged or destroyed. For example, if a business owns a van, it has an insurable interest in that van. If the van were stolen or destroyed in an accident, the business would suffer a financial loss. People who use a building for storage have an insurable interest in the property they house in the building, even though they do not own the building. A fire could destroy their property in the building, causing financial loss. The amount of a policyholder's insurable interest in the property to be insured is usually specifically indicated in the policy and forms the basis for the insurance rate.

DEDUCTIBLES

Many insurance contracts include deductibles. A **deductible** is the amount the insured party pays for a loss before the insurance company pays anything. A deductible makes the insured responsible for part of the loss in return for a lower premium. For example, if a vehicle insurance policy has a $500 deductible

Technology *tip*

A major risk to companies conducting business on the Internet is information security. The technology used to protect transactions as they are transmitted over the Internet is Secure Sockets Layer (SSL). SSL "encrypts" confidential data (converts it into an unreadable form) to ensure that it cannot be viewed or modified as it moves between the customer and the business's Web site. The online order form is secured with a "digital certificate." Customers see a closed lock at the bottom of the Web page when the transaction is secure.

and a $1,500 loss occurs, the insurer pays $1,000 and the insured is responsible for $500 of the loss (the amount of the deductible). If the loss is only $400, the insured would bear the entire loss, and the insurer would pay nothing.

To reduce their premiums, people often choose to include a higher deductible in their policy if they can afford to pay the amount of the deductible in case of a loss. For example, the premium for an auto insurance policy with a $200 deductible may be $850 a year. The premium for a $500 deductible policy may be $600. Having the $500 deductible policy saves the policyholder $250 a year. Of course, if there is a loss, the policyholder must pay $500 rather than $200.

CHECKPOINT

What do insurance companies do with the premiums they collect?

Noninsurable Risks

Businesses are also concerned with risks for which there is no insurance. The discussion below focuses on some of these noninsurable risks.

1. Companies produce products because they expect to sell them. However, fashions, styles, and product features constantly change. If consumer tastes change, the business may suffer a loss if it can't sell its products or it must drastically reduce prices. A company with a large stock of outdated products not only will have trouble selling the products but will develop a negative image among consumers.

2. Old buildings, equipment, and technology can also cause customers to avoid a business. A business that is modern and uses the latest technology may attract customers away from an established business unless the latter works to keep up-to-date.

3. Improved methods of transportation may give one type of business an advantage over another. For instance, private parcel services originally took a great deal of the parcel business away from the U.S. Postal Service. The Postal Service now offers Priority Mail, Express Mail, guaranteed delivery, and other services to try to recapture some of the lost parcel business. Pickup and delivery services, weekend schedules, and special services such as packing are all ways that parcel services try to meet customer needs better than their competitors do.

4. Changes in the weather can cause serious business risks. For example, a long winter season may prevent manufacturers and retailers from selling spring clothing. A rainy summer may slow business at resorts if people stay home. A lack of rain can result in crop failures for farmers who have invested large amounts of money in seed, fertilizer, and equipment. A lack of snow may reduce sales of skis and snowmobiles.

5. Changes in economic conditions present another serious risk. Rising unemployment rates cause people to be more careful when spending their money. Higher gasoline prices add to business costs and may cause customers to spend less on luxuries. Some of those risks can be overcome to some extent by studying business forecasts and planning carefully in anticipation of changes in the economy. Others require an adjustment in operations to save costs in one area when they are increasing in others. Therefore, a knowledge of economics and business trends is essential.

6. Within any business community, there are numerous local risks. For example, the relocation of highways may cause customers to change their shopping behavior. The development of new highways or new regional shopping centers may take customers to larger communities to do their shopping. Street improvements may make one location more attractive than another and draw customers away from an old location. The establishment of no-parking zones may have a negative effect on certain types of businesses. Population shifts may make it necessary for businesses to move.

No insurance can protect businesses from these and similar risks. Unless businesspeople recognize trends and take action, they may find their businesses totally or partially destroyed. Noninsurable risks pose a great challenge to managers.

CHECKPOINT
List several noninsurable risks that businesses should anticipate and prepare for.

18.3 Assessment

UNDERSTAND MANAGEMENT CONCEPTS

Determine the best answer for each of the following questions.

1. The possible financial loss that a policyholder will suffer if property is damaged or destroyed is
   a. a risk
   b. an insurable interest
   c. an insurance policy
   d. a deductible

2. Which of the following would *not* be an example of a noninsurable risk?
   a. poor weather conditions that result in lower-than-expected sales
   b. a road closure that makes it difficult for customers to get to a business
   c. the theft of expensive jewelry from a jewelry store
   d. old buildings, equipment, and technology that make a business appear out-of-date to customers

THINK CRITICALLY

Answer the following questions as completely as possible.

3. What could happen to a business if the owners decide to put money into a savings account to pay for possible losses rather than purchase insurance?

4. What changes are occurring in your city that may have a negative effect on businesses but are not insurable? What actions could businesses take to reduce the impact of the changes?

18.4 Types of Business Insurance

Goals

- Describe several types of property and vehicle insurance that businesses need.
- Identify the types of insurance businesses should consider carrying on the people associated with the business.
- Describe additional insurance that businesses may need to cover special types of risks.

Terms

- insurance agents
- no-fault insurance
- health insurance
- disability insurance
- life insurance
- beneficiaries
- liability insurance
- malpractice insurance
- bonding

Selecting and Buying Insurance

Most insurance contracts are purchased from insurance agents. **Insurance agents** represent insurance companies and sell insurance to individuals and businesses. Some agents represent several different insurance companies and can provide many types of insurance for a business. Other agents represent only one company or may sell only one type of insurance, such as life or auto insurance.

Most communities have reputable agents offering all types of insurance. There are often differences in the policies and services offered by different insurance companies and agents. A businessperson should discuss insurance needs with two or three agents before selecting a company and the type and amount of insurance. It is usually not the best business practice to select an agent just because he or she is able to offer the lowest rates. The service another agent and company provide if a loss occurs may more than make up for slightly higher insurance premiums. Figure 18-7 (see p. 496) describes important factors to consider when choosing an insurance company and an agent.

The primary objectives when purchasing insurance are (1) to get the proper coverage of risks at a reasonable cost, and (2) to make certain that the insurance company will pay the claim in the event of loss. For example, a business that needs fire insurance wants to be sure that the insurance company that issues the policy will pay a claim promptly so that business activities will not be interrupted. A business that buys liability insurance wants to be sure that if a person is injured, the insurance company will help determine the business's responsibility and make a fair settlement with the injured person. Business owners should consider the areas where major losses could occur when planning the purchase of insurance.

PROPERTY INSURANCE

A business may obtain various types of insurance to fit its needs in protecting its property. The major types of property insurance that a business might have are

FIGURE 18-7 Important Factors in Selecting an Insurance Company and Agent

1. Can the company that the insurance agent represents furnish the right kind of insurance?
2. Does the insurance agent have a proper knowledge of insurance?
3. Are the policies understandable?
4. Are the company's rates reasonable?
5. What kind of service does the agent furnish?
6. What kind of reputation does the agent have for helping when losses occur?
7. What reputation does the company have for settling claims?
8. Can the company help in reducing risks?

Of the top four most expensive catastrophes for the insurance industry in the United States, three were natural events and one was the result of terrorism. The most expensive was Hurricane Katrina in 2005. The estimated total of insured property losses was $40.6 billion. The next three most expensive disasters were Hurricane Andrew in 1992 ($21.6 billion), the World Trade Center and Pentagon terrorist attacks in 2001 ($20.7 billion), and the Northridge, California, earthquake in 1994 ($16.5 billion).

(1) fire insurance, (2) burglary and robbery insurance, (3) business income insurance, (4) transportation insurance, and (5) vehicle insurance.

Fire insurance provides funds to replace such items as buildings, furniture, machinery, raw materials, and inventory destroyed by fire. Fire insurance on a building may not cover the equipment, machinery, and materials in the building. Separate policies may be required to protect the contents as well as the building itself from fire loss. The owners of a building should obtain insurance to protect their investment. The occupants of a rented building should look into insurance to protect their property inside the building. You should know exactly what the policy covers when buying fire insurance.

Some basic fire insurance policies may be extended to cover additional risks, such as wind, hail, and hurricanes. Additional protection beyond the primary peril is called *extended coverage*. It is obtained by paying an additional premium and adding a special clause to the contract. Because extended coverage costs more, businesses generally buy it only if the additional perils are fairly common in their area. For example, West Coast businesses may buy earthquake insurance because earthquakes occur there, but Midwest businesses usually do not need this coverage. In some areas of the country, insurance companies will not sell extended coverage for some perils because the chance of loss is too high. For example, insurance companies may not be willing to sell flood insurance to cover homes built in an area where flooding regularly occurs. In such cases, businesses and individuals may be able to purchase insurance from the state or federal government.

Burglary and robbery insurance provides protection from loss resulting from the theft of money, inventory, and various other business assets. Because of the differences in types of businesses and operating methods, the risks vary considerably, as do premium rates. Burglary and robbery insurance does not cover the loss of products and equipment taken by employees or shoplifted merchandise. Separate insurance is available to cover these losses, but it is often very expensive. Businesses usually spend a great deal on security equipment and training to prevent these types of losses. However, they may purchase insurance as well to protect against unusually large losses from shoplifting or theft.

Business income insurance (also known as *business interruption insurance*) is designed to compensate firms for loss of income during the time required to restore damaged property. For instance, after a hurricane, a damaged store suffers an additional loss because it cannot earn an income until its facilities are restored and it can start selling merchandise again. Some of its expenses continue even though the business cannot operate, such as interest on loans, taxes, rent, insurance payments, advertising, telephone service, and some salaries.

Transportation insurance protects against damage, theft, or complete loss of goods while they are being shipped. Although the transportation company may be responsible for many losses during the shipment of goods, some losses may be the responsibility of the seller or buyer. The seller can purchase insurance, or the transportation company may provide insurance as part of the cost of transportation. Anytime businesses ship products, they should find out if the goods are insured and who is paying the cost of the insurance.

VEHICLE INSURANCE

Many businesses own a large number of vehicles, including cars, trucks, and special vehicles for moving inventory and loading trucks, train cars, and airplanes. Several different kinds of vehicle insurance are needed for protection against theft, property damage, and personal injury. Several common types of vehicle insurance are available.

Collision insurance provides protection against damage to the insured's own vehicle when it is in a collision with another car or object.

Comprehensive insurance, included in most basic vehicle policies, covers loss caused by something other than collisions, such as rocks hitting a windshield, fire, theft, storm damage, and vandalism.

Vehicle liability insurance provides protection against damage caused by the insured's vehicle to other people or their property. Most states require all vehicle owners to carry a minimum amount of liability insurance.

Medical payments insurance covers medical, hospital, and related expenses caused by injuries to any occupant of the vehicle. These payments are made regardless of the legal liability of the policyholder.

Normally, the insurance company of the person responsible for an accident must pay the costs of damages. However, some states have passed no-fault insurance laws. Under **no-fault insurance**, each insurance company is required to pay the losses of its insured when an accident occurs, regardless of who was responsible for the accident. The intent of no-fault insurance is to reduce automobile insurance costs that result from legal actions taken to determine fault and obtain payment for losses.

PHOTO: © GETTY IMAGES/PHOTODISC.

What is the intent of no-fault insurance?

CHECKPOINT

What are the major types of property insurance that businesses need?

Insuring People

People are important to the success of all businesses. Owners and managers, employees, people working for suppliers or other businesses, and customers influence the financial success of the business. There are economic risks that involve all those people. Insurance is available to protect businesses from those risks. The primary types of insurance related to employees are health, disability, life, and liability insurance as well as employee bonding.

HEALTH AND DISABILITY INSURANCE

Health insurance provides protection against the expenses of individual health care. Typically, businesses offer three categories of coverage to their employees: (1) medical payments, (2) major medical, and (3) disability. *Medical payments insurance* covers normal health care and treatment costs. *Major medical insurance* provides additional coverage for more critical illnesses or treatments that are particularly extensive and expensive.

Disability insurance offers payments to employees who are not able to work because of accidents or illnesses. Insurance companies typically do not pay disability claims unless the injured employee is unable to perform any work for the company. Then it usually pays a portion of the salary the employee was earning before the disability.

Because the health and wellness of employees are important to both the business and the employee, both often share the cost of health insurance. Most businesses offer a group insurance policy. Under this type of plan, all employees can obtain insurance at a reasonable cost, regardless of their health, and the cost is typically lower than if they purchased coverage individually.

Health insurance has become an important concern for American businesses, individuals, and government. Because of the high costs of medical care, insurance costs have increased to the point that many people and even companies cannot afford them. Alternatives have been considered to control costs and provide basic coverage to as many people as possible.

One alternative to health insurance for employees is a health maintenance organization (HMO). An HMO is a cooperative agreement between a business and a group of physicians and other medical professionals to provide for the health care needs of the business's employees. The HMO receives a regular payment for each employee that covers a complete set of medical services. To receive coverage, employees must obtain treatment only from the health care providers in the HMO. The goal of the HMO is to keep people healthy rather than waiting until they become sick and then treating the illnesses. Health services are planned and performed in a way that carefully controls health costs.

Some people prefer to receive health care services from a physician and hospital they select rather than from the assigned health care practitioners in an HMO. To fill this need, insurance companies offer another alternative: the preferred provider organization (PPO). A PPO is an agreement among insurers, health care providers, and businesses that allows employees to choose from a list of physicians and health care facilities. The insurance company negotiates with a number of physicians and hospitals for a full range of health care services. The contracts establish the costs that the insurer will pay for those services to control costs while still offering consumers a choice of providers.

The alternative health plans being used by many companies today, such as HMOs and PPOs, have not resulted in the anticipated cost savings. In fact, health care and health insurance costs are two of the most rapidly growing expenses of many businesses today. Most are looking for alternatives, and many are shifting more and more of the cost to employees or are reducing benefits. The costs and methods of health insurance are one of the areas of employee benefits that both businesses and the federal government are studying closely.

LIFE INSURANCE

Another common form of insurance on people is life insurance. **Life insurance** pays money upon the death of the insured to a person or persons identified in the insurance policy, known as **beneficiaries**. With life

NET Bookmark

Floods are one of the major risks many businesses and homeowners fail to insure. Flood insurance is usually not offered as part of home and business policies but is sold through a cooperative agreement between the federal government and private insurance companies and agents. Point your browser to www.thomsonedu.com/school/bpmxtra. Play the flood-risk scenarios that demonstrate how flooding can affect people in various parts of the country. Decide which of the scenarios could affect people in your community. Prepare a short speech you would give to businesses and consumers to convince them of the importance of buying flood insurance.

www.thomsonedu.com/school/bpmxtra

insurance, individuals can provide some financial protection for their families in the event of their death. Some companies provide a specific amount of life insurance as a standard part of employee benefits. Others offer the opportunity for employees to purchase life insurance but the employees must pay most or all of the cost.

Many businesses insure the lives of owners and key managers because of their importance to the financial success of the business. In the case of sole proprietorships, owners usually find it easier to borrow money if they carry adequate life insurance on themselves. Life insurance has an especially important place in partnerships. Generally, a partnership is dissolved upon the death of one partner. Each partner usually carries life insurance on the other partner, so that if one dies, the other will receive, as beneficiary of the insurance policy, sufficient money to buy the other's share of the business.

CHECKPOINT

What is the difference between health insurance and disability insurance?

Other Business Insurance Needs

In addition to insuring business operations and people, businesses often buy insurance to cover special types of risk. Two such special needs are liability insurance and bonding.

BUSINESS OPERATIONS

Businesses face many risks that result from the operation of the business. People may get hurt while on the job, products may cause damage or injury, and employees may do things that damage people or their property. Liability insurance protects against losses from injury to people or their property that result from the products, services, or operations of the business. For example, if a toy injures a child, the child's parents may sue the toy manufacturer. Liability insurance would protect the company in such circumstances.

Clients sometimes sue professionals, such as lawyers and physicians, who provide personal services. Malpractice insurance is a type of liability insurance that protects against financial loss arising from suits for negligence in providing professional services. Malpractice claims are a major cost to professionals. Even if the businessperson is not guilty of malpractice, the legal fees can be very high.

Some businesses need a special type of insurance protection called bonding. Bonding pays damages to people whose losses are caused by the negligence or dishonesty of an employee or by the failure of a business to complete a contract. Bonding is often required for contractors hired to construct large buildings, highways, or bridges, and for companies such as Wells Fargo that transport large sums of money between businesses and financial institutions.

INSURANCE FOR INTERNATIONAL OPERATIONS

Many businesses operate or sell products in other countries. Insurance policies typically do not cover losses or liability resulting from international operations. Special coverage may be available at additional cost within existing insurance policies. Businesspeople should keep in mind that the insurance laws of the country in which the business is operating apply to loss situations. To encourage international business with developing countries, the U.S. government formed the *Overseas Private Investment Corporation.* The corporation provides insurance coverage for businesses that suffer losses or damage to foreign investments as the result of political risks. Although coverage is expensive, companies can even purchase insurance that covers losses suffered if the purchasers of exports do not pay for their purchases. Companies that are just beginning to engage in international trade or have not worked with a specific international company before may want to consider such insurance. Businesses shipping products to other countries should also obtain special transportation insurance, because several different companies and transportation methods may be involved as the products move from country to country.

CHECKPOINT

What types of businesses require malpractice insurance?

18.4 Assessment

UNDERSTAND MANAGEMENT CONCEPTS

Determine the best answer for each of the following questions.

1. Payments to employees who cannot work because of accidents or illnesses are offered through _____ insurance.
   a. health
   b. malpractice
   c. disability
   d. liability

2. A special type of insurance that pays damages to people whose losses are caused by the negligence or dishonesty of an employee or by the failure of the business to complete a contract is
   a. bonding
   b. beneficiary
   c. agent
   d. preferred provider

THINK CRITICALLY

Answer the following questions as completely as possible.

3. If you are choosing among employers for a full-time job and one offers health insurance and the other does not, how important would that be in deciding which job to choose? Why?

4. How does having life insurance policies on the owners of a partnership help protect the business in case of the death of one of the partners?

CHAPTER CONCEPTS

- To accept credit cards, a business must establish a relationship with a bank and a credit card company. Some firms both offer their own store credit card and accept credit cards. Others offer installment plans.

- Debit cards are a way to make electronic payments by immediately withdrawing cash from the cardholder's bank account and crediting the payment to the seller's account. They can be used to buy products and withdraw cash from ATMs. Smart cards can perform all the functions of credit, debit, and ATM cards.

- Businesses obtain information on customers' creditworthiness from credit applications and credit bureau ratings. Ratings are based on the four Cs: character, capacity, capital, and conditions.

- Effective collection procedures and aging of accounts receivable are two ways to manage credit sales. As a last resort, businesses may work out alternative payment plans with delinquent customers, use a collection agency, or take legal action.

- Managers must find ways to identify and reduce risks. Businesses may purchase property insurance, vehicle insurance, insurance on people, liability insurance, bonding, and international insurance.

- Many risks, such as weather and economic conditions, cannot be insured. Managers must be prepared to respond to noninsurable risks.

REVIEW TERMS AND CONCEPTS

Write the letter of the term that matches each definition. Some terms will not be used.

1. Measure of a credit applicant's current financial worth or ability to pay based on assets
2. Credit plan in which customer agrees to make a stated number of payments over a fixed period of time at a specified interest rate
3. Persons who represent the insurance company and sell insurance to individuals and businesses
4. Possible financial loss that a policyholder will suffer if the property is damaged or destroyed
5. Insurance that protects against losses from injury to people or their property that result from a business's products, services, or operations
6. Private company that acts as an intermediary between a business and credit card companies to establish and maintain credit services
7. Risk management tool that limits financial loss from uncontrollable events in exchange for regular payments
8. Insurance plan in which each insurance company must pay the losses of its insured when an accident occurs, regardless of who was responsible for the accident
9. Clearinghouse for information on the creditworthiness of individuals or businesses
10. Credit cards associated with specific organizations and offered to people affiliated with those organizations

a. affinity credit cards
b. aging of accounts
c. bonding
d. capacity
e. capital
f. character
g. co-branded credit cards
h. credit agency
i. debit card
j. disability insurance
k. installment credit
l. insurable interest
m. insurance
n. insurance agents
o. liability insurance
p. malpractice insurance
q. merchant account provider
r. no-fault insurance
s. smart card

DETERMINE THE BEST ANSWER

11. Which of the following would *not* be an efficient way for a business to accept all major credit cards?
    a. Work with each major company to establish a credit account.
    b. Seek a merchant account provider.
    c. Establish a private credit card system that also accepts other cards.
    d. All are appropriate ways.

12. A person using revolving credit is approved to
    a. make charges at any time
    b. charge less than the approved amount
    c. pay off the full amount by the end of the billing period without a finance charge
    d. all of the above

13. _____ cards are used by businesses for computer security, in cable and satellite television receivers, and in cell phones.
    a. Credit
    b. Debit
    c. Affinity
    d. Smart

14. To determine the creditworthiness of people or organizations, businesses apply the
    a. four Cs of credit
    b. 80/20 rule
    c. "keep it simple" policy
    d. minimum approval rate standard

15. Which of the following is an objective managers try to meet when establishing credit procedures?
    a. Give customers extra time to pay if they request it.
    b. Immediately drop customers who cannot meet payment deadlines.
    c. Use procedures that retain the goodwill of the customer.
    d. None of the answers is correct.

16. Businesses use aging of accounts to
    a. study the effectiveness of accounts receivable collection
    b. determine which accounts payable to pay first
    c. decide when equipment needs to be replaced
    d. send credit customers thank-you cards on the anniversary of the date they opened their accounts

17. Which of the following is *not* a fact on which the concept of insurance is based?
    a. It is difficult for a business to predict whether it will have specific losses or the amount of those losses.
    b. Many businesses face the same type of perils.
    c. Insurance companies can accurately estimate the probability of certain types of losses.
    d. Insurance companies insure against both predictable and unpredictable losses.

APPLY WHAT YOU KNOW

18. Based on the Reality Check scenario at the beginning of the chapter, what types of business insurance would you recommend for Sandra? Divide your recommendations into three categories: (a) must have, (b) should have, (c) probably doesn't need. Justify your decisions.

19. Identify several possible future uses for smart cards: (a) for financial transactions, (b) for other personal uses, (c) for other business uses. What problems do you anticipate might result for the widespread use of smart cards carrying a large amount of personal information?

20. Although the use of credit usually leads to increased sales for retailers, when could credit sales actually lead to decreased profits? What can business owners and managers do to reduce that possibility?

21. If you owned a restaurant in your community how would you try to identify noninsurable risks that might have a negative effect on the business? Identify several things that are more likely to have a negative effect on a restaurant than on other types of businesses.

MAKE CONNECTIONS

22. **Teamwork** Assume you are the credit manager of a major retail store. A customer of several years, who has an excellent credit background, now has a $4,600 unpaid balance. The customer has made no payments in several months. You learn from your credit bureau that she is not currently behind on other accounts but the credit balances on all her accounts are increasing. She recently lost her job. Form a team of three students to propose three realistic ways you, as the credit manager, might handle this customer. Which of the options would result in a collection and maintain the customer's goodwill?

23. **Research** Find an Internet site that provides quotes for life insurance. Determine what a $100,000 term life insurance policy would cost for a male, 45 years of age. Then determine the cost for the same amount of insurance for a female of the same age. Report the costs of insurance from three insurance companies. Present your results in a table. If the costs differ for the companies and for males and females, identify possible reasons for those differences.

24. **Technology** Use a computer spreadsheet program and the following information on unpaid purchases to prepare a credit report dated November 30 on the accounts receivable for a business that offers 30-day credit terms. The report should contain an aging of accounts receivable, similar to the one shown in Figure 18-4, and the percentage of delinquent accounts in relation to the total accounts receivable.

> Sykes purchased $600 on November 15.
> Sanford purchased $1,500 on November 19.
> Jenkins purchased $2,100 on November 12.
> Sanchez purchased $900 on October 17.
> Godowski purchased $600 on October 10.
> Yamamoto purchased $300 on September 25.

CASE IN POINT

CASE 18-1: Is Credit for Everyone?

Alissa, a recent college graduate, has just accepted a job in the credit department of Kriall's, a fashion-oriented clothing store with an exclusive image. Alissa feels that even though most customers can pay for their merchandise with cash, check, or debit card, credit is very convenient. Alissa met Tay-Von at the new-employee orientation meeting when they both started working for Kriall's. Tay-Von is in the management training program. He worked in the collections department of a discount store while in college and formed some strong opinions about the use of credit by consumers.

Over lunch one day, Alissa and Tay-Von discussed their views on credit. Tay-Von started the conversation by saying that he couldn't understand why a store like Kriall's, which attracted exclusive, well-to-do customers, had to offer credit. The customers certainly had enough money to pay cash, and the cost of the credit operations reduced the business's profits.

Tay-Von said, "I just reviewed the aging-of-accounts report for our store. I'm amazed at how many customers are always late paying their bills. And the notes accompanying the report usually say the customer simply forgot to pay. Yet even when they're late with their payments, we continue to offer them credit just to keep them from getting upset with our store. Why, one of our customers, who is the CEO of a large company, is now 60 days late paying for two very expensive suits he purchased."

"I'm sure it was just an oversight," Alissa said. "I expect he is very busy or traveling and just hasn't remembered to pay the bill."

"Not so," said Tay-Von. "We've sent him two notices 30 days apart by certified mail. It's no oversight. He just knows he can pay whenever he wants." Tay-Von could not resist adding, "Now that you've been working here, do you still believe credit is so great for everyone? If the well-to-do can't pay on time, what about the people who don't have that much money? How do they pay their bills? Credit encourages people to buy over their heads. Without credit, everyone would be better off. Stores wouldn't have to worry about collecting debts, and customers would buy only what they need."

"And you and I wouldn't have jobs," Alissa retorted. "People shop in this store because we offer credit. And we charge interest if they don't pay on time, so when they do pay we cover our costs. Credit is good for business and good for consumers. Both rich and poor people can learn to use credit wisely."

THINK CRITICALLY

1. Do you agree more with Tay-Von or Alissa? Justify your choice.
2. Do you feel that people tend to take advantage of the credit offered by businesses even when they have the money to pay?
3. Do businesses have a responsibility to help their customers use credit wisely? Why or why not?

CASE 18-2: Costs versus Risk

Xavier and Olivia Sanchez are making final plans to open the small antiques shop they have been planning for several years. They have bought and sold antiques as a hobby for many years. They would purchase one or two pieces, clean and repair them as needed, then display them at local flea markets and crafts fairs. They have many customers who know them very well and who regularly call them for help in locating specific pieces they are looking for. They are viewed by many as real experts in the antiques business.

In the beginning, buying and selling antiques was just a hobby the Sanchezes enjoyed. Gradually they decided to turn their hobby into a full-time business. They have taken several steps to realize their dream. They rented an older store building in the downtown area, spent the last six months going to auctions and making some very good purchases, and worked with their banker to develop a business plan for their shop. With the help of the SBA, they obtained a six-month loan to pay the initial costs they cannot cover from their personal savings.

Now they are ready to open the business. They have little money left other than the money they have put aside for their living expenses until the business starts to make a profit. All the money they borrowed is tied up in inventory, display equipment, advertising, and a reserve for operating expenses, including the first six months of rent. They are running the shop themselves so will have no employee expenses. They are confident they can get by on the money they have saved. They expect that advertising will bring many customers into the store.

As they review their budget and bank account balances one last time, Olivia reminds Xavier that they have not purchased any business insurance as their banker recommended. She is worried that they face several risks that could result in serious financial problems for them and their business. However, Xavier believes that because the money from their loan is already committed and the money in their personal savings is very limited, they will have to do without insurance until the business starts making a profit. "After all," he reasons, "we're renting the building, so we don't need fire insurance. If there is a fire, the landlord's policy will cover us. And we don't have any employees, so we don't need health or life insurance. Why should we waste money right now on unnecessary insurance?"

THINK CRITICALLY

1. Do you agree that if the owner of the building has a fire insurance policy, the Sanchezes will not need to purchase their own fire insurance for their antiques? Why or why not?
2. What types of insurable risks in addition to those identified by Xavier should the Sanchezes consider when deciding whether to purchase insurance?
3. What noninsurable risks might the Sanchezes face? What do you recommend they do to reduce the impact of those risks?

MY BUSINESS, INC.

Credit and insurance decisions are important for every business. New businesses in particular should consider whether to accept credit and which credit system to use. They should also study the types of insurable and noninsurable risks the business will likely face. In this project segment, you will study and determine credit policies and insurance needs for your company.

DATA COLLECTION

1. Visit a bank and determine the differences between the credit and debit cards that the bank offers. Identify the cost to a business to accept each type of card from customers. Determine what information the bank will need from a new business to decide whether it will give the business approval to accept credit and debit cards.
2. Obtain a credit application from a business. Review it and determine what information the business collects from the form. Categorize the information according to the four Cs of credit.
3. Interview an insurance agent to determine the types of insurance coverage available for small businesses, the protection provided, and the cost of each type of insurance.
4. Review newspapers for several days and identify the types of risks and reported losses suffered by businesses. Identify which companies appeared to be insured and which were not.

ANALYSIS

1. Many small businesses are beginning to accept debit cards in the same way they accept cash but do not accept credit cards. Decide whether you will accept debit or credit cards for purchases in your business or operate on a cash-only basis. Develop a written justification for your decision, then develop one or more policy statements for the business based on your decision.
2. Consider the procedures you will follow to collect receivables from customers who do not pay their accounts on time. List the steps you will follow to attempt to collect. What action will you take if the account proves to be uncollectible? Write two collection letters you would send to customers at the end of 30 days and at the end of 60 days if the account is unpaid.
3. Design a spreadsheet or database for keeping your customers' credit and payment data. Determine the types of information you need to maintain and label the columns according to the data they will contain.
4. Make a list of each type of insurance you believe you will need to carry on your business. Identify the amount of insurance you will carry, the estimated annual cost of each policy, and the company or insurance agent you plan to use to purchase the insurance.
5. Make a list of five uninsurable risks you believe your business will face. For each, describe what you will do to minimize the negative impact on your business.

Career Cluster
Financial Manager

Managing finances and making financial decisions affect every part of a business. Financial managers develop budgets, manage investments, monitor financial resources, prepare and file government reports, and analyze the effects of business activities on the business's financial condition. The goal is to support top executives and other managers in using financial resources effectively and increasing the company's profits. Most financial managers work in private industry, insurance, banking, and financial services with opportunities in government and other public organizations.

Needed Skills

- Must have a bachelor's degree in finance, accounting, or a related field at a minimum; master's degree in business administration, economics, or finance preferable.
- Courses in business law, economics, accounting, finance, mathematics, and statistics desirable.
- Must be analytical, pay attention to detail, be able to work under pressure, manage time effectively.

Employment Outlook

Financial management jobs will grow as fast as or faster than most jobs over the next decade. The number of financial jobs is closely tied to changes in the economy. However, the increasing importance of financial information as well as increasing financial regulation affecting businesses will result in a higher demand for people skilled in financial management.

PHOTO: © DIGITAL VISION.

Working in Financial Services

As the cash manager for a large service business, Emily monitors cash receipts and disbursements in the day-to-day operations. She ensures that adequate cash is available to fund short-term operations and excess cash is invested. She makes cash flow projections and tracks the use of cash against projections to improve the company's cash management decisions.

Job Titles

Controller
Treasurer
Finance officer
Credit manager
Risk and insurance manager

Career Assessment

Check your library or the Internet for information about financial managers to identify the many diverse roles they play in business. Describe what you like and don't like about financial management careers.

Case Study

AGING OF "BOOMERS" LEADS TO POTENTIAL INVESTMENT OPPORTUNITIES

Baby boomers, people born between 1946 and 1964, have the potential to strongly impact the health care and retirement planning systems. According to the Census Bureau, there are 76 million baby boomers. This group will make up 20 percent of the population by 2030. The wants and needs of aging baby boomers provide a wide range of investment opportunities.

Boomers spend more than $1 trillion a year, according to an estimate from *American Demographics*. Industries producing boomer-friendly products and services offer attractive investment opportunities. Top boomer "niche" industries include travel, leisure, and recreation; senior living; health care services companies; chronic disease management; generic pharmaceuticals; "vanity" products and services; and financial services.

The money that baby boomers spend on travel, leisure, and recreation will help the industries related to cruises, motor homes, high-end hotels, at-home entertainment systems, health clubs, and golf.

Companies that provide senior housing services will benefit as boomers enter retirement. Home improvement will benefit as boomers retrofit their homes to accommodate their changing needs. Assisted living is another industry that will cater to aging baby boomers, and nursing homes could see a dramatic increase in demand as people live longer.

Boomers' consumption of health care products and services is rising. Specialty pharmaceutical and biotechnology companies that develop drugs for diabetes, arthritis, osteoporosis, cancer, heart disease, and Alzheimer's will experience greater demand from an aging population. Pharmaceutical prices will continue to spur the growth of generic drugs. Higher demand for pharmaceuticals will increase the need for benefit service managers.

Baby boomers had the highest rate of cosmetic procedures of all age groups, according to the American Society for Aesthetic Plastic Surgery. Industries linked to cosmetic procedures and personal-care products will benefit from boomers' attention to their appearance.

Advice and guidance in the areas of wealth management and trust services are increasingly important to boomers as they move into their golden years. The aging of the baby boom generation could provide investors with a variety of attractive investment opportunities.

THINK CRITICALLY

1. What investment opportunities arise from the needs of an aging population?
2. Why are baby boomers an attractive customer base?
3. Give an example of how aging baby boomers affect the housing industry.
4. How can financial services offered at banks be adjusted to the needs of individuals in assisted care centers?

Desktop Publishing Event

The banking industry has become increasingly competitive. First Bank has hired your team to develop a newsletter using a desktop-publishing program to advertise their services. You and a partner have two hours to prepare the document. It should include graphics, text, creative layout, and appropriate fonts and type sizes.

Team members may use two computers for this assignment. You are allowed to use a scanner and/or clip art. No other equipment may be used. The finished product may be submitted in black-and-white or in color on plain paper. Word division manuals and dictionaries may be used as reference materials for this project.

Your desktop-publishing document should advertise the bank's 20 convenient locations throughout the city. Ten of the banks are located in supermarkets. The bank is open seven days a week for customers' convenience. The Visa card offered at the bank carries a low 8.9 percent interest rate for qualified customers. No fee is charged for checks if customers maintain at least $500 in their accounts. When customers use their debit cards, 1 percent of each transaction amount is donated by First Bank to a school chosen by the customer.

PERFORMANCE INDICATORS EVALUATED

- Create, design, and produce usable copy on a computer using desktop-publishing software.

- Demonstrate an understanding and mastery of basic desktop terminology and concepts.

- Produce accurate work that has been proofread carefully.

- Communicate a clear, effective message for a business.

- Manage information effectively for a desktop-publishing document.

For more detailed information about performance indicators, go to the DECA Web site.

THINK CRITICALLY

1. How can a newsletter be designed to increase the number of customers who read it?
2. Why is accuracy so important for a bank newsletter?
3. What is the benefit of using graphics in a desktop-publishing document?

http://www.fbla-pbl.org/

Production and Marketing Management

CHAPTERS

"It is the fate of most companies to see a competitor come out with something new that they should have thought of. Worse, the idea may have been kicking around in their organization without ever surfacing at a level where it could have been seized and launched. Good ideas are in the air, and what separates the masters from the plodders is how well organized they are to capture and evaluate ideas, and then to develop and launch them successfully."

Phillip Kotler

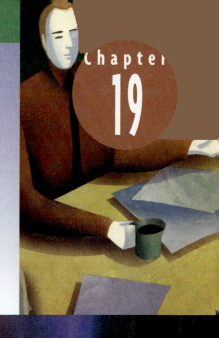

Product Planning and Production Management

19.1 Developing New Products

19.2 Planning a Manufacturing Business

19.3 Service Businesses

REALITY CHECK

Adventures in Shopping

Laresa walked through the door of her home and collapsed on the couch. She and her friend, Desiree, had just returned from a shopping trip to a new store called Millennium. It was promoted as "the shopping experience for the 21st century," and "the alternative to the American mall." Although she was tired, she couldn't wait to tell her mother about the experience.

"It's the biggest store I've ever seen—bigger than the discount warehouses. The store seemed to have every product you could want and a lot of products I've never seen before."

Noticing how tired Laresa appeared, her mother asked, "With such a big store and so many products, do people really enjoy shopping there? I would think it would be confusing and exhausting."

Laresa replied, "It's really easy and fun. You don't have to walk. Instead, you can stand on slowly moving walkways, like the ones you see in airports, that move you up and down the aisles. There are huge video displays that identify the types of products in each area of the store as well as smaller computer screens you touch to find the products you want, see demonstrations of the products, and get answers to your questions. You don't have to carry any packages. If you see something you want to buy, you enter the information in the computer. They guarantee that if the product isn't in stock, it will be delivered to your home within 24 hours. All of your purchases are packaged and waiting for you when you're ready to leave. At the checkout, the clerk reviews your order, processes your payment, and even has the packages delivered to the curb so you can drive up with your car."

19.1 Developing New Products

Goals

- Describe the steps in new-product development.
- Describe the differences between alternative manufacturing processes.

Terms

- product development
- consumer panel
- pure research
- applied research
- manufacturing
- mass production
- continuous processing
- repetitive production
- intermittent processing
- custom manufacturing

Product Development

Laresa's experience demonstrates that businesses are constantly trying to find better ways to please customers. As consumers, we are offered a growing number of choices of products and services to satisfy our wants and needs. Businesses compete to develop and sell the products that consumers want. If consumers in Laresa's city decide that the new business offers them a better shopping experience, other stores will have to change in order to compete. As shown in Figure 19-1, before a business can offer new products to consumers, it must do the following:

1. Develop an idea for a new product that consumers want to buy.
2. Turn the idea into a workable product design.
3. Produce the product and make it available to consumers at a price they are willing to pay.

If any one of the steps cannot be completed successfully, the product will fail.

Developing new products for sale is a very difficult and expensive task. For example, a national fast-food restaurant spent over a million dollars on research to develop a new sandwich for its menu. Then it spent additional millions of dollars developing a production process that would maintain a consistent taste and quality for the sandwich, no matter where the customer purchased it. In this case, the sandwich was popular with consumers as soon as it was introduced, so the company was able to recover all of its costs and make a profit. However, companies sometimes spend that much money and more, only to find that not enough customers want the product. Their new product fails, and they lose all of the money they spent to develop it.

Only a small number of new product ideas ever reach the market. Even for those that do, over half do not survive in the market for five years. Therefore, producers risk large amounts of money in buildings, equipment, materials, and personnel to provide the products that we consume.

Product development is the process of creating or improving a product or service. As a result of many factors, products are continuously changing—old products go out of use or are improved, and new products appear. Most of the products you will be using in 10 years are not available today. For a company to

FIGURE 19-1 The Steps in Product Development

1. Develop an idea for a new product that customers want to buy.
   - Conduct consumer research.
   - Conduct product research.

2. Turn the idea into a workable product design.
   - Build and test models of the product.
   - Determine what resources will be needed to produce large quantities of the product.
   - Determine the costs of producing the product and compare them to the product's price.

3. Be able to produce the product and make it available to consumers at a price they are willing to pay.
   - Build or remodel manufacturing facilities, if necessary.
   - Purchase raw materials.
   - Train employees.
   - Promote, distribute, and sell the product.

survive, it must continually search for ways to improve even its most successful products and regularly develop new products. Product development drives other business activities. Before a company can market, advertise, distribute, and sell a product, it must create and produce it. Think of the millions of dollars that were invested to develop the new store, Millennium, described at the beginning of the chapter. The investors in that business are excited by the new business idea, but to earn a return on their investment, the product must succeed.

CREATING PRODUCT IDEAS

The first step in product development is to come up with a good new product idea. You have probably seen a new product and said to yourself, "I could have thought of that." But developing successful product ideas is not easy. The process for coming up with product ideas is both creative and scientific.

Ideas for new products can come from many sources. People inside and outside the company may suggest new product ideas. A company may get ideas from salespeople and production personnel, from other businesspeople, and from research projects. Many companies employ people whose primary responsibility is to create and test new products.

CONSUMER RESEARCH Many companies gather information to help in product development by contacting the people who are likely to purchase the product. One of the best sources of ideas for product improvements or new products is a company's customers. They have used the company's products and know what they like and don't like, and what new products they would like to have. Companies can get this information from customers in many ways. Some companies send questionnaires to people who recently bought a product, asking for their opinions. Others have telephone numbers that customers can call or e-mail addresses they can use when they have questions or problems.

PHOTO: © GETTY IMAGES/PHOTODISC.

Why might a company use its customers to help in the process of product development?

J. D. Power and Associates is an internationally recognized marketing information firm. Automotive studies are the product for which the company is best known. These consumer opinion studies measure customer satisfaction from vehicle purchase through five years of ownership. Automobile manufacturers are provided with information that helps them anticipate and respond to changes in the time-sensitive automobile industry.

Salespeople can also gather information from customers. Because salespeople regularly talk to customers, they collect valuable information that can help the company improve its products. Managers should encourage salespeople to learn as much as they can about customer likes and dislikes. Many companies have specific procedures and forms for salespeople to use when they gather important information from customers. The procedures ensure that the information is communicated to the people responsible for product development.

If a company wants to get a great deal of information from consumers about possible new products, it might form a **consumer panel**—a group of people who offer opinions about a product or service. The panel consists of several people who have bought or are likely to buy the company's products. Panel members meet with trained interviewers to discuss their feelings about new products and what they think the company can do to improve its current products.

Have you ever been shopping in a mall when someone asked you to participate in a short interview or product review? Companies often conduct research in places where customers shop. The research may involve asking customers a short series of questions about their experiences with products or a more complicated process in which consumers are shown samples of new products and asked detailed questions about them. The developers of Millennium, the large store described earlier that was so exciting to Laresa, likely used a great deal of consumer research to design the best combination of products, services, and store layout to meet customer needs.

PRODUCT RESEARCH Product research is performed by engineers and other scientists to develop new products or to discover improvements for existing products. There are two types of product research—pure research and applied research. **Pure research** is done without a specific product in mind. Researchers in many companies are continually searching for new processes, materials, or ideas. They are experts in specific areas, such as biology, chemistry, robotics, electronics, or energy sources. They conduct experiments and tests in order to make discoveries that might lead to new products.

Many products we use today have been developed as a result of such research. The latest computer technology, life-saving drugs, energy-efficient appliances and homes, and improved food products have resulted from pure research projects. Many of the products we consume have been changed and improved through chemical research. Some examples are low-calorie sweeteners, meat substitutes made from soybean products, and vitamin-enhanced soft drinks. Insulation used in beverage coolers and nonstick surfaces on cooking utensils and razor blades are products that have been developed through research conducted by scientists involved in the space program.

Universities, medical research facilities, and government-sponsored research programs are heavily involved in pure research. Because of those efforts, we will likely see products in the near future that use energy more efficiently, apply laser technology, provide more effective treatments for diseases, and result in improved prediction and control of the weather.

Applied research is research that studies existing product problems or possible design improvements for current products. Improvements in electric battery storage and the mechanics of engines are resulting in a new type of fuel-efficient automobile that combines a small combustion engine with a battery that can recharge while you drive. Fiber-optics research continues to increase the amount of voice and data communications that can move on the same transmission line while maintaining security and quality. Digital video technology improves the quality of the images we see on our televisions and allows us to select from among hundreds of channels to develop a personal viewing package at any time of the day or night.

To be successful for a long time, products must be constantly changed and improved. Many types of improvements result from product research. Changes can be made in the physical product, or new features can be added to existing products. Researchers may discover new uses for the product or ways to make the product easier to use. Sometimes changes in the package itself—without actual product changes—can improve a product.

DESIGNING NEW PRODUCTS

In planning and producing a new product, businesses should involve all major departments, including production, finance, human resources, and marketing. The product should be designed to meet customer needs. Customers should be able to identify features of the new product that are different from and better than those of competing products. Also, products must be safe and easy to use. They must meet all state and federal laws for product quality and environmental and consumer safety.

If research results in a new product idea that has a good chance for consumer acceptance, the company begins to design the product. In this step, engineers and researchers build models of the product and test them to be sure that the company can produce a quality product. The design process should include factors such as durability, ease of use, and a pleasing appearance. Usually a great deal of testing is conducted to ensure that the product meets all requirements for success before the company makes the large investment needed to produce it.

Once a model has been built and tested, the company must determine what resources it will need to produce the product in large quantities. It may have to buy production facilities and equipment or modify those it is currently using to produce other products. If the company can use existing facilities and equipment, it must develop a production schedule that shows how it can produce the new products without disrupting the production of current products.

The company will have to determine the costs of producing the product and compare those costs to the price it will charge for the product. It is possible that the product cannot be sold at a price that will cover all the research, design, and production costs. In this case, the company will decide not to produce the product. If the company makes the decision to halt development at this point, it will incur less financial loss than if it produces a large quantity that goes unsold or must be sold at a loss.

CHECKPOINT
List the three steps a business must perform in order to offer new products to consumers.

Producing the Product

If the new product has survived the research and design process, the company can begin producing for sale. This is an expensive step. The company may have to build or remodel its manufacturing facilities. It must purchase raw materials and hire and train enough employees to produce the product. Then it must promote, distribute, and sell the product. However, if the company has carefully planned and produced the product, the product has a better chance of succeeding and earning a profit for the company when customers purchase it.

As you learned in Chapter 1, production is making a product or providing a service. **Manufacturing** is a form of production in which raw and semifinished materials are processed, assembled, or converted into finished products.

Manufacturing is a complex process, even when only one product is produced. Examine any product you purchased recently. Very likely, it is made of several parts. The company must either manufacture those parts or purchase them from other companies. The manufacturer must store the parts until it needs them. Then people and machinery must assemble the parts. Once assembled, the product must be packaged. Many products are packed together for shipping and then stored in a warehouse for delivery to the businesses that will sell them.

In addition to the activities just described, the manufacturing process involves many other tasks. The manufacturer must maintain equipment, purchase supplies, and train people to operate the equipment. And often, manufacturers produce many products at the same time.

DIFFERENT TYPES OF MANUFACTURING PROCESSES

When you think of a manufacturing business, you may have an image of a large factory with a long assembly line. Workers perform specific activities on the assembly line as the product moves past. Many products, all looking exactly alike, are produced on assembly lines each day. But assembly lines are only one of several ways to manufacture products (see Figure 19-2).

MASS PRODUCTION **Mass production** is an assembly process that produces a large number of identical products. It usually involves an assembly line in which employees at each workstation continuously perform the same task to assemble the

---

FIGURE 19-2 Different Types of Manufacturing

TYPE OF MANUFACTURING	WHAT HAPPENS IN THE PROCESS
Mass Production	An assembly process produces a large number of identical products
Continuous Processing	Raw materials move through special equipment that changes their form to make them more usable for consumption or further manufacturing
Repetitive Production	The same thing is done over and over to produce a product
Intermittent Processing	Short production runs are used to make predetermined quantities of different products
Custom Manufacturing	A unique product is designed and built to meet the purchaser's specific needs

product. Many products you use are assembled through mass production. Automobiles, cameras, home appliances, and many brands of computers are mass-produced.

Mass production enables companies to manufacture products at a low cost and in large quantities. But many changes have occurred in mass production since Henry Ford first used assembly lines to produce cars in the early 1900s. Now manufacturers often train assembly line workers to perform several different activities. Workers can then switch tasks periodically to make the job more interesting. Teams of workers and supervisors meet regularly to identify problems and develop solutions. Computers monitor the assembly process to ensure that needed parts and materials are available at the right time and the right place. Robots stationed at many places along assembly lines complete tasks such as painting, welding, and quality-control testing.

PHOTO: © GETTY IMAGES/PHOTODISC.

How has mass production changed since its first use in the early 1900s?

CONTINUOUS PROCESSING Raw materials usually need to be processed before they can be consumed. With ==continuous processing==, raw materials constantly move through specially designed equipment that changes their form to make them more usable for consumption or further manufacturing. Steel mills, for example, convert iron ore into steel to be used by other manufacturers. Oil refineries change crude oil into a variety of petroleum products, including gasoline and heating oil. Cereal manufacturers process many different kinds of grain into the cereals you eat for breakfast. Production runs may last days, weeks, or months without equipment shutdowns.

REPETITIVE PRODUCTION In ==repetitive production==, the same thing is done over and over to produce a product. The activity is usually rather simple and can be completed in a short time. The repetitive process may use modules (preassembled parts or units) in the assembly process. For example, the repetitive process is used to produce washing machines. First, the motor is assembled as a separate module. Then it is installed in the frame, which has been assembled separately. Controls, hoses, and other features may be added in yet another process. Mobile homes and recreational vehicles are often assembled using repetitive production. Individual sections are constructed and then brought together for final assembly on the frame or chassis.

INTERMITTENT PROCESSING ==Intermittent== processing uses short production runs to make predetermined quantities of different products. The most common form of intermittent processing is the manufacturing or assembly of a specific product to meet a customer's order or specifications. An example of a business using intermittent manufacturing is a printing company. Each printing job varies in quantity, type of printing process, binding, color of ink, and type of paper. When the company receives an order, the

NETBookmark

The International Organization for Standardization (ISO) has done a remarkable job of ensuring that companies around the world meet quality standards across a number of products. Their latest standards are helping to ensure that companies meet environmental standards as well. Point your browser to www.thomsonedu.com/school/bpmxtra. Read the overview of the ISO system and the ISP 9000 and 14000 standard. Explain how these standards are helping companies, customers, and the general public worldwide. Would a company want to compete in the world market without meeting these standards?

www.thomsonedu.com/school/bpmxtra

printer assigned to the job assembles the necessary materials, selects the correct printing equipment, and completes the printing. A bakery uses intermittent processing, as does a company that roasts, blends, and grinds many varieties of coffee beans to order.

CUSTOM MANUFACTURING Often there is a need to build only one unit or a very limited number of units of a product. The product may be very large or complex and take a long time to build. **Custom manufacturing** is the process used to design and build a unique product to meet the specific needs of the purchaser. Buildings, bridges, and computer programs are all examples of custom manufacturing. If a company needs a special piece of equipment built, it hires a custom manufacturer.

A custom manufacturer must be able to work with a customer to develop a unique product. The company must be flexible enough to build a different product each time, and it may need to build part of a product or the entire product at a new location each time.

CHECKPOINT

Describe five alternative ways a product can be manufactured.

19.1 Assessment

UNDERSTAND MANAGEMENT CONCEPTS

Circle the best answer for each of the following questions.

1. Research done without a specific product in mind is called
   a. applied research
   b. product research
   c. pure research
   d. scientific research

2. An assembly process that produces a large number of identical products is called
   a. continuous processing
   b. intermittent processing
   c. mass production
   d. repetitive production

THINK CRITICALLY

Answer the following questions as completely as possible.

3. Describe where new product ideas come from.

4. Explain the differences between the alternative ways of manufacturing.

Xtra! Study Tools
thomsonedu.com/school/bpmxtra

19.2 | Planning a Manufacturing Business

Goals

- Discuss the important considerations in locating a manufacturing business.
- Describe the factors that influence the organizing and production process.

Terms

- inventory management
- human resource planning
- production scheduling
- quality management
- computer-aided design (CAD)
- computer-integrated manufacturing

Establishing a manufacturing business requires a number of important decisions. The company must be able to get the materials it needs to build products. It must have buildings designed and built. The company must purchase specialized machinery and equipment and arrange it in the buildings so that it can produce quality products rapidly and at a low cost. The company must hire people with the skills to perform the many activities needed to produce the products. If it cannot find people with the needed skills, it must train others. Finally, after manufacturing the products, the company must store them until it can sell and distribute them to customers.

Technology *tip*

Just-in-time inventory (JIT) systems use computer communication to connect manufacturers' inventory levels to suppliers. Suppliers are notified to deliver inventory just in time for its use in manufacturing. This reduces the cost to manufacuturers because they don't need to carry large amounts of inventory.

Locating the Business

One of the first decisions a manufacturing company must make is where to locate the business. Although it might seem that a business could locate anywhere it wants to, finding the best location is a very complicated procedure. Several factors influence the decision of where to locate a manufacturing business.

AVAILABILITY OF RAW MATERIALS

If a manufacturer must process raw materials as part of the production process, it must have a reliable supply of those materials. Also, the cost of the raw materials must be as low as possible. The manufacturer may therefore choose to locate close to the source of the raw materials to keep the cost of transporting them as low as possible. Furniture and textile manufacturers, steel mills, and food-processing companies are examples of industries that locate close to the source of needed raw materials. Consider what the most important raw materials are for each of these manufacturers and where the manufacturers are likely to locate because of the need for these materials.

TRANSPORTATION METHODS

The company must decide how to obtain the materials needed to manufacture the products and how it will ship the products to customers. The choice of transportation method can determine whether the company will receive materials and deliver products on time. The major transportation methods include

air, rail, truck, water, and pipeline. Each has specific advantages based on time, cost, and convenience. Very bulky, fragile, or perishable products need special transportation. Companies may decide to locate close to a railroad, an interstate highway system, or a major airport to be able to conveniently access the type of transportation needed. If the company is involved in international business, it may need to locate near a variety of transportation sources.

SUPPLY AND COST OF ENERGY AND WATER

The costs and supply of energy that manufacturers use is an important consideration in production planning. The company must have an uninterrupted supply of energy (such as electricity, gasoline, or coal) at a reasonable cost. There have been times in recent years when several types of energy, including electricity and gasoline, have been in short supply. Energy prices can change dramatically in a short time, making it difficult to control costs. As a result, companies had to switch to other forms of energy or reduce operations.

Water supplies are limited in many parts of the United States as well as in other countries. Governments tightly control access to water as well as the requirements for treatment and discharge of wastewater. Cities and states have passed environmental laws that regulate access to water and energy resources and where specific types of businesses can and cannot locate. A company must be sure to locate where it will have enough energy and water to be able to operate for many years.

LAND AND BUILDING COSTS

Some companies can operate in small buildings, but others may need several hundred acres of land. Companies can purchase or lease land and buildings. Constructing a large manufacturing building costs many millions of dollars. A company will need a source of financing for the construction and will normally pay the cost of the building over many years.

As a business grows, it must plan for possible future expansion. Many companies have had to expand several times since they started business. Expansion is easier if enough land is available close to the existing buildings and buildings are designed to be flexible and allow for expansion.

Companies must carefully consider how the manufacturing process will affect other people and organizations in the same area. Businesses with production processes that create odors or high noise levels may be severely restricted in where they can locate or may face lawsuits from adjoining neighborhoods.

LABOR SUPPLY

Well-trained employees are an important part of most manufacturing operations. Few businesses can operate effectively today without well-educated employees. In selecting a location, a company should look at the available supply of workers, the training they might need, and the cost of the labor. The choice of location depends on whether the company needs highly skilled employees or unskilled labor. The days of easily available and inexpensive labor providing the skills a company needs are over. Businesses are working with government agencies, colleges, and universities to design training programs to ensure a competitive workforce.

LOCATION OF CUSTOMERS

Just as some companies need to locate near the source of raw materials, others may consider the location of their customers. This is an important factor when most of the customers can be found in one part of the country, when they need the products regularly and rapidly, or when transportation costs of the finished products will be very high.

Manufacturers that supply parts for the auto industry usually locate near the automobile production facilities. Some companies locate near seaports if they have important markets in other countries. Because soft drink companies must provide a regular, fresh supply of their product to many stores and businesses, they have bottling plants and distribution centers in most cities to reduce transportation costs.

Today some states are developing large air freight centers. These are airports that are surrounded by efficient distribution centers and have easy access to interstate highways and rail lines. Air freight centers are being created to attract manufacturing businesses that need to ship products quickly by air.

PHOTO: © GETTY IMAGES/PHOTODISC.

What factors influence the location of a manufacturing business?

ECONOMIC AND LEGAL FACTORS

A company also considers the type and amount of taxes it must pay in the location of its manufacturing facilities. Some cities offer reduced tax rates or may even waive some taxes for several years to encourage new businesses to locate there. Others have taxes on inventory and equipment that increase the costs of business operations. Most towns and cities use zoning laws to restrict where businesses can locate and how they can operate. Environmental regulations control the use of water and energy as well as require businesses to avoid polluting the water, air, and land.

CHECKPOINT
Why have some U.S. manufacturers relocated to China?

Production Planning

Developing a production plan can be compared to planning a meal. All the ingredients must be available in the right quantities and at the right time. Cooking utensils need to be assembled. Some foods require longer cooking times than others, so preparation of each item must begin at the correct time. If scheduled and completed correctly, all the dishes can be served at the same time.

When planning production, the company identifies all the resources required to produce the product and estimates when each will be needed and in what quantity. Because production occurs over a period of time and in a sequence, the company will not need all resources at once. If the company receives the materials before it needs them, it will have to use both space and money for storage. On the other hand, if the company can't get the resources when it needs them, it will have to delay production and spend money on nonproductive employee time until the necessary materials arrive.

Three important activities are part of production planning. **Inventory management** is planning the quantities of materials and supplies needed for production and the number of finished products required to fill customer orders. **Human resource planning** is determining the types of jobs required for each part of production, the number of people needed for each job, and the skills each person will need in order to do the job. **Production scheduling** is identifying the steps required in a manufacturing process, the time required to complete each step, and the sequence of the steps. Managers use sophisticated planning systems to develop production schedules. Computers are very useful in scheduling production and monitoring progress toward meeting production schedules.

BUILDING LAYOUT

A manufacturer must organize its facilities, equipment, and materials to produce products efficiently. Products have to move through the building, parts must be added, and employees must be able to work on the product easily and safely. The manufacturer must have cost-effective methods for receiving and storing raw materials, parts, and supplies. Once products are finished, the manufacturer must store them or load them for shipment.

The type of layout a manufacturer uses depends on the product and the assembly process. For example, one company that builds tractors has a continuous assembly line that is nearly a mile long. Many of the parts have to be stored long distances from the place they are needed. The parts are delivered to the assembly line with overhead conveyor belts and chains.

A small company that builds electric motors delivers all needed parts to each assembler's work area. The assembler puts the parts together to finish the motor. The motor then moves to the shipping area for packaging and storing for delivery.

A company that manufactures desktop computers organizes its manufacturing employees in teams with their own work areas. Each team orders the parts it needs and keeps them in easy-to-reach bins around its workspace. The entire team works on the assembly, tests each computer to make sure it works, and packages it for delivery. This procedure allows the company to quickly build a customized computer for each customer's order.

In addition to the type of product and the assembly process used, other factors influence the layout of the business. The layout should be designed to make product assembly easy and safe. Employees may need areas to test and repair products. Products and people must be able to move around the building. Employees need food services and break areas. Other activities that support the manufacturing process, such as purchasing, information management, training, and administrative services, require space as well.

For most companies, the layout should be flexible so they can add new machinery and equipment. Also, companies may need to expand the layout as the company grows or change it to produce new products.

Focus On...

Global Quality–ISO Standards

Global trade has created a variety of problems for companies, along with opportunities to reach new customers with their products and services. One of the greatest challenges has been the lack of standardization among the products produced by different companies. Consider the problems that a company creates when it produces machinery that cannot be sold in another country because it is not compatible with the machinery that customers in that country already use. What if a company needs to make repairs and the available parts don't match the broken parts?

The International Organization for Standardization (ISO) was organized to deal with the standardization issue, which is a barrier to international trade. The two primary goals of this international organization are:

- to develop agreements on production designs to increase compatibility among products that are used with each other, and
- to establish standards to ensure quality and reliability when one company purchases the products of another company.

Over 130 countries participate in the voluntary organization. Because of the agreements developed by the ISO, products such as credit cards can be used in cash machines in any country and batteries produced in one country will work in a CD player produced in another country. If an airline needs to replace a bolt in an engine mount while the plane is in another country, it can be assured that the bolt produced in that country will fit.

Standards known as ISO 9000 establish very specific requirements for manufacturing processes and product specifications. Any business that works with another ISO-certified business can trust that the requirements have been met. A newer set of standards, ISO 14000, describes specific requirements for environmental management. A company that agrees to these standards assures that it will follow rigorous guidelines in the use of resources and protection of the environment.

Many government agencies and individual companies do not purchase products from a company that is not ISO certified. Companies spend a great deal of time and undertake expensive training programs to make sure that their products and processes meet ISO requirements. The result is much more efficient trade among businesses and countries, plus a higher quality of products and operations in thousands of companies.

The International Organization for Standardization has had a big impact on the ways businesses interact with each other. It continues its work as new technologies emerge and as manufacturing problems are identified to make the process of international trade easier.

Think Critically

1. What are some examples of products that are not standardized, resulting in problems using one brand with another?
2. Why would a company refuse to work with other companies that are not ISO certified?
3. Why might a company decide not to meet the standards established by ISO?
4. Use the Internet to locate companies that identify themselves as ISO certified. Find Web sites that provide additional information or that describe specific ISO standards.

IMPROVING PRODUCTION PROCESSES

Improving quality and productivity has been one of the most important challenges facing businesses in the last decade. Increasing global competition has resulted in a larger number of products from which customers can choose. Businesses have found that customers buy the best product available for the price they can afford, resulting in increased pressure to improve quality while holding down costs and prices.

As you learned in Chapter 1, for many years companies were more interested in production efficiency than in quality. As early as the 1950s, Dr. W. Edwards Deming was encouraging businesses to focus on quality as the most important company goal, but his ideas were largely ignored in the United States. Today, however, because of the success of companies that have adopted Deming's ideas, most manufacturers use principles of quality management. **Quality management** is the process of assuring product quality by developing standards for all operations and products and measuring results against those standards. For quality management to succeed, the company must believe that no defects are acceptable and that all employees are responsible for quality. Everyone must be able to identify problems and take responsibility for correcting them. Rewards must be based on achieving the quality standards rather than meeting a certain level of production.

To encourage American companies to improve quality, Congress created the Malcolm Baldrige National Quality Award in 1987. To win the award, a company must demonstrate that it has implemented a program to develop and maintain quality in all of its products and activities. Companies compete for the award because customers are more likely to buy from companies that can prove their commitment to quality by winning this honor.

Technology has contributed to the improvement of manufacturing for many years. Computers have dramatically improved the quality and speed of production and have reduced costs. Robots now perform many of the routine and repetitive tasks previously done by low-skilled employees. Fewer people are now needed to accomplish the same level of production. However, those people must be skilled in computer operations and modern production processes.

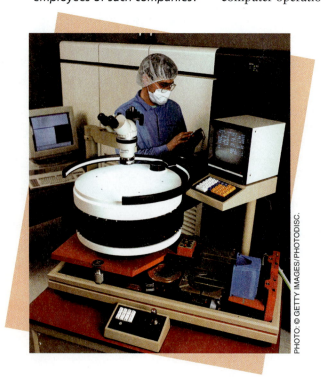

Technology has greatly contributed to the improvement of manufacturing. What effect have computers had on the employees of such companies?

PHOTO: © GETTY IMAGES/PHOTODISC.

In addition to routine tasks, computer technology can also accomplish more difficult and challenging tasks. Using a computer application known as **computer-aided design** (CAD), engineers can design and test products before they are even built. They can view a design from various angles, study possible modifications, and test the products for strength and durability.

The most extensive use of computers in manufacturing is a system known as **computer-integrated manufacturing**. In this process, all manufacturing systems are designed and managed with computers. Design work, planning and scheduling, resource management, and control are all tied together through computers. When someone makes a change in one area, computers determine the impact of the change on other areas and communicate that information to the affected work units.

The Internet has become a powerful resource in improving the speed and quality of manufacturing. Some of the uses of the Internet are very basic but have an amazing impact on how a business operates. As an example, it used to be a very expensive and time-consuming process for companies to get approval from the Food and Drug Administration when they wanted to produce a new food product or drug. They had already spent months and often years developing and testing the product. Then they had to prepare, print, and ship volumes of reports to the FDA for approval. Today that entire process can be managed on the Web. Companies can transmit reports instantly, research questions online, send answers to the FDA by e-mail, and conduct meetings on computer screens. The approval process time has been cut in half, and the cost of approval has gone down substantially.

An automobile manufacturer with plants in many countries around the world is improving the automobile design process using the Internet. Product designers come together in cyberspace to share ideas and plan new products. If one factory identifies design or manufacturing problems, it can immediately share information about the problems with every other facility and cooperatively develop a solution. The system is resulting in cost savings because there are fewer design problems and good designs are now being used over and over in many locations. Also, the manufacturer benefits from greater creativity in developing new automobile models as people from around the world share their ideas.

CHECKPOINT

Describe the factors companies consider when they plan production.

19.2 Assessment

UNDERSTAND MANAGEMENT CONCEPTS

Circle the best answer for each of the following questions.

1. All of the following should be considered when deciding where to locate a manufacturing company except
   a. availability of raw materials
   b. transportation methods
   c. supply and cost of energy and water
   d. international competition

2. Production planning includes all of the following except
   a. building planning
   b. human resource planning
   c. inventory management
   d. production scheduling

THINK CRITICALLY

Answer the following questions as completely as possible.

3. Explain why a company would need to consider the supply and cost of energy and water.

4. Explain why quality standards are important for manufacturing businesses.

Xtra!
Study Tools
thomsonedu.com/school/bpmxtra

19.3 Service Businesses

Goals
- Identify the characteristics of services that make them different from products.
- Describe the ways businesses maintain product and service quality.

Terms
- intangible
- tangibles
- reliability
- responsiveness
- assurance
- empathy

Service businesses are the fastest-growing segment of our society. More than two-thirds of the U.S. labor force is now employed in service-producing businesses or service jobs. Over 70 percent of economic activity in the United States is service related. Therefore, the United States is changing from the world's leading manufacturing economy into its leading service economy. Many service businesses are quite small and employ only a few people, and others have total sales of millions of dollars each year and employ thousands of people.

The Nature of Services

Figure 19-3 illustrates that services are very different from tangible products. As you learned in Chapter 1, services are activities of value that do not result in the ownership of anything tangible. Traditional service businesses include theaters, travel agencies, beauty and barbershops, lawn care businesses, and insurance agencies. New types of services are emerging as well, such as online music and video download services, comprehensive financial services, information management, and human resource management.

HOW SERVICES DIFFER FROM PRODUCTS

Services have important characteristics that make them different from products. These differences in form, availability, quality, and timing require unique operating procedures for service businesses.

FORM Services are intangible. Intangible services do not have a physical product, they cannot be seen or examined before purchase, and they do not exist after the consumer uses them. When you go to a theater to see a play, you rely on a review in the newspaper or what you have heard from others to decide if it is something you want to attend. If a company hires a carpet-cleaning business for its offices, it will need to bring them back when the carpets must be cleaned again.

AVAILABILITY A service cannot be separated from the person or business supplying it. Dental care requires a dentist, a concert requires an orchestra, and tax preparation requires an accountant. People who purchase services are also purchasing

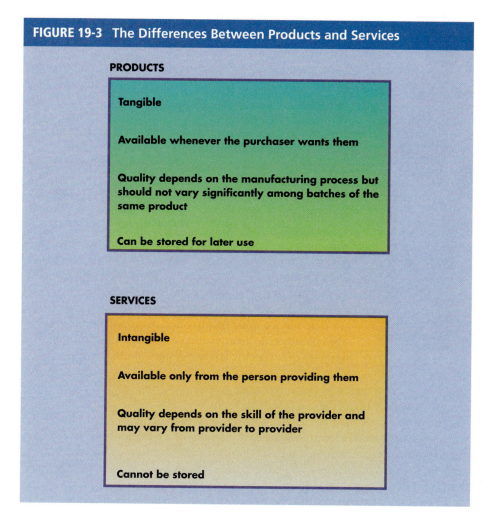

FIGURE 19-3 The Differences Between Products and Services

PRODUCTS

Tangible

Available whenever the purchaser wants them

Quality depends on the manufacturing process but should not vary significantly among batches of the same product

Can be stored for later use

SERVICES

Intangible

Available only from the person providing them

Quality depends on the skill of the provider and may vary from provider to provider

Cannot be stored

the availability and the skill of the person performing the service. If a business or individual is unable to deliver a service, customers must go without. Trading in the stock market using the Internet has become popular as investors bypass traditional stockbrokers. However, in several instances, a business offering Internet stock trading had serious hardware or software problems that prevented customers from accessing accounts to buy and sell stocks.

QUALITY The quality of the service depends on who provides it as well as where and when that service is provided. Removing 10 inches of snow from a parking lot may be more effective with a tractor and a dump truck than with a small snow blower. A hairstylist who has not completed training recently may not be able to offer the latest hair designs. A service provider who is tired, untrained, or unconcerned about the customer may not provide the same quality of service each time. Understanding these factors makes it easier for a business to control the quality of services and ensure that customers get the same quality time after time.

TIMING A service cannot be stored or held until needed. After a movie starts, it is no longer available in its complete form until it is replayed. If the courts in a tennis club are full, no one else can play tennis at that time. Likewise, the owner of a taxi company must have cars and drivers available at all times, even if no one is using a taxi at a specific time.

facts & figures

The Ritz-Carlton Hotel Company is the only two-time recipient of the Malcolm Baldrige National Quality Award in the service category. Their strategy is to achieve 100 percent customer loyalty. The company set a target of "defect-free" experiences for guests, implementing a system to chart progress toward elimination of all customer problems—no matter how minor. Any employee can spend up to $2,000 to immediately correct a problem or handle a complaint.

How can employees of service businesses do a better job of meeting customers' needs?

OPERATING A SERVICE BUSINESS

By understanding the unique characteristics of services, managers in charge of planning services can do a better job of meeting customer needs. Consider the planning that must be done by the managers of Millennium, the new store described at the beginning of the chapter. They must make sure the business offers the best level of customer service possible to the thousands of people who shop there.

Because a service is intangible, service providers must find ways to describe their service to prospective customers. They may have to demonstrate how they will provide the service and the benefits the customers will receive. To help overcome this problem, service businesses sometimes provide a product to customers as part of the service. Insurance companies provide policy documents and leather cases to hold the documents, tour services provide travel bags, and hotels provide small gifts in their rooms to remind their guests of the service and the service provider.

The service must be provided in an acceptable way to the customer. A client visiting a barbershop may want the services of a specific barber. A person completing a bank transaction may want to talk with a teller rather than use an ATM. Airline travelers may prefer not to stand in long lines to check their luggage and get a boarding pass for their flight.

The people providing the service must be well trained. They must be able to work with customers, identify needs, and provide the appropriate service. They must recognize that customer satisfaction is directly related to how well they perform. In turn, customers will expect the same quality of service each time they purchase it.

The supply of a service must be matched to the demand. If a bus company expects a large number of customers to ride its buses on the Saturday of a home football game, it may have to schedule more buses. If a snowstorm is anticipated, companies that clear parking lots and driveways may need to find additional equipment and operators. During a particularly cool and rainy summer, the operator of a swimming pool will probably need to schedule fewer lifeguards and pool attendants.

CHECKPOINT

Describe the four basic characteristics of a service business.

Ensuring Service Quality

Just as manufacturers are constantly improving their products and processes to better satisfy customers, service businesses also look for better ways to provide services. Some of those ways include hiring and training employees more carefully, thoroughly planning how to maintain service quality standards, and using technology to improve the availability and delivery of services. The Internet is

PHOTO: © BANANASTOCK.

providing both opportunities and challenges for service businesses. For example, it is easier to get information to customers using the Internet. Pizzas, CDs, and videotapes can now be ordered online. However, when customers can download movies via the Internet or place grocery orders at their favorite supermarket and have products delivered to their door, traditional businesses must consider the potential impact on their sales and profits.

SERVQUAL

Business researchers have developed a means of measuring service quality, the SERVQUAL survey. This survey measures five dimensions that customers consistently rank as important to service quality:

- **Tangibles:** the appearance of physical facilities, equipment, personnel, and promotional material
- **Reliability:** the ability to perform the promised service dependably and accurately
- **Responsiveness:** the willingness to help customers and provide prompt service
- **Assurance:** the knowledge and courtesy of employees and their ability to convey trust and confidence
- **Empathy:** the caring and individualized attention the business provides its customers

The SERVQUAL survey measures service quality perceptions of customers, service providers (individuals who deal directly with customers), and managers. Researchers look at the differences, or gaps, between these groups to identify differences in expectations and service quality perceptions.

STANDARDIZING SERVICES

Franchises for service businesses are becoming quite common. Franchising allows a service to be provided in a variety of locations while maintaining a consistent image and level of quality. Examples of franchised service businesses include car repair, video rentals, tax preparation and legal services, and house-cleaning businesses.

Service businesses are responding to the specific needs of customers. Extended hours, more service locations, a greater variety of services, and follow-up activities with customers to ensure satisfaction are all ways that businesses are attempting to meet customer needs. Managers of service businesses are learning that they must plan their service processes as carefully as manufacturers plan their production processes. In both cases, customers expect a quality product or service delivered in a timely fashion at a fair price.

CHECKPOINT

Explain how a business can ensure service quality.

19.3 | Assessment

UNDERSTAND MANAGEMENT CONCEPTS

Circle the best answer for each of the following questions.

1. Which of the following describes a service business accurately?
   a. Services are tangible.
   b. A service is separate from the person or business.
   c. Service businesses do not need to worry about quality.
   d. A service cannot be stored or held.

2. The SERVQUAL survey measures all of the following except:
   a. intangibles
   b. reliability
   c. responsiveness
   d. assurance

THINK CRITICALLY

Answer the following questions as completely as possible.

3. Explain how services are different from tangible products.

4. Explain why the SERVQUAL survey collects data from customers, service providers, and managers.

Xtra!
Study Tools
thomsonedu.com/school/bpmxtra

CHAPTER CONCEPTS

- Businesses are continually looking for new product ideas that meet consumer needs and ways to improve their current products. Product development is based on consumer and product research.

- During product design, models are tested to make sure they meet consumer needs and will be safe and durable. The company then determines the resources and facilities needed and if a product will be profitable.

- Products are manufactured in several different ways: mass production, continuous processing, repetitive production, intermittent processing, and custom manufacturing.

- Decisions about where to locate a business are based on the location and availability of raw materials, transportation methods, supplies of energy and water, the costs of land and buildings, the labor supply, the location of customers, and any economic and legal factors that may affect the business.

- Production planning involves inventory management, human resource planning, and production scheduling. Quality management sets standards for products and operations and ways to measure results.

- Service businesses are the fastest-growing segment of the U.S. economy. Services are different from products in form, availability, quality, and timing.

REVIEW TERMS AND CONCEPTS

Write the letter of the term that matches each definition. Some terms will not be used.

1. Process of creating or improving a product or service
2. Research that studies existing product problems or possible design improvements for current products
3. Planning the quantities of materials, supplies, and finished products required to meet customer orders
4. Computer application engineers use to design and test products before they are built
5. Group of people who offer opinions about a product or service
6. Form of production in which raw and semifinished materials are processed, assembled, or converted into finished products
7. Process in which all manufacturing systems are designed and managed using computers
8. Assuring product quality by developing standards and measuring results against those standards
9. Identifying the steps required in a manufacturing process, the time required to complete each step, and the sequence of the steps
10. Manufacturing process that uses short production runs to make predetermined quantities of different products
11. Research done without a specific product in mind
12. Process used to design and build a unique product to meet the specific needs of the purchaser

a. applied research
b. computer-aided design (CAD)
c. computer-integrated manufacturing
d. consumer panel
e. continuous processing
f. custom manufacturing
g. intermittent processing
h. inventory management
i. manufacturing
j. product development
k. production scheduling
l. pure research
m. quality management
n. repetitive production

DETERMINE THE BEST ANSWER

13. Human resource planning determines all of the following *except*
    a. the types of jobs required for each part of production
    b. the number of people needed for each job
    c. the salaries of each worker
    d. the skills each person will need in order to do the job

14. Companies use this process do the same thing over and over to produce a product.
    a. customer manufacturing
    b. intermittent processing
    c. mass production
    d. repetitive production

15. Buildings, bridges, and computer programs are all examples of
    a. custom manufacturing
    b. intermittent processing
    c. mass production
    d. repetitive production

16. To encourage American companies to improve quality, Congress in 1987 created the
    a. American National Quality Award
    b. ISO National Award
    c. Malcolm Baldrige National Quality Award
    d. Total Quality Management Award

17. The major transportation methods include
    a. rail, truck, and water
    b. air, rail, truck, and water
    c. air, rail, truck, water, and freight
    d. air, rail, truck, water, and pipeline

18. The International Organization for Standardization (ISO) was organized to
    a. deal with global standardization issues
    b. develop agreements on production designs and compatibility
    c. establish standards to ensure quality and reliability
    d. all of the above

19. The manufacturing process that produces a large number of identical products and usually involves an assembly line where employees at workstations continuously perform the same task to assemble the product is called
    a. custom manufacturing
    b. intermittent processing
    c. mass production
    d. repetitive production

APPLY WHAT YOU KNOW

20. Explain why a company would use both consumer research and product research when developing new product ideas.
21. Describe the methods used by product developers to collect data for research. Explain how technology can be used in research.
22. Describe the circumstances in which a company might decide to go ahead with the production of a new product rather than spend time developing and testing a model.
23. Explain why companies would compete for the Malcolm Baldrige Award.
24. Describe the economic and legal factors that might affect the location of a manufacturing business.

MAKE CONNECTIONS

25. **Math** The Neveau Corporation spent $8,937,250 on research last year. It spent 30 percent on consumer research, 25 percent on pure research, and the remainder on applied research. The company's annual sales for the last year were $297,550,000.
    a. What percentage of sales did the company spend on research?
    b. How much did the company spend on each of the three types of research?
26. **Research** Join a team with several other students in your class. Your teacher may assign you to a specific group and topic. Use the Internet or your library to gather information on one of the following topics: Dr. W. Edwards Deming, the Malcolm Baldrige National Quality Award, the ISO, Total Quality Management, or Continuous Quality Improvement. Prepare an oral report. Include slides developed with computer presentation software. Provide at least three Internet addresses (URLs) where you found useful information on the topic.
27. **Writing** Place yourself in the role of your city's economic development director. Evaluate your city against the criteria that manufacturers consider in locating their facilities. Write a letter that you would use to convince a manufacturer to locate in your city.
28. **Speaking** Participate in a debate with other students in your class. Your teacher will provide instructions on how the debate will be organized. Do research to gather information in support of your position. The two positions to be debated are:
    a. Cities and states should encourage economic development and provide better jobs for their citizens by reducing the amount of regulation on where manufacturing businesses can locate.
    b. Cities and states should increase the regulation on where businesses can locate to protect the environment and its citizens.

CASE IN POINT

CASE 19-1: Maintaining Quality in a Competitive Market

TaeMark, a major software development company, is facing increasing competition from many new businesses. It prides itself on staying in touch with its customers and carefully testing all new software products and upgrades to ensure that they are easy to use and free of "bugs" before distributing them for sale. That process is both time-consuming and expensive. It often takes more than a year to get a new type of software on the market. The cost of the research and testing makes the company's software among the most expensive on the market.

TaeMark has noticed a new trend in software development in the past several years. Small and large competitors are flooding the market with new software. Many of the new products never achieve a high level of sales and often are removed from the market after a few months. However, it appears the competitors are willing to develop many products that don't sell with the hope that a few will be very successful and profitable. Also, most of the new software products are introduced without much testing to ensure quality. The new software developers believe that customers will put up with problems as long as the company quickly puts out a new edition of the software that corrects the problem. Competitors may put out two or three editions of a product in the time it takes TaeMark to develop and test one product. Because of the way the new software developers operate, they can price their software much lower than TaeMark can. TaeMark is also finding a change in customer attitudes about software developers. Customers express growing dissatisfaction with quality and say they are not willing to pay high prices for software when they know they will have to upgrade the software frequently.

THINK CRITICALLY

1. Why do you believe some companies are willing to forgo the time and cost of research and testing in order to get products on the market faster?
2. Why do you believe customers appear to have negative attitudes toward software developers yet are still willing to purchase their products?
3. The new competitors are allowing customers to identify problems with their software. Then they develop new editions that correct the problems. Is this really a form of research? Why or why not?
4. Would you advise TaeMark to change its product development process to be more like that of new competitors, or to continue the process it has used in the past? What are the advantages and disadvantages of each choice?
5. Explain how TaeMark could use the SERVQUAL survey to improve the quality of its software. Would ISO certification help TaeMark sell its software?

CASE 19-2: Delivering a Quality Vacation Experience

Rebecca and Jacob DeNucci vacation with their family each summer on an island just off the coast of North Carolina. The island is a popular tourist area, with several large hotels and a ferry boat that brings people from the mainland to the island for day-long visits. Rebecca and Jacob began to think about ways they could use their time to make money during the summer. They considered the needs of the tourists visiting the island and decided to begin a guide service for people who wanted to explore the hills and forests of the island.

They spent some time planning two different tours. The short tour would last one hour. It would be for people who wanted to see some of the beautiful spots on the island but were not prepared for extensive hiking. The long tour would take half a day and would include hiking over 5 miles. It was designed for more experienced outdoors people who wanted to study the plants, trees, and wildlife unique to the island. Rebecca and Jacob would provide the short tour to groups of 10 to 15 people at a rate of $2 per person. The long tour would serve four to eight people and would cost $10 per person.

After planning, Rebecca and Jacob developed small posters and some business cards that described their guide service, listed the days and hours the tours were available, and gave their home phone number. They distributed their materials to the hotels and restaurants on the island and the mainland.

THINK CRITICALLY

1. Do you think Rebecca and Jacob have done effective planning for their service business? What are some additional things they may want to consider before beginning the business?
2. Suggest ways that the DeNuccis can (a) help prospective customers understand the type and quality of their service, (b) ensure that customers get a high-quality service each time, and (c) provide the service to customers at an appropriate time and location.
3. Explain how Rebecca and Jacob can ensure they are providing quality service.
4. During the second summer, the DeNuccis' business became extremely successful, and more tours were requested than they could personally lead. Now they are considering hiring other teenagers who also vacation on the island to lead the tours. What recommendations would you make concerning the qualifications and training of the new employees?
5. Describe what the DeNuccis can include in their advertising to convince potential customers that they are offering a quality experience.

MY BUSINESS, INC.

NEW PRODUCT PLANNING

Two important elements of product planning for a new retail business are (1) gathering information from potential customers about their attitudes toward the product, and (2) scheduling the activities to be completed in organizing the business. You will complete those two activities in this section of the project.

DATA COLLECTION

1. Identify five people who represent potential customers for your business. They are your consumer panel, so select people who represent different ages, income levels, occupations, and interests. If possible, meet with them as a group. If that is not possible, then meet with them individually. During the meeting, describe your business idea and provide them with a survey that asks for their reactions. Have them recommend what they would like to see in the products, prices, and location. They might also recommend some effective ways to promote the business. After you have met with the panel, write a report that summarizes its recommendations.
2. Identify and complete a detailed analysis of as many different juice drinks and related products as you can find in the town or city in which you live. For those that seem to be most popular, try to identify what product features (including factors such as the package) make them successful. Also identify any product features that you believe should be improved. Prepare a survey questionnaire to test your analysis of the product features. Your goal is to find out what features your customers really want. Ask at least 10 people (who are not classmates) to complete your survey.

ANALYSIS

1. Prepare a written analysis of the recommendations you collected from your consumer panel. Select the recommendations that you would implement and give your reasons.
2. Prepare a written analysis of the data you collected from your product survey. Summarize your conclusions about what product features your customers want.
3. Search the Internet to find a list of the recommended steps for opening a new business. Then develop a schedule that lists the activities in the order you would complete them for your business. Prepare a timetable for the completion of each activity, making certain you allow enough time for each one. Project the date you will be able to open your business.
4. Because your juice business relies on effective service, prepare a list of services you will provide to customers. Then prepare a step-by-step procedure for each service to ensure high-quality delivery each time.

Nature and Scope of Marketing

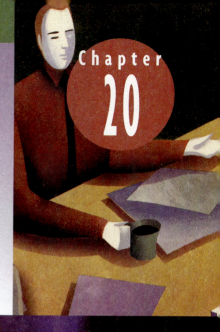

REALITY CHECK

The Supply-vs.-Demand Dilemma

Tony Taylor looked back on the previous week with amazement. He remembered that on Monday he sat through his economics class learning about the concept of supply and demand. As he listened, he thought, "This doesn't apply to me. At most, it might affect some very large businesses. I wonder why we're studying it." But what a week!

He and three friends had wanted to see a certain movie for several weeks but could not find a time when they could all go together. Finally, everyone was available after school on Tuesday to catch the 4:00 matinee. Tony rushed out of school and down to the bank to withdraw some money for the movie and snacks. When he entered the bank, he encountered a long line of customers waiting for the bank tellers. A computer problem had shut down all the ATMs, so everyone had to do their banking in person.

By the time Tony got his cash, he was already late for the movie. As he dashed up to the theater, he saw his friends standing outside. Attendance for the movie they wanted to see had recently fallen off, so the theater was no longer showing that movie.

Then, on Wednesday, Tony heard that his favorite music group would be performing locally and tickets would go on sale this weekend. Promoters announced that due to the expected high demand for tickets, a $15 surcharge was being added to the price of each ticket. Tony thought the tickets were already expensive and didn't see why he should have to pay more when several other, less popular groups had played with no surcharge added.

But today had been the most frustrating day. Tony's parents owned a small landscaping business, and Tony always helped them find high school students to work during the summer. He had never had problems getting enough applicants for the available jobs. However, few people he talked with today were interested. They told him that because the unemployment rate was so low, many jobs were available that paid more and were not as hard work as landscaping. Now Tony thought back through his week's experiences and remembered Monday's economics discussion. "Maybe supply and demand affect my life more than I realize," he reflected.

20.1 Nature of Marketing

Goals

- Discuss the importance of marketing and its role in the economy.
- Describe the factors that are part of the nature of marketing.

Terms

- retailers
- wholesalers
- buying
- selling
- transporting
- storing
- financing
- researching
- risk taking
- grading and valuing
- production oriented
- sales oriented
- customer oriented
- marketing concept

Importance Of Marketing

In our private-enterprise economy, it is not always easy to match production and consumption. Individual businesspeople make decisions about what they will produce, and individual consumers make decisions about what they want to purchase. For the economy to work well, producers and consumers need information to help them make their decisions, so that producers can provide the types and amounts of products and services that consumers are willing and able to buy. Marketing activities, when performed well, help to match production and consumption. As you learned in an earlier chapter, *marketing* is a set of activities that gets products from producers to consumers. From that very basic definition, you may think that marketing is simply transporting products. However, it is much more than that. It includes packaging, developing brand names, and determining prices. Marketing even involves financing and storing products until customers purchase them. Also, most products require some type of promotion. Marketing is involved in all of these activities and many more.

A more detailed definition will provide a better description of modern marketing. The American Marketing Association defines *marketing* as an organizational function and a set of processes for creating, communicating, and delivering value to customers and for managing customer relationships in ways that benefit the organization and its stakeholders. Because marketing is the key tool in matching supply and demand, it can be viewed in another way as well. If marketing is successful, businesses can sell their products and services and consumers can purchase the things they want. Therefore, the goal of effective marketing is to create and maintain satisfying exchange relationships between buyers and sellers.

Every consumer comes into daily contact with marketing in one form or another. Whenever you see an advertisement on television or on the Internet, notice a truck being unloaded at a warehouse, or use a credit card to purchase a product, you are seeing marketing at work. Each retail store location, each form of advertising, each salesperson, and even each package in which a product is sold is a part of marketing. A great deal of business activity centers on marketing.

Millions of businesses worldwide engage in marketing as their primary business activity. Those organizations include **retailers**—businesses that sell directly to final consumers—and **wholesalers**—businesses that buy products from businesses and sell them to other businesses. The thousands of businesses that sell services, rather than products, are also included. In addition, advertising agencies provide promotional services, finance companies offer loans and other financial services, and transportation companies handle and move products. All of these types of business as well as many others that support the marketing efforts of other businesses are directly involved in marketing.

Many manufacturers have marketing departments with employees who do marketing tasks. For example, marketing department employees do market research, design products, and sell the products. Other types of marketing jobs involve advertising and sales promotion, customer service, credit, and insurance. The many jobs range from clerk to vice president in charge of all marketing activities. Well over one-third of all people employed in the United States work in a marketing job or a marketing business.

It is estimated that the average consumer sees about 1 million marketing messages a year—about 3,000 a day. One trip to the supermarket alone can expose you to more than 10,000 marketing messages.

CHECKPOINT

List the three primary business organizations that engage in marketing.

Nature of Marketing

When many people think of marketing, they think only of advertising and selling. However, many marketing activities must occur before a product can be advertised and sold. To better understand marketing, we will examine the major marketing activities, the cost of marketing activities, and the role of marketing in business.

MARKETING ACTIVITIES

The following are the most common marketing activities:

- **Buying** Obtaining a product to be resold; involves finding suppliers that can provide the right products in the right quality and quantity at a fair price.
- **Selling** Providing personalized and persuasive information to customers to help them buy the products and services they need.
- **Transporting** Moving products from where they were made to where consumers can buy them.
- **Storing** Holding products until customers need them, such as on shelves, in storage rooms, or in warehouses.
- **Financing** Providing money to pay for the various marketing activities, such as by obtaining credit when buying and extending credit when selling.
- **Researching** Studying buyer interests and needs, testing products, and gathering facts needed to make good marketing decisions.
- **Risk taking** Assuming the risk of losses that may occur from fire, theft, damage, or other circumstances.
- **Grading and valuing** Grouping goods according to size, quality, or other characteristics, and determining an appropriate price for products and services.

COST OF MARKETING

Whether the product is paper clips for offices or huge generators for utility companies, businesses must perform all eight marketing activities just described

Storing is a common marketing activity. What are some others?

as the product moves from producer to customer. Because performing these activities requires many people and special equipment, the cost of marketing a product is sometimes higher than the cost of making that product. Therefore, perhaps half or more of the price you pay for a product may result from marketing expenses. Although this amount may appear high, the well-spent marketing dollar contributes much to the success of products and businesses as well as to the satisfaction of customers. Good marketing makes the product or service available to customers when and where they want it.

ROLE OF MARKETING

Marketing's role changes as environmental conditions change. Marketing has not always been an important part of business. In the early 1900s, business conditions were much different than they are now. Customers had only a few products to choose from and a limited amount of money to spend. Usually only a few producers manufactured a product, and the manufacturing process was not very efficient. Demand for most products was greater than the supply. As a result, most producers concentrated on making more kinds of products in greater quantities. Under these conditions, firms were **production oriented**—that is, decisions about what and how to produce received the most attention. Businesses did not have to worry a great deal about marketing.

When production becomes efficient and more businesses offer similar products, competition among businesses increases. Each business has to work harder to sell its products to customers when customers see they have many choices. Companies must emphasize distribution to get their products to more customers. In addition, advertising and selling become important marketing tools as businesses try to convince customers that their products are the best. Production may be considered the most important activity, but it is not enough for a business to be successful. Under these conditions, businesses may become **sales oriented**; that is, they emphasize widespread distribution and promotion to sell their products.

In many product categories today, consumers realize they can choose from a wide range of goods and services. Many businesses are competing with each other to sell the same product. But companies realize that it is not enough just to produce a variety of products; they must produce the *right* products. Companies that produce what customers want and make buying easy for customers will be more successful than those that do not.

Today, more and more businesses are focusing on customer needs. They have become **customer oriented**—they direct the activities of the company toward satisfying customers. Keeping the needs of the consumer uppermost in mind during the design, production, and distribution of a product is called the **marketing concept**.

A company that has adopted the marketing concept has a marketing manager who is part of top management and is involved in all major decisions, as illustrated in Figure 20-1. Marketing personnel work closely with the other people in the business to make sure the company keeps the needs of customers in mind in all operations. The company's success is determined by more than current profits. Profit is important, but long-term success depends on satisfying customers so that they will continue to buy from the company.

FIGURE 20-1 When a company is customer oriented, the marketing manager is part of top management.

PRESIDENT

OPERATIONS MANAGER

MARKETING MANAGER

FINANCE MANAGER

CHECKPOINT

List the eight most common marketing activities.

20.1 Assessment

UNDERSTAND MANAGEMENT CONCEPTS

Circle the best answer for each of the following questions.

1. Marketing department employees do which of the following?
   a. market research
   b. product design
   c. product sales
   d. all of the above

2. A business that focuses on widespread distribution and promotion is
   a. production oriented
   b. sales oriented
   c. customer oriented
   d. market oriented

THINK CRITICALLY

Answer the following questions as completely as possible.

3. Explain why marketing is an important activity in an economy.

4. Explain why the costs of marketing a product are justified.

Xtra!
Study Tools
thomsonedu.com/school/bpmxtra

20.2 Elements of Marketing

Goals

- Describe the role that market determination plays in marketing.
- Define basic marketing concepts and the four elements of the marketing mix.

Terms

- market
- market research
- target markets
- marketing mix
- product
- price
- distribution (place)
- promotion

Market Determination

Before a company decides to make and distribute a product, it must determine the market it wants to serve. Here, market refers to the types of buyers a business wishes to attract and where those buyers are located. All companies need to clearly identify their markets.

WHOM TO SERVE

There are many potential customers for a product. Some people may be searching for the product, whereas others do not currently want the product and will have to be convinced to buy it. Some people are very easy to reach, but others are more difficult. For cost reasons, it is usually unwise to try to reach all potential customers. Therefore, a business identifies several groups of potential customers and then decides which group or groups will be the best markets for its product.

Marketers often develop customer profiles based on population characteristics, such as age, gender, family status, education, income, and occupation, in which to group consumers. A clothing manufacturer, for example, could handle women's or men's clothing, clothing for children or adults, casual clothing or the latest high fashion, and so on. The producer of cellular telephones may want to attract families, people concerned about their safety, or businesspeople. A business can decide to serve one or more markets. Companies choose a market based on the opportunities for success that the market presents. For example, an attractive market may have few existing competitors, a large number of customers with a need for the product, and customers with sufficient money to spend on such a product. If the business has the ability to produce a product that will satisfy the needs of that market, then it is a good market for the business to serve.

WHERE TO SERVE

Producers often limit the scope of their business operations to certain geographic areas. Marketing managers study sections of a city, state, country, or continent to determine whether their product might sell more successfully in one area than another. Climate, for example, may cause a small producer of air conditioners to concentrate its marketing efforts on countries with hot and humid climates, whereas the maker of snow skis may concentrate on areas with cold winters and mountains. Some products may sell better on the coasts than in the middle of the country, or in rural areas better than in cities. Finding the best marketing locations enables a business to achieve the most sales for its marketing dollar.

IDENTIFYING TARGET MARKETS

Companies can produce goods and services that meet consumers' needs better if they know who their customers are, where they are located, and what they want and need. Many companies spend a great deal of money on market research before they begin to develop products. Market research is the study of a company's current and prospective customers.

Companies use market research to identify their target markets. Target markets are groups of customers with very similar needs to whom the company plans to sell its product. If the company can find a group of people with very similar needs, it can more easily produce a product that will satisfy everyone in the group. On the other hand, if people in the group have needs that are quite different, it will be almost impossible to develop a product that will satisfy each of them.

Imagine developing a product like a bicycle. It can be made in a variety of sizes and shapes with a number of special features. No one bicycle will satisfy everyone's needs. Long-distance racers want something very different from what the weekend rider desires. However, if you could find a group of people with very similar needs, you could successfully design a bicycle for that group. If you identified the groups depicted in Figure 20-2, each with unique needs for your product, your bicycle company could choose to design a slightly different product for each group.

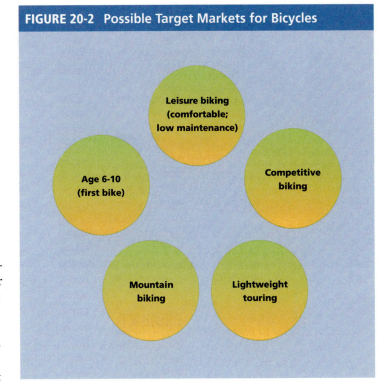

FIGURE 20-2 Possible Target Markets for Bicycles

- Leisure biking (comfortable; low maintenance)
- Competitive biking
- Age 6-10 (first bike)
- Mountain biking
- Lightweight touring

CHECKPOINT

List six customer profile characteristics that can be used to identify markets.

The Marketing Mix

Marketing managers have many decisions to make. These decisions center on four elements of marketing: (1) the *product*, (2) its *price*, (3) *distribution* (sometimes referred to as *place*), and (4) *promotion*. Planning each element involves answering some important questions. For example, assume that you want to market a new product. You must answer the following questions related to the four elements of marketing: (1) Will you make the product in one size and color, or in several? (2) Will you price the product high, medium, or low? (3) Will you sell the product in retail stores or over the Internet? (4) Will you use newspaper, radio, television, or Internet advertising?

The blend of all decisions related to the four elements of marketing—product, price, distribution, and promotion—is called the marketing mix. The marketing mix for a new product may be to design the item for young adults, give it a low

price, sell it through retail stores, and advertise it on the radio. Or it could be to produce a medium-priced item to be advertised on television and sold door-to-door to senior citizens. Can you identify the marketing mix for one of the businesses that Tony Taylor thought about in the chapter-opening scenario?

Several companies marketing the same product may use very different marketing mixes, because they made different decisions. Furthermore, they must review their decisions frequently, because conditions change constantly. Changes in general economic conditions, changes in consumer needs, and the development of new or improved products by competitors are factors that may require a change in the marketing mix. Next, you will learn about the decisions involved in each marketing mix element.

Coffeehouses are a popular place for people to meet and socialize. Which elements of the marketing mix should a new competitor focus on to attract customers?

PRODUCT

The first marketing mix element is the product. **Product** can be defined as all attributes, both tangible and intangible, that customers receive in exchange for the purchase price. For example, when consumers buy a computer, they are also buying the company's customer service and technical support as well as other intangibles, such as the prestige of the brand name. All of these attributes are part of the product. Products include services as well as physical goods. A critical question relating to the product is: What do customers want? Product planning and development deal with finding answers to that question.

By identifying the target market for a product and knowing what customers in that market want, the company can design a product to fit those customers. Market information can help marketers develop a product strategy that includes decisions such as:

1. The *number* of items to produce.
2. The *physical features* the product should possess, such as size, shape, color, and weight.
3. The *quality* preferred by the target market.
4. The *number of different models* and the *features* of each model needed to serve the various markets the company wants to attract.
5. The *packaging features* of the item, such as the color and the shape of the package, as well as the information printed on it.
6. The *brand name*.
7. Product *guarantees* and *services* the customers would like.
8. The *image* to be communicated to customers by the product's features, packaging, and brand name.

PRICE

The second mix element around which marketing decisions are made is price. **Price** is the amount of money given to acquire a product. The many decisions a company makes during product development influence the price. First, the price must be high enough to cover the costs of producing and marketing the product. If the company decides to manufacture a high-quality product, it would likely have to set a higher price to cover its costs than it would for a low-quality product.

Ethics *tip*

Marketing may have one of the worst ethical reputations in business, often because marketing is seen as pushing products on people who may not need them, promoting products with half-truths, and pricing products unfairly. Today marketers concerned about maintaining long-term relationships must act ethically.

The number of competing products and their prices, the demand for the product, and whether the product will be sold for cash or credit are some of the many other factors that influence price decisions.

When making price decisions, a company must do more than just set a price that customers will pay for the product. It must decide what price to charge other companies that buy and resell the product. Will the company offer coupons, discounts, or other promotional bonuses to attract customers? Will it allow customers to bargain for a lower price or trade in a used product for a new one? As you can see, pricing is not an easy marketing decision.

DISTRIBUTION

The third element around which marketing decisions are made is distribution. Distribution decisions relate to the economic concept of *place utility*, which you studied in Chapter 3. *Place utility* means that the product must be in a place where customers need or want it. Distribution (or place), therefore, is the set of activities required to transport and store products and make them available to customers.

Marketing managers must select businesses to handle products as they move from the producer to the consumer. Many manufacturers prefer to use other businesses to sell their products rather than try to reach consumers directly. Therefore, they may sell their products to retailers or to wholesalers, which then sell to retailers. Choosing the various routes that products will follow as they are distributed and the businesses that will sell them to consumers are important marketing decisions.

Planning distribution also includes the actual physical handling of the products and the customer service provided when orders are processed. Have you ever opened a product you purchased, only to find it damaged or missing pieces? Have you ordered something from a catalog or the Internet and received the wrong merchandise or no merchandise at all? Each of these examples describes a problem with a company's distribution system and will result in dissatisfied customers as well as a loss of sales and profits for the company.

PROMOTION

The fourth marketing mix element for which decisions must be made is promotion. Promotion means providing information to consumers that will assist them in making a decision and persuade them to purchase a product or service. The major methods of promotion are advertising and personal selling. You will learn about other types of promotion in a later chapter.

Promotional decisions for a digital camera might involve selecting advertising as the main vehicle and deciding whether to advertise in magazines or by direct mail to prospective customers. Marketing managers decide when and how frequently to advertise. Then they must decide whether to stage product demonstrations in stores or at consumer electronics shows. Managers must also decide the type of information to communicate to consumers and whether to try to communicate directly with each customer or use more impersonal messages that can reach a larger audience at a time.

business *note*

Consumers see a relationship between product benefits and the product price. This is called value. There is a mathematical formula for this relationship: Product Benefits/Price = Value. A product is seen as having greater value if it offers more benefits for the same price or the same benefits at a lower price. One product may have more features or a better brand image but a higher price. Another product may be cheaper but have fewer benefits. Marketers often try to persuade consumers that a product has many benefits, justifying a higher price. Often those benefits are intangible, such as high social value or status. Consumers may be willing to pay a higher price to be "cool."

The type of product and its price influence promotional decisions. The strategy for promoting an expensive piece of jewelry will be much different from that for promoting tennis shoes.

Although the product and its price provide general guides for promotion, marketing managers must consider many other factors before developing the actual promotions. For example, the company will budget only a certain amount of money for promotion. Managers must decide when to spend the money and how much to spend on advertising, displays, and other types of promotion. They must consider what promotions competitors are using and what information consumers need in order to decide to buy.

CHECKPOINT
List the elements of a marketing mix.

20.2 Assessment

UNDERSTAND MANAGEMENT CONCEPTS

Circle the best answer for each of the following questions.

1. Groups of customers with very similar needs to whom the company plans to sell its product are called the
   a. target customers
   b. target consumers
   c. target market
   d. target groups

2. The four elements of the marketing mix include all of the following except
   a. product
   b. price
   c. customer
   d. promotion

THINK CRITICALLY

Answer the following questions as completely as possible.

3. Explain how companies identify their markets.

4. Describe what a customer receives in exchange for a purchase price.

20.3 Marketing Plan

Goals
- Explain the four stages of the product life cycle.
- Identify the consumer goods classifications.

Terms
- marketing plan
- product life cycle
- introduction stage
- growth stage
- maturity stage
- decline stage
- industrial goods
- consumer goods
- convenience goods
- shopping goods
- specialty goods
- unsought goods

All the marketing decisions for a particular product must work together for the product to succeed. For example, advertising may be timed to coincide with a product's introduction. To help coordinate marketing activities, businesses develop marketing plans. The **marketing plan** is a detailed written description of all marketing activities that a business must accomplish in order to sell its products. It describes the goals the business wants to accomplish, the target markets it wants to serve, the marketing mixes it will use for each product, and the tactics that make up the marketing strategy. It identifies the ways in which the business will evaluate its marketing to determine if the activities were successful and the goals were accomplished. The marketing plan is written for a specific time period (often one year).

The top marketing executive develops the marketing plan, based on information from many other people. Market research is very important in developing a marketing plan. Once a written plan is completed, all of the people involved in marketing activities can use it to guide their decisions about each marketing mix element and to coordinate their efforts as they complete the planned activities.

The marketing plan is influenced by a product's life cycle stage and the nature of the competition. These factors influence the development of a marketing mix.

The Product Life Cycle

Successful products move through fairly predictable stages throughout their product lives. They are introduced, and then their sales and profits increase rapidly to a point at which they level off. Eventually, both profits and sales decline as newer products replace the old ones. The **product life cycle** consists of the four stages of sales and profit performance through which all brands of a product progress: introduction, growth, maturity, and decline. The product life cycle usually describes an industry's progression. Figure 20-3 (see p. 548) is a graphical depiction of sales and profits at different stages of the product life cycle.

INTRODUCTION

In the **introduction stage**, a brand-new product enters the market. Initially, there is only one brand of the product available for consumers to purchase. The new product is quite different from, and expected to be better than, products customers are currently using. Examples of products that were recently in

FIGURE 20-3 Sales and profits follow a predictable pattern as products progress through each stage of the product life cycle.

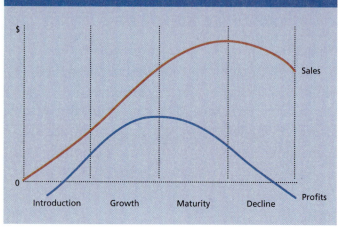

the introduction stage include Web-ready cellular telephones, high-definition television (HDTV), and portable audio players that can download digital music files from the Internet.

When a company introduces a product, it is concerned about successfully producing and distributing it. The company needs to inform prospective customers about the brand-new product and its uses, because people will be unfamiliar with it. There is no competition from the same type of product, but customers are probably using other, older products. The company must show customers how the new product is better than the products they are currently using. Initially, only a few customers will buy the product, but their experience will often determine whether other people will want to buy it as well.

The costs of producing and marketing a new product are usually very high, resulting in a loss or very low profits for the firm initially. The company is counting on future sales to make a profit. If a product is successfully introduced, an increasing number of consumers will accept it, sales will rise rapidly, and profits will grow.

GROWTH

When competitors see the success of the new product, they will want to get into that market as well. When several brands of the new product are available, the market moves into the **growth stage** of the life cycle. If customers like the new product, they will begin buying it regularly and telling others about it, so more and more customers become regular purchasers.

In the growth stage, each company tries to attract customers to its own brand. Companies attempt to improve their brands by adding features that they hope will satisfy customers. They also add to their distribution to make the product more readily available to the growing market. Most companies make a profit in this stage. Profits are likely to increase as companies sell enough of the product to cover the research and development costs. Examples of products that have been in the growth stage recently are digital video cameras, personal digital assistants (PDAs), and wireless computers.

How might a fast-food company respond to the maturity stage of the product life cycle?

PHOTO: © GETTY IMAGES/PHOTODISC.

MATURITY

A product in the maturity stage has been purchased by large numbers of customers and has become quite profitable. In the **maturity stage**, the product is competing with many other brands with very similar features. Customers have a hard time identifying differences among the brands but may have developed a loyalty to one or a very few brands.

In this stage, companies emphasize the promotion of their brand name, packaging, a specific image, and often the price of the product. Because there are so many customers, each business has to distribute the product widely, adding to their costs. Competition becomes intense. Companies must spend a lot on promotion and reduce prices, because customers have many brands from which to choose. Profits usually fall even though sales may still rise. Products in the maturity stage include automobiles, desktop computers, personal-care products such as toothpaste and deodorant, and many other products that you use regularly and purchase without a great deal of thought.

One way that businesses respond to the maturity stage of the life cycle is to look for new markets. Businesses often move into international markets as competition increases in their home countries. As several fast-food companies found fewer and fewer attractive locations for new stores in the United States, they began to open outlets in Canada, Europe, and Mexico. Now they are expanding into South America and even into Russia and China.

DECLINE

Many products stay in the maturity stage of the life cycle for a long time. However, sooner or later products move into a decline stage. The decline stage occurs when a new product is introduced that is much better or easier to use and customers begin to switch from the old product to the new product. As more and more customers are attracted to the new product, the companies selling the old product see declines in profits and sales. The companies may not be able to improve the older products enough to compete with the new products, so they drop them from the market when declining profits no longer support their existence.

Some companies have been able to move old products out of the decline stage by finding new uses for them. For example, petroleum vapor rubs are being used for fungus infections, and baking soda is used to remove odors from refrigerators and cat litter boxes. If companies cannot save a product from the decline stage, they attempt to sell their remaining inventory to the customers who still prefer it. However, they spend as little money as possible on marketing the product and do not produce any more.

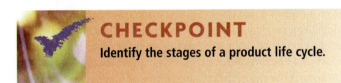

CHECKPOINT
Identify the stages of a product life cycle.

Product Categories

When making marketing decisions, marketers need to understand how customers shop for and use products. Products can be classified as either industrial goods or consumer goods. Industrial goods are products designed for use by another business. Frequently, industrial goods are purchased in large quantities, are made to special order for a specific customer, or are sold to a selected group of buyers within a limited geographic area. Examples of industrial goods include bricks purchased by a building contractor, aluminum purchased by an aircraft manufacturer, and computers and computer supplies purchased by accounting firms. Many, but not all, industrial goods are used to produce other products or are incorporated into the products being produced. Some are used in the operation of the business.

Consumer goods are products designed for personal or home use. Jewelry, furniture, magazines, soft drinks, and computer games are some of the many products used by consumers. Consumer goods require careful marketing attention, because there are so many products and brands available and so many possible customers throughout the world.

Technology tip

The Internet is changing the way individuals shop for specialty goods. The Internet allows a person to shop at many stores in a very short period of time. Even luxury items such as diamonds are sold online. Individuals can check many sites, compare prices, and buy as if a luxury specialty item were a more common consumer good.

PHOTO: © DIGITAL VISION.

How are specialty goods different from other types of goods?

Depending on who is making the purchase and how they will use it, a product may be both a consumer good and an industrial good. Gasoline and laptop computers, for instance, may be purchased by consumers in small quantities or by businesses in large quantities.

TYPES OF CONSUMER PRODUCTS

To look at the attributes of consumer goods more specifically, marketers group them into four categories: convenience goods, shopping goods, specialty goods, and unsought goods. The categories are based on (1) how important the product is to the customer and (2) whether the customer is willing to spend time to compare products and brands before making a decision to buy. Companies make different marketing decisions, depending on which category of consumer goods they are selling.

CONVENIENCE GOODS Convenience goods are inexpensive items that consumers purchase regularly without a great deal of thought. Consumers are not willing to shop around for these products because they purchase them often, the many competing products do not differ much from each other, and they don't cost much money. Therefore, marketers must sell their convenience goods through many retail outlets that are conveniently located close to where people work and live. Products that are usually treated as convenience goods are candy, milk, soft drinks, pencils, soap, and many other inexpensive household items.

SHOPPING GOODS Products that consumers purchase less frequently than convenience goods, usually have a higher price, and require some buying thought are called shopping goods. Customers see important differences between brands in terms of price and features. Therefore, they are willing to shop at several businesses and compare products and brands before they make a purchase. Shopping goods do not have to be sold in as many places as convenience goods. They need effective promotion so customers can make informed decisions. Cars, furniture, large appliances, and houses are all examples of shopping goods for most people.

SPECIALTY GOODS Specialty goods are products that customers insist on having and are willing to search for until they find them. Customers who decide that only one product or brand will satisfy them will shop until they locate and buy that brand. Marketers place their specialty goods in fewer businesses within a shopping area, price them higher than competing products and brands, and need not promote them as much as other types of consumer products. Examples of specialty goods are designer clothing, expensive jewelry, and certain brands of cameras, computers, and automobiles.

UNSOUGHT GOODS Customers do not shop for some products because they do not have a strong need for them. Such products are known as unsought goods, and they present a difficult marketing problem. Life insurance, cemetery plots, and funeral services are unsought by most consumers. A company marketing unsought goods usually has to go to the customer and use personal selling to discuss the need for the product. Unless the customer recognizes a need that the product can satisfy, the product will remain unsold.

facts & figures

Marketing to children continues to be a controversial issue. The Federal Trade Commission's Children's Online Privacy Protection Act requires publishers of children's Web sites to post comprehensive privacy policies on their sites. In addition, the sites must notify parents about their information practices and obtain parental consent before collecting any personal information from children under age 13.

SUCCESSFUL MARKETING STRATEGIES

Marketing managers cannot afford to guess about which types of marketing mixes to use. Marketing is too expensive and customers have too many choices for businesses to risk making mistakes. Marketers use concepts such as the product life cycle and consumer goods categories to plan effective marketing mixes. For example, if a product is in the growth stage, the mix will be quite different than if it is in the maturity stage. If consumers view a product as a specialty good, marketers will emphasize different mix elements than if it is a convenience good. Marketers study markets and competition and use their knowledge of marketing to make decisions that will satisfy customer needs and result in a profit for the company.

Many consumer complaints today involve marketing activities. Misleading advertisements, poor customer service, high prices, and poor delivery are all marketing problems. Businesses must be as careful in making marketing decisions as they need to be in producing a quality product. In the next two chapters, we will examine each part of the marketing mix in more detail. You will learn how businesses plan products and use marketing activities to satisfy customers and attract them away from competing businesses.

CHECKPOINT

List the four different categories of consumer goods.

20.3   Assessment

UNDERSTAND MANAGEMENT CONCEPTS

Circle the best answer for each of the following questions.

1. The product life cycle stage in which there is only one brand of a product available for consumers to purchase is the
   a. introduction stage
   b. growth stage
   c. maturity stage
   d. decline stage

2. Products that customers insist on having and are willing to search for until they find them are called
   a. convenience goods
   b. shopping goods
   c. specialty goods
   d. unsought goods

THINK CRITICALLY

Answer the following questions as completely as possible.

3. Explain why a product's life cycle stage influences marketing strategy.

4. Describe the factors that influence consumer goods classification.

Xtra!
Study Tools
thomsonedu.com/school/bpmxtra

Focus On...

Retail Strategy–Retailers that Changed Business

Most manufacturers of consumer goods rely on retailers to provide the connection with the customers who will purchase their products. The retailers purchase the products from the manufacturer, stock them in stores that are close to where customers live, advertise and sell the products, and often offer delivery of the products and many customer services. Retailers provide these important marketing functions for manufacturers.

A few retailers have changed the way business is done. Because of their ideas, they forced their competitors to respond or risk going out of business.

One of the first was Sears Roebuck. In the late 1800s and early 1900s, some of the largest retailers reached their customers by mail. They sent catalogs to people all over the country and filled customer orders by mail or by shipping in trucks and trains. Sears decided customers wanted faster service and the opportunity to examine merchandise before making a purchase. The company began building large stores filled with a wide variety of products. Customers flocked to the stores, and Sears became the largest retailer in the world.

Sears stores were located in large and mid-size cities. Sam Walton saw opportunities in the thousands of small communities around the country. Wal-Mart grew because of its emphasis on carefully chosen locations, working with manufacturers to buy at the lowest prices, developing an efficient product distribution system, and creating a friendly shopping experience. Because of those efforts, Wal-Mart could offer lower prices than most other retailers. With this new philosophy of retailing, Wal-Mart replaced Sears as the world's largest retailer.

Today, a new form of retailing is developing, led by Jeff Bezos. Mr. Bezos recognized the potential of Internet commerce. By developing an easy-to-use Web site and offering customers secure online transactions, rapid product delivery, and effective customer service, Amazon.com developed into the largest e-retailer, with revenues approaching $1 billion.

In each example, the success of the companies resulted from finding new ways to offer products and services to consumers. By performing marketing activities more effectively than its competitors, each company has become a leading retailer.

Think Critically

1. Why were major retailers using catalogs and mail order in the late 1800s and early 1900s to sell products to their customers? What changes were occurring in the United States that provided the opportunity for Sears Roebuck to change the way products were sold?
2. Review the eight marketing activities described in the chapter and suggest which of the activities were most important to the success of Wal-Mart. Why were many of Wal-Mart's competitors not able to offer the same low prices to customers?
3. Do you believe that an e-retailer like Amazon.com will ever replace Wal-Mart as the world's largest retailer? Why or why not?

CHAPTER CONCEPTS

- Marketing helps to balance the supply of products with the demand for those products. The goal of effective marketing is to create and maintain satisfying exchanges between buyers and sellers. Every business is involved in marketing. It is the primary activity of retailers and wholesalers.

- Marketing involves eight activities: buying, selling, transporting, storing, financing, researching, risk taking, and grading and valuing.

- A business may be production oriented, sales oriented, or customer oriented. The marketing concept focuses on the needs of consumers during the design, production, and distribution of a product.

- Businesses use marketing research to identify target markets—customers with very similar needs that the business wants to serve.

- The four elements of the marketing mix are product, price, distribution, and promotion. Marketing decisions center on these four elements. A written marketing plan coordinates the many decisions and activities involved in marketing.

- The product life cycle consists of four stages: introduction, growth, maturity, and decline.

- Consumer goods can be classified as convenience, shopping, specialty, or unsought goods, based on their importance to consumers and how much time they are willing to spend making buying decisions.

REVIEW TERMS AND CONCEPTS

Write the letter of the term that matches each definition. Some terms will not be used.

1. Businesses that sell directly to final consumers
2. Keeping the needs of the consumer uppermost in mind during the design, production, and distribution of a product
3. Emphasizing widespread distribution and promotion to sell products
4. Types of buyers a business wishes to attract and where those buyers are located
5. The study of a company's current and prospective customers
6. Groups of customers with very similar needs to whom the company plans to sell its product
7. All attributes, both tangible and intangible, that customers receive in exchange for the purchase price
8. Detailed written description of all marketing activities that a business must accomplish to sell its products
9. Set of activities required to transport and store products and make them available to customers
10. Blend of all decisions related to the four elements of marketing—product, price, distribution, and promotion
11. Amount of money given to acquire a product
12. Product life cycle stage in which several brands of the new product are available

a. customer oriented
b. distribution (place)
c. growth stage
d. market
e. market research
f. marketing concept
g. marketing mix
h. marketing plan
i. maturity stage
j. price
k. product
l. retailers
m. sales oriented
n. target markets

DETERMINE THE BEST ANSWER

13. Businesses that buy products from businesses and sell them to other businesses are called
    a. industrial companies
    b. marketers' retailers
    c. wholesalers
    d. retailers

14. A _____ producer concentrates on making more kinds of products in greater quantities.
    a. production-oriented
    b. sales-oriented
    c. market-oriented
    d. product-oriented

15. The four stages of sales and profit performance through which a product progresses are called the
    a. product categories
    b. marketing mix
    c. product life cycle
    d. product evolutionary cycle

16. In the _____ stage, a brand-new product enters the market and there is only one brand of the product available for consumers to purchase.
    a. introduction
    b. growth
    c. maturity
    d. decline

17. In the _____ stage, there are many competing brands with very similar features and customers have a hard time identifying differences among the brands.
    a. introduction
    b. growth
    c. maturity
    d. decline

18. Inexpensive items that consumers purchase regularly without a great deal of thought are called
    a. convenience goods
    b. consumer goods
    c. shopping goods
    d. specialty goods

19. Providing money for various marketing activities, such as by obtaining credit when buying and extending credit when selling, is called
    a. granting credit
    b. setting price
    c. financing
    d. risk taking

APPLY WHAT YOU KNOW

20. Describe the ways that trucking companies, banks, and warehouses are marketing businesses.

21. Explain why it is important to conduct market research to determine the markets to be served before deciding what to produce and sell.

22. Describe how customers might know if a company has a customer orientation rather than a sales orientation.

23. What are some examples of goods or services that would sell well only in specific geographic locations?

24. Describe how the price is influenced by the other three elements of the marketing mix. What could a marketing manager do with other mix elements to increase or decrease a product's price?

MAKE CONNECTIONS

25. **Math** Complete the following table for the four products listed by determining the total cost of each product and the percentage of the final product price that was spent on marketing.

	Product 1	Product 2	Product 3	Product 4
Retail Price	$45.20	$576.00	$32,750.00	$4.80
Raw Materials	6.20	28.00	12,650.00	.78
Other Product Costs	3.80	56.50	2,500.00	.14
Operating Expenses	4.30	74.00	4,825.00	.32
Marketing Expenses	14.90	96.50	3,500.00	2.50

26. **Research** Interview 10 people to determine how they purchase jeans. Ask each of them the following questions: Where do you usually buy your jeans? What product features are important to you? How important is price in your decision to purchase jeans? Do you usually buy one brand? Do you usually look in several stores before you buy a pair of jeans?

    Based on each person's answers, determine whether he or she is treating jeans as a convenience, shopping, specialty, or unsought good. Write a short report discussing your findings and your conclusions. Include a chart or graph illustrating your findings.

27. **Speaking** Participate in a debate with other class members. Your teacher will assign you to one side of the issue or the other and will give you specific instructions and guidelines. The issue is: Marketing causes people to spend money for things they otherwise would not buy and do not need. Do you agree or disagree?

28. **Technology** Use the Internet to find examples that illustrate each of the four elements of the marketing mix—product, price, distribution, and promotion. Use presentation software such as PowerPoint to link to examples and to the concept of a marketing mix.

CASE IN POINT

CASE 20-1: Computer Life Cycle

The personal-computer market has become very competitive, and it is more and more difficult for computer manufacturers to make a profit. Technology changes rapidly, so if a company has not sold its inventory of one model when a competitor introduces a newer, faster, more powerful model, it often has to sell its older model at a loss. Many computer purchasers are not brand-loyal and either look for a lower price or expect the manufacturer to include related products, such as a monitor, printer, scanner, or several types of software with the new computer.

Online computer sellers have created considerable competition for traditional store outlets. Many consumers today do not feel they need much technical help with computers. Businesses are also buying online because they can configure computers to meet their needs.

Newer computer products are entering the market. These include wireless portable computers and personal digital assistants. Even cellular telephones are gaining computer functionality.

One computer manufacturer began a new marketing program that offered customers a free computer. The computer was not the manufacturer's latest model, however. The offer also did not include a large monitor or additional equipment or software. Instead, the manufacturer required the customer to sign a contract to use the manufacturer's Internet service for at least three years, at a cost of $24.95 a month. Typically, consumers could buy the same service for as little as $14.95 a month from other companies.

THINK CRITICALLY

1. Which stage of the product life cycle do you believe computers are in, based on the case information? Why?
2. Explain how this stage affects the price of computers.
3. Are computers industrial or consumer products? Explain your answer.
4. In which consumer product category do you believe consumers classify computers, based on the case information? Why?
5. How does your product category choice in question #4 fit with companies' ability to sell computers on the Internet? Explain your answer.
6. Describe the target market that you believe might be attracted to the manufacturer's offer of a free computer.
7. Explain why a consumer may or may not find the Internet/computer package an appealing offer.
8. What are the advantages and disadvantages of offering consumers a computer that is not the company's latest model?

CASE 20-2: Appliance Marketing Mix

The Willomette Company manufactures small household appliances, such as toasters, blenders, and food processors. Ron Willomette started the company 20 years ago as a sole proprietorship. Initially, Mr. Willomette reconditioned and resold used appliances that other companies had manufactured. Now he has incorporated the business and has two manufacturing plants that produce his own brand of appliances. The Willomette Company has a full line of over 50 models of products that are sold throughout the United States.

Willomette appliances are higher priced than many other national brands and imported products. They are usually sold through smaller non-chain-store outlets. Willomette usually advertises in kitchen design magazines and other media that cater to higher-income consumers.

In the past five years, competition from foreign companies in the small-appliance market has increased. The competition hasn't hurt Willomette yet, but company executives don't want to wait until sales and profits start to decline before acting. One vice president recommended that Willomette begin a program of international marketing. Based on the traveling she has done, she believes that the demand for Willomette's appliances would be very strong in Europe and several countries in Africa and South America. Because there has been strong customer acceptance of the company's products in the United States, she believes Willomette should have no trouble selling the same products in other countries.

THINK CRITICALLY

1. Which stage of the product life cycle do you believe Willomette is in, based on the case information? Why?
2. In which consumer product category do you believe consumers would classify Willomette's products, based on the case information? Why?
3. Describe the elements of Willomette's marketing mix.
4. Describe the target market that you believe might be attracted to Willomette appliances.
5. Which of the major marketing activities would Willomette have to perform to sell its products in international markets?
6. How does the marketing concept relate to the decision Willomette must make about entering international markets?
7. Do you agree that products that are successful in the United States will also be successful in other countries? Explain.
8. What would Willomette have to do if it wanted to increase the demand for its products in the United States by selling industrial products?

MY BUSINESS, INC.

To market your products effectively, you will need to identify the target market for your business. Then you must determine how customers will view your product as they make decisions to buy. The activities in this section of the project will help you understand your customers so you can develop an effective marketing mix.

DATA COLLECTION

1. Locate books, newspaper and magazine articles, Web resources, and other information sources that describe people who are interested in healthy lifestyles and nutrition. Make a list of the sources of information that will help you describe possible target markets for your juice bar and provide brief descriptions of the information in each of the sources you list.
2. Review advertisements from other businesses that might compete with your juice bar. For each business, prepare a description of the target market it appears to be appealing to and the key part of its marketing mix that it is advertising.
3. Using library or Internet resources, locate several marketing-oriented magazines or trade journals that you could consult for information. Also identify some marketing-related professional organizations or trade associations that might be helpful to you.

ANALYSIS

1. Using the categories of consumer goods listed in the chapter, determine if customers will treat your product as a convenience, shopping, specialty, or unsought good. Describe how that decision will influence the way you market your products.
2. Markets are made up of many segments of people with one or more similar characteristics. Segments of a market can be identified that have one or more strong needs or wants in common. What market segment(s) can you identify for your product?
3. Develop a detailed customer profile of one or more target markets that you can serve successfully. Make sure that your profile description includes both an identification of the target market and the important needs of the market that are related to your product.
4. Develop a set of questions that you would use to collect information from your target market so that you can be market oriented in your marketing offerings.
5. Prepare a general description of the marketing mix you believe would satisfy the consumers in your target market. Develop a marketing plan that describes the goals your business should accomplish, the target market you want to serve, the marketing mix you will use, and the tactics that make up your marketing strategy.

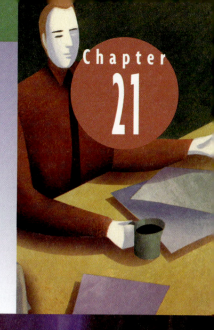

Product Development and Distribution

21.1 Product

21.2 Distribution

21.3 Channel Design

REALITY CHECK

Decisions, Decisions

Alexis Converse sat at her computer in the purchasing office late into the night. She was challenged by a crisis facing her company. A major piece of manufacturing equipment had failed today and could not be repaired. Each day that the equipment was not operational would cost the company several thousand dollars in lost production and sales.

The machine was over 10 years old, and it had worked well for most of the time the company owned it. In discussing its replacement with the production manager, Alexis agreed that they should replace the machine with the same brand. However, there were now two new models to consider. Alexis could purchase the equipment directly from the manufacturer in Italy or from an equipment distributor located two states away. It would take the manufacturer eight days to deliver, whereas the distributor could have one model available in two days and the other in four.

Alexis was concerned about installation and maintenance. She wanted to make sure the new machine would not break down. The manufacturer had a specialist who would travel to the plant to install the equipment and make sure it was working. The manufacturer also included a five-year warranty with onsite service, but the warranty added 25 percent to the cost of the equipment. Alexis had heard that the distributor could help with the installation but did not provide an additional warranty or service. Delays or problems in installation would only add to the company's losses.

All Alexis wanted to do was to get the equipment replaced and the company back into production. Why did these decisions have to be so difficult?

Product

Goals

- Explain how products, product lines, and product assortments are developed.
- Discuss how product selection, packaging, and branding improve product sales and customer satisfaction.

Terms

- basic product
- enhanced product
- extended product
- product line
- product assortment
- brand

You learned in Chapter 20 that companies develop a marketing mix to satisfy customers and make a profit. The marketing mix is made up of the product, distribution, price, and promotion plans. Offering products that meet the needs of customers would seem to be a company's most important responsibility. The product is important, but it must be carefully coordinated with each of the other mix elements. In this chapter, we will examine how companies plan products and make distribution decisions.

Product Development

As you learned in Chapter 20, a *product* consists of all attributes, both tangible and intangible, that customers receive in exchange for the purchase price. It includes both physical goods and services. Some products are very simple and easy for the customer to understand and use, and others are very complex. Because of the variety of customer needs, the uses for products, and the number of competing companies producing and selling products, product development decisions must be made carefully. If companies produce the wrong products in the wrong quantities without the features and services customers need, they will have invested a great deal of time and money with no chance to sell the products at a profit. They will quickly lose out to competitors who make better product decisions.

Businesspeople and consumers usually hold very different perceptions of a product. Businesspeople think of their products as what they have to offer to customers. Consumers, on the other hand, are more likely to think of products as ways to satisfy their needs. The company that manufactures the machine Alexis needed to purchase at the beginning of the chapter designed a product to perform a specific production function. The company is expert in the technology of equipment design, so it builds what it believes to be a good product that customers will prefer over the alternatives. Alexis wants a good piece of equipment but is also very concerned about delivery, installation services, maintenance, and cost. If the equipment manufacturer does not carefully consider all of Alexis's needs, it probably won't make the sale.

Even the simplest products are made up of several components. An inexpensive handheld calculator consists of the operating unit to make the calculations, a case, display, and keys. It may be battery operated or use solar power or electricity. It could have a backlight to illuminate the display in the dark. It could be pocket- or desk-sized and be capable of special mathematical functions. Also, it might come in a variety of colors and include a protective case and an instruction manual. Given the combination of features, the price of the calculator could range from a few dollars to as much as $50 or more. If you were the person responsible for designing a calculator to sell, what combination of design features would you include? This example shows that product planning can be very complex. Businesses have many choices in designing products. In developing their product strategy, marketers pay close attention to their customers' needs and wishes.

PHOTO: © GETTY IMAGES/PHOTODISC.

Why should a company make product development decisions very carefully?

PRODUCT DESIGN LEVELS

There are three levels of product design—a basic product, an enhanced product, and an extended product. The **basic product** is the physical product in its simplest form. It should be easy for consumers to understand and see how it can meet a need. The basic product of one company is usually similar to that of its competitors.

The basic product will meet an important consumer need. However, most consumers are attempting to satisfy several needs at one time with a purchase, or they have very specific needs different from those of other consumers. In that case, the basic product will not be satisfactory. Therefore, a business develops an **enhanced product**. An enhanced product offers different features and options for the consumer. For example, a basic computer can be produced in desktop or notebook form. It can have different screen and hard-drive sizes and offer DVD, an advanced speaker system, and many other features. If you visit the Web site of an online computer manufacturer, you can see the many options available to prospective purchasers. Choices are grouped by categories of customers, such as business, home office, education, and family, making it easier for customers to design the computer system they need.

The third level of product development is to plan extended products. An **extended product** includes additional features that are not part of the physical product but increase its usability. Examples are customer service, information on effective use of the products, and even additional products that improve the use of the original purchase. If you purchase a new digital video camera, you will need tapes to begin filming. In addition, a tripod may be helpful to make sure the video images are not shaky. Editing software, instructional videotapes, and even lens filters to create special effects may be useful to some but not all customers. The right combination of choices allows customers to get just the right product to meet very specialized needs.

Companies may offer a warranty (a statement from the seller about the product's qualities or performance) or a guarantee (an assurance from the seller that a product will perform to your satisfaction for a certain period of time). This can help reassure the customer about the product.

CHECKPOINT

List and define the three levels of product design.

Product Selection

After designing the product, companies must make another set of decisions to plan the product mix element. The first decision is whether to offer a product line. A **product line** is a group of similar products with obvious variations in the design and quality to meet the needs of distinct customer groups. New and small companies may begin by offering only one category of product to its customers. That product may have choices of features, options, and enhancements, but the basic product is the same for all customers. With more experience and resources, the company may decide to expand its product line.

One of the obvious ways to expand a product line is to offer different sizes of the product. That can be done with the serving sizes of food items, as well as with the sizes of automobiles. As an example, when sports utility vehicles (SUVs) were first introduced, most manufacturers produced one midsize model, such as the Chevy Blazer or Ford Explorer. As the popularity of SUVs grew, manufacturers began to appeal to other market segments with smaller models, such as the Toyota RAV4, and then very large models, including the Mercury Mountaineer and Cadillac Escalade. Rising gas prices opened a market for fuel-efficient SUVs, such as Honda's CR-V. Some companies offer only one model size, but others have a model in each size category for a full product line.

Another way to develop a product line is to offer variations in quality and price. If you visit an appliance store, you will usually find low-, mid-, and high-priced choices for each type of appliance, such as refrigerators, dishwashers, and microwaves. The price differences are based on the construction, quality of materials, and available features and options. A person buying a microwave for a college dorm room probably does not want the most expensive, full-featured choice, and so will be drawn to the lower-priced end of the product line. On the other hand, a gourmet chef making a purchase for a new kitchen may want only the highest quality and latest features.

Once a company has made decisions about a product line, it continues planning by determining the product assortment. A **product assortment** is the complete set of all products a business offers to a market. A product assortment can have depth, breadth, or both. A company offering a deep product assortment carries a large number of choices of features for each product category it handles. Walk into a Bath and Body Works store and look at the variety of fragrances, colors, bottle sizes, and packages for any of the major products sold there. That is an example of a deep assortment. Compare that to the choices of bath lotions that you might find in a small drugstore, where the assortment would be limited.

With a broad product assortment, a business offers a large number of different but often related products to its customers. If you visit a garden center, you may find many different types of products for lawns and gardens, ranging from plants, shrubs, and trees to lawn mowers, hoses, and patio furniture. There may not be a wide range of choices within every product category, but customers should be able to satisfy most of their outdoor home needs at one location. As shown in Figure 21-1, businesses can choose any combination of depth and breadth for their product assortment. Some will be very small and specialized,

It is often difficult to identify the total number of product lines a store carries by walking through the store. But product lines are often used to organize a customer's online shopping experience. Point your browser to www.thomsonedu.comschoolbpmxtra. Look at the tabs in the Web site. How do these indicate product lines? Click on the "See All" tab. Describe how this shows Wal-Mart's online product assortment. Based on your research, how does the online site differ from Wal-Marts you have visited?

www.thomsonedu.com/school/bpmxtra

and others will offer a wide variety of many different products.

PACKAGING

Two important product mix decisions are packaging and branding. Neither decision is directly related to the actual physical product itself, but each can be an important influence on purchase decisions.

Most companies package their products before selling them. The package can serve four different purposes. First, it protects the product while it is being shipped and stored. Products can easily be damaged when they are grouped together for shipment from the factory to the retail store. Boxes and containers are needed for protection. The actual container or wrapping in which the individual product is packaged also offers protection on the store shelf and may provide security to keep the product from being lost or stolen.

Second, the package can provide important information to customers on product composition, special features, and proper use. Boxes and containers also provide information to shippers on appropriate handling, storage, and delivery.

A package can be designed to make the product easier to use. A plastic bottle of soda is less likely to be broken if dropped. An easy-opening lid or a container that fits the hands of the consumer makes product handling easier. Window cleaner that is premixed in a spray bottle is much more convenient than one that must be poured into a bucket and applied with a sponge.

Finally, especially for consumer products, the package is often an important promotional tool. A well-designed, attractive package calls attention to itself on the store shelf, helps the customer recall previously seen advertising, and provides a reminder of the needs that the product will satisfy if purchased.

Figure 21-1 Businesses build product assortment to meet their customers' needs.

PRODUCT BREADTH

	More	Less
More (PRODUCT DEPTH)	A BROAD VARIETY OF MANY PRODUCTS	A LARGE VARIETY IN FEW PRODUCT CHOICES
Less	MANY PRODUCTS WITH LIMITED VARIETY	LIMITED PRODUCT CHOICES AND VARIETY

BRANDING

Can you name the brands of clothing, pizza, and toothpaste you prefer? Do you and your friends regularly shop at certain stores but not others? Product and store brands play a major role in buying decisions. A **brand** is a name, symbol, word, or design that identifies a product, service, or company.

Why are brands so important to consumers? Have you ever shopped in a store that had generic (nonbranded) products or that sold only unfamiliar brands? With no information to guide you, it is difficult to make a product selection with which you are comfortable. You and people you trust have had experiences with various brands. If a particular company's products consistently meet your needs, you will likely buy from that company again. If you have a negative experience, however, you are likely to avoid similar purchases in the future. If you are satisfied with one product from a company, you are likely to have confidence in a different product sold under the same brand. Businesses recognize that brand recognition is an important influence in increasing sales. The levels of consumer brand awareness are shown in Figure 21-2 (see p. 564).

What different purposes could the packaging of this product serve?

PHOTO: © COMSTOCK IMAGES.

facts & figures

Corporate identity refers to a company's name or logo—its visual expression or its "look." *Corporate image* is the public's perception of a company. *Corporate branding*, by contrast, is a business process—one that is planned, strategically focused, and integrated throughout the organization.

FIGURE 21-2 The Five Levels of Consumer Brand Awareness

- Consumers are unable to identify the brand.

- Consumers can identify the brand but it has little influence on their purchase decision.

- Consumers can identify the brand but will not purchase it because of its brand.

- Consumers easily recognize the brand and will choose it if it is available.

- Consumers view the brand as the most satisfying and will not purchase a different brand.

CHECKPOINT

Name four purposes of packaging.

21.1 Assessment

UNDERSTAND MANAGEMENT CONCEPTS

Circle the best answer for each of the following questions.

1. A(n) _____ product offers different features and options for the consumer.
   a. augmented
   b. basic
   c. enhanced
   d. extended

2. A group of similar products with obvious variations in design and quality to meet the needs of distinct customer groups is called a
   a. product assortment
   b. product mix
   c. product line
   d. product design

THINK CRITICALLY

Answer the following questions as completely as possible.

3. Describe the different perceptions of a product that are usually held by businesspeople and consumers.

4. Explain how a business can expand its product line.

Xtra! Study Tools
thomsonedu.com/school/bpmxtra

21.2 | Distribution

Goals

- Discuss the important factors to be considered when selecting channels of distribution.
- Describe the different channels of distribution.

Terms

- economic discrepancies
- economic utility
- channels of distribution
- channel members
- direct distribution
- indirect distribution
- telemarketing
- administered channel
- channel integration

Purposes of Distribution

Our economic system relies on the successful exchange of products and services between businesses and consumers. But no matter how good a product is, this exchange will not occur successfully unless the company fills orders correctly and delivers the product undamaged and on time to the correct locations. These functions are all part of effective distribution. Successful exchanges are not easy. In fact, most of the problems consumers and businesses face in our economy occur during the exchange process.

Economic discrepancies are the differences between the business's offerings and the consumer's requirements. Marketers are concerned about four important economic discrepancies:

1. Differences between the *types* of products produced and the *types* consumers want.
2. Differences between the *time* of production and the *time* consumers want the products.
3. Differences between the *location* where products are produced and the *location* where consumers want them.
4. Differences between the *quantities* produced and the *quantities* consumers want.

Producers manufacture large quantities of one or a very few products; consumers want small quantities of a variety of products. Producers manufacture products at a specific time and in a particular location; that time and location do not typically match the time and place consumers need the product. Distribution systems are designed to get the types and quantities of products customers want to the locations where and when they want them.

ECONOMIC UTILITY

Businesses create customer satisfaction by providing economic utility. **Economic utility** is the amount of satisfaction received from using a product or service. Businesses create economic utility and customer satisfaction by designing the form, time, place, and possession of a product.

Businesses create *form utility* by designing a product that is better or easier to use. Creating a product that is durable, has important features, or is sold in the size or quantity desired enhances form utility.

Distribution creates both time and place utility. *Time utility* is created when consumers are able to purchase a product when they need it. Time utility is enhanced when a customer can obtain a product at a convenient time and does not have to wait for delivery. Distribution creates *place utility* by having products and services available at a convenient location so customers do not have to drive a long distance to find them or are unable to purchase several related items at the same location.

Possession utility is created by developing a product that consumers can afford to purchase. Businesses can increase possession utility by extending credit, allowing the customer to make several payments for the purchase over a period of time.

CHECKPOINT

Describe the four types of economic discrepancies.

Channels of Distribution

The routes products follow while moving from producer to consumer, including all related activities and participating organizations, are called **channels of distribution**. Businesses that participate in activities that transfer goods and services from the producer to the user are called **channel members**.

Channel members are generally retailers and wholesalers. As you learned in Chapter 20, a retailer sells directly to the consumer. A wholesaler, on the other hand, buys from and sells to other businesses or organizations rather than to final consumers. Wholesalers, retailers, and other channel members serve important and specific roles in the exchange process.

Determining the number and type of businesses and the activities they will perform in a channel of distribution is an important decision. Adding businesses to the channel makes the channel more complex and difficult to control. However, using businesses that have particular expertise in transportation, product handling, or other distribution activities may result in improved distribution or actual cost savings. The activities that need to be performed as a product moves from producer to consumer help to determine the number and types of businesses in the channel.

Customers influence the development of a distribution channel. When developing a channel, businesses must consider the location of customers, the number of customers wanting the product, and the ways in which customers prefer to purchase and consume the product.

business *note*

Marketers take a systems perspective when they design channels of distribution. This means that they look at how all parts of a distribution system work together to meet customers' needs at the lowest possible cost. Businesses use their distribution systems to gain competitive advantages.

In some industries, such as retailing, distribution is so important that top managers specialize in this field. The last two chief executive officers of Wal-Mart, David Glass and Lee Scott, both had expertise in distribution. Why would the retail industry consider channels of distribution a top priority? Why would Wal-Mart hire CEOs with a background in distribution?

Producers need distribution channels whether they make products for consumers or for other businesses. The channels that products follow may be quite simple and short or long and complex. The shortest path is for the producer to sell directly to the user; the longest path can include a retailer, a wholesaler, and even other businesses.

When producers sell directly to the ultimate consumer, it is called **direct distribution**. When distribution takes place through channel members, it is called **indirect distribution**. Figure 21-3 illustrates different types of distribution channels.

DIRECT DISTRIBUTION

Direct distribution (sometimes called *direct marketing*) is accomplished in a number of ways. One way is for sales representatives to call on users in person. This is the primary method businesses use when selling to other businesses. Another popular form of direct distribution is the use of the mail. Businesses send letters and advertising brochures or catalogs to prospective customers through the mail or e-mail. Customers can use a mail-order form, telephone, fax, or online order form to make purchases directly from the manufacturer.

Today, one of the most popular methods of direct distribution is telemarketing. **Telemarketing** is marketing goods and services by telephone. It combines telephone sales with computer technology. Salespeople at computer terminals make and receive calls to and from prospective customers. Some telemarketing simply involves taking orders from customers who have seen merchandise advertised on television or in direct-mail advertising. When making a sale, the salesperson completes an order form displayed on the terminal screen, then routes the form to the company's distribution center for shipment. Telemarketing is an extremely efficient method of direct marketing, although its misuse by some consumer-marketing companies has given it a bad name. Poorly prepared salespeople and calls placed at an inconvenient time for products that customers don't want are not elements of effective business practices.

An increasingly popular method of direct distribution is through the Internet. A manufacturer can develop a Web site on which to feature its products. Customers order the products online from the site, and the company ships the products directly to the purchaser. Internet sales are expected to become a large

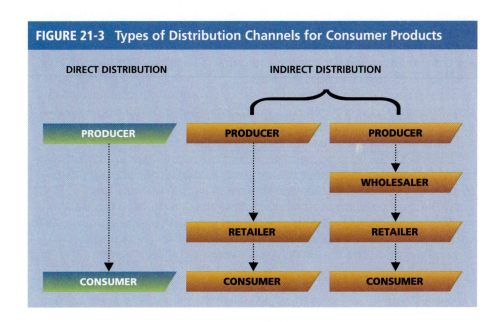

FIGURE 21-3 Types of Distribution Channels for Consumer Products

DIRECT DISTRIBUTION

INDIRECT DISTRIBUTION

PRODUCER

PRODUCER

PRODUCER

WHOLESALER

RETAILER

RETAILER

CONSUMER

CONSUMER

CONSUMER

What are some of the positive and negative aspects of telemarketing?

part of sales for many companies because of the speed and efficiency of this distribution method.

INDIRECT DISTRIBUTION

When producers cannot or choose not to perform all marketing activities, they need an indirect channel of distribution. Manufacturers can simplify many of their marketing operations by selling to retailers. They will need fewer salespeople, because they sell to a small number of retail customers rather than to a very large number of final consumers. They can share advertising with the retailers, and the retailers will be responsible for much of the product storage, consumer credit management, and other activities. Retailers specialize in marketing activities, and this allows producers to specialize in manufacturing activities. As you learned in Chapter 1, specialization leads to improved efficiency, which benefits consumers through lower prices and added or improved services.

Retailers benefit consumers in several ways. Unlike producers, retailers can be conveniently located near consumers and can provide the products of many manufacturers in one place, thereby permitting consumers to make comparisons among a variety of types and brands of products. Furthermore, retailers can offer several kinds of products that consumers may need, making it possible for consumers to do all their shopping at one or a few locations. Retailers offer convenient shopping hours, credit terms, merchandise exchanges, and other special services to encourage customers to shop in their businesses.

Retail businesses range from large department stores that stock a broad variety of merchandise to small retailers specializing in a limited variety. Also, there is a growing number of nonstore retailers. They sell products to customers in a number of ways that do not require a shopping trip to a store. Those ways include vending machines; direct marketing by retailers through telephone, catalog, or online ordering services; in-home parties and sales presentations; and shopping channels on cable television.

Producers prefer to sell products to retailers that buy in large quantities, such as department and discount stores and supermarkets. Smaller retailers are usually not able to deal directly with the manufacturer, so they must buy from other channel members. They turn to wholesalers, who consolidate the orders of a number of smaller businesses and then place the larger orders with manufacturers. Also, many wholesalers offer credit terms to retailers and provide help in planning promotions and sales strategies.

Wholesalers sell business products as well as consumer products. Many small businesses cannot purchase in the quantities required by large manufacturers or meet their terms of sale. They seek the service of a wholesaler, often called an industrial distributor, to purchase the products they need.

Wholesalers are an important part of international marketing today. Those that have developed international customers and distribution systems offer an effective way for companies to enter those markets. International wholesalers can also import products from other countries to sell to their customers.

Wholesalers provide valuable services that producers may not provide. They sell to retailers in small quantities and can usually deliver goods quickly.

INTEGRATED MARKETING CHANNELS

Usually the businesses involved in a channel of distribution are independent businesses. They make their own decisions and provide the activities they believe

Ethics *tip*

Telemarketing has been a very popular form of direct marketing, but not everyone likes it. Many states have created no-call lists. Any telemarketer calling a phone number on the list can be fined. Telemarketers are also not likely to make a sale to a home that wants to block calls.

their customers want. It is not unusual for businesses in a distribution channel to have conflicts with each other. One way for channels to work together more effectively is for a large business in the channel to take responsibility for planning, coordination, and communication. The business organizes the channel so that each participant benefits and helps the other businesses perform their functions successfully. An **administered channel** is one in which one organization takes a leadership position to benefit all channel members.

Cooperation is difficult among businesses that operate at different levels of a channel and have very different responsibilities. Some very large businesses attempt to solve that problem through channel integration. **Channel integration** occurs when one business owns the organizations at other levels of the channel. A manufacturer may purchase the businesses that provide wholesaling or retailing functions. A large retailer may decide to buy a wholesaler or even several small manufacturing businesses. Each business can still perform the specific functions needed for a successful channel, but having one owner for all businesses avoids the conflicts that occur in other channels.

CHECKPOINT

List three factors businesses must consider when developing a channel of distribution.

21.2 Assessment

UNDERSTAND MANAGEMENT CONCEPTS

Circle the best answer for each of the following questions.

1. The routes products follow while moving from producer to consumer, including all related activities and participating organizations, are called
   a. routes of distribution
   b. methods of distribution
   c. channels of distribution
   d. the marketing route

2. When producers sell directly to the ultimate consumer they are using:
   a. direct distribution
   b. indirect distribution
   c. indirect marketing
   d. Internet marketing

THINK CRITICALLY

Answer the following questions as completely as possible.

3. Explain how economic discrepancies are related to economic utility.

4. Describe the differences between direct and indirect channels.

Xtra!
Study Tools
thomsonedu.com/school/bpmxtra

Focus On...

TELEMARKETING—DOING IT RIGHT!

Telemarketing employs more people in the U.S. than any other form of direct marketing. Over 1 million people work directly in telemarketing, and their work creates over 8 million additional jobs in order processing, distribution, and related support positions. Companies spent $58 billion on telemarketing in the late 1990s, compared to $37 billion on direct mail. However, telemarketing often has a negative image. Telemarketers sometimes bother people, are rude or unprepared, or mislead customers into thinking they are participating in a survey.

The responsibility for ethical business practices is shared by individual businesses, professional business associations, federal and state governments, consumer groups, and individual consumers. Each is responsible for enforcing laws and regulations when companies violate established fair business practices.

Business associations create codes of ethics that, although not enforceable by law, provide guidelines for ethical practices for member businesses. The associations enforce the code of ethics by publicizing the information to consumers, asking customers to identify unethical businesses, and removing businesses from the association if they violate the code.

The following are some key features of the American Teleservices Association Code of Ethics for Telemarketing:

- Companies should not call people who are unlikely to be interested.
- Calls should be monitored by the company to ensure quality service.
- The product and delivery should be exactly as promised, and consumers should be informed of their options if service is unsatisfactory.
- All calls should clearly identify the name of the organization making the call and the purpose of the call.
- Guarantees and warranties should be clearly disclosed and copies made available on request.
- Merchandise should not be sent without clear customer permission.
- All calls should be made during reasonable hours.

Think Critically

1. Why do you believe telemarketing is such a successful direct marketing tool yet continues to receive a large number of consumer complaints?
2. Based on your experience with telemarketing, do telemarketers generally follow the ethics statements listed above? Which are most often followed and which are not?
3. What responsibilities do you believe consumers have in dealing with ethical problems they encounter with telemarketing? Should they do anything when they encounter ethical treatment from businesses?
4. Prepare several statements of ethical practices that should apply to Internet marketing.

Source: www.ataconnect.org (The American Teleservices Association, Inc.); www.the-dma.org (Direct Marketing Association's Telephone Marketing)

21.3 Channel Design

Goals
- Discuss the factors that affect a producer's choice of distribution channel.
- Describe the characteristics of major forms of transportation used to distribute products.
- Give examples of product-handling procedures that improve product distribution.

Terms
- piggyback service
- containerization
- bar codes
- warehouses
- distribution center

Selecting a Channel of Distribution

From the available channels of distribution, ranging from direct and simple to indirect and complex, producers must decide which channel or channels will best fit their needs. Producers generally prefer to use as few channels and channel members as possible. Sometimes producers need to use more than one channel to get the widest distribution for their product. Products such as books, candy, pens, and soap are purchased by many people in a variety of locations. Such items require several channels to reach all of the possible consumers. The manufacturers may sell directly to national discount stores that can sell large quantities of the product. To reach other markets, the manufacturers may sell to large wholesalers that, in turn, sell to supermarkets, convenience stores, vendors, or other types of businesses.

Selling to different types of customers requires different channels of distribution. For example, a magazine publisher may sell magazines through retail stores, news agencies, newsstands, and magazine subscription agencies, as well as directly through the mail or Internet to subscribers. Figure 21-4 summarizes these different channels (see p. 572).

Producers must consider many factors when deciding which channel or channels to select for distributing their products. Some of the main factors are:

- *Perishability of the product.* Highly perishable articles, such as bread, fresh flowers, and ice cream, require rapid and careful handling. Those products are usually marketed directly to the consumer or through very few channel members.
- *Geographic distance between producer and consumer.* Many products are now sold internationally as well as throughout the country in which they are produced. If the market is very close to the point of production, there is less need for channel members. Generally, more businesses participate in handling a product as the distance from producer to consumer increases.
- *Need for special handling of the product.* If the product requires costly procedures or equipment for handling, it is likely to pass through as few channel members as possible. Gasoline, which requires pipelines, special tanks, and trucks for handling, is moved from the refiner to the retailer

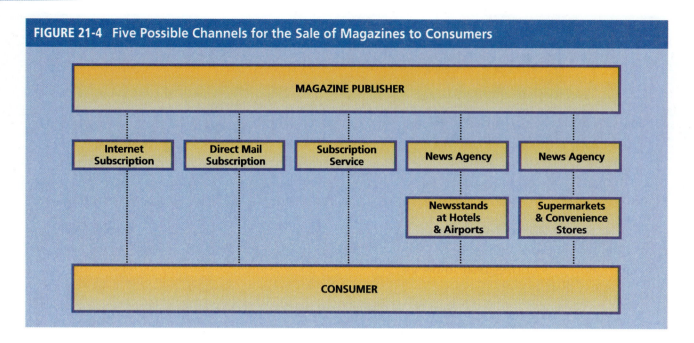

FIGURE 21-4 Five Possible Channels for the Sale of Magazines to Consumers

MAGAZINE PUBLISHER

| Internet Subscription | Direct Mail Subscription | Subscription Service | News Agency | News Agency |

Newsstands at Hotels & Airports — Supermarkets & Convenience Stores

CONSUMER

as directly as possible. Refiners own some gasoline retail outlets. Products that are highly complex and need experts to install and repair also require short channels. Manufacturers of large computer systems, for example, sell directly to users.

- *Number of users.* The greater the number of users of a product, the more channel members there probably are. For instance, a manufacturer of steel is likely to sell directly to a few large users, whereas a shoe manufacturer may sell to wholesalers that then distribute to a variety of retail businesses.

- *Number of types of products manufactured.* A producer with only one product, such as pottery, will probably sell to a wholesaler. It is too expensive to maintain a sales force large enough to contact all retailers in the country. But if a producer manufactures a large number of electrical products, such as coffeemakers, clocks, heaters, and toasters, it might sell directly to large retailers that handle all of these products. The marketing costs can be distributed over many products.

- *Financial strength and interests of the producer.* Large companies that are strong financially are better able to perform the marketing activities required to move goods from producer to consumer through the least number of channel members. They may find it more profitable to handle the marketing activities within the company rather than using other businesses. They also have more control over the channel rather than relying on others to perform many of the activities.

Channel decisions, like other marketing decisions, require careful study and are subject to change. With all the recent advances in technology, transportation and storage facilities, and retail methods, producers are constantly looking for more efficient ways to market their goods.

CHECKPOINT

List six factors that producers consider when deciding which channel or channels to select for distributing their products.

Transportation Decisions

Selecting the channel members that will help sell the product to the consumer is only one of the distribution decisions a company must make. Another important decision is how to physically transport the products from producer to consumer.

Buyers and sellers face several common problems related to transportation. One problem deals with the types of products to be shipped. Factors to consider in shipping include the size, shape, and weight of the goods. Also, certain goods are fragile and may need special care in handling. Transporting 100 tons of steel, for example, requires very different treatment from that required to move a carton of glassware.

Another transportation problem is the time needed for delivery. Some buyers expect or need shipment within a matter of hours, and others may not need or expect delivery for several weeks. Still another shipping problem is cost. In addition to the basic transportation charges, there are the costs of packaging products for shipment, insurance, and often storing products before, during, and after delivery to the buyer. Producers that do not perform their own shipping activities must first decide on their products' distribution requirements, then select the transportation method and companies that meet these requirements.

Both consumers and businesses are concerned about the quality of products at the time of purchase. They also want products available where and when they need them and at a reasonable cost. Because distribution activities affect all of these concerns, businesses plan them carefully.

COMMON TRANSPORTATION METHODS

The most commonly used methods of transporting goods are by railroad, truck, and airplane. A business may use more than one type of transportation, depending on the requirements for the shipment.

Railway transportation is one of the most common forms of shipping in the United States. Over a third of the volume of products shipped in the United States goes by rail car. The principal advantage of rail transportation is the low cost of moving heavy and bulky items long distances. However, products move slowly on long train routes as cars are added or dropped off. For bulky products or large quantities, the cost of shipping by rail is usually lower than by other methods.

Trucks are frequently used for short-distance shipping. Trucks are essential to smaller communities and rural areas that other transportation methods do not serve. Industries such as agriculture, mining, and lumber depend on trucks to move products from the source of production to the processing location.

Much long-distance shipping is also done by truck. For products that need to be moved rapidly, in smaller quantities than can be economically shipped by rail, or where rail is not accessible, trucks are the typical transportation choice. Some transportation companies load truck trailers and place them on railroad cars to be shipped close to the final destination. This service is called **piggyback service**. Many trucking companies now use computer systems to track customer orders and reroute trucks for rapid pickup and delivery. This flexibility is important for businesses that are trying to keep inventories low while maintaining high service levels.

Airplanes provide the most rapid form of transportation, but their rates are much higher than those for other methods. Airplanes can move products quickly over long distances. Items can move across a country in a few hours and around the world in a day, if necessary. The majority of air shipments involve items of relatively small bulk, high value, or quick perishability. Packages and mail are moved regularly on passenger airlines as well as by air parcel companies. Airlines are also used for shipping cut flowers, high-fashion clothing, seafood, film,

facts & figures

United Parcel Service is the world's largest package distribution company. It transports more than 3.75 billion parcels and documents annually. The company uses more than 575 aircraft, 92,000 vehicles, and over 1,700 facilities to provide service in more than 200 countries and territories.

Technology tip

A new technology based on tiny radio frequency identification (RFID) tags allows businesses to track products without bar codes. These small chips can be placed in or on product packaging and emit a radio code when scanned. They are used to track inventory in warehouses and allow for scanless purchasing.

PHOTO: © GETTY IMAGES/PHOTODISC.

and jewelry. Air shipments are very important for items needed in emergencies, such as medicine and blood, parts for machines needing quick repairs, or important documents.

Increasingly, businesses are shipping large and bulky items on special cargo planes designed for easy loading and unloading. Regional air freight terminals are being constructed so products can be moved rapidly into and out of airports without interfering with passenger travel. As rapid and efficient transportation becomes more important to businesses and consumers, more products are being shipped by air, even though the cost is higher. People pay more for the transportation that meets their requirements.

OTHER TRANSPORTATION METHODS

Water transportation (ocean, lake, and river) is the slowest method of transporting goods. However, it is

How does containerization improve shipping services?

also the cheapest for bulky goods, such as coal, iron ore, oil, lumber, grain, and cotton. Those are the principal items transported by water. Many products that are produced in large volume for international markets, such as automobiles and large pieces of equipment, are shipped across the oceans. At any large harbor on a coast you can see hundreds of types of products being loaded and unloaded from ships.

In the United States, as well as in many other countries, networks of thousands of miles of pipelines have been built. Pipelines mostly transport petroleum and natural gas. In many countries, however, pipelines are important methods of moving water for irrigation and human consumption.

One way to improve shipping services is through **containerization**. Products are packed in large shipping containers at the factory and are then shipped by a number of transportation methods before being unpacked. The containers can easily be loaded and unloaded from trucks to rail cars, ships, and cargo planes, and back to trucks. This method reduces the amount of product handling and product damage.

CHECKPOINT

Compare the three principal methods of transporting products.

Product Handling

Lost, late, or damaged products are of little value to customers. Product handling is an important part of the distribution process. Most products are handled several times on their way from producer to consumer. Each time a product is handled adds to the cost of distribution, increases delivery time, and increases the chances that damage will occur. Businesses evaluate their product-handling procedures to find ways to improve the process. Improvements may include more secure packaging, more efficient procedures for packing and unpacking, and better equipment for handling and storing products.

TRACKING PRODUCTS

An important part of product handling is keeping track of the products. Businesses and customers want to know where products are in the distribution channel and when they will be delivered. The record keeping required is often a very time-consuming task. Businesses now use bar coding to track products during distribution. **Bar codes** are product identification labels containing a unique set of vertical bars that computer scanning equipment can read. Each product or container has a bar code. The scanning equipment can read the code at any time during distribution to track the product's progress.

PRODUCT STORAGE

Manufacturers or channel members often must store products at points along the way from producer to consumer. Usually, consumers do not buy products as soon as they are produced. Producers and channel members may want to accumulate a large quantity of products to make shipping more efficient. Also, consumers buy some products more during one time of the year than another. Lawn mowers, air conditioners, snowmobiles, and skis are examples of such products. Most companies produce those products throughout the year to make production more efficient. They then store the products until they are ready to distribute them for sale.

Warehouses are buildings used to store large quantities of products until they can be sold. They are usually large buildings with racks, shelves, or bins for storing products. Warehouse operators may control temperature or humidity if the stored products need special protection. They must carefully handle and store the products to prevent damage. Warehouse personnel keep computerized records of where each product is stored in the warehouse. When they receive an order, the computer displays the quantity of the product available and its location in the warehouse.

Handling products and storing them for a long time is expensive. Also, moving them around increases the chances for damage. For more efficient handling with less risk of damage, many companies use mechanical equipment and robots to handle the products in their warehouses. Computers control both the equipment and the robots as products are moved into storage and subsequently removed for shipment.

Large wholesalers and retailers that handle a variety of products and sell them through a number of outlets have replaced traditional warehouses with distribution centers. A **distribution center** is a large building designed to accumulate and redistribute products efficiently. A wholesaler or retailer usually buys products from a number of manufacturers. Each manufacturer ships these products to the distribution center in large quantities. Center workers then repackage the products into smaller quantities, combine them with products from other manufacturers, and ship them to stores that sell that bundle of products to consumers. Distribution centers can save businesses a great deal of money. They reduce transportation and storage costs and provide individual stores with the products they need quickly. Individual stores can order smaller quantities than if they had to order merchandise from each manufacturer, so products will not become outdated as easily.

How are bar codes used in product handling?

ORDER PROCESSING

Customers place orders in person or by mail, telephone, computer, or fax. When an order reaches the business, employees must process the paperwork to fill the order and bill the customer. If customers have questions or problems with the order, employees must handle them in a friendly and courteous fashion. Some employees are responsible for tracking orders until they reach the customers to make sure the customers receive what they expect.

Most companies have automated some or all of the order-processing system. Orders entered into a computer system can be easily tracked. Some companies make computer records available to channel members and customers so they can also track orders at any time from their own computers.

CHECKPOINT
Describe how manufacturers or channel members store products at points along the way from producer to consumer.

21.3 Assessment

UNDERSTAND MANAGEMENT CONCEPTS
Circle the best answer for each of the following questions.

1. The transportation method in which truck trailers are placed on railroad cars is called
   a. railback
   b. piggyback
   c. truck to rail
   d. trainback

2. Buildings used to store large quantities of products until they can be sold are called
   a. distribution centers
   b. storage houses
   c. warehouses
   d. wholesalers

THINK CRITICALLY
Answer the following questions as completely as possible.

3. Describe some of the common problems related to transportation.
4. Why is product handling an important part of the distribution process?

Xtra!
Study Tools
thomsonedu.com/school/bpmxtra

CHAPTER CONCEPTS

- Businesses think of their products as what they have to offer to consumers. Consumers are more likely to think of products as ways to satisfy needs.

- Businesses develop products on three levels: basic product, enhanced product, and extended product. Also, businesses must decide whether to offer product lines and product assortments.

- Packaging adds value by protecting the product during shipping and storage; providing information about product composition, features, use, and proper handling; making the product easier to use; and promoting the product.

- Branding gives customers confidence in making a purchase. If they recognize a brand name and have had good experiences with that brand, they will be more likely to buy the brand again.

- Effective distribution gets the correct products to customers at the right place and time and in the correct form.

- Channels of distribution can be either direct (from manufacturer directly to purchaser) or indirect (using retailers and sometimes wholesalers to handle some of the marketing activities). Telemarketing is a type of direct distribution.

- Distribution activities include product handling and storing, transporting and tracking the product, order processing, and customer service.

REVIEW TERMS AND CONCEPTS

Write the letter of the term that matches each definition. Some terms will not be used.

1. Physical product in its simplest form
2. Product that includes additional features that are not part of the physical product but increase its usability
3. Group of similar products with obvious variations in the design and quality to meet the needs of distinct customer groups
4. Routes products follow while moving from producer to consumer, including all related activities and participating organizations
5. Complete set of all products a business offers to a market
6. Differences between a business's offerings and the consumer's requirements
7. Businesses that participate in activities that transfer goods and services from the producer to the user
8. Distribution in which producers sell directly to the ultimate consumer
9. Distribution that takes place through channel members
10. Channel in which one organization takes a leadership position to benefit all channel members

a. administered channel
b. bar codes
c. basic product
d. brand
e. channel integration
f. channel members
g. channels of distribution
h. direct distribution
i. distribution centers
j. economic discrepancies
k. extended product
l. indirect distribution
m. product assortment
n. product line

DETERMINE THE BEST ANSWER

11. A product that offers different features and options for the consumer is a(n)
    a. augmented product
    b. branded product
    c. enhanced product
    d. total product

12. One of the most popular methods of direct distribution combines telephone sales with computer technology and is called
    a. direct marketing
    b. online marketing
    c. phone sales
    d. telemarketing

13. A distribution channel in which one business owns organizations at other levels of the channel is a(n)
    a. administered channel
    b. channel integration
    c. channel captain
    d. channel linkage

14. Packing products in large shipping containers at the factory and shipping them by a variety of transportation methods is
    a. multishipping
    b. containerization
    c. factory shipping
    d. piggybacking

15. Which of the following are functions of packaging?
    a. protecting products
    b. providing information to customers
    c. making the product easier to use
    d. All of the above are functions of packaging.

16. The type of distribution in which a sales rep calls on a person or a company sends material directly to a customer is called
    a. direct distribution
    b. indirect marketing
    c. telemarketing
    d. database marketing

17. The preferred low-cost transportation system used to move heavy and bulky items is
    a. air freight
    b. ocean freight
    c. rail
    d. trucks

APPLY WHAT YOU KNOW

18. Identify a company with a product that has an extensive product line. Identify specific products that are part of the product line. Then describe the differences among those products and why they meet different customers' needs.

19. For a product with which you are familiar, describe ways that the packaging improves sales and usability. Now identify examples of packaging that interferes with sales and usability.

20. Make a list of products you have purchased that were probably stored for a length of time before you purchased them. Then make a similar list of products that were not stored or were stored only a short time before you purchased them. Discuss the differences among the products.

21. Provide examples showing that the ways in which consumers purchase a product influence the type of distribution channel used.

22. Discuss the problems businesses and consumers might encounter with product distribution and order processing when the Internet is used for selling and buying.

MAKE CONNECTIONS

23. **Math** An appliance store can purchase a certain brand of electric heater for $45.00 from a firm in City A or for $48.50 from another firm in City B. The transportation cost from City A is $3.88 per heater. From City B, the transportation cost is $2.77 per heater. What is the difference in cost between the two firms if the appliance store buys 500 heaters? What factors other than cost should the appliance store consider when deciding from which firm to make the purchase?

24. **Technology** A student organization to which you belong has decided to sell containers of bottled water at after-school activities, athletic events, and other functions as a fund-raiser. Your organization made an agreement with the supplier that allows you to design a unique package for the water bottle. Use a computer graphics program, like Microsoft's Paint, to design a package that will meet the four different purposes of packaging described in the chapter.

25. **Writing** Assume you work for a company located in Utah that manufactures children's toys and games. Your potential customers are located throughout the world. Write a one-page report stating the ways in which you can use each of the following methods to improve customer service or profitability: (a) Internet sales, (b) containerization, and (c) bar coding.

26. **Research** Use the Internet to identify two companies that specialize in shipping products. List the services they offer and describe how they specialize. Compare your answers to those of other students.

CASE IN POINT

CASE 21-1: A Photographic Assortment

Aisha Muran has been a part-time photographer for many years. She has specialized in individual family portraits for most of her business. Her customers learn of her primarily via word of mouth or when they see her portraits in other people's homes. She enjoys the work but doesn't make enough money to do it full-time.

Part of Aisha's problem involves changes in technology. Many people are now buying inexpensive digital cameras and printers. This equipment allows individuals to take their own pictures, send copies over the Internet or by disk, and print high-quality images.

She has discussed the issue with several business advisers, who suggested she consider expanding beyond portrait photography. They recommended expanding into weddings and special events; taking photos of landscapes, buildings, animals, and other subjects that would meet the needs of a broader audience; or purchasing and reselling home accessories that would complement the purchase of pictures and portraits. They have also mentioned that she could learn to enhance and improve the quality of digital photos taken by her clients and then print them using a professional-quality printer.

Aisha is unsure of what direction to take with her business. She has considered spending money to advertise. She is also not sure that she wants to get involved with digital photography.

THINK CRITICALLY

1. Describe a basic product, enhanced product, and extended product that you would recommend to Aisha for expanding her business.
2. List the elements in Aisha's current product assortment. Develop a new product assortment that she could offer. Identify which of these two assortments would be most appealing to potential customers.
3. If Aisha decided to purchase and resell home accessories, how could she use the concept of a product line to effectively market those products?
4. Describe how the Internet has made possible a new distribution system for photographic images. Explain how digital photography would enhance Aisha's product offerings.
5. Construct a grid like the one shown in Figure 21-1 for Aisha, illustrating how she could develop a business that would fit into each of the four quadrants. Describe the types of products she could offer for each of the four positions on the grid.
6. Should Aisha spend any money on advertising before she has made her product decisions? Explain your answer.

CASE 21-2: A Direct-Marketing Dilemma

The Elegant Affair is a specialty retail shop. It sells assorted gift boxes of various meats, cheeses, nuts, jams, and jellies. The business is located in a midwestern city and is facing declining sales due to the city's economic difficulties. One major manufacturing plant has closed, and layoffs from other businesses have caused many people to move from the area in search of new jobs.

The president of the company has been studying a number of alternative distribution methods. She has considered moving her retail business to another city. This would require a large investment and hiring and re-training a new set of employees. She has also considered closing the retail shop and finding other stores to carry her products. This would lower her profit per box but could increase the total number of boxes sold. She has also considered direct marketing as a way to increase sales without having to move the store or build a new store in an area with a more attractive economic climate.

Direct-marketing alternatives she has considered include using the Internet and telemarketing. She believes that by using salespeople and a computerized telemarketing system, the company can sell gift boxes to people throughout the United States. She also believes that the cost of those sales will actually be lower than the cost of selling the products to people who come into the store. However, she is concerned about the increasing use of no-call lists. The Internet could open sales across the country, but will require an investment in technology and new personnel.

THINK CRITICALLY

1. List each of the alternative distribution systems that The Elegant Affair is considering. List the advantages and disadvantages of each of these alternatives.
2. What types of activities would The Elegant Affair have to do to start a telemarketing system?
3. How can the company identify prospective customers for its telemarketing salespeople to call?
4. What types of activities would The Elegant Affair have to do to start an Internet-based marketing system?
5. Identify two distribution methods that The Elegant Affair might use for the products it sells through telemarketing or the Internet. What are the advantages and disadvantages of each?
6. Develop a brief script for the telemarketing salespeople to use to introduce the company and its products to prospective customers.
7. How could the increasing use of no-call lists impact the telemarketing strategy? What types of customers are likely to be on a no-call list?
8. Do you believe an online system for customer ordering might be a better method for the company than telemarketing? Why or why not?

MY BUSINESS, INC.

DEVELOPING YOUR PRODUCT AND DISTRIBUTION STRATEGY

Two important marketing decisions for your new business are the type and assortment of products you will offer and how to distribute them. Some new businesses have very limited product choices, and others offer an extensive set of enhanced and extended products. Most retail businesses purchase products and supplies from other channel members, so they are part of an indirect channel of distribution. An important part of distribution is to select a good location for the business that makes it convenient for customers to find the business and purchase your product. In this project segment, you will study product development and distribution decisions for your new juice business.

DATA COLLECTION

1. Identify your basic physical product. It will be very similar to that offered by many competitors. Study as many competitors as you can and identify the possible extended and enhanced product choices for this type of business.
2. Study competitors and collect additional information about this type of business from magazines and the Internet. List possible product lines and product assortments that seem appropriate for the juice products.
3. Collect examples of the packages and brand names used by the primary competitors selling these products in your community.
4. Develop a simple map of the area of your town or city where you might locate your new business. Mark on the map the locations of the businesses that offer the same types of products you are considering.

ANALYSIS

1. Develop a product strategy that identifies the products, product lines, and product assortments you plan to offer during your first six months in operation. Justify your choices.
2. Review a business directory from your community or on the Internet. Identify at least four manufacturers or suppliers from whom you might purchase the products and supplies you will need for your business.
3. Design the basic juice cup or container you will use to package your product. If possible, contact a supplier and determine the cost of various sizes of cup or container. Identify any other packaging you will need.
4. Once your facility has been determined, analyze any immediate and long-term improvements needed for the facility. Develop a sales presentation on your products. Videotape it or present it to your class.
5. Develop a distribution plan. Include the methods you plan to use to store products and supplies and transport them to your stores. Also list other possible channels for distributing your products.

Career Cluster
Marketing Manager

The objective of any business is to market its products or services profitably. Marketing managers develop the business's detailed marketing strategy. They determine the demand for products and services, identify potential consumers, develop a pricing strategy, monitor trends in new products and services, and oversee product development and promotion.

Employment Outlook

Marketing manager jobs will grow at an average rate over the next 10 years. The greatest demand will be for sales managers, marketing managers, advertising and promotions managers, and public relations managers.

Job Titles

Marketing assistant
Marketing manager
Area or territory marketing manager
Marketing vice president

Needed Skills

- College or graduate degree in business administration with an emphasis in marketing preferable.
- Courses in business law, economics, accounting, finance, mathematics, and statistics desirable.

- Must be creative, motivated, able to handle stress, able to communicate persuasively (both orally and in writing).
- Must have computer skills to conduct advertising, marketing, promotion, public relations, and sales activities on the Internet.

Working in Marketing

PHOTO: © CORBIS.

John works as a marketing assistant to a marketing-division vice president. He must act as a jack-of-all-trades in marketing. He has been assigned jobs that include creating marketing presentations, conducting research, working with sales teams, developing promotional material, and helping to develop strategies for product lines. His boss is being considered for a corporate vice president's role. This would allow John to move to a marketing manager's position, where he would be in charge of a variety of marketing projects.

Career Assessment

Check your library or the Internet for resources about marketing managers. Identify the roles that marketing managers play in a business. Specify what you like and dislike about this career area.

Pricing and Promotion

22.1 The Business Buying Decision

22.2 Pricing & Costs

22.3 Promotion

REALITY CHECK

Why Pay More?

Michi and Arturo walked out of Windzors, a sporting goods store that had just opened in the new Regency Park shopping plaza. "I can't believe that store will be successful," said Michi. "I've never seen sports equipment priced that high!"

"The products really were expensive," agreed Arturo. "But it certainly isn't a normal sporting goods store. The salesperson said they would help design your own set of personalized golf clubs and that you would get five hours of lessons with the golf pro at the Regency Sports Center if you purchased a set of clubs."

"Did you see the area where they sold downhill skis?" asked Michi. "They had a moving slide like an escalator where you could actually ski. They also had a machine that formed molds around your feet for custom-fitting ski boots. They sponsor a ski club and organize vacations to the mountains in the United States and even to other countries. I've never seen that in a sporting goods store."

"Why would people want to pay that much?" Arturo wondered. "Sure, they have the top brand names and unique services. But you can get the same type of products for 40 to 50 percent less at other stores."

"I don't know," said Michi. "They certainly have effective advertising, sales brochures, and customer service. And the store was filled with people. Maybe the owners are on to something."

A business is successful when it brings buyers and sellers together and they are both satisfied with the exchange. To be successful, businesses must offer the type and quality of products and services that meet the needs of their customers. The products must be priced so that buyers consider them a good value for the money.

Whether the buyers are businesses purchasing raw materials to use in manufacturing, equipment to operate the business, or products for resale, or consumers buying products for their own use, they must have information to make their decisions. Buyers must be aware of the products, how the products will meet their needs, and where they can buy them. Then buyers and sellers must agree on a price and method of payment. In this chapter, you will learn about the last two elements of the marketing mix: pricing and promotion.

22.1 The Business Buying Decision

Goals
- Discuss how businesses make their buying decisions.
- Describe the steps in the business buying process.

Terms
- business buying process
- new task purchase
- modified rebuy
- straight rebuy

Planning a Business Purchase

When planning a purchase, businesses actually make several specific decisions. They must decide what to purchase, when to purchase, from whom to purchase, and how much to purchase.

WHAT TO PURCHASE

To be successful, a business must keep the right kind of products in stock. Manufacturers buy products to use in producing products to sell to their customers. Wholesale or retail businesses purchase products for resale or for use in the operation of their businesses. In all cases, the most important consideration in making purchases is the customers' needs. Businesses that do not satisfy customers will not thrive. Businesses must consider both quality and assortment of products in deciding what to purchase.

Some buyers try to sell more products than their competitors do by offering low-quality products at a low price. They believe that price is so important to customers that they will accept lower quality to save money. This strategy can backfire. Customers compare price and quality to make the best possible decision. They usually do not select the absolute cheapest product if it is of inferior quality, nor do they always pay the highest price even if quality is superior.

Two factors influence a business's selection of product assortment. The first is competition. A new store will have a hard time attracting customers if it carries only the same products or brands that are carried by local businesses that are already successful. A business needs to emphasize the products customers want but offer some differences from competitors' products.

The second factor in choosing a product assortment is the financial strength of the business. It costs a great deal to keep a wide selection of products available. Businesses can stock a limited variety of products while still offering customers a good selection. Product variety is a difficult decision. Businesses need to stock items that customers want, but their budget has limits.

Businesses have several sources of assistance in determining what to purchase. Catalogs and salespeople are valuable tools. Trade associations and their publications can also help. Businesses should listen carefully to their customers in determining what to purchase. They should also review company records of previous sales and regularly study what products sell well and not so well for competitors.

When planning a purchase, what decisions does a business typically make?

PHOTO: © GETTY IMAGES/PHOTODISC.

WHEN TO PURCHASE

The types of products, the types and locations of suppliers, and other factors such as style and price trends influence the decision about when to purchase. For a manufacturer, raw materials and component parts must be available when needed for production, or the business will not be able to maintain its production schedule. Wholesalers and retailers need an adequate supply of products when customers want to buy. Businesses often must place orders well in advance for products to be available when their customers need them. For example, retail clothing stores often order summer fashions in January or earlier. Whether a buyer believes the prices of products will fall or rise also influences when product orders are placed.

business *note*

Marketing uses many theories and concepts from a number of other fields. These include psychology, sociology, social psychology, and economic psychology. These fields help marketers understand both individual and business buying processes and motives. How can these "ologies" help marketers understand the needs of their customers? What classes could you take that would help improve the selling process?

FROM WHOM TO PURCHASE

Part of the purchasing decision is to choose the right suppliers. Businesses consider the reputation of each supplier in such areas as dealing with customers, filling orders rapidly and exactly as requested, and providing necessary services. Other considerations are the supplier's price and credit terms.

Businesses must decide whether to make purchases from only one supplier or to spread the orders among several suppliers. Most businesses concentrate their buying among a few suppliers. This practice usually develops better relationships between the suppliers and the purchaser. Better prices, credit terms, and service are also likely to result. However, relying on one supplier leaves the purchaser vulnerable when that business experiences problems.

HOW MUCH TO PURCHASE

A business should have sufficient products available to meet customer demand. If customers cannot purchase the products they want when they want, they will go elsewhere. If a manufacturing business runs out of the necessary raw materials and parts, they must delay production.

On the other hand, if businesses have a much larger inventory than they need, they are tying up large amounts of money in inventory that they could use in other ways to make a profit. The large inventory also requires extra storage space. If businesses keep only small quantities in stock, they reduce the risk of loss from spoilage, changes in design, or changes in demand. Many suppliers are now able to fill orders quickly, making it easier for companies to carry lower quantities of many of the products they sell.

CHECKPOINT
List the specific decisions businesses must make when planning a purchase.

Ethics _tip_

Ethics is an important issue in purchasing. A "kickback" is a payment from a vendor to a buyer for the purpose of improperly obtaining favorable treatment in the issuance of a contract or purchase order. Other actions that are considered unacceptable include the showing of excessive favoritism toward a vendor and the solicitation or acceptance of gifts from the vendor by the purchaser.

Business Buying Process

Businesses typically follow a set of formal procedures when they decide to purchase a product. This process is called the **business buying process**, as outlined in Figure 22-1. Businesses do not always go through every step of this process. There are three different types of buying processes.

FIGURE 22-1 The Business Buying Process

Problem Recognition
A business buying need is recognized.

Product Specification
Specific details about the product needs are developed.

Supplier Search
Suppliers are requested to submit bids showing how specifications are met and at what price.

Supplier Selection
Suppliers are evaluated to determine if they are able to meet needs.

Submit Order
Order is placed with quantity needs, delivery date, return policies, warranties, etc.

Review Performance
The suppliers are reviewed on an ongoing basis.

Businesses must conduct a **new task purchase** process when they are purchasing a product, inventory item, or supply for the first time. Businesses typically purchase a large quantity of products and face larger risks than consumers making purchases. For example, if a supplier is unable to supply inventory items, a business could lose sales or have idle workers, resulting in higher costs. To lower these risks, businesses conduct careful searches for suppliers, following all the steps in Figure 22-1. Depending on the purchase, new task purchases can take over a year to complete.

In a **modified rebuy**, a business purchases a new or modified product from established suppliers. In this case, a business may submit new specifications or ask for bids from new suppliers to ensure they are getting the best price for their needs.

Many purchase decisions are low risk and can be made without modifications. This is often the case when a business is engaged in a **straight rebuy**. For example, when a business needs more paper for copiers or printers, it often repurchases from suppliers it has used before.

CHECKPOINT

List the three levels of the business buying process.

22.1 Assessment

UNDERSTAND MANAGEMENT CONCEPTS

Circle the best answer for each of the following questions.

1. Businesses use which of the following sources of assistance in determining what to purchase?
   a. company records
   b. salespeople
   c. trade associations
   d. all of the above

2. When a business is purchasing a new or modified product from established suppliers, it is engaging in
   a. a new task purchase
   b. a modified rebuy
   c. a straight rebuy
   d. an established purchase

THINK CRITICALLY

Answer the following questions as completely as possible.

3. Describe the factors that influence a business's decision about when to purchase.

4. Explain the differences between the three purchase processes used by businesses.

Xtra!
Study Tools
thomsonedu.com/school/bpmxtra

22.2 Pricing & Costs

Goals

- Distinguish between various types of discounts and price components.
- Describe factors involved in establishing product prices and common pricing strategies.
- Discuss ways that companies try to control costs that can lead to higher prices.

Terms

- list price
- discounts
- trade discount
- quantity discount
- seasonal discount
- cash discount
- selling price
- cost of goods sold
- operating expenses
- margin (gross profit)
- net profit
- markup
- markdown

Payment Terms and Discounts

Businesses establish a price at which they would like to sell a product. The initial price that the seller posts on a product is its list price. Often, however, customers do not pay the list price. The terms of sale offered by the seller or requested by the buyer affect the actual price paid. The terms of sale identify delivery conditions, when invoices must be paid, and whether the buyer can receive credit or discounts.

The buyer may specify requirements the seller must meet. The buyer and seller discuss those requirements and then negotiate any changes before a final decision is made. The buyer and seller discuss price, quantity, and delivery, and agree on the terms of the sale. The supplier then receives the buyer's purchase order or contract, which details the form, quantity, and price of the products to be supplied.

PAYMENT TERMS

Companies that sell to other businesses often extend credit to their customers. They list their credit terms on the invoice. Invoices often state credit terms in a form such as *net 30 days*, which means that the buyer must pay in full within 30 days from the date on the invoice. Some businesses offer longer payment terms, such as net 60 days. The longer the term, the better for the buyer, who then has a chance to sell the goods by the time payment is due or earn interest on the money that otherwise would be paid to the supplier.

DISCOUNTS

Suppliers may offer discounts on products that their business customers purchase. Discounts are reductions from a product's list price designed to encourage customers to buy. Common types of discounts are trade, quantity, seasonal, and cash discounts.

A trade discount is a price reduction that manufacturers give to their channel partners, such as wholesalers or retailers, in exchange for additional services. For example, a manufacturer may give retailers a 30 percent discount but may give wholesalers a 45 percent discount from the list price (or 15 percent more

PHOTO: © GETTY IMAGES/PHOTODISC.

Why might a business offer a seasonal discount for its products?

than retailers). In this case, the manufacturer expects the wholesalers to perform additional marketing activities beyond those expected from retailers.

A **quantity discount** is a price reduction offered to customers that buy in quantities larger than a specified minimum. For example, a retail paint store that orders 200 gallons of paint from a wholesaler pays a certain price per gallon. However, the wholesaler may lower the price per gallon if the store orders at least 1,000 gallons at one time. The purpose of the discount is to encourage customers to buy in large quantities. The manufacturer can afford to sell the larger quantity for a lower price because that sale reduces the cost of inventory, the amount of storage space needed, the insurance costs, and the administrative costs of product handling. Quantity discounts may be based on the number of units purchased or on the dollar value of the order.

A **seasonal discount** is a price reduction offered for ordering or taking delivery of products in advance of the normal buying period. It encourages the buyer to purchase earlier than necessary or at a time when orders are normally low. An example is a discount on snowmobiles purchased in the summer. The seasonal discount is a way the manufacturer attempts to balance production and inventory levels throughout the year for products that are normally purchased at a few specific times during the year.

To encourage early payment, many businesses offer a cash discount. A **cash discount** is a price reduction given for paying by a certain date. A cash discount is usually stated as a percentage of the purchase price (for example, 2 percent). Businesses offer cash discounts with various dating and credit terms. For example, the terms of a purchase may be net 30 days with a 2 percent discount for payment within 10 days. If the invoice is dated May 1, the buyer can deduct 2 percent from the total price when paying on or before May 11. Otherwise, the buyer must pay the full amount by May 31. Businesses express terms like these in this form: 2/10, n/30.

COMPONENTS OF PRICE

The prices businesses charge can make the difference between the success and failure of their products. Customers must view the product as a good value for the price. The price must be competitive with prices of competitors' products, yet high enough for the business to make a profit on the sale.

The **selling price** is the actual price customers pay for the product. The selling price is determined by subtracting any discounts from the list price. Businesses often set list prices higher than the price at which they end up selling the products. To make a profit, businesses must plan for discounts when setting their list prices.

Figure 22-2 illustrates the components that marketing managers consider when setting prices. To make a profit, marketers must set prices high enough to more than cover all costs. The income remaining after deducting costs from the selling price is the net profit for that sale.

The largest cost that the price must cover is the cost of goods sold. The **cost of goods sold** is the cost to produce the product or buy it for resale. For manufacturers, the cost of goods sold is the total cost of the materials, operations, and personnel used to make the product. For wholesalers and retailers, it is the price they pay their supplier to buy the product plus the cost of transporting it to their location for resale to their customers. For example, if the invoice price of an item is $55 and the transportation charge is $5, the cost of goods sold is $60.

Operating expenses are the costs of operating a business. They do not include costs involved in the actual production or purchase of merchandise, which would be part of the cost of goods sold. Most costs involved in the day-to-day running of a business fall into this category. Figure 22-3 (see p. 592) lists some common operating expenses.

The **margin** or **gross profit** is the difference between the selling price and the cost of goods sold. In Figure 22-2, the margin is 40 cents. Marketers think of the margin as the percentage of sales available to cover operating expenses and provide a profit. For example, a business may operate on a 25 percent margin. If operating expenses are more than 25 percent of sales, the company will lose money.

Net profit is the difference between the selling price and all costs and expenses of the business. Net profit can be calculated using the following formula:

Net profit = selling price − cost of goods sold − operating expenses.

Markup is the amount added to the cost of goods sold to determine the selling price. It is similar to margin. When stated in dollars and cents, markup and margin are identical. For example, in Figure 22-2, the markup is also 40 cents. Often businesses express the markup as a percentage of the cost of goods sold or as a percentage of the selling price. Thus, the markup in Figure 22-2 is 66 2/3 percent of cost (40 cents/60 cents). Expressed as a percentage of the selling price, it is 40 percent (40 cents/100 cents).

Some consumers confuse the markup percentage with profit. They believe that if a business has a 50 percent markup, it is making a profit of 50 percent of the selling price. However, markup must cover operating expenses. If the business with a 50 percent average markup on its products has operating expenses of 45 percent of sales, it will have a profit of 5 percent of total sales.

Markdown is any amount by which the original selling price is reduced before the item is sold. Companies use markdowns when their inventory is not selling at a satisfactory rate. Because the costs associated with the products remain the same, markdowns reduce profits, so companies want to avoid them.

Around 80 percent of car buyers use Internet services that provide information on cars and car prices, and locate cars from multiple dealers in a given area. The dealers often offer discounted prices because they know consumers can easily comparison-shop.

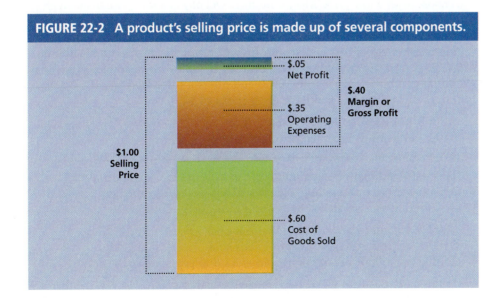

FIGURE 22-2 A product's selling price is made up of several components.

FIGURE 22-3 Businesses consider operating expenses such as these when setting a product's price.

Rent	Taxes
Interest paid on borrowed money	Repairs and maintenance
Salaries, wages, and benefits	Supplies
Telephone service	Inventory losses due to theft, spoilage, or breakage
Depreciation expense	
Furniture, fixtures, and equipment	Customer service expenses
Uncollected accounts and collection expense	Advertising
	Donations
Delivery costs	Utilities
Insurance	Cost of business services

CHECKPOINT
Explain how net profit is calculated.

Pricing Strategies

Because businesses operate for profit, they must set prices that will entice customers to buy the products yet will make a profit after costs are deducted. Businesses can use different strategies to achieve this goal. For example, a business can establish a high price. Fewer customers will buy at a high price than a low price, but the company will make a greater gross profit per item sold. On the other hand, a business can choose to set a low price. More customers will buy at a low price than a high price, but the company will make less gross profit per item sold. In this case, the company hopes to make a satisfactory profit by selling a large number of items.

No one strategy is best in all cases. Either of these strategies can result in a satisfactory profit for the company. Consider the following example:

Business A buys a product for $500 and offers it for sale at $1,000. It sells four of these in a month, making a gross profit of $2,000:

$1,000 × 4 items = $4,000 revenue from sales
$500 × 4 items = $2,000 cost of goods sold
$4,000 revenue − $2,000 cost of goods sold = $2,000 gross profit

Business B, selling the same product, thinks it can make a better profit by setting a lower price and selling a greater quantity. It offers the item for $800. In one month it sells six items, for a gross profit of $1,800:

$800 × 6 items = $4,800 revenue from sales
$500 × 6 items = $3,000 cost of goods sold
$4,800 − $3,000 cost of goods sold = $1,800 gross profit

In this case, Business A's strategy made the higher profit. However, either strategy could result in the higher profit. The challenge is to choose the strategy that works best for the situation.

Both of these companies made a gross profit, but they must deduct operating expenses to arrive at their net profit. If Business A's operating expenses are much greater than Business B's, then Business B might make the greater net profit, even though its gross profit was lower.

Businesses must be careful about setting extremely high or extremely low prices. With extremely high prices, the business may not sell a sufficient quantity to yield a net profit. With extremely low prices, the business may not be able to cover its costs no matter how many products it sells. Between these two extremes is a reasonable price that satisfies customers and allows a reasonable profit. Next you will learn about some of the strategies marketing managers use to set a reasonable price.

PRICING TO MEET COMPETITION

The amount of competition among companies handling similar products or services is an important factor in establishing prices. If one company has much higher prices than its competitors for the same products, some of the company's customers are likely to buy from the competitors. Even similar businesses in separate locations may compete for the same customers. If prices are too high in one area, many people will travel elsewhere to purchase goods or services. For example, if a service station in one neighborhood is selling a certain brand of gasoline for $2.39 a gallon and a station 2 miles away is selling the same brand for $1.99, customers may be willing to travel to buy where the price is lower.

The Internet has had a major impact on pricing, because it makes price comparison easy for customers. Some Web sites search for the lowest prices for specific products. Customers who value low prices over service may buy from the lowest-priced competitor.

A business may need to offer some of its merchandise at a price that does not allow a profit because a competitor has established an even lower price. However, it is not always necessary to have a lower selling price than competitors. If a company has a loyal group of customers and offers a product with some distinct advantages, or provides services that customers want and other companies do not offer, the company may be able to charge a higher price without losing customers. Remember that the cost of providing higher-quality products or more services may be expensive, so profits may not be higher just because prices are higher. Windzors, the exclusive sporting goods store in the chapter-opening case, was relying on unique products, exclusive services, and an interesting shopping experience to justify much higher product prices.

When competition is intense, some companies may have to set some of their prices at or below the actual costs of doing business. In such a competitive situation, only the most efficient businesses make a net profit. Even when competition is not strong, if a company sets its prices too high, people will try to do without its products or find substitutes rather than pay prices that seem to give that company an unduly large profit.

PRICING TO EARN A SPECIFIC PROFIT

When introducing a new product, many businesses base their selling price on a specific profit they want to make. The business first determines the costs of

Why has the Internet had a major effect on pricing?

PHOTO: © GETTY IMAGES/PHOTODISC.

producing and marketing the product, as well as all related operating expenses. It then sets the price by adding the amount necessary to make the target profit. But even setting prices based on a target profit won't guarantee that the company will make that profit. Customers must like the product well enough to buy it at that price. Also, competitors selling the same product might sell for less, luring away customers. In either case, the company may have to mark down its price to attract more buyers, reducing profit below its target.

PRICING BASED ON CONSUMER DEMAND

The owner of a business that carries fashion merchandise knows that at certain times the products will be in great demand, and at other times the demand will be very low. Swimsuits sell quickly early in the season but slowly late in the season, unless the retailer greatly reduces the prices. Because a retailer cannot accurately predict the exact number of suits it will sell, it will set a selling price at the beginning of the season that should ensure a net profit on the entire inventory of swimsuits, even though it may have to drastically reduce prices later in the season.

A manufacturer of a product that suddenly becomes popular may want to sell at a high price while the demand is great. When new competitors enter the market or customers tire of the product and demand begins to decline, the manufacturer will need to sell the product at a much lower price.

The introduction of new products in the market presents an interesting study in price decisions. High-definition televisions (HDTVs) are growing in popularity. In the beginning, a few brands were priced extremely high—several thousand dollars—compared to standard televisions. As customer demand increased, many more competitors entered the market, and prices began to drop to between $1,000 and $2,000. Eventually prices will drop even lower.

PRICING TO SELL MORE PRODUCTS

How do extra customer services affect pricing?

PHOTO: © JEFF GREENBERG/PHOTOEDIT.

Products that are priced higher usually sell more slowly than those that cost the same but are priced lower. For example, a product that cost $40 may be priced at $60 but may not sell for two months. A similar product that also cost $40 may be priced at $48 and sell in two weeks. If the second product continues to sell at that pace, the business will sell more of it and achieve a larger net profit over the course of the year. The business must be careful that the lower price is high enough to cover operating costs and still contribute to profit. Otherwise, using the lower price is a poor decision. For example, if the product priced at $48 had a cost of goods sold of $40 and must cover $10 worth of operating expenses, then the business will never make a net profit on the product no matter how many it sells.

If a business has a low rate of inventory turnover, it must charge higher prices to cover the cost of the inventory and the operating expenses of the business. For instance, many items in an exclusive jewelry store may be sold and replenished at the rate of once a year or less. The jeweler, therefore, must mark the retail price of the products very high in relation to their cost to make a reasonable profit.

PRICING TO PROVIDE CUSTOMER SERVICES

A business that offers credit, free delivery, or 24-hour emergency service will have higher operating expenses than one that offers no services. Higher operating expenses require a higher selling price to yield the same net profit as that earned by a business with lower expenses. If a business's customers expect a high level of service, or if the business is using the extra service to appear different from competitors, it will have to set prices higher to achieve a profit.

CHECKPOINT
List five different pricing strategies that businesses use.

Controlling Costs

Businesses are not always able to increase prices just because they are not making a profit. The costs of merchandise and operating expenses often increase, but prices charged to customers cannot be raised due to competition. Businesses have to make careful purchasing and operating decisions to avoid unnecessary expenses. Three important areas that can affect costs are (1) markdowns, (2) damaged or stolen merchandise, and (3) merchandise returns.

MARKDOWNS

In many cases, businesses are forced to sell some products at lower prices than they had planned. This can happen because they purchase products that customers do not want or that go out of style. Businesses must also sell products at lower prices when they overestimated demand and bought too many products, when competition increases, or when competitors lower prices.

Businesses cannot always avoid markdowns, but they can usually control them. Careful purchasing can eliminate many markdowns. Proper product handling and marketing practices can also reduce the number of markdowns.

DAMAGED OR STOLEN MERCHANDISE

Some products may be damaged so much that they cannot be sold. Other products may be stolen by shoplifters or employees. These situations have a serious effect on profits.

Assume that a product with a selling price of $5.00 is damaged or stolen. The product cost the business $4.00, and operating expenses amounted to $.75 for each product. Expected net profit was $.25. In order to recover the cost of that one damaged or stolen product, the business will have to sell 16 more products than originally planned (16 products x $.25 = $4.00). It will have to sell another three products to cover operating expenses. The business will not earn a profit on the sale of the 19 products if just one product out of 20 is damaged or stolen. To reduce the amount of damaged and stolen merchandise, companies may take actions such as employing security guards or installing surveillance cameras and training employees to handle merchandise carefully.

NET**Bookmark**

The Internet is gaining in popularity with advertisers. This new medium facilitates the targeting of individuals with customized ads. But companies must learn how to use this medium. The Internet Advertising Bureau provides information to help companies develop e-mail, wireless, and interactive television strategies. Point your browser to www.thomsonedu.com/school/bpmxtra. Identify the benefits of membership in the IAB. Evaluate the information provided on the IAB site. How does the IAB help companies?

www.thomsonedu.com/school/bpmxtra

RETURNED MERCHANDISE

If customers are not satisfied with their purchases, they may return the products for a refund. This adds to expenses in two ways. If the business can resell the merchandise, it will have to sell it at a reduced price. Also, many expenses are involved in handling and reselling the returned merchandise, which increases operating expenses. Some returned merchandise cannot be resold.

To make a profit, businesses must consider their record of returned merchandise when buying and pricing merchandise. They must try to buy just the type and quality of merchandise that customers prefer in order to help reduce returns. Salespeople should be trained to sell products that customers need rather than attempting to convince customers to buy things they do not need. Offering customer service and support to help customers use the products properly and resolve their problems also reduces the amount of merchandise returned.

When managers give close attention to the three problem areas of markdowns, damaged or stolen merchandise, and returns, they can keep operating expenses to a minimum. As a result, they can maintain profits while lowering the markup percentage. In that way, both the businesses and their customers benefit.

CHECKPOINT

List three purchasing and operating areas in which a business can control costs.

22.2   Assessment

UNDERSTAND MANAGEMENT CONCEPTS

Circle the best answer for each of the following questions.

1. A purchase that is net 60 days with a 3 percent discount for payment within 30 days would be indicated by
    a. 3/60, n/30
    b. 30/60, n/3
    c. 30/3, n/60
    d. 3/30, n/60

2. What is it called when a business sells a product at a price lower than planned?
    a. markup
    b. markup on price
    c. markdown
    d. price discount

THINK CRITICALLY

Answer the following questions as completely as possible.

3. Explain how competition influences pricing strategy.

4. Explain why stolen merchandise can have a strong impact on a company's profits.

22.3 Promotion

Goals

- Discuss the purpose of promotion in meeting business and consumer needs.
- Discuss how businesses use advertising to promote their products.
- Explain the parts of the selling process and how each is used to help customers make buying decisions that meet their needs.
- Describe the different types of sales promotions.

Terms

- advertising
- advertising media
- full disclosure
- substantiation
- cease-and-desist order
- corrective advertising
- personal selling
- buying motives
- objections
- sales promotions
- self-service merchandising

Promotion as Marketing Communication

To be successful, a business must interest people in buying its products and services. Even good products will not sell automatically. Consumers need to know the product is available and where they can purchase it. They must be able to easily see the differences among brands and determine which brand will best meet their needs.

Consumers generally follow five steps in progressing toward a purchase decision. Figure 22-4 (see p. 598) summarizes the steps in the consumer decision-making process. Although the five steps are common to all consumers, each consumer has different needs and gathers information in different ways to satisfy those needs. Some customers spend a great deal of time and consult many information sources before deciding to buy or not to buy. Other consumers might not be as careful or use the same methods. Therefore, businesses must provide appropriate information to help consumers move through the decision-making process to select the product that meets their needs.

Promotion is the primary way that businesses communicate with prospective customers. Businesses use promotion to inform consumers about the features and benefits of their products and services and to encourage them to buy.

Effective promotion is based on effective communication. You learned about the elements of a communication model in Chapter 10. In promotion, the company that develops the promotion is the sender. The information in the promotion is the message, and the method of promotion (advertising, personal selling, sales promotion) determines the communication medium. The prospective consumer is the receiver. Feedback from the receiver helps the sender determine if the promotion was successful and adjust the message, if necessary. Forms of promotion that businesses commonly use to communicate with customers are advertising, personal selling, and sales promotions, such as coupons, sampling, and in-store displays.

FIGURE 22-4 Steps in the Consumer Decision-Making Process

PROBLEM RECOGNITION

The consumer identifies a need to satisfy or a problem to solve.

INFORMATION SEARCH

The consumer gathers information about alternative solutions for the need or problem.

ALTERNATIVE EVALUATION

The consumer weighs the options to determine which will best satisfy the need or solve the problem.

PURCHASE

If the consumer identifies a suitable and affordable choice, he or she makes the purchase.

POST-PURCHASE EVALUATION

The consumer uses the product or service and evaluates how well it met the need or solved the problem.

CHECKPOINT

List the three different methods of promoting a product.

Advertising

Advertising is any form of paid promotion that delivers a message to many people at the same time. Because the message is designed to appeal to many people, it is rather impersonal. However, because the message reaches thousands of people, the cost of communicating with each person is very low.

Organizations spend more money each year in the United States on advertising than on any other type of promotion. The average business spends less than 2 percent of total sales annually on advertising, but some businesses spend over 20 percent. Companies in industries such as beverages, cosmetics, and electronics rely heavily on advertising and spend a significant amount throughout the year to keep their brand names in front of consumers.

ADVERTISING PURPOSES AND MEDIA CHOICES

Advertising is a powerful tool because it can help a business accomplish a variety of objectives. Companies must consider carefully what they want to communicate to consumers and plan specific advertising to accomplish that communication goal. The major purposes of advertising are shown in Figure 22-5.

Most businesses use some form of advertising to attract prospective customers. However, the methods of reaching consumers—the advertising media—vary a great deal. **Advertising media** are the methods of delivering the promotional

facts & figures

In 2005, the U.S. corporation that spent the most dollars on advertising was Procter & Gamble, which spent over $3.2 billion.

message to the intended audience. The most widely used forms of advertising media are classified by categories in Figure 22-6 (see p. 600).

PLANNING AND MANAGING ADVERTISING

Businesses have many choices of media to use to communicate information to customers. However, planning an advertising program involves more than selecting the media. Advertising should be planned to support other promotion and marketing decisions. Most businesses that spend a significant amount of money for advertising throughout the year develop an advertising plan. The plan outlines communication goals and specifies an advertising budget, a calendar of advertising activities, and how the advertising will be evaluated.

Small businesses often need help in developing their advertising plans and writing their advertisements. A printing company may have specialists who can write the copy and design the

FIGURE 22-5 Advertising can accomplish many purposes. Businesses carefully plan each ad to focus on a specific purpose.

1. To inform and educate consumers.
2. To introduce a new product or business.
3. To announce an improvement or product change.
4. To reinforce important product features and benefits.
5. To increase the frequency of use of a product.
6. To increase the variety of uses of a product.
7. To convince people to enter a store.
8. To develop a list of prospects.
9. To make a brand, trademark, or slogan familiar.
10. To improve the image of a company or product.
11. To gain support for ideas or causes.

advertisement for a direct-mail piece. The people who sell advertising space may offer suggestions for preparing newspaper ads. Radio and television station marketing people may also help plan advertising.

As the business grows, the owner has the option of hiring someone to handle the advertising or of placing all of the company's advertising planning in the hands of an advertising agency. Full-service agencies provide all the services related to planning and producing advertisements for all media and buying the space or time for the ads in the media. Most agencies also offer research services to determine customers' product and information needs. For their services, advertising agencies usually charge a percentage of the total amount spent for the advertising, but some may charge for the actual costs of developing and placing the ads.

Some very large companies have a complete advertising department that performs all the functions of an ad agency. Because of the amount of advertising large companies do and its cost, it is more efficient for those companies to have their own advertising personnel than to pay an ad agency.

THE ADVERTISING BUDGET Companies allot an amount for advertising when they develop their overall company budget. Most businesses plan the advertising program for one year or less. Of course, emergencies may arise that require a quick decision, but planning helps avoid budget misuse. If the company is developing a new product, it will usually prepare an advertising budget to support the new product's introduction into the market.

Large businesses often develop separate advertising budgets for new products, product lines, customer groups, or market regions. Separate budgets make it easier to determine the effects of specific advertising on sales and profits.

The amount a business spends on advertising depends more on the characteristics of the product and target market than on the competition. A business with a loyal group of customers and a product that has been in the market for a long time may need to spend less than a business with a new or very complex product or one positioned in an extremely competitive market. A business that relies on advertising for the majority of its promotion will, of course, spend a larger percentage of sales on advertising than a business that has a balanced promotional program of advertising, personal selling, and sales promotion.

FIGURE 22-6 Types of Advertising Media by Categories

PUBLICATION ADVERTISING

newspapers, general and special interest magazines, business and professional journals, and directories

MASS MEDIA ADVERTISING

radio, network and local television, cable television

OUTDOOR ADVERTISING

billboards, signs, posters, vehicle signage, and electronic displays

DIRECT ADVERTISING

sales letters, catalogs, brochures, inserts, telemarketing, fax messages, and computer databases

DISPLAY ADVERTISING

window, counter, and aisle displays; special signage; self-service merchandising; trade show displays

INTERNET ADVERTISING

static banner, interactive banner, buttons, sponsored site, cooperative site listings, e-mail list development

TIMING OF ADVERTISING Advertising is more effective at some times than others. Companies determine the times when potential customers are most willing and able to buy the products or services advertised. Many products and services are seasonal, with the majority of sales concentrated in a few months of the year. Companies spend more advertising dollars during those times when consumers are considering the purchase of the product than during times when customers are less likely to buy. For example, advertising for ski resorts or ocean cruises increases during the winter months, and advertising for air conditioners and lawn mowers appears mostly in the spring and summer.

Occasionally, companies advertise to increase purchases at times customers do not traditionally consider buying the product. By emphasizing new product development and advertising, turkey producers and processors have increased the sale of turkey products throughout the year. Those businesses had previously sold almost all of their products near the Thanksgiving holiday and one or two other holiday times during the year.

A single advertisement may produce temporary results, but regular advertising is important in building a steady stream of customers. If advertising does not appear often enough, customers tend to forget about the business or product. To keep their name and brands fresh in consumers' minds, businesses often spread their advertising over the entire year. Only when the company wants an immediate impact, such as for a new-product introduction or for a special event, would it consider a large, one-time expenditure.

ADVERTISING EVALUATION Advertising effectiveness is evaluated in a number of ways. Researchers measure which advertisements a market sees, what they remember from the ads, and whether or not the ads have influenced their attitudes or feelings about a product.

A number of companies specialize in advertising evaluations. The A. C. Nielsen Company uses people meters to record who in a family watches what television shows. The Arbitron Company has people record in a diary which radio programs they listen to throughout a day.

TRUTH IN ADVERTISING AND SELLING

Laws and regulations protect consumers from unfair promotional practices. Nationally, the Federal Trade Commission (FTC) and the Federal Communications Commission (FCC) are responsible for regulating promotion. As you learned in Chapter 7, false advertising is a violation of the law. False advertising is defined by federal law as "misleading in a material respect" or in any way that could influence the customer's purchase or use of the product.

To protect consumers, advertisers are required to make full disclosure, providing all information necessary for consumers to make an informed decision. They must also provide substantiation—that is, be able to prove all claims they make about their products and services in promotions.

If a business violates laws and regulations in its advertising, it may face three types of penalties from the regulating agencies: (1) The agency may impose a cease-and-desist order, which requires the company to stop using specific advertisements. (2) If the advertising has harmed consumers, the company may be required to spend a specified amount of its advertising budget to run corrective advertising. Corrective advertising is new advertising designed to change the false impression left by the misleading information. (3) In unusual situations, the company may have to pay a fine to the government or to the consumers harmed by its illegal advertising.

Long-term business success is built on honesty and fair practices. A businessperson may occasionally be tempted to exaggerate or to imitate a competitor who seems to be stretching the truth. In the long run, however, it does not pay to destroy customers' confidence. If customers do not get what they believed was promised to them in advertisements or by salespeople, they will likely not return to the business. On the other hand, a satisfied customer is often an important source of promotion for a business.

CHECKPOINT

List the components of an advertising plan.

Personal Selling

Personal selling is promotion through direct, personal contact with a customer. The salesperson usually makes direct contact with the customer through a face-to-face meeting. There are many types of customers, and a salesperson must be able to adjust to each type. Some customers know exactly what they want, but others are in the early stages of decision making. A critical sales skill is understanding the customer's motivations.

STUDYING THE WANTS OF CUSTOMERS

Individuals are motivated to buy for different reasons. **Buying motives** are the reasons people buy. Some common consumer buying motives are listed in Figure 22-7. To be successful, the salesperson must determine a particular customer's buying motive and then tailor the sales presentation to appeal to that motive. In many cases, the salesperson can appeal to more than one buying motive. For instance, a laundry company representative attempting to sell laundry services to a working couple with three children may talk about the comfort and convenience of having the laundry done outside the home rather than doing it themselves. The salesperson may also explain that it is less expensive to send the laundry to a professional service because of all the expenses involved in doing laundry at home.

Suppose this same salesperson calls on the owner of a barbershop or beauty salon. The salesperson can emphasize the special sterilizing treatment given to towels, capes, and uniforms and the speedy delivery of the laundered items. Both the family and the business owner might find individually scheduled pickup and delivery services attractive. Providing customer satisfaction through a sale is the ultimate goal of a salesperson. This method of selling does not require high-pressure selling; it requires intelligent customer-oriented selling.

FIGURE 22-7 Understanding common buying motives of consumers is an important selling skill.

Status	Ease of use	Affection
Appetite	Love of beauty	Wealth
Comfort	Amusement	Enjoyment
Desire for bargains	Desire for good health	Pride of ownership
Recognition	Friendship	Fear

PRESENTING AND DEMONSTRATING THE PRODUCT

Customers are interested in what the product will do for them and how they can use it. Salespeople must have a thorough knowledge of the product so they can provide accurate information and answer questions. For example, customers might ask: "How much paint will I need for a bathroom 12 feet by 8 feet?" "Which vinyl is best for a concrete basement floor?" "Why is this pair of shoes $68 and that pair $55?" Different customers value different types of information about the same product. Salespeople should study the products they sell as well as the competition's products, so they can be prepared to answer any questions customers might ask. Nothing is more frustrating than to listen to a salesperson talk at length about product information that is of no interest to the customer.

In addition to giving customers information, salespeople should be able to demonstrate the use of the product so that customers can determine whether or not the product will meet their needs. It is usually a good idea for salespeople to show the product and its uses at the same time that they provide information about it. The salesperson can then focus the customer's attention on the product while explaining its features and advantages. Whenever possible, salespeople should encourage the customer to participate. When a customer is directly involved and becomes comfortable using the product, initial interest can change to desire to own the product.

In certain selling situations, such as selling very large or bulky products or selling services, salespeople demonstrate without having the actual product. They use items such as photographs, charts, catalogs, videotapes, or computer displays. Such situations make it more difficult for the customer to get a true feeling for the use of a product, so the salesperson must rely on effective communication to increase understanding and desire to purchase the product.

ANSWERING CUSTOMER QUESTIONS

A customer usually has many questions during the salesperson's presentation and demonstration. The salesperson should not be concerned by the questions but should view them as an opportunity to better understand the customer's needs and help the customer make the best decision.

When customers are not certain the product is suitable for them, they may raise objections. **Objections** are concerns or complaints expressed by the customer. Objections may represent genuine concerns, or they may simply be an effort to avoid making a decision to purchase. It is difficult to second-guess a customer to determine if the objection is real or not. The salesperson should listen carefully to the objection, then help the customer make the best decision.

CLOSING THE SALE

For many salespeople, the most difficult part of the selling process is asking the customer to buy. As you saw in Figure 22-4, a decision to purchase involves several steps, and each customer moves through those steps in a different way and at a different speed.

If the salesperson has involved the customer in the sales presentation and has listened carefully to the customer's needs, the customer's interest in buying should be rather apparent. Typically, effective salespeople give the customer the opportunity to buy several times during the sales presentation by asking for a decision on a specific model, color, price, or type of payment. If the customer continues to ask questions, the salesperson answers the questions and continues the discussion until the customer appears satisfied. Then the salesperson attempts to close the sale again.

Many sales, particularly for expensive products, take several meetings between the salesperson and the customer. In business-to-business selling, teams of salespeople and company specialists may meet several times with teams of buyers from the customer's company. Several people will likely make the final decision. Salespeople should continue to work with the customers until it is clear that they do not want the product or until the sale is made.

FOLLOW-UP

The selling process is not complete just because the customer agrees to purchase a product. Selling is successful only when the customer is satisfied. Satisfied customers lead to repeat sales that help the company remain profitable in the future.

A plan for retaining customers includes several follow-up activities after the sale. The salesperson should check with the customer to make sure that the order is correct, that the customer knows how to use the product, and that the product

Focus On...

Global Sales–Chaebol–A South Korean E-commerce Club

Combine a unique cultural buying motive, the technology of the Internet, and effective pricing and you have a rapidly growing sales tool in South Korea. In 1998, the South Korean company Samsung tried to find a way to help its 185,000 employees through a difficult economic time by developing a group-purchasing program over the Internet. Employees purchasing products offered by the company on their Internet "cybermall," known as Chaebol, were given a 15 percent discount on the price of the products.

A unique aspect of the South Korean culture is a strong commitment to group purchasing. Employee groups, groups of professionals, and even alumni of schools encourage each other to purchase from Internet sites set up specifically for their group. In addition to providing products for sale, the cyber communities offer chat rooms, bulletin boards, group information and news, and personal home pages. These cyber groups reduce the amount of promotion required and also allow companies to sell products at a lower cost because of the greater volume resulting from group purchasing.

Even Samsung was surprised by the success of Chaebol. The Internet site increased its membership to 1.2 million customers within two years and expects to add at least another million in the third year. Sales are expected to top $1 billion by 2005, with net profits of $45 million.

For years, many social networks in South Korea have formed around employee groups. So it has been much easier to extend buying club services to those existing groups. Samsung now establishes similar Internet services for many businesses. It has formed a partnership with Freechal. com to open a site called Samsung Mall that is available to anyone. However, it still uses purchasing clubs as the primary method of signing up customers, continuing to build on the cultural need to belong to a group. The next step for Samsung is to develop an agreement with one of South Korea's largest parcel delivery services to be able to guarantee 24-hour delivery of products ordered on the Internet.

Think Critically

1. Why do you believe Internet shopping grew so rapidly among Samsung employees in the first two years of the new cybermall business?
2. What causes Internet sales to increase when Samsung develops specialized cyber communities and includes chat rooms, information services, and home pages developed specifically for a particular group of consumers?
3. Do you think U.S. culture would support the same approach to developing Internet shopping groups as was done in South Korea? Why or why not? Are there examples of successful shopping groups in the United States that have developed without the use of the Internet? For those you can identify, what has made them successful?

Source: BusinessWeek Online, March 20, 2000 (http://www.businessweek.com/ 2000)

meets the customer's needs. If there are problems, they should be corrected immediately. If following up with each customer is impractical, the business could periodically conduct a customer satisfaction survey. This could be done with an in-store, mailed, or e-mailed questionnaire or through phone calls to random customers. The follow-up contact will remind satisfied customers where they made their purchases, so they may choose to buy from the business again.

CHECKPOINT

Name the five areas that salespeople must master to be successful.

Sales Promotions

Sales promotions are any promotional activities other than advertising and personal selling intended to motivate customers to buy. Some sales promotions are designed to encourage customers to buy immediately. Others are designed to display the products in an attention-getting or attractive way to encourage customers to examine the products.

Coupons are a type of sales promotion used extensively to promote consumer products. Coupons are an effective method of increasing sales of a product for a short time. They are used principally to introduce a new product or to maintain and increase a company's share of the market for established brands. Coupons usually appear in newspaper and magazine advertisements, but they are also distributed by direct mail and are now even available on the Internet. A coupon packaged with a product the customer just purchased may encourage the customer to buy the same brand the next time. Or the enclosed coupon may be for another product from the same company, to encourage the customer to try it.

Manufacturers often cooperate with wholesalers and retailers by providing promotional materials. Some of these materials, commonly furnished without cost or at a low price, include window displays, layouts and illustrations for newspaper ads, direct-mail inserts, display materials, and sales presentation aids.

When producers are introducing a new product, they may distribute samples through the mail. The purpose of this activity is to familiarize people with the products to create a demand for them in local businesses. Coupons often accompany the samples to encourage consumers to go to a local store and buy the product.

Producers and distributors also cooperate with retailers by arranging special displays and demonstrations within stores. For example, demonstrators may cook and distribute samples of a new brand of hot dog to customers in a grocery store. This practice usually helps the retailers sell the new product. The retailer, of course, gives this merchandise preference over other competing

How do businesses use coupons as a sales promotion tool?

PHOTO: © GETTY IMAGES/PHOTODISC.

products because of this special promotion. Sometimes distributors pay merchants for the privilege of giving demonstrations or offer special prices for the opportunity.

Today, store designs, displays, labels, and packaging promote products so well that many stores let these promotions alone sell the products, rather than employ many salespeople. In **self-service merchandising**, customers select the products they want to purchase, take them to the checkout counter, and pay for them, without much help from salespeople. The display of merchandise in self-service stores attracts attention and makes it convenient for the shopper to examine the merchandise. The labels on the merchandise provide adequate information about the merchandise for the shopper to make a decision.

CHECKPOINT

Name at least five different types of sales promotion.

22.3 | Assessment

UNDERSTAND MANAGEMENT CONCEPTS

Circle the best answer for each of the following questions.

1. Any form of paid promotion that delivers a message to many people at the same time is called
   a. advertising
   b. promotion
   c. sales
   d. sales promotion

2. Customer objections in a sales situation are typically the result of
   a. real customer concerns
   b. avoiding decisions
   c. neither a nor b
   d. both a and b

THINK CRITICALLY

Answer the following questions as completely as possible.

3. Explain why a good salesperson studies a customer's buying motive.

4. Describe the major goals of sales promotion.

Xtra!
Study Tools
thomsonedu.com/school/bpmxtra

CHAPTER CONCEPTS

- Businesses must decide what to buy, when to buy, from whom to buy, and how much to buy. Mistakes result in unsold products, dissatisfied customers, and losses rather than profits.

- When setting a product's price, businesspeople consider payment terms, discounts, and the elements that make up a product's price. Pricing strategies include pricing to meet the competition, to earn a specific profit, to sell more products, and to provide customer services.

- Businesses attempt to control costs by establishing practices that help reduce markdowns, damaged or stolen merchandise, and customer returns.

- The most common methods of promotion are advertising, personal selling, and sales promotion.

- Advertising is paid promotion directed at a large number of people at the same time. An advertising plan outlines communication goals, timing, budget, and evaluation criteria. The FTC and the FCC protect consumers from unfair and illegal promotion. Companies must be able to prove all claims made in ads and can be asked to stop using illegal ads, run corrective advertising, or pay a fine.

- Personal selling is selling through direct personal contact. Salespeople study buying motives, demonstrate the product, answer customer questions, and close the sale when customers are prepared to make a purchase decision. The sale is complete when the salesperson follows up with the customer to determine if he or she is satisfied with the purchase.

REVIEW TERMS AND CONCEPTS

Write the letter of the term that matches each definition. Some terms will not be used.

1. Initial price that the seller posts on a product
2. Price reduction given for paying by a certain date
3. Cost to produce a product or buy it for resale
4. Difference between the selling price and the cost of goods sold
5. Promotion through direct, personal contact with a customer
6. Methods of delivering a promotional message to the audience
7. The reasons people buy
8. Any promotional activities other than advertising and personal selling intended to motivate customers to buy
9. Difference between the selling price and all costs and expenses of the business
10. Providing all information necessary for consumers to make an informed decision
11. Ability to prove all claims made about a product or service in promotions
12. Requiring a company to stop using specific advertisements

a. advertising media
b. buying motives
c. cash discount
d. cease-and desist-order
e. cost of goods sold
f. discounts
g. full disclosure
h. list price
i. margin (gross profit)
j. markdown
k. net profit
l. personal selling
m. sales promotions
n. substantiation

DETERMINE THE BEST ANSWER

13. A price reduction that manufacturers give to their channel partners, such as wholesalers or retailers, in exchange for additional services is a
    a. manufacturer's discount
    b. trade discount
    c. sales promotion
    d. wholesale discount

14. Reductions taken from the price of a product to encourage customers to buy is known as a
    a. selling price
    b. markdown
    c. markup
    d. trade discount

15. A price reduction offered for ordering or taking delivery of products in advance of the normal buying period to encourage buyers to purchase earlier than necessary or at a time when orders are normally low is called a(n)
    a. quantity discount
    b. seasonal discount
    c. annual discount
    d. special discount

16. The costs of operating a business, not including costs involved in the actual production or purchase of merchandise, are the
    a. cost of goods sold
    b. normal expenses
    c. operating expenses
    d. operating costs

17. If a company violates federal law by "misleading in a material respect" or in any way that could influence the customer's purchase or use of the product, it could be forced to
    a. cease and desist
    b. use corrective advertising
    c. pay a fine
    d. all of the above

18. Subtracting any discounts from a product's list price yields the actual price customers pay for the product, or its
    a. actual price
    b. sale price
    c. selling price
    d. trade price

19. Advertising designed to change false impressions left by misleading information is called
    a. corrective advertising
    b. false advertising
    c. normal advertising
    d. misleading advertising

APPLY WHAT YOU KNOW

20. Explain why it is important for businesses to consider both the customer and the business when planning the sale of products.
21. Using the formula for calculating net profit, suggest several ways that a business can increase the net profit from the sale of a product.
22. Which advertising media do you believe are most effective for the products you purchase? Why? Would the same media be most effective for advertising the products your parents buy? Why or why not?
23. Explain why high-technology products are often sold initially at very high prices but later at prices that have dropped dramatically.
24. Why do you believe that closing the sale is the most difficult step of the selling process for many salespeople? As a customer, what would you recommend to salespeople to make that step easier and more successful?

MAKE CONNECTIONS

25. **Math** A book and gift store with average annual sales of $700,000 spends 3 percent of its sales for advertising. The store's advertising budget is divided as follows: catalogs, 30 percent; calendars and other sales promotions, 7 percent; window displays, 15 percent; newspaper advertising, 15 percent; direct mail, 20 percent; and miscellaneous, 13 percent.
    a. How much is the average annual advertising budget?
    b. What is the amount spent on each type of advertising?
26. **Research** Use the Internet to identify the cost of ad placement in a number of media. Identify the cost per thousand (cost/1,000 people reached) for each medium. Identify which media have a higher cost. Specify why these media are able to charge a higher price.
27. **Technology** Use the Internet to find online examples of each of the following types of advertising: static banner, interactive banner, button, sponsored site, and affiliate listing with another Internet site. Using a screen capture, take an example of each online advertisement you find and prepare a slide show of the various types of Internet advertising.
28. **Speaking** Assume that you are a salesperson in a furniture store. Develop a list of the buying motives you believe might be prompting each of the following types of customers to consider buying a sofa sleeper: (a) a college student who is buying furniture for a one-bedroom apartment, (b) a family that is outfitting a family room they are remodeling, and (c) a motel owner who is deciding between a less expensive sofa and the sofa sleeper for 50 rooms. Prepare and present a sales presentation to the class that you would use for each of these customers.

CASE IN POINT

CASE 22-1: Advertising: The Root of All Evil?

Peter and Torrie were watching television. During a commercial they discussed how companies use advertising.

Peter: *Companies spend too much money on advertising. If they would spend less, the prices of products would be a lot lower. I heard that companies that advertise on the Super Bowl program spend more than $1 million for one ad.*

Torrie: *Companies are not only placing ads in the middle of shows, they're also putting them into movies and television shows. I think they should remove ads from television and radio. I usually switch between channels during commercials anyway.*

Peter: *It seems like advertising is everywhere. No matter where you go or what you do, you see products promoted. My parents bought a TiVo, so I don't even see commercials on our system.*

Torrie: *It seems that companies advertise to get people to buy products they don't want. I've bought some things just because of the ad and regretted it later. Companies with good products shouldn't have to advertise. People will find out about them from others who try the products and like them.*

Peter: *The worst thing about advertising is that businesses can say anything they want to about products, even if the statements are untrue. They often criticize their competitors, making you think there's something wrong with the other product. After watching or listening to an ad, you're more confused than ever about what to buy.*

THINK CRITICALLY

1. Do you believe product prices would decrease if companies did not advertise? Explain.
2. Explain why some companies would pay $1 million to advertise during the Super Bowl.
3 What would happen to television and radio if advertising support was dropped?
4. Do good products need to be advertised? Why or why not?
5. What types of controls are there on what a business can say in its advertising? What can consumers do if they believe they have been misled by advertising?
6. Do you believe advertising results in more confusion than help for consumers? Justify your answer.
7. Do you think that the high level of advertising creates needs rather than simply informing the customer of product benefits? Explain your answer.
8. How do channel surfing and TiVo affect the effectiveness of advertising? How are companies shifting strategy in this new environment?
9. Develop an argument to convince Peter and Torrie that advertising is a vital part of a marketing strategy.

DEVELOPING A PRICING AND ADVERTISING STRATEGY

A businessperson must set prices on products that will provide a reasonable net profit. In addition, a new business needs to plan promotion to introduce people to the business and its products and to encourage customers to try the products.

DATA COLLECTION

1. Use the Internet to locate sources of information on start-up expenses for small businesses and develop a list of the common types of expenses and the range of costs you might expect when you begin your business.
2. Interview one or two small-business owners in your community. Ask them to explain the terms and policies of some of the vendors they deal with.
3. Ask one or two small-business owners to explain the types of promotion they use, what assistance they get with promotional planning, and how they estimate the amount of money they can spend on promotional activities.
4. Collect samples of advertising and promotion that local small businesses are using. Analyze their effectiveness in communicating with prospective customers. Analyze the publicity's potential impact. Prepare possible strategies for dealing with it.
5. Check with several media that offer advertising in your community (newspapers, television, radio, etc.). Obtain a price list that indicates the costs of advertising in each medium, based on the size, type, and frequency of the advertising.

ANALYSIS

1. Assume that, in an average month, your sales will include 700 small drinks, 800 large drinks, 900 supplement additions to the drinks (beyond any free supplements), and 2,000 high-energy snack bars. First, determine the price you will charge for each product, being realistic about what you believe customers are willing to pay. Then estimate your monthly expenses. Have several people review your estimates to determine if they are realistic. Then calculate your estimated monthly profit or loss.
2. Is your estimated monthly net profit adequate? If not, consider what changes you could make to improve it. (Don't make any price changes at this time.) Which of the possible changes are most likely to be successful? Which are least likely to be implemented?
3. Being as creative as possible, list several ways of promoting your new business that would be (a) informative, (b) unique, and (c) affordable. Consider methods in addition to advertising.
4. Develop a three-month promotional plan for your new business. Include methods, media to be used, time schedule, budget, and samples of the promotions.

Case Study

NEW PRODUCTS AND INCENTIVES COUNTER RISING GAS PRICES

Rising gas prices have spurred the production of hybrid cars and of ethanol, a plant-based alcohol fuel that may help reduce U.S. dependence on foreign oil. In 2005, President Bush signed an energy bill that encourages greater use of ethanol as an ecologically sound fuel additive. Government incentives along with high gas prices have led to a mini-boom in ethanol plant construction in major corn-growing states like Iowa and Nebraska. Thirty-three ethanol plants were under construction a year after the president signed the bill, and 8 of the 95 plants in operation were being expanded. The ethanol supply is expected to double to 9.8 billion gallons by 2015.

Ethanol makers received a boost not only from the energy bill but from Detroit automakers who are promoting vehicles that can burn E85, a blend of 85 percent ethanol and 15 percent gasoline. The more common gasohol consists of 10 percent ethanol.

Several well-known corporations are supporting the move toward more fuel-efficient cars. Driving a hybrid already means free parking at meters in one Connecticut city and reserved parking spots near the front door of a New Hampshire company. Bank of America is offering incentives to individuals who buy hybrid vehicles. Some Bank of America employees receive $3,000 cash if they buy a fuel-efficient vehicle. The company offered its incentive program to 21,000 employees in Boston, Los Angeles, and Charlotte, joining other companies and communities nationwide in pushing the hybrids. Bank of America offers a rebate to any employee who buys a hybrid vehicle and lives within 90 miles of the three cities. Google, the Internet giant based in Mountain View, California, offers $5,000 cash to individuals who purchase low-emission cars that get at least 45 miles per gallon and $2,500 to those who lease them.

THINK CRITICALLY

1. Give two examples of public relations benefits achieved by the Bank of America incentive program.
2. What two products have benefited from higher fuel costs?
3. Why would farmers be interested in the trends covered in this article?
4. Why is it wise for automakers in Detroit to get involved in this special project?

Retail Merchandising Series Event

The purpose of the Advertising Campaign Event is to provide an opportunity for the participants to prepare an advertising campaign of any length for a real product, service, company, or business and to present the campaign to a prospective client/advertiser. Participants will also create an appropriate budget and select media for the advertising campaign. This event consists of outline fact sheets, the written comprehensive exam, and the oral presentation. You will be focusing on the outline fact sheets and oral presentation for this assignment.

The body of your outline fact sheets will be limited to 10 numbered pages, not including the title page and table of contents. Your oral presentation may be up to 20 minutes long. You will have 15 minutes to present your advertising campaign and 5 minutes to field questions from judges. Your outline fact sheets should include: an executive summary; a description of the product, service, or business; a description of the client; objectives of the campaign; identification of the target market (primary and secondary); a list of advertising media necessary for the campaign; a budget; schedules of all advertising planned; schedules of all sales promotion activities planned; and a statement of benefits to the client.

You have been hired by a local restaurant that serves home-cooked food in a community with a population of 20,000 people. Over the past year, Subway, Pizza Hut, and Wendy's have opened outlets in the community. Your advertising campaign must attract business from both residents and visitors. Your client wants a fresh promotional strategy for each month of the year.

PERFORMANCE INDICATORS EVALUATED

- Understand the value of an effective advertising campaign.
- Analyze the competition to determine company strengths.
- Produce promotions that will increase customer traffic.
- Communicate an advertising campaign that wins the approval of the client.
- Prepare a realistic budget for an advertising campaign.

For more detailed information about performance indicators, go to the DECA Web site.

THINK CRITICALLY

1. Why should a local restaurant that has been around for a long time be concerned with advertising?
2. What disadvantage is faced by a local restaurant competing with national fast-food restaurants?
3. Why should the advertising campaign pay attention to customer loyalty from residents in the community?

http://www.deca.org/

Human Resources Management

"People make change happen. Today's successful companies have recognized that only by investing in their most important assets—their people—can a true company transformation become a reality. People, using their knowledge and skills, are the only effective change agents for any company. "

Daniel R. Tobin

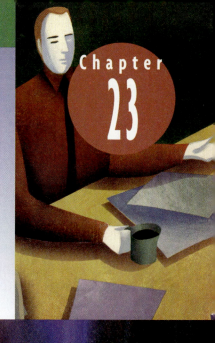

Managing Human Resources

REALITY CHECK

A Hard Decision

Patrick Gomez and his parents were discussing two job offers he had received. Both jobs were in marketing research, the area of business in which he wanted to work. One job was with a contract research organization, and the second was in the marketing department of an international manufacturer. He thought he would enjoy working for either company.

The major difference between the job offers was the rate of pay and the benefits. In the first job, Patrick would be considered a contract employee. He would receive $15 per hour. He would work a minimum of 35 hours per week and most weeks would work a full 40 hours. However, there were no benefits such as insurance or paid holidays.

The second job paid an annual beginning salary of $21,000. Patrick would work a minimum of 40 hours per week, with occasional weekend work during busy times. He would receive two weeks' paid vacation plus five additional holidays. The company would contribute $150 per month and Patrick would pay $55 per month for health and dental insurance. He would also have a company-paid life insurance policy worth twice his annual salary. Each year the company would contribute an amount equal to 5 percent of Patrick's salary to a retirement plan. If Patrick stayed with the company for five years, he would become part of the retirement plan and would be entitled to the money upon retirement.

As Patrick considered the choices, he was impressed with the possibility of earning over $31,000 per year at the first company if he worked 40 hours per week for the entire year. He had a number of school loans to pay off, and the extra money would come in handy.

However, his parents reminded him that he was not guaranteed all of those hours and could take no vacations if he expected to earn that much money. Although he had no major health problems, any illness could be expensive and would be covered by the health insurance of the second company but not by the first. And, even though Patrick was only 22 years old, beginning to save for retirement at an early age was an important consideration. Patrick knew he had a difficult decision to make. He had never considered how salary and benefits could affect a job decision.

23.1 Human Resources in Business

Goals
- Identify the reasons human resources management is important to businesses and employees.
- Identify and describe each of the major human resources activities.

Terms
- human resources management (HRM)
- 360-degree feedback
- employee assistance programs

The Need for Human Resources

Of all the resources used by a business, probably the most important to its success is people. People are responsible for the effective use of all other resources in the business. People make decisions, operate equipment, maintain records, and deal with customers. Because of their value to the business, managing people is a critical function.

All managers work with people. However, **human resources management (HRM)** consists of all activities involved with acquiring, developing, and compensating the people who do the company's work. HRM is sometimes called *personnel management*. Employees' pay, training, benefits, work environment, and many other factors contribute to their productivity, performance quality, and willingness to stay with the company. The people who work in human resources management perform the tasks that help the business keep the skilled, productive, and satisfied employees it needs to succeed.

To begin human resources planning, companies must determine the number of people they will need in order to perform all tasks as well as the skills those people will need. Then they must recruit, hire, and train those employees. Once on the job, the employees will need equipment and other resources to accomplish their jobs. Directions provided through descriptions of job duties, policies, and procedures help the organization operate effectively. Human resources employees take part in all of these activities.

Businesses must be sure that employees are satisfied with their jobs and motivated to perform well. They need to be concerned about employee safety and health, working conditions, wages, and benefits. Employees who are doing a good job need to be recognized and rewarded, and those who are not must be given training and support to improve their performance. In some cases, employees must be removed from their jobs if their performance does not improve or if there are major changes in company operations. As you can see, working with people involves many responsibilities.

Most companies have a department that is responsible for human resources management. Large companies may have several specialized divisions within the department, each of which deals with a specific area in human resources. Some human resources activities may be performed in other departments across the organization but are planned and coordinated through the human resources (HR) department. Most managers regularly use the services of the human resources department as they work with their employees. Employees also receive a variety of services from the people who work in human resources.

CHECKPOINT

What do the people who are involved in human resources management do?

Human Resources Activities

The important human resources services common to many businesses are illustrated in Figure 23-1 and are described next.

EMPLOYMENT

Employment is the one area most people associate with human resources management. The employment function of human resources involves all activities required to maintain an adequate number of qualified employees in the company. Employment activities include determining the need to hire employees, recruiting applicants, determining the qualifications of applicants, and hiring the most qualified applicants to fill the available jobs. In addition, transfers, promotions, retirements, dismissals, and other job changes are part of the employment function.

WAGES AND BENEFITS

The amount a company pays employees directly and spends to provide employee benefits such as insurance and vacation time is a major part of its operating

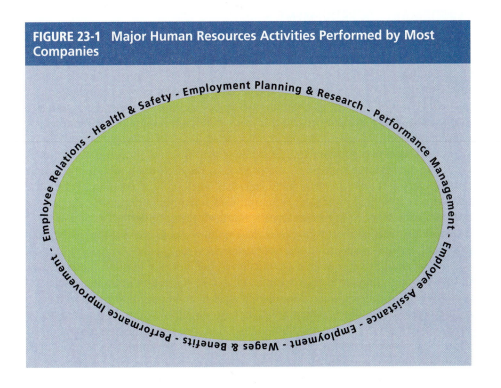

FIGURE 23-1 Major Human Resources Activities Performed by Most Companies

budget. The level of wages and benefits, especially when compared to that of competitors, helps to determine who will apply for job openings and whether they are likely to make a long-term commitment to the company or will be looking for higher-paying jobs. When performing the wages-and-benefits function, human resources employees plan and manage the financial and nonfinancial rewards available to employees.

Wages and benefits must be carefully controlled. Employee productivity (the amount of work accomplished) compared to the pay and benefits will determine whether the company can be profitable or not. It is important that employees view the system for determining pay as fair and that there is a reasonable relationship between the amount paid to an employee and the value of that employee's work to the company. Human resources is typically responsible for developing a pay system that classifies jobs according to levels and pay ranges. When a person is hired, promoted, or given a pay increase, human resources performs or monitors the procedures to ensure that the employee gets paid the correct amount.

Companies offer benefits to their employees in addition to wages. Some benefits, such as Social Security and Medicare, are required by law. Others, such as insurance and vacations, are not legally required, but many companies provide them. Often benefit plans are different for full-time than for part-time employees or are based on the length of time the employee has worked for the company. People who work in human resources study what benefits can be offered, determine the current and future costs of each type of benefit, and help management develop the benefits plan. They also provide information to employees about each type of benefit and make sure that employees recognize the value of the benefits to them.

Some companies offer employees choices of benefits, so helping employees make the best decisions and keeping track of each person's choices can be quite complicated. Once employees make their decisions, human resources employees complete the necessary paperwork or enter the data into the company's computer system. Each benefit program must be monitored to control costs and to make sure employees receive the benefits to which they are entitled.

Why is it important for businesses to carefully plan the package of wages and benefits offered to employees?

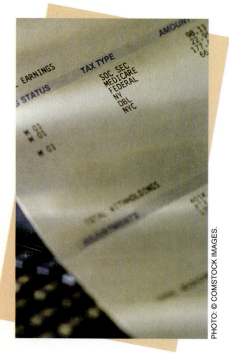

PHOTO: © COMSTOCK IMAGES.

PERFORMANCE IMPROVEMENT

Companies cannot continue to compete effectively if employees' skills are the same today as they were the day they were hired. Employees must improve their skills and learn new ones on the job. The role of human resources in performance improvement involves training and educating employees to ensure high quality and efficient work. Often the human resources department plans and manages performance improvement programs in cooperation with managers and individual employees.

Most businesses conduct several types of training and education programs. Once hired, employees receive an orientation to the company and initial training to make sure they are successful in the new job. Then, as equipment or procedures change, the company must prepare employees for those changes. Finally, when evaluations indicate that an employee is not performing as well as expected, the company provides support to improve the employee's performance so that it does not result in poor-quality products or customer service.

Employees may be promoted or transferred to a new job in the company. Part of the process of preparing employees for possible promotions or moving current employees to new jobs is a continuing education and training program. Many companies also allow employees to participate in education programs for their own personal development, believing that such programs increase employee motivation and productivity. Companies sometimes reimburse employees for some or all of the costs of education as an employee benefit.

Finally, if the company cuts back on the number of employees, eliminates a department, or undergoes a major change in its business activities, it may help the employees who will be terminated prepare for new jobs. Some of those jobs may be in other parts of the company that are adding employees, but the education and training may be for jobs in other companies. It may seem strange that companies would spend money to educate employees to work for other companies. However, progressive employers view these programs as a responsibility to employees who have contributed to the company's past success. They also believe that people are more likely to work for a company that demonstrates this level of commitment to its employees.

EMPLOYEE RELATIONS

Human resources plays a major role in employee relations by ensuring effective communication and cooperation between management and employees. If a labor union is organized within a company, a very formal set of relationships exists between employees and management. The human resources workers responsible for employee relations assist in negotiating labor contracts with the union and deal with employee activities and problems that relate to the contract. If employees are not represented by a union, human resources still performs the same types of activities, but usually in a less formal way.

The flattened organizations of today mean fewer managers. Businesses expect employees to take more responsibility for their own work. Work teams made up of employees and managers are taking responsibility for many decisions once made only by managers. These decisions include hiring, determining how work will be performed, and improving work procedures. Human resources personnel help to prepare people for their new responsibilities and develop supporting materials, training, and computerized forms and procedures to help the teams successfully perform their new tasks.

Another important area of employee relations is assuring that the company complies with all equal-employment and affirmative-action laws. In addition, human resources personnel work with employees and managers to prepare people for future job openings and promotions, as well as help them work cooperatively with each other despite individual differences. Companies are most successful when all employees have access to any job for which they are qualified and when discrimination is not a part of employment decisions or the daily work environment.

HEALTH AND SAFETY

Illnesses and injuries among employees are expensive for companies. If employees are unhealthy or injured, they may not be able to work. Other employees will have to complete that work, or the company must hire temporary employees to do it. Also, the cost of insurance and health care rises as the number of employee illnesses and injuries increases. Expensive insurance is harmful to both the employee and the company.

Substance abuse can greatly increase injuries on the job. Workers under the influence of illegal drugs or alcohol have reduced dexterity and impaired judgment. As a result, they may ignore safety procedures or be unable to perform them properly. Substance abuse also lowers worker productivity and increases absenteeism.

The human resources department is responsible for maintaining safe work areas and work procedures, enforcing laws and regulations related to safety and health, and providing adequate education and training in health and safety.

Teamwork *tip*

HR employees must be aware that the importance of each of their services is different for managers, new employees, employees with families, and employees nearing retirement. Each manager and employee needs to be treated as an individual client with specific needs. HR must work as a team to provide the range of specialized services required by everyone in the business.

PHOTO: © GETTY IMAGES/PHOTODISC.

Why might a company provide a benefit such as fitness programs for employees?

Most human resources departments provide regular safety training, place safety posters and materials in the workplace to remind workers to follow safety procedures, and monitor procedures to identify and correct possible safety problems. They also collect and report data on work-related injuries and illnesses to be sure the company and employees are well informed about the level of safety in the company and in each department. Companies often reward work units that operate for a specific amount of time without a job-related injury.

Companies sometimes promote good health by maintaining a smoke-free environment and offering help for employees to stop smoking through education programs, support groups, and even financial bonuses. To reduce employee absences and cut insurance costs, many companies organize wellness and fitness programs, build and staff fitness centers, and pay for employees to enroll in health education classes.

PERFORMANCE MANAGEMENT

Managers regularly evaluate their employees' performance to determine how well it is meeting expectations. They identify employees' strengths and reward them for superior performance. If they discover performance problems, they must help their employees improve and provide training, if needed.

Individual managers are responsible for evaluating the employees they supervise and using the results of the evaluation to improve performance. The role of human resources in performance management is to develop the evaluation system and materials and to educate managers and employees on the proper methods for evaluating and improving performance. Human resources personnel work with managers and experienced employees to design the performance management system and then prepare the forms and materials needed. They then train the managers to evaluate employees objectively, complete the evaluation forms, and conduct evaluation conferences with the employees. They also help employees understand their role in the evaluation process. The human resources department usually maintains the results of the evaluations in each employee's personnel file.

A newer method of performance evaluation, **360-degree feedback**, uses performance feedback gathered from a broad range of people with whom the employee works rather than from just the employee's manager. People who are peers of the employee contribute performance feedback. For example, a manager gathers feedback from other managers who work at the same level; employees receive feedback from coworkers. In addition, the 360-degree feedback system includes information from people who report to the person being reviewed. Sometimes even suppliers and customers are asked for feedback.

In the 360-degree feedback system, people completing the reviews fill out a detailed questionnaire about the person's performance. The responses are anonymous, so the person evaluated does not know who specifically provided the information. The information is summarized, a report is prepared, and a performance improvement conference is held with an evaluation expert to ensure that the employee and the manager interpret the information correctly and know how to use it to improve future performance.

EMPLOYEE ASSISTANCE PROGRAMS

Today, businesses recognize that employees have many important responsibilities in addition to their jobs. Personal and family concerns may interfere with an employee's work. Issues ranging from financial problems to marriage and family issues and alcohol or drug abuse are increasingly common among employees.

Employee assistance programs provide confidential personal problem-solving, counseling, and support services for employees. For the most part, participating in the services is voluntary, and employees can choose to receive assistance whenever they need the help and support. For serious problems that are interfering with work, managers can refer employees to specific assistance services, but, again, the employee can choose not to accept the assistance. For these types of employee assistance programs, the company hires specialists such as counselors, psychologists, and medical personnel to provide the services.

Some employee assistance programs have expanded to provide services needed by single-parent or two-working-parent families, or by employees in transition because of job changes or moving to a new location. Even special financial services such as short-term loans or financial assistance for education may be offered. Human resources personnel involved in employee assistance programs may arrange day-care services for children or elderly parents, help with short-term housing needs, plan carpooling or other transportation services, and facilitate many other activities that help employees balance their work and personal lives.

EMPLOYMENT PLANNING AND RESEARCH

You can see from the human resources services described above that maintaining an effective workforce is very complex. Companies change rapidly, but it may take weeks and months to hire new people, design training programs, or complete performance reviews. Federal and state employment laws as well as company policies and procedures require a great deal of information about each employee to be collected and maintained.

A major human resources function involves researching and maintaining the information that managers need to determine personnel needs and manage the workforce. The people working in this area of human resources gather information, use computer programs to analyze that information, and maintain and review employee records as well as company and competitive employment information. They then distribute this information to managers to alert them to problems, the need for changes, and ways to improve employee productivity.

business *note*

Every business is responsible for its employees' health and safety. The costs to business of workplace injuries now exceed $50 billion per year. The most common causes of injury are improper lifting, pushing, pulling, or carrying and accidental tripping or falling.

Human resources has an important role in reducing workplace accidents and injuries. The first strategy is careful design of the work area and planning of work procedures. Work areas should be well lighted, have no slippery surfaces, and be free of clutter. Tools, equipment, and storage areas that reduce the need for heavy or awkward lifting and carrying should be available. Work procedures should be designed to make sure they are safe.

A second responsibility of HR in workplace safety is employee training. New employees should complete training in how to handle products, tools, and equipment safely and lift, move, and carry materials correctly. A very important part of training is to make sure each employee is committed to following safe procedures and watching out for the safety of others. Most businesses place signs, warnings, and even alarms in the workplace as reminders. They also reward departments and employees with good safety records.

CHECKPOINT

What are the major human resources activities performed by most companies?

What tasks are involved in the research function of human resources management?

PHOTO: © GETTY IMAGES/PHOTODISC.

23.1 | Assessment

UNDERSTAND MANAGEMENT CONCEPTS

Determine the best answer for each of the following questions.

1. Another name for human resources management is
   a. operations management
   b. supervision
   c. personnel management
   d. training

2. Providing confidential personal problem-solving, counseling, and support services for employees is called
   a. performance management
   b. employee assistance
   c. employee relations
   d. performance improvement

THINK CRITICALLY

Answer the following questions as completely as possible.

3. Why are benefits considered to be as important as the amount of wages or salary to many employees?

4. What are some possible advantages and disadvantages of using a 360-degree system for performance evaluation?

Xtra!
Study Tools
thomsonedu.com/school/bpmxtra

23.2 The Employment Process

Goals
- Describe the steps a business should follow to hire an employee.
- Discuss effective procedures for promoting, transferring, and discharging employees.

Terms
- job description
- job specification
- promotion
- transfer
- discharge
- layoff
- employee turnover
- exit interview

Selecting Personnel

Hiring new employees is an expensive but very important activity for every business. Effective selection means hiring people with the right skills for each job. Hiring people who do not meet specific job qualifications results in high training costs, dissatisfied employees and customers, and poor performance. This section discusses some essential procedures for selecting personnel in a company with a human resources department.

ESTABLISHING A NEED

As a first step in the process of hiring a new employee, managers must establish that they actually need a new employee. Normally, the need develops to replace an employee who has left the company, been promoted, or retired. If the company or department is growing, new employees are needed to handle the extra work. Changes in the operations of a department or the use of new procedures or equipment may require that employees be hired to perform those duties.

After identifying a need, the department manager typically works with human resources specialists to complete the hiring process. The human resources department must have detailed and accurate information about the position in order to screen applicants and choose only the most qualified people to interview. To compile the needed information, companies prepare a job description and job specification for each position in the company. A **job description** is a list of the basic tasks that make up a job. A **job specification** is a list of the qualifications a worker needs to do that job. The two documents are important in helping to identify the qualifications and skills of the new employee. They also help applicants understand what will be required of them in their new jobs.

Human resources employees work with managers and employees who are currently doing each job to prepare job descriptions and specifications. This information is maintained in the human resources department and is updated regularly as job requirements and activities change. The data are used in a variety of ways, but in the selection process, the information is used to recruit a pool of qualified applicants and to help determine the best candidate for the job.

PHOTO: © GETTY IMAGES/PHOTODISC.

Why is it important to hire employees with the right skills for each job?

Technology *tip*

Many company Web sites allow applicants to submit their résumés as an e-mail attachment or by copying and pasting it into a résumé submission form. Be careful when using the copy-and-paste feature if your résumé has unique styles and formatting. The formatting may be lost when it is submitted, resulting in a résumé that does not look professional or may even be confusing to the receiver.

RECRUITING APPLICANTS

After the human resources department has received a request to fill a position and reviewed the job description and specifications, it must identify applicants for the opening. An effective recruitment process will result in a number of applicants from which a well-qualified person can be selected. If the pool of qualified applicants is too small, the chances of finding someone who is well qualified decreases. If the pool is too large, the process of selecting the most qualified applicant takes longer and adds to the company's costs.

There are many sources of prospective employees. The human resources department must be aware of those sources and use those most likely to yield qualified applicants. Some of the most commonly used sources of prospective employees are current employees, unsolicited applications, employment agencies, and other sources.

CURRENT EMPLOYEES Companies should make information about all job vacancies available to everyone in the company and give current employees the first opportunity to apply. There are many reasons for using this source. The job may be a promotion for some employees, which can serve as an incentive to work harder. If it is not a promotion, allowing an employee to change jobs may provide better work hours, working conditions, or pay. The new job may be a better match for the employee's interests and abilities. Placing a current employee in a job opening is also good practice for companies that are anticipating employee cutbacks.

Current employees may also recommend people they know for open positions in the company. Employees will need specific information about job openings and the procedures they should use to nominate people for openings. They must also know that the people recommended will be treated fairly and in the same way as other job applicants.

UNSOLICITED APPLICATIONS A business that has a reputation as a good employer is likely to have people applying for jobs at all times. Most large companies take applications regularly, even when they currently have no openings that fit the applicants. As applications arrive, human resources screens them for minimum qualifications and classifies them according to job categories in the company. Then they maintain the applications in an active file for a period of time, such as six months, and review them when openings occur.

EMPLOYMENT AGENCIES Employment agencies are businesses that actively recruit, evaluate, and help people prepare for and locate jobs. Many employment agencies are private businesses and receive a fee from the applicant or from the employer when a successful placement is made. All states maintain an employment service supported by state and federal taxes. Public employment offices are usually located in several cities throughout each state. They offer testing services, job listings, and help in preparing applications and developing interviewing skills. They work with businesses to publicize available jobs and identify qualified candidates for job openings.

OTHER SOURCES Colleges and universities, career and technical schools, and an increasing number of high schools have placement offices to assist graduates in obtaining jobs. Businesses can use those offices to obtain lists of potential employees and, in some cases, to obtain résumés and other information about the school's graduates. The offices may provide assistance in scheduling interviews with a number of applicants to help the recruiting business.

Advertising is a common method of attracting job applicants. Companies frequently advertise in local newspapers or on television or radio when they need a large number of employees or they must fill an opening quickly. For longer-term needs or more specialized jobs, companies may place advertising in industry magazines or other specialized publications. Human resources employees carefully write employment advertisements to attract only qualified applicants rather than large numbers of unqualified people.

The Internet has become a popular resource for recruiting personnel. Web sites such as monster.com and careerbuilder.com provide thousands of job listings that job seekers can search by job category, location, company, or salary expectations. Most of the top employment sites on the Web also allow people seeking employment to post their résumés. Some sites provide services such as help in résumé preparation and tips for a successful job search. Most major Internet employment sites make it possible for applicants to submit their résumés to prospective employers online. Today, companies that regularly hire employees place a link to employment opportunities on their home page so that prospective employees can obtain an up-to-date listing of available jobs.

PROCESSING APPLICATIONS

Most job seekers fill out an application form, which must ask only for information necessary to make the best selection for the job. The form must not ask for inappropriate, illegal, or discriminatory information. Then, a number of steps are followed to complete the selection process and choose the best candidate for the job:

1. Human resources employees review the applications to eliminate the people who do not meet minimum qualifications. Those qualifications would typically include level of education, specific training, certifications, or licenses. Applicants are often eliminated at this stage because they filled out the application form incorrectly, did not fully complete the application, or had very poor written communication skills.

2. A human resources employee interviews the remaining applicants to confirm information on the application, to gather information on oral communication and human relations skills, and to provide more information to the applicants about the company and the job.

3. A human resources employee checks the information supplied on the application form and through the interview for accuracy by contacting schools attended, previous employers, and listed references. Careful questioning of a reference can often reveal important information about an applicant's strengths, work habits, and human relations skills.

4. Human resources employees administer tests to the applicants remaining in the pool to determine if they have the needed knowledge and skills for the specific job. To be legal, the tests must measure only characteristics important for success on the job.

5. The manager or a work team of the department that has the opening interviews the top applicants. The interview allows more specific questioning related to the duties and qualifications for the job, can offer applicants detailed information about the job and the department, and gives applicants the opportunity to ask questions. By understanding the job and its requirements, applicants are in a better position to determine if the job would satisfy them.

6. The final selection is made by comparing information gathered with the job requirements. The decision should be made carefully and objectively. Many businesses require prospective employees to pass a physical exam, including drug screening. They also check for a possible criminal record. Some companies require drug screening and a criminal background check

The Small Business Administration reports that for every $1 an employer invests in screening new employees, the business saves $5 to $16 in reduced absenteeism, turnover, insurance, and employer liability.

early in the employment process; others complete it as one of the last steps before a finalist is hired.

7. When an applicant is hired, human resources employees walk the new employee through filling out the necessary paperwork, such as tax forms and insurance enrollment forms. They then help the new employee get a good start with an orientation program and initial training. After the new employee has been at work for several weeks, the human resources department may follow up to see whether the right person was selected in order to improve employment procedures.

CHECKPOINT
What are some commonly used and effective sources of prospective employees?

Promoting, Transferring, and Releasing Employees

The amount of time and money invested in recruiting, hiring, and training a new employee is very high. Because of the expense, once the company finds a good employee, it should attempt to keep that person as long as possible. Offering opportunities for promotion and transfer can help retain good employees. The company also needs a procedure for dealing with employees who are not performing satisfactorily and for reducing the number of employees if changing economic conditions require downsizing.

CHANGES IN EMPLOYMENT STATUS

A **promotion** is the advancement of an employee within a company to a position with more authority and responsibility. Usually, a promotion includes an increase in pay and may include greater prestige and benefits. Promotion opportunities occur when another person vacates a job (through promotion or retirement, for example) or when the company creates a new position.

Whenever possible, a business should fill vacancies by promotion. If the company has an effective selection procedure, it should have well-qualified employees who, with training and experience, could be promoted. Every employee should have an equal opportunity to receive promotions for which they are qualified. Employees need to know the job to which they can advance and the factors considered in promotion. Many companies now provide career counseling services for employees. Through career counseling, employees can plan career paths, determine the education and training required for the jobs in the career path, and develop plans to prepare for the jobs they want. You will learn more about employee development in Chapter 25.

A **transfer** is the assignment of an employee to another job in the company that, in general, involves the same level of responsibility and authority as the person's current work. There are many reasons for transfers.

- Employees being trained for management positions may be transferred among several positions to gain experience.
- Employees may be transferred to give them a better opportunity for promotion.
- Employees may be transferred to new departments or new company locations due to growth or reduction of the size of departments.

- Employees may choose to transfer to jobs that better meet their current interests and needs.
- Employees may be transferred to overcome difficulties resulting from poor performance or conflicts with other people on the job.

Some situations require employees to leave the company. Some employee separations are permanent, and others are temporary. They may result from a downturn in the economy or in the company's fortunes. Employees may also be released because they have violated company policies or have been unsuccessful at improving unsatisfactory job performance.

A <mark>discharge</mark> is the release of an employee from the company due to inappropriate work behavior. In ordinary language, this means that the employee is fired. Careful procedures must be followed to make sure the reasons for the discharge are a clear violation of company rules and policies and have been communicated to the employee. A <mark>layoff</mark> is a temporary or permanent reduction in the number of employees because of a change in business conditions. After a layoff, employees may be called back to work when jobs become available again. When a company plans a large number of layoffs, the human resources department should help employees plan for them. HR may help locate other jobs, offer personal and career counseling, or provide retraining for other jobs within the company.

EMPLOYEE TURNOVER

<mark>Employee turnover</mark> is the rate at which people enter and leave employment in a business during a year. The rate of turnover is important to a business because the loss of experienced employees means that new employees have to be hired and trained. New employees will not be as productive as experienced ones for some time. Between the time an experienced employee leaves and a new employee is hired, the remaining employees are often called on to get the work done. Most companies watch their employee turnover rate carefully and make every effort to keep it low.

Two common formulas for computing the rate of employee turnover are shown in Figure 23-2. An example will illustrate the difference between the two methods. Suppose that over the last year 150 employees left their jobs in a company. The company hired 120 new employees to replace those who had left. The average number of employees during the year was 1,000. According to the first formula,

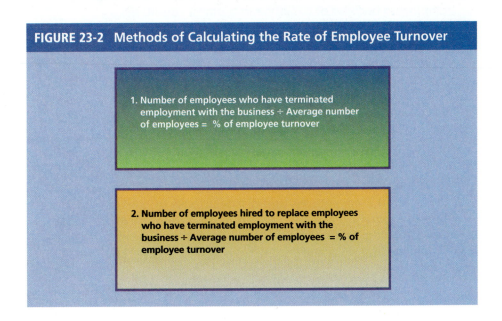

FIGURE 23-2 Methods of Calculating the Rate of Employee Turnover

1. Number of employees who have terminated employment with the business ÷ Average number of employees = % of employee turnover

2. Number of employees hired to replace employees who have terminated employment with the business ÷ Average number of employees = % of employee turnover

the employee turnover was 15 percent (150/1,000). According to the second formula, it was 12 percent (120/1,000). To make it easier to study employee turnover trends, the company should use the same formula from year to year.

EXIT INTERVIEWS

Whenever an employee leaves the company, interviewing the person can gain some important feedback. An **exit interview** is a formal interview with an employee who is leaving the company to determine his or her attitudes about the company and suggestions for improvement. The exit interview provides an opportunity to learn about the causes of employee turnover and gain feedback about the company's policies and procedures, management, and operations. The interview procedure should be carefully planned to get important information in a way that is comfortable for the person being interviewed and to accurately record the information so it can be used to improve operations and employment procedures.

CHECKPOINT

What are the differences between promotion, transfer, and discharge?

23.2 Assessment

UNDERSTAND MANAGEMENT CONCEPTS

Determine the best answer for each of the following questions.

1. The first step in the employment process is
   a. preparing a job description and job specifications
   b. recruiting a pool of applicants
   c. asking applicants to take a drug test
   d. reviewing applications that are on file

2. A _____ is a temporary or permanent reduction in the number of employees because of a change in business conditions.
   a. transfer
   b. discharge
   c. layoff
   d. promotion

THINK CRITICALLY

Answer the following questions as completely as possible.

3. Why should the human resources department take most of the responsibility for the steps in the application process rather than allowing the employing department to complete them?

4. What are the advantages and disadvantages of having managers identify specific employees for promotions and transfers rather than opening up the process to all company employees?

Xtra!
Study Tools
thomsonedu.com/school/bpmxtra

Focus On...

Social Responsibility–Increasing Employment Opportunities through the ADA

Many companies search to fill increasingly technical and complex jobs with qualified applicants. Some employment divisions report screening hundreds of applications to find one person who meets the necessary job requirements. At the same time, businesses have overlooked millions of Americans who have the necessary job qualifications for many jobs. Why? They have disabilities that many employers mistakenly believe will prevent them from performing job duties effectively.

Because of the widespread misunderstanding, stereotypes, and discrimination faced by disabled Americans in the workplace, a law to correct the discrimination was enacted in 1990. The Americans with Disabilities Act (ADA) prohibits employment discrimination against individuals with physical and mental handicaps or chronic illnesses if they are able to perform the basic functions of the job. Under ADA, employers must provide the opportunity for all disabled applicants who are otherwise qualified to compete for available jobs. A qualified applicant is a person who has the required education and experience and can perform the work if the employer provides "reasonable accommodation."

Providing reasonable accommodation means making facilities, equipment, procedures, and activities accessible and usable; restructuring jobs and work tasks when possible; and providing access to the same benefits and privileges available to other employees. The word *reasonable* is used to ensure that employers do not have to make changes that result in a severe financial hardship for the business or that alter the job so that required work cannot be completed. Studies done in businesses in preparation for implementing the ADA found that, with careful planning, many accommodations for disabled employees could be accomplished at no additional cost. Other changes could be made at relatively low cost by implementing creative solutions. Although some organizations are concerned about the impact and cost of complying with the Americans with Disabilities Act, many others have found that it has encouraged them to consider a group of productive employees they had previously ignored.

Think Critically

1. Why do you believe it was necessary for the federal government to pass the ADA legislation?
2. If you were a businessperson, how would you respond to the ADA requirements?
3. Using your school as an example, in what ways have the facilities, equipment, and materials been modified to meet the needs of disabled students, faculty, and staff? Are there areas in the school where you believe other reasonable accommodations can be made?

23.3 | Employment Law

Goals

- Describe several ways that employees are protected through federal and state employment legislation.
- Discuss the steps that government and businesses have taken to remove discrimination in employment opportunities.

Terms

- Fair Labor Standards Act (FLSA)
- Occupational Safety and Health Act (OSHA)
- Social Security
- Medicare
- workers' compensation
- unemployment insurance

Regulating Employment Conditions and Benefits

State and federal governments have been concerned for years about employee/employer relationships and the protection of employees. They have passed several laws to protect employees, improve their health and safety, and provide minimum employee benefits. The federal Department of Labor (DOL) administers and enforces more than 180 laws related to employment and workplace safety. The laws cover about 10 million employers and 125 million workers. HR departments are responsible for understanding the laws and ensuring that the business complies with their requirements. The major laws regulating employment are reviewed next.

THE FAIR LABOR STANDARDS ACT

The **Fair Labor Standards Act (FLSA)** prescribes standards for wages and overtime pay. FLSA affects most private and some public employers. It requires employers to pay covered employees at least the federal minimum wage and overtime pay of one-and-one-half times the regular rate of pay. Most managers and other types of salaried employees are exempt from FLSA regulations. Also, businesses that are not involved in interstate commerce but conduct all their activities within one state may not be covered. However, many states have their own minimum-wage laws.

THE OCCUPATIONAL SAFETY AND HEALTH ACT

The **Occupational Safety and Health Act (OSHA)** regulates safety and health conditions in most businesses. Employers have a duty to provide their employees with a workplace free from unsafe working conditions and other hazards. The act is enforced through workplace inspections and investigations.

SOCIAL SECURITY AND MEDICARE

Social Security is a social insurance program funded through payroll contributions. The formal title of the program is the Federal Old-Age and Survivors Insurance Trust Fund and the Federal Disability Insurance Trust Fund (OASDI). The largest component of OASDI is the payment of retirement benefits. Throughout a person's life, contributions are made by both the employer and employee. The Social Security Administration keeps track of the contributions. Upon retirement, the person can begin to receive payments from the account. The amount of the monthly benefit depends on the earnings record and the age at which benefits begin. A worker who becomes totally disabled, regardless of his or her age, can also receive benefits under the Social Security law. There are also provisions for payments to survivors after the death of a person who has made contributions.

Medicare provides supplemental health insurance for retirement-age people as well as others with specified disabilities. There are three parts to Medicare coverage—hospital insurance, medical insurance, and prescription drug coverage. The required contribution rates for Social Security in effect as of 2005 are 6.20 percent for employers and employees for all earnings up to $90,000. In addition, a Medicare contribution of 1.45 percent of all earnings is required by the employer and employee. People who are self-employed must pay a total combined rate of 15.30 percent for Social Security and Medicare.

NETBookmark

Social Security contributions are made by employees and employers each pay period. Although you can see the amount deducted from your paycheck and the total amount contributed each pay period, it is difficult to realize the amount of benefits you will receive upon retirement. The Social Security Administration has developed a simple calculator that anyone can use to estimate the amount of benefits they will receive based on the wages they earn, the number of years they plan to work, and the age at which they plan to retire. Point your browser to www.thomsonedu.com/school/bpmxtra. Open the Quick Calculator and experiment by inputing different estimates of income and retirement options to see the impact on potential retirement payments. What factors other than income and retirement age may affect the benefits you receive?

www.thomsonedu.com/school/bpmxtra

WORKERS' COMPENSATION AND UNEMPLOYMENT INSURANCE

All states have workers' compensation laws. **Workers' compensation** requires employers to provide insurance for the death, injury, or illness of employees that result from their work. Some states maintain the insurance programs, but many offer coverage through private insurance companies. **Unemployment insurance** is a state-managed program that provides temporary income to individuals who have been laid off from their jobs. Specific requirements must be met in terms of the length of employment and steps taken to regain employment. Employers make contributions to the state unemployment fund based on the number of employees and their employment history.

FAMILY AND MEDICAL LEAVE ACT

The Family and Medical Leave Act (FMLA) requires that employers covered by the law must allow an eligible employee up to a total of 12 weeks of leave during a year for one of the following reasons:

- the birth, adoption, or foster-care placement of a child of the employee
- caring for an immediate family member (spouse, child, or parent) with a serious health condition
- medical leave for a serious health condition

CHECKPOINT

What employment laws are administered by states rather than the federal government?

Equal Opportunity in Employment

In recent years, many businesses have taken positive steps to correct discrimination in employment. Those steps include the development of written plans for fair employment practices, a review of recruitment and selection procedures, improved access to job training to qualify employees for promotion who may have been excluded in the past, diversity training for all managers and employees, and improved performance evaluation procedures that reduce bias. Companies that have taken a sincere and active interest in improving the diversity of their workforce and eliminating discrimination have found that diversity improves decision making by bringing a rich array of ideas and perspectives to company planning and problem solving.

Government has also played a role in reducing discrimination and increasing employment opportunities for everyone. The laws related to equal employment are described in Figure 23-3.

FIGURE 23-3 Laws that Expand Employment Opportunities

The Civil Rights Act

This act prohibits discrimination in hiring, training, and promotion on the basis of race, ethnicity, gender, religion, or national origin.

Equal Pay Act

This act prohibits unequal pay for men and women who are doing substantially the same work.

Age Discrimination in Employment Act

This act prohibits discrimination in conditions of employment or job opportunities for persons over 40 years old.

Immigration Reform and Control Act

This act requires employers to verify that potential employees are not aliens unauthorized to work in the United States and prohibits employment discrimination because of national origin or citizenship status.

Americans with Disabilities Act

This act prohibits discrimination against qualified people with disabilities in employment, public services, transportation, public accommodations, and telecommunications. It requires employers to make reasonable accommodations to support the employment of disabled employees.

facts & figures

Supply and demand cause the compensation for some jobs to be higher than for others even when the jobs are of similar difficulty, responsibility, and so on. The level of compensation is also influenced by what competing firms pay for similar jobs. However, laws and regulations also affect the level of compensation by ensuring there is no discrimination based on gender, age, or disability.

CHECKPOINT

List the important laws that regulate employment discrimination and equal employment.

PHOTO: © DIGITAL VISION.

Which employment laws are designed to protect this worker?

23.3 Assessment

UNDERSTAND MANAGEMENT CONCEPTS

Determine the best answer for each of the following questions.

1. The federal law that prescribes standards for wages and overtime pay is the
   a. Fair Labor Standards Act
   b. Occupational Safety and Health Act
   c. Federal Old-Age and Survivors Insurance Trust Fund
   d. Medicare Act

2. Which of the following is *not* provided protection from employment discrimination by federal law?
   a. age
   b. income
   c. gender
   d. citizenship status

THINK CRITICALLY

Answer the following questions as completely as possible.

3. Why do you believe federal and state governments have taken a specific interest in wages, working conditions, and the health and safety of employees?

4. What are some ways a prospective employee can determine if an employer provides equal employment opportunity or continues practices that discriminate in hiring and promotions?

Xtra!
Study Tools
thomsonedu.com/school/bpmxtra

thomsonedu.com/school/bpmxtra

CHAPTER CONCEPTS

- Human resources personnel perform the tasks that help a business keep the skilled, productive, and satisfied employees it needs to succeed.

- The HR employment function involves all activities required to maintain an adequate number of qualified employees in the company. HR is also responsible for wages and benefits, performance improvement, employee relations, health and safety, performance management, employee assistance programs, and employment planning and research.

- Effective selection means hiring people with the right skills for each job. Hiring people who do not meet specific job qualifications results in high training costs, dissatisfied employees and customers, and poor performance.

- Companies can retain good employees by offering opportunities for promotion and transfer. Procedures are also needed to deal with employee discharges and layoffs.

- HR departments are responsible for understanding federal and state employment laws and ensuring that the business complies with them.

- Employee diversity improves organizations by bringing a rich array of ideas and perspectives to a company. Companies must be aware of and follow laws related to equal opportunity and discrimination.

REVIEW TERMS AND CONCEPTS

Write the letter of the term that matches each definition. Some terms will not be used.

a. 360-degree feedback
b. employee assistance programs
c. employee turnover
d. exit interview
e. Fair Labor Standards Act
f. human resources management
g. job description
h. job specification
i. layoff
j. Medicare
k. Occupational Safety and Health Act
l. promotion
m. Social Security
n. transfer
o. unemployment insurance
p. workers' compensation

1. Confidential personal problem-solving, counseling, and support services for employees
2. State-managed program that provides temporary income to individuals who have been laid off from their jobs
3. Advancement of an employee within a company to a position with more authority and responsibility
4. Employer-provided insurance for the death, injury, or illness of employees that result from their work
5. Temporary or permanent reduction in the number of employees because of a change in business conditions
6. Performance feedback gathered from a broad range of people with whom an employee works rather than from just the employee's manager
7. Federal law that prescribes standards for wages and overtime pay
8. Rate at which people enter and leave employment in a business during a year
9. List of the qualifications a worker needs to do a specific job
10. All activities involved with acquiring, developing, and compensating the people who do the company's work
11. Supplemental health insurance for retirement-age people and others with specified disabilities
12. Social insurance program funded through payroll contributions

DETERMINE THE BEST ANSWER

13. Of all the resources used by a business, probably the most important to its success is its
    a. technology
    b. capital
    c. people
    d. raw materials

14. Which of the following is *not* a situation in which HR should provide training in an organization?
    a. when an employee is first hired
    b. when an employee is promoted or transferred
    c. when layoffs occur, to help employees prepare for new jobs
    d. All are situations in which HR should provide training.

15. Job descriptions and job specifications are used in the employment process to
    a. get the largest pool of applicants possible
    b. provide information to applicants so they can understand the job for which they are applying
    c. allow managers to describe jobs in a way that fits the qualifications of the person they want to hire
    d. all of the above

16. Which of the following statements about the effective use of job transfers is *not* true?
    a. Employees may transfer to new departments or new company locations due to growth or reduction in the size of departments.
    b. Employees may transfer to jobs that better meet their current interests and needs.
    c. Employees may be transferred to overcome difficulties resulting from poor performance or conflicts with other people on the job.
    d. Employees may be transferred after a clear violation of company rules or inappropriate work behavior.

17. Medicare provides retirees with which of the following benefits?
    a. hospital insurance
    b. health insurance
    c. prescription drug coverage
    d. all of the above

18. Employers are expected to make reasonable accommodations in work procedures, facilities, and equipment as part of the
    a. Americans with Disabilities Act
    b. Age Discrimination in Employment Act
    c. Civil Rights Act
    d. Social Security Act

APPLY WHAT YOU KNOW

19. Based on the Reality Check scenario at the beginning of the chapter, which job would you choose if you were Patrick? What are the reasons for your choice? Why is the other choice less desirable?

20. Businesses must be sure employees are satisfied with their jobs and motivated to perform well. What are the most important activities that human resources departments perform that you believe support that goal? Justify your choices.

21. What would you like and dislike about the 360-degree feedback system if your employer used it to evaluate your work performance?

22. Why should a company eliminate applicants who are careless and make errors in completing an application even if they are otherwise well qualified for a job?

23. In some businesses, experienced employees have a higher accident rate than new employees. What actions would you recommend to increase employee attention to safety and accident prevention?

24. If you were a manager, what steps would you take to create a work environment that is diverse, expands employment opportunities, and does not discriminate?

MAKE CONNECTIONS

25. **Writing** Think of a job that interests you and would fit your current skills and education. Prepare a job description for the ideal job. Then write an advertisement that a company could place in a newspaper to recruit applicants for the job. Find examples and information on the Internet and local newspapers if necessary. Share your finished products with a classmate and ask for feedback on whether the job description and ad provide clear and adequate information for an applicant.

26. **Role-Playing** You are a manager meeting with a new employee who is at the end of the six-week probationary period. You must discharge the employee due to an attendance problem and the inability to complete many work assignments on time. Ask another student to play the role of the employee. Your goal is to have a positive meeting to communicate the reasons for the termination and to encourage the person to work on the weaknesses for future jobs.

27. **Visual Arts** Identify a safety concern in your school that might result in an accident that injures people or damages property. Prepare a poster that encourages people to follow safe procedures related to the safety concern.

28. **Law** Review newspapers and magazines to locate an article related to the violation of employment law by an employer. Study the information and write a one-page report on the issue. Describe the law or laws related to the violation, the specific circumstances that led to the violation, and the actions that were taken against the business if the violation was proven.

CASE IN POINT

CASE 23-1: Did Charles Have a Chance?

Charles Morgan was hired five weeks ago to work in the mailroom of the Teletron Trading Corporation. His job was to collect mail twice daily from each office in the building, sort and process outgoing mail, deliver outgoing mail to the post office, and pick up incoming mail from the post office. He learned the job in one day by working with the outgoing employee, Tomika Williams. Tomika had been hired by another company and had only one day left with the company by the time Charles was hired.

After one month, Charles thought that he was doing well. Some of the first few days had been rather rough, but things seemed to be going more smoothly now. He rarely saw his supervisor, but when he did the supervisor always greeted him pleasantly.

A week later he received notice that he was being discharged at the end of his six-week probationary period. There was no explanation for the discharge, and Charles was not aware of the probationary period. He went to the human resources office immediately. The employment manager pulled a folder from the file and began reading notes that had been placed there during the past month. Charles responded truthfully to each item.

a. An hour late to work on May 15: "My car wouldn't start, but I called to say that I would be in as soon as possible. I worked an extra hour at the end of the day to finish my duties."

b. Two offices complained that the mail had not been picked up on the second of the month: "It was my second day on the job, and I couldn't remember all of the stops. After the second day, I made a schedule and I haven't missed an office since."

c. The Research Department complained that an important document was sent by regular mail when it should have been sent by express mail: "I didn't know the policy for deciding when and how to send items until I was told I had done it wrong. I asked the supervisor, who gave me a procedures manual to study. Tomika Williams had not told me about the manual."

Several other similar complaints were included in the file. Charles readily admitted to but explained each one. According to the employment manager, Charles was being discharged in keeping with company policy. The policy stated that any employee who received five or more complaints about work procedures during the probationary period was automatically discharged.

THINK CRITICALLY

1. What is your opinion of what happened to Charles? What responsibility should he take for what happened? Justify your opinion.

2. Develop several reasons to justify the probationary and discharge policy of the company. Describe what you believe the company should do to improve the policy.

3. Why do you believe Charles was prepared for his job in the way he was? What role should the human resources department play when employees receive that type of training? What recommendations can you make to improve the company's training procedures?

CASE 23-2: What Can We Cut?

The executive team of the Drindel Corporation was facing a crisis. International competition was putting tremendous pressure on the company. Several longtime competitors in the United States had already either been purchased by foreign companies or had moved most of their production operations to other countries to take advantage of lower wage rates and production costs. Drindel had operated in the United States for more than 80 years. Managers wanted to keep their U.S. operations and continue to provide jobs for their current employees. However, they also knew they had to find ways to reduce costs to be able to remain competitive and profitable. They had already cut all the costs they could in production and operations and now were turning to a major cost area—personnel. Drindel had always prided itself on paying competitive wages and offering a comprehensive set of benefits, including insurance, vacations, employee assistance programs, and ongoing training. As a result, Drindel employees were very loyal and the company had one of the lowest turnover rates in the industry. However, the cost of wages, benefits, and human resources services was the one remaining area that Drindel executives felt they had to examine carefully. These were the choices they considered:

a. Ask all employees, including managers, to take a 10 percent reduction in wages and salaries to bring those costs near the industry average.

b. Ask employees to pay the full cost of health insurance. Currently the company paid 80 percent and employees 20 percent. The total monthly cost of health insurance through the company was lower than what employees would have to pay if they purchased it individually.

c. Give each employee $200 per month to spend on any benefits they chose. That would reduce the company's cost of benefits by nearly half and allow employees to pick those most important to them. If employees chose no benefits, they would be paid the $200.

d. Reduce the size and cost of the human resources department by eliminating all employee assistance programs and the personnel who provided them and by cutting the amount of training by 50 percent.

THINK CRITICALLY

1. Why do you believe Drindel executives were attempting to protect their company by cutting personnel costs rather than choosing their competitors' strategy—moving operations to another country?
2. Evaluate each of the choices in terms of its possible effect on the company and its immediate and long-term cost savings.
3. If you were a Drindel employee, which option would you choose? Why? If you were an executive, which choice would be best for the company? Why?

Because a small business has only a few employees, each employee is very important to the success of the company. When you begin to hire employees for your business, you will need procedures designed to hire excellent employees. You will also need to develop effective human resources policies and procedures that will encourage employees to be productive and help you keep them working for you.

DATA COLLECTION

1. Review the employment ads in your local newspaper for several days. Identify ads for employment in small service businesses. Study the qualifications required and descriptions of duties listed.

2. Interview the owner of a small business. Discuss each of the human resources activities described in lesson 23-1. Identify the problems the business has in managing human resources. Ask the owner if substance abuse among employees is a problem, and how he or she deals with the problem.

3. Investigate Internet resources for checking the backgrounds of job applicants for criminal records. Write down your thoughts about doing these kinds of checks.

4. Obtain and study the security policies of two local businesses. Then write a policy statement to help provide security for your employees.

5. Search the Internet to identify recommendations on benefit plans for small businesses. Sites such as the Small Business Administration and the Department of Labor are excellent starting points for your research.

ANALYSIS

1. Develop a job description and job specifications for an employee you would hire. Then write the copy for a newspaper or Internet advertisement you would use to recruit potential employees.

2. Develop a specific set of procedures for hiring and orienting new employees. Include a statement of nondiscrimination in hiring that complies with applicable laws.

3. Develop a specific set of procedures for promoting, laying off, and discharging employees.

Chapter 24

Rewarding and Developing Employees

24.1 Compensation Planning

24.2 Employee Benefits

24.3 Improving Employee Performance

REALITY CHECK

Changing an Employee Reward System

The HR planning board of Petro Services, Inc., was meeting to review a proposed change in the compensation plan the company used for all its employees. For 25 years, the company had had a bonus system. The board of directors approved a specific amount of money to be used at the end of the year for employee bonuses. The bonuses were determined by division managers based on their review of each employee's performance. Bonus amounts varied considerably across the business. Some managers awarded large bonuses—several thousand dollars—to a very few employees. Other managers awarded smaller bonuses—only a couple of hundred dollars—to a large number of employees. A growing number of complaints were heard by HR and the board about the seeming unfairness of the bonus system. Also, the board wasn't sure that the bonuses actually improved the company's performance.

The new plan being proposed took a different approach than the bonus system. Money to reward employees at the end of the year would be allocated as a small percentage of the profits Petro Services earned for the year. If the company was not profitable, money would not be available for the reward program. If there was a profit, every company employee would receive a monetary reward in the form of profit sharing. The amount of the reward would be based on employees' job classifications and the number of years they had worked for the company. It was expected that in a typical year when the company made a profit, the reward for each employee would range between $250 and $1,000. In very profitable years, those amounts could triple.

The goal of the program was to encourage all employees to take responsibility for the profitability of the company. The more profitable the company, the higher the end-of-year reward. The process would also seem fairer to employees. However, people who had earned large bonuses in the past might be upset, and all employees would be unhappy if there was no profit.

24.1 Compensation Planning

Goals
- Describe several types of compensation systems and the reasons each is used.
- Discuss important factors that affect pay levels in a business.

Terms
- compensation
- wage
- salary
- compensation plan
- time plan
- commission plan
- piece-rate plan
- combination plan
- bonus
- minimum wage law

Compensation Plans

One of the important reasons people work is to earn money. But money is just one valuable benefit that employees receive for their labor. Other benefits include such things as paid vacations, company-sponsored health insurance, and employee assistance programs. The pay and other benefits employees receive in exchange for their labor are called **compensation**.

The method used to determine pay can be an important factor in attracting employees to the company, motivating them to give their best efforts, and retaining good employees. Therefore, the compensation system must pay employees fairly, in a way that encourages them to work for the company while using the company's resources efficiently.

Many factors affect the amount of pay an employee receives. These include the skill required for the job, the work conditions, the amount of education and experience the person has, the supply and demand for that type of worker, and economic conditions.

A **wage** is pay based on an hourly rate. **Salary** is pay based on a time frame other than hourly, such as weekly or monthly. Salaries are most often paid to executives, supervisors, professionals, and others who do not have a fixed number of hours to work each week. Companies develop compensation plans to determine how employees will be paid. A **compensation plan** is a system of policies and procedures for calculating the wages and salaries in an organization.

Because businesses vary a great deal in terms of what they produce and the qualifications of their employees, many different methods are used to determine how employees are paid. Under some plans, employees with the same qualifications and experience are paid the same no matter what job they do or whether one is more productive than another. Other systems determine pay levels by the type of work, the amount produced, or the quality of the work. Commonly used compensation plans are time plans, performance plans, and combination plans.

TIME PLANS

The most common payment method is a **time plan**, which pays a certain amount for a specified period of time worked. Wages are a time-based plan. For example, an employee might earn $8.50 per hour. A salary is also based on time worked. For example, a company may pay an employee a salary of $2,800 per month,

facts & figures

The cost of living is a major factor in determining the real value of your total compensation. For example, a person who earns $40,000 in Anchorage, Alaska, would need to earn only $24,000 in Little Rock, Arkansas, to maintain the same standard of living. A $55,000 salary in Raleigh, North Carolina, is equal to $71,000 in Miami, Florida.

whereas another company may set an employee's salary at $43,800 per year. In either case, the employee receives a regular paycheck, often on a semiweekly or monthly basis, with the payment based on the time worked and the wage or salary rate established for that person or job.

Time plans are easy to administer because pay is based directly on the amount of time worked. However, time plans do not financially reward employees who provide extra effort or do outstanding work. Changes in the total compensation paid by the business can be made by scheduling employees for fewer or more hours and by adjusting wage and salary rates. Employees are neither rewarded nor penalized with compensation based on their efforts. The only way to earn more money is to work additional time periods if available. If the hours of work are reduced through no fault of the employee, compensation is reduced as well.

PERFORMANCE PLANS

Two types of plans pay employees for the amount of work they produce. A **commission plan** pays employees a percentage of the volume of sales for which they are responsible. For example, a salesperson may earn a commission of 5 percent on total sales. If the salesperson makes sales worth $10,000 during one week, he or she would earn $500 that week. The commission system provides a direct incentive to employees because their efforts directly determine their pay. Also, the business can control the relationship between compensation and costs because pay relates directly to the amount of sales. A negative result of the commission plan is that it encourages the salesperson to concentrate on activities that lead to the largest commissions. A salesperson may try to sell products a customer doesn't need, may concentrate on larger customers while ignoring smaller but important customers, and may not attend to work that detracts from selling time.

A similar type of performance pay system is the piece-rate plan. The **piece-rate plan** pays the employee a fixed rate for each unit produced. An individual employee's pay in this case is based directly on the amount of work the employee produces. For example, if an employee earns 30 cents for each unit and produces 250 units in a day, the employee earns $75 for the day.

Although piece-rate plans were first used in factories to encourage employees to increase production, companies also pay other types of employees on the basis of units of work completed. They may pay billing clerks based on the number of invoices processed, data-entry personnel according to the number of lines of copy entered, order pickers based on the number of items they pull from inventory to fill orders, and market researchers based on the number of phone interviews they complete.

Well-designed pay plans based on productivity usually result in increased performance, at least in the short run. However, performance plans can make it difficult for new employees to earn a reasonable amount because they are inexperienced and cannot work as efficiently as experienced workers. Performance plans may also encourage experienced employees to find shortcuts to increase their production, resulting in quality or safety problems.

Performance plans are a bit more difficult to control than other compensation plans. It is difficult to predict the quantity of work that one employee or a group of employees can actually complete when their goal is to increase the amount of pay they will earn. Production may increase to a much higher level than expected, resulting in more products than can be sold.

How might receiving a salary versus a commission affect the way a salesperson works with customers?

PHOTO: © GETTY IMAGES/PHOTODISC.

Costs are then higher than budgeted and profits are reduced. But if a company tries to limit the level of production or cut the piece rate to hold down costs, employees will be upset.

Some companies are developing innovative ways to compensate performance on specific, short-term projects that motivate employees while not adding greatly to the organization's costs. The reward is often in the form of a product or service the employee values rather than a direct wage or salary payment. Under one such plan, managers reward employees who have performed well or have accomplished a specific, challenging goal. When an individual or a work team achieves the established goal, the manager provides rewards such as tickets for an upcoming athletic event or concert, gift certificates for employees to take their family out for a night on the town, or some other reward that is meaningful to the employees in recognition of their efforts.

COMBINATION PLANS

To get the advantages of various types of pay systems, some companies use combination plans. A **combination plan** is a pay plan that provides each employee a small wage or salary and adds incentive pay based on performance. Such a plan assures the employee a specified amount of money but allows the person to earn an additional amount based on effort. It is particularly effective for jobs that require a number of activities that do not directly result in increased production or sales. Some companies provide the incentive based on the performance of a work team or group rather than on the individual's performance, in order to encourage cooperation and group effort.

A variation of the combination plan is the use of bonuses. A **bonus** is money paid at the end of a specific but long period of time (3, 6, or 12 months) for performance that exceeds the expected standard for that period. Bonuses relate employee rewards to achievement of important department or company goals or to the overall organizational performance for the time period. If the work unit or company does well, employees share in the financial success. The bonus system is used to encourage employees to focus on long-term performance rather than on day-to-day efforts only. It also encourages them to consider the overall success of the business and how their individual job and the work of their department contribute to that success. To receive a bonus, everyone in the department and organization must do well.

CHECKPOINT

Describe the differences in the three major types of compensation plans.

Factors Affecting Pay Levels

Determining the amount of wages and salaries is an important business decision. In addition to the type of pay plan, companies consider other factors when determining wages and salaries. For example, employees who bring more skills to the job may be more valuable to the company and therefore receive greater pay than other employees in the same job. Also, some jobs may be more important to the company than others, justifying greater pay. The company may pay more

Increasing your value to your employer through training may result in an increase in your compensation.

PHOTO: © GETTY IMAGES/PHOTODISC.

for greater experience or more years worked for the company. The supply and demand for that type of labor, current economic conditions, and the prevailing wage rates in the community and the industry also affect the rate of pay. Companies may choose to provide a range of employee benefits as an alternative to high wages. Finally, federal and state labor laws, such as laws that set minimum wages, affect employee pay.

THE IMPORTANCE OF COMPENSATION PLANNING

Human resources departments are usually charged with developing and maintaining a company's compensation system. Because compensation is often one of the largest expenses of a company, it is important that the total compensation paid is consistent with the sales and other income earned by the business. If compensation costs are too high, the company will be unable to earn a profit. On the other hand, if wages and salaries are too low, the company will be unable to attract the number of employees needed with the skills required to perform the company's work. In either case, the company will be at a competitive disadvantage.

Usually human resources departments of large companies employ economists and other specialists to develop pay plans and to help determine the total amount of money that should be spent on employee compensation, including benefits. Smaller companies usually attempt to compare the wages and salaries they offer to those offered by competitors so as not to lose valuable employees to other companies as a result of low wages. Compensation plans are reviewed frequently to make sure they are accomplishing the goals for which they were established, to make sure that they are fair to various categories of employees, and to evaluate the total amount of compensation in relation to the company's financial performance.

Changing a total compensation plan or even parts of the plan is a very difficult task but must be done from time to time. Before changing the plan, human resources needs the approval of executives and should involve employee groups in reviewing proposed changes and determining the effects of the changes on employees. The actual changes, the reasons for the changes, and the effects of the changes on compensation should be carefully explained to employees. Employees should be given time to adjust to the changes, especially if the changes may result in a lower level of pay or fluctuations in the amount the employee earns from pay period to pay period.

MEETING LEGAL REQUIREMENTS

Employers must be sure that compensation plans meet all federal and state laws. For the most part, laws do not identify the amount that must be paid to any employee. One exception is minimum wage laws. However, they do mandate that employers do not discriminate in the way compensation is determined.

MINIMUM WAGE A **minimum wage law** specifies that it is illegal for employers to pay less than an identified wage rate to any employee. Minimum wage laws have been developed as both social and economic policies in many countries. They suggest that workers should not be exploited by employers and that the country wants its citizens to receive at least a minimum level of financial resources for their work. Most businesses and jobs are covered by minimum wage laws, but there are some exceptions.

The Unites States first established a federal minimum wage in the 1930s. At that time, the minimum hourly rate was set at $.25. It has been increased from time to time, usually after significant political debate. In 2006 the federal minimum wage rate was $5.15, unchanged since 1997. Most states have established minimum wage rates that apply to most businesses within those states. Only six states do not have their own minimum wage. As with all states, the federal minimum wage law still applies. Many states set their minimum wage rate at the same level as the federal rate. However, in recent years, more and more states have established a higher minimum wage than the federal level. Figure 24-1 shows the states with the highest minimum wage rates in 2006.

COMPENSATION DISCRIMINATION Employers must also follow laws establishing fair levels of compensation. One category of compensation law deals with equal compensation. It states that employers may not pay unequal wages to men and women who perform jobs that require substantially equal skill, effort, and responsibility and are performed under similar working conditions within the same business. It is legal to have compensation differences based on seniority, merit, or the quantity or quality of production. More broadly, employers are prevented from using compensation plans that result in unfair differences in compensation levels based on race, color, religion, gender, national origin, age, or disability.

COMPETITIVE PRESSURES

Businesses are influenced by their competitors when establishing pay rates. Prospective employees will usually consider several businesses when deciding on a job and will be attracted to those that offer the best combination of compensation, benefits, working conditions, and possibilities for advancement. So businesses must offer compensation that is competitive with that of similar businesses. On the other hand, if compensation levels are much higher than competitors', it will be difficult for the company to control costs, prices, and profits. If wage and salary rates are high, the company will need employees who are more productive and maintain a high level of quality in their work.

As businesses respond to more and more international competition, it is no longer possible to compare compensation levels with those of competitors in the same state or country. U.S. businesses have been forced to compete with companies in countries that have much lower wage rates. As a result, many companies have moved some of their operations to those countries to take advantage of lower

FIGURE 24-1 Minimum Wage Rates of Selected States, 2006

State	Minimum Wage
Washington	$7.63
Oregon	$7.50
Connecticut	$7.40
Vermont	$7.25
Alaska	$7.15
Rhode Island	$7.10
District of Columbia	$7.00

wages. For example, a comparison of average wage rates of several countries shows that for every dollar U.S. workers earn on average, a worker in Korea earns $.50, a Hungarian worker earns $.25, and a Mexican worker earns $.11. There are also differences in the productivity of and training costs for workers from various countries. Some companies that moved operations to other countries expecting great savings in labor costs have found that other costs are higher than expected.

CHECKPOINT

List several factors that should be considered by a company when establishing a compensation plan.

24.1 | Assessment

UNDERSTAND MANAGEMENT CONCEPTS

Determine the best answer for each of the following questions.

1. Which performance plan pays employees a percentage of the volume of sales for which they are responsible?
   a. wage plan
   b. bonus plan
   c. commission plan
   d. piece-rate plan

2. Which of the following is *not* a factor that can be used to determine discrimination in equal compensation laws?
   a. skill level
   b. quantity of work
   c. effort required
   d. responsibility

THINK CRITICALLY

Answer the following questions as completely as possible.

3. Why do you believe most jobs are paid on a time plan rather than a performance plan? Which type of compensation plan would you prefer and why?

4. Why would some states choose to have a higher minimum wage rate than the one established by the federal government? What effect might the higher rate have on businesses that operate in several states?

Xtra!
Study Tools
thomsonedu.com/school/bpmxtra

24.2 Employee Benefits

Goals
- Recognize how employee benefits add to the total compensation received.
- Describe several ways companies can improve HR services while controlling costs.

Terms
- employee benefits
- pension plan
- tax deferred
- flex-time
- job sharing
- profit-sharing plan
- cafeteria plan

Customary Employee Benefits

In addition to pay, employees often receive other valuable benefits from their employer as part of their total compensation. When employees make decisions about which employer to work for or whether to accept a promotion, the wage or salary level is often considered the most important factor in the decision. However, the total compensation package is probably more important. One job may pay significantly more than another, but if the second job provides a number of benefits and the company pays most or all of the cost of those benefits, the total compensation may be higher for the second job. Having insurance, paid vacations, medical leave, and contributions to a retirement plan can make an otherwise lower-paying job more attractive.

Employee benefits are all forms of compensation and services that a company provides to employees in addition to salaries and wages. Employee benefits can significantly increase the total compensation an employee receives. It can also increase the costs to the employer. On average, companies spend an additional 20 to 40 percent of employee wages and salaries on benefits. Assume that a company employs 300 people at an average salary of $30,000. In addition to the $9,000,000 in salaries, the cost of benefits may be as much as $3,600,000. In the same way, rather than earning $30,000, the average employee receives as much as $42,000 in total compensation. If employees did not receive those benefits, they would have to pay the total cost from their wages and salaries if they needed to obtain insurance, establish a retirement fund, or take a day off for illness.

CUSTOMARY EMPLOYEE BENEFITS

INSURANCE Many businesses make it possible for their employees to obtain insurance at lower costs through group insurance policies. Health, vision, dental, life, and disability insurance are common types of coverage provided. In many cases, the company pays part or all of the employee's insurance costs. Most business insurance plans offer coverage for the employee's family members. Although employees usually must pay the additional cost for family coverage, they pay a much lower rate than if they purchased the same insurance privately.

RETIREMENT PLANS As employees get older and begin to consider retirement, they become increasingly concerned about the income they will have once they stop working. Retirement plans are designed to meet that need. A pension plan is a company-sponsored retirement plan that makes regular payments to employees after retirement. Companies with a pension plan put a percentage of employees' salaries into a pension fund. The money is invested and earnings are used to make pension payments to retired employees. In a few pension plans, the employer makes the entire contribution, but in most plans the employee makes a contribution as well or pays the entire cost of the contribution. Employee contributions to many retirement plans can be tax-deferred, meaning the contribution is made before taxes are calculated on the employee's income. Tax deferment reduces the amount of income taxes to be paid. When the employee retires, benefits received are taxed, but usually at a lower rate than when the contribution was made. Figure 24-2 summarizes the differences among common types of retirement plans.

VACATIONS AND TIME OFF After employees have worked for a company for a specified time, often one year, they may begin to earn vacation days. Most companies pay the employees' regular salary during vacations. In addition to earned vacations, some companies are closed for holidays and may pay their employees for those days. Other common benefits are paid or unpaid absences for personal illness, the illness or death of family members, and the birth or adoption of a child.

REQUIRED BENEFITS Federal and state laws require companies to offer a number of benefits to employees, including Social Security and Medicare contributions, workers' compensation, and unemployment insurance. Companies employing 50 or more people must offer unpaid family and medical leave. These benefits were described in Chapter 23.

FIGURE 24-2 Common Types of Retirement Plans

TYPE OF PENSION	DESCRIPTION
Pension Plan	A retirement plan in which the company invests a specific amount of money for each employee, based on his or her pay, and uses the earnings to make regular payments to retirees. The company owns and manages the investments.
401k Plan	A company-sponsored retirement plan in which employees may choose to have a percentage of their pay contributed to one of several alternative investment plans selected by the employer. Investment companies, rather than the employer, manage the investments, but employees own their accounts.
IRA Plan	A retirement plan that is not company-sponsored in which employees contribute a percentage of their pay, up to a specified legal limit, in any investment plan of their choice. The employer is not involved in selecting or controlling the employees' investments. The law allows only people who are not covered by an employer's retirement plan to have an IRA.
Keogh Plan	A retirement plan designed for self-employed people, who may contribute an amount of their earnings into an investment fund managed by an investment company. Keogh plans are open to people involved in sole proprietorships or partnerships.

HOURS OF WORK

To respond to the changing lifestyles of workers and the operating needs of businesses, some companies have experimented with changes in the standard 40-hour, five-day workweek. One such change involves scheduling employees to work 10 hours a day for four days per week. Another variation, **flex-time**, lets employees choose their own work hours within specified limits. **Job sharing** allows two people to share one full-time job. Each person works half the time, either half days or alternate days of the week.

Companies may also stagger the workweek by having some employees start their week on days other than Monday. In this way, the business can operate seven days a week without having employees work more than five days, thereby obtaining maximum use of facilities and equipment while controlling labor costs. It is also a way to reduce traffic congestion or demands on employee services, such as parking and food services, at specific times.

PHOTO: © GETTY IMAGES/PHOTODISC.

Some companies include a generous retirement plan in the benefits package as one way to attract and retain good employees. How important is a retirement plan to you?

OTHER BENEFITS

The benefits described above are most common and are available to employees in many companies. Increasingly, businesses are providing other types of benefits for employees. Many companies provide free or low-cost parking, food services and cafeterias, and discounts on the purchase of products produced or sold by the company. Many businesses contribute to the cost of college classes or other educational programs completed by employees. More and more companies are providing parents time off to visit their children's schools. Some companies today even offer unique services, such as hiring someone to do gift shopping or take clothing to a dry cleaner for busy employees and offering transportation to employees who carpool but need to go home due to an emergency.

Free or low-cost professional services for employees, including the services of financial and investment advisers, lawyers, accountants, and counselors, are offered by many benefit plans today. An increasingly important benefit for employees with young children is the availability of day-care facilities. That same benefit is being extended to families with elderly parents living with them, in the form of elder-care programs.

Some companies offer a **profit-sharing plan**, which pays employees a small percentage of the company's profits at the end of the year. Profit sharing encourages employees to do things that increase company profits in order to obtain the benefit.

As you can see, the range of employee benefits is quite broad. Companies offer new benefits as employee needs change and as companies compete to attract and keep good employees. Because individual needs can be quite different, businesses have a difficult time providing the right set of benefits for every employee. Some companies have attempted to solve that problem by letting employees choose from among a number of available benefits. A program in which employees can select the benefits that meet their personal needs is known as a **cafeteria plan**. In this program, each employee can choose among benefits with equal value or give up certain benefits and receive their cost as additional compensation.

CHECKPOINT

On average, what percentage of employee wages and salaries do companies spend on benefits?

NETBookmark

The Bureau of Labor Statistics conducts annual surveys of the compensation and benefits offered by U.S. employers and posts summaries at an easy-to-use Web site. Point your browser to www.thomsonedu.com/school/bpmxtra. Choose several categories of data and click on "Retrieve Data" to review the information. Now go to the "Other Surveys" drop-down menu at the top of the page and select another category. After reviewing the information, suggest how it would be helpful to employers, HR personnel, and employees.

www.thomsonedu.com/school/bpmxtra

Improving Human Resources Services

Companies are looking at ways to improve human resources services while controlling the costs of providing those services. They are finding many ways to use technology to reduce paperwork and streamline the process of maintaining and distributing information to employees. Some companies are also employing outside companies to perform some human resources tasks.

USE OF TECHNOLOGY

Managing human resources requires a great deal of information pertaining to every employee in the organization. Much of the cost of managing human resources goes into the paperwork needed to gather and update this information. Employees must fill out forms. Then HR employees must make copies, store them, and retrieve them when needed. Whenever a change occurs, the process must be repeated.

Computers have greatly improved the way companies gather and store employment information. Companies now store employment data electronically, making access and updates easy. When an employee gets a raise or moves to a new home, HR employees can easily make these changes in the computer system. To keep records confidential, companies take security precautions, such as requiring a password to access employees' files.

The Internet has also made HR activities more efficient. The Internet provides a way for employers and job seekers to exchange information. Companies can use the Internet to communicate new policies or new benefit options to employees throughout the company and the world. Companies may even set up information kiosks in cafeterias and break rooms, so employees can easily check on benefits and other employment information. People participating in employee evaluation, such as the 360-degree feedback process, can complete their evaluation forms online.

Screening job applicants is one task an HR department might outsource. What are others?

PHOTO: © DIGITAL VISION.

OUTSOURCING SERVICES

Some companies are now outsourcing some or all of their HR services. *Outsourcing* is hiring an outside firm to perform specialized tasks. For example, a company may hire an outside employment agency to perform all of its employment activities, including recruiting, selecting, and even training. A second common use of outsourcing in human resources is to contract with an information systems company to manage all the personnel data required to manage human resources.

INCREASING VALUE OF HUMAN RESOURCES

Human resources management is very important in all types of businesses. Managers faced with the task of improving the effectiveness and profitability of a business are always looking for ways to improve employee performance. As employees' needs continue to change and the cost of providing employee services and benefits increases, managers must emphasize building and maintaining effective employee relations. Several areas are of special concern to companies that value their employees: legal responsibilities identified by employment laws, equal opportunity for all employees, and improvements in the way HR services are provided and managed.

CHECKPOINT

Identify ways that companies are reducing the costs of human resources management.

24.2 Assessment

UNDERSTAND MANAGEMENT CONCEPTS

Determine the best answer for each of the following questions.

1. On average, companies spend an additional _____ percent of employee wages and salaries on benefits.
   a. 0 to 10
   b. 10 to 20
   c. 20 to 40
   d. 40 to 60

2. Which of the following is *not* one of the ways companies are attempting to control the rising costs of benefits?
   a. outsourcing HR services to other companies
   b. using technology such as the Internet
   c. reducing the amount of paperwork
   d. cutting the number of benefits offered to employees

THINK CRITICALLY

Answer the following questions as completely as possible.

3. How can cafeteria plans actually reduce the total cost of benefit plans for employers?

4. What types of problems might companies that outsource many of their HR activities encounter? As an employee, how would you feel about other companies having access to your personal information?

Xtra!
Study Tools
thomsonedu.com/school/bpmxtra

Focus On...

Employer/Employee Relations–Employees Lose Jobs and Retirement

When Enron declared bankruptcy in 2002, its estimated 21,000 employees were hurt in two ways. Not only did most lose their jobs, but a large percentage also lost all of their retirement savings. They had invested in 401k retirement plans offered by the company. Enron's contributions to the retirement plans consisted entirely of company stock. Employees were encouraged by executives to purchase Enron stock with their individual contributions to their retirement funds. Because the stock was regularly increasing in value, often at a rate much higher than that of most other investment choices, it seemed to be a good decision, especially with the support of executives. The value of many employees' retirement accounts was nearing or surpassing $1 million, and employees were looking forward to a very comfortable retirement. Then reality hit.

When executives were accused of gross mismanagement and illegal activities that manipulated the stock price, Enron stock dropped quickly from $90 to $9 per share, then to $.30. The retirement plan did not allow employees to sell the stock the company had invested until they reached the age of 50, so they were forced to hold on to their shares as the price plummeted. At the same time, Enron executives changed the administrator of the retirement funds and employees were prevented from accessing or changing any of their investments. In the end, employees who had hoped to retire as millionaires were left with a retirement fund worth nothing. Lawsuits have been filed to recover the money lost as a result of the illegal activities of Enron executives. However, because the company's total losses are estimated at $60 billion to $80 billion, and the losses in retirement funds of Enron employees and other retirement funds that had invested in Enron stock are estimated at $1.5 billion, no one realistically expects to recover anything of value.

Traditional pension funds of corporations that pay a specified monthly amount to retirees are insured by the Pension Benefit Guaranty Corporation. This federal agency was created in 1974 to provide protection to employees if their company's pension fund or the company itself failed. It currently pays benefits to about 683,000 retirees in 3,595 pension plans. However, the protection does not extend to retirement plans that are investment based without guaranteed benefits, such as 401k plans. So employees such as those of Enron who thought they were building good retirement "nest eggs" now find themselves with no money on which to retire.

Think Critically

1. Even though the Enron executives acted unethically and illegally, do Enron employees share any responsibility for their losses? Why or why not?
2. Could a similar situation occur in another company today? What can employers and employees do to protect retirement funds? Should the government have any role in protecting these types of retirement plans? Justify your answer.

24.3 Improving Employee Performance

Goals
- Describe the procedures for reviewing employee performance.
- Discuss several important training needs of businesses.

Terms
- formal training
- informal training

Companies depend on effective and satisfied employees. Just as a company cannot operate if equipment is outdated or regularly needs repair, it must have employees with up-to-date skills who perform their jobs accurately and efficiently. Two requirements for maintaining a high-quality workforce are an effective system for performance review and well-designed training and development programs.

Employee Performance Review

Companies must make sure employees are performing as well as they possibly can. As you learned in Chapter 11, a performance review is the process of assessing how well employees are doing their jobs. Companies use the information obtained from performance reviews for career planning, determining increases in wages and salaries, and planning training programs. Continuing poor performance reviews may lead to employee transfer, demotion, or even discharge.

CONDUCTING A PERFORMANCE REVIEW

The first step in developing a performance review process is to determine what to evaluate. Each job should have a complete description of duties and performance expectations, and the review should focus on these duties and expectations. Next, the human resources department prepares forms and procedures for performance reviews. Those materials should be designed to make the review process as easy and objective as possible.

Managers conduct formal performance reviews of all employees usually once or twice a year. The formal review is based on regular observations of the employee's performance throughout the year, checking the quality and quantity of the work the employee has produced, and seeking feedback from others who have worked with the employee. Some managers fail to conduct regular reviews of each employee's work and so base their formal evaluation on the most recent work, general observations, or even biases. That procedure is certainly unfair to the employee and does not result in an accurate evaluation or provide the chance to recognize positive performance and improve employee performance in weaker areas.

To be most objective, managers should use observation forms and record information on the employee's performance. Those forms and records should be specific to each employee's job and based on the employee's job description and job responsibilities. They should also take into account the employee's experience

653

business *note*

People do better work when they are praised rather than criticized. Yet, in a recent survey, nearly 60 percent of employees reported they had received no praise at work during the past year. Whether you are a manager, team leader, or coworker, here are some tips for offering praise to others. You may be surprised at the positive effect it has. You might even start receiving praise in return.

Praise something specific the other person has done well. Identify the action and why it was important.

Say "thank you" frequently. People like to hear appreciation for their efforts and contributions.

Recognize the things people do that really make improvements. When people are doing what they are supposed to do, praise will remind them to keep focused on the important things.

Recognize the small things as well as the big ones. Praise steps in the right direction rather than waiting for the final results. Encouragement keeps people going in the right direction.

Personalize the praise when possible. Connect the praise to something you know about the person that is important to them.

Spread praise around. Be careful not to ignore people you don't know as well or who haven't performed well in the past. Find everyone doing something well and recognize it. It will usually result in more positive actions as people seek recognition.

and training. If observations are too general or do not consider any unique requirements or expectations, they will not be fair, can be legally challenged, and will not contribute to specific performance improvement.

Based on the information collected, the manager fills out an evaluation form about the employee's performance. The process in many companies also requires the employee to complete a self-evaluation using the same form. Some companies use 360-degree feedback, as discussed in Chapter 23, to obtain feedback from other people.

Employees should be just as careful and objective in completing their self-evaluation as they expect their supervisor to be. Some employees find it difficult to specifically identify their strengths and the things they do well. They are not used to giving themselves praise. But being specific and honest in the self-assessment is important if the goal is to be recognized for positive efforts and results as well as to identify ways to improve performance. In the same way, the employee should not cover up skills or work that have not been up to standard. If the supervisor believes the employee is not being honest, it will be difficult for him or her to recognize the positive parts of the self-evaluation.

PREPARING FOR A PERFORMANCE REVIEW CONFERENCE

After the manager and employee have completed the performance evaluation forms, they should discuss the information in a performance review conference. The conference is scheduled soon after the performance review so the information is fresh in their minds. The goals of the meeting are to review all evaluation information, discuss the employee's performance and the reasons for the ratings, recognize areas of strengths as well as those needing improvement, and agree on a plan for performance improvement, including the support the manager will provide to the employee.

An upcoming performance review conference is often a source of anxiety for both managers and employees. However, if carefully planned, the evaluation meeting can be a positive experience. The following guidelines for managers can help in achieving that goal:

1. Schedule enough time for the discussion and plan for it in advance by reviewing the employee's job requirements, previous evaluations, and career plans. Inform the employee well in advance and provide copies of the information that will be reviewed so the employee can be well prepared as well and won't be surprised.
2. Focus the discussion on the employee's performance, not on the employee. Feedback should be based on objective information, not opinions.
3. Allow the employee opportunities to discuss his or her performance and views of the job, working conditions, and available support. The employee should also be positive and objective and focus on the job, not on other individuals.

4. Discuss strengths as well as areas that need improvement. Identify how the strengths can contribute to the employee's career goals and specific ways the employee can develop needed skills and improve performance.

5. Agree on a specific development plan for the next work period, how the employee can improve, what rewards he or she will receive for meeting improvement goals, and the types of support that will be provided.

If performance is so far below standard that the employee will be penalized or even terminated, the manager should plan particularly carefully for that conference. The employee should not be surprised by the negative information. The decision should be based on previous evaluations as well as personal discussions the manager has held with the employee. Specific and objective reasons based on company policies and job requirements should be presented and discussed. The employee should have the opportunity to offer information but the discussion must remain positive rather than turn into an argument. The manager should give the employee specific information on the penalties or termination procedures and arrange a meeting for the employee with the appropriate human resources personnel. Although the conference will not be easy, the manager should maintain a positive tone and thank the employee for the contributions made during his or her time in the department and with the company.

INFORMAL REVIEWS

In addition to the formal performance review procedures, managers should regularly provide informal feedback, support, and encouragement to every employee. Employees also can conduct regular self-assessments or ask managers, coworkers, or others who know them well for feedback. These informal reviews can be very helpful to employees in understanding how well they are performing their jobs and what needs to be done to improve performance or to prepare for promotions and career advancement.

CHECKPOINT
Describe the steps that should be taken to conduct a positive performance review conference.

Planning Training and Development

Businesses spend a great deal of money on training activities designed to improve the productivity of their employees. Training is divided into two categories, based on how it is organized and delivered. **Formal training** is carefully planned instruction with a specific curriculum and instructor. It may be conducted by supervisors, experienced employees, or professional trainers. Formal training may be offered by the company, professional and trade associations, schools and colleges, or private companies. Formal training can be delivered in traditional classrooms, training centers, laboratories, or organized areas in the workplace. It is increasingly delivered using such technology as computers, the Internet, and training simulators.

Informal training is unstructured and unplanned instruction developed for specific situations or individuals. Informal training is often delivered by a supervisor, coworker, or mentor in one-on-one situations with an individual employee or a small group of employees. For example, a coworker might show a new employee how to perform a specific job, or a vendor might demonstrate a new piece of equipment to employees who will use it. Informal training also includes self-study by individual employees and coaching provided by a supervisor or mentor.

Studies estimate that U.S. companies spend $50–60 billion each year on formal training programs. Informal training may cost businesses as much as an additional $200 billion each year. Beyond the costs of training, many companies pay some or all of the costs of college courses that employees take as part of preparing for promotions and career advancement or as an employee benefit. The large allocation of money for training and development can be justified if the result is employees who are able to perform more and higher-quality work.

EFFECTIVE TRAINING

As companies recognize the value of training, they are working to develop more effective training procedures. On the average, companies spend several hundred dollars on every employee each year for training. Therefore, they want to be sure the training is effective at improving employees' performance. Trainers use many techniques to improve employee performance. Figure 24-3 summarizes several characteristics of effective training.

IDENTIFYING TRAINING NEEDS

An important activity for all companies is determining the need for employee training. Some training needs are quite obvious. When the company buys new equipment, begins new operations, or introduces new procedures, employees must be trained for the changes. Also, when new employees are hired or experienced employees are promoted to new jobs, they do not have all the skills they need to begin work immediately. In these cases, companies should offer the needed training.

Other training needs are not as obvious. In some instances, poor work performance can be a symptom of insufficient training. Conflicts among employees, areas of customer dissatisfaction, or work hazards and employee injuries often signal the need for training. Unless companies are aware of problems and try to determine whether training can help solve them, the problems likely will not disappear.

In some companies, each department forms a problem-solving group made up of managers and employees. Those groups can identify training needs in addition to their other responsibilities. Because they work regularly with the equipment and the procedures of the department, the groups are in a good position to identify performance problems and help design training programs.

FIGURE 24-3 Characteristics of Effective Training Programs

TO BE EFFECTIVE, TRAINING SHOULD:

1. Be interesting to the trainee.
2. Be related to knowledge the trainee already has developed.
3. Explain why as well as how something is done.
4. Progress from simple to more difficult steps.
5. Let the trainee learn complicated procedures in small steps.
6. Allow plenty of practice time.
7. Let the trainee concentrate on becoming comfortable with a new procedure before worrying about accuracy.
8. Provide regular and positive feedback to the trainee on progress being made.
9. Be done in short time blocks using a variety of activities.
10. Involve the learner in training activities as much as possible.

TYPES OF TRAINING

The Bureau of Labor Statistics reports on the common types of training provided by U.S. employers. They are:

- Basic-skills training: training in reading, writing, arithmetic, and language skills, including English as a second language
- Occupational-safety training: information on safety hazards, regulations, and safe working procedures

- Employee health and wellness training: information and guidance on personal health issues such as stress reduction, substance abuse, nutrition, and smoking cessation
- New-employee orientation training: introduction to the organization, coworkers, personnel, and workplace rules and procedures; development of beginning job skills
- Awareness training: information and guidelines on policies and practices that affect employee relations or the work environment, including Equal Employment Opportunity practices, affirmative action, workplace diversity, and sexual harassment
- Communication, employee development, and quality training: training in public speaking, conducting meetings, writing, time management, leadership, working in groups or teams, employee involvement, total quality management, change management, and job reengineering
- Job skills training: training in specific skills for different types of jobs in the organization, including management, technical and professional jobs, computer work, clerical and administrative operations, sales and customer service, production, manufacturing, and construction.

CHECKPOINT
What is the difference between formal and informal training?

24.3 Assessment

UNDERSTAND MANAGEMENT CONCEPTS
Determine the best answer for each of the following questions.

1. The process of assessing how well employees are doing their jobs is
   a. a career plan
   b. a performance review
   c. a training plan
   d. an employee evaluation
2. Which of the following is *not* a characteristic of formal training?
   a. based on a specific curriculum
   b. taught by an instructor
   c. planned
   d. unstructured

THINK CRITICALLY
Answer the following questions as completely as possible.

3. Why are managers and employees often anxious before a performance review? What would you do as a manager to help reduce an employee's anxiety?
4. Why do you believe companies deliver more informal training than formal training? Is one is more effective than the other? Why?

Xtra!
Study Tools
thomsonedu.com/school/bpmxtra

CHAPTER CONCEPTS

- Factors that affect the amount of pay an employee receives include the skill required for the job, working conditions, education and experience, supply and demand for that type of worker, and economic conditions.

- Companies develop compensation plans to determine how employees will be paid. Common compensation plans are time plans, performance plans, and combination plans.

- Companies may choose to provide a range of employee benefits in addition to wages. Employers must be sure that compensation plans meet all federal and state laws.

- On average, companies spend between 20 and 40 percent of employee wages and salaries for benefits. Customary benefits include insurance, retirement plans, vacations and time off, as well as benefits required by law.

- Performance reviews assess how well employees are doing their jobs. Procedures should be followed for evaluation as well as for possible penalties or termination.

- The large amount of money companies spend on formal and informal training can be justified if the result is more effective and productive employees.

REVIEW TERMS AND CONCEPTS

Write the letter of the term that matches each definition. Some terms will not be used.

a. bonus
b. cafeteria plan
c. combination plan
d. commission plan
e. compensation
f. compensation plan
g. employee benefits
h. flex-time
i. formal training
j. informal training
k. job sharing
l. minimum wage law
m. performance review
n. pension plan
o. piece-rate plan
p. profit-sharing plan
q. salary
r. tax deferred
s. time plan
t. wage

1. Process of assessing how well employees are doing their jobs
2. All forms of compensation and services a company provides to employees in addition to salaries and wages
3. Payment method that pays a certain amount for a specified period of time worked
4. Carefully planned instruction with a specific curriculum and instructor
5. Payment method that pays the employee a fixed rate for each unit produced
6. Arrangement in which employees choose their own work hours within specified limits
7. Law that specifies it is illegal for employers to pay less than an identified wage rate to any employee
8. Pay based on an hourly rate
9. Program in which employees can select the benefits that meet their personal needs
10. Company-sponsored retirement plan that makes regular payments to employees after retirement
11. Pay and other benefits employees receive in exchange for their labor
12. Pay based on a time frame other than hourly, such as weekly or monthly

DETERMINE THE BEST ANSWER

13. Which of the following is *not* a factor companies should use to determine the amount of pay an employee receives?
    a. the skill required for the job
    b. the age and gender of the employee
    c. the work conditions
    d. economic conditions
14. Which of the following is *not* a benefit that companies are required to offer based on federal laws?
    a. a minimum wage
    b. Social Security
    c. Medicare
    d. paid family and medical leave
15. At the end of a performance review conference, the manager and employee should agree on
    a. an increase in salary
    b. each of the ratings of employee performance
    c. a specific development plan for the next work period
    d. all of the above
16. Which of the following statements is true about employee training?
    a. Businesses spend more money on formal training than informal training.
    b. An example of formal training is a coworker showing a new employee how to perform a specific procedure.
    c. On average, companies spend several hundred dollars on every employee for training each year.
    d. Employees should always identify their own training needs.

APPLY WHAT YOU KNOW

17. Based on the Reality Check scenario at the beginning of the chapter, do you believe the proposed compensation system will be fairer to employees than the previous system? Do you believe it is a better system for the company? Why?
18. What are the advantages and disadvantages of time and performance pay plans? How do combination plans emphasize the advantages and reduce the disadvantages of each plan?
19. Offer some examples of jobs for which salaries have recently been affected by supply and demand. How should a company respond when it finds that employees are leaving to obtain higher wages and salaries at other companies?
20. What do you believe would be the most important employee benefits to a young, beginning employee? To an experienced, married employee with children? To an older employee nearing retirement? Are there any benefits you believe all three types of employees would value?

21. How can the way employee performance reviews and conferences are conducted affect employee morale? What are reasons both managers and employees have negative feelings about performance reviews and conferences? How can companies work to change those feelings?

22. Some of the best-performing companies also spend the most on employee training. Why would a successful company want to devote more time and money to training? Why do you believe low training budgets can affect a company's sales and profitability?

MAKE CONNECTIONS

23. **History** Use the library and the Internet to research the history of minimum wage legislation in the United States. Prepare a two-page report on the history, including the reasons some people support regular increases in the minimum wage and other people oppose them.

24. **Mathematics** A telemarketing firm has a complex pay structure for its salespeople. Each person is given a base salary and a quota (minimum expected sales). In addition to the base salary, the company pays the following commissions on sales:

   4 percent for all sales up to $75,000
   5 percent for sales of $75,001 to $150,000
   6 percent for any sales above $150,000

   Any salesperson who exceeds the assigned quota is paid a bonus of $5,000. Complete the following table using the information given.

Salesperson	Base Salary	Commission	Bonus	Total Salary
Egan	_____	_____	_____	_____
Ranelle	_____	_____	_____	_____
Chen	_____	_____	_____	_____

   Egan has a base salary of $20,000, sales of $80,000, and a quota of $75,000.
   Ranelle has a base salary of $28,000, sales of $140,000, and a quota of $150,000.
   Chen has a base salary of $31,000, sales of $220,000, and a quota of $200,000.

25. **Visual Arts** After providing employee training, businesses often place posters in the workplace as reminders of important procedures. Design an attractive poster that could be placed in a computer lab in your school to remind students and teachers of procedures they should follow when using the equipment.

26. **Research** Use the Internet to gather information on education and training programs delivered via the Internet. Prepare a chart that compares the advantages and disadvantages of that delivery method in terms of cost and effectiveness.

CASE IN POINT

CASE 24-1: The Benefit of Benefits

Joanne Wilkens and Teresa Soto were exercising on stationary bicycles in the health and fitness center of the Wainwright Company. The company added the fitness center a year ago and both employees have used it extensively ever since. They use the equipment and take several fitness classes taught by on-site fitness personnel. In addition, they have completed a number of health-and-wellness programs the company has started offering. Joanne and Teresa are both pleased with the effects on their overall health and fitness levels. Today, however, as they exercised, they discussed an article in the company's online newsletter.

Joanne: *The article said that the average employee in the company receives total compensation of $36,500 a year. I can't believe that. I think I'm close to the average in salary, and I'll only take home a little more than $28,000 this year.*

Teresa: *That's right. What they don't say is that we have a lot of money deducted from our checks each month for taxes, insurance, and the retirement plan.*

Joanne: *As a matter of fact, the article says the company contributes an additional $9,000 on average for each employee to pay for benefits. That makes over $17,000 difference between what I take home and what the company says I receive in compensation and benefits. I can't imagine what benefits we get that cost that much money. There must be a mistake in those figures.*

Teresa: *Let's stop in at the human resources office when we're finished here. Maybe they can explain the difference.*

THINK CRITICALLY

1. If the newsletter information is accurate and if Joanne is paid about the average amount for all employees, can you explain the difference between the compensation figures?
2. Should employees consider the amount that is taken out of their paychecks each month for taxes, insurance, and pensions as part of their compensation? Why or why not?
3. If you worked in the human resources department, how would you explain the difference between the salary and benefits the company says it pays and the amount of money Joanne and Teresa take home in their paychecks?
4. Although the company's fitness facility and programs are a benefit for employees, should they be considered part of the employees' benefits costs? Why or why not? How do employees and the company benefit from the addition of a fitness center and health-and-fitness programs?
5. Why do you believe that many employees are like Joanne and Teresa and don't recognize the total cost of employee benefits? What should a company do to avoid that problem?

CASE 24-2: Changing a Business Image

This Car's-4-U is a used-auto dealership owned by Fred Anderson and Julia Parente as a partnership. They recognize that many people are wary of used-car dealers, believing the dealership and salespeople are dishonest and will do anything to make a sale. The view of many is that used cars are a risk because the customer doesn't know the vehicle's history and the dealership will not disclose any known defects or problems. Then the customer may end up stuck with a vehicle that brings nothing but headaches and repair expenses.

Fred and Julia are determined to change the image of their dealership. They want customers to feel good about the purchases they make and return to the dealership for service and future purchases. They have developed a used-car business that is more like the new-car dealerships customers are used to. They have a modern facility with a large showroom and a well-lighted lot to display their used cars. They have established an up-to-date service center to take care of the cars they sell, with highly qualified technicians using the latest technology.

The final area of concern is the sales process. They are aware that most auto dealerships pay salespeople commissions on sales volume. They know that many customers view salespeople negatively, expecting them to use high-pressure tactics to make a sale. Fred and Julia do not want customers dissatisfied because of the actions of their salespeople. However, they also know that they need sales to make a profit, so the salespeople must be able to convince prospective customers to buy the used cars. They are willing to hire the best people and offer them the necessary training. But they also believe the compensation system may be part of the solution.

The partners are considering several compensation options: (a) an attractive hourly wage, with hours assigned to each salesperson based on his or her sales history; (b) a small weekly salary and a reasonable commission based on the number of cars sold; (c) an attractive salary that is not tied to sales but a careful, regular performance review by the sales manager to determine the effectiveness of the sales and customer service skills of the salesperson; or (d) a combination plan of a reasonable monthly salary, a small commission on each car sold, and a bonus based on the satisfaction level of customers after they have purchased a car.

THINK CRITICALLY

1. Do you believe the changes the partners have already implemented for their dealership will result in a different image for their business? Why or why not?
2. What are the advantages and disadvantages of each compensation option in meeting the partners' goals for a different image for the business and for a profitable business?
3. How do you believe each option will be viewed by the company's salespeople?
4. Which compensation plan would you recommend the partners adopt? Why?

project: MY BUSINESS, INC.

COMPENSATING AND PREPARING EMPLOYEES

Small businesses are usually at a disadvantage when developing pay and benefit plans for employees. They usually cannot compete in terms of wages or salaries and benefits. Small-business owners must be creative in developing ways to attract and retain employees.

DATA COLLECTION

1. Use the Internet to find data on the average wages and benefits paid to employees in service industries related to your business. Also determine whether your state and city have a higher or lower cost of living than average.
2. Contact two small-business owners in your area and discuss the types of benefits they offer to employees, why they decided to offer or not offer benefits, and how they believe the wages and benefits they offer affect their ability to attract and retain employees.
3. Search the Internet for recommendations on benefit plans for small businesses. Sites such as the Small Business Administration and the Department of Labor are excellent starting points for your research.
4. Talk with several of your classmates, friends, and family members who work for small businesses. Discuss why they chose to work for a small business, whether they believe their wages and benefits are competitive with those of larger businesses, and how important benefits are to them currently and in the future when deciding which jobs to accept.
5. Use a telephone directory, business directory, local newspapers, and the Internet to identify schools, colleges, government agencies, and other public and private organizations that are sources of employee training and training resources for small businesses in your area.

ANALYSIS

1. Identify the advantages and disadvantages of two pay plans you would consider using for employees. Then select the plan you would use and establish the wage or salary rate for full- and part-time employees.
2. Identify the benefits you will provide for employees, including those required by federal and state law and any additional benefits, if any, you will provide. Attempt to calculate the cost of each benefit for one employee.
3. Make a list of the types and number of employees you will employ in the first six months of your business operations. Expand the list to the types and numbers of employees you believe you will employ by the end of the second year. Develop a budget of salary and benefits costs for each time period.

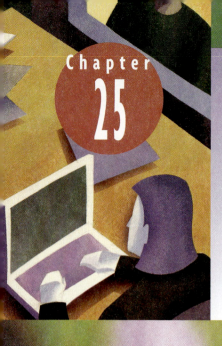

Chapter 25

Developing an Effective Organization

25.1 The Changing Organizational Environment

25.2 Managing Organizational Change

25.3 Career Development

25.4 Personal Career Planning

REALITY CHECK

The End of an Era

James Lane had a good life. Since graduating from high school, he had worked for Alliance Industries, a company that produced steel and steel products for the auto industry. In the 23 years of his employment, he had enjoyed most workdays, had a great group of friends at the company, and earned a comfortable living for his family. His career had progressed at Alliance from a basic maintenance position to machine operator, and then eight years ago to supervisor of machining. During that time he had completed a two-year degree in supervision and management at a community college to be well prepared for his new job.

Like many companies, Alliance Industries was being challenged by competition and changes in the auto industry such as the switch from steel to other metals and plastics. Changes in technology required major investments in new equipment, and competition was forcing cost cutting. Alliance was trying to develop new markets for its steel both in the United States and abroad. But international competition was forcing steel prices down dramatically, making it difficult for the company to make money even when it found new customers. Alliance was also interested in purchasing smaller companies to expand the types of products it could offer its customers, including newer composite materials that were stronger and lighter than steel. But those companies were not interested in being part of an older company that many viewed as slower to respond to the new business environment and hampered by traditional management practices.

James now faced an important decision. Alliance was reducing its workforce, eliminating many supervisory positions. The company offered James the opportunity to go back to a machinist position, but it would require additional training and a reduction in pay. James didn't know how he would be accepted if he went back to work with the people he had been supervising and if he would be happy with that work. If he chose not to accept the job change, Alliance would provide career counseling and other services to help him find another job, but there was no guarantee that there would be a job for which he was qualified in his community.

25.1 The Changing Organizational Environment

Goals
- Describe challenges facing businesses that require major organizational changes.
- Discuss the two important components of an organizational development program.

Terms
- job security
- free-trade agreements
- organizational development
- career development

The New Employment Environment

In the last part of the 20th century, many companies faced global competitive pressures unlike those they had seen before. That competition forced companies to reconsider their organizational size, structure, and operations. Many were forced to downsize their operations by cutting the number of employees, reducing product offerings, or cutting costs in other ways. Other companies restructured their operations to work and use resources more efficiently. Some large companies reduced employment by thousands of people. Like the problem facing James Lane with Alliance Industries, employees who had spent many years with the same company (some nearing retirement) suddenly found themselves without a job.

Many employees who lost their jobs when businesses cut back have been unable to find satisfying employment. Some have had to accept lower-level jobs or jobs that pay less or offer fewer benefits. Those who were able to keep their jobs are not certain of their job security, the likelihood of being employed by the same company in the future. They may distrust their employer, believing that the actions of businesses today demonstrate a lack of commitment to employees.

ECONOMIC AND POLITICAL CHANGES

Now, in the 21st century, the focus is on developing a whole new generation of businesses. The Internet has led to the creation of many new organizations that look quite different from traditional businesses. They may have only a few employees, and the employees may not work in the same building or even in the same city. Internet companies may rely on other businesses to perform many of the traditional business functions, and the owners may have more skill and experience with technology than with organizing and managing a business. As traditional businesses observed the impact of the Internet, most began to experiment with the new technology and integrate Internet services and resources into their own companies. The new Internet businesses were forced to become more effective in both business operations and management or they were forced out of business. Today, few businesses rely on the Internet only, and most have incorporated some Internet-based operations within their more traditional operations.

International competition has grown dramatically as large firms expand into new markets, develop cooperative agreements with foreign firms, or purchase competing businesses that allow them to expand their operations for greater

PHOTO: © DIGITAL VISION.

influence and control in the marketplace. Governments as well as businesses and economic associations are attempting to reduce existing barriers to international trade by reorganizing relationships among countries and negotiating free-trade agreements. **Free-trade agreements** eliminate almost all trade restrictions and subsidies between individual countries and groups of countries.

Probably the most significant change in political structure affecting business competition and trade was the development of the European Union (EU) in 1967. The European Union was the first and most important international market system in the world. It was formed to increase the economic and political power of the countries of Western Europe in the face of growing global competition. The EU agreements support the free movement of goods, services, capital, and labor across all member countries. The EU parliament also develops and coordinates economic, social, and environmental policies among members. In 2006, the European Union expanded to 25 countries.

Human resources personnel help employees prepare for changes in the organization and changes in their own careers. Why is it important for employees to focus on the future of the company as well as on their personal plans?

HUMAN RESOURCES' RESPONSES TO CHANGE

Today, we see dramatic changes in both traditional and new businesses. Dealing with the results of those changes presents challenges to both employees and managers. Much of the pressure to maintain a strong organization falls on the human resources department. Whether it is a traditional business that has gone through a major restructuring or a new business attempting to build a unique type of organization, human resources personnel must help the organization be effective and successful.

Two major responsibilities have emerged for the human resources department in today's organizations. **Organizational development** refers to carefully planned changes in the structure and operation of a business to adjust to a competitive business environment. **Career development** is a program that matches the career plans of employees with the employment needs of the business. This chapter focuses on these two human resources programs. We will discuss how companies can make changes in the way they are organized while maintaining positive management-employee relations. We will also examine how individuals can take responsibility for their own career development through effective career planning.

CHECKPOINT

What are the two major responsibilities that have emerged for human resources departments in today's organizations?

The Role of Human Resources in Change

Consider all the ways that employees can contribute to the success or failure of a business. Employees play a major role in product quality, customer satisfaction, equipment maintenance, and efficient use of materials to limit waste. You can probably think of many other ways that employees can help or hurt the business for which they work.

The ways businesses organize work and provide resources also affect their success. Inefficient work processes, delays in receiving needed materials, and problems within channels of distribution all hinder a business's ability to meet customer needs. Because of such problems, companies are now paying a great deal of attention to the way in which they structure their organization, how work flows through the business, and how employees work together and with their managers. Today, businesses are making important changes in their organizations to make sure they continue to be successful.

Two important ways that businesses are changing are making improvements in work processes and building effective working relationships. Improving work processes means improving the way work is accomplished. The goal of work process improvement is to eliminate errors, improve quality, and reduce costs.

The focus of the second element of organizational development is on the people who complete the work. Studies have shown that employees who believe they are an important part of the organization will be committed to its success and will work to achieve the company's goals. Several important relationships contribute to an effective organization: the relationships among a company's personnel, including management-employee relationships, and relationships with people in other organizations with whom the company works as well as with the company's customers.

IMPROVING WORK PROCESSES

One of the focuses of organizational development is to improve the way work is accomplished. This includes the materials and resources used, the organizational structure and relationships among work units, the job duties assigned to individuals and groups, and work procedures and operations. Most of the emphasis on improving work processes is directed inside the company. But improving work processes also involves the way businesses work with each other as part of product development, production, distribution, sales, and customer service.

Improving the way work is accomplished may require using new technologies, rearranging work areas, changing relationships between departments and work groups, and modifying procedures for completing tasks. Remember the concerns James Lane had about the changes Alliance Industries was planning. The company was changing to new products, equipment, and procedures that would be quite different from what he and other employees had experienced. They had to find ways to reduce costs while keeping quality high.

It is not easy for any company to make these types of changes when people are reluctant to use new technologies or change the way they have been doing things for many years. It may even be difficult to identify new ways to organize and accomplish work, because people in the company are familiar only with the way things have been done in the past. Often organizational development programs bring in experts from outside the company to help identify and study new work processes and to work with employees to help them accept and respond positively to the changes.

business note

Besides e-mail, two other types of interpersonal communication on the Internet are newsgroups and blogs. Newsgroups are online bulletin boards developed around a specific subject. People can post current news related to the subject, comments, and replies to other people's comments and questions. Special programs called newsreaders are used to read newsgroups.

The term blog is a shortened version of *weblog*. A blog is usually created by someone who offers expertise or opinion on current events or an area of special interest. Blogs can be like personal journals or business newsletters. Most blogs encourage readers to respond.

Newsgroups and blogs are useful places to find answers to questions or to interact with people with similar interests. These online groups can be formal or informal. Some are created for entertainment; others are devoted to career, professional, and business topics.

Newsgroups and blogs are visited by all sorts of people. Because postings can be read by thousands of participants, it is important to be thoughtful, concise, and considerate. Before organizing a blog or participating in a newsgroup, check company policies. Remember not to give out personal or confidential business information.

IDENTIFYING THE NEED FOR CHANGE

The history of business is filled with stories of organizations that experienced years of success, only to fall on hard times and ultimately fail. The causes of a business failure may be that competitors were able to improve their products and services, customers did not receive the service they expected, costs were not controlled, or the organizational structure did not adjust to new conditions. No matter what the specific cause, the reason for the failure of a previously successful business is most likely the inability to change. It may be that the executives of the company did not recognize the need for change, believed the company did not need to change, or were unable to plan and manage the needed change.

Throughout this textbook, you have learned that the environment faced by businesses today is very different from that in the past. The differences occur both outside the business (the *external environment*) and inside the business (the *internal environment*). Today, the external factors most likely to result in problems for an organization are changes in workforce demographics, the nature of competition, customer expectations, and technology. Several important internal factors that affect a company's success are quite similar. They include changes in the makeup of the company's workforce, employee expectations, outdated work processes and technology, ineffective organizational structure, and poor management practices.

Figure 25-1 shows several key indicators that an organization may be experiencing problems requiring major change. Every organization should pay careful attention to its external and internal environment to monitor those indicators. Companies that do not pay attention often recognize problems too late to take the necessary action. When sales and profits decline and the business has not recognized the need for change or invested in new technology and procedures, it is often too late.

When a business tries to solve a problem, it often discovers that the problem results from a fundamental flaw in operations. Organizational development programs must identify and resolve the underlying operational problem in order to fix the original problem. For example, one company found that production levels had declined significantly during June, July, and August. When company managers studied the problem, they discovered that employee absences were almost double on Mondays and Fridays what they were on the other days of the week. Production was delayed on both of those days because work teams were not full or temporary employees brought in on those days were not as efficient. To solve the production problem, the employee absence issue had to be resolved. Working with employees, the managers learned that the way vacation days were scheduled encouraged employees to take off Mondays and Fridays to create short summer vacations. A revised policy allowed employees to schedule two- or three-day vacations in the middle of the week. This change reduced Monday and Friday absences and solved the production problem.

FIGURE 25-1 Important Indicators That an Organization Needs to Make Changes

- New competitors entering the market
- Introduction of new technologies by other businesses
- Changes in laws and regulations affecting the business
- Major changes in products and services offered or in markets served
- Rapid growth by the business
- Loss of market share
- Increasing customer complaints
- Poor relationships with business partners
- Increasing operating costs
- Decreasing revenues or profits
- Decline in employee morale and increasing employee turnover
- Conflicts among departments or other work units
- Participation in a merger or acquisition

Another company experienced an increasing number of customer complaints regarding late deliveries of products. The company had used the same parcel delivery service to make deliveries to customers for more than 20 years. A study of the problem revealed that the delivery company had changed its distribution procedures. It was using larger trucks and making fewer trips to many cities to cut its costs. To improve customer service, the company stopped using that parcel service and contracted with a new, smaller delivery company that used a computerized delivery scheduling system. This change allowed the company to schedule product delivery with customers when they made the purchase and reduced late deliveries by more than 80 percent. Fixing the underlying delivery service problem resolved the issue of customer complaints.

CHECKPOINT

Identify the two important elements of an effective organizational development program.

25.1 | Assessment

UNDERSTAND MANAGEMENT CONCEPTS

Determine the best answer for each of the following questions.

1. Which of the following is one of the major responsibilities of a human resources department in responding to organizational change?
   a. financial restructuring
   b. organizational development
   c. personnel cutbacks
   d. all of the above

2. The goal of work process improvement includes all of the following *except*:
   a. eliminating errors
   b. improving quality
   c. reducing costs
   d. terminating employees

THINK CRITICALLY

Answer the following questions as completely as possible.

3. How does the formation and expansion of the European Union benefit companies in those countries? Do you see any negative effects on those companies?

4. Why do you believe that many managers and employees have a difficult time adjusting to the changes businesses are making?

Xtra!
Study Tools
thomsonedu.com/school/bpmxtra

25.2 Managing Organizational Change

Goals

- Summarize the major steps in planning and implementing an organizational development program.
- Discuss three job design strategies that can increase employee satisfaction.

Terms

- performance standards
- job design
- job enlargement
- cross training
- job enrichment

Planning Organizational Development Programs

As soon as the company identifies a problem or a need for change, it should plan and implement an organizational development program. Because almost all important changes in a business involve or affect employees, the human resources department should have an important role in the program. The changes may involve developing new employee skills or increasing or decreasing the size of the workforce. A change or major reorganization may affect management-employee relationships. The company may decide to change the pay or benefits plans to encourage employee participation or to reduce costs.

The major steps in planning and implementing an organizational development program are the following:

1. Affirm the mission and goals of the organization. There must be agreement within the company about the purpose of the business and the criteria used to determine if the company is successful. A company should not easily change its mission or goals but may need to change them in response to the external and internal environment.

2. Identify the important markets that will be the company's primary focus and the products and services needed to serve those markets. This step will require establishing customer service standards. You have learned that a *standard* is a specific measure against which something is judged. Customer service standards, then, are measures against which the company judges its performance in meeting customer expectations. Those standards may include the minimum acceptable levels of product quality, delivery speed, order-fulfillment accuracy, and customer support and follow-up.

3. Determine the organizational changes required to achieve the company's mission, goals, and customer service standards, and prepare a plan for implementing the changes. These will usually involve one or more of the following factors: work processes, the organizational structure, work relationships, and employee skills. Also, the plan should include performance standards, which are specific statements of the expected results from critical business activities. Most organizational development changes require a long time to implement successfully. Implementation may take many months, and the company may not see results for a year or more.

PHOTO: © GETTY IMAGES/PHOTODISC.

Competition requires that all businesses constantly look for ways to change and improve. How have changes in manufacturing procedures affected the jobs of factory workers?

4. Build commitment within the organization for the changes. Successful organizational change requires the understanding and support of managers and employees. That understanding and support will be given only if all employees are fully informed of (a) the change, (b) the reasons change is necessary, (c) the likely results if the change is not made, (d) how employees will be affected by the change, and (e) how the organization and its employees will benefit if the change is successful. Successful organizational development usually results when company personnel are involved early in the process and when they have a role in designing the plan.

5. Follow through on the organizational development plan. Employees are more likely to support the plan if they see that the organization is committed to it and that change is occurring. Managers should keep employees informed of results of the changes even if they are not always positive at the beginning. Unless something occurs that makes it clear that the plan will not work, the organizational development plan should continue until it achieves the stated goals.

6. Make the new process part of the organization's culture. If people believe the change is not important or is only temporary, they will not commit to its success. When the new process is implemented and supported, the organization has changed, and the old procedures are no longer appropriate, the organizational development program is complete.

Alliance Industries, discussed in the opening scenario, needed to implement an organizational development program for the major changes it was planning. Can you find evidence that Alliance used any of the six steps you just studied?

Success *tip*

Managers who tap into employees' need to grow in their jobs are more likely to retain talented people. A manager should set a *direction* for each employee that aligns with the company's vision and mission, *listen* to employee ideas on ways to improve the business, *guide* the employee in meeting the business's goals, and *measure progress and give feedback* through employee performance evaluations.

CHECKPOINT

What is the evidence that an organizational development program is complete?

Improving the Work Environment

The needs and expectations of workers today are very different from those of workers in the past. Work is just one part of an employee's life. Of course, employees want jobs that provide a reasonable wage or salary. But the amount of money earned is not always the most important thing. Today, employees are concerned about a variety of factors related to their work, including the work schedule and working conditions. Vacations, insurance, pensions, and other benefits are also important to most people. They also want an interesting and challenging job as well as recognition for their work. Both personal and financial needs are important to employees, and managers must recognize those needs in order to maintain an effective workforce.

Satisfied employees are more productive, have fewer absences, and are more likely to want to stay with the company. Therefore, managers spend considerable time working with employees to make the work environment as satisfying as possible. Studies have found that employees are most satisfied with their work when they (1) perform interesting work, (2) feel responsible for the work, (3) receive recognition for good work, and (4) have a feeling of achievement.

It is surprising to many managers that although the amount of compensation is important to employees, it is not necessarily more important than other factors related to the job. Because of these studies, companies are directing their organizational development efforts toward the design of the work environment and jobs to better meet employee needs. **Job design** refers to the kinds of tasks that make up a job and the way workers perform these tasks in doing their jobs.

JOB ENLARGEMENT

Organizations try to make work more meaningful and motivating for employees. One way to do this is through **job enlargement**, or making a job more interesting by adding variety to the tasks. For example, three workers on an assembly line might be responsible for three separate tasks, each one performing one task over and over. With job enlargement, each worker is given responsibility to complete all three tasks. In this way they can perform a greater variety of tasks, making the work less monotonous and boring. Also, the company now has three people who can perform all of the work rather than three specialized employees who can perform only one part of a complex job.

Employees should be involved in making the decision to change the job and in redesigning the job. Employees also need training and adequate time and practice to develop the new skills. Companies should not enlarge jobs just to reduce the number of employees or to get employees to do more work. If employees believe that these are the real reasons for enlarging their jobs, they will not accept the changes willingly.

CROSS TRAINING

Another use of job design to increase employee effectiveness and motivation is cross training. With **cross training**, employees are trained to perform more than one job in the company, even though they typically perform only one. Employees can be rotated to other jobs when an absence or illness occurs, while a replacement employee is being trained, when a significant increase or decrease in the amount of work occurs for a specific job, or simply to provide change and variety for employees. Cross training makes an employee more valuable to the company because that person can perform a broader set of work tasks. Employees

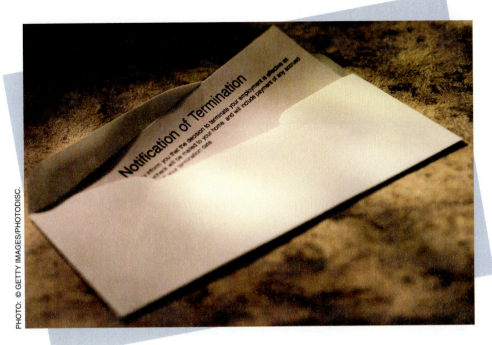

What effects does the termination of some employees have on those who remain?

learn more about the work performed in the organization as they learn multiple jobs and increase their skills.

JOB ENRICHMENT

Another way to use job design to improve employee satisfaction is to involve employees in decision making. Job enrichment gives employees the authority to make meaningful decisions about their work. For example, managers may allow workers to make choices about how to do their jobs. Managers may ask employees for advice on how to improve performance or reduce errors. Job responsibilities may be changed so employees can solve problems themselves without checking with their supervisor. For example, in one major hotel chain, employees are authorized to immediately take the necessary steps to resolve a customer problem or complaint at a cost of up to $200 without consulting a manager.

As you learned in earlier chapters, some companies have work teams that are responsible for the entire assembly of a product, performance of a service, or operation of a small unit in the business. The team helps with goal setting, shares all tasks, and is responsible for the results. Companies using this system have found that team members develop a strong loyalty to the other members and take personal responsibility for the effective operation of the team and the quality of its work.

Some companies expand the duties and responsibilities of employees for the wrong reasons. To save money, the companies cut the number of personnel and divide the additional work among the remaining employees. Sometimes that is done without providing additional training or any recognition or rewards for employees who are required to take on the additional work. Employees are already upset about losing coworkers and concerned that they might also lose their jobs. If they feel forced to take on additional responsibilities that may require longer work hours and greater job pressure, they will not have positive feelings about the changes.

An improved work environment and worker involvement are important goals of organizational development. Improving management and employee relationships, making work more meaningful, and developing effective work teams are all important organizational development programs. They affect the internal environment of the business. In addition, some organizational development programs work to improve relationships in the external environment, including the way employees interact with other businesses in the distribution channel and with customers. Many businesses involve personnel from cooperating businesses in solving problems and developing new procedures. They frequently consult customers in order to consider their needs and perceptions in planning organizational changes.

CHECKPOINT
What is the difference between job enlargement and job enrichment?

25.2 | Assessment

UNDERSTAND MANAGEMENT CONCEPTS

Determine the best answer for each of the following questions.

1. The first step in planning and implementing an organizational development program is
   a. affirming the mission and goals of the organization
   b. identifying important markets, products, and services for the company
   c. determining the organizational changes required to meet the company goals
   d. none of the above

2. Giving employees the authority to make meaningful decisions about their work is known as
   a. job design
   b. job enlargement
   c. job enrichment
   d. cross training

THINK CRITICALLY

Answer the following questions as completely as possible.

3. If you were an employee in a company undergoing change, would you want to be informed of and involved in the planning even if it requires additional work time and responsibilities? Why or why not?

4. If you were a manager, would you be in favor of the increased use of work teams among your employees? How would your job change as a result? What new problems do you believe you would encounter?

Xtra!
Study Tools
thomsonedu.com/school/bpmxtra

25.3 Career Development

Goals
- Describe the requirements for a career development program.
- Identify the specific career development responsibilities of various groups in a business.

Terms
- career path
- individual career plan
- career centers

The Importance of Career Development

In the past, many companies were short-sighted when they planned for their employment needs. When a position was vacant, they would begin the recruitment and selection process. If they no longer needed certain employees, they might terminate those employees without considering future employment needs. Those procedures were based on the belief that companies could easily find the employees they needed. Those companies did not view employees as a particularly valuable resource.

CHANGING VIEWS OF EMPLOYEES

Successful businesses view their relationships with employees very differently today. They realize that it is not easy to find employees with the required qualifications. It is also very expensive to hire and train a new employee. Companies invest in employees and want to get the greatest value from them. That occurs when companies hire employees with skills that closely match the needs of the job, train them, and then keep them happy, so they will stay with the company for a long time. Companies following this new philosophy recognize that the knowledge and performance of their employees are major factors in their success.

Changing technology requires employees to update their skills. For example, not many years ago, businesses processed most information manually, using typewriters and calculators. Today, companies process information with computers. Auto mechanics used to rely on hand tools and their own knowledge and observational skills to repair automobiles. Now they have access to a variety of electronic tools, machines, and computerized diagnostic equipment. Every business has similar examples of new skills that are required of employees. It is not possible to be successful with the old equipment and old skills. To get the needed skills, businesses offer training to current employees when new technology requires it and search for new employees with up-to-date skills to fill vacancies.

In the scenario at the beginning of the chapter, James Lane had been a very valuable employee to Alliance Industries for many years. Even though the company was undergoing major changes, it was attempting to include James in its plans by offering him another job and the needed training to prepare for that job.

CAREER DEVELOPMENT PLANNING

A *career development program* is a plan for meeting the company's future employment needs by systematically preparing current employees for future positions in the company. Human resources personnel are responsible for implementing the career development program, but they need the support of all parts of the company for the program to be successful. A career development program requires a long-term organizational plan, career paths, effective employee performance reviews, career counseling, and training and development for employees.

LONG-TERM PLANS Career development starts with the job opportunities in a company. Companies must determine what jobs will be available in the future, how many people will be needed in each job, and the knowledge and skills those employees will require. In the previous section, you learned that companies study their external and internal environments to identify business opportunities and needed changes in the organization. One part of that study includes employment needs. The HR department works with that information to project specific job opportunities in each part of the company and the requirements employees must meet for each job.

CAREER PATHS A career path is a progression of related jobs with increasing skill requirements and responsibility. Career paths provide opportunities for employees to advance within the company, make additional contributions, and receive greater satisfaction from their work.

Traditionally, a career path moved an employee from an entry-level position into management. However, companies also offer career paths that allow employees to advance into nonmanagement positions. Some people do not want to be managers, and companies usually have relatively few management positions. Therefore, companies often make other opportunities available so that employees do not get locked into one job if they choose not to become managers or are unable to qualify for management positions. Examples of a management career path and a nonmanagement path are shown in Figure 25-2. Companies should identify a variety of career paths. Each job should be part of a career path, and employees should be aware of the paths available to them.

PERFORMANCE REVIEWS Employees need accurate information on their skills and abilities to make good career decisions. When employees know how well they are performing, they can determine what skills they need to improve to meet current job requirements or to qualify for another job in a career path. In an effective career development program, the manager carefully evaluates an employee's performance and regularly reviews the information with the employee. The manager and employee can determine whether the employee needs additional training to improve performance and to advance in the organization. The results of performance reviews should be compared to new job requirements as the company makes changes, so that employees know what is expected of them.

CAREER COUNSELING For career development to be effective, employees must be aware of opportunities and plan their career paths. The human resources department offers career information and counseling services as part of the career development program. Many companies have made career counseling part of every employee's performance review conference. Managers are often trained to provide career information to the employees they supervise.

Career counseling may result in an individual career plan, which identifies the jobs that are part of the employee's career path, the training needed to advance

Success *tip*

Employees need to take responsibility for their own performance improvement. They should focus on (1) committing to achieving performance goals, (2) soliciting performance feedback and coaching, (3) communicating openly and regularly with the manager, (4) collecting and reviewing performance data, and (5) preparing for and participating effectively in performance review conferences.

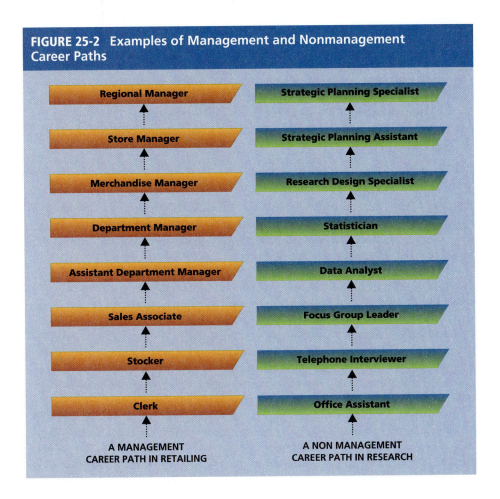

FIGURE 25-2 Examples of Management and Nonmanagement Career Paths

A MANAGEMENT CAREER PATH IN RETAILING	A NON MANAGEMENT CAREER PATH IN RESEARCH
Regional Manager	Strategic Planning Specialist
Store Manager	Strategic Planning Assistant
Merchandise Manager	Research Design Specialist
Department Manager	Statistician
Assistant Department Manager	Data Analyst
Sales Associate	Focus Group Leader
Stocker	Telephone Interviewer
Clerk	Office Assistant

along the career path, and a tentative schedule for the plan's activities. The plan is jointly developed by the employee, a human resources specialist, and possibly the employee's manager.

Some companies have **career centers**, facilities where human resources employees manage career development activities. Employees visit the center to obtain career information (computer programs, Internet sites, books, pamphlets, DVDs, and so on), consult career counselors, and schedule career-planning workshops or testing.

TRAINING AND DEVELOPMENT The final part of a career development program is helping employees obtain the training and education they need for changing job requirements and new jobs. With careful planning, companies can develop training programs and other educational opportunities to prepare employees for new job requirements before the need arises. In that way, the business can be assured that it will have well-trained employees to fill job needs and employees will be trained for job changes.

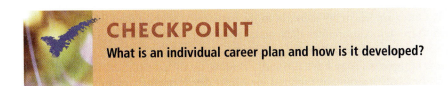

CHECKPOINT
What is an individual career plan and how is it developed?

Implementing a Career Development Program

Career planning does not just happen. It also cannot be considered the responsibility of employees alone. Businesses that want to match employees and jobs successfully must do several things to ensure that the career development program works well. Everyone in the company has specific responsibilities for career development.

CAREER DEVELOPMENT RESPONSIBILITIES

Responsibility for organizing and managing the career development program is usually assigned to the human resources department. The department does much of the initial planning and puts together the people, materials, and procedures needed for the program.

Everyone in the business must be educated about the career development program and his or her role in career planning. Managers need to identify career opportunities in their departments and work with human resources personnel when changes are planned in their departments that will affect the career plans of employees. Managers also have specific responsibilities in a career development program. They evaluate employee performance and include career planning in follow-up conferences. They help identify employees who are ready for career advancement. They serve as coaches and mentors to help each worker make effective career choices.

Employees should be aware of career development resources and how the career-planning process works. They are responsible for much of their individual career planning and development but must know where to get help when they need it. Employees use performance reviews and evaluation conferences to gather information to make career plans. They can then schedule assessments, counseling, and training to prepare for career advancement.

The human resources department manages the career development program. Specialists provide career counseling, training, and help in understanding the performance review process. They continually remind managers and employees of the importance of supporting career planning and development, evaluate the effectiveness of the company's program, and make sure the career development program is aligned with the company's mission and goals.

SPECIAL CAREER DEVELOPMENT PROGRAMS

Companies that offer career development programs should make the services available to all employees, from the newest to the most experienced. However, there are situations in which specific individuals or groups of employees participate in programs designed to meet specific needs in the company. Those programs may not be available to all employees.

Most large businesses offer career planning, training, and counseling to employees selected to be managers. These employees receive testing services, obtain experience in all parts of the business, and often are assigned to an experienced manager who serves as role model and mentor.

Nonmanagement jobs can be targeted for specific career development programs as well. For example, many jobs are more frequently held by men than women or women than men. Companies may make extra efforts to encourage and prepare people from the underrepresented gender for those jobs.

Some companies may have difficulty finding qualified candidates for certain jobs. Those positions may be targeted for career development attention. Employees

Large organizations find it difficult to train the many employees often located in different communities and countries. Many are expanding the use of the Internet to deliver training programs. Technology allows training to be conducted in much the same way as traditional face-to-face training. Early results show as much as a 50 percent reduction in the time required to train as well as savings in training costs based on reduced expenses for travel and training facilities.

who are interested in or have the skills to qualify for hard-to-fill jobs are encouraged to participate in the special programs. For example, if a company is having difficulty recruiting computer programmers or product design specialists, it may undertake a career development program to encourage current employees to complete the necessary training for those jobs. These efforts demonstrate the company's commitment to its current employees. They provide opportunities for promotion and advancement that serve as a strong motivator for employees and encourage them to make a career with the business rather than look for opportunities outside the company. Finally, developing current employees who have already selected the company and have demonstrated their abilities is usually less expensive and more reliable than recruiting outside the company.

CHECKPOINT

In what situations might a company offer special career development programs that are not open to all employees?

25.3 | Assessment

UNDERSTAND MANAGEMENT CONCEPTS

Determine the best answer for each of the following questions.

1. A progression of related jobs with increasing skill requirements and responsibility is a career
   a. goal
   b. review
   c. plan
   d. path

2. Career development programs are managed by
   a. the human resources department
   b. each employee
   c. company executives
   d. specially trained consultants hired by the company

THINK CRITICALLY

Answer the following questions as completely as possible.

3. What evidence would you look for in a business that would demonstrate it believes in the importance of career development?

4. How can a business believe in equal opportunity for all employees and still have special career development programs that are not open to all employees?

Xtra!
Study Tools
thomsonedu.com/school/bpmxtra

Focus On...

Innovation—Ideas for Sale

Most businesses are faced with the need to change, so it is not surprising that people are starting new businesses to help other businesses manage change. One of the most unusual new business concepts is selling ideas. The BrainStore in Biel, Switzerland, offers just such a service. Its owners refer to their business as an "idea factory." In fact, they believe companies cannot rely on the typical way that new ideas are generated. Using a brainstorming session or just thinking about a problem will not achieve the needed results when businesses are faced daily with problems and challenges. The BrainStore has broken down the process of idea generation into a specific sequence of activities.

The process starts in the *creativity lab.* The lab is an open room with pens, paper, scissors, crayons, beads, and other "toys." These are the tools that support creativity. The room looks more like an elementary school classroom than a place where businesspeople meet. The atmosphere encourages play, experiments, and "completely unrealistic thoughts." The result is usually a large number of creative ideas that can then be processed through the idea factory. The next step in the idea sequence is *compression*, where ideas are sorted, compared, and narrowed to the few judged as best. Then the idea moves through *testing*, where research is done to determine if the idea will work and can be implemented. Often models or prototypes of solutions are built for review and further testing. The final step is called *finishing.* Here the idea that has been successfully tested is prepared for implementation. This step may include developing marketing and communications strategies or the actual development of products, services, or processes that will support the needed change or solve the problem.

Initially the BrainStore worked with large businesses to create new products, develop marketing programs, or solve challenging problems. However, the owners now believe their ideas can help individual consumers as well, so they have opened a retail version of the business. For about $20, they will provide ideas for home decorating, improving a personal relationship, or writing an important speech.

Think Critically

1. Do you believe ideas can actually be developed in the same way that a company might manufacture a product? Why or why not?
2. What are the advantages of creating a room that looks like an elementary school classroom for the first step in idea generation? How do you think the results would be different if the company used a typical business office for that activity?
3. After working with the BrainStore, what other activities should an organization perform to implement the ideas that were developed?

Goals
- Describe the variety of career opportunities in business, including international business careers.
- Outline the steps in preparing an individual career plan.

Terms
- entry-level occupations
- career-level occupations
- specialist occupations
- supervisor/management occupations
- executive/entrepreneur occupations
- career portfolio

Business Careers

Business careers are appealing because of the number and variety of jobs available and the opportunities for advancement. No matter what your interests, skills, or level of education and experience might be, there is a job in business that matches them. Once you have obtained your first job and gained both experience an knowledge of business procedures, many opportunities open up. You can advance with additional education or with continuing experience and training on the job.

You can identify career paths in almost any business. If you begin work in a clerical position, you may progress to more specialized jobs in information management or office administration. You can then advance from assistant manager to department manager or to a highly specialized position in either area. Some people progress to the very top of the company as executives. Similar career paths are available to people who begin as counter workers in fast-food restaurants, supply clerks in factories, or bell staff in hotels.

Because common areas of knowledge and skills are important to many types of businesses, you are not limited to one career path, one type of business, or one geographic area. People who begin in banking may change to an insurance career. Someone who is a salesperson for a computer products company may decide to move to a pharmaceutical company for a higher salary or more responsibilities. If job prospects are not particularly good in one part of the country, a skilled businessperson can probably find employment in another region. Career paths in business are usually very flexible.

LEVELS OF EMPLOYMENT

When you first enter the workforce, you will most likely begin in an entry-level position. Many people get their first job in business while still in high school, with little prior work experience and only a beginning understanding of business principles and operations. The top positions in large corporations are held by people with many years of experience. Executives usually have worked in several areas of the business and often have experience in several businesses. Most business executives today have a college degree and, increasingly, graduate degrees.

There is still a gender gap in salaries for technology jobs, but it is narrower than the gap in other career areas and is getting smaller. The average annual salary of tech workers in 2005 was $69,000 for men and $63,000 for women. The nearly 10 percent difference has declined almost 4 percent in just over a year and is much lower than the national average gender wage gap in all occupations—24 percent.

Businesses have several levels of employment, based on the amount of education and experience required. Common levels are entry, career, specialist, management, and executive/entrepreneur.

Entry-level occupations usually involve routine activities and require little training. These jobs are open to people with little or no previous business education or experience. If you have not worked in business before, this is where you might begin. People hold entry-level jobs for only a short time until they have developed enough experience and skill for promotion. Examples of entry-level jobs are cashier, counter person, clerk, receptionist, and operator.

Career-level jobs require more complex duties. People in **career-level occupations** have the authority to control some of their work and make some decisions. To be successful, they should have a basic understanding of business and skills in the areas in which they are working. They usually view their work as more than a job and have an interest in the area of business as a potential career. Career-level jobs include sales associate, reservations agent, word processor, bank teller, and customer service representative.

Specialist occupations require a variety of skills in one or more business functions and extensive understanding of the operations of a specific company or industry. Specialists are the people considered the most skilled or expert in the activities they perform on the job. Specialists in businesses include buyers, researchers, Web designers, programmers, analysts, professional salespeople, technicians, machine operators, and people in similar technical or skilled positions.

Supervisors/managers hold the first levels of management positions. They must have a high level of knowledge in the parts of the organization that they supervise. They also must be effective decision makers and have strong leadership ability. People in **supervisor/management occupations** are responsible for specific units in a business and must make decisions about operations and personnel. The job titles associated with this level of employment are supervisor, assistant manager, and manager. The people who perform management tasks within work teams are often called *team leaders*.

Executives/entrepreneurs perform all the management tasks associated with owning a business or managing a major function, a large unit in a company, or the entire company. People who work in **executive/entrepreneur occupations** are fully responsible for the success or failure of the company. They must possess a comprehensive understanding of business and management. They spend most of their time planning and evaluating the work of the organization. The positions held by executives/entrepreneurs are vice president, president, chief executive, and owner.

CAREERS IN INTERNATIONAL BUSINESS

The growth of trade between countries and increasing global competition provide continuing evidence of the importance of international business. It has never been easier to travel to other countries, communicate with people around the world, buy products produced in other places, and sell products and services abroad. The Internet makes access to almost any business and millions of customers only a mouse-click away. We are members of a global community generally, and a global business community specifically. As businesses expand into international markets, so do the opportunities for international business careers.

International business careers have all the advantages of a career in one country plus more. In addition to the excitement and challenges that accompany any business career, international careers usually offer additional job choices and the chance to develop new skills, travel, and interact with a wide variety of people from different cultures.

The international businessperson should know something about the culture of the country in which the business will operate or to which the company's products and service are directed. The economic environment of countries is another important area of study. Currently, English is the international language of business. However, there is no substitute for understanding the language of the country in which you will work. People are favorably impressed when you take the trouble to learn their language. It is difficult to predict which languages will be the most important in your future. Your commitment to study and learn a second language will impress employers as well as your international contacts. You will also find it easier to learn an additional language if needed later. Your selection of international courses in high school and college, travel opportunities, and interactions with people from other countries and cultures are all valuable experiences if you would like to work in international business.

PHOTO: © GETTY IMAGES/PHOTODISC.

What are some advantages of international business careers?

CHECKPOINT

List the levels of business employment in order of least experience and education to most.

Preparing for a Business Career

Preparing for a career in business may seem like trying to negotiate a maze. People who are not familiar with business may have difficulty determining what preparation they need and how to obtain the job they want. If you talk to people who have worked in business for many years, you will find that some did not plan or prepare for the job they currently hold. They often ended up there after starting in another part of the business or in an entirely different occupation.

Today, a person is less likely to enter a business career without specific preparation. In your study of business, you have seen that a business career requires a great deal of knowledge and skill in a number of areas. People who understand the requirements and carefully plan to develop the necessary skills are more likely to succeed in business. In some ways, preparing for a business career is complicated, but in other ways it is really quite simple. It is often a matter of matching your personal qualities, education, and experience with a career path in business.

Good business education programs are offered in high schools as well as in community and junior colleges and career and technical schools. Business is usually one of the largest degree programs in colleges and universities. You can complete a general business preparation or specialize in a specific area, such as accounting, computer science, marketing, or even e-commerce. Many businesses offer education and training programs for their employees or pay for some or all of the costs of college coursework. You can also attend conferences and seminars sponsored by businesses and professional associations.

Experience in business is always an advantage. Experience in working with people in any way can give you confidence and develop important communication and interpersonal skills. Even if you have not worked part-time or full-time in a business, other types of experiences are useful. Working on projects in an organization, writing for the yearbook or school newspaper, forming a Junior Achievement company, or helping in a parent's business are all examples of experiences that can develop skills important in business.

Most employers value experience when they hire employees. It is relatively easy to find an entry-level job if you are not particularly concerned about type of work or working conditions. These entry-level jobs provide the work experience that will qualify you for the jobs you prefer. Even though the pay may not be as high as you would like and work schedules are sometimes difficult to manage with school and extracurricular activities, it is important to have a good work record at your first jobs.

Beginning employees who stay with one employer for a length of time and receive favorable evaluations will find it easier to receive promotions or be hired by an employer offering a better job. Employees who take advantage of training, opportunities for leadership, or the chance to supervise other employees or contribute to team activities will have an excellent employment record to use when applying for promotions or advanced jobs in other companies.

DEVELOPING AN INDIVIDUAL CAREER PLAN

Many people do little planning, even for the things that are most important to them. You know from your study of business that planning is an important skill. Businesses that plan are much more successful than those that do not. Likewise, people who plan their careers are more likely to achieve their career goals than those who do not plan. By developing a career plan, you will be able to practice an important business skill. In addition, you can show your plan to potential employers to demonstrate your ability to plan.

The following steps provide an outline for developing your own career plan.

1. *Develop an understanding of business concepts and the different types of business careers.* Study careers in depth to determine the industries, businesses, and jobs that most interest you and the types of career paths related to those jobs.
2. *Complete a self-assessment of your knowledge, skills, and attitudes that are related to those needed in business careers.* Ask a counselor to assist you with appropriate interest and aptitude tests that can help you with your assessment. Get feedback from people who know you well (family, friends, teachers, and employers) about their perceptions of the important skills, knowledge, and attitudes you have identified.
3. *Identify the education and experience requirements for business careers that interest you.* Compare those career requirements with your current

Technology *tip*

If you are interested in a technology career in business, the top four skills business recruiters look for in information technology applicants are applications development, information security, project management, and help-desk skills. A big problem faced by recruiters is finding the right skills in the right locations. Well-qualified applicants willing to move will continue to have many choices of information technology jobs.

preparation, and determine the additional education and experience you will need to qualify for those careers.

4. *Discuss the education and experience you will need with people (counselors or businesspeople) who are familiar with education programs and employment opportunities.* Ask them to help you select those that fit your career plans and qualifications.

5. *Develop a career plan that identifies the knowledge and skills needed for the career you have chosen and how you will develop them through a combination of education and experience.* The plan can identify the jobs in a career ladder, the schools or educational programs you plan to attend, the length of time it will take you to ascend each step of the career ladder, and the ultimate career goal you would like to achieve.

PREPARING A CAREER PORTFOLIO

Artists, models, and advertising people have used portfolios for many years to demonstrate their abilities and present examples of their work. You may already have been asked to develop an education portfolio to document your work in several of your classes. A career portfolio is an organized collection of information and materials you develop to represent yourself, your preparation, and your accomplishments. You might want to create a portfolio to help with career planning and to represent yourself when you apply for jobs or for admission to an educational institution.

Your portfolio should provide clear descriptions of your preparation, skills, and experience. Those descriptions can include examples of projects you have completed in school and on the job or for organizations to which you belong. They can even be work you have done as a hobby that demonstrates an important business skill. You can include evaluations of your skills and work evidenced through tests, checklists of competencies you have mastered, and performance reviews from employers. Also, you might ask people who know you well to write recommendations that relate to your skills and abilities or critiques of your projects or work.

You can develop your portfolio over a long period of time. You might start it now and continue to add to it as you complete high school, go on for additional education, or move through jobs in your career ladder. You should prepare a portfolio that allows you to add and remove items. Put your materials in a binder or other protective covering to keep them in good condition. As you become increasingly skilled with computer technology, you might want to develop a digital version of your portfolio. You can scan printed materials and photograph objects and add digital video and audio files to your digital portfolio. Whether in digital or print form, make and keep backup copies of your important materials in a secure place.

The portfolio should include your best and most recent materials. Many people develop a personal Web site that includes a summary of their career portfolio and some examples of recent accomplishments. It provides an efficient way to share information

NETBookmark

Many fun and informative career planning resources can be found on the Internet. ACT is an independent, not-for-profit organization that provides a variety of career assessment, research, and information resources. An interesting tool for matching personal interests with jobs is ACT's World of Work Map. Point your browser to www.thomsonedu.com/school/bpmxtra. Use the tool to see what types of careers match your personal interests. Did you identify careers that you had not considered in the past?

www.thomsonedu.com/school/bpmxtra

about themselves with a prospective employer or mentor or an educational institution to which they are applying. If you decide to use the Internet for this purpose, be careful to protect personal and confidential information.

A portfolio is a good way to identify important materials that will help you with your self-assessment. It also keeps materials organized so you can show them to others to demonstrate achievement, or as you apply for educational programs and jobs. Because it must communicate your preparation and skills effectively, it should be well organized, professional, and easy for others to review and understand.

CHECKPOINT

How can a career portfolio help you in career planning?

25.4 Assessment

UNDERSTAND MANAGEMENT CONCEPTS

Determine the best answer for each of the following questions.

1. People in ____ occupations are responsible for specific units in a business and must make decisions about operations and personnel.
   a. entry-level
   b. career-level
   c. supervisor/management
   d. specialist

2. An organized collection of information and materials developed to represent yourself, your preparation, and your accomplishments is a
   a. résumé
   b. career portfolio
   c. job application
   d. career plan

THINK CRITICALLY

Answer the following questions as completely as possible.

3. Why is it fairly easy for businesspeople who work in one company or industry to move to a job in a different company, industry, or country?

4. How can a well-developed career portfolio provide an advantage for an applicant for a new job?

Xtra!
Study Tools
thomsonedu.com/school/bpmxtra

CHAPTER CONCEPTS

- The dramatic changes facing both traditional and new businesses present challenges to both employees and managers. Human resources personnel can help businesses respond to those changes by establishing organizational development programs.

- Two important elements of an effective organizational development program are improving work processes and building effective working relationships. The goal is to eliminate errors, improve quality, and reduce costs.

- Successful businesses value their employees. They use job enlargement, cross training, and job enrichment to improve employee satisfaction.

- Career development programs meet a company's future employment needs by systematically preparing current employees for future positions in the company. A successful career development program requires a long-term organizational plan, career paths, employee performance reviews, career counseling, and training and development.

- Common levels of business employment are entry, career, specialist, supervisor/management, and executive/entrepreneur. Career paths exist in all types of businesses. Following career-planning procedures will help you obtain a job that is both satisfying and rewarding.

REVIEW TERMS AND CONCEPTS

Write the letter of the term that matches each definition. Some terms will not be used.

1. Training employees to perform more than one job in the company, even though they typically perform only one
2. Occupations in which employees have the authority to control some of their work and make some decisions
3. Likelihood of being employed by the same company in the future
4. Facilities where human resources employees manage career development activities
5. Progression of related jobs with increasing skill requirements and responsibility
6. Program that matches the career plans of employees with the employment needs of the business
7. Making a job more interesting by adding variety to the tasks
8. Organized collection of information and materials developed to represent yourself, your preparation, and your accomplishments
9. Occupations that involve routine activities and require little training
10. Carefully planned changes in the structure and operation of a business to adjust to a competitive business environment
11. The kinds of tasks that make up a job and the way workers perform these tasks in doing their jobs
12. Occupations fully responsible for the success or failure of a company

a. career centers
b. career development
c. career-level occupations
d. career path
e. career portfolio
f. cross training
g. entry-level occupations
h. executive/entrepreneur occupations
i. individual career plan
j. job design
k. job enlargement
l. job enrichment
m. job security
n. organizational development
o. performance standards
p. specialist occupations
q. supervisor/management occupations

DETERMINE THE BEST ANSWER

13. The responsibility for planning and managing organizational development and career development programs is usually given to
    a. managers
    b. individual employees
    c. consultants
    d. the human resources department

14. Studies have found that employees are most satisfied with their work based on all of the following factors except
    a. performing interesting work
    b. being paid more than their coworkers
    c. receiving recognition for good work
    d. all of the above

15. Which of the following is *not* a requirement of an effective career development program?
    a. long-term company plans to determine job opportunities
    b. career paths leading to both management and nonmanagement positions
    c. regular employee performance reviews
    d. All are needed for an effective career development program.

16. Web designers, programmers, analysts, professional salespeople, technicians, machine operators, and similar technical or skilled positions are all examples of _____ occupations.
    a. entry-level
    b. career-level
    c. specialist
    d. supervisor/management

APPLY WHAT YOU KNOW

17. Based on the Reality Check scenario at the beginning of the chapter, how can James Lane use career planning to help make the best decision for his future? What kinds of help and assistance should Alliance Industries provide to James and other employees to help them prepare for the upcoming changes?

18. In what ways is the employment environment today different from the environment 10 years ago, and in what ways is it similar? What changes do you predict will occur in the employment environment over the next 10 years?

19. How can work processes be improved without changing the technology or equipment used to complete the work?

20. What are some valuable sources of information that managers can use to identify possible changes in the external environment?

21. Using jobs with which you are familiar, suggest some ways organizations could use job enlargement and job enrichment to increase employee satisfaction and motivation.

22. Some companies believe that each employee should be totally responsible for his or her career development. Why is it likely that career development will not be successful in those companies?

23. In what ways would planning for a career in international business be similar to or different from planning for a career in one's home country?

MAKE CONNECTIONS

24. **Teamwork** Form a team with several classmates. Identify one problem related to the "work" environment or "work" relationships of your school. Identify why the problem exists and how the school would be better if the problem were solved. Then propose several solutions and analyze each to determine its advantages and disadvantages. Select the one solution your group believes could be implemented and would be acceptable to administrators, teachers, and students. Prepare a written report from your group that identifies the problem, the proposed solution, and the key steps to successfully implementing the solution.

25. **Math** Yarcho and Slayton, Inc. has been training employees to prepare them for a changeover in computer technology. A report on the training program reveals the following data:

Date of Training	Number of Participants	Cost of Training	Department
2-04	45	$ 900	Marketing
7-26	26	3,120	Information
1-13	11	495	Management
4-05	58	870	
9-29	32	960	Operations
5-30	65	3,250	
11-08	29	435	Accounting
3-19	12	900	and Finance
7-12	38	760	
12-01	19	855	

   a. Calculate the cost per participant of each training session.
   b. Determine the average cost of training per participant for the entire company.
   c. If the company has a total of 206 employees with 45 in Marketing, 58 in Information Management, 65 in Operations, and 38 in Accounting and Finance, determine the average amount spent on each employee for training for each department and for the entire company.

26. **Career Planning** Identify a management or nonmanagement specialist job that interests you. Using career information from your school counseling center, library, or the Internet, prepare a description of the education and experience requirements for the job. Identify an entry-level job and at least two other related jobs with more advanced requirements and responsibilities that could form a career path for you. Write a job description for each job. List your current skills and experience that prepare you for the career path. Identify the skills, education, and experience you will need to progress along the career path.

CASE IN POINT

CASE 25-1: Encouraging Employee Involvement

The Orion Corporation recently implemented employee involvement teams as part of an organizational development program. The employees in the customer support department of the engineering division were excited about the chance to participate in solving a problem they had been facing for some time. Fourteen of the 20 employees had school-age children. Several times during the year, the employees needed time off from work to attend parent-teacher conferences, help with projects in their child's school, or attend an important school activity involving their children. Orion had no policy that allowed employees time away from work. The employees either had to miss the school activities or call in sick. Most of the employees felt uncomfortable about taking a "sick day" when they really were not sick.

The employee team worked carefully and developed the following plan: Each employee could have up to two half-day absences for school-related activities during the year. The absence would have to be scheduled at least one week in advance and only one employee could be absent at a time. The other employees would complete the work of the absent employee before they left for the day without additional pay. The department manager could cancel the absence with one day's notice if the department had special assignments or extra work.

The employee team submitted its plan to the department manager. The manager rejected the employee recommendation. She identified two reasons for rejecting the plan: (1) The company could not have different policies concerning employee absences for each department. (2) Not all employees in the department had school-age children, so the policy would be unfair to those employees who did not.

THINK CRITICALLY

1. Do you believe the manager made the right decision about the team's recommendation? Why or why not? What should the manager do now, based on her decision not to accept the team's recommendation? If you were the manager, how would you respond to the team's recommendation?
2. How do you believe the employees will feel about the organization, based on the manager's response to their proposal? What would you recommend the employees do, based on the responses of the manager?
3. How can the Orion Corporation improve the way it organizes and uses teams in the future? Should the manager's role change now that employee involvement teams are being formed?

CASE 25-2: Getting Serious about Career Planning

Felicia Bendine is starting her senior year of high school. She wants her last year in school to be enjoyable, but she also knows she has to get serious about her future. Many of her friends have already submitted applications for admission to colleges and universities, and a few have decided on military careers. Some intend to obtain full-time jobs right after high school, and others are going on to a community college for specialized technical training. Felicia is open to all those ideas but hasn't really decided on any particular one.

Felicia has always wanted to own a business, preferably a collectibles shop that relates to her hobby. Felicia has collected rare dolls since she was a little girl. She has more than 200 dolls in her collection, a few of which are worth several hundred dollars. She has them displayed in their original boxes in her bedroom and frequently attends collectible shows in the area. She has made both sales and purchases to add to her collection.

For the past three years, Felicia has worked for Mr. and Mrs. Abbott in their antique shop in her neighborhood. She had visited the Abbotts' store one day, and when they found out about her doll collection, they gave her a 1930s doll from their inventory. She volunteered to help out in the store, and it turned into a part-time job. She has given them several ideas about business operations from the courses she has taken in school and even set up a simple Web site where they can advertise their business. It has brought many out-of-town visitors to the store.

The Abbotts have suggested to Felicia that someday, when they decide to retire, they would love to see her take over the business. Felicia expects that their retirement is many years away but is intrigued by the idea. However, she doesn't know if she wants to wait that long to own her own business or what she should do after graduating from high school to prepare for that opportunity or another route to her goal of being an entrepreneur. She does know that she has to do some serious planning in the next few months.

THINK CRITICALLY

1. What education beyond high school do you believe Felicia will need to be a successful small-business owner? What types of business experience would help her prepare to own and operate a business?
2. What are the advantages and disadvantages to Felicia of waiting for the Abbotts' retirement and then buying their business? What information about the business and the Abbotts' plans does Felicia need to help her with that decision?
3. If you were Felicia's friend, what would you recommend she do during her senior year to plan for her future? Justify your recommendations.

MY BUSINESS, INC.

DEVELOPING AN EFFECTIVE ORGANIZATION

Even new businesses must be concerned about change and maintaining an effective work environment and work processes. One of the serious problems faced by small businesses is how to provide a motivating and rewarding experience for employees so they will continue to work for the business even though wages and benefits may be less than they can obtain in larger businesses. The following activities will help you consider how to maintain an effective organization and prepare for your role as a small-business owner.

DATA COLLECTION

1. Review magazine and newspaper articles and Internet information about small-business operations. Identify issues small businesses face that often lead to major problems or failure.
2. Identify a small number of people who have worked in a small business for a short time and then changed jobs due to dissatisfaction with the job. Also identify a small number who have worked in a small business and are satisfied with their jobs. Ask each group the reasons for their satisfaction or dissatisfaction. Ask them to identify which of the reasons are directly related to the size of the business.
3. Review information on innovative small businesses and analyze how they are responding to local and global competition, changes in technology, and improvements in work procedures.
4. Identify the business operations, management, and interpersonal skills you will need to develop as the manager of a small business. Gather information from the library or the Internet about opportunities for formal education, professional self-improvement, and life-long learning that could help you improve your skills as a business owner.

ANALYSIS

1. Compile a list of things you could do as the owner of a new small business to develop a work environment that would motivate employees while encouraging effective performance. Try to list things that would not be particularly expensive to implement.
2. Assume that your business has been receiving an increased number of customer complaints. When you question your employees, they tell you that they are unsure of how to deal with difficult customers. Identify employee attitudes that result in customer satisfaction. Develop a procedure your employees could use in complex situations, including follow-up techniques.
3. List the jobs in a career path you can follow to develop the experience and skills you will need to own and operate your own business. Describe the formal education and informal education you will need.

Career Cluster
Human Resources Specialist

Human resources specialists provide a link between management and employees. They recruit and interview prospective employees and advise on hiring decisions in accordance with policies and requirements that are consistent with employment laws. They also help prepare employees for their jobs, provide training, and prepare both managers and employees for performance review procedures. They are involved in career planning and efforts to improve the work environment.

Employment Outlook

Human resources specialists are employed in virtually every industry. Some are self-employed consultants to public and private employers. The private sector accounts for about 80 percent of salaried HR jobs. The growing importance of occupational safety and health, equal employment opportunity, wages, health care, pensions, and organizational change will increase the demand for many types of human resources specialists.

PHOTO: © GETTY IMAGES/PHOTODISC.

Job Titles

Employment Manager
Manager of Diversity and Equal Opportunity Programs
Training and Development Specialist
Compensation and Benefits Specialist

Needed Skills

- Must have a college degree, generally with a major in human resources, personnel, or industrial and labor relations.
- Advanced education and training in areas such as law, counseling, education, or change management preferred.
- Must have excellent communication and human relations skills.

Working in Human Resources

Evelyn is an instructional designer in the training department. She works with managers and experienced employees to determine training needs for a department or job area. Expert employees help her identify the correct procedures for completing job tasks and operating any special equipment. Working with other specialists, she develops instruction that can be delivered in a laboratory, classroom, or over the Internet. Her training programs are carefully tested and improved before they are used by the company.

Career Assessment

Check your library or the Internet for information on HR careers and career paths. Which HR jobs might you consider, and why?

Case Study

DO NICE EMPLOYEES FINISH LAST?

Business is not an easy game to play. Individuals are sometimes tempted to put their interests above those of others. Unethical individuals capitalize on the misfortune of fellow workers. The *Harvard Business Review* found that personal feelings toward an individual are more significant in the formation of productive work relationships than the person's competence. The ability to connect with others is increasingly important, as the global business environment requires individuals who can collaborate with diverse teams of employees and outside contacts. Companies expect staff members to work on project-based teams more frequently in the next 10 to 15 years. Individuals who are pleasant and personable will have the greatest success in forming productive professional partnerships.

A positive, friendly disposition can be a valuable career asset. There is a difference between being nice and being a pushover, however. People who try too hard to be liked may seem disingenuous or out of touch with reality. Some professional situations simply require individuals to take a stand, even when it would be easier to ignore the circumstances. Being overly accommodating can result in shouldering a disproportionate amount of work, losing out on promotion opportunities, and suffering from burnout. For example, offering to stay late to help a colleague finish a project before she leaves on vacation is a gesture that may build goodwill and increase the likelihood that the coworker will lend you a hand when you need it. Being too nice, on the other hand, occurs when you stay late every night because you have a hard time telling colleagues that your plate is full. The result is burnout from not being able to balance work and leisure.

Another example of being nice is receiving kudos from a satisfied client for a job well done and forwarding the message to those who worked on the project with you to let them know that everyone's effort was appreciated. The entire team receives a morale boost. Receiving praise from a satisfied customer and giving all the credit to everyone else on your team because you don't want to seem self-serving is an example of being too nice. Your accomplishments go unnoticed and your superiors do not realize the true value you bring to the firm.

THINK CRITICALLY

1. What is the fine line between being nice and too nice at work?
2. Why is it important to give colleagues the credit they deserve?
3. What is the danger faced by efficient employees who willingly take on responsibilities and complete projects on time?
4. How would an unethical employee handle praise for a task successfully completed by a team?

Human Resources Management Event

You have 30 minutes to prepare a speech for the employees of a successful clothing store called Latest Edition. Your speech will be seven minutes long, and the audience has three minutes to ask questions.

Salary and benefits are very important to Latest Edition's employees. Full-time employees' salaries are based totally on commission. They earn 14 percent of all sales during the year. Latest Edition sells expensive clothing and it is not unusual for the top sales associates to sell $10,000 worth of merchandise on a weekend shift during the busy holiday season. On a summer weekday, however, sales can be slow to nonexistent. Full-time employees receive four weeks of paid vacation and 80 percent of their health insurance. Part-time employees earn $8.50 an hour and no commission or fringe benefits.

You must report the latest pay and benefits package for part-time and full-time employees. Latest Edition must watch its total budget carefully to compete with national department stores like Macy's and Nordstrom. Full-time employees will now be paid a base salary of $20,000 and 10 percent commission on all sales. They will still have four weeks of paid vacation, and the company will cover 90 percent of their health insurance. Part-time employees will earn $7.00 per hour plus 8 percent commission on sales, with no benefits. All employees will receive a 40 percent discount on clothing they purchase for themselves. You must give this information a positive twist, because the level of concern among employees has been raised with the changes.

PERFORMANCE INDICATORS EVALUATED

- Demonstrate knowledge of human resources management and management concepts.
- Apply critical-thinking skills to interpret personnel policies.
- Demonstrate effective oral communication skills.
- Demonstrate effective persuasive and informative communication and presentation skills.
- Discuss compensation, benefits, and incentive programs.

For more detailed information about performance indicators, go to the BPA Web site.

THINK CRITICALLY

1. Why are compensation and benefits difficult topics to present to employees?
2. Name advantages and disadvantages of paying commission on sales.
3. How do you think the change of compensation for part-time employees will affect their sales performance?

http://www.bpa.org/

Glossary

A

accountability The obligation to accept responsibility for the outcomes of assigned tasks.

accounting equation Assets = Liabilities + Capital

accounts payable record A record showing money owed and payments made by the business.

accounts receivable record A record showing what each customer owes and pays.

achievement need In McClelland's theory, the need to take personal responsibility for work, set personal goals, and have immediate feedback on work.

actuaries Persons who calculate insurance rates.

administered channel A channel in which one organization takes a leadership position to benefit all channel members.

advertising All forms of paid promotion that deliver a message to many people at the same time.

advertising budget A plan of the amount of money a firm should spend for advertising based on estimated sales.

advertising media The methods of delivering the promotional message to the intended audience.

affiliation need In McClelland's theory, motivation related to relationships with others and fitting in with a group.

affinity credit cards Cards associated with specific organizations and offered to people affiliated with those organizations.

aging the accounts Analyzing customers' account balances within categories based upon the number of days each customer's balance has remained unpaid.

application software Software which consists of instructions for performing various types of tasks.

applied research Research that studies existing product problems or possible design improvements for current products.

assessed valuation The value of property determined by tax officials.

assets Things owned, such as cash and buildings.

assurance SERVQUAL dimension; the knowledge and courtesy of employees and their ability to convey trust and confidence.

authority The right to make decisions about work assignments and to require other employees to perform assigned tasks.

autocratic leader One who gives direct, clear, and precise orders with detailed instructions as to what, when, and how work is to be done.

automatic teller machine (ATM) A computer that enables bank customers to deposit, withdraw, or transfer funds by using a bank-provided plastic card.

avoidance strategy A strategy for resolving conflict that takes a neutral position or agrees with another person's position even though it differs from your personal belief.

B

baby boom The high birth rate period from 1945 to 1965.

baby bust The low birth rate period following the baby boom period.

balance of payments Accounting statement in which all international transactions are recorded; consists of current account and capital account.

balance sheet (statement of financial position) A financial statement that lists the assets, liabilities, and capital of a business.

bank A financial institution that accepts demand deposits, makes consumer and commercial loans, and buys and sells currency and government securities.

bankruptcy A legal process that allows selling assets to pay off debts.

banner ad A Web advertising unit, like a placement ad in a newspaper.

bar codes Product identification labels containing a unique set of vertical bars that can be read using computer scanning equipment.

basic product The physical product in its simplest form.

beneficiaries Persons who receive a life insurance payment on the death of an insured person.

board of directors (directors or board) Ruling body of a corporation.

bond A long-term written promise to pay a definite sum of money at a specified time.

bonding The process which provides payment of damages to people who have losses resulting from the negligence or dishonesty of an employee or from the failure of the business to complete a contract.

bonus Money paid at the end of a specific period of time for performance that exceeds the expected standard.

book value The value of a share of stock that is found by dividing the net worth (assets minus liabilities) of the corporation by the total number of shares outstanding.

brainstorming A group discussion technique that is used to generate as many ideas as possible for solving a problem.

brand A name, symbol, word, or design that identifies a product, service, or company.

bricks-and-click businesses Businesses that use the Internet to support their bricks-and-mortar businesses.

bricks-and-mortar businesses Businesses that complete most of their business activities at a physical location rather than through the Internet.

browser A program that permits you to navigate and view Web pages.

budget A financial plan usually extending for one year.

building codes Codes that regulate physical features of structures.

business An organization that produces or distributes a good or service for profit.

business buying process A set of formal procedures followed by a business when it decides to purchase a product.

business cycles A pattern of irregular but repeated expansion and contraction of the GDP.

business ethics A collection of principles and rules of conduct based on what is right and wrong for an organization.

business plan (1) A written description of the business and its operations with an analysis of the opportunities and risks it faces. (2) A written guide that helps the entrepreneur during the design and start-up phases of the business.

buying Obtaining goods to be resold.

buying motives The reasons people buy.

C

cafeteria plan A benefit program in which employees can select the benefits that meet their personal needs.

capacity Earning power.

capital (net worth, owner's equity, stockholders' equity) (1) What a business is worth after subtracting liabilities from assets. (2) A measure of the credit applicant's current financial worth or ability to pay based on assets.

capital account An account that records investment funds coming into and going out of a country.

capital budget A financial plan for replacing fixed assets or acquiring new ones.

capital formation The production of capital goods.

capital goods Buildings, tools, machines, and other equipment that are used to produce other goods but do not directly satisfy human wants.

capitalism An economic-political system in which private citizens are free to go into business for themselves, to produce whatever they choose to produce, and to distribute what they produce as they please.

capital stock (or simply stock) The general term applied to the shares of ownership of a corporation.

career centers Facilities where career development activities are managed.

career development A program that provides a long-term focus on a company's employment needs combined with support for employees so they can prepare for future jobs in the company.

career-level occupations An occupation in which the employee has the authority to control some of their work and make some decisions.

career path A progression of related jobs with increasing skill requirements and responsibility needed to advance along the career path, and a tentative schedule for the plan's activities.

career portfolio An organized collection of information and materials you develop to represent yourself, your preparation, and your accomplishments.

carpal tunnel syndrome (CTS) Type of injury that can occur from repetitive motion such as using a computer keyboard or playing video games.

cash budget An estimate of cash received and paid out.

cash discount A discount given if payment is received by a certain date.

cash flow The movement of cash into and out of a business.

cease-and-desist order Legal penalty requiring that a company stop using specific advertisements.

centralized organization Business structure in which a few top managers do all the major planning and decision making.

certificate of deposit (CD) A savings account that requires an investor to deposit a specified sum for a fixed period at a fixed interest rate.

certified public accountant (CPA) A person who has met a state's education, experience, and examination requirements in accounting.

channel integration When one business owns the organizations at other levels of the channel.

channel members Businesses that participate in activities transferring goods and services from the producer to the user.

channel of communication The means by which a message is conveyed.

channels of distribution (marketing channels) The routes products and services follow, including the activities and participating organizations, while moving from the producer to the consumer.

character An indication of one's moral obligation to pay debts.

charter (certificate of incorporation) An official document granted by a state giving power to run a corporation.

check A written order on a financial institution to pay previously deposited money to a third party on demand.

chief information officer (CIO) The top computer executive.

close corporation (closely held corporation) A corporation that does not offer its shares of stock for public sale.

co-branded credit cards Credit cards cosponsored by two companies which have benefits and rewards designed specifically for their joint customers.

code of ethics A formal, published collection of values and rules used to guide the behavior of an organization toward its various stakeholders.

collateral Property a borrower pledges to assure repayment of a loan.

combination plan A pay plan that provides each employee a small wage or salary and adds incentive pay based on the person's performance.

command economy An economic system in which the method for determining what, how, and for whom goods and services are produced is decided by a central planning authority.

commercial businesses Firms engaged in marketing, in finance, and in furnishing services.

commercial loan A loan made to a business.

commission plan A compensation plan in which employees are paid a percentage of the volume of business for which they are responsible.

common stock Ownership that gives holders the right to participate in managing the business by having voting privileges and by sharing in the profits (dividends) if there are any.

communication The sharing of information which results in a higher degree of understanding between the message sender and receiver.

communication network A structure through which information flows in a business.

communism Forced socialism where all or almost all the productive resources of a nation are owned by the government.

comparable worth Paying workers equally for jobs with similar but not identical job requirements.

comparative advantage theory A theory which states that to gain a trade advantage, a country should specialize in products or services that it can provide more efficiently than other countries.

compensation The money and other benefits people receive for work.

compensation plan A system of policies and procedures for calculating the wages and salaries in an organization.

competition Rivalry among sellers for consumers' dollars.

compromise strategy A strategy in which everyone involved in a conflict agrees to a mutually acceptable solution.

computer A machine that processes and stores data according to instructions stored in it.

computer-aided design (CAD) Computer application that allows engineers to design and test products before they are even built.

computer-integrated manufacturing Process in which all manufacturing systems are designed and managed with computers.

conditions Economic and other matters, such as the economic health of a community or nation and the extent of business competition, that affect credit decisions.

conflict A situation that develops when one person interferes with the achievement of another's goals.

consultant An expert who is called upon to study a special problem and offer solutions.

consumer goods Products produced for sale to individuals and families for personal use.

consumer goods and services Goods and services that satisfy people's economic wants directly.

consumer loan A loan made to an individual.

consumer panel A group of people who offer opinions about a product or service.

Consumer Price Index (CPI) A measure of the average change in prices of consumer goods and services typically purchased by people living in urban areas.

containerization A process in which products are packed in large shipping containers at the factory and then

shipped using a number of transportation methods before being unpacked.

continuous processing Manufacturing process in which raw materials constantly move through specially designed equipment that changes their form to make them more usable for consumption or further manufacturing.

controlling Evaluating results to determine if the company's objectives have been accomplished as planned.

convenience goods Inexpensive items that consumers purchase regularly without a great deal of thought.

cookies Files of information about a user that some Web sites create and store on the user's own computer.

cooperative A business owned and operated by its user-members for the purpose of supplying themselves with goods and services.

copyright Sole right given to an author by the federal government to reproduce, publish, and sell literary or artistic work for the life of the author plus 70 years.

corporation A business owned by a group of people and authorized by the state in which it is located to act as though it were a single person.

corrective advertising New advertising designed to change the false impression left by misleading information.

cost of goods sold The cost to produce a product or buy it for resale.

credit agency A clearinghouse for information on the creditworthiness of individuals or businesses.

creditors Those to whom money is owed.

creditworthiness A measure of a person's ability and willingness to repay a loan.

cross training A process in which employees are trained to perform more than one job in the company even though they typically perform only one.

culture (1) The shared values, beliefs, and behavior existing in an organization. (2) The customs, beliefs, values, and patterns of behavior of the people of a country or group.

current account An account that records the value of goods and services exported and those imported from foreigners, as well as other income and payments.

custom manufacturing Process used to design and build a unique product to meet the specific needs of the purchaser.

customer oriented Term referring to businesses that direct company activities at satisfying customers.

D

data Original facts and figures that businesses generate.

data-processing center A business that processes data for other businesses for a fee.

database A collection of data organized in a way that makes data easy to find, update, and manage.

debentures Bonds that are not secured by assets but based upon the faith and credit of the corporation that issues them.

debit card A card which allows a person to make cash withdrawals from ATMs, pay bills by phone from bank accounts, and pay for on-site purchases such as food and household items.

debt capital (creditor capital) Capital loaned to a business by others.

decentralized organization A business which is divided into smaller operating units where managers are given almost total responsibility and authority for the operation of those units.

decision support system (DSS) A system that helps managers consider alternatives in making specific decisions.

decline stage A time period when a new product is introduced that is much better or easier to use than the old one, and customers begin to switch from the old product to the new product.

deductible An arrangement that permits the insured to bear part of the loss in return for a lower premium.

demand The number of similar products that will be bought at a given time at a given price.

demand deposit Money put into a financial institution by depositors which can be withdrawn at any time without penalty.

democratic leader One who encourages workers to share in making decisions about work-related problems.

depreciation Decrease in the value of an asset due to wear and age.

depression A long and severe drop in the GDP.

direct deposit Electronic transfer of a paycheck directly from the employer's bank account into the employee's bank account.

direct distribution When producers sell directly to the ultimate consumer.

disability insurance Insurance which offers payments to employees who are no longer able to work because of accidents or illnesses.

discharge The release of an employee from the company due to inappropriate work behavior.

discounts Reductions taken from the price of the product to encourage customers to buy.

distortion The conscious or unconscious way people change messages.

distraction Anything that interferes with the sender's creating and delivering a message and the receiver's getting and interpreting a message.

distribution (place) The set of activities required to transport and store products and make them available to customers.

distribution center A large building designed to accumulate and redistribute products efficiently.

dividends Profits distributed to stockholders on a per-share basis.

domain name A Web site owner's unique Internet address.

domestic goods Products made by firms in the United States.

dot-com business A company that does almost all of its business activities through the Internet.

downsize To cut back on the goods and services provided and thereby shrink the size of a firm and the number of employees.

dumping The practice of selling goods in a foreign market at a price that is below cost or below what the business charges in its own home country.

E

e-commerce Doing business online.

economics The body of knowledge that relates to producing and using goods and services that satisfy human wants.

economic discrepancies Differences between the offerings of a business and the requirements of a consumer.

economic growth Occurs when a country's output exceeds its population growth.

economic system An organized way for a country to decide how to use its productive resources; that is, to decide what, how, and for whom goods and services will be produced.

economic utility The amount of satisfaction received from using a product or service.

economic wants The desire for scarce material goods and services.

effectiveness Making the right decisions about what products or services to offer customers and the best ways to produce and deliver them.

efficiency Producing products and services quickly, at low cost, without wasting time and materials.

electronic funds transfer (EFT) Transferring money by computer rather than by check.

electronic shopping carts Specialized programs that keep track of shoppers' selections as they shop, provide an order form for them to complete, and submit the form to the company through the Internet.

embargo A process in which the government bars companies from doing business with particular countries.

emoticons Facial expressions created with keyboard symbols and used to express feelings in e-mail messages.

empathy SERVQUAL dimension; the caring and individualized attention the business provides its customers.

employee assistance programs Employer programs that provide confidential personal problem-solving, counseling, and support services for employees.

employee benefits All forms of compensation and services the company provides to employees in addition to salaries and wages.

employee turnover The rate at which people enter and leave employment in a business during a year.

empowerment Letting workers decide how to perform their work tasks and offer ideas on how to improve the work process.

endorsement The signature—usually on the back—that transfers a negotiable instrument.

enhanced product A product that offers different features and options for the consumer.

entrepreneur A person who starts, manages, and owns a business.

entry-level occupations Occupations which usually involve routine activities and require little training.

equity capital (owner capital) Money invested in the business by its owner or owners.

ergonomics The science of adapting equipment to the work and health needs of people.

ethics The code of moral conduct that sets standards for what is valued as right or wrong behavior for a person or group.

euro The currency of the European Union.

European Union (EU) A trading bloc consisting of 15 European countries.

exchange rate The value of one country's currency expressed in the currency of another.

excise tax A sales tax that applies only to selected goods and services, such as gasoline.

executive A top-level manager who spends almost all of his or her time on management functions.

executive/entrepreneur occupations Occupations in which the employees are fully responsible for the success or failure of the company.

executive information system (EIS) Information system that combines and summarizes ongoing transactions within the company to provide top-level executives with information needed to make decisions about company goals and direction.

exit interview A formal interview with an employee who is leaving a company to determine the person's attitudes and feelings about the company's policies and procedures, management, and operations.

expert power Power given to people who are considered the most knowledgeable.

exporting When a company sells its goods and services to a foreign country.

extended product A product that includes additional features that are not part of the physical product but increase its usability.

extranet A private network that companies use to share certain information with selected people outside the organization.

F

factors of production Land, labor, capital goods, and management—the four basic resources that are combined to create useful goods and services.

Fair Labor Standards Act (FLSA) Prescribes standards for wages and overtime pay.

false advertising Advertising that is misleading in a material respect or in any way that could influence the customer's purchase or use of the product.

Federal Deposit Insurance Corporation (FDIC) A federal agency that insures deposits in banks and savings institutions up to approximately $100,000 per depositor account.

Federal Reserve System (Fed) The central bank of the United States.

feedback A receiver's response to a sender's message.

file server (or simply server) A computer in a LAN that stores data and application software for all PC workstations.

finance Business activity that deals with all money matters related to running a business.

financial records (accounting records) Organized summaries of a business's financial information and activities.

financial statements Reports that summarize financial data over a period of time.

financing Providing money that is needed to perform various marketing activities, such as obtaining credit when buying and extending credit when selling.

firewall A system using special software that screens people who enter or exit a network by requesting passwords.

fixed assets Expensive assets of a business that are expected to last and be used for a long time.

fixed interest rate An interest rate that does not change throughout the life of the loan.

flame An electronic message that contains abusive, threatening, or offensive content that may violate company policy or public law.

flattened organization An organization with fewer levels of management than traditional structures.

flex-time A plan that lets employees choose their own work hours, within specified limits.

foreign goods Products made by firms in other countries.

formal communication network System of official channels that carry organizationally approved messages; flows upward, downward, and across the organization in a prescribed manner.

formal training Carefully planned instruction with a specific curriculum and instructor.

franchise A legal agreement between a company and a distributor to sell a product or service under special conditions.

franchisee The distributor of a franchised product or service.

franchisor The parent company of a franchise agreement that provides the product or service.

free-trade agreements International agreements that eliminate almost all trade restrictions and subsidies between individual countries and groups of countries.

Frost Belt The colder northern half of the United States.

full disclosure Providing all information necessary for consumers to make an informed decision.

G

Generation X People in the post-baby-boom generation.

glass ceiling An invisible barrier to job advancement.

global competition The ability of profit-making organizations to compete with other businesses in other countries.

goal A specific statement of a result the business expects to achieve.

grading and valuing Grouping goods according to size, quality, or other characteristics, and determining an appropriate price for products and services.

grapevine An informal communication system that develops among workers.

gross domestic product (GDP) The total market value of all goods produced and services provided in a country in a year.

growth stage Stage of the product life cycle when several brands of the new product are available.

H

hardware Equipment that makes up a computer system.

health insurance Insurance which provides protection against the expenses of health care.

high-context culture A culture in which communication occurs through non-verbal signs and indirect suggestions.

home country The country in which a multinational corporation has its headquarters.

host country The foreign country where a multinational firm has production and service facilities.

human capital Accumulated knowledge and skills of human beings; the total value of each person's education and acquired skills.

human relations How well people get along with each other when working together.

human resources management (HRM) All activities involved with acquiring, developing, and compensating the people who do the company's work.

human resources planning Determining the types of jobs that are required for each part of the production process and the number of people needed for each job.

hygiene factors Job factors that dissatisfy when absent but do not contribute to satisfaction when they are present.

hyperlink A Web page address embedded in a word, phrase, or graphic that, when clicked, transports users to that address.

I

identity power Power given to people because others identify with and want to be accepted by them.

implementing Helping employees to work effectively.

importing Buying goods or services made in a foreign country.

income statement (profit and loss statement) A financial document that reports total revenue and expenses for a specific period.

income tax A tax levied against the profits of business firms and against earnings of individuals.

indirect distribution Distribution that takes place through channel members.

individual career plan Identifies the jobs that are part of the employee's career path, the training needed to advance along the career path, and a tentative schedule for the plan's activities.

industrial businesses Firms that produce goods that are often used by other businesses or organizations to make things.

industrial goods Products designed for use by another business.

industry Term often used to refer to all businesses within a category.

inflation A rapid rise in prices caused by an inadequate supply of goods and services.

informal communication network Unofficial ways of sharing information in an organization.

informal training Training and instruction that is unstructured and unplanned but developed for specific situations or individuals.

information Data that has been processed in some way that is useful to decision makers.

information liability Responsibility for physical or economic injury arising from incorrect data or wrongful use of data.

information system A computer system used to process data for the purpose of generating information from that data.

innovation Something entirely new.

installment credit Credit used when a customer makes a sizable purchase and agrees to make payments over an extended but fixed period of time.

insurable interest Any interest in property that will suffer a possible financial loss if there is a loss of or damage to the property.

insurance A risk management tool that limits financial loss from uncontrollable events in exchange for regular payments.

insurance agents People who represent the insurance company and sell insurance to individuals and businesses.

insurance rate The amount charged for a certain value of insurance.

intangible When applied to services, having no physical form, visibility, or existence after consumer has used the service.

intermittent processing Manufacturing process that uses short production runs to make predetermined quantities of different products.

international business Business activities that occur between two or more countries.

international licensing Arrangement in which one company allows a different company in another country to make and sell its products according to certain specifications.

International Monetary Fund (IMF) International institution that helps financially strapped countries pay for imports or repay loans.

Internet (Net) A worldwide network of linked computers that allows data and information to be transferred among computers.

Internet domain A registered Web site.

Internet Service Provider (ISP) A service that provides Internet access.

interstate commerce Business operations and transactions that cross over state lines.

intranet A private company network that allows employees to share resources no matter where they are located.

intrapreneur An employee who is given funds and freedom to create a special unit or department within a company in order to develop a new product, process, or service.

intrastate commerce Business transacted within a state.

introduction stage Stage of the product life cycle when a brand-new product enters the market.

inventory management Planning the quantities of materials and supplies needed for production and the number of finished products required to fill customer orders.

investment The use of money to make more money.

investment bank An organization that helps businesses raise capital through the sale of stocks and bonds.

J

job description A list of the basic tasks that make up a job.

job design The kinds of tasks that make up a job and the way workers perform these tasks.

job enlargement Making a job more interesting by adding variety to the tasks.

job enrichment Encouraging employee participation in decision making.

job security The likelihood that employment will not be terminated.

job sharing An employment plan that allows two people to share one full-time job.

job specification A list of the qualifications a worker needs to do a job.

joint venture Two or more businesses that agree to provide a good or service, sharing the costs of doing business and also the profits.

just-in-time (JIT) inventory controls A method in which the company maintains very small inventories and obtains materials just in time for use.

K

knowledge workers People who work with information.

L

labor The human effort, either physical or mental, that goes into the production of goods and services.

labor force Most people aged 16 or over who are available for work, whether employed or unemployed.

labor participation rate The percentage of the labor force either employed or actively seeking employment.

layoff A temporary or permanent reduction in the number of employees resulting from a change in business conditions.

leader A manager who earns the respect and cooperation of employees to effectively accomplish the organization's work.

leadership The ability to influence individuals and groups to achieve organizational goals.

leadership style The general way a manager treats and directs employees.

lease A contract that allows the use of an asset for a fee.

liabilities Claims against assets or things owed—the debts of a business.

liability insurance Insurance which provides protection for risks involved in operating a business.

licensing A way to limit and control those who plan to enter certain types of businesses.

life insurance Insurance that pays money on the death of the insured to a person or people identified in the insurance policy.

limited liability company (LLC) A special type of corporation that is taxed as if it were a sole proprietorship or partnership.

limited partnership Partnership in which a partner's liability is limited to the amount of the partner's investment.

line of credit The authorization to borrow up to a maximum amount for a specified period of time.

line organization Business structure in which all authority and responsibility may be traced in a direct line from the top executive down to the lowest employee level.

line-and-staff organization The addition of staff specialists to a line organization.

list price The original price that the seller posts on the product.

local area network (LAN) An electronic system that allows computer information to move over short distances between or among different computers.

long-term debt Capital that is borrowed for longer than a year.

low-context culture A culture in which people communicate directly and explicitly.

M

malpractice insurance A type of liability insurance that protects against financial loss arising from suits for negligence in providing professional services.

management The process of accomplishing the goals of an organization through the effective use of people and other resources.

management information system (MIS) Integrates data from various departments to make it available to help managers with daily business operations.

manager A person who completes all four management functions on a regular basis and has authority over other jobs and people.

manufacturing Form of production in which raw and semifinished materials are processed, assembled, or converted into finished products.

margin (gross profit) The difference between the selling price and the cost of goods sold.

markdown Any amount by which the original selling price is reduced before an item is sold.

market The types of buyers a business wishes to attract and where such buyers are located.

market economy An economic system that determines what, how, and for whom goods and services are produced by coordinating individual choices through arrangements that aid buying and selling goods and services.

market research The study of a company's current and prospective customers.

market value The value at which stock is bought and sold on any given day.

marketing The process of planning and executing the conception, pricing, promotion, and distribution of ideas, goods, and services to create exchanges that satisfy individual and organizational objectives.

marketing concept Keeping the needs of the consumer uppermost in mind during the design, production, and distribution of a product.

marketing mix The blending of all decisions that are related to the four elements of marketing.

marketing plan A detailed written description of all marketing activities that a business must accomplish in order to sell a product.

markup The amount added to the cost of a product to determine its selling price.

mass production Assembly process that produces a large number of identical products; usually involves an assembly line.

matrix organization An organization which combines workers into temporary work teams to complete specific projects.

maturity date Date on which a loan must be repaid.

maturity stage Stage of the product life cycle when there are many competing brands with very similar features.

Medicare Supplemental health insurance for retirement-age people as well as others with specified disabilities.

merchandise inventory Goods purchased to sell to customers at a profit.

merchant account provider A private company that acts as an intermediary between businesses and one or more credit card companies to establish and maintain credit services.

mid-manager A manager who completes all of the management functions but spends more time on one of the functions or is responsible for a specific part of the company's operations.

minimum wage law A law that specifies that it is illegal for employers to pay less than an identified wage rate to any employee.

mission statement A short, specific statement of the purpose and direction of the business.

mixed economy An economic system that uses aspects of a market and a command economy to make decisions about what, how, and for whom goods and services are produced.

modem An electronic device inside or outside the computer that enables it to send data over phone lines or cable.

modified rebuy When a business purchases a new or modified product from established suppliers.

money market account A type of savings account in which the deposits are invested in short-term, government-backed securities.

monopoly Situation created when only one company provides a product or service without competition from other companies.

Moore's Law The prediction that the amount of data that can be processed by a computer chip will double about every 18 months.

motivation The set of factors that cause a person to act in a certain way.

motivators Factors that increase job satisfaction.

multinational firm A business that owns or controls production or service facilities outside the country in which it is based.

mutual fund Company that pools the money of many small investors for the purchase of stocks and bonds.

N

natural monopoly Type of monopoly that usually involves providing public services, such as public utilities, which have a fairly stable demand and are costly to create.

natural resources Anything provided by nature that affects the productive ability of a country.

Net Generation Those persons born between 1977 and 1997.

net profit The difference between the selling price and all costs and expenses of the business.

new task purchase Process when a business is purchasing a product, inventory item, or supply for the first time.

no-fault insurance Each insurance company is required to pay the losses of its insured when an accident occurs, regardless of who might have been responsible for the loss.

nominal group technique (NGT) Group problem-solving method in which group members write down and evaluate ideas to be shared with the group.

nonbank Financial institution whose primary purpose is to offer financial products and services other than deposits and loans.

noneconomic wants Desires for non-material things that are not scarce.

nongovernmental organizations (NGOs) Group problem-solving method in which group members write down and evaluate ideas to be shared with the group.

nonprofit corporation An organization that does not pay taxes and does not exist to make a profit.

nontariff barriers Barriers other than tariffs that restrict imports.

nonverbal communication Delivering messages by means other than speaking or writing.

North American Free Trade Agreement (NAFTA) A trading bloc consisting of the United States, Canada, and Mexico.

O

objections Concerns or complaints expressed by the customer.

Occupational Safety and Health Act (OSHA) Federal law that regulates safety and health conditions in most businesses.

officers Top executives who are hired to manage the business.

open corporation (publicly owned corporation) A corporation that offers its shares of stock for public sale.

open leader A manager who gives little or no direction to workers.

operating budget A plan showing projected sales, costs, expenses, and profits for the ongoing operations of a business.

operating expenses The costs of operating a business.

operating system software A master control program that manages the computer's internal functions and file system.

operational planning Short-term planning that identifies specific activities for each area of the business.

organization chart A visual device that shows the structure of an organization and the relationships among workers and divisions of work.

organizational development Carefully planned changes in the structure and operation of a business so it can adjust successfully to the competitive environment.

organizing Determining how plans can most effectively be accomplished; arranging resources to complete work.

output The quantity, or amount, produced within a given time.

outsourcing Hiring an outside firm to perform specialized tasks for a business.

P

Pacific Rim Countries located on the western edge of the Pacific Ocean.

par value (stated value) A dollar value shown on a share of stock, which is an arbitrarily assigned amount that is used for bookkeeping purposes.

parent firm A company that controls another company.

partnership A business owned by two or more persons.

patent An agreement in which the federal government gives an inventor the sole right for 20 years to make, use, and sell an invention.

pension plan A company-sponsored retirement plan that makes regular payments to employees after retirement.

performance review The process of assessing how well employees are doing their jobs.

performance standards Specific statements of the expected results from critical business activities.

personal digital assistant (PDA) A small, computer-like device that can send and receive messages wirelessly.

personal property tax A tax on such items as furniture, machinery, and equipment.

personal selling Promotion through direct, personal contact with a customer.

piece-rate plan A compensation plan that pays the employee a fixed rate for each unit of production.

piggyback service A distribution method where truck trailers are loaded and placed on railroad cars to be shipped close to their final destination.

pixel One or more dots that act as the smallest unit on a video display screen.

planning Analyzing information and making decisions about what needs to be done.

policies Guidelines used in making decisions regarding specific, recurring situations.

position power Power that comes from the position the manager holds in the organization.

power The ability to control behavior.

power need In McClelland's theory, desire to influence and control others and to be responsible for a group's activities.

preferred stock Ownership that gives holders preference over the common stockholders when distributing dividends or assets.

price The amount of money given to acquire a product.

price discrimination Setting different prices for different customers.

prime rate The lowest rate of interest; the rate at which large banks loan large sums to the best-qualified borrowers.

private property Items of value that individuals can own, use, and sell.

privatization Transfer of authority to provide a good or service from a government to individuals or businesses.

problem A difficult situation requiring a solution.

procedure A list of steps to be followed for performing certain work.

process improvement Efforts to increase the effectiveness and efficiency of specific business operations.

producer Anyone who aids in creating a utility.

product All attributes that customers receive in exchange for the purchase price.

product assortment The complete set of all products a business offers to a market.

product development Process of creating or improving a product or service.

product life cycle The four stages of sales and profit performance through which all brands of a product progress.

product life cycle theory Theory that companies look for new markets when products are in the maturity and decline stages of the product life cycle.

product line A group of similar products with obvious variations in the design and quality to meet the needs of distinct customer groups.

production Making a product or providing a service.

production oriented Term referring to businesses that emphasize decisions about what and how to produce and then how to sell the products.

production scheduling Identifying the steps required in a manufacturing process, the time required to complete each step, and the sequence of the steps.

productivity Producing the largest quantity in the least time by using efficient methods and modern equipment.

profit the incentive, as well as the reward, for producing goods and services.

profit-sharing plan A benefit plan that pays employees a small percentage of the company's profits at the end of the year.

progressive tax Tax based on the ability to pay.

promissory note An unconditional written promise to pay a certain sum of money, at a particular time or on demand, to the order of one who has obtained the note.

promotion (1) Providing information to consumers that will assist them in making a decision to purchase a product or service. (2) The advancement of an employee within a company to a position with more authority and responsibility.

property tax A levy on material goods owned.

proportional tax (flat tax) Tax rate that remains the same regardless of the amount on which the tax is imposed.

proprietor The owner-manager of a business.

prospectus A formal summary of the chief features of the business and its stock offering.

proxy A written authorization for someone to vote on behalf of the person signing the proxy.

public franchise A contract that permits a person or organization to use public property for private profit.

pure research Research done without a specific product in mind.

Q

quality standard Describes expected consistency in production or performance.

quantity discount Discount used by sellers to encourage customers to buy in large quantities.

quantity standard Establishes the expected amount of work to be completed.

quasi-public corporation A business that is important but lacks the profit potential to attract private investors and is often operated by local, state, or federal government.

quotas Limits placed on the quantity or value of units permitted to enter a country.

R

real property tax A tax levied on land and buildings.

recession A decline in the GDP that continues for six months or more.

recycling The reuse of products or product packaging whenever possible.

regressive tax Taxation wherein the actual tax rate decreases as the taxable amount increases.

reliability SERVQUAL dimension; the ability to perform the promised service dependably and accurately.

repetitive production Manufacturing process in which the same thing is done over and over to produce a product.

researching Studying buyer interests and needs, testing products, and gathering facts needed to make good marketing decisions.

responsibility The obligation to do an assigned task.

responsiveness SERVQUAL dimension; the willingness to help customers and provide prompt service.

retailers Businesses that sell directly to final consumers.

retained earnings Profits that are put aside to run a business.

revolving credit A credit plan that combines the features of regular charge credit and installment credit.

reward power Power based on the ability to control resources, rewards, and punishments.

risk taking Assuming the risk of losses that may occur from fire, theft, damage, or other circumstances.

Rust Belt The north central and northeastern states where major manufacturing centers were once dominant.

S

salary Compensation paid on a basis other than hourly, such as weekly or monthly.

sales budget A forecast of the sales for a month, a few months, or a year.

sales oriented Term referring to businesses that emphasize distribution and promotion to sell their products.

sales promotions Any promotional activities other than advertising and personal selling intended to motivate customers to buy.

sales tax A tax levied on the retail price of goods and services at the time they are sold.

sanctions A milder form of embargo that bans specific business ties with a foreign country.

savings account An account that allows the customer to make deposits, earn interest, and make withdrawals at any time without financial penalties.

savings bonds Non-negotiable securities sold by the U.S. Treasury in small denominations to individual investors.

schedule A time plan for reaching objectives.

search engine A program that assists in locating information on the Internet.

seasonal discount Discount given to the buyer for ordering or taking delivery of goods in advance of the normal buying period.

secured loan (collateral loan) A loan that requires the borrower to pledge something of value as security.

self-directed work team A team in which members together are responsible for the work assigned to the team.

self-service merchandising Customers select the products they wish, take them to a cashier or checkout counter, and pay for them.

self-understanding An awareness of your attitudes and opinions, leadership style, decision-making style, and relationships with other people.

selling Providing personalized and persuasive information to customers to help them buy the products and services they need.

selling price The actual price paid for a company's products by the customer.

service businesses Businesses that use mostly labor to offer mostly intangible products to satisfy consumer needs.

shares Equal parts of the division of ownership of a corporation.

shopping goods Goods that are bought less frequently than convenience goods, usually have a higher price, and require some buying thought.

short-term debt Borrowed capital that must be repaid within a year, and often in 30, 60, or 90 days.

situational leader One who understands employees and job requirements and matches actions and decisions to the circumstances.

Small Business Administration (SBA) Government-supported agency that counsels, assists, and protects the interests of small businesses.

Small Business Development Centers (SBDCs) Centers through which the SBA offers free consulting assistance.

smart card A credit and debit card with a memory that stores financial, health, credit, and other kinds of data that can be read by computers.

socialism An economic-political system in which the government controls and regulates the means of production.

social networking Virtual communities for people interested in sharing information about themselves with others.

social responsibility The duty of a business to contribute to the well-being of society.

Social Security A social insurance program funded through payroll contributions.

software Special instructions computers are provided to perform tasks.

sole proprietorship (proprietorship) A business owned and managed by one person.

spam Unsolicited advertising via e-mail.

span of control The number of employees who are directly supervised by one person.

specialist occupations Occupations that require a variety of skills in one or more business functions and extensive understanding of the operations of a specific company or industry.

specialty goods Products that customers insist upon having and are willing to shop for until they find them.

stakeholders The owners, customers, suppliers, employees, creditors, government, general public, and other groups who are affected by a firm's action.

standard A specific measure by which something is judged.

start-up budget Budget that projects income and expenses from the beginning of a new business until it becomes profitable.

sticky floor syndrome The inability of workers to move up from low-paying jobs requiring little skill and education.

stockholders (shareholders) Owners of a corporation.

stock index An average of the prices of selected stocks considered to be representative of a certain class of stocks or of the economy in general.

stock option A right granted by a corporation that allows current stockholders to buy additional shares when issued at a fixed price for a specific period of time.

storing Holding goods until needed by consumers, such as on shelves, in storage rooms, or in warehouses.

straight rebuy A repurchase from previously used suppliers.

strategic alliances Arrangements in which firms agree to cooperate on certain aspects of business while remaining competitors on other aspects.

strategic planning Long-term planning that provides broad goals and directions for the entire business.

Subchapter S corporation Special type of corporation allowed by states that is taxed as if it were a sole proprietorship or partnership.

subordinate Someone who is subject to the authority and control of another person.

subsidiaries Foreign branches of a business, registered as independent legal entities.

substantiation Being able to prove all claims made about products and services in promotions.

Sun Belt The warmer southern half of the nation.

supervisor A manager whose main job is to direct the work of employees.

supervisor/management occupations Occupations involving responsibility for specific units in a business and for decisions about operations and personnel.

supply The number of similar products that will be offered for sale at a particular time and at a particular price.

SWOT analysis An examination of an organization's internal strengths and weaknesses as well as opportunities and threats from its external environment.

symptom A sign or indication of something that appears to be the problem.

T

360-degree feedback A method of performance evaluation that uses performance feedback gathered from a broad range of people with whom the employee works, both inside and outside the organization.

tangibles SERVQUAL dimension; the appearance of physical facilities, equipment, personnel, and promotional material.

target markets Groups of customers with very similar needs to whom the company can sell its product.

tariff A tax on foreign goods to protect domestic industries and earn revenue.

tax-deferred Term referring to contributions made before taxes are calculated on the employee's income.

team building Getting people to believe in the goals of the company and work well together to accomplish them.

team organization Business structure that divides employees into permanent work teams.

telecommunications (data communications) A system involving the electronic movement of information from one location to another location.

telecommute Working from home or on the road, staying in contact with the employer electronically.

telemarketing Marketing goods and services by telephone.

term loan Medium- or long-term financing used for operating funds or the purchase or improvement of fixed assets.

time deposits (certificates of deposit or CDs) Deposits made for a specified period of time that cannot be withdrawn early without some financial penalty.

time plan A compensation plan which pays a certain amount for a specified period of time worked.

trade credit Short-term financing obtained by buying goods and services that do not require immediate payment.

trade discount A special deduction from the list price that is given to certain types of buyers, such as wholesalers or retailers, because the buyers perform certain functions for the seller.

trademark A distinguishing name, symbol, or special mark placed on a good or service that is legally reserved for the sole use of the owner.

trading bloc An arrangement between two or more countries to remove all restrictions on the sale of goods and services among them while imposing barriers to trade and investment with countries that are not part of the bloc.

transfer The assignment of an employee to another job in the company that involves the same type of responsibility and authority.

transporting Moving goods from where they were made to where consumers can buy them.

Treasury instruments Securities issued by the U.S. government.

U

underground economy Income that is not recorded in the GDP.

Unemployment insurance A state-managed program that provides temporary income to individuals who have been laid off from their jobs.

unity of command A law or guideline which states that no employee has more than one supervisor at a time.

unlimited financial liability Liability of each member of a partnership for all the debts of the business.

unsecured loan A loan that is not backed by collateral.

unsought goods Products that many customers will not shop for because they do not have a strong need for the product.

utility The ability of a good or service to satisfy a want.

V

variable interest rate An interest rate that can increase or decline based on the factors used to adjust the rate.

variance The difference between current performance and the standard.

venture capital Financing obtained from an investor or investment group that lends large sums of money to promising new or expanding small companies.

virtual corporation A network of companies that form alliances among themselves to take advantage of fast-changing market conditions.

vision A broad, lasting, and often inspirational view of a company's reason for existing.

VoIP (Voice over Internet Protocol) Using the Internet for telephone services.

W

wages Compensation paid on an hourly basis.

warehouses Buildings used to store large quantities of products until they can be sold.

Web-hosting service A private business that maintains the Web sites of individuals and organizations on its computers for a fee.

what-if decisions Explore the consequences of specific choices using computer software.

wholesalers Businesses that buy products from businesses and sell them to retailers or other businesses.

wholly owned subsidiary When a firm sets up a business abroad on its own without any partners.

wide area network (WAN) A network of linked computers that covers a wide geographic area.

win/lose strategy A strategy in which no one compromises, thereby resulting in one person winning and one losing.

work coach Experienced manager who meets regularly with a new manager to provide feedback and advice.

work rules Regulations created to maintain an effective working environment.

work schedules Schedules identifying the tasks to be done, employees assigned to the work, and the time frame for completion of each task.

work team A group of individuals who cooperate to achieve a common goal.

workers' compensation Insurance provided by employers for the death, injury, or illness of employees that result from their work.

working capital The difference between current assets and current liabilities.

World Bank International institution that provides low-cost, long-term loans to less-developed countries to develop basic industries and facilities.

World Trade Organization (WTO) International organization that creates and enforces rules governing trade among countries.

World Wide Web (WWW, Web) Makes the Internet accessible to the average person.

Z

zoning Regulations that specify which land areas may be used for homes and which areas may be used for different types of businesses.

Index

Index